, California ✧ Archives of the Mormon

aterial culture ✧ Eli H. Peirce Collection,

is of the Cha[illegible] [illegible]estern

erforming a[illegible] [illegible]oeder

ecial Collections, Harold B. Lee Library,

✧ Foundation for Ancient Research and

✧ Family History Library of The Church

e City, Utah ✧ Mormon emigration trails

folklore ✧ Historical Department of

Saints, Salt Lake City, Utah ✧ Beinecke

rary, San Marino, California ✧ literature

rary, University of Utah ✧ photoarchives

Archives and Record Services, Salt Lake

hurch of Jesus Christ of Latter Day Saints,

ical Society, Salt Lake City, Utah ✧ science,

l Collections, Merrill Library, Utah State

State University ✧ Weber State University

Mormon Americana

Mormon Americana

A Guide to Sources and Collections in the United States

Edited by David J. Whittaker

Published by BYU Studies

Provo, Utah

1995

BYU Studies Monographs

B. H. Roberts, *The Truth, the Way, the Life*

The Journals of William E. McLellin, 1831-1836

Hearts Turned to the Fathers: A History of the Genealogical Society of Utah, 1894-1994

We Rejoice in Christ: A Bibliography of LDS Writings on Jesus Christ and the New Testament

Mormon Americana: A Guide to Sources and Collections in the United States

Library of Congress Cataloging-in-Publication Data

Mormon Americana: A guide to sources and collections in the United States / edited by David J. Whittaker.

p. cm. — (BYU Studies monographs)

Includes bibliographical references and index.

ISBN 0-8425-2315-4 : $29.95

1. Mormons—United States—Archival resources. 2. Mormons—United States—Library resources. 3. Mormon Church—United States—Archival resources. 4. Mormon Church—United States—Library resources. 5. Church of Jesus Christ of Latter-day Saints—Archival resources. 6. Church of Jesus Christ of Latter-day Saints—Library resources. 7. Libraries—Special collections—Mormons. 8. Libraries—Special collections—Mormon Church. 9. Libraries—Special collections—Church of Jesus Christ of Latter-day Saints. I. Whittaker, David J. II. Series.

E184.M8M67 1994 94-29931

026'.2893—dc20 CIP

Printed in the United States of America

10 9 8 7 6 5 4 3 2 1

This volume is dedicated to
the editors and staff of BYU Studies,
past and present

Table of Contents

Part IV: Special Topics in Mormon Americana

Part V: Conclusion

Acknowledgements

In the time it has taken to bring *Mormon Americana* to press, many people have contributed to all stages of production. To the authors of the various essays I owe a special thanks; their professionalism and patience during the long process of production have been greatly appreciated. Likewise, the cooperation and responses to my letters and personal visits by librarians and archivists throughout the United States have been of great assistance in bringing this project to fruition.

The editors and staff of BYU Studies have rendered invaluable encouragement and practical assistance since I proposed the project to Edward Geary in 1987. Having worked for twelve years with the BYU Studies staff, first as Book Review Editor and then as an Associate Editor, I have a special appreciation for the countless contributions and often unacknowledged hard work required to bring an idea into print. Thus this volume is dedicated to the editors and staff as a partial thank you to everyone who has worked in the BYU Studies office over the years.

Edward A. Geary encouraged this effort as it grew from the original four essays, to a special issue, and finally to a separate volume. Linda Hunter Adams and Doris R. Dant have also supported this project from its inception. John W. Welch saw the project's potential for a separate book and has seen it through to completion as a volume in the new BYU Studies Monograph series.

Special thanks go to the BYU Studies editorial staff for assistance in editing, typing, proofreading, footnote checking, and the dozens of other tasks that lie behind book production: Angela Ashurst-McGee, Daryl R. Hague, Doris R. Dant, I. Andrew Teasdale, I. LaPriel Brimhall, John W. Welch, Karl F. Batdorff, Marny K. Parkin, and Nancy R. Lund. Interns at BYU Studies who assisted with these tasks include Alison McCreadie, Angela Clyde, Anissa J. Wall, Austin Gray, Becky R. Petersen, Boley T. Thomas, Brandy Vogel, Camera Palmer, Catherine F. Cvetko, Chad Poulson, Chandler Childs, David Cannell, David Pace, David Wootton, Debbie Peart, Doug Larsen, Douglas C. Waddoups, Emily Buhrley, Gayle S. Kunz, Heather Fitzgerald, Heidi A. Biehl, Jane Young, Jason S. Izatt, Jennifer Day, Jennifer Hurlbut, Jennifer Nyland, Jennifer Rasmussen Wallace, John Miner, Jonathan D. Lofgren, Julie Swindler,

Karen Beckstead, Kelli Robison, Kim Malouf, Kirsten Sorenson, Kristina Labadie, Laura Hunter, Laurel Davis, Lillian Chaves, Mandy Dalton, Melinda Brockett, MeLínda Evans Jeffress, Michelyn Lyster, Nathan Oman, NiCole M. Baker, Ron Hampton, Rosalyde Frandsen, Sarah Hatch, Sara Pfister, Scott Curtis, Shelly M. Rime, Stacy Chaney, Stacy Wiker, Steve Hansen, Steve Harper, Tamary Reynolds, Tanya Levin, Tanya M. Burrell, Travis Jacobsen, and Troy Blair. Thanks also to Howard A. Christy, Elizabeth Watkins, and Jennifer Harrison at Scholarly Publications for their reading of the manuscript.

Sterling J. Albrecht, the University Librarian at Brigham Young University, has been supportive of my work, as has A. Dean Larsen, former Associate University Librarian for Collection Development. My colleagues in the Department of Special Collections and Manuscripts in the Harold B. Lee Library at BYU have encouraged this project in various ways and have provided a collegial atmosphere where I could discuss this project at various stages in its development. Our department chairman, Scott H. Duvall, has encouraged my work on this project, as have my associates in the Archives: Dennis Rowley, James D'Arc, and Harvard Heath. Chad J. Flake, Curator of Rare Books at BYU, has also provided friendship and has been an example of a tireless Mormon bibliographer in his own right.

Finally, I would like to thank my wife Linda who has encouraged and actively supported my scholarly work for over thirty years. No one knows better than she the incredible number of hours that a project like this demands. She has sacrificed time with her husband and has been patient as other things necessarily got postponed. As a friend and advisor in all things, she manages to provide encouragement, balance, and a wonderful home environment for my work in Mormon studies. All of this she does in addition to her own full-time work as an administrative assistant to an Associate Academic Vice President at BYU, not to ignore her important roles as a mother of four and grandmother of three. No one could ask for a more complete companion.

—David J. Whittaker

Part I:
Introduction

Introduction to *Mormon Americana*

David J. Whittaker

Rodney Stark, a non-Mormon sociologist of American religion, recently challenged his colleagues throughout the country to begin paying more attention to the history and development of The Church of Jesus Christ of Latter-day Saints. Stark's own studies have led him to conclude that the numerical growth of the Mormon Church, both in the past and as projected for the years ahead, makes it a world religion. He has specifically challenged scholars, who, for the first time in history, have a unique opportunity to study the birth and development of a new world religion.[1] Jan Shipps, another non-Mormon student of Latter-day Saint history, has argued that Mormonism is a "new religious tradition," providing explanations for her contention that go beyond the demographic material and straight-line projections of Stark.[2]

From its beginnings in 1830, the Church has attracted serious observers. Travel and curiosa accounts of the nineteenth century, the perceptive observations of Richard Burton in the 1860s and Eduard Meyer in the 1910s, and a host of commentary in more recent times by such outside scholars as William F. Albright and Thomas F. O'Dea—all these manifest to the continuing attraction of the Mormon Church and its people.[3] While most of these students have registered fascination in their descriptions of the Mormon movement, Sydney Ahlstrom voices his fascination most clearly in his award-winning *A Religious History of the American People*, "One cannot even be sure if the object of our consideration is a sect, a mystery cult, a new religion, a church, a people, a nation, or an American subculture; indeed, at different times and places it is all of these."[4]

Probably no American-born religion is as richly documented as The Church of Jesus Christ of Latter-day Saints.[5] From personal journals to institutional records, the rich treasures of manuscripts and printed materials have yet to be fully mined by students of the Latter-day Saint experience. But because of the sheer volume of these sources, students of Mormon history can easily lose their way. One of the purposes of this special volume is to assist researchers in identifying the major repositories and sources of Mormon material.

Even before the Church was organized in April 1830, Joseph Smith gave to the world a new volume of scripture, the Book of Mormon, that claimed to carefully chronicle families led by God to the Americas. The Book of Mormon tells of successive prophet-record-keepers who maintained accounts of their own ministries in addition to the more secular events of their people.[6] One such leader counseled his son about the importance of maintaining records by explaining records' role in "enlarg[ing] the memory of [the] people" (Alma 37:8). No doubt the Book of Mormon influenced Joseph's record keeping by providing an example of the key role records played in the societies mentioned within its pages. Thus on the day the Church was organized, a revelation specifically commanded that a "record" should be kept.[7] Subsequent revelations and directives broadened the duties of those individuals given responsibility for record keeping.[8] Throughout the Church's formative years, Joseph Smith led the movement to create and preserve the historical resources of the Church and its members. He recognized the need to document all aspects of the Church and particularly understood the role accurate records could play in strengthening the administrative structure of the Church. He also invited individual members to keep records, both genealogical and personal, that would document their role in the great events of the Restoration movement.[9]

Record keeping and its related activity of compiling source material continued after Joseph Smith's death in 1844. The institutional need to more fully document Joseph's life was surely a key factor in the continuing activities of individuals such as Willard Richards, Thomas Bullock, and even later of Andrew Jenson.[10] Others followed,[11] and despite the large number of published works of Mormon history and biography, the real core of Mormon studies remains unpublished in the journals and personal papers of the members.

Mountains of primary sources document all aspects of the Latter-day Saint experience. The only book-length guide to this material listed almost 2,900 items or collections,[12] but as with most pioneering works it made mistakes. And because the guide is about twenty years old, it does not document the large number of collections that have been cataloged or have surfaced during the last two decades. While a new edition of this important work is clearly needed, until it is revised students of Mormon history must search the repositories themselves, or at least become more aware of the growing, national computer databases.

To more fully assist students of things Mormon, this volume of the BYU Studies Monograph Series has been assembled. It had its origin in the Annual Meeting of the Pacific Coast Branch, American

Historical Association, held at Occidental College in Southern California in August, 1987. One session, "Mormon Archivists Access Their Holdings," was organized by Guy Bishop, then of the Los Angeles County Museum of Natural History. The session met at the Henry E. Huntington Library and consisted of presentations by George Miles of the Beinecke Library at Yale University; Bonnie Hardwick of the Bancroft Library at the University of California, Berkeley; Peter Blodgett of the Huntington Library; and myself, representing the Archives at Brigham Young University. In subsequent discussions the participants decided to gather the initial papers together for publication. As the process of revision and rewriting was underway, the original four presentations expanded to include other significant libraries and archives throughout the United States. During the process of editing these essays for publication, it became apparent that students of Mormon history would be served more fully by essays devoted to specific topics in addition to special repositories. Thus various scholars were invited to prepare extended source essays focusing on their areas of expertise. This volume is the final product of a broad cooperative effort made by many archivists, librarians, and researchers throughout the country who have responsibility for or knowledge of significant Mormon resources.

David J. Whittaker is the editor of *Mormon Americana: A Guide to Sources and Collections in the United States.* He is also Senior Librarian and Curator of the Archives of the Mormon Experience, Harold B. Lee Library, Brigham Young University.

NOTES

[1]"The Rise of a New World Faith," *Review of Religious Research* 26 (September 1984): 18–27.

[2]*Mormonism: The Story of a New Religious Tradition* (Urbana: University of Illinois Press, 1985).

[3]For early curiosa accounts see Howard C. Searle, "Early Mormon Historiography: Writing the History of the Mormons, 1830–1858" (Ph.D. diss., UCLA, 1979), 29–51; Edwina Jo Snow, "Singular Saints: The Image of the Mormons in Book-Length Travel Accounts, 1847–1857" (master's thesis, George Washington University, 1972); and Snow, "British Travelers View the Saints, 1847–1877," *BYU Studies* 31 (Spring 1991): 63–81. Burton's observations are in his *The City of the Saints* (London, 1861). For Eduard Meyer, see *The Origin and History of the Mormons, with Reflections on the Beginnings of Islam and Christianity* (1914), translated from German by Heinz F. Rahde and Eugene Seaich (Salt Lake City:

University of Utah, 1961). More recently see William F. Albright, "Archaeology and Religion," *Cross Currents* 9 (Spring 1959): 111; Thomas F. O'Dea, *The Mormons* (Chicago: University of Chicago Press, 1957). See also *Reflections on Mormonism, Judaeo-Christian Parallels,* ed. Truman G. Madsen, vol. 4 in Religious Studies Monograph Series (Provo, Utah: Religious Studies Center, Brigham Young University, 1978).

[4]Sydney Ahlstrom, *A Religious History of the American People* (New Haven: Yale University Press, 1972), 508.

[5]Basic works on the history of The Church of Jesus Christ of Latter-day Saints include B. H. Roberts, *A Comprehensive History of the Church of Jesus Christ of Latter-day Saints, Century One,* 6 vols. (Salt Lake City: Deseret News Press, 1930); James B. Allen and Glen M. Leonard, *The Story of the Latter-day Saints,* rev. ed. (Salt Lake City: Deseret Book, 1992); Leonard J. Arrington and Davis Bitton, *The Mormon Experience: A History of the Latter-day Saints* (New York, Alfred A. Knopf, 1979); and Daniel H. Ludlow, ed., *The Encyclopedia of Mormonism,* 5 vols. (New York: Macmillan, 1992).

[6]Studies suggesting this include John Sorenson, *An Ancient American Setting for the Book of Mormon* (Salt Lake City: Deseret Book and F.A.R.M.S., 1985), 50–56; and Richard L. Bushman, "The Book of Mormon in Early Mormon History," in *New Views of Mormon History: A Collection of Essays in Honor of Leonard J. Arrington,* ed. Davis Bitton and Maureen Ursenbach Beecher (Salt Lake City: University of Utah Press, 1987), 3–18.

[7]D&C 21:1 in current editions; Chapter 22 in 1833 Book of Commandments.

[8]D&C 47:1–4; 69:2, 3, 8; 85:1–2 (with Oliver Cowdery letter to David Whitmer, January 1833, MS in Cowdery Letterbook, Henry E. Huntington Library, San Marino, Calif.); 20:82–84; 107:5–9; 123; 128:2–8.

[9]See the excellent overview in Dean C. Jessee, "Joseph Smith and the Beginning of Mormon Record Keeping," in *The Prophet Joseph: Essays on the Life and Mission of Joseph Smith,* ed. Larry C. Porter and Susan Easton Black (Salt Lake City: Deseret Book Co., 1988), 138–60.

[10]See Howard C. Searle, "Willard Richards as Historian," *BYU Studies* 31 (Spring 1991): 41–62; Jerald F. Simon, "Thomas Bullock as an Early Mormon Historian," *BYU Studies* 30 (Winter 1990): 71–88; and Keith W. Perkins, "A Study of the Contributions of Andrew Jenson to the Writing and Preservation of LDS Church History" (master's thesis, Brigham Young University, 1971).

[11]For overviews see Leonard J. Arrington, "The Search for Truth and Meaning in Mormon History," *Dialogue: A Journal of Mormon Thought* 3 (Summer 1968): 56–66; David J. Whittaker, "Historians and the Mormon Experience: A Sesquicentennial Perspective," in *The Eighth Annual Sidney B. Sperry Symposium, January 20, 1980* (Provo, Utah: Brigham Young University Press for the Church Educational System, 1980), 293–327; Thomas G. Alexander, "Toward the New Mormon History: An Examination of the Literature on the Latter-day Saints in the Far West," in *Historians and the American West,* ed. Michael P. Malone (Lincoln: University of Nebraska Press, 1983), 344–68; and Davis Bitton and Leonard J. Arrington, *Mormons and Their Historians* (Salt Lake City: University of Utah Press, 1988).

[12]Davis Bitton, *Guide to Mormon Diaries and Autobiographies* (Provo, Utah: Brigham Young University Press, 1977).

Sources for the Study of Joseph Smith

Dean C. Jessee

In December 1894, a service commemorating Joseph Smith's birth was held in the old Sixteenth Ward meetinghouse in Salt Lake City. Bathsheba W. Smith, one of the dwindling generation of Latter-day Saints who knew the Prophet, spoke to the assembly. The aging matriarch mentioned that she had been personally acquainted with Joseph and that she prided herself as a judge of handsome men. Then, referring to cherished paintings of the Prophet adorning the walls of the chapel, she commented that they were "but little better than cartoons"; they were nothing but "libels" and "ought to be burned."[1]

In the absence of photography, contemporary paintings and drawings were made of Joseph Smith which time has enshrined with an aura of respectability and reverence, but the historical value of those renditions is only as good as the skill of the artists who produced them. Age does not necessarily guarantee accuracy. This point raises a question: if nineteenth-century artistic skills failed to secure an accurate visual image of the Prophet, did writing skills preserve a more dependable literary image? A look at the sources suggests that Bathsheba Smith's observation regarding the paintings could well apply to a substantial part of the historical records that provide the resources for the study of Joseph Smith.

Born in a log cabin in the town of Sharon, Vermont, in 1805, Joseph Smith is widely known as the prophet-founder of Mormonism. When he was eleven, his family moved to Palmyra, New York. There, amidst the religious turmoil of the "burned-over district," Joseph became concerned for the welfare of his "immortal soul." That concern resulted in a series of visions in which he was told that "the covenant which God made with ancient Israel was at hand to be fulfilled, that the preparatory work for the second coming of the Messiah was speedily to commence; that the time was at hand for the gospel, in all its fulness to be preached in power, unto all nations that a people might be prepared for the millennial reign," and that he was "chosen to be an instrument in the hands of God to bring about some of his purposes in this glorious dispensation."[2]

Joseph Smith Jr., Carter Collection. Courtesy LDS Church Archives.

The publication of the Book of Mormon and the organization of the Church in 1830 propelled the young prophet onto the stage of public controversy. Then, after fourteen years of contending for his message in a hostile world and trying to establish a gathering place for his followers, first in New York, then in Ohio, Missouri, and Illinois, he was shot to death by a mob with blackened faces who stormed the jail at Carthage, Illinois, where he was being detained.

This article introduces to the general reader, as well as to the historical researcher, the crucial historical sources that make up the raw materials for the study of the Prophet. The sources are diverse and widely scattered. For purposes of description, they may be divided into six general categories: Joseph Smith's own papers; institutional sources; newspapers; the records of people who knew Joseph Smith; secondary sources; and beyond these, although not directly contributing to the narrative of Joseph's life, works that help to illuminate the world in which he lived.

Joseph Smith's Papers

The sources that most clearly reveal Joseph Smith are his own papers, the bulk of which are located in the archives of The Church of Jesus Christ of Latter-day Saints in Salt Lake City, Utah, and the Reorganized Church of Jesus Christ of Latter Day Saints at Independence, Missouri. Significant materials in lesser quantity are found at other repositories, including Brigham Young University, Chicago Historical Society, Huntington Library, Illinois State Historical Library, Iowa Historical Society, University of Utah, Utah State Historical Society, and Yale University.

The Joseph Smith papers cover a sixteen-year period beginning in 1828 during his work on the Book of Mormon and ending at his death in June 1844.[3] The papers include the following:

- approximately one hundred manuscript revelations.

- a dozen diaries and journals beginning with the year 1832 and continuing, with substantial gaps, to the end of his life.
- three copybooks containing correspondence, revelations, and other documents dated between 1829 and 1843.
- less than a thousand items of loose papers consisting primarily of correspondence as well as some financial records, reports of discourses, autobiographical writings, and other documents.
- manuscripts pertaining to the Book of Mormon, the books of Abraham and Moses, and a Bible revision.
- some Egyptian papyrus.
- manuscripts for a history of the Church.
- a few drawings and paintings of Joseph produced during his lifetime.

The Smith papers are not voluminous in comparison with those of other prominent Americans currently being edited for publication. A comprehensive edition of Joseph's works will probably not exceed eight volumes.[4]

Institutional Sources

In addition to his own papers, other sources useful for the study of the Prophet are the records of early Church and civic organizations that report his activities as Church President, town mayor, municipal court judge, and militia commander. These records include

- "The Conference Minutes, and Record Book, of Christ's Church of Latter Day Saints," commonly referred to as the Far West Record, a book containing minutes of Church meetings between 1830 and 1844.[5]
- John Whitmer's early history of the Church, 1831–38.[6]
- the Kirtland Council Minute Book, 1832–37.
- the Nauvoo High Council Minute Book, 1839–40.
- the Nauvoo Municipal Court Docket, 1841–45.
- "A Record of the Proceedings of the City Council of the City of Nauvoo," 1841–45.
- the Nauvoo Legion Minute Book, 1841–44.
- "A Record of the Organization and Proceedings of the Female Relief Society of Nauvoo," 1842–44.
- records of the Council of Fifty.[7]

Newspapers

The most extensive public source of information about Joseph Smith during his lifetime was the newspaper. A recent study shows the importance of newspapers as an avenue of communication in the United States and the rapid spread of that medium due to the increase of mail service during Joseph Smith's lifetime. In 1824 some six hundred newspapers existed in the United States; seven years later nearly half that many existed in New York state alone. In 1800, five years before the Prophet's birth, the United States had nine hundred post offices and more than twenty thousand miles of postal roads. By the time Joseph was fifteen, the year of his first vision, forty-five hundred post offices and seventy-two thousand miles of postal roads existed. Ten years later, the year Joseph established the Church, mail transportation had mushroomed to fifteen million miles, and by 1833 had surpassed twenty-three million miles. By that same year, reportedly 11,800,000 newspapers were passing through the New York City post office annually, and the postmaster of a small New York town reported processing 14,262 newspapers in one week. This extensive promulgation of news was encouraged by a 1792 postal law that set the rate for sending a newspaper at one-and-a-half cents, compared to as much as twenty-five cents for a one-page letter. Between newspaper offices, the paper could be sent free.[8]

Newspaper editors regularly copied from each other. Consequently, when Joseph Smith became a subject of public notice following the appearance of the Book of Mormon in Palmyra, New York, in 1830, and as the Latter-day Saints moved to Ohio, Missouri, and Illinois, news about the Prophet became available throughout the country.[9] Among the newspapers that played a prominent role in formulating public opinion about him were the *Reflector* (Palmyra, New York), *Painesville Telegraph* (Painesville, Ohio), *Sangamo Journal* (Springfield, Illinois), and *Warsaw Signal* (Warsaw, Illinois). At the same time, Latter-day Saint papers also played a role in disseminating information from their perspective. Church publications included *The Evening and the Morning Star* (Independence, Missouri, 1832–34), *The Latter-day Saints' Messenger and Advocate* (Kirtland, Ohio, 1834–37), the *Wasp* (Nauvoo, Illinois, 1842–43), the *Nauvoo Neighbor* (Nauvoo, Illinois, 1843–45), and the *Times and Seasons* (Nauvoo, Illinois, 1839–46).

People Who Knew Joseph Smith

The writings of people who knew Joseph Smith are another important source of information about him. Of these papers, those of his family and closest associates are fundamental. Because members of the Smith family knew him best and were the first to believe his message, their writings are preferred sources for measuring his credibility. The biography written by his mother contains insight to his family heritage and details recorded by no one else.[10] And although Joseph's father kept no personal record, lines from his father's patriarchal blessing book address Joseph's religious claims and character.[11] Furthermore, the autobiography of Joseph and Emma's oldest son gives valuable insight from the perspective of one of his children.[12]

In addition to the foregoing, Joseph's limited correspondence with his wife Emma opens a small but revealing window into his domestic life as husband and father and substantiates statements of some who observed the Smith family in their home over extended periods of time.[13] John Bernhisel, for example, who was a boarder with the Smith family for more than nine months, had abundant opportunity to observe Joseph in the intimate confines of his home. Bernhisel observed:

> in the gentle charities of domestic life, as the tender and affectionate husband & parent, the warm and sympathising friend, . . . the prominent traits of his [Joseph's] character are revealed, and his heart is felt to be keenly alive to the kindest and softest emotions of which human nature is susceptible, and I feel assured that his family and friends formed one of the greatest consolations to him, while the vials of wrath were poured upon his head, while his footsteps were pursued by malice and envy, and reproach and slander were strewed in his path.[14]

The writings of a number of Joseph Smith's close associates illuminate segments of his life where his own records are silent. One of these associates was Willard Richards, who arrived late on the Mormon scene and served as private secretary and Church historian during the last year and a half of the Prophet's life. Richards's prime contribution was keeping the Prophet's journal for him and writing a substantial amount of Joseph's correspondence. Richards also produced a diary of his own which contains, among other information, a record of progress in compiling the manuscript of the *History of the Church* during his Nauvoo involvement in that work and the only contemporary eyewitness account of events at the Carthage jail that culminated with the murder of Joseph and Hyrum Smith.[15]

Along with the writings of Richards, the diary of English convert William Clayton provides a valuable parallel account of the Prophet's late Nauvoo years from Clayton's perspective as land agent, deputy recorder of deeds, Nauvoo Temple recorder, and close confidant. In addition to writing his own personal diary, Clayton took the place of Willard Richards in keeping Joseph Smith's journal when Richards took an extended absence from Nauvoo.[16]

Another diarist who contributes to the knowledge of Joseph Smith was Wilford Woodruff, who first met the Prophet in Kirtland, Ohio, in 1834. Woodruff was the only Mormon diarist who kept a consecutive record during the last ten years of Joseph Smith's life. Hence, when not absent on proselyting and other assignments, Woodruff adds significantly to the understanding of Joseph Smith. Woodruff's diary contains reports of several discourses of the Prophet recorded by no one else.[17]

Still other associates and participants have supplied missing or corroborative detail. For example, writings of Oliver Cowdery, David Whitmer, Martin Harris, John Whitmer, and Joseph Knight are important for the understanding of Joseph Smith's early experiences connected with the beginnings of Mormonism.[18] In 1833, for instance, Cowdery recalled the conferral of priesthood upon him and Joseph Smith by a divine messenger four years earlier:

> he [Joseph] was ordained by the angel John, unto the lesser or Aaronic priesthood, in company with myself, in the town of Harmony, Susquehannah County, Pennsylvania, on Fryday, the 15th day of May, 1829, after which we repaired to the water, even to the Susquehannah River, and were baptized, he first ministering unto me and after I to him. But before baptism, our souls were drawn out in mighty prayer to know how we might obtain the blessings of baptism and of the Holy Spirit, according to the order of God, and we diligently saught for the right of the fathers and the authority of the holy priesthood, and the power to admin[ister] in the same: for we desired to be followers of righteousness and the possessors of greater knowledge, even the knowledge of the mysteries of the kingdom of God. Therefore, we repaired to the woods, even as our father Joseph said we should, that is to the bush, and called upon the name of the Lord, and he answered us out of the heavens, and while we were in the heavenly vision the angel came down and bestowed upon us this priesthood; and then, as I have said, we repaired to the water and were baptized. After this we received the high and holy priesthood.[19]

In addition to those above, other important gap-filling writings, such as the records of George A. Smith, Heber C. Kimball, and

Wilford Woodruff, help clarify the march of Zion's Camp in 1834.[20] Furthermore, the writings of Parley P. Pratt, Hyrum Smith, and Alexander McRae are invaluable for the Prophet's Missouri jail experience of 1838–39.[21] Finally, the records of John Taylor, Cyrus Wheelock, Dan Jones, and John S. Fullmer help piece together the chaotic final days at Carthage, Illinois.[22]

Besides the foregoing, other individuals made occasional observations or heard the Prophet speak. These observers' records shed light on Joseph Smith as a person and on isolated incidents in his life. Converts and others often recorded their first impressions or occasional instances of seeing or hearing him. These writings provide a wide range of descriptions and anecdotes.[23] In 1835, for example, new convert Jonathan Crosby arrived in Kirtland, Ohio, and decided "to go & see the Prophet of God first of all." Knocking at the Prophet's door, Crosby found him entertaining guests, but nevertheless, "he bade me come in, and be seated . . . and made me welcom. There was quite a little company in that evening. . . . We had a pleasant time, drank pepper and sider and had supper." Reflecting on the experience, Crosby noted, "I thought he was a quear man for [a] prophet, at first, he didn't appear exactly as I expected to see a Prophet of God, however, I was not stumbled at all. I found him to be a friendly cheerful pleasant agreable man. I could not help likeing him."[24]

Personal reactions to the Prophet were not limited to his admirers. And although much of the attention he received in the public press was negative, adding considerable distortion to the historical record, such materials occasionally contribute to the understanding of his life and thought beyond identifying the nature of his opposition. In this context, John C. Bennett's exposé of Mormonism (published after his 1842 excommunication) is the earliest known source for sentiments attributed to the Prophet in an 1842 letter he presumably wrote to Nancy Rigdon.[25] And although John Corrill left the Church in Missouri in 1838 and published a history in which he explained his reasons for leaving, his work gives useful insight into Joseph Smith and a period of Mormon history badly lacking in primary sources.[26]

Secondary Sources

In addition to the primary sources that pertain to Joseph Smith, an increasing amount of research on Mormonism has produced a substantial array of secondary material. Much of this research has been fostered in the last thirty years by a number of organizations and publishing outlets that address topics of LDS concern. Of particular note are organizations like the Mormon History Association, the LDS Historical Department, the Joseph Fielding Smith Institute for Church History (Brigham Young University), the Religious Studies Center (Brigham Young University), the John Whitmer Historical Association, and the Sunstone Foundation; publications such as *BYU Studies, Dialogue, Journal of Mormon History, Sunstone,* and *Utah Historical Quarterly;* and the following publishers: Deseret Book Company, Signature Books, the University of Illinois Press, and the University of Utah Press.

Secondary works dealing with Joseph Smith cover a wide range of topics pertaining to his life and times. Because Mormonism is based upon the religious experiences and claims of Joseph Smith, much attention in the secondary literature has been given to Joseph's early visions and the coming forth of the Book of Mormon. During the last sixty years, three full-length biographies of Joseph Smith, written from widely differing viewpoints, have appeared: Fawn Brodie's humanistic *No Man Knows My History* (New York: Knopf, 1945), and more sympathetic studies by Donna Hill, *Joseph Smith: The First Mormon* (Midvale, Utah: Signature Books, 1977), and Francis Gibbons, *Joseph Smith, Martyr, Prophet of God* (Salt Lake City: Deseret Book, 1977). (For a more complete listing of secondary works dealing with Joseph Smith, see David J. Whittaker, "Joseph Smith in Recent Research: A Selected Bibliography," which follows this essay.)

Scholarly Works about Joseph's World

Besides the sources directly relating to Joseph Smith's life, extensive scholarly output illuminates the world in which he lived. The convincing biography of the Prophet will be the one that not only pieces together the story of his life, but also effectively relates him to the American religious, economic, social, and political environment of the first half of the nineteenth century. The historical profession, in producing a large and ever-increasing volume of information covering almost every facet of nineteenth-century American life, has indirectly enriched the understanding of Joseph Smith.[27]

Problems with the Joseph Smith Sources

The study of Joseph Smith, like that of other figures of the past, is one of locating and interpreting the sources. But the circumstances of early Mormon record keeping, as well as the nature of the sources that have a bearing upon the study of his life, have complicated the process of understanding him. In the first place, the gradual development of a record-keeping enterprise among the Latter-day Saints and disruptive conditions due to persecution and the frequent movement of the Church in the early decades of its history limited the amount and quality of records that were kept.[28]

One of the largest factors affecting the understanding of Joseph Smith from the historical sources is the extreme hostility of the public press. Those who study the Prophet must not ignore Moroni's warning that Joseph's name would be known "for good and evil among all nations, kindreds, and tongues . . . that it should be both good and evil spoken of among all people."[29] This warning indicates that the historical sources concerning the Prophet will be highly polarized. Indeed, his motivation for writing his history was a response "to the many reports which have been put in circulation by evil disposed and designing persons in relation to the rise and progress of the Church . . . , to disabuse the public mind, and put all inquirers after truth into possession of the facts."[30] He later added, "so embittered was the public mind against the truth, that the press universally had been arrayed against us."[31]

The first public notice of Joseph Smith in the news media was a June 1829 announcement of the forthcoming publication of the Book of Mormon.[32] In the years that followed, newspapers played a major role in formulating the picture of the Prophet that would generally prevail. At first the public reaction toward him was one of caution and curiosity, but it soon gave way to antagonism and hostility. Palmyra, New York, newspaper editors Pomeroy Tucker (*Wayne Sentinel*), J. A. Hadley (*Palmyra Freeman*), and Abner Cole (*Reflector*) became the creators of a grotesque image that would characterize Joseph Smith in much of the public mind for decades to come.[33] These men orchestrated themes that were perpetuated and enlarged upon by others, including Eber D. Howe, John C. Bennett,[34] and Thomas Sharp,[35] resulting in an inordinate amount of distortion seeping into the stream of historical sources pertaining to Joseph Smith.

Abner Cole introduced the cartoon character "Jo Smith" to the world, describing him as "tall and slender . . . having but little expression of countenance, other than that of dulness [*sic*]; his mental powers appear to be extremely limited." Even after publishing the Book of Mormon, Jo Smith was "profoundly ignorant" of the meaning of many of its words. Cole added that all of the Smiths were noted for their "ignorance and stupidity" and their "propensity to superstition and a fondness for every thing marvelous;" they were a family taken to nocturnal treasure digging, "too lazy or idle to labor for bread in the day time." Cole went on to place the Book of Mormon in a context of nighttime money digging, evil spirits with long beards, peep stones, mineral rods and balls, rusty swords, and stuffed toads—a story that did not come close to Joseph Smith's explanation or the economic history of the Smith family in New York but appealed to the mentality of many of his contemporaries.[36]

Cole's thesis of unprincipled Smiths gained momentum in 1834 when ex-Mormon, Doctor Philastus Hurlbut, who had been cut off from the Church for immorality, became involved with a committee of anti-Mormons in Kirtland, Ohio. The committee sent Hurlbut to gather information to disparage the Smith family, divest the Prophet of "all claims to the character of an honest man," and place him at an "immeasurable distance from the high station he pretends to occupy." Hurlbut collected numerous derogatory statements he attributed to former townspeople of the Smiths in New York and Pennsylvania, which were published by Eber D. Howe in *Mormonism Unvailed* (Painesville, Ohio, 1834). Howe's work, which picked up on the Cole thesis in order to belittle the Smith character, also introduced the Spaulding theory to explain the Book of Mormon's origin. *Mormonism Unvailed* became a popular source for subsequent critics of the Prophet.[37]

Another element that has had an impact upon the understanding of the Mormon Prophet in the historical sources stems from his own philosophy of record keeping. He once stated that a great man must shun trivia, by which he meant that prophets should not be their own scribes.[38] As a result of this philosophy, a substantial number of Joseph's writings, including almost the entire content of his journals after 1836, were the product of other men's minds. Therefore, researchers have a clouded view of Joseph when a definition of his personality and thoughts is important.[39]

This clouded view is illustrated by the failure of many people to understand Joseph Smith both during and after his lifetime. Central to understanding him is a definition of his religious mission. That is, one must consider the nature of his prophetic call—his divine mandate—and the way his lifetime performance related to it.[40] An 1830 revelation declared that Joseph was "inspired to move the cause of Zion in mighty power for good."[41] And a short time later he was told, "Thou shalt devote all thy service in Zion; and in this thou shalt have strength," but "in temporal labors thou shalt not have strength, for this is not thy calling."[42] What were the features of this program for Zion? The answer is not concisely stated in any one place in the Prophet's writings; it must be gleaned from throughout his papers.

At Nauvoo, Joseph Smith privately introduced key elements of his plan for Zion. But the necessity for secrecy and the delegation of his journal keeping tended to obscure the nature and significance of his work there. People heard his religious pronouncements and were aware of the private practice of plural marriage and of temple ordinances. They saw his business dealings, his involvement in politics, his selling goods at his store, his presiding as judge of the municipal court, his deliberations as mayor with town leaders about community affairs, his buying and selling of land, his preoccupation with military affairs, his playfulness with people young and old, and his efforts to avoid the snares of his enemies. But people did not see the thread that connected all these activities to "the cause of Zion." Consequently, outsiders regarded him as an eccentric or a religious fanatic, and dissidents saw him as a fallen prophet.

Joseph's journal entries illustrate how secrecy and his delegation of journal writing create an unclear picture of his purposes. On May 28, 1843, secretary Willard Richards cryptically wrote, "5 P.M. - adjourned council met in upper room. . . . Joseph & J. Adams [shorthand symbol]." The following day Richards noted,

> 9 A.M. - met pursuant to adjournment. Joseph, Hyrum, Brigham, Willard, & Sis Thompson [shorthand symbol].- & Heber & Newel K. present also Joseph & James Adams singing & prayer by Elder Brigham Young - Conversation & instruction - & teaching concerning the things of God. had a pleasant interview.

These two entries are practically meaningless as they stand and are easily passed over. Even when one translates Richards's shorthand to discover the words "were married," the record makes no sense because the people referred to had already been married. Not until other sources are consulted does one learn that Richards had recorded the first eternal marriage sealings, an important ordinance connected with the temple and the building of the latter-day Zion.

Still engaged in keeping Joseph Smith's journal on March 10, 1844, Richards recorded a meeting of the Twelve and others at the Nauvoo Mansion, where letters of Lyman Wight "about removing to the Table Lands of Saxet [Texas] &c &c -" were read. Joseph asked, "Can this council keep what I say, not make it Public? all held up their hands." Richards then jotted disconnected phrases: "copy the constitution of the U.S.," "hands of a select committee," "No law can be enacted but what every man can be protected from.-" "grant their petition, go ahead concerning the indians & southern states &c." There was talk of sending men to Santa Fe "and if Notsuoh [Houston] will embrace the gospel.-"

> can amend that constitution & make it the voice of Jehovah and shame the U.S. Parley Pratt in favor. Hyrum concurred.- said Joseph. let us adjourn till after supper - to the school room.-

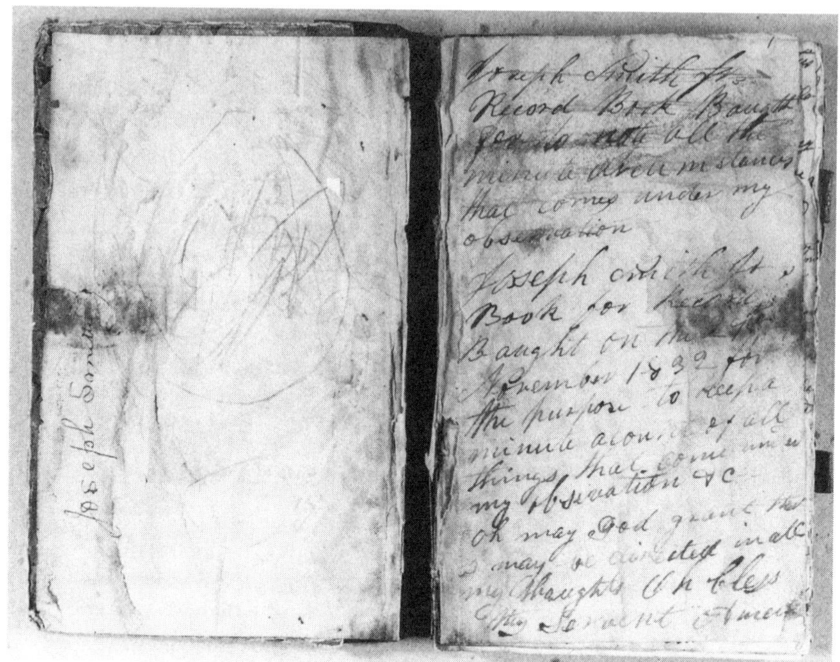

Joseph Smith Jrs
Record Book Baught
for to note all the
minute circumstances
that comes under my
observation
Joseph Smith Jrs
Book for Record
Baught on the 27th of
November 1832 for
the purpose to keep a
minute account of all
things that come under
my observation &c
Oh may God grant that
I may be directed in all
my thaughts Oh bless
thy Servent Amen

Joseph Smith Jr.'s beginning journal entry, November 27, 1832, written in his own hand. Courtesy LDS Church Archives.

Saturday May 27. 1843
2 P.M. the twelve were in Council on B. Winchester. Joseph. Hyrum. & Young. Adams. & [illegible] Whitney & Sister Emma. Adams & [illegible] & G. J. Adams & others. Winchester was silenced. See minutes of the twelve. adjourned to Monday 6 P.M. A tremendous rain storm. all day commencing with thunder in the morning. Joseph instructed the Twelve to call up the whole Philadelphia Church— while in the council

Sunday May 28.
Cloudy & rain.— cold.—
5 P.M.— adjourned council met in the upper Room. attened to ordinances and counselled and prayed that James Adams might be delivered from his enemies &c. O. P. Rockwell, & the twelve be prospered in collecting means to build the Nauvoo House Joseph— & J. Adams or o[illegible] &c [illegible].—

Joseph Smith Jr. journal, May 27–28, 1843, in the handwriting of Willard Richards. Courtesy LDS Church Archives.

> 7 eve assembled at the assembly room over the store, Joseph. Hyrum. Brigham 12. Temple committee. Phelps. A. Fielding, J. Phelps. Wasson, Evening - in council over the store.

The following day, March 11, the council met again: "At home 9. AM. in council in Lodge room . . . P.M. in council same place.-" These entries document the beginnings of the Council of Fifty, another feature in Joseph Smith's plan for Zion.[43] But clearly other sources are needed to make them meaningful.

Missing from the report of these events is not only information to properly identify what is taking place, but also explanations that relate them to "the cause of Zion." The absence of Joseph Smith's own expressions from a key historical record bearing his name means that the one voice central to historical understanding is unavailable. Furthermore, the absence of Joseph's voice magnifies the voices of hostility that were loudly proclaiming against him and distorting his agenda.[44]

Published Editions of Joseph Smith's Papers

A study of Joseph Smith sources would not be complete without a look at published editions of his personal papers. Historical editing, as it has developed in recent decades, is the process of reproducing in type a person's writings, sometimes with explanatory annotations and footnotes to help the reader better understand original sources in their historical context. The value of documentary editions lies in making the sources more accessible and understandable. During the one hundred and fifty years since Joseph Smith's death, several works have been published or are in the process of publication:

Smith, Joseph, Jr. *History of The Church of Jesus Christ of Latter-day Saints.* Ed. by James Mulholland, Robert B. Thompson, William W. Phelps, Willard Richards, George A. Smith, Wilford Woodruff, and later, B. H. Roberts. 6 vols. Salt Lake City: Deseret Book, 1912.

Smith, Joseph Fielding, comp. and ed. *Teachings of the Prophet Joseph Smith.* Salt Lake City: Deseret News Press, 1938.

Nelson, Leland R., comp. *The Journal of Joseph: The Personal Diary of a Modern Prophet by Joseph Smith, Jr.* Provo, Utah: Council Press, 1979.

Ehat, Andrew F., and Lyndon W. Cook., comps. and eds. *The Words of Joseph Smith: The Contemporary Accounts of the Nauvoo Discourses of the Prophet Joseph.* Provo, Utah: Religious Studies Center, Brigham Young University, 1980.

Cook, Lyndon W. *The Revelations of the Prophet Joseph Smith.* Provo, Utah: Seventy's Mission Bookstore, 1981.

Jessee, Dean C., comp. and ed. *Personal Writings of Joseph Smith.* Salt Lake City: Deseret Book, 1984.

Faulring, Scott H., comp. and ed. *An American Prophet's Record: The Diaries and Journals of Joseph Smith.* Salt Lake City: Signature Books, 1987.

Jessee, Dean C., comp. and ed. *The Papers of Joseph Smith.* 2 vols. to date. Salt Lake City: Deseret Book, 1989–.

The *History of the Church* was the first major attempt to publish Joseph Smith's papers at least in part. The work, which began in 1838 under Joseph's direction, used materials from his diaries, correspondence, revelations, reports of discourses, and other documents of importance. It was compiled and edited largely by Willard Richards, George A. Smith, and Wilford Woodruff.[45] The *History* continues to be the single most important published source for the study of Joseph Smith's life.

The daily diary-type narrative of the *History* primarily follows the Prophet's own autobiographical writings and journals. However, the compilers bridged gaps in the Smith journals by using other persons' diaries or writings, sometimes changing them from third person to first person to maintain the style of personal Joseph Smith authorship. Editorial methods of the time not only permitted such liberty, but allowed for other alteration and modernization of original textual material such as correcting grammar, spelling, and punctuation, and in some instances adding to and deleting from the original content. Furthermore, the editors did not always distinguish material written personally by the Prophet from that written by others for him. Consequently, while the *History* remains a valuable work for the study of Joseph Smith, the original sources upon which it is based must be consulted for questions involving accuracy of the text and the degree of Joseph Smith's personal involvement.

The *History* was originally published serially beginning in the *Times and Seasons* and *LDS Millennial Star* in 1842, during Joseph Smith's lifetime, and continued in the *Deseret News* and *Millennial Star* after his death. The serialized installments of the *History* were later edited by B. H. Roberts at the beginning of the twentieth century for publication in their present multivolume format.

Teachings of the Prophet Joseph Smith is a chronological compilation of primarily doctrinal statements excerpted from sermons, letters, and other writings of Joseph Smith. The materials in this volume were taken mainly from the *History of the Church* but also include extracts from other early Church works including the *Evening and the Morning Star, LDS Messenger and Advocate,* "Far West Record," *Times and Seasons,* the Journal History of the Church, and a few manuscript sources. *Teachings* was produced to provide a more comprehensive collection of the Prophet's doctrinal statements than was contained in Edwin F. Parry's little compilation, *Joseph Smith's Teachings: A Classified Arrangement of the Doctrinal Sermons and Writings of the Great Latter-day Prophet* (Salt Lake City: Deseret News, 1912). Consequently, "historical matters and incidental or unimportant matters"[46] were left out of *Teachings,* as were revelations and articles readily available to the Latter-day Saints, such as Joseph Smith's account of his early visions that had been published in tract form and in the Pearl of Great Price. To facilitate topical study, *Teachings* provided subject headings in the text and an "exhaustive index."[47]

The Journal of Joseph claims to present "the personal journal or diary of Joseph Smith Junior"[48] containing "Joseph's own personal account of his feelings, revelations, persecutions, disappointments, accomplishments and day-to-day happenings."[49] The compiler claims to have assembled together "into one handy volume the great majority of Joseph's personal journal entries."[50] In reality, the volume is not a publication of Joseph Smith's original journals; rather, it is a republication of daily entries extracted from the *History of the Church* and suffers the limitations which that work imposes.[51]

The Words of Joseph Smith, as stated in the book's subtitle, is a collection of speeches given by the Prophet during the Nauvoo years (1839–44). Because no written drafts or verbatim reports of the speeches exist, *The Words of Joseph Smith* depends upon written reports by clerks or witnesses. The reports vary in completeness and accuracy. When the speeches were prepared for publication in the *History of the Church,* the editors did their best to flesh out and refine the original reports. In some instances, the speeches as published in the *History* closely parallel the original reports; in others, editors inserted phrases and sentences to bridge disconnected thoughts. In instances where more than one report of a discourse existed, the reports were carefully compared and amalgamated to produce the published version. *The Words of Joseph Smith* is an attempt to publish the original longhand reports as they read before being edited for publication in the *History.* The editors promise "a faithful copy of the original reports," including "original spelling, punctuation, and paragraphing."[52] A comparison of the published work with original sources shows general compliance with this editorial rule. The volume also contains valuable explanatory notes.

The Revelations of the Prophet Joseph Smith is a historical and biographical commentary of all Doctrine and Covenants revelations. The volume does not contain the text of the revelations, nor does it include revelations not in the Doctrine and Covenants. Each person mentioned in the Doctrine and Covenants is identified with a substantial biographical summary. Furthermore, historical background is provided for each section.

The Personal Writings of Joseph Smith is an attempt to publish everything written in Joseph Smith's own hand. In addition, the volume contains other material Joseph is known to have dictated. Because most of the writings bearing Joseph Smith's name were written by others for him, *Personal Writings* contains that portion of his papers that most clearly reflects his own mind and personality. These papers include the first two of his twelve journals, four autobiographical writings, and eighty-eight pieces of correspondence. Some of these writings were not available when the *History of the Church* was produced. In essence, *Personal Writings* is a one-volume collection of core material from the projected multivolume *Papers of Joseph Smith* and includes photographs of all Joseph Smith holographic material. Based upon the assumption that a person's handwriting—including punctuation and spelling—is the fullest expression of personality, *Personal Writings* presents the text of original manuscripts as accurately as typography will allow. Annotations, explanatory notes, photographs, and maps help place the sources in their historical context. Researchers should know, however, that six documents included in this volume were later determined to be Mark Hofmann forgeries.[53]

An American Prophet's Record is an attempt to publish the original handwritten journals of Joseph Smith as they read before being edited for the *History of the Church.* However, because the editor produced the work from a microfilm copy without access to the original manuscripts housed in the LDS Church Archives, the volume comes short of its goal, both in completeness and accuracy. The edition does not include a large 1842 journal that was missing from the microfilm source. The editor sought to present the diaries in a "readable format,"[54] which included correcting and altering spelling, punctuation, and capitalization—a procedure that leaves some uncertainty as to how the original text actually reads. To compensate for the journal missing from the microfilm, the editor copied selections from *Personal Writings, The Words of Joseph Smith,* and *History of the Church* to approximate the missing text. The volume identifies prominent people and provides a useful chronology of Joseph Smith's life. Suggesting that some documentary publications "display an inordinate, unwarranted amount of document annotation,"[55] the editor has reserved "for the interested reader the task of providing supplementary historical and biographical context."[56] The first 158 pages published here, which include the Prophet's 1832 History and the first two of his diaries, were previously published in *Personal Writings.*

The Papers of Joseph Smith is projected to be a comprehensive edition of Joseph's papers including his diaries and journals, his correspondence, revelations, discourses, and other papers. Volume 1 contains autobiographical and historical documents either written personally by Joseph, dictated to his clerks, or written by others from material Joseph provided. This volume covers events of his early life, his early religious experiences, and history of the Church. Volume 2 contains the Prophet's journals covering the period 1832 through 1842, including the 1842 journal not included in *An American Prophet's Record.* Volume 3 will include the remainder of the Joseph Smith journals to the end of his life, 1842 through 1844. The editorial rules governing this work are essentially the same as in *Personal Writings.* In addition to annotations, footnotes, maps, and charts, each volume contains a biographical register in which an attempt has been made to identify persons mentioned in the original sources. Once completed, *Papers* will contain everything that has been published in the editions listed above, with the exception of the non-Joseph Smith materials published in *History of the Church,* and the facsimile reproductions of Joseph Smith holographic material that appeared in *Personal Writings.*

To whatever extent that accuracy in preserving original sources was not a criterion for publishing them, accuracy is a problem facing those who use the modern editions of the Joseph Smith material as a substitute for the original manuscripts. Imprecise editorial rules, or the failure to use or adequately compare original manuscripts in transcribing and proofing texts, renders some modern editions less than dependable. Consequently, to determine whether or not a given edition provides an acceptable standard of accuracy, the user should compare the edited version with an original manuscript or two.

In conclusion, if the modern literary portrait of Joseph Smith is to be more accurate than the early graphic images of him that graced the walls of the old Salt Lake City meetinghouse, the material that pertains to the study of Joseph Smith, whether original sources or edited publications, presents a number of challenges that the user must consider in order to obtain the best picture the sources will allow.

Dean C. Jessee is Senior Research Historian with the Joseph Fielding Smith Institute for Church History at Brigham Young University.

NOTES

[1]*Salt Lake Herald,* December 24, 1894. Patriarch John Smith and Angus M. Cannon, who also spoke on the occasion, echoed Bathsheba Smith's observation. Others in the nineteenth century were equally unimpressed by the pictorial record. Alfred B. Lambson noted of Joseph, "there are no pictures that do justice to him." See "Alfred Boaz Lambson," *Utah Genealogical and Historical Magazine* 6 (1915): 148.

On the visual image of Joseph Smith, see Marba C. Josephson, "What Did the Prophet Joseph Smith Look Like?" *Improvement Era* 56 (May 1953): 311-15, 371-75; Doyle Green, "Are These Portraits of the Prophet Joseph Smith?" *Improvement Era* 69 (December 1966): 1074-77; Lewis Taylor, "Joseph the Prophet: A Self-Portrait," *Ensign* 3 (June 1973): 40-44; Ephraim Hatch, "What Did Joseph Smith Look Like?" *Ensign* 11 (March 1981): 65-73; William B. McCarl, "The Visual Image of Joseph Smith" (master's thesis, Brigham Young University, 1962); and Lorie Winder, "In Search of the Real Joseph Smith," *Sunstone* 5 (November/December 1980): 30-34.

[2]"Church History," *Times and Seasons* 3 (March 1, 1842): 707; see also Dean C. Jessee, ed., *The Personal Writings of Joseph Smith* (Salt Lake City: Deseret Book, 1984), 214.

[3]See Jeffery O. Johnson, *Register of the Joseph Smith Collection in the Church Archives* (N.p., 1973).

[4]By contrast, the Abraham Lincoln legal papers alone contain more than sixty thousand items. The James Madison papers are projected for 60 volumes; the Jefferson Papers, 83 volumes; the George Washington Papers, 75 volumes; and the Papers of Benjamin Franklin, 50 volumes. *The Papers of Joseph Smith* are currently being published by Deseret Book, Salt Lake City, under the direction of the Joseph Fielding Smith Institute for Church History at Brigham Young University.

[5]See Donald Q. Cannon and Lyndon W. Cook, eds., *Far West Record: Minutes of The Church of Jesus Christ of Latter-day Saints, 1830-1844* (Salt Lake City: Deseret Book, 1983).

[6]John Whitmer, "The Book of John Whitmer," RLDS Church Archives, Independence, Missouri. The Whitmer manuscript is published in F. Mark McKiernon and Roger D. Launius, *An Early Latter Day Saint History: The Book of John Whitmer* (Independence, Mo.: Herald House, 1980).

[7]With the exception of the John Whitmer History, all of the foregoing records are in the Archives Division, Church Historical Department, The Church of Jesus Christ of Latter-day Saints, Salt Lake City (LDS Church Archives).

[8]Walter A. Norton, "Comparative Images: Mormonism and Contemporary Religions as Seen by Village Newspapermen in Western New York and Northeastern Ohio, 1820-1833" (Ph.D. diss., Brigham Young University, 1991), 33-35, 42, 44-45.

[9]Norton, "Comparative Images," 48-50.

[10]Lucy Smith, *Biographical Sketches of Joseph Smith the Prophet and His Progenitors for Many Generations* (Liverpool: Published for Orson Pratt by S. W. Richards, 1853). Also informative is William Smith, *William Smith on Mormonism* (Lamoni, Iowa: Herald Steam Book and Job Office, 1883).

[11]In a father's blessing dated December 9, 1834, the elder Smith stated, among other things:

> The Lord thy God has called thee by name out of the heavens: thou hast heard his voice from on high from time to time, even in thy youth. The hand of the angel of his presence has been extended toward thee by which thou hast been lifted up and sustained; yea, the Lord has delivered thee from the hands of thine enemies . . . , thou hast sought to know his ways, and from thy childhood thou hast meditated much upon the great things of his law. Thou hast suffered much in thy youth; and the poverty and afflictions of thy father's family have been a grief to thy soul. Thou hast desired to see them delivered from bondage, for thou hast lov'd them with a perfect love. Thou hast stood by thy father. . . . Thou hast been an obedient son: the commands of thy father and the reproofs of thy mother, thou hast respected and obeyed. . . . Thou hast been called, even in thy youth to the great work of the Lord: to do a work in this generation which no other man would do as thyself. ("The Book of Patriarchal Blessings, 1834," p. 3, LDS Church Archives.)

[12]Richard P. Howard, ed., *The Memoirs of President Joseph Smith III (1832-1914): A Photo-Reprint Edition of the Original Serial Publication as Edited by Mary Audentia Smith Anderson and Appearing in the Saints' Herald (November 6, 1934-July 31, 1937)* (Independence, Mo.: Herald House, 1979).

[13]Correspondence of Joseph Smith to his wife Emma is in Jessee, *Personal Writings;* see also the Emma Hale Smith Papers at the RLDS Archives in Independence, Missouri.

[14]John M. Bernhisel to Thomas Ford, June 14, 1844, Bernhisel Collection, LDS Church Archives; see also *History of the Church* 6:467-68.

[15]For information about Richards's work in writing the *History of the Church,* see Dean C. Jessee, "The Writing of Joseph Smith's History," *BYU Studies* 11 (Summer 1971): 439-73. Richards's diary is in the Willard Richards Papers, LDS Church Archives. For his work in writing Joseph Smith's journals, see *Papers of Joseph Smith* 2:334-35.

[16]The Clayton diary is in the LDS Church Archives. For Clayton's writing in Joseph Smith's journal, see *The Papers of Joseph Smith* 2:395-506. See also James B. Allen, *Trials of Discipleship: The Story of William Clayton, a Mormon* (Urbana: University of Illinois Press, 1987).

[17]The Woodruff diary is in the LDS Church Archives; see also Wilford Woodruff, *Wilford Woodruff's Journal, 1833-1898 Typescript,* ed. Scott G. Kenney, 9 vols. (Midvale, Utah: Signature Books, 1983-84). See also Thomas G. Alexander, *Things in Heaven and Earth: The Life and Times of Wilford Woodruff, a Mormon Prophet* (Salt Lake City: Signature Books, 1991).

[18]See the Papers of Oliver Cowdery, LDS Church Archives; see also, Lyndon W. Cook, ed., *David Whitmer Interviews* (Orem, Utah: Grandin Book, 1991); and Dean C. Jessee, "Joseph Knight's Recollection of Early Mormon History," *BYU Studies* 17 (Autumn 1976): 29-39. The most comprehensive study of the sources pertaining to pre-1830 events involving the Book of Mormon

witnesses is Richard L. Anderson, *Investigating the Book of Mormon Witnesses* (Salt Lake City: Deseret Book, 1981).

[19]"The Book of Patriarchal Blessings, 1834," pp. 8–9, LDS Church Archives; see also the Papers of Oliver Cowdery.

[20]See the following sources in the LDS Church Archives: George A. Smith, "Memoirs of George Albert Smith"; Heber C. Kimball, "The Journal and Record of Heber Chase Kimball"; Diary of Wilford Woodruff; and Wilford Woodruff, "The History and Travels of Zion's Camp."

[21]See Parley P. Pratt, *History of the Late Persecutions Inflicted by the State of Missouri upon the Mormons* (Detroit: Dawson and Bates, Printers, 1839); papers of Hyrum Smith, LDS Church Archives and Harold B. Lee Library, Brigham Young University, Provo, Utah; Alexander McRae, "Incidents in the History of Joseph Smith," *Deseret News,* November 2 and 9, 1854.

[22]John Taylor's account of the last days at Carthage was first published in Richard F. Burton, *The City of the Saints and across the Rocky Mountains to California* (London: Longman, Green, Longman, and Roberts, 1862); see also *History of the Church* 7:55–126; Cyrus Wheelock to George A. Smith, December 29, 1854, LDS Church Archives; Dan Jones, "The Martyrdom of Joseph and Hyrum Smith," January 20, 1855, LDS Church Archives; and John S. Fullmer, *Assassination of Joseph and Hyrum Smith, the Prophet and the Patriarch of The Church of Jesus Christ of Latter-day Saints, also a Condensed History of the Expulsion of the Saints from Nauvoo* (Liverpool, 1855).

[23]A non-Mormon reaction is the letter of Mathew L. Davis to his wife, February 6, 1840, published in *History of the Church* 4:78–80. Other accounts of this genre are in Hyrum L. Andrus and Helen Mae Andrus, *They Knew the Prophet* (Salt Lake City: Bookcraft, 1974); Milton V. Backman Jr., comp., with Keith Perkins, "Writings of Early Latter-day Saints and Their Contemporaries: A Database Collection," Brigham Young University; and Davis Bitton, *Guide to Mormon Diaries and Autobiographies* (Provo, Utah: Brigham Young University Press, 1977).

[24]"A Biographical Sketch of the Life of Jonathan Crosby Writen [*sic*] by Himself," 13–14, Utah State Historical Society, Salt Lake City.

[25]*Sangamo Journal,* August 19, 1842. The letter began, "Happiness is the object and design of our existence, and will be the end thereof if we pursue the path that leads to it; and this path is virtue, uprightness, faithfulness, holiness, and keeping all the commandments of God." See also Jessee, *Personal Writings,* 506–9, 689; and *History of the Church* 5:134–36.

[26]John Corrill, *Brief History of the Church of Christ of Latter Day Saints* (St. Louis: By the author, 1839).

[27]In this vast literature are such diverse studies as David Freeman Hawke, *Everyday Life in Early America* (New York: Harper and Row, 1988); Eric Sloane, *Diary of an Early American Boy: Noah Blake, 1805* (New York: Ballantine Books, 1965); Paul W. Gates, *The Farmer's Age: Agriculture 1815–1860* (New York: Holt, Rinehart, and Winston, 1962); Robert H. George, "Life on a New Hampshire Farm, 1825–1835," *Historical New Hampshire* 22 (Winter 1967): 3–16; Jon Butler, "Magic, Astrology, and the Early American Religious Heritage, 1600–1760," *American Historical Review* 84 (April 1979): 317–46; Sarah F. McMahon, "A Comfortable Subsistence: The Changing Composition of Diet in Rural New England, 1620–1840," *William and Mary Quarterly* 42 (January 1985): 26–65; Russell M. Jones, "American Doctors and the Parisian Medical World, 1830–1840,"

Bulletin of the History of Medicine 47 (January-February 1973): 40-65; and Elizabeth Casper Brown, "The Bar on a Frontier: Wayne County, 1796-1836," *American Journal of Legal History* 14 (April 1970): 136-56.

[28]See Dean C. Jessee, "Joseph Smith and the Beginning of Mormon Record Keeping," in *The Prophet Joseph Smith: Essays on the Life and Mission of Joseph Smith,* ed. Larry C. Porter and Susan Easton Black (Salt Lake City: Deseret Book, 1988); and Dean C. Jessee, "Priceless Words and Fallible Memories: Joseph Smith as Seen in the Effort to Preserve His Discourses," *BYU Studies* 31 (Spring 1991): 19-40.

[29]*Papers of Joseph Smith* 1:277-78; and *History of the Church* 1:11-12.

[30]*Papers of Joseph Smith* 1:267; and *History of the Church* 1:1. Joseph justified the writing of his history to Oliver Cowdery in 1834 stating, "I have learned that many of the opposers of those principles which I have held forth to the world, profess a personal acquaintance with me though when [not] in my presence, represent me to be another person in age, education, and stature, from what I am." Joseph Smith to Oliver Cowdery, *Latter Day Saints' Messenger and Advocate* 1 (December 1834): 40; see also *Papers of Joseph Smith* 1:13.

[31]*Papers of Joseph Smith* 1:384; and *History of the Church* 1:273.

[32]*The Wayne Sentinel* (Palmyra, New York), June 26, 1829.

[33]Norton, "Comparative Images," 244. During the 1829 printing of the Book of Mormon at the Egbert B. Grandin press in Palmyra, New York, local newspaper editor Abner Cole used the same press during off hours to publish his *Reflector.* Having access to the print shop, Cole also saw printed pages of the Book of Mormon before its March 1830 publication. He took the liberty to pirate pages and print them in his paper in January 1830. After being forced by Joseph Smith's threat of a lawsuit to desist from his unauthorized publishing venture, Cole lashed back in the pages of his paper with a disparaging attack against the Prophet. Cole characterized Joseph as ignorant and lazy and portrayed the Book of Mormon as a product of magic and superstition. His work established him as the father of anti-Mormon literature. On Cole, see Joseph W. Banner, "Obediah Dogberry: Rochester Free-Thinker," *Rochester History* 36 (July 1974): 1-24.

[34]Bennett relied heavily upon the Hurlbut/Howe material before adding his own dimension. See John C. Bennett, *History of the Saints: An Exposé of Joe Smith and Mormonism* (Boston: Leland and Whiting, 1842).

[35]Thomas Sharp's vitriolic reaction to Joseph Smith is in the pages of his *Warsaw* (Illinois) *Signal* in 1843-44.

[36]See Smith, *Biographical Sketches,* 148-50; and *Reflector* (Palmyra, New York), June 12, July 7, 1830; February 1, 14, 28, 1831.

[37]For an assessment of the Hurlbut/Howe evidence, see Richard Lloyd Anderson, "Joseph Smith's New York Reputation Reappraised," *BYU Studies* 10 (Spring 1970): 283-314.

[38]Journal of Joseph Smith, March 4, 1843; see also *History of the Church* 5:289.

[39]See Jessee, "Priceless Words and Fallible Memories."

[40]On Joseph Smith's mission, see Ronald K. Esplin, "Joseph, Brigham, and the Twelve: A Succession of Continuity," *BYU Studies* 21 (Summer 1981): 301-41; Ronald K. Esplin, "Joseph Smith's Mission and Timetable: 'God Will Protect Me until My Work Is Done,'" in *The Prophet Joseph Smith,* 280-319; and Ronald K. Esplin, "The Significance of Nauvoo for Latter-day Saints," *Journal of Mormon History* 16 (1990): 71-86.

[41]Doctrine and Covenants 21:7; and Book of Commandments 22:8.

[42]Doctrine and Covenants 24:7, 9; and Book of Commandments 25:12–14.

[43]For clarification here, see D. Michael Quinn, "The Council of Fifty and Its Members, 1844–1945," *BYU Studies* 20 (Winter 1980): 163–97.

[44]Absent from Joseph Smith's Nauvoo journals is the personal dimension illustrated in his holograph writings, such as this one: "I was awoke by Brother Davis knocking at my door saying Brother Joseph come git up and see the signs in the heavens and I arrose and beheld to my great Joy the stars fall from heaven yea they fell like hail stones a litteral fullfillment of the word of God as recorded in the holy scriptures and a sure sign that the coming of Christ is clost at hand Oh how marvellous are thy works Oh Lord and I thank thee for thy mercy unto me thy servent Oh Lord save me in thy kingdom for Christ sake Amen." See Diary of Joseph Smith, November 13, 1833; and *Papers of Joseph Smith* 2:10–11.

[45]On the writing and publication of the history, see Jessee, "Writing of Joseph Smith's History"; and Jessee, "The Reliability of Joseph Smith's History," *Journal of Mormon History* 3 (1976): 23–46; see also Howard C. Searle, "Early Mormon Historiography: Writing the History of the Mormons, 1830–1858" (Ph.D. diss., UCLA, 1979); and Howard C. Searle, "Willard Richards as Historian," *BYU Studies* 31 (Spring 1991): 41–62.

[46]Smith, *Teachings,* 3.

[47]Smith, *Teachings,* 3.

[48]Nelson, *Journal of Joseph,* ii.

[49]Nelson, *Journal of Joseph,* ii.

[50]Nelson, *Journal of Joseph,* ii.

[51]See Howard C. Searle, "The Authorship of the History of Joseph Smith: A Review Essay," *BYU Studies* 21 (Winter 1981): 101–22.

[52]Ehat and Cook, *Words of Joseph,* xxiii.

[53]The six Hofmann forgeries in *Personal Writings* are the Note on Anthon Transcript, February 1828, pp. 223–25; Joseph Smith to Emma Smith, March 6, 1833, pp. 277–78; Joseph Smith to Hyrum Smith, May 25, 1838, pp. 358–59; the Joseph Smith III Blessing, January 17, 1844, pp. 565–66; Joseph Smith to Maria and Sarah Lawrence, June 23, 1844, p. 598; and Joseph Smith to Jonathan Dunham, June 27, 1844, pp. 616–18.

Summaries of the Hofmann case are in Richard E. Turley Jr., *Victims: The LDS Church and the Mark Hofmann Case* (Urbana: University of Illinois Press, 1992); Linda Sillitoe and Allen D. Roberts, *Salamander: The Story of the Mormon Forgery Murders* (Salt Lake City: Signature Books, 1988); Robert Lindsey, *A Gathering of Saints: A True Story of Money, Murder, and Deceit* (New York: Simon and Schuster, 1988); see also David J. Whittaker, "The Hofmann Maze: A Book Review Essay with a Chronology and Bibliography of the Hofmann Case," *BYU Studies* 29 (Winter 1989): 67–124.

[54]Faulring, *An American Prophet's Record,* xv.

[55]Faulring, *An American Prophet's Record,* xx.

[56]Faulring, *An American Prophet's Record,* xx.

Joseph Smith in Recent Research: A Selected Bibliography

David J. Whittaker

The Records of His Life

Diaries and Holographic Writings

Berrett, LaMar C. "An Impressive Letter from the Pen of Joseph Smith." *BYU Studies* 11 (Summer 1971): 517–23. Letter to Emma dated June 6, 1832, Greenville, Indiana.

Bushman, Richard L. "The Character of Joseph Smith: Insights from His Holographs." *Ensign* 7 (April 1977): 10–13.

Faulring, Scott H., ed. *An American Prophet's Record: The Diaries and Journals of Joseph Smith.* Salt Lake City: Signature Books in association with Smith Research Associates, 1989.

Jessee, Dean C. *The Papers of Joseph Smith.* 2 vols. Salt Lake City: Deseret Book, 1989, 1992. Ongoing project.

———. *The Personal Writings of Joseph Smith.* Salt Lake City: Deseret Book, 1984.

Jessee, Dean C., and William G. Hartley. "Joseph Smith's Missionary Journal." *New Era* 4 (February 1974): 34–36.

King, Arthur Henry. "Joseph Smith as a Writer." In *The Abundance of the Heart,* 198–205. Salt Lake City: Bookcraft, 1986.

Partridge, Elinore H. "Characteristics of Joseph Smith's Style and Notes on the Authorship of the Lectures on Faith." In *Task Papers in LDS History,* no. 14, 1–29. Salt Lake City: Historical Department of The Church of Jesus Christ of Latter-day Saints, 1976. See also Partridge, "Nineteenth-Century Spelling: The Rules and the Writers." *Ensign* 5 (August 1975): 74–80.

Revelations

Clark, James R. *The Story of the Pearl of Great Price.* Salt Lake City: Bookcraft, 1955.

Cook, Lyndon W. *The Revelations of the Prophet Joseph Smith.* Provo, Utah: Seventy's Mission Bookstore, 1981.

Howard, Richard P. *Restoration Scriptures: A Study of Their Textual Development.* Independence, Mo.: Herald House, 1969.

Jessee, Dean C. "The Original Book of Mormon Manuscript." *BYU Studies* 10 (Spring 1970): 259–78.

Larson, Stan. "A Study of Some Textual Variations in the Book of Mormon. . . ." Master's thesis, Brigham Young University, 1974.

Matthews, Robert J. *"A Plainer Translation": Joseph Smith's Translation of the Bible, a History and Commentary.* Provo, Utah: Brigham Young University Press, 1975.

Nibley, Hugh W. "A New Look at the Pearl of Great Price." *Improvement Era* 71–73 (January 1968–May 1970).

Reynolds, Noel B., ed. *Book of Mormon Authorship.* Provo, Utah: Religious Studies Center, Brigham Young University, 1982.

Sorenson, John L. *An Ancient American Setting for the Book of Mormon.* Salt Lake City: Deseret Book; Provo, Utah: F.A.R.M.S., 1985.

Stocks, Hugh G. "The Book of Mormon, 1830–1979: A Publishing History." Master's thesis, UCLA, 1979.

Vogel, Dan, ed. *The Word of God: Essays on Mormon Scripture.* Salt Lake City: Signature Books, 1990.

Whittaker, David J. "Substituted Names in the Published Revelations of Joseph Smith." *BYU Studies* 23 (Winter 1983): 103–12.

Woodford, Robert J. "The Historical Development of the Doctrine and Covenants." Ph.D. diss., Brigham Young University, 1974.

Sermons/Discourses

Burton, Alma P., comp. *Discourses of the Prophet Joseph Smith.* 3d ed. Salt Lake City: Deseret Book, 1968. Arranged topically.

Cannon, Donald Q., Larry E. Dahl, and John W. Welch. "The Restoration of Major Doctrines through Joseph Smith." Parts 1 and 2. *Ensign* 19 (January 1989): 26–33; (February 1989): 6–13.

Dahl, Larry E., and Charles D. Tate Jr., eds. *The Lectures on Faith in Historical Perspective.* Religious Studies Center Monograph Series, vol. 15. Provo, Utah: Religious Studies Center, Brigham Young University, 1990.

Ehat, Andrew F., and Lyndon W. Cook, eds. *The Words of Joseph Smith: The Contemporary Accounts of the Nauvoo Discourses of the Prophet Joseph.* Provo, Utah: Religious Studies Center, Brigham Young University, 1980. Texts of 173 addresses.

Godfrey, Kenneth W. "A New Look at an Alleged Little Known Discourse by Joseph Smith." *BYU Studies* 9 (Autumn 1968): 49–53. Compare Lawrence Foster, "A Little-Known Defense of

Polygamy from the Mormon Press in 1842." *Dialogue: A Journal of Mormon Thought* 9 (Winter 1974): 21-34.

Jessee, Dean C. "Joseph Smith's 19 July 1840 Discourse." *BYU Studies* 19 (Spring 1979): 390-94.

———. "Priceless Words and Fallible Memories: Joseph Smith as Seen in the Effort to Preserve His Discourses." *BYU Studies* 31 (Spring 1991): 19-40.

King Follett Discourse [April 7, 1844]: see the articles in *BYU Studies* 18 (Winter 1978): 179-225.

Madsen, Truman G., ed. *The Concordance of the Doctrinal Statements of Joseph Smith.* Salt Lake City: I.E.S. Publishing, 1985.

Millet, Robert L., ed. *Joseph Smith: Selected Sermons and Writings.* Mahwah, N.J.: Paulist Press, 1989.

Smith, Joseph Fielding, comp. *Teachings of the Prophet Joseph Smith.* Salt Lake City: Deseret Book, 1938. Arranged chronologically.

"History of Joseph Smith"

Jessee, Dean C. "The Reliability of Joseph Smith's History." *Journal of Mormon History* 3 (1976): 23-46.

———. "The Writing of Joseph Smith's History." *BYU Studies* 11 (Summer 1971): 439-73.

Searle, Howard C. "Authorship of the History of Joseph Smith: A Review Essay." *BYU Studies* 21 (Winter 1981): 101-22.

———. "Early Mormon Historiography: Writing the History of the Mormons, 1830-1858." Ph.D. diss., UCLA, 1979.

Visual Portrayals

Anderson, Lavina Fielding. "139-Year-Old Portraits of Joseph and Emma Smith." *Ensign* 11 (March 1981): 62-64.

Green, Doyle L. "Are These Portraits of the Prophet Joseph Smith?" *Improvement Era* 69 (December 1966): 1074-77.

Hatch, Ephraim. "What Did Joseph Smith Look Like?" *Ensign* 11 (March 1981): 65-73.

Josephson, Marba C. "What Did the Prophet Joseph Smith Look Like?" *Improvement Era* 56 (May 1953): 311-15, 371-75.

McCarl, William B. "The Visual Image of Joseph Smith." Master's thesis, Brigham Young University, 1962.

Taylor, J. Lewis. "Joseph the Prophet: A Self-Portrait." *Ensign* 3 (June 1973): 40-44.

Winder, Lorie. "The Search for the Real Joseph Smith." *Sunstone* 5 (November/December 1980): 30-34.

His Life and Times

Historiography

Alexander, Thomas G. "The Place of Joseph Smith in the Development of American Religion: A Historiographical Inquiry." *Journal of Mormon History* 5 (1978): 3-17.

Anderson, Richard Lloyd. "Joseph Smith's New York Reputation Reappraised." *BYU Studies* 10 (Spring 1970): 283-314.

Green, Arnold H., and Lawrence P. Goldrup. "Joseph Smith, an American Muhammad? An Essay on the Perils of Historical Analogy." *Dialogue* 6 (Spring 1971): 46-58.

Hill, Marvin S. "Joseph Smith the Man: Some Reflections on a Subject of Controversy." *BYU Studies* 21 (Spring 1981): 175-86.

———. "The 'Prophet Puzzle' Assembled; or, How to Treat Our Historical Diplopia toward Joseph Smith." *Journal of Mormon History* 3 (1976): 101-5.

Shipps, Jan. "The Prophet Puzzle: Suggestions Leading toward a More Comprehensive Interpretation of Joseph Smith." *Journal of Mormon History* 1 (1974): 3-20.

Joseph Smith's America

Anderson, Richard Lloyd. "The Mature Joseph Smith and Treasure Searching." *BYU Studies* 24 (Fall 1984): 489-560.

Backman, Milton V., Jr. *American Religions and the Rise of Mormonism.* Salt Lake City: Deseret Book, 1965.

Brooke, John L. *The Refiner's Fire: The Making of Mormon Cosmology, 1644-1844.* Cambridge UK: Cambridge University Press, 1994.

———. "'Of Whole Nations Being Born in One Day': Marriage, Money, and Magic in the Mormon Cosmos, 1830-1846." *Social Science Information* 30 (March 1991): 107-32.

Brown, Richard D. *Knowledge Is Power: The Diffusion of Information in Early America, 1700-1865.* New York: Oxford University Press, 1989.

Butler, Jon Magic. "Astrology, and the Early American Religious Heritage, 1600-1760." *American Historical Review* 84 (April 1979): 317-46.

———. "The Dark Ages of American Occultism, 1760-1848." In *The Occult in America: New Historical Perspectives,* ed. by Howard Kerr and Charles L. Crow, 58-78. Urbana: University of Illinois Press, 1983.

Cross, Whitney R. *The Burned-Over District: The Social and Intellectual History of Enthusiastic Religion in Western New York, 1800–1850.* 1950. Reprint, New York: Harper and Row, 1965.

Davis, David Brion. "Some Ideological Functions of Prejudice in Ante-Bellum America." *American Quarterly* 15 (Summer 1963): 115–25.

Feldberg, Michael. *The Turbulent Era: Riot and Disorder in Jacksonian America.* New York: Oxford University Press, 1980.

Foster, Lawrence. *Religion and Sexuality: Three American Experiments in the Nineteenth Century.* New York: Oxford University Press, 1981.

Gilmore, William J. *Reading Becomes a Necessity of Life: Material and Cultural Life in Rural New England, 1780–1835.* Knoxville: University of Tennessee Press, 1989.

Grimstead, David. "Rioting in Its Jacksonian Setting." *American Historical Review* 77 (April 1972): 361–97.

Hill, Marvin S. *Quest for Refuge: The Mormon Flight from American Pluralism.* Salt Lake City: Signature Books, 1989.

Hughes, Richard T., ed. *The American Quest for the Primitive Church.* Urbana: University of Illinois Press, 1988.

Ludlum, David M. *Social Ferment in Vermont, 1791–1850.* 1939. Reprint, New York: AMS Press, 1966.

Norton, Walter A. "Comparative Images: Mormonism and Contemporary Religions as Seen by Village Newspapermen in Western New York and Northeastern Ohio, 1820–1833." Ph.D. diss., Brigham Young University, 1991.

Pessen, Edward. *Jacksonian America: Society, Personality, and Politics.* Rev. ed. Homewood, Ill.: Dorsey Press, 1978.

Paul, Robert. "Joseph Smith and the Manchester (New York) Library." *BYU Studies* 22 (Summer 1982): 333–56.

Quinn, D. Michael. *Early Mormonism and the Magic World View.* Salt Lake City: Signature Books, 1987.

Reinders, Robert. "Militia and Public Order in Nineteenth Century America." *Journal of American Studies* 11 (April 1977): 81–101.

Ricks, Stephen D., and Daniel C. Peterson. "Joseph Smith and 'Magic': Methodological Reflections on the Use of a Term." In *"To Be Learned Is Good If . . .,"* ed. by Robert L. Millett, 129–47. Salt Lake City: Bookcraft, 1987.

Saum, Lewis O. *The Popular Mood of Pre-Civil War America.* Contributions in American Studies, no. 46. Westport, Conn.: Greenwood Press, 1980.

Sellers, Charles G. *The Market Revolution: Jacksonian America, 1815-1846.* New York: Oxford University Press, 1991.

Shipps, Jan. *Mormonism: The Story of a New Religious Tradition.* Urbana: University of Illinois Press, 1985.

Taylor, Alan. "The Early Republic's Supernatural Economy: Treasure Seeking in the American Northeast, 1780-1830." *American Quarterly* 38 (Spring 1986): 6-34.

———. "Rediscovering the Context of Joseph Smith's Treasure Seeking." *Dialogue* 19 (Winter 1986): 18-28.

Tyler, Alice Felt. *Freedom's Ferment: Phases of American Social History from the Colonial Period to the Outbreak of the Civil War.* Minneapolis: University of Minneapolis Press, 1944.

Vogel, Dan. *Indian Origins and the Book of Mormon: Religious Solutions from Columbus to Joseph Smith.* Salt Lake City: Signature Books, 1986.

———. *Religious Seekers and the Advent of Mormonism.* Salt Lake City: Signature Books, 1988.

Walker, Ronald W. "Joseph Smith: The Palmyra Seer." *BYU Studies* 24 (Fall 1984): 461-72.

———. "The Persisting Idea of American Treasure Hunting," *BYU Studies* 24 (Fall 1984): 429-59.

Whittaker, David J. "Almanacs in the New England Heritage of Mormonism." *BYU Studies* 29 (Fall 1989): 89-113.

———. "The Religious Context of Mormon History: A Bibliography for the American Setting." *Mormon History Association Newsletter,* no. 45 (November 1980): 8-17.

Wiebe, Robert H. *The Opening of American Society: From the Adoption of the Constitution to the Eve of Disunion.* New York: Knopf, 1984.

Wood, Gordon S. "Evangelical America and Early Mormonism." *New York History* 61 (October 1980): 359-86.

Family

Anderson, Mary Audentia Smith. *Ancestry and Posterity of Joseph Smith and Emma Hale.* Independence, Mo.: Herald House, 1929.

Anderson, Richard Lloyd. "The Alvin Smith Story: Fact and Fiction." *Ensign* 17 (August 1987): 58-72.

———. "Heritage of a Prophet." *Ensign* 1 (February 1971): 15-19.

———. "Joseph Smith's Brothers: Nauvoo and After." *Ensign* 9 (September 1979): 30-33.

———. "Joseph Smith's Home Environment." *Ensign* 1 (July 1971): 56-59.

———. *Joseph Smith's New England Heritage: Influences of Grandfathers Solomon Mack and Asael Smith.* Salt Lake City: Deseret Book, 1971.

———. "The Reliability of the Early History of Lucy and Joseph Smith." *Dialogue* 4 (Summer 1969): 12–28.

———. "What Were Joseph Smith's Sisters Like, and What Happened to Them after the Martyrdom?" *Ensign* 9 (March 1979): 42–44.

Backman, Milton V., Jr., and James B. Allen. "Membership of Certain of Joseph Smith's Family in the Western Presbyterian Church of Palmyra." *BYU Studies* 10 (Summer 1970): 482–84.

Bennett, Archibald F. "Solomon Mack and His Family." *Improvement Era* 58–59 (September 1955–May 1956). Ongoing series.

Bushman, Richard L. *Joseph Smith and the Beginnings of Mormonism.* Urbana: University of Illinois Press, 1984.

Cannon, Donald Q. "Topsfield, Massachusetts: Ancestral Home of the Prophet Joseph Smith." *BYU Studies* 14 (Autumn 1973): 56–76.

Corbett, Pearson H. *Hyrum Smith, Patriarch.* Salt Lake City: Deseret Book, 1976.

Enders, Donald L. "A Snug Log House: A Historical Look at the Joseph Smith Sr. Family Home in Palmyra, New York." *Ensign* 15 (August 1985): 14–23.

Grant, Carter E. "The Joseph Smith Home." *Improvement Era* 62 (December 1959): 898–99, 976–80.

Launius, Roger. *Joseph Smith III, Pragmatic Prophet.* Urbana: University of Illinois Press, 1988.

McGavin, E. Cecil. *The Family of Joseph Smith.* Salt Lake City: Bookcraft, 1963.

Newell, Linda King, and Valeen Tippetts Avery. *Mormon Enigma: Emma Hale Smith, Prophet's Wife, Elect Lady, Polygamy's Foe, 1804–1879.* Garden City, New York: Doubleday, 1984.

Smith, Lucy Mack. *Biographical Sketches of Joseph Smith the Prophet, and His Progenitors for Many Generations.* London: Published for Orson Pratt by S. W. Richards, 1853. Available in many reprintings.

Wells, Junius F. "The Smith Family in Vermont." *Improvement Era* 14 (December 1910): 95–102.

First Vision

Allen, James B. "Eight Contemporary Accounts of Joseph Smith's First Vision—What Do We Learn From Them?" *Improvement Era* 73 (April 1970): 4–13.

Allen, James B. "Emergence of a Fundamental: The Expanding Role of Joseph Smith's First Vision in Mormon Religious Thought." *Journal of Mormon History* 7 (1980): 43-61.

———. "The Significance of Joseph Smith's First Vision in Mormon Thought." *Dialogue* 1 (Autumn 1966): 28-45.

Anderson, Richard Lloyd. "Circumstantial Confirmation of the First Vision through Reminiscences." *BYU Studies* 9 (Spring 1969): 373-404.

Backman, Milton V., Jr. "Confirming Witnesses of the First Vision." *Ensign* 16 (January 1986): 32-37.

———. *Joseph Smith's First Vision.* 2d ed. Salt Lake City: Bookcraft, 1980. Contains the texts of the eight known contemporary accounts, in addition to being a study of the historical context of the Vision.

———. "Joseph Smith's Recitals of the First Vision." *Ensign* 15 (January 1985): 8-17.

Bushman, Richard L. "The First Vision Revisited." *Dialogue* 4 (Spring 1969): 82-93.

Cheesman, Paul R. "An Analysis of the Accounts Relating to Joseph Smith's Early Visions." Master's thesis, Brigham Young University, 1965.

Crawley, Peter. "A Comment on Joseph Smith's Account of His First Vision and 1820 Revival." *Dialogue* 6 (Spring 1971): 106-7.

Enders, Donald L. "The Sacred Grove." *Ensign* 20 (April 1990): 14-17.

Foster, Lawrence. "First Visions: Personal Observations on Joseph Smith's Religious Experience." *Sunstone* 8 (September-October 1983): 39-43.

Hill, Marvin S. "The First Vision Controversy: A Critique and Reconciliation." *Dialogue* 15 (Summer 1982): 31-46.

———. "A Note on Joseph Smith's First Vision and Its Import in the Shaping of Early Mormonism." *Dialogue* 12 (Spring 1979): 90-99.

Howard, Richard P. "Joseph Smith's First Vision: The RLDS Tradition." *Journal of Mormon History* 7 (1980): 23-29.

Jessee, Dean C. "Early Accounts of Joseph Smith's First Vision." *BYU Studies* 9 (Spring 1969): 275-94.

Kimball, Stanley B. "A Footnote to the Problem of Dating the First Vision." *Dialogue* 5 (Winter 1970): 121-23.

Lambert, Neal E., and Richard H. Cracroft. "Literary Form and Historical Understanding: Joseph Smith's First Vision." *Journal of Mormon History* 7 (1980): 31-42.

McCollum, Adele Brannon. "The First Vision: Re-Visioning Historical Experience." In *Literature of Belief: Sacred Scripture and*

Religious Experience, ed. by Neal E. Lambert, 177–96. Provo, Utah: Religious Studies Center, Brigham Young University, 1981.

Nibley, Hugh W. "Censoring the Joseph Smith Story." *Improvement Era* 64 (July 1961): 490–92, 522, 524, 526, 528; (August 1961): 577–79, 605–9; (October 1961): 724–25, 736, 738, 740; and (November 1961): 812–13, 865–69. Also in *Tinkling Cymbals and Sounding Brass,* vol. 11 of *The Collected Works of Hugh Nibley,* 55–101. Salt Lake City: Deseret Book; Provo, Utah: F.A.R.M.S., 1991.

Olsen, Steven L. "Joseph Smith and the Structure of Mormon Identity." *Dialogue* 14 (Autumn 1981): 89–99.

Walters, Wesley P. "Joseph Smith's First Vision Revisited." *Journal of Pastoral Practice* 4 (Summer 1980): 92–109.

———. "New Light on Mormon Origins from the Palmyra Revival." *Bulletin of the Evangelical Theological Society* 10 (Fall 1967): 227–44.

Whittaker, David J. "Joseph Smith's First Vision: A Source Essay." *Mormon History Association Newsletter,* no. 42 (November 1979): 7–9.

Coming Forth of the Book of Mormon

Anderson, Richard Lloyd. "Confirming Records of Moroni's Coming." *Improvement Era* 73 (September 1970): 4–8.

———. "By the Gift and Power of God." *Ensign* 7 (September 1977): 79–85.

———. "Gold Plates and Printer's Ink." *Ensign* 6 (September 1976): 71–76.

———. *Investigating the Book of Mormon Witnesses.* Salt Lake City: Deseret Book, 1981.

———. "The Trustworthiness of Young Joseph Smith." *Improvement Era* 73 (October 1970): 82–89.

Backman, Milton V., Jr. *Eyewitness Accounts of the Restoration.* Orem, Utah: Grandin Books, 1983.

Bushman, Richard L. "The Book of Mormon and the American Revolution." *BYU Studies* 17 (Autumn 1976): 3–20.

Cook, Lyndon W., ed. *David Whitmer Interviews: A Restoration Witness.* Orem, Utah: Grandin Books, 1991.

Gunn, Stanley R. *Oliver Cowdery, Second Elder and Scribe.* Salt Lake City: Bookcraft, 1962.

Kirkham, Francis. *A New Witness for Christ in America.* Rev. ed. 2 vols. Salt Lake City: Utah Printing Co., 1959.

Metcalfe, Brent Lee, ed. *New Approaches to the Book of Mormon, Explorations in Critical Methodology.* Salt Lake City: Signature Books, 1993. Note *Review of Books on the Book of Mormon* 6, no. 1 (1994). Whole issue.

Van Wagoner, Richard, and Steven C. Walker. "Joseph Smith: 'The Gift of Seeing.'" *Dialogue* 15 (Summer 1982): 49-68.

Walker, Ronald W. "Martin Harris: Mormonism's Early Convert." *Dialogue* 19 (Winter 1986): 29-43.

Personal

Allen, James B. "Joseph Smith as a Young Man." *New Era* 1 (January 1971): 19-21.

Anderson, Richard L. "Joseph Smith's New York Reputation Reappraised." *BYU Studies* 10 (Spring 1970): 283-314.

Arrington, Leonard J. "The Human Qualities of Joseph Smith, the Prophet." *Ensign* 1 (January 1971): 35-38.

———. "Joseph Smith and the Lighter View." *New Era* 6 (August 1976): 8-13.

Conkling, J. Christopher. *A Joseph Smith Chronology.* Salt Lake City: Deseret Book, 1979.

Crawley, Peter. "The Passage of Mormon Primitivism." *Dialogue* 13 (Winter 1980): 26-37.

Hill, Marvin S. "Joseph Smith and the 1826 Trial: New Evidence and New Difficulties." *BYU Studies* 12 (Winter 1982): 223-33.

Jessee, Dean C. "Joseph Smith's Reputation among Historians." *Ensign* 9 (September 1979): 56-61.

———. "Spirituality of Joseph Smith." *Ensign* 8 (September 1985): 14-20.

———. "'Walls, Grates, and Screeking Iron Doors': The Prison Experience of Mormon Leaders in Missouri, 1838-1839." In *New Views of Mormon History: Essays in Honor of Leonard J. Arrington,* ed. by Davis Bitton and Maureen Ursenbach Beecher, 19-42. Salt Lake City: University of Utah Press, 1987.

Madsen, Gordon A. "Joseph Smith's 1826 Trial: The Legal Setting," *BYU Studies* 30 (Spring 1990): 91-108.

Madsen, Truman G. "Joseph Smith's Reputation among Theologians." *Ensign* 9 (September 1979): 61-63.

Proper, David R. "Joseph Smith and Salem." *Essex Institute Historical Collections* 100 (April 1964): 88-97.

Wirthlin, LeRoy S. "Joseph Smith's Boyhood Operation: An 1813 Surgical Success." *BYU Studies* 21 (Spring 1981): 131-54; and Wirthlin, "Nathan Smith (1762-1828): Surgical Consultant to Joseph

Smith," *BYU Studies* 17 (Spring 1977): 319-37. See also Reed C. Durham Jr., "Joseph Smith's Own Story of a Serious Childhood Illness." *BYU Studies* 10 (Summer 1970): 480-82; and Richard L. Anderson, "The Trustworthiness of Young Joseph Smith," *Improvement Era* 73 (October 1970): 82-89.

Institutional/Doctrinal

Allen, James B. "Was Joseph Smith a Serious Candidate for the Presidency of the United States?" *Ensign* 3 (September 1973): 21-22.

———. "Why Did People Act that Way?" *Ensign* 8 (December 1978): 21-24. On early Mormon persecution, see also *Sunstone* 4 (July-August 1979): 42-46; and Leonard J. Arrington and Davis Bitton. *The Mormon Experience,* 44-64. New York: Alfred A. Knopf, 1979.

Allen, James B., Ronald K. Esplin, and David J. Whittaker. *Men With a Mission: The Quorum of the Twelve Apostles in the British Isles, 1837-1841.* Salt Lake City: Deseret Book, 1992.

Anderson, Richard Lloyd. "Joseph Smith and the Millenarian Time Table," *BYU Studies* 3 (Spring-Summer 1961): 55-66.

Andrew, Laurel B. *The Early Temples of the Mormons: The Architecture of the Millennial Kingdom in the American West.* Albany: State University of New York Press, 1978.

Arrington, Leonard J., Feramorz Y. Fox, and Dean L. May. *Building the City of God: Community and Cooperation among the Mormons.* Salt Lake City: Deseret Book, 1976. See especially chapter 2 on consecration.

Bachman, Danel W. "A Study of the Mormon Practice of Plural Marriage before the Death of Joseph Smith." Master's thesis, Purdue University, 1975.

Beecher, Maureen Ursenbach, and Lavina Fielding Anderson, eds. *Sisters in Spirit: Mormon Women in Historical and Cultural Perspective.* Urbana: University of Illinois Press, 1987.

Brink, T. L. "Joseph Smith: The Verdict of Depth Psychology." *Journal of Mormon History* 3 (1976): 73-83.

Cook, Lyndon W. *Joseph Smith and the Law of Consecration.* Orem, Utah: Grandin Books, 1985.

Crawley, Peter, and Richard Lloyd Anderson. "The Political and Social Realities of Zion's Camp." *BYU Studies* 14 (Summer 1974): 406-20.

Derr, Jill Mulvay, Janath Russell Cannon, and Maureen Ursenbach Beecher. *Women of Covenant: The Story of the Relief Society.* Salt Lake City: Deseret Book, 1992.

Ehat, Andrew F. "'It Seems Like Heaven Began on Earth': Joseph Smith and the Constitution of the Kingdom of God," *BYU Studies* 20 (Spring 1980): 253-79.

———. "Joseph Smith's Introduction of Temple Ordinances and the 1844 Mormon Succession Question." Master's thesis, Brigham Young University, 1982.

Ellsworth, S. George. "A History of Mormon Missions in the United States and Canada, 1830-1860." Ph.D. diss., University of California, Berkeley, 1951.

Esplin, Ronald K. "The Emergence of Brigham Young and the Twelve to Mormon Leadership, 1830-1841." Ph.D. diss., Brigham Young University, 1981.

Gayler, George R. "The 'Expositor' Affair: Prelude to the Downfall of Joseph Smith." *Northwest Missouri State College Studies* 25 (February, 1961): 3-15.

Godfrey, Kenneth W. "Joseph Smith and the Masons." *Journal of the Illinois State Historical Society* 64 (Spring 1971): 79-90.

———. "The Zelph Story," *BYU Studies* 29 (Spring 1989): 31-56.

Hansen, Klaus J. *Quest for Empire: The Political Kingdom of God and the Council of Fifty in Mormon History.* Ann Arbor, Mich.: Michigan State University Press, 1967.

Hartley, William G. "'Upon You My Fellow Servants': Restoration of the Priesthood." In *The Prophet Joseph: Essays on the Life and Mission of Joseph Smith,* ed. by Larry C. Porter and Susan Easton Black, 49-72. Salt Lake City: Deseret Book, 1988.

Hill, Marvin S., C. Keith Rooker, and Larry T. Wimmer. "The Kirtland Economy Revisited: A Market Critique of Sectarian Economics." *BYU Studies* 17 (Summer 1977): 391-472.

Hogan, Mervin B. "The Milieu of Mormonism and Freemasonry at Nauvoo: An Interpretation." *Transactions: The American Lodge of Research, Free and Accepted Masons* 13 (1976): 188-202.

"Joseph Smith Papyri." See *Dialogue* 3 (Summer 1968); *Sunstone* 4 (December 1979); and *BYU Studies* 11 (Summer 1971).

McMurrin, Sterling. *The Theological Foundation of the Mormon Religion.* Salt Lake City: University of Utah Press, 1965.

Millet, Robert L. "Joseph Smith and Modern Mormonism: Orthodoxy, Neoorthodoxy, Tension, and Tradition," *BYU Studies* 29 (Summer 1989): 49-68.

Oaks, Dallin H., and Joseph I. Bentley. "Joseph Smith and Legal Process: In the Wake of the Steamboat Nauvoo." *BYU Law Review* (1976): 735-82. Reprinted in *BYU Studies* 19 (Winter 1979): 167-99.

Olsen, Steven L. "Joseph Smith and the Structure of Mormon Identity." *Dialogue* 14 (Autumn 1981): 89-100.

Paul, [Erich] Robert. "Joseph Smith and the Plurality of Worlds Idea." *Dialogue* 19 (Summer 1986): 13-36.

Peterson, Paul H. "An Historical Analysis of the Word of Wisdom." Master's thesis, Brigham Young University, 1972.

Poll, Richard D. "Joseph Smith and the Presidency, 1844." *Dialogue* 3 (Autumn 1968): 17-21.

Quinn, D. Michael. "The Council of Fifty and its Members, 1844-1945." *BYU Studies* 20 (Winter 1980): 163-97.

———. "The Evolution of the Presiding Quorums of the LDS Church." *Journal of Mormon History* 1 (1974): 21-38.

———. "Joseph Smith III's Blessing and the Mormons of Utah." *John Whitmer Historical Association Journal* 1 (1981): 12-27. Also in *Dialogue* 15 (Summer 1982): 69-80. The Blessing document turned out to be a Hofmann forgery.

———. *The Mormon Hierarchy: Origins of Power.* Salt Lake City: Signature Books in association with Smith Research Associates, 1994.

———. "The Mormon Succession Crisis of 1844." *BYU Studies* 16 (Winter 1976): 187-233.

Underwood, Grant. *The Millenarian World of Mormonism.* Urbana: University of Illinois Press, 1993.

Whittaker, David J. "The 'Articles of Faith' in Early Mormon Literature and Thought." In *New Views of Mormon History: Essays in Honor of Leonard J. Arrington,* ed. by Davis Bitton and Maureen Ursenbach Beecher, 63-92. Salt Lake City: University of Utah Press, 1987.

———. "The Book of Daniel in Early Mormon Thought." In *By Study and Also By Faith: Essays in Honor of Hugh W. Nibley on His Eightieth Birthday,* ed. by John M. Lundquist and Stephen D. Ricks, 155-201. Vol. 1. Salt Lake City: Deseret Book; Provo, Utah: F.A.R.M.S., 1990.

Zucker, Louis C. "Joseph Smith as a Student of Hebrew," *Dialogue* 3 (Summer 1968): 41-55.

Biographical Studies

Andrus, Hyrum L. *Joseph Smith, the Man and the Seer.* Salt Lake City: Deseret Book, 1960.

Andrus, Hyrum L., and Helen Mae Andrus. *They Knew the Prophet.* Salt Lake City: Bookcraft, 1974.

Anderson, Karl Ricks. *Joseph Smith's Kirtland: Eyewitness Accounts.* Salt Lake City: Deseret Book, 1989.

Brodie, Fawn M. *No Man Knows My History: The Life of Joseph Smith.* 1946; New York: Alfred A. Knopf. 2d ed. 1971. Note the review essays by Marvin S. Hill: "Secular or Sectarian History? A Critique of 'No Man Knows My History,'" *Church History* 43 (March 1974): 78-96; and "Brodie Revisited: A Reappraisal," *Dialogue* 7 (Winter 1972): 72-85.

Cannon, George Q. *Life of Joseph Smith the Prophet.* Salt Lake City: Deseret Book, 1964. Originally published in 1888. Written with Frank Cannon.

Evans, John Henry. *Joseph Smith: An American Prophet.* Salt Lake City: Deseret Book, 1966. Originally published in New York in 1933.

Hill, Donna. *Joseph Smith: The First Mormon.* Garden City, N.Y.: Doubleday, 1977.

Jenson, Andrew. "Joseph Smith the Prophet." *The Historical Record* 7 (January 1888): 353-576.

Madsen, Truman G. *Joseph Smith among the Prophets.* Salt Lake City: Deseret Book, 1965.

———. *Joseph Smith the Prophet.* Salt Lake City: Bookcraft, 1989.

Roberts, B. H. *Joseph Smith, the Prophet-Teacher.* Princeton: The Deseret Club of Princeton University, 1967. Originally published in 1908.

Smith, Lucy Mack. *History of Joseph Smith by His Mother.* Salt Lake City: Bookcraft, 1958. Originally published in 1853. A good introduction to this history is Howard C. Searle "Early Mormon Historiography. . . ." Ph.D. diss., UCLA, 1979, pp. 358-428. See also Jan Shipps *Mormonism: The Story of a New Religious Tradition,* chapter 5. Urbana: University of Illinois Press, 1985.

Tullidge, Edward W. *Life of Joseph the Prophet.* New York, 1878; 2d ed. 1880. The first edition ended with Joseph Smith's death, but the second edition followed the history of the RLDS Church, which he had joined, to 1880.

Widtsoe, John A. *Joseph Smith: Seeker after Truth, Prophet of God.* Salt Lake City: Bookcraft, 1957.

Essay Collections

Black, Susan Easton, and Charles D. Tate Jr., eds. *Joseph Smith: The Prophet, the Man.* Provo, Utah: Religious Studies Center, Brigham Young University, 1993.

Porter, Larry C., and Susan Easton Black, eds. *The Prophet Joseph: Essays on the Life and Mission of Joseph Smith.* Salt Lake City: Deseret Book, 1988.

Mark Hofmann Forgeries of Early Mormon Manuscripts

Sillitoe, Linda, and Allen D. Roberts. *Salamander: The Story of the Mormon Forgery Murders.* Salt Lake City: Signature Books, 1988.

Turley, Richard E., Jr., *Victims: The LDS Church and the Mark Hofmann Case.* Urbana: University of Illinois Press, 1992.

Whittaker, David J. "The Hofmann Maze: A Book Review Essay with a Chronology and Bibliography of the Hofmann Case." *BYU Studies* 29 (Winter 1989): 67-124.

The Martyrdom

Anderson, Richard Lloyd. "Joseph Smith's Prophecies of Martyrdom." In *Sidney B. Sperry Symposium, January 26, 1980: A Sesquicentennial Look at Church History,* 1-14. Provo, Utah: Brigham Young University College of Religious Instruction, 1980.

Bernauer, Barbara Hands. "Still 'Side by Side'—the Final Burial of Joseph and Hyrum Smith." *John Whitmer Historical Association Journal* 11 (1991): 17-33.

Bitton, Davis. "The Martyrdom of Joseph Smith in Early Mormon Writings." *John Whitmer Historical Association Journal* 3 (1983):29-39.

———. *The Martyrdom Remembered: A One-Hundred-Fifty Year Perspective on the Assassination of Joseph Smith.* Salt Lake City: Aspen Books, 1994.

Ellsworth, Paul D. "Mobocracy and the Rule of Law: American Press Reaction to the Murder of Joseph Smith." *BYU Studies* 28 (Fall 1979): 71-82.

Esplin, Ronald K. "Joseph, Brigham, and the Twelve: A Succession of Continuity." *BYU Studies* 21 (Summer 1981): 301-41.

———. "The Significance of Nauvoo for Latter-day Saints." *Journal of Mormon History* 16 (1990): 71-86.

Gayler, George R. "Governor Ford and the Death of Joseph and Hyrum Smith." *Journal of the Illinois State Historical Society* 50 (Winter 1957): 391-411.

Godfrey, Kenneth W. "Non-Mormon View of the Martyrdom: A Look at Some Early Published Accounts." *John Whitmer Historical Association Journal* 7 (1987): 12-20.

Hampshire, Annette P. *Mormonism in Conflict: The Nauvoo Years.* Studies in Religion and Society, Vol. 11. New York: Edwin Mellen, 1985.

Hampshire, Annette P. "Thomas Sharp and Anti-Mormon Sentiment in Illinois." *Journal of the Illinois State Historical Society* 72 (May 1979): 82-100.

———. "The Triumph of Mobocracy in Hancock County, 1844-1846." *Western Illinois Regional Studies* 5 (Spring 1982): 17-37.

Huntress, Keith. "Governor Thomas Ford and the Murderers of Joseph Smith." *Dialogue* 4 (Summer 1969): 41-52.

———. *Murder of an American Prophet.* San Francisco: Chandler Publishing Co., 1960.

Jessee, Dean C. "Return to Carthage: Writing the History of Joseph Smith's Martyrdom." *Journal of Mormon History* 8 (1981): 3-19.

Jolley, Clifton H. "The Martyrdom of Joseph Smith: An Archetypal Study." *Utah Historical Quarterly* 44 (Fall 1976): 329-50.

Jones, Dan. "The Martyrdom of Joseph Smith and His Brother Hyrum." Introduction and translation from Welsh by Ronald D. Dennis. *BYU Studies* 24 (Winter 1984): 79-109.

Kimball, Stanley B. "Thomas L. Barnes: Coroner of Carthage." *BYU Studies* 11 (Winter 1971): 141-47.

Launius, Roger D., ed. "Anti-Mormonism in Illinois: Thomas C. Sharp's Unfinished History of the Mormon War, 1845." *Journal of Mormon History* 15 (1989): 27-45.

Oaks, Dallin H., and Marvin S. Hill. *Carthage Conspiracy: The Trial of the Accused Assassins of Joseph Smith.* Urbana: University of Illinois Press, 1975.

Poulsen, Richard C. "Fate and the Persecutors of Joseph Smith: Transmutations of an American Myth." *Dialogue* 11 (Winter 1978): 63-70.

Shipps, Jan, ed. "A Little Known Account of the Murders of Joseph and Hyrum Smith," *BYU Studies* 14 (Spring 1974): 389-92.

Van Wagoner, Richard, and Steven C. Walker. "The Joseph/Hyrum Smith Funeral Sermon [by William W. Phelps]." *BYU Studies* 23 (Winter 1983): 3-18.

The Study of Mormon History: A Guide to the Published Sources

David J. Whittaker

The study of Mormon history and culture has experienced a virtual renaissance in the last twenty-five years. The professionalization of Mormon studies is one aspect of this development, which has seen the founding of the Mormon History Association (1965) and the appearance or revitalization of a variety of professionally edited magazines and journals that regularly print articles on Mormon history. These publications include *Dialogue: A Journal of Mormon Thought,* the *Journal of Mormon History,* the *John Whitmer Historical Society Journal, Sunstone,* and, of course, *BYU Studies*. In addition, professional publications issued throughout the United States have given increased attention and space to Mormon topics. The 1992 appearance of the multivolume *Encyclopedia of Mormonism,* ed. Daniel H. Ludlow (New York: Macmillan) testifies to the increasing sophistication of the academic study of Mormon culture. It also suggests the growing interest in things Mormon by the larger culture.

This essay surveys the growing body of Mormon studies by focusing on those works that are most useful for serious students; it also gives special attention to the bibliographical works that are especially valuable for researchers. With few exceptions, this survey concentrates on published works and is, out of necessity, selective. The reader is also referred to the more specialized topical essays in *Mormon Americana*.

General Histories

In many ways, the six-volume history issued in 1930 as part of the Church's centennial remains indispensable for LDS history: B. H. Roberts, *A Comprehensive History of the Church of Jesus Christ of Latter-day Saints, Century 1* (1930; reprint, Provo, Utah: Brigham Young University Press, 1965). Two one-volume histories were prepared for the sesquicentennial of the Church; both are excellent in their presentations. James B. Allen and Glen M. Leonard, *The Story of the Latter-day Saints,* 2d ed., rev. and enl. (Salt Lake City: Deseret Book,

1992) takes the reader chronologically through the history of the Church and also provides extensive and excellent bibliographical guides. Leonard J. Arrington and Davis Bitton, *The Mormon Experience: A History of the Latter-day Saints* (New York: Alfred A. Knopf, 1979) takes an interpretive, topical approach, somewhat in the tradition of Catholic sociologist Thomas F. O'Dea's still important *The Mormons* (Chicago: University of Chicago Press, 1957). The most up-to-date textbook prepared for use in the Church Educational System is *Church History in the Fulness of Times: The History of The Church* (Salt Lake City: The Church of Jesus Christ of Latter-day Saints, 1989). A history for young adults is Dean Hughes, *The Mormon Church: A Basic History* (Salt Lake City: Deseret Book, 1986).

Of the histories of Mormon-dominated Utah, the most comprehensive and bibliographically useful is the multiauthored *Utah's History,* ed. Richard D. Poll, Thomas G. Alexander, Eugene E. Campbell, and David E. Miller (Provo, Utah: Brigham Young University Press, 1978). Older and still useful are Orson F. Whitney, *History of Utah,* 4 vols. (Salt Lake City: George Q. Cannon and Sons, 1892–1904) [vol. 4 is biographical]; Noble Warrum, ed., *History of Utah Since Statehood,* 4 vols. (Chicago: S. J. Clarke Publishing, 1919–20) [vols. 2–4 are biographical]; and Wain Sutton, ed., *Utah: A Centennial History,* 3 vols. (New York: Lewis Historical Publishing, 1949) [vol. 3 is biographical]. Gustive O. Larson, *Outline History of Utah and the Mormons,* 3d ed. (Salt Lake City: Deseret Book, 1965) is still helpful. However, Dean L. May, *Utah: A People's History* (Salt Lake City: University of Utah Press, 1987) is more interpretative and was produced as a companion volume for a public television series on the history of Utah. Published in honor of Utah's 1996 statehood centennial is the *Utah History Encyclopedia,* ed. Allan Kent Powell (Salt Lake City: University of Utah Press, 1994). Also underway for the centennial are a multivolume, multiauthored history of Utah; a series of county histories; and other important projects.

Source and Essay Collections

The major archival repositories and libraries are surveyed in this volume. The best single published guide to individual items is Davis Bitton, *Guide to Mormon Diaries and Autobiographies* (Provo, Utah: Brigham Young University Press, 1977). Valuable published sources of Mormon history include William E. Berrett and Alma P. Burton, *Readings in L.D.S. Church History,* 3 vols. (Salt Lake City: Deseret Book, 1953–1958); William Mulder and A. Russell Mortensen, eds., *Among the Mormons: Historic Accounts by Contemporary Observers* (1958; reprint, Lincoln: University of Nebraska Press, 1973); Elden J.

Watson, comp., *The Orson Pratt Journals* (Salt Lake City: By the comp., 1975); Kenneth W. Godfrey, Audrey M. Godfrey, and Jill Mulvay Derr, *Women's Voices: An Untold History of the Latter-day Saints, 1830-1900* (Salt Lake City: Deseret Book, 1982); Dean C. Jessee, ed., *Letters of Brigham Young to His Sons* (Salt Lake City: Deseret Book, 1974); and Donald Q. Cannon and Lyndon W. Cook, eds., *The Far West Record: Minutes of The Church of Jesus Christ of Latter-day Saints, 1830-1844* (Salt Lake City: Deseret Book, 1983). Earlier, professionally edited manuscripts appeared in the *Utah Historical Quarterly.* Also valuable are the published volumes of the journals of William E. McLellin: Jan Shipps and John W. Welch, eds., *The Journals of William E. McLellin, 1831-1836* (Provo, Utah: BYU Studies and Urbana: University of Illinois Press, 1994); John D. Lee: Robert Glass Cleland and Juanita Brooks, eds., *A Mormon Chronicle: The Diaries of John D. Lee, 1848-1876,* 2 vols. (1955; reprint, Salt Lake City: University of Utah Press, 1983); Hosea Stout: Juanita Brooks, ed., *On the Mormon Frontier: The Diary of Hosea Stout, 1844-1861,* 2 vols. (Salt Lake City: University of Utah Press and Utah State Historical Society, 1964); Charles L. Walker: Andrew Karl Larson and Katharine Miles Larson, eds., *The Diary of Charles Lowell Walker,* 2 vols. (Logan, Utah: Utah State University Press, 1980); and Charles Ora Card: *The Diaries of Charles Ora Card: The Canadian Years, 1886-1903,* ed. Donald G. Godfrey and Brigham Y. Card (Salt Lake City: University of Utah Press, 1993). Signature Books of Salt Lake City has been issuing limited editions of various Mormon journals, beginning with their nine-volume edition of *Wilford Woodruff's Journal,* ed. Scott G. Kenney (Midvale, Utah: Signature Books, 1983-84). Other volumes include the diaries of Heber C. Kimball, John Henry Smith, and William Clayton.

Essay collections of importance include F. Mark McKiernan, Alma R. Blair, and Paul M. Edwards, eds., *The Restoration Movement: Essays in Mormon History* (Lawrence, Kans.: Coronado Press, 1973); Marvin S. Hill and James B. Allen, eds., *Mormonism and American Culture* (New York: Harper and Row, 1972); Donald Q. Cannon and David J. Whittaker, eds., *Supporting Saints: Life Stories of Nineteenth-Century Mormons* (Provo, Utah: Religious Studies Center, Brigham Young University, 1985); and Davis Bitton and Maureen Ursenbach Beecher, eds., *New Views of Mormon History: A Collection of Essays in Honor of Leonard J. Arrington* (Salt Lake City: University of Utah Press, 1987).

Reference Works

The above mentioned *Encyclopedia of Mormonism* is currently the most comprehensive and authoritative reference work on all aspects of The Church of Jesus Christ of Latter-day Saints. A large percentage of the entries were written by students of the specific topic and most entries include bibliographic references. These, combined with excellent graphics, maps, and photographs, offer the student a kind of "Encyclopedia Judaica" for Mormon history, religion, and culture.

There have been other reference works which remain valuable for students. Nineteenth-century works which attempt to provide a handbook to Mormonism include George A. Smith, *The Rise, Progress, and Travels of The Church of Jesus Christ of Latter-day Saints . . .* (Salt Lake City: Printed at the Deseret News Office, 1869); Franklin D. Richards, *Compendium* (London: LDS Book Depot, 1857); John Jaques, *The Church of Jesus Christ of Latter-day Saints: Its Priesthood, Organization, Doctrines, Ordinances and History* (Salt Lake City: Deseret News, 1882); and Abraham H. Cannon, *A Hand-book of Reference to the History, Chronology, Religion, and Country of the Latter-day Saints . . .* (Salt Lake City: Juvenile Instructor Office, 1884). The first historical periodical in the Church was Andrew Jenson, *The Historical Record: A Monthly Periodical Devoted Exclusively to Historical, Biographical, Chronological, Autobiographical, and Statistical Matters,* 9 vols. (Salt lake City: By the author, 1882–90). Works that have appeared in the twentieth century include Andrew Jenson, *Encyclopedic History of the Church of Jesus Christ of Latter-day Saints* (Salt Lake City: Deseret News Press, 1941); Jenson, *Church Chronology,* 2d. ed., rev. and enl. (Salt Lake City: Deseret News, 1914); Melvin Brooks, *LDS Reference Encyclopedia,* 2 vols. (Salt Lake City: Bookcraft, 1960–65, 1971); John W. Van Cott, *Utah Place Names* (Salt Lake City: University of Utah Press, 1990); and Thomas K. Martin, Tim B. Heaton, and Stephen J. Bahr, eds., *Utah in Demographic Perspective* (Salt Lake City: Signature Books, 1986). The *Deseret News Church Almanac* (generally published annually from 1974 to the present) is a very useful compilation of facts and statistics about the Church. The *Church News* section of *Deseret News* is a weekly report on various activities of the Church throughout the world.

A useful atlas of Mormonism is now available: *Historical Atlas of Mormonism,* S. Kent Brown, Donald Q. Cannon, Richard H. Jackson, eds. (New York: Simon and Schuster, 1994). The student will also find the following work useful: Wayne L. Wahlquist and others, *Atlas of Utah* (Ogden, Utah: Weber State College, 1981). The student of Mormon history will benefit from the recent work of cultural geographers: D. W. Meinig, "The Mormon Culture Region: Strategies and Patterns in the Geography of the American West, 1847-1964," *Annals of the Association of American Geographers* 55 (June 1965): 191-220; Lowell C. "Ben" Bennion, "Mormon Country a Century Ago: A Geographer's View," in *The Mormon People: Their Character and Traditions,* ed. Thomas G. Alexander, Charles Redd Monographs in Western History, no. 10 (Provo, Utah: Brigham Young University Press, 1980), 1-26; Dean R. Louder and Lowell C. Bennion, "Mapping the Mormons across the Modern West," in *The Mormon Role in the Settlement of the West,* ed. Richard H. Jackson, Charles Redd Monographs in Western History, no. 9 (Provo, Utah: Brigham Young University Press, 1978), 135-69; and Dean R. Louder, "A Distributional and Diffusionary Analysis of the Mormon Church, 1850-1970," (Ph.D. diss., University of Washington, 1972).

Guidebooks to historic sites include three volumes by Richard Neitzel Holzapfel and T. Jeffery Cottle: *Old Mormon Palmyra and New England: Historic Photographs and Guide* (Santa Ana, Calif.: Fieldbrook Productions, 1991); *Old Mormon Kirtland and Missouri...* (Santa Ana, Calif.: Fieldbrook Productions, 1991); and *Old Mormon Nauvoo, 1839-46 . . .* (Provo, Utah: Grandin Books, 1990). Older guides include R. Don Oscarson and Stanley B. Kimball, *The Travelers' Guide to Historic Mormon America* (Salt Lake City: Bookcraft, 1965); Stanley B. Kimball, *Historic Sites and Markers along the Mormon and Other Great Western Trails* (Urbana: University of Illinois Press, 1988); and James and Lavelle Moss, *Historic Sites of The Church of Jesus Christ of Latter-day Saints in the British Isles* (Salt Lake City: Publishers Press for The Church of Jesus Christ of Latter-day Saints, 1987).

Bibliography

Students of Mormon history and culture have a rich variety of bibliographical aids to assist them. "Mormon Bibliography," an annual listing of Mormon publications, has appeared regularly in *BYU Studies* since 1960. *Dialogue* issued the bibliographical "Among the Mormons" from 1977 to 1986; it provided specialized articles on a variety of topics. The Mormon History Association *Newsletter* has included a variety of bibliographical essays on both period and topical subjects. In July 1954, Wayne Stout completed but never published "A Bibliography on Mormonism," a pioneering bibliography of 1041 typed pages. A bound copy is in Special Collections, Harold B. Lee Library, Brigham Young University.

A massive (about 10,000 items) key-worded guide to scholarly literature on Mormonism is in the final stages of preparation by James B.

Allen, Ronald W. Walker, and David J. Whittaker. The guide will be entitled "Studies in Mormon History: A Bibliography, with Index and a Guide to Further Research." It is anticipated that this two-volume work will be available in 1996 from the University of Illinois Press.

A bibliographical listing of graduate studies on Mormonism was published by the College of Religious Instruction, Brigham Young University, in 1971: *A Catalogue of Theses and Dissertations concerning the Church of Jesus Christ of Latter-day Saints, Mormonism and Utah*. The same college issued a small, mimeographed "Additions" list in 1974. A list and discussion of dissertations is in Leonard J. Arrington, "Scholarly Studies of Mormonism in the Twentieth Century," *Dialogue* 1 (Spring 1966): 15–32. See also Ruth M. Jones and Robert N. McMillan, "Utah, the Mormons, and the West: A Bibliography and Check List of Theses at the University of Utah," *Utah Historical Quarterly* 23 (January 1955): 79–85; Ida-Marie Clark Logan, "A Bibliography of Theses and Dissertations concerning Utah or the Mormons Written outside the State of Utah" (master's thesis, Utah State University, 1956), which also appears as a series in *Utah Historical Quarterly* 27 (January 1959): 85–100 and 27 (April 1959): 169–90; William V. Nash, "Library Resources for the Study of Mormons and Mormonism," (Urbana: Graduate School of Library Science, University of Illinois, 1960); Kip Sperry, *A Guide to Indexes to Mormon Works, Mormon Collections, and Utah Collections* (Salt Lake City: Historical Department of The Church of Jesus Christ of Latter-day Saints, 1974); Gordon Irving, "Utah Since 1847: A Guide to Bibliographies, Finding Aids, and Major Source Repositories" (typescript available in various Utah libraries); David L. Laughlin, "A Selective, Evaluative, and Annotated Bibliography on Mormonism," *Bulletin of Bibliography* 48 (June 1991): 75–101; Armand L. Mauss and Jeffrey R. Franks, "Comprehensive Bibliography of Social Science Literature on the Mormons," *Review of Religious Research* 26 (September 1984): 73–115; James B. Allen, "Since 1950: Creators and Creations of Mormon History," in *New Views of Mormon History*, ed. Davis Bitton and Maureen Ursenbach Beecher (Salt Lake City: University of Utah Press, 1987), 407–38; Milton V. Backman Jr., comp., *Selected Bibliography of LDS Church History* (Provo, Utah: College of Religion, Brigham Young University, 1987); Susan L. Fales and Chad J. Flake, comps., *Mormons and Mormonism in U.S. Government Documents: A Bibliography* (Salt Lake City: University of Utah Press, 1989); Mark L. Grover, *The Mormon Church in Latin America: A Periodical Index, 1830–1976* (Provo, Utah: Brigham Young University Press, 1977); Russell T. Clement, comp., *Mormons in the Pacific: A Bibliography* (Laie, Hawaii: The

Institute for Polynesian Studies, BYU—Hawaii Campus, 1981); Samuel E. Burggraaf, Mark L. Chamberlain, and James N. Gilson, *Guide to Mormon Audio/Visual Materials: An Indexed Listing of Audio/Visual Material Produced by, for, or about The Church of Jesus Christ of Latter-day Saints* (Provo, Utah: Harold B. Lee Library and the David O. McKay Institute of Education, 1983); and Susan L. Fales and Lanell M. Reeder, "Mormonism: Bibliography of Bibliographies," *Mormon History Association Newsletter,* no. 72 (April 1989): 5-8 and no. 74 (October 1989): 4-7. The best guide to date to the personal records of Mormons is Davis Bitton, ed., *Guide to Mormon Diaries and Autobiographies* (Provo, Utah: Brigham Young University Press, 1977).

Mark W. Hofmann was not the first person to forge LDS historical texts, but he is the best known. An introduction and guide to his extensive deceit is David J. Whittaker, "The Hofmann Maze: A Book Review Essay with a Chronology and Bibliography of the Hofmann Case," *BYU Studies* 29 (Winter 1989): 67-124. See also Richard E. Turley Jr., *Victims: The LDS Church and the Mark Hofmann Case* (Urbana: University of Illinois Press, 1992).

Historiography

Record keeping has characterized the Mormon movement from its earliest days; few American religions have the rich manuscript record of their history that Mormons do. An excellent discussion of the origins of this concern is Dean C. Jessee, "Joseph Smith and the Beginning of Mormon Record Keeping," in *The Prophet Joseph: Essays on the Life and Mission of Joseph Smith,* ed. Larry C. Porter and Susan Easton Black (Salt Lake City: Deseret Book, 1988), 138-60. See also Howard C. Searle, "Early Mormon Historiography: Writing the History of the Mormons, 1830-1858" (Ph.D. diss., UCLA, 1979); and Charles P. Adams and Gustive O. Larson, "A Study of the LDS Church Historian's Office, 1830-1900," *Utah Historical Quarterly* 40 (Fall 1972): 370-88. Useful surveys of the history of Mormon historical writing include Leonard J. Arrington, "The Search for Truth and Meaning in Mormon History," *Dialogue* 3 (Summer 1968): 56-66; David J. Whittaker, "Historians and the Mormon Experience: A Sesquicentennial Perspective," in *Sidney B. Sperry Symposium, January 26, 1980: A Sesquicentennial Look at Church History* (Provo, Utah: Brigham Young University, College of Religious Instruction, 1980), 293-327; and Davis Bitton and Leonard J. Arrington, *Mormons and Their Historians* (Salt Lake City: University of Utah Press, 1988). See also S. George Ellsworth, "Utah History: Retrospect and Prospect," *Utah Historical Quarterly* 40 (Fall

1972): 342-67. An early scholarly evaluation is Marvin S. Hill, "Survey: The Historiography of Mormonism," *Church History* 28 (December 1959): 418-26; and a more recent collection of essays is George D. Smith, ed., *Faithful History: Essays on Writing Mormon History* (Salt Lake City: Signature Books, 1992). A guide to the extensive literature on the more recent discussions on Mormon historiography is Louis C. Midgley and David J. Whittaker, "Mapping Contemporary Mormon Historiography: An Annotated Bibliography" (a working draft has been deposited in Special Collections, Harold B. Lee Library, Brigham Young University). See also John Phillip Walker, ed., *Dale Morgan on Early Mormonism: Correspondence and a New History* (Salt Lake City: Signature Books, 1986).

Historical Periods

The growing professionalization of Mormon studies is best seen in the outpouring of scholarly works detailing more limited period or regional studies. The following suggest the more important scholarly monographs the serious researcher will wish to consult. Most of the published studies include bibliographies.

Mormon Origins and the New England Background. The most complete study of the earliest events leading to the organization of the Church in April 1830 is Richard L. Bushman, *Joseph Smith and the Beginnings of Mormonism* (Urbana: University of Illinois Press, 1984). See also Richard Lloyd Anderson, *Joseph Smith's New England Heritage* (Salt Lake City: Deseret Book, 1971); Milton V. Backman Jr., *Joseph Smith's First Vision: Confirming Evidences and Contemporary Accounts,* 2d ed. (Salt Lake City: Bookcraft, 1980); Larry C. Porter, "A Study of the Origins of the Church of Jesus Christ of Latter-day Saints in the States of New York and Pennsylvania, 1816-1831" (Ph.D. diss., Brigham Young University, 1971); Leonard J. Arrington, "Mormonism: From Its New York Beginnings," *New York History* 61 (October 1980): 387-410; Richard Lloyd Anderson, *Investigating the Book of Mormon Witnesses* (Salt Lake City: Deseret Book, 1981); and D. Michael Quinn, *Early Mormonism and the Magic World View* (Salt Lake City: Signature Books, 1987).

Important studies of Joseph Smith's first vision are by James B. Allen: "The Significance of Joseph Smith's 'First Vision' in Mormon Thought," *Dialogue* 1 (Autumn 1966): 29-45; "Emergence of a Fundamental: The Expanding Role of Joseph Smith's First Vision in Mormon Religious Thought," *Journal of Mormon History* 7 (1980): 43-61; and "Eight Contemporary Accounts of Joseph Smith's First

Vision—What Do We Learn From Them?" *Improvement Era* 73 (April 1970): 4-13. Specialized studies of the priesthood restoration are Larry C. Porter, "Dating the Restoration of the Melchizedek Priesthood," *Ensign* 9 (June 1979): 5-10; William G. Hartley, "'Upon You My Fellow Servants': Restoration of the Priesthood," in *The Prophet Joseph: Essays on the Life and Mission of Joseph Smith,* ed. Larry C. Porter and Susan Easton Black (Salt Lake City: Deseret Book, 1988), 49-72; and Gregory A. Prince, *Having Authority: The Origins and Development of Priesthood during the Ministry of Joseph Smith* (Independence, Mo.: Independence Press for the John Whitmer Historical Association Monograph Series, 1993). Two short bibliographical essays on this period are by David J. Whittaker: "Joseph Smith's First Vision: A Source Essay," *Mormon History Association Newsletter,* no. 42 (November 1979): 7-9; and "Sources on Mormon Origins in New York and Pennsylvania," *Mormon History Association Newsletter,* no. 43 (March 1980): 8-12. See also Mark Grover, "Bibliographic Essay on Works about the New York Period of Mormon History (1965-1975)," *Gradalis Review* 2 (Spring 1974): 24-39 [the *Review* was a publication of the Brigham Young University Graduate Student Association of Library and Information Science].

Ohio Period. The most accessible study is Milton V. Backman Jr., *The Heavens Resound: A History of the Latter-day Saints in Ohio, 1830-1838* (Salt Lake City: Deseret Book, 1983). See also Robert Kent Fielding, "The Growth of the Mormon Church in Kirtland, Ohio" (Ph.D. diss., Indiana University, 1957); Max H. Parkin, "Conflict at Kirtland: The Nature and Causes of External and Internal Conflict of the Mormons in Ohio between 1830 and 1838" (master's thesis, Brigham Young University, 1966); Marvin S. Hill, *Quest for Refuge: The Mormon Flight from American Pluralism* (Salt Lake City: Signature Books, 1989), which offers a different perspective than Klaus J. Hansen, *Quest for Empire: The Political Kingdom of God and the Council of Fifty in Mormon History* (East Lansing: Michigan State University Press, 1967); Stanley B. Kimball, "Sources on the History of the Mormons in Ohio: 1830-1838 (Located East of the Mississippi)," *BYU Studies* 11 (Summer 1971): 524-40; Karl R. Anderson, *Joseph Smith's Kirtland: Eyewitness Accounts* (Salt Lake City: Deseret Book, 1989); Marvin S. Hill, Larry T. Wimmer, and C. Keith Rooker, "The Kirtland Economy Revisited: A Market Critique of Sectarian Economics," *BYU Studies* 17 (Summer 1977): 391-472 [issued as a separate volume by Brigham Young University Press in 1978]; and Davis Bitton, "The Waning of Mormon Kirtland," *BYU Studies* 12 (Summer 1972): 455-64.

Missouri Period. There is no adequate one volume history of the Mormon experience in Missouri. For the Jackson County period (1831-33), see Warren A. Jennings, "Zion Is Fled: The Expulsion of the Mormons from Jackson County, Missouri" (Ph.D. diss., University of Florida, 1962); Richard Lloyd Anderson, "Jackson County in Early Mormon Descriptions," *Missouri Historical Review* 65 (April 1971): 270-93; Warren A. Jennings, "The Expulsion of the Mormons from Jackson County, Missouri," *Missouri Historical Review* 64 (October 1969): 41-63; and Jennings, "The City in the Garden: Social Conflict in Jackson County, Missouri," in F. Mark McKiernan and others, eds., *The Restoration Movement: Essays in Mormon History* (Lawrence, Kans.: Coronado Press, 1973), 99-119. An important source of this early period is *The Journals of William E. McLellin, 1831-1836,* eds., Jan Shipps and John W. Welch (Provo, Utah: BYU Studies and Urbana: University of Illinois Press, 1994.)

For the Clay and Ray County period (1833-37), see Max H. Parkin, "A History of the Latter-day Saints in Clay County, Missouri, from 1833 to 1837" (Ph.D. diss., Brigham Young University, 1976); and Peter Crawley and Richard Lloyd Anderson, "The Political and Social Realities of Zion's Camp," *BYU Studies* 14 (Summer 1974): 406-20.

For the Daviess and Caldwell County experience, see Leland H. Gentry, "A History of the Latter-day Saints in Northern Missouri from 1836 to 1839" (Ph.D. diss., Brigham Young University, 1965); Stephen C. LeSueur, *The 1838 Mormon War in Missouri* (Columbia: University of Missouri Press, 1987), whose emphasis on sinister Danite activity ought to be balanced with David J. Whittaker, "The Book of Daniel in Early Mormon Thought," in *By Study and Also By Faith: Essays in Honor of Hugh Nibley,* ed. John M. Lundquist and Stephen D. Ricks, 2 vols. (Salt Lake City: Deseret Book and Foundation for Ancient Research and Mormon Studies, 1990), 1:155-201; Clark V. Johnson, ed., *Mormon Documents of the 1833-1838 Missouri Conflict* (Provo, Utah: Religious Studies Center, Brigham Young University; Salt Lake City: Bookcraft, 1992); Leland H. Gentry, "Adam-ondi-Ahman: A Brief Historical Survey," *BYU Studies* 13 (Summer 1973): 553-76; Richard Lloyd Anderson, "Atchison's Letters and the Causes of Mormon Expulsion from Missouri," *BYU Studies* 26 (Summer 1986): 3-47; and Dean C. Jessee, "'Walls, Grates and Screeking Iron Doors': The Prison Experience of Mormon Leaders in Missouri, 1838-1839," in *New Views of Mormon History,* ed. Davis Bitton and Maureen Ursenbach Beecher (Salt Lake City: University of Utah Press, 1987), 19-42. See also Stanley B. Kimball, "Missouri Mormon Manuscripts: Sources in Selected Societies," *BYU Studies* 14 (Summer 1974): 458-87.

Illinois Period. Several good bibliographical essays are available on this period: Richard D. Poll, "Nauvoo and the New Mormon History: A Bibliographical Survey," *Journal of Mormon History* 5 (1978): 105–23; Glen M. Leonard, "Recent Writing on Mormon Nauvoo," *Western Illinois Regional Studies* 11 (Fall 1988): 69–93; and Leonard, "Remembering Nauvoo: Historiographical Considerations," *Journal of Mormon History* 16 (1990): 25–39. Histories of the Nauvoo experience include Robert B. Flanders, *Nauvoo: Kingdom on the Mississippi* (Urbana: University of Illinois Press, 1965); and David E. Miller and Della S. Miller, *Nauvoo: The City of Joseph* (Santa Barbara: Peregrine Smith, 1974). Glen M. Leonard's history of the Nauvoo experience (building on the earlier work of T. Edgar Lyon) is nearing completion and promises to be the definitive study. While nothing substitutes for a personal visit to the restored Nauvoo, the work of Nauvoo Restoration Incorporated is shown in Janath R. Cannon, *Nauvoo Panorama: Views of Nauvoo before, during and after Its Rise, Fall, and Restoration* (Nauvoo, Ill.: Nauvoo Restoration, 1991); and in James L. Kimball Jr., "J. LeRoy Kimball, Nauvoo Restoration Pioneer: A Tribute," *BYU Studies* 32 (Winter and Spring 1992): 5–12.

The Charter for the city of Nauvoo is studied in James L. Kimball Jr., "The Nauvoo Charter: A Reinterpretation," *Journal of the Illinois State Historical Society* 64 (Spring 1971): 66–78; and Kimball, "A Wall to Defend Zion: The Nauvoo Charter," *BYU Studies* 15 (Summer 1975): 491–97. The Nauvoo Legion is the subject of two valuable studies: Hamilton Gardner, "The Nauvoo Legion, 1840–1845: A Unique Military Organization," *Journal of the Illinois State Historical Society* 54 (Summer 1961): 181–97; and John Sweeney Jr., "A History of the Nauvoo Legion in Illinois" (master's thesis, Brigham Young University, 1974). Dennis Rowley looks at the larger economics of Nauvoo in two articles: "Nauvoo: A River Town," *BYU Studies* 18 (Winter 1978): 255–72; and "The Mormon Experience in the Wisconsin Pineries, 1841–1845," *BYU Studies* 32 (Winter and Spring 1992): 119–48. The Nauvoo Temple is described in Stanley B. Kimball, "The Nauvoo Temple," *Improvement Era* 66 (November 1963): 974–76, 978–84; and Don F. Colvin, "A Historical Study of the Mormon Temple at Nauvoo, Illinois" (master's thesis, Brigham Young University, 1962). The significance of this temple in early Mormon history is discussed in Ronald K. Esplin, "The Significance of Nauvoo for Latter-day Saints," *Journal of Mormon History* 16 (1990): 71–86.

Especially valuable for understanding the emergence of the Quorum of the Twelve Apostles as the second most powerful quorum in the Church is Ronald K. Esplin, "The Emergence of Brigham Young and the Twelve to Mormon Leadership, 1830–1841" (Ph.D. diss., Brigham Young University, 1981); and Esplin, "Joseph, Brigham and the Twelve: A Succession of Continuity," *BYU Studies* 21 (Summer 1981): 301–41. For a good summary of the current understanding of the role of the Council of Fifty in early Mormon history, and a view that seriously questions the interpretations of Klaus Hansen, see D. Michael Quinn, "The Council of Fifty and Its Members, 1844 to 1945," *BYU Studies* 20 (Winter 1980): 163–97. See also Andrew F. Ehat, "'It Seems like Heaven Began on Earth': Joseph Smith and the Constitution of the Kingdom of God," *BYU Studies* 20 (Spring 1980): 253–79. The events surrounding the death of Joseph Smith in June 1844 are treated in Dallin H. Oaks and Marvin S. Hill, *Carthage Conspiracy: The Trial of the Accused Assassins of Joseph Smith* (Urbana: University of Illinois Press, 1975). Annette P. Hampshire takes a sociological perspective in examining the growing conflicts of the Nauvoo period in *Mormonism in Conflict: The Nauvoo Years,* Studies in Religion and Society, vol. 11 (New York: The Edwin Mellen Press, 1985). A good overview, in addition to those cited above by Ronald Esplin, of the historical and administrative issues of who could have been Joseph Smith's successor is D. Michael Quinn, "The Mormon Succession Crisis of 1844," *BYU Studies* 16 (Winter 1976): 187–233. See also Andrew F. Ehat, "Joseph Smith's Introduction of Temple Ordinances and the 1844 Mormon Succession Question" (master's thesis, Brigham Young University, 1982). A study which looks at Mormons in Philadelphia and on the east coast during the Nauvoo era is David J. Whittaker, "East of Nauvoo: Benjamin Winchester and the Early Mormon Church" (forthcoming in the *Journal of Mormon History*).

Aspects of the martyrdom of Joseph Smith are considered in the following works: Keith Huntress, "Governor Ford and the Murderers of Joseph Smith," *Dialogue* 4 (Summer 1969): 41–52; Ronald K. Esplin, "Joseph Smith's Mission and Timetable: 'God Will Protect Me until My Work is Done'," in *The Prophet Joseph: Essays on the Life and Mission of Joseph Smith,* ed. Larry C. Porter and Susan Easton Black (Salt Lake City: Deseret Book, 1988), 280–319; Dean C. Jessee, "Return to Carthage: Writing the History of Joseph Smith's Martyrdom," *Journal of Mormon History* 8 (1981): 3–19; Clifton H. Jolley, "The Martyrdom of Joseph Smith: An Archetypal Study," *Utah Historical Quarterly* 44 (Fall 1976): 329–50; Richard C. Poulsen, "Fate and the Persecutors of Joseph Smith: Transmutations of an American Myth," *Dialogue* 11 (Winter 1978): 63–70; and Davis Bitton, "The Martyrdom of Joseph Smith in Early Mormon Writings," *John Whitmer Historical Association Journal* 3 (1983): 29–39. A useful guide to the major sources of the Nauvoo experience gathered at one university is Stanley B. Kimball, *Sources of Mormon History in Illinois, 1838-1848: An Annotated Catalog of the Microfilm Collection at Southern Illinois University* (Carbondale, Ill.: Central Publications, 1966); and John C. Abbott, "Sources of Mormon History in Illinois, 1839-48, and a Bibliographic Note," *Dialogue* 5 (Spring 1970): 76-79.

Iowa and the Exodus West. Mormon knowledge of the American West prior to and after their exodus from Nauvoo began in February 1846 is the subject of two studies by Lewis Clark Christian: "A Study of Mormon Knowledge of the American Far West Prior to the Exodus (1830-February 1846)" (master's thesis, Brigham Young University, 1972); and "A Study of the Mormon Western Migration between February 1846 and July 1847 with Emphasis on and Evaluation of the Factors that Led to the Mormons' Choice of Salt Lake Valley as the Site of Their Initial Colony" (Ph.D. diss., Brigham Young University, 1976). See also Ronald K. Esplin, "'A Place Prepared': Joseph, Brigham and the Quest for a Promised Refuge in the West," *Journal of Mormon History* 9 (1982): 85-111.

The best study of the Mormon movement across Iowa Territory and the establishment of their temporary settlements along the Missouri River (near the Council Bluffs area today) is Richard E. Bennett, *Mormons at the Missouri, 1846-52: 'And Should We Die'* (Norman, Okla.: University of Oklahoma Press, 1987), although the focus of the volume is limited to 1846-47. See also Stanley B. Kimball, "The Iowa Trek of 1846: The Brigham Young Route from Nauvoo to Winter Quarters," *Ensign* 2 (June 1972): 36-45; and Kimball, "The Mormon Trail Network in Iowa, 1838-1863: A New Look," *BYU Studies* 21 (Fall 1981): 417-30.

The story of the initial movement to the Salt Lake Valley is told in Wallace Stegner, *The Gathering of Zion: The Story of the Mormon Trail* (New York: McGraw-Hill, 1964). A useful, day-by-day account of the 1847 pioneers is Hal Knight and Stanley B. Kimball, *111 Days to Zion* (Salt Lake City: Deseret News, 1978). See also Richard H. Jackson, "Myth and Reality: Environmental Perception of the Mormons, 1840-1865, an Historical Geosophy" (Ph.D. diss., Clark University, 1970); and John D. Unruh Jr., *The Plains Across: The Overland Emigrants and the Trans-Mississippi West, 1840-60* (Urbana: University of Illinois Press, 1979).

The enlistment and history of the Mormon Battalion was first told in a book-length account by participant Daniel Tyler, *A Concise History of the Mormon Battalion in the Mexican War* (1881; reprint, Chicago: Rio Grande Press, 1964). More recently see John Yutinus,

"A Ram in the Thicket: The Mormon Battalion in the Mexican War" (Ph.D. diss., Brigham Young University, 1975); and Stanley B. Kimball, "The Mormon Battalion March, 1846-47," *Ensign* 9 (July 1979): 57-61.

Early Pioneer Period (1847–1869). The most recent study of these years is Eugene E. Campbell, *Establishing Zion: The Mormon Church in the American West, 1847-1869* (Salt Lake City: Signature Books, 1988). Older but still useful studies include Hubert Howe Bancroft, *History of Utah, 1540-1886* (1889; reprint, Salt Lake City: Bookcraft, 1964); Levi Edgar Young, *The Founding of Utah* (New York: Charles Scribners' Sons, 1923); Andrew Love Neff, *History of Utah, 1847 to 1869* (Salt Lake City: Deseret News Press, 1940); Leland H. Creer, *The Founding of an Empire: The Exploration and Colonization of Utah, 1776-1856* (Salt Lake City: Bookcraft, 1947); Dale L. Morgan, *The Great Salt Lake* (Indianapolis: Bobbs-Merrill, 1947); Nels Anderson, *Desert Saints: The Mormon Frontier in Utah* (Chicago: University of Chicago Press, 1942); Howard R. Lamar, *The Far Southwest: 1846-1912, a Territorial History* (New Haven: Yale University Press, 1966); Charles S. Peterson, *Utah: A Bicentennial History,* The States and the Nation Series (New York: W. W. Norton for the American Association for State and Local History, 1977); and the early volumes of Orson F. Whitney, *History of Utah,* 4 vols. (Salt Lake City: George Q. Cannon and Sons, 1892-1904).

Special topics are treated in the following works: Dale L. Morgan, "The State of Deseret," *Utah Historical Quarterly* 8 (April-October 1940): 65-239; Peter Crawley, "The Constitution of the State of Deseret," *BYU Studies* 29 (Fall 1989): 7-22; William G. Hartley, "Mormons, Crickets, and Gulls: A New Look at an Old Story," *Utah Historical Quarterly* 38 (Summer 1970): 224-39; Paul H. Peterson, "The Mormon Reformation" (Ph.D. diss., Brigham Young University, 1981); Juanita Brooks, *The Mountain Meadows Massacre* (Stanford: Stanford University Press, 1950); Norman F. Furniss, *The Mormon Conflict, 1850-1859* (New Haven: Yale University Press, 1960); LeRoy R. and Ann W. Hafen, eds., *The Utah Expedition, 1857-58: A Documentary Account* (Glendale, Calif.: Arthur H. Clark, 1958); Donald R. Moorman and Gene A. Sessions, *Camp Floyd and the Mormons* (Salt Lake City: University of Utah Press, 1992); E. B. Long, *The Saints and the Union: Utah Territory during the Civil War* (Urbana: University of Illinois Press, 1981); and Thomas G. Alexander and James B. Allen, *Mormons and Gentiles: A History of Salt Lake City* (Boulder, Colo.: Pruett Publishing, 1984).

See also the following bibliographical works: Thomas G. Alexander and James B. Allen, "The Mormons in the Mountain West:

A Selected Bibliography," *Arizona and the West* 9 (Winter 1967): 365-84; Philip A. M. Taylor, "Recent Writing on Utah and the Mormons," *Arizona and the West* 4 (Autumn 1962): 249-60; S. Lyman Tyler, *Greater Utah, the Mormons, et al.: The Region and the Record* (Salt Lake City: American West Center, University of Utah, 1981); Tyler, *The Historiography of Utah, the Mormons, and the West: A Personal Approach* (Salt Lake City: American West Center, University of Utah, 1978); J. Cecil Alter, "Bibliographers' Choice of Books on Utah and the Mormons," *Utah Historical Quarterly* 24 (July 1956): 214-31; Frank H. Jonas, "Bibliography on Utah Politics," in "Bibliography on Western Politics," *The Western Political Quarterly* 11, supplement (December 1958): 132-51; and Thomas G. Alexander, "Toward the New Mormon History: An Examination of the Literature on the Latter-day Saints in the Far West," in *Historians and the American West,* ed. Michael P. Malone (Lincoln: University of Nebraska Press, 1983), 344-68.

Later Pioneer Period (1869–1896). The period from the coming of the transcontinental railroad in 1869 to Utah statehood in 1896, a period of retrenchment, stress, and persecution, is discussed in a number of good works. Leonard J. Arrington, *Great Basin Kingdom: An Economic History of the Latter-day Saints, 1830-1900* (Cambridge: Harvard University Press, 1958) is essential. Gustive O. Larson, *The "Americanization" of Utah for Statehood* (San Marino, Calif.: Huntington Library, 1971) provides a useful overview of the major events. A more recent study which shows more attention to the behind-the-scenes saga is Edward Leo Lyman, *Political Deliverance: The Mormon Quest for Utah Statehood* (Urbana: University of Illinois Press, 1986). See also Robert Joseph Dwyer, *The Gentile Comes to Utah,* 2d ed. (1941; reprint, Salt Lake City: Western Epics, 1971); Jean Bickmore White, "Utah State Elections: 1895-1899" (Ph.D. diss., University of Utah, 1968); Edward Leo Lyman, "Isaac Turmbo and the Politics of Utah Statehood," *Utah Historical Quarterly* 41 (Spring 1973): 128-49; and Jan Shipps, "The Mormons in Politics: The First Hundred Years" (Ph.D. diss., University of Colorado, 1965). Studies focusing on the polygamy issues of this period are noted below.

Early Twentieth Century. The best place to begin is Thomas G. Alexander, *Mormonism in Transition: A History of the Latter-day Saints, 1890-1930* (Urbana: University of Illinois Press, 1986). See also the 1953 dissertation of Milton R. Merrill, *Reed Smoot, Apostle in Politics* (Logan: Utah State University Press and Department of Political Science, 1990), which work must be supplemented by M. Paul Holsinger, "For God and the American Home: The Attempt to Unseat Senator Reed Smoot, 1903-1907," *Pacific Northwest Quarterly* 60

(July 1969): 154-60; Thomas G. Alexander, "Reed Smoot, the LDS Church, and Progressive Legislation, 1903-1933," *Dialogue* 7 (Spring 1972): 47-56; Jan Shipps, "The Public Image of Sen. Reed Smoot, 1902-1932," *Utah Historical Quarterly* 45 (Fall 1977): 380-400; Harvard S. Heath, "Reed Smoot, the First Modern Mormon" (Ph.D. diss., Brigham Young University, 1990); and Jan Shipps, "Utah Comes of Age Politically: A Study of the State's Politics in the Early Years of the Twentieth Century," *Utah Historical Quarterly* 35 (Spring 1967): 91-111. See also Leonard J. Arrington and Thomas G. Alexander, *A Dependent Commonwealth: Utah's Economy from Statehood to the Great Depression* (Provo, Utah: Brigham Young University Press, 1974); and Richard O. Cowan, *The Church in the Twentieth Century* (Salt Lake City: Bookcraft, 1985).

Depression to World War II. Useful places to begin, in addition to the histories cited above, are Wayne K. Hinton, "Some Historical Perspectives on Mormon Responses to the Great Depression," *Journal of the West* 24 (October 1985): 19-26; and Hinton, "The Economics of Ambivalence: Utah's Depression Experience," *Utah Historical Quarterly* 54 (Summer 1986): 268-85.

The beginnings of the modern welfare program are discussed in Leonard J. Arrington and Wayne K. Hinton, "Origin of the Welfare Plan of The Church of Jesus Christ of Latter-day Saints," *BYU Studies* 5 (Winter 1964): 67-85; Albert L. Fisher, "Mormon Welfare Programs: Past and Present," *Social Science Journal* 15 (April 1978): 75-99; Jessie Embry, "Relief Society Grain Storage Program, 1876-1940" (master's thesis, Brigham Young University, 1974); and Jill Mulvay Derr, "Changing Relief Society Charity to Make Way for Welfare," in *New Views of Mormon History,* ed. Davis Bitton and Maureen Ursenbach Beecher (Salt Lake City: University of Utah Press, 1987), 242-72.

The Church during World War II is treated in the histories cited above and particularly in Richard O. Cowan, *The Church in the Twentieth Century* (Salt Lake City: Bookcraft, 1985) and in James B. Allen and Glen M. Leonard, *The Story of the Latter-day Saints,* 2d ed., rev. and enl. (Salt Lake City: Deseret Book, 1992). Useful studies which focus on individual experiences are Joseph M. Dixon, "Mormons in the Third Reich: 1933-1945," *Dialogue* 7 (Spring 1972): 70-78; William G. Hartley, "War and Peace and Dutch Potatoes," *Ensign* 8 (July 1977): 18-23; and Alan F. Keele and Douglas F. Tobler, "The Fuhrer's New Clothes: Helmuth Huebner and the Mormons and the Third Reich," *Sunstone* 5 (November/December 1980): 20-29.

The Internationalization of the Church. An excellent place to begin studying the growth of the Church is Dean R. Louder,

"A Distributional and Diffusionary Analysis of the Mormon Church, 1850–1970" (Ph.D. diss., University of Washington, 1972). An introductory overview of the history of Mormon missionary work is James R. Moss, R. Lanier Britsch, James R. Christianson and Richard O. Cowan, *The International Church* (Provo, Utah: Brigham Young University Press, 1982); Bruce A. Van Orden is currently rewriting this volume. See also the references below under Missiology.

Late Twentieth Century. For an excellent overview of more recent developments, see James B. Allen and Glen M. Leonard, *The Story of the Latter-day Saints,* 2d ed., rev. and enl. (Salt Lake City: Deseret Book, 1992), chapters 19–21, and the related bibliographies.

Economic History

The most important single work on this topic is Leonard J. Arrington, *Great Basin Kingdom: An Economic History of the Latter-day Saints, 1830–1900* (Cambridge: Harvard University Press, 1958). Much of Arrington's professional work has concentrated on Mormon and western economic history; a guide to his extensive bibliography is David J. Whittaker, "Leonard James Arrington: A Bibliography," in *New Views of Mormon History,* ed. Davis Bitton and Maureen Ursenbach Beecher (Salt Lake City: University of Utah Press, 1987), 439–69. An especially valuable work providing more detailed analysis of specific topics and communities and carrying this story into the twentieth century is Arrington, Feramorz Y. Fox, and Dean L. May, *Building the City of God: Community and Cooperation among the Mormons,* rev. ed. (Urbana: University of Illinois Press, 1992). See also Mario DePillis, "The Development of Mormon Communitarianism, 1826–1846" (Ph.D. diss., Yale University, 1960); Lyndon W. Cook, *Joseph Smith and the Law of Consecration* (Provo, Utah: Grandin Books, 1985); Dean L. May, "Body and Soul: The Record of Mormon Religious Philanthropy," *Church History* 57 (September 1988): 322–36; and Garth L. Mangum and Bruce D. Blumell, *The Mormons' War on Poverty: A History of LDS Welfare 1830–1990* (Salt Lake City: University of Utah Press, 1993).

Information on the history of Church finances can be gleaned from the following sources: Leonard J. Arrington, *Great Basin Kingdom: An Economic History of the Latter-day Saints, 1830–1900* (Cambridge: Harvard University Press, 1958); Leonard J. Arrington and Davis Bitton, "The Temporal Foundation," in *The Mormon Experience: A History of the Latter-day Saints* (New York: Alfred A. Knopf, 1979), 262–83; Bill Beecham and David Briscoe, "Mormon Money and How It's Made," *Utah Holiday,* 5 (March 22, 1976): 4–11; "Change Comes to

Zion's Empire," *Business Week,* November 23, 1957, 103–16; Jeffrey Kaye, "An Invisible Empire: Mormon Money in California," *New West,* May 8, 1978, 36–41; Robert Gottlieb and Peter Wiley, *America's Saints: The Rise of Mormon Power* (New York: Putnam's Sons, 1984), 95–128; H. Henderson, "Managing the Mormon Millions," *Executive* 18 (November 1976); 32–35; Randall Hatch, "The Mormon Church: Managing the Lord's Work," *MBA* (June 1977): 33–37; Fred Esplin, "The Saints Go Marching On: Learning to Live with Success," *Utah Holiday* 10 (June 1981): 33–48; Arrington, "The Six Pillars of Utah's Pioneer Economy," *Encyclia: The Journal of the Utah Academy of Sciences, Arts, and Letters* 54, part 1 (1977): 9–24; Arrington, "Mormondom's Financial Records," *This People* 12 (Summer 1991): 46–47; David James Croft, "The Private Business Activities of Brigham Young, 1847–1887," *Journal of the West* 16 (October 1977): 36–51; Arrington, "The Mormon Tithing House: A Frontier Business Institution," *Business History Review* 28 (March 1954): 24–58; John Heinerman and Anson Shupe, *The Mormon Corporate Empire* (Boston: Beacon Press, 1985); and the series on the Church's finances in the *Arizona Republic,* 1991, reprinted in various other newspapers. See, for example, the *Salt Lake Tribune,* June 30, 1991, and *Deseret News,* July 2–3, 1991. The student must remember that since 1952 the Church has not made public its financial records, thus no fully reliable account of its finances is available.

Administrative History

No comprehensive study of the organizational history of the Mormon Church is available, but there are a growing number of very good specialized studies upon which such a work will be constructed. D. Michael Quinn has written a number of these: "Organizational Development and Social Origins of the Mormon Hierarchy, 1832–1932: A Prosopographical Study" (master's thesis, University of Utah, 1973); "The Mormon Hierarchy, 1832–1932: An American Elite" (Ph.D. diss., Yale University, 1976); "The Evolution of the Presiding Quorums of the LDS Church," *Journal of Mormon History* 1 (1974): 21–38; "From Sacred Grove to Sacral Power Structure," *Dialogue* 17 (Summer 1984): 9–34; and *J. Reuben Clark: The Church Years* (Provo, Utah: Brigham Young University Press, 1983). Neil K. Coleman, "A Study of the Church . . . as an Administrative System: Its Structure and Maintenance," (Ph.D. diss., New York University, 1967) is also useful. Among William G. Hartley's essays on administrative history, the following are especially valuable: "Nauvoo Stake, Priesthood Quorums, and the Church's First Wards," *BYU Studies* 32 (Winter and Spring 1992):

57-80; "Ordained and Acting Teachers in the Lesser Priesthood, 1851-1883," *BYU Studies* 16 (Spring 1976): 375-98; "The Seventies in the 1880s: Revelations and Reorganizing," *Dialogue* 16 (Spring 1983): 62-88; "The Priesthood Reorganization of 1877: Brigham Young's Last Achievement," *BYU Studies* 20 (Fall 1979): 3-36; and "The Priesthood Reform Movement, 1908-1922," *BYU Studies* 13 (Winter 1973): 137-56. A short bibliographical note is David J. Whittaker, "An Introduction to Mormon Administrative History," *Dialogue* 15 (Winter 1982): 14-20. A useful history of leadership changes is Reed C. Durham Jr. and Steven H. Heath, *Succession in the Church* (Salt Lake City: Bookcraft, 1970). A history focusing on the Quorum of the Twelve Apostles is Wilburn D. Talbot, *The Acts of the Modern Apostles* (Salt Lake City: Randall Book, 1985). The Seventies are studied in James N. Baumgarter, "The Role and Function of the Seventy in L.D.S. Church History" (master's thesis, Brigham Young University, 1960). A valuable chronological compilation of documents on the history of the Seventies is an unpublished work by John L. Lund, "An Extensive Annotated Bibliography [to 1970] of Literature Related to the Office and Calling of the Seventy," manuscript in Special Collections, Harold B. Lee Library, Brigham Young University.

The central role of Mormon lay bishops is discussed in D. Gene Pace, "Community Leadership on the Mormon Frontier: Mormon Bishops and the Political, Economic and Social Development of Utah before Statehood" (Ph.D. diss., Ohio State University, 1983); Pace, "The LDS Presiding Bishop, 1851-1888: An Administrative Study" (master's thesis, Brigham Young University, 1978); and Dale F. Beecher, "The Office of Bishop," *Dialogue* 15 (Winter 1982): 103-15.

On the office of patriarch, see Irene May Bates, "Transformation of Charisma in the Mormon Church: A History of the Office of Presiding Patriarch, 1833-1979" (Ph.D. diss., UCLA, 1991).

The correlation program, the most important administrative development in recent years, can be studied through Carol H. Cannon, comp., "Correlation Chronology As Reflected in Minutes of Correlation Executive Committee Meetings, 1960-1971," copy in Church Library, The Church of Jesus Christ of Latter-day Saints, Salt Lake City; Bruce D. Blumell, "Priesthood Correlation, 1960-1974," copy in Church Historical Department, The Church of Jesus Christ of Latter-day Saints, Salt Lake City; Dale C. Mouritsen, *A Defence and a Refuge: Priesthood Correlation and the Establishment of Zion* (Brigham Young University Press, 1972); Jerry "J" Rose, "The Correlation Program of the Church . . . during the Twentieth Century," (master's thesis, Brigham Young University, 1973); and John P. Fugal, comp.,

A Review of Priesthood Correlation (Provo, Utah: Brigham Young University Press, 1968). An outsider's perception is presented in Robert Gottlieb and Peter Wiley, *America's Saints: The Rise of Mormon Power* (New York: Putnam's Sons, 1984), 56-64, much of which appears as "The Lee Revolution and the Rise of Correlation," *Sunstone* 10, no. 1 (1984-85): 18-22.

Students of the LDS Church must be aware of the publications addressing its governance. These include the turn-of-the-century guidebooks of Joseph B. Keeler; John A. Widtsoe, comp., *Priesthood and Church Government* (Salt Lake City: Deseret Book, 1939); Harold Glen Clark, *The Art of Governing Zion* (Provo, Utah: Extension Publications, Brigham Young University, 1966); Richard O. Coman and Wilson K. Andersen, *The Living Church: The Unfolding of the Programs and Organization of The Church of Jesus Christ of Latter-day Saints during the Twentieth Century* (Provo, Utah: Brigham Young University Printing Service, 1974); and the various volumes of James R. Clark's *The Messages of the First Presidency,* 6 vols. (Salt Lake City: Bookcraft, 1965-1975). The best way to follow recent developments is through the Church's internally produced *Priesthood Bulletin* (1965-74) [six times per year]; and *Bulletin* (1980-present); and the *General Handbook of Instructions* (1976-1989).

A bibliographical guide to the judicial system of the Church is David J. Whittaker, "The LDS Judicial System: A Selected Bibliography," *Mormon History Association Newsletter,* no. 59 (October 1985): 8-10. See also Edwin Brown Firmage and Richard Collin Mangrum, *Zion in the Courts: A Legal History of the Church of Jesus Christ of Latter-day Saints, 1830-1900* (Urbana: University of Illinois Press, 1988); and Lester Bush Jr., "Excommunication and Church Courts: A Note from the General Handbook of Instructions," *Dialogue* 14 (Summer 1981): 74-98.

The revelation extending the priesthood to all worthy males (June 1978) is treated in a volume of essays: Lester E. Bush Jr. and Armand L. Mauss, eds., *Neither White Nor Black: Mormon Scholars Confront the Race Issue in a Universal Church* (Midvale, Utah: Signature Books, 1984). This volume also contains an extensive bibliography.

Mormons and American Society

The treatment of Mormons in the periodical press has received scholarly attention and is worth noting because of the bibliographical content in each. See Fay Ollerton, "The American Periodicals Treatment of Mormonism Since 1850" (master's thesis, Columbia University,

1947); Herbert N. Morris, "An Analysis of References to the Church of Jesus Christ of Latter-day Saints in General Magazines of the United States during Selected Periods between 1847 and 1953" (master's thesis, Brigham Young University, 1958); David G. Wright, "A Content Analysis of References to the Church of Jesus Christ of Latter-day Saints in General Magazines in the United States between 1953 and 1964" (master's thesis, Brigham Young University, 1964); Dale P. Pelo, "Mormonism in National Periodicals, 1961–70" (master's thesis, Brigham Young University, 1973); Richard O. Cowan, "Mormonism in National Periodicals" (Ph.D. diss., Stanford University, 1961); and Dennis L. Lythgoe, "The Changing Image of Mormonism in Periodical Literature" (Ph.D. diss., University of Utah, 1969).

The rather negative image of the Mormons apparent throughout American history has been studied from a variety of perspectives. An important study of the early negative newspaper coverage is Walter A. Norton, "Comparative Images: Mormonism and Contemporary Religions as Seen by Village Newspapermen in Western New York and Northeastern Ohio, 1820–1833" (Ph.D. diss., Brigham Young University, 1991).

Specific studies of those individuals and published works critical of the Mormons include the following: Richard Lloyd Anderson, "Joseph Smith's New York Reputation Reappraised," *BYU Studies* 10 (Spring 1970): 283–314; Jon Haupt and Leonard J. Arrington, "The Missouri and Illinois Mormons in Ante-Bellum Fiction," *Dialogue* 5 (Spring 1970): 37–50; Arrington and Haupt, "Intolerable Zion: The Image of Mormonism in Nineteenth Century American Literature," *Western Humanities Review* 22 (Summer 1968): 243–60; Lester E. Bush Jr., "The Spalding Theory Then and Now," *Dialogue* 10 (Autumn 1977): 40–69; David Brion Davis, "Some Themes of Counter-Subversion: An Analysis of Anti-Masonic, Anti-Catholic, and Anti-Mormon Literature," *Mississippi Valley Historical Review* 47 (September 1960): 205–24; Marvin S. Hill, "Cultural Crisis in the Mormon Kingdom: A Reconsideration of the Causes of Kirtland Dissent," *Church History* 49 (September 1980): 286–97; Kenneth W. Godfrey, "Causes of Mormon-Non-Mormon Conflict in Hancock County, Illinois, 1839–1846" (Ph.D. diss., Brigham Young University, 1967); Annette P. Hampshire, "Thomas Sharp and Anti-Mormon Sentiment in Illinois, 1842–1845," *Journal of the Illinois State Historical Society* 72 (May 1979): 82–100; Hampshire, "The Triumph of Mobocracy in Hancock County, 1844–1846," *Western Illinois Regional Studies* 5 (1982): 17–37; Rebecca Foster Cornwall and Leonard J. Arrington, "Perpetuation of a Myth: Mormon Danites in Five Western Novels,

1840-1890," *BYU Studies* 23 (Spring 1983): 147-65; Merle W. Wells, *Anti-Mormonism in Idaho, 1872-1892* (Provo, Utah: Brigham Young University Press, 1978); David Brudnoy, "A Decade in Zion: Theodore Schroeder's Initial Assault on the Mormons," *Historian* 37 (1975): 241-56; Scott Faulring, "An Oral History of the Modern Microfilm Co., 1959-1982" (Senior Seminar Paper, Department of History, Brigham Young University, 1983) [an extensive oral history with Sandra Tanner and an exhaustive bibliography of the publications of Modern Microfilm Company—now Utah Lighthouse Ministry—the most active contemporary anti-Mormon publisher]; Lawrence Foster, "Career Apostates: Reflections on the Works of Jerald and Sandra Tanner," *Dialogue* 17 (Summer 1984): 35-60; Stephen W. Stathis and Dennis L. Lythgoe, "Mormonism in the Nineteen-Seventies: The Popular Perception," *Dialogue* 10 (Spring 1977): 95-113; and Stathis, "Mormonism and the Periodical Press: A Change is Underway," *Dialogue* 14 (Summer 1981): 48-73.

The graphic image of the Latter-day Saints has been studied in Gary L. Bunker and Davis Bitton, *The Mormon Graphic Image, 1834-1914* (Salt Lake City: University of Utah Press, 1983). Film images are the subject of the following studies by Richard Alan Nelson: "A History of Latter-day Saint Screen Portrayals in the Anti-Mormon Film Era, 1905-1936" (master's thesis, Brigham Young University, 1975); "From Antagonism to Acceptance: Mormons and the Silver Screen," *Dialogue* 10 (Spring 1977): 59-69; and "Commercial Propaganda in the Silent Film: A Case Study of 'A Mormon Maid' (1917)," *Film History: An International Journal* 1 (1987): 149-62. See also Stuart W. Hyde, "The Anti-Mormon Drama in the United States," *Western Humanities Review* 9 (Spring 1955): 177-81; and Fred C. Esplin, "The Church as Broadcaster," *Dialogue* 10 (Spring 1977): 25-45.

Important critiques of the recent anti-Mormon film *The Godmakers* are found in *Dialogue* 18 (Summer 1985): 14-39; and Gilbert W. Scharffs, *The Truth about* The Godmakers (Salt Lake City: Publishers Press, 1986). For responses to a persistent charge of evangelical Christians, see Stephen E. Robinson, *Are Mormons Christians?* (Salt Lake City: Bookcraft, 1991) and Daniel C. Peterson and Stephen D. Ricks, *Offenders for a Word* (Salt Lake City: Aspen Books, 1992).

Klaus J. Hansen, *Mormonism and the American Experience* (Chicago: University of Chicago Press, 1981) attempts to place Mormonism in its larger American setting. The American religious context for Mormonism is discussed in Whitney R. Cross, *The Burned-Over District* (1950; reprint, New York: Harper and Row, 1965); Milton V. Backman Jr., *American Religions and the Rise of Mormonism,* rev. ed. (Salt Lake City: Deseret Book, 1970). See also Gordon S. Wood, "Evangelical America and Early Mormonism," *New York History* 61 (October 1980): 359–86; Timothy L. Smith, "The Book of Mormon in a Biblical Culture," *Journal of Mormon History* 7 (1980): 3–21; Marvin S. Hill, "The Shaping of the Mormon Mind in New England and New York," *BYU Studies* 9 (Spring 1969): 351–72; and Hill, "The Rise of Mormonism in the Burned-Over District: Another View," *New York History* 61 (October 1980): 411–30.

Significant outside observers who have written about Mormonism include Eduard Meyer, *The Origin and History of the Mormons with Reflections on the Beginnings of Islam and Christianity,* trans. Heinz F. Rahde and Eugene Seaich (1912; reprint, Salt Lake City: University of Utah, [1961]); Wallace Stegner, *Mormon Country* (New York: Duell, Sloan and Pearce, 1942); Thomas F. O'Dea, *The Mormons* (Chicago: University of Chicago Press, 1957); Mark P. Leone, *Roots of Modern Mormonism* (Cambridge: Harvard University Press, 1979); Jan Shipps, *Mormonism: The Story of a New Religious Tradition* (Urbana: University of Illinois Press, 1985); R. Laurence Moore, *Religious Outsiders and the Making of Americans* (New York: Oxford University Press, 1986), especially chapter 1; Martin E. Marty, "Two Integrities: An Address to the Crisis in Mormon Historiography," *Journal of Mormon History* 10 (1983): 3–19; John G. Gager, "Early Mormonism and Early Christianity: Some Parallels and Their Consequences for the Study of New Religions," *Journal of Mormon History* 9 (1982): 53–60; and the rather chaotic discussion by Harold Bloom, *The American Religion: The Emergence of the Post-Christian Nation* (New York: Simon and Schuster, 1992), section two. See also Truman G. Madsen, ed., *Reflections on Mormonism: Judaeo-Christian Parallels,* Religious Studies Center Monograph Series, vol. 4 (Provo, Utah: Religious Studies Center, Brigham Young University, 1978).

Observations by various "visitors" to Mormon communities are valuable for both their views and the larger impact they had. Among the first was Nancy Towle, who reported her observations of Mormon Kirtland in *Vicissitudes: Illustrated in the Experiences of Nancy Towle in Europe and America* (Charleston, 1832). Charlotte Haven's perceptions of Nauvoo are in "Charlotte Haven Writes Home from Nauvoo," in *Among the Mormons: Historic Accounts by Contemporary Observers,* ed. William Mulder and A. Russell Mortensen (1958; reprint, Lincoln: University of Nebraska Press, 1973), 116–23, and "'Great Events Have Transpired': Politics and Polygamy," 124–27; Richard Burton's visit to Utah was detailed in his *City of the Saints* (1861; reprint, New York: Alfred A. Knopf, 1963). Especially valuable is

Elizabeth Wood Kane, *Twelve Mormon Homes Visited in Succession on a Journey through Utah to Arizona* (1874; reprint, Salt Lake City: University of Utah Press, 1974).

Useful scholarly studies of the travel and curiosa literature include Fawn M. Brodie, "Sir Richard F. Burton: Exceptional Observer of the Mormon Scene," *Utah Historical Quarterly* 38 (Fall 1970): 295–311; D. L. Ashliman, "The Image of Utah and the Mormons in Nineteenth-Century Germany," *Utah Historical Quarterly* 35 (Summer 1967): 209–27; Ashliman, "Mormonism and the Germans: An Annotated Bibliography, 1848–1966," *BYU Studies* 8 (Autumn 1967): 73–94; Wilfried Decoo, "The Image of Mormonism in French Literature, [Parts I and II]," *BYU Studies* 14 (Winter 1974): 157–75, and 16 (Winter 1976): 265–76; Edwina Jo Snow, "Singular Saints: The Image of the Mormons in Book-Length Travel Accounts, 1847–1857" (master's thesis, George Washington University, 1972); Snow, "William Chandless: British Overlander, Mormon Observer, Amazon Explorer," *Utah Historical Quarterly* 54 (Spring 1986): 116–36; Snow, "British Travelers View the Saints, 1847–1877," *BYU Studies* 31 (Spring 1991): 63–81; Michael W. Homer, "The Church's Image in Italy from the 1840s to 1946: A Bibliographic Essay," *BYU Studies* 31 (Spring 1991): 83–114; Homer, "'Recent Psychic Evidence': The Visit of Sir Arthur Conan Doyle to Utah in 1923," *Utah Historical Quarterly* 52 (Summer 1984): 264–74; and Howard C. Searle, "Early Mormon Historiography" (Ph.D. diss., UCLA, 1979), 29–51.

Perceptive studies on the relationship of Mormonism to its host culture include Thomas F. O'Dea, "Mormonism and the American Experience of Time," *Western Humanities Review* 8 (Summer 1954): 181–90; O'Dea, "Mormonism and the Avoidance of Sectarian Stagnation: A Study of Church, Sect, and Incipient Nationalism," *American Journal of Sociology* 60 (November 1954): 285–93; O'Dea, "Sources of Strain in Mormon History Reconsidered," in *Mormonism and American Culture,* ed. Marvin S. Hill and James B. Allen (New York: Harper and Row, 1972), 147–67; Klaus J. Hansen, "Mormon Sexuality and American Culture," *Dialogue* 10 (Autumn 1976): 45–56; James L. Clayton, "The Challenge of Secularism," *Dialogue* 3 (Autumn 1968): 63–76; John Sorenson, "Mormon World View and American Culture," *Dialogue* 8 (Summer 1973): 17–29. See also Kenneth H. Winn, *Exiles in a Land of Liberty: Mormons in America* (Chapel Hill: University of North Carolina Press, 1989); and Armand L. Mauss, *The Angel and the Beehive: The Mormon Struggle with Assimilation* (Urbana: University of Illinois Press, 1994).

Valuable studies which examine the attitudes of Church members and leaders regarding war include Robert Jeffrey Stott, "Mormonism and

War: An Interpretative Analysis of Selected Mormon Thought regarding Seven American Wars" (master's thesis, Brigham Young University, 1974); D. Michael Quinn, "The Mormon Church and the Spanish-American War: An End to Selective Pacifism," *Pacific Historical Review* 43 (August 1974): 342-66; and Ronald W. Walker, "Sheaves, Bucklers and the State: Mormon Leaders Respond to the Dilemmas of War," *Sunstone* 7 (July-August 1982): 43-56. See also Richard T. Maher, "For God and Country: Mormon Chaplains during World War II" (master's thesis, Brigham Young University, 1975); and Joseph F. Boone, "The Roles of The Church of Jesus Christ of Latter-day Saints in Relation to the United States Military, 1900-1975" (Ph.D. diss., Brigham Young University, 1975).

Studies which seek to examine Mormonism in an international context include Spencer J. Palmer, *An Expanding Church* (Salt Lake City: Deseret Book, 1978); Palmer, *The Church Encounters Asia* (Salt Lake City: Deseret Book, 1970); F. LaMond Tullis, ed., *Mormonism: A Faith for All Cultures* (Provo, Utah: Brigham Young University Press, 1978); R. Lanier Britsch, *Unto the Islands of the Sea: A History of the Latter-day Saints in the Pacific* (Salt Lake City, Deseret Book, 1986); Garth N. Jones, "Expanding LDS Church Abroad: Old Realities Compounded," *Dialogue* 13 (Spring 1980): 8-22; Jones, "Spreading the Gospel in Indonesia: Organizational Obstacles and Opportunities," *Dialogue* 15 (Winter 1982): 79-90; Brigham Y. Card and others, eds., *The Mormon Presence in Canada* (Logan: Utah State University Press, 1990); F. LaMond Tullis, *Mormons in Mexico: The Dynamics of Faith and Culture* (Logan: Utah State University Press, 1987); Leonard J. Arrington, "Historical Development of International Mormonism," *Religious Studies and Theology* 7 (January 1987): 9-22; Mark L. Grover, "Mormonism in Brazil: Religion and Dependency in Latin America" (Ph.D. diss., Indiana University, 1985); David Knowlton, "Missionaries and Terror: The Assassination of Two Elders in Bolivia," *Sunstone* 13 (August 1989): 10-15; and James B. Allen, "On Becoming a Universal Church: Some Historical Perspectives," *Dialogue* 25 (March 1992): 13-36.

Missiology

There is no one-volume history of Mormon missionary activity. A survey of the extensive literature is presented in a three-part guide organized by country in David J. Whittaker, "A Bibliography of LDS Missions and Missionary Work," *Mormon History Association Newsletter,* no. 69 (July 1988): 5-8; no. 70 (October 1988): 4-8; and no. 71 (January 1989): 3-4. The essential studies include S. George Ellsworth, "A History of Mormon Missions in the United States and Canada, 1830-1860," (Ph.D. diss., University of California, Berkeley, 1951); Barbara Joan McFarlane Higdon, "The Role of Preaching in the Early Latter-day Saint Church, 1830-1846" (Ph.D. diss., University of Missouri, 1961); James B. Allen, Ronald K. Esplin, and David J. Whittaker, *Men with a Mission: The Quorum of the Twelve Apostles in the British Isles, 1837-1841* (Salt Lake City: Deseret Book, 1992); Gordon Irving, "Numerical Strength and Geographical Distribution of the LDS Missionary Force, 1830-1974," *Task Papers in LDS History*, no. 1 (Salt Lake City: Historical Department of The Church of Jesus Christ of Latter-day Saints, 1975); and Brad Morris, "The Internationalization of the Church of Jesus Christ of Latter-day Saints," manuscript copy in the Church Library.

Also useful are Calvin S. Kunz, "A History of Female Missionary Activity in the Church of Jesus Christ of Latter-day Saints, 1830-1898" (master's thesis, Brigham Young University, 1976); and Tancred I. King, "Missiology and Mormon Missions," *Dialogue* 16 (Winter 1983): 42-50.

Biography

In 1888, Andrew Jenson issued his first *Biographical Encyclopedia* as a supplement to his *Historical Record*. He expanded the effort into four volumes: *LDS Biographical Encyclopedia* (Salt Lake City: Jenson History, 1901-1936). Also useful is Frank E. Esshom, *Pioneers and Prominent Men of Utah* (Salt Lake City: Utah Pioneers Book Publishing, 1913). Volume four of Orson F. Whitney's *History of Utah* (Salt Lake City: George Q. Cannon and Sons, 1904) is a biographical appendix to his larger project. The most comprehensive aid to students seeking biographical information on Mormons is Marvin Wiggins, *Mormons and their Neighbors: An Index to over 75,000 Biographical Sketches from 1820 to the Present,* 2 vols. (Provo, Utah: Harold B. Lee Library, Brigham Young University, 1984). Biographical sketches of Church leaders are in Lawrence R. Flake, *Mighty Men of Zion* (Salt Lake City: Karl D. Butler, 1974). Interpretative essays on the strengths and weaknesses of Mormon biography, as well as works that evaluate the historiography of Mormon biographical efforts, include Davis Bitton, "Mormon Biography," *Biography: An Interdisciplinary Quarterly* 4 (Winter 1981): 1-16; Ronald W. Walker, "The Challenge and Craft of Mormon Biography," *BYU Studies* 22 (Spring 1982): 179-92; and David J. Whittaker, "The Heritage and Tasks of Mormon Biography," in *Supporting Saints: Life Stories of Nineteenth Century Mormons,* ed. Donald Q. Cannon and David J. Whittaker (Provo, Utah: Religious Studies Center, Brigham Young University, 1985), 1–16. See also the insightful study by Susan Hendricks Swetnam, *Lives of the Saints in Southeast Idaho: An Introduction to Mormon Pioneer Life Story Writing* (Moscow: University of Idaho Press, 1991).

Biographies of the men who have served as President of the LDS Church, as well as of those individuals who worked closely with them are uneven and, with few exceptions, written for a popular audience rather than with careful concern for research and objectivity. The exceptions are worth noting. A good place to begin is with the multi-authored collection of essays on each of the Presidents: Leonard J. Arrington, ed., *The Presidents of the Church* (Salt Lake City: Deseret Book, 1986).

The founder, Joseph Smith, still awaits a definitive biography. The widely touted study by Fawn M. Brodie, *No Man Knows My History: The Life of Joseph Smith, the Mormon Prophet,* rev. ed. (New York: Alfred Knopf, 1971), is seriously flawed by Brodie's refusal to see any of Joseph Smith's religious claims or experiences as anything more than the result of environmental or psychological factors. Such a secular portrait of a religious man must be seen as inadequate; for a critique of Brodie's work along this line, see Marvin S. Hill, "Brodie Revisited: A Reappraisal," *Dialogue* 7 (Winter 1972): 72-85; and Hill, "Secular or Sectarian History? A Critique of *No Man Knows My History,*" *Church History* 43 (March 1974): 78-96. A useful overview of Joseph Smith is Thomas G. Alexander, "The Place of Joseph Smith in the Development of American Religion: A Historiographical Inquiry," *Journal of Mormon History* 5 (1978): 3–17. The first published biography in LDS history was by Joseph's mother, Lucy Mack Smith, *Biographical Sketches of the Prophet Joseph Smith, and His Progenitors for Many Generations,* rev. ed. (1853; reprint, Salt Lake City: Bookcraft, 1945). The most recent attempt to treat Joseph's whole life with sensitivity to his religious claims is Donna Hill, *Joseph Smith: The First Mormon* (Garden City, New York: Doubleday, 1977). For a biographical study of his first wife, see Linda King Newell and Valeen Tippetts Avery, *Mormon Enigma: Emma Hale Smith, Prophet's Wife, "Elect Lady," Polygamy's Foe* (Garden City, New York: Doubleday, 1984). A detailed study of the introduction of plural marriage during Joseph Smith's lifetime is Danel W. Bachman, "A Study of the Mormon Practice of Plural Marriage before the Death of Joseph Smith" (master's thesis, Purdue University, 1975). Two useful collections of essays on Joseph Smith are Larry C. Porter and Susan Easton Black, eds., *The Prophet Joseph: Essays on the Life and Mission of Joseph Smith* (Salt Lake City: Deseret Book, 1988);

and Susan Easton Black and Charles D. Tate Jr., eds., *Joseph Smith: The Prophet, the Man* (Provo, Utah: Religious Studies Center, Brigham Young University, 1993).

The best biography of Brigham Young is Leonard J. Arrington, *Brigham Young: American Moses* (New York: Alfred Knopf, 1985). See also Dean C. Jessee, "The Writings of Brigham Young," *Western Historical Quarterly* 4 (June 1973): 273–94; Ronald W. Walker and Ronald K. Esplin, "Brigham Himself: An Autobiographical Recollection," *Journal of Mormon History* 4 (1977): 19–34; Lester E. Bush Jr., "Brigham Young in Life and Death: A Medical Overview," *Journal of Mormon History* 5 (1978): 79–103; Leonard J. Arrington, "The Settlement of the Brigham Young Estate, 1877–1879," *Pacific Historical Review* 21 (February 1952): 1–20; Eugene England, *Brother Brigham* (Salt Lake City: Bookcraft, 1980); and Ronald K. Esplin, "From the Rumors to the Records: Historians and the Sources for Brigham Young," *BYU Studies* 18 (Spring 1978): 453–65. Particularly valuable essays on Young's leadership and oratory are Leonard J. Arrington and Ronald K. Esplin, "Building a Commonwealth: The Secular Leadership of Brigham Young," *Utah Historical Quarterly* 45 (Summer 1977): 216–32; Gordon Irving, "Encouraging the Saints: Brigham Young's Annual Tours of Mormon Settlements," *Utah Historical Quarterly* 45 (Summer 1977): 233–51; and Ronald W. Walker, "Raining Pitchforks: Brigham Young as Preacher," *Sunstone* 8 (May–June 1983): 5–9. Young's close friend and counselor in the First Presidency is the subject of Stanley B. Kimball, *Heber C. Kimball, Mormon Patriarch and Pioneer* (Urbana: University of Illinois Press, 1981). Biographical studies of contemporaries of Young include Juanita Brooks, *John D. Lee: Zealot-Pioneer, Builder-Scapegoat* (Glendale, Calif.: Arthur H. Clark, 1962); James B. Allen, *Trials of Discipleship: The Story of William Clayton, a Mormon* (Urbana: University of Illinois Press, 1987); Andrew Karl Larson, *Erastus Snow: The Life of a Missionary and Pioneer for the Early Mormon Church* (Salt Lake City: University of Utah Press, 1971); Breck England, *The Life and Thought of Orson Pratt* (Salt Lake City: University of Utah Press, 1985); Leonard J. Arrington, *Charles C. Rich: Mormon General and Western Frontiersman* (Provo, Utah: Brigham Young University Press, 1974); Arrington, *From Quaker to Latter-day Saint: Bishop Edwin D. Woolley* (Salt Lake City: Deseret Book, 1976); and Gene A. Sessions, *Mormon Thunder: A Documentary History of Jedediah Morgan Grant* (Urbana: University of Illinois Press, 1982).

John Taylor is the subject of Samuel W. Taylor, *The Kingdom or Nothing: The Life of John Taylor, Militant Mormon* (New York: Macmillan, 1976). Unfortunately, this biography is flawed by an anti-Brigham

Young bias that sees Young as the Dark Ages and Taylor as the Renaissance of Mormonism; such a view is clearly unfair to both men, and seems to be more a reflection of Samuel Taylor's filial-pietistic bias that here creates misunderstandings of Mormon history. Still useful is B. H. Roberts, *The Life of John Taylor* (1892; reprint, Salt Lake City: Bookcraft, 1963). Manuscript material by John Taylor is hard to come by, but see Dean C. Jessee, "The John Taylor Nauvoo Journal," *BYU Studies* 23 (Summer 1983): 1-105.

Wilford Woodruff is the subject of Thomas G. Alexander, *Things in Heaven and Earth: The Life and Times of Wilford Woodruff, a Mormon Prophet* (Salt Lake City: Signature Books, 1991). Studies of Woodruff's contemporaries include Bruce Van Orden, *Prisoner for Conscience' Sake: George Reynolds* (Salt Lake City: Deseret Book, 1992); and David S. Hoopes and Roy Hoopes, *The Making of a Mormon Apostle: The Story of Rudger Clawson* (Lanham, Md.: Madison Books, 1990).

For studies about Lorenzo Snow, see Eliza R. Snow, *Biography and Family Record of Lorenzo Snow* (1884; reprinted, Salt Lake City: Zion's Book Store, 1975); and Thomas C. Romney, *The Life of Lorenzo Snow* (Salt Lake City: Nicholas G. Morgan Sr., 1955).

For studies about Joseph F. Smith, see Joseph Fielding Smith, *Life of Joseph F. Smith* (Salt Lake City: Deseret Book, 1938); and *From Prophet to Son: Advice of Joseph F. Smith to His Missionary Sons,* ed. Hyrum M. Smith III and Scott G. Kenney (Salt Lake City: Deseret Book, 1981).

Francis M. Gibbons's *Heber J. Grant: Man of Steel, Prophet of God* (Salt Lake City: Deseret Book, 1979) gives an essential outline. Ronald W. Walker has published a variety of essays on Grant, but has yet to finish what will be the definitive biography. Biographical studies of Grant's colleagues include John R. Talmage, *The Talmage Story: Life of James E. Talmage—Educator, Scientist, Apostle* (Salt Lake City: Bookcraft, 1972); Dale C. Mouritsen, "A Symbol of New Directions: George Franklin Richards and the Mormon Church, 1861-1950" (Ph.D. diss., Brigham Young University, 1982); Truman G. Madsen, *Defender of the Faith: The B. H. Roberts Story* (Salt Lake City: Bookcraft, 1980); Frank W. Fox, *J. Reuben Clark: The Public Years* (Salt Lake City: Deseret Book; Provo, Utah: Brigham Young University Press, 1980) and D. Michael Quinn, *J. Reuben Clark: The Church Years* (Salt Lake City: Deseret Book; Provo, Utah: Brigham Young University Press, 1983).

George Albert Smith is the subject of Francis M. Gibbons, *George Albert Smith: Kind and Caring Christian, Prophet of God* (Salt Lake City: Deseret Book, 1990); Merlo J. Pusey, *Builders of the*

Kingdom: George A. Smith, John Henry Smith, and George Albert Smith (Provo, Utah: Brigham Young University Press, 1981); and Glen R. Stubbs, "A Biography of George Albert Smith, 1870 to 1951" (Ph.D. diss., Brigham Young University, 1974).

David O. McKay is treated in a biography by his son in David Lawrence McKay, *My Father, David O. McKay* (Salt Lake City: Deseret Book, 1989). Close associates are studied in G. Homer Durham, *N. Eldon Tanner: His Life and Service* (Salt Lake City: Deseret Book, 1982); and Eugene E. Campbell and Richard D. Poll, *Hugh B. Brown: His Life and Thought* (Salt Lake City: Bookcraft, 1975).

The most recent leaders of the Church are the subjects of the following biographies: Joseph Fielding Smith Jr. and John J. Stewart, *The Life of Joseph Fielding Smith . . .* (Salt Lake City: Deseret Book, 1972); L. Brent Goates, *Harold B. Lee: Prophet and Seer* (Salt Lake City: Bookcraft, 1985); Edward L. Kimball and Andrew W. Kimball, *Spencer W. Kimball . . .* (Salt Lake City: Bookcraft, 1977); Sheri L. Dew, *Ezra Taft Benson: A Biography* (Salt Lake City: Deseret Book, 1987); and Eleanor Knowles, *Howard W. Hunter* (Salt Lake City: Deseret Book, 1994).

Emigration and Colonization

The idea of gathering new converts to a central location was a fundamental notion in nineteenth-century Mormonism. For a discussion see William Mulder, "Mormonism's 'Gathering': An American Doctrine with a Difference," *Church History* 23 (September 1954): 248-64. For the essential story of the major Mormon emigration agency see Gustive O. Larson, "The Story of the Perpetual Emigration Fund," *Mississippi Valley Historical Review* 18 (September 1931): 184-94, which is based on Larson's 1926 master's thesis at Brigham Young University; and Larson, *Prelude to the Kingdom: Mormon Desert Conquest, a Chapter in American Cooperative Experience* (Francistown, N.H.: Marshall Jones, 1947). See also William G. Hartley, "Coming to Zion: Saga of the Gathering," *Ensign* 5 (July 1975): 14-18. The two most productive areas of Mormon immigrants in the nineteenth-century are studied in Philip A. M. Taylor, *Expectations Westward: The Mormons and the Emigration of Their British Converts in the Nineteenth Century* (Ithaca: Cornell University Press, 1965); Richard L. Jensen and Malcolm R. Thorp, eds., *Mormons in Early Victorian Britain* (Salt Lake City: University of Utah Press, 1989); and William Mulder, *Homeward to Zion: The Mormon Migration from Scandinavia* (Minneapolis: University of Minnesota Press, 1957). An extended study of Norway is Gerald M. Haslam, *Clash of Cultures: The Norwegian Experience with*

Mormonism, 1842-1920, American University Studies Series 9, History, vol. 7 (New York: Peter Lang, 1984). Mormon sea travel is the subject of two important works by Conway B. Sonne, *Saints on the Seas: A Maritime History of Mormon Migration, 1830-1890* (Salt Lake City: University of Utah Press, 1983); and *Ships, Saints, and Mariners: A Maritime Encyclopedia of Mormon Migration, 1830-1890* (Salt Lake City: University of Utah Press, 1983). An excellent short piece by Sonne is "Under Sail to Zion," *Ensign* 21 (July 1991), 6-14. See also William Mulder, "Mormon Sources for Immigration History," *The Immigration History Newsletter* 10 (November 1978): 1-8. Perhaps the best known aspect of the Mormon gathering is told in LeRoy R. Hafen and Ann W. Hafen, *Handcarts to Zion: The Story of a Unique Western Migration, 1856-1860* (Glendale, Calif.: Arthur H. Clark, 1960). See also Philip A. M. Taylor, "The Mormon Crossing of the United States, 1840-1870," *Utah Historical Quarterly* 25 (October 1957): 319-37; Ronald D. Dennis, *The Call of Zion: The Story of the First Welsh Mormon Emigration* (Provo, Utah: Religious Studies Center, Brigham Young University, 1987); Richard L. Jensen, "Steaming Through: Arrangements for Mormon Emigration from Europe, 1869-1887," *Journal of Mormon History* 9 (1982): 3-23; and Jensen and Gordon Irving, "The Voyage of the Amazon: A Close View of One Immigrant Company," *Ensign* 10 (March 1980): 16-19.

Studies of the Mormon emigration trails are many. The best single volume is Stanley B. Kimball, *Historic Sites and Markers along the Mormon and Other Great Western Trails* (Urbana: University of Illinois Press, 1988). See also Stanley B. Kimball, *Discovering Mormon Trails: New York to California, 1831-1868* (Salt Lake City: Deseret Book, 1979); and Kimball's essay in *Mormon Americana.* Studies of the Mormon colonizing trails within the Great Basin are harder to find. Most of the Utah period histories cited above contain essential information, but see B. Gene Ramsey, "Scientific Exploration and Discovery in the Great Basin from 1831-1891" (Ph.D. diss., Brigham Young University, 1972); and Rick J. Fish, "The Southern Utah Expedition of Parley P. Pratt, 1849-1850" (master's thesis, Brigham Young University, 1992).

The basic story of Mormon colonization is presented in Milton R. Hunter, *Brigham Young: The Colonizer,* 4th ed. (1940; reprint, Santa Barbara, Calif.: Peregrine Smith, rev., 1973). Two essays have suggested Hunter's shortcomings as well as encouraged new directions for future study: Eugene E. Campbell, "Brigham Young's Outer Cordon—a Reappraisal," *Utah Historical Quarterly* 41 (Summer 1973): 221-53; and Richard Sherlock, "Mormon Migration and Settlement after 1875," *Journal of Mormon History* 2 (1975): 53-68.

A valuable overview of the literature on Mormon colonization is Wayne L. Wahlquist, "A Review of Mormon Settlement Literature," *Utah Historical Quarterly* 45 (Winter 1977): 4–21. Lowry Nelson, *The Mormon Village: A Pattern and Technique of Land Settlement* (Salt Lake City: University of Utah Press, 1952) remains a classic. A useful introduction to the Mormon settlement in southern Utah and surrounding areas is Andrew Karl Larson, *"I Was Called to Dixie": The Virgin River Basin, Unique Experiences in Mormon Pioneering* (Salt Lake City: Deseret News Press, 1961). Edward A. Geary, *The Proper Edge of the Sky: The High Plateau Country of Utah* (Salt Lake City: University of Utah Press, 1992) is an excellent history combining both literary skills and good historical research. On the Mormon village as physical space and design, see Richard H. Jackson, "The Mormon Village: Genesis and Antecedents of the City of Zion Plan," *BYU Studies* 17 (Winter 1977): 223–40. See also Richard V. Francaviglia, *The Mormon Landscape: Existence, Creation, and Perception of a Unique Image in the American West* (New York: AMS Press, 1978). Among Dean L. May's studies, the following are particularly useful: "The Making of Saints: The Mormon Town as a Setting for the Study of Cultural Change," *Utah Historical Quarterly* 45 (Winter 1977): 75–92; "A Demographic Portrait of the Mormons, 1830–1980," in *After 150 Years: The Latter-day Saints in Sesquicentennial Perspective,* ed. Thomas G. Alexander and Jessie L. Embry (Provo, Utah: Charles Redd Center for Western Studies, Brigham Young University, 1983); and "People on the Mormon Frontier: Kanab's Families of 1874," *Journal of Family History* 1 (December 1976): 169–92.

Valuable discussions on the continuity of Mormon community are Douglas D. Alder, "The Mormon Ward: Congregation or Community?" *Journal of Mormon History* 5 (1978): 61–78; and Mario S. DePillis, "The Persistence of Mormon Community into the 1990s," *Sunstone* 15 (September 1991): 28–49. *The Mormon Role in the Settlement of the West,* ed. Richard H. Jackson (Provo, Utah: Brigham Young University Press, 1978) contains a number of valuable essays. Larry M. Logue, *A Sermon in the Desert: Belief and Behavior in Early St. George, Utah* (Urbana: University of Illinois Press, 1988) and Michael Scott Raber, "Religious Polity and Local Production: The Origins of a Mormon Town" (Ph.D. diss., Yale University, 1978) suggest some of the new directions of Mormon studies.

Two recent works suggest the possibilities of community studies in Mormon-dominated areas: Lavina Fielding Anderson, ed., *Chesterfield: Mormon Outpost in Idaho* (Bancroft, Idaho: Chesterfield Foundation, 1982); and Gary B. Peterson and Lowell C. Bennion, *Sanpete*

Scenes: A Guide to Utah's Heart (Eureka, Utah: Basin/Plateau Press, 1987). Charles S. Peterson has reflected on the impact of the Mormon Village in several essays: "A Mormon Town: One Man's West," *Journal of Mormon History* 3 (1976): 3-12; "Life in a Village Society, 1877-1920," *Utah Historical Quarterly* 49 (Winter 1981): 78-96; and *Take Up Your Mission: Mormon Colonization along the Little Colorado River, 1870-1900* (Tucson: University of Arizona Press, 1973). See also David J. Whittaker, "Mormon Social History: A Selected Bibliography," *Mormon History Association Newsletter,* no. 61 (April 1986): 2-5; Douglas D. Alder, "Writing Southern Utah History: An Appraisal and a Bibliography," *Journal of Mormon History* 20 (Fall 1994): 156-78; and William A. Wilson, "A Bibliography of Studies in Mormon Folklore," *Utah Historical Quarterly* 44 (Fall 1976): 389-94. An important history of a contemporary LDS ward on the east coast of the United States is Susan Buhler Taber, *Mormon Lives: A Year in the Elkton Ward* (Urbana: University of Illinois Press, 1993).

The challenge of maintaining a unique identity while adjusting to the larger culture is examined in several essays. These include those appearing in the special issue of *Dialogue* 3 (Autumn 1968) on "Mormons in the Secular City" and several essays by Armand Mauss: "Saints, Cities, and Secularism: Religious Attitudes and Behavior of Modern Urban Mormons," *Dialogue* 7 (Summer 1972): 8-24; "The Angel and the Beehive: Our Quest for Peculiarity and Struggle with Secularization," *BYU Today* 37 (August 1983): 12-15; and "Assimilation and Ambivalence: The Mormon Reaction to Americanization," *Dialogue* 22 (Spring 1989): 30-67. See also Armand L. Mauss, *The Angel and the Beehive: The Mormon Struggle with Assimilation* (Urbana: University of Illinois Press, 1994).

Mormons and Medicine

A good overview is Robert T. Divett, *Medicine and the Mormons: An Introduction to the History of Latter-day Saint Health Care* (Bountiful, Utah: Horizon Publishers, 1981). See also Lester E. Bush Jr., "The Mormon Tradition," in *Caring and Curing: Health and Medicine in the Western Religious Traditions,* ed. Ronald L. Numbers and Darrel W. Amundsen (New York: Macmillan, 1986), 397-420; Bush, "A Peculiar People: The Physiological Aspects of Mormonism, 1850-1975," *Dialogue* 12 (Fall 1979): 61-83; Bush, "Birth Control among the Mormons: Introduction to an Insistent Question," *Dialogue* 10 (Autumn 1976): 12-44; and, most fully, Bush, *Health and Medicine among the Latter-day Saints: Science, Sense, and Scripture* (New York: Crossroad Publishing, 1993).

Historical studies of the Mormon health code include Paul H. Peterson, "An Historical Analysis of the Word of Wisdom" (master's thesis, Brigham Young University, 1972); Lester E. Bush Jr., "The Word of Wisdom in Early Nineteenth-Century Perspective," *Dialogue* 14 (Autumn 1981): 46–65; Dennis Lancaster, "Dixie Wine" (master's thesis, Brigham Young University, 1972); and Thomas G. Alexander, "The Word of Wisdom: From Principle to Requirement," *Dialogue* 14 (Autumn 1981): 78–88.

Women

The first scholarly effort to survey the sources on this topic was Carol Cornwall Madsen and David J. Whittaker, "History's Sequel: A Source Essay on Women in Mormon History," *Journal of Mormon History* 6 (1979): 123–45. More recently see Patricia Lyn Scott and Maureen Ursenbach Beecher, "Mormon Women: A Bibliography in Process, 1977–1985," *Journal of Mormon History* 12 (1985): 113–27; and Karen Purser Frazier, comp., *Bibliography of Social Scientific, Historical, and Popular Writings about Mormon Women* (Provo, Utah: Womens' Research Institute, Brigham Young University, 1990), which lists about 1,150 items organized into thirty topical categories. Three particularly useful essay collections are Claudia L. Bushman, ed., *Mormon Sisters: Women in Early Utah* (Cambridge, Mass.: Emmeline Press Limited, 1976); Vicky Burgess-Olsen, ed., *Sister Saints* (Provo, Utah: Brigham Young University Press, 1978); and Maureen Ursenbach Beecher and Lavina Fielding Anderson, eds., *Sisters in Spirit: Mormon Women in Historical and Cultural Perspective* (Urbana: University of Illinois Press, 1987). More recent developments are suggested in Maxine Hanks, ed., *Women and Authority: Reemerging Mormon Feminism* (Salt Lake City: Signature Books, 1992). An excellent history of the Relief Society organization is Jill Mulvay Derr, Janath R. Cannon, and Maureen Ursenbach Beecher, *Women of Covenant: The Story of Relief Society* (Salt Lake City: Deseret Book, 1992).

The controversy surrounding the Equal Rights Amendment illuminates a variety of issues relating to women in the contemporary Church. See the following for a variety of perspectives: Dixie Snow Huefner, "Church and Politics at the IWY Conference," *Dialogue* 11 (Spring 1978): 58–75; O. Kendall White Jr., "'A Feminist Challenge': Mormons for ERA as an Internal Social Movement," *Journal of Ethnic Studies* 13 (Spring 1985): 29–50; White, "Overt and Covert Politics: The Mormon Church's Anti-ERA Campaign in Virginia," *Virginia Social*

Science Journal 18 (Winter 1980): 10–16; White, "Mormonism and the Equal Rights Amendment," *Journal of Church and State* 31 (Spring 1989): 249–67; D. Michael Quinn, "The LDS Church's Campaign against the Equal Rights Amendment," *Journal of Mormon History* 20 (Fall 1994): 85–155; and Rex E. Lee, *A Lawyer Looks at the Equal Rights Amendment* (Provo, Utah: Brigham Young University Press, 1980).

Mormon Family

Historical studies of the Mormon family have begun to appear, although none are fully satisfactory. A sampling includes Michael Guy Bishop, "The Celestial Family: Early Mormon Thought on Life and Death, 1830–1846" (Ph.D. diss., Southern Illinois University, 1981); Bishop, "Eternal Marriage in Early Mormon Marital Beliefs," *Historian* 52 (Autumn 1990): 76–88; Bishop, "Preparing to Take the Kingdom: Childrearing Directives in Early Mormonism," *Journal of the Early Republic* 7 (Fall 1987): 275–90; Lawrence Foster, "Between Heaven and Earth: Mormon Theology of the Family in Comparative Perspective, the Shakers, the Oneida Perfectionists, the Mormons," *Sunstone* 7 (July–August 1982): 6–13; Bruce L. Campbell and Eugene E. Campbell, "The Mormon Family," in *Ethnic Families in America,* ed. Charles H. Mindell and Robert W. Habenstein (New York: Elsivier, 1981), 369–416; and E. Campbell and B. Campbell, "Divorce among Mormon Polygamists: Extent and Explanations," *Utah Historical Quarterly* 46 (Winter 1978): 4–23. See also "The Mormon Family in the Modern World," *Dialogue* 2 (Autumn 1967): 41–108; Harold T. Christensen, "Stress Points in Mormon Family Culture," *Dialogue* 7 (Winter 1972): 20–34; Darwin L. Thomas, "Family in Mormon Experience," in *Families and Religions: Conflict and Change in Modern Society,* ed. W. D'Antonio and J. Aldous (Beverly Hills, Calif.: Sage Publications, 1983), 267–88; Darwin L. Thomas, ed., *The Religion and Family Connection: Social Science Perspectives,* Religious Studies Center Specialized Monograph Series, no. 3 (Provo, Utah: Religious Studies Center, Brigham Young University, 1988); O. Kendall White Jr., "Ideology of the Family in Nineteenth-Century Mormonism," *Sociological Spectrum* 6 (1986): 289–306; and Howard M. Bahr and Renata Tonks Forste, "Toward a Social Science of Contemporary Mormondom," *BYU Studies* 26 (Winter 1986): 73–121. An especially valuable collection of essays, some of which focus on the LDS family, is Marie Cornwall, Tim B. Heaton, and Lawrence A. Young, eds., *Contemporary Mormonism: Social Science Perspectives* (Urbana: University of Illinois Press, 1994).

Polygamy

The first scholarly bibliographical essay on this topic was Davis Bitton, "Mormon Polygamy: A Review Article," *Journal of Mormon History* 4 (1977): 101-18. An updated listing by Patricia Lyn Scott is "Mormon Polygamy: A Bibliography, 1977-92," *Journal of Mormon History* 19 (Spring 1993): 133-55. Book-length histories include Kimball Young, *Isn't One Wife Enough?* (New York: Holt, 1954); Lawrence Foster, *Religion and Sexuality: Three American Communal Experiments of the Nineteenth Century* (New York: Oxford University Press, 1981); Richard S. Van Wagoner, *Mormon Polygamy: A History,* 3d ed. (Salt Lake City: Signature Books, 1992); Jessie L. Embry, *Mormon Polygamous Families: Life in the Principle* (Salt Lake City: University of Utah Press, 1987); Rex Eugene Cooper, *Promises Made to the Fathers: Mormon Covenant Organization* (Salt Lake City: University of Utah Press, 1990); and B. Carmon Hardy, *Solemn Covenant: The Mormon Polygamous Passage* (Urbana: University of Illinois Press, 1992). Two important studies focusing on post-Manifesto plural marriage are Kenneth L. Cannon II, "Beyond the Manifesto: Polygamous Cohabitation Among LDS General Authorities after 1890," *Utah Historical Quarterly* 46 (Winter 1978): 24-36; and D. Michael Quinn, "LDS Church Authority and New Plural Marriages, 1890-1904," *Dialogue* 18 (Spring 1985): 9-105.

On the history of the Mormon fundamentalist practice of plural marriage, see Martha S. Bradley, "Changed Faces: The Official LDS Position on Polygamy, 1890-1990," *Sunstone* 14 (February 1990): 26-33; Ken Driggs, "After the Manifesto: Modern Polygamy and Fundamentalist Mormons," *Journal of Church and State* 32 (Spring 1990): 367-89; Driggs, "Twentieth-Century Polygamy and Fundamentalist Mormons in Southern Utah," *Dialogue* 24 (Winter 1991): 44-58; D. Michael Quinn, "Plural Marriage and Mormon Fundamentalism," *Fundamentalisms and Society: Reclaiming the Sciences, the Family, and Education,* ed. Martin E. Marty and R. Scott Applegate, Fundamentalist Project sponsored by the American Academy of Arts and Sciences, vol. 2 (Chicago: University of Chicago Press, 1993), 240-93; and Martha Sonntag Bradley, *Kidnapped from That Land: The Government Raids on the Short Creek Polygamists,* Publications in Mormon Studies, vol. 9 (Salt Lake City: University of Utah Press, 1993).

Mormon Thought

The best place to begin is with the official publications of the Church. Particularly useful are the official reports of Church conference addresses: the *Journal of Discourses,* 26 vols. (Salt Lake City and

Liverpool, 1854–1886); and *Conference Reports,* issued generally twice per year since 1898. A compilation of the official statements of the First Presidency through 1952 is James R. Clark, *The Messages of the First Presidency,* 6 vols. (Salt Lake City: Bookcraft, 1965–75). A guide to the publications (most are considered unofficial) of the General Authorities of the Church is Gary Gillum, "Out of the Books Which Shall Be Written," *Dialogue* 12 (Summer 1979): 99–123. An important study of the themes of the general conferences of the Church as indices to changes is Gordon Shepherd and Gary Shepherd, *A Kingdom Transformed: Themes in the Development of Mormonism* (Urbana: University of Illinois Press, 1984).

No one can address the topic of Mormon doctrine without seriously considering the sermons and writings of Joseph Smith. Dean C. Jessee has published the most important works on the Joseph Smith manuscripts: "The Early Accounts of Joseph Smith's First Vision," *BYU Studies* 9 (Spring 1969): 275–94; "Joseph Smith's 19 July 1840 Discourse," *BYU Studies* 19 (Spring 1979): 390–94; the series "Joseph Smith Jr.: In His Own Words," *Ensign* 14 (December 1984): 22–31, 15 (January 1985): 18–24, and 15 (February 1985): 6–13; "The Original Book of Mormon Manuscript," *BYU Studies* 10 (Spring 1970): 259–78; "The Writing of Joseph Smith's History," *BYU Studies* 11 (Summer 1971): 439–73; "The Reliability of Joseph Smith's History," *Journal of Mormon History* 3 (1976): 23–46; *The Personal Writings of Joseph Smith* (Salt Lake City: Deseret Book, 1984); and the first two volumes of the comprehensive edition now in process, *The Papers of Joseph Smith* (Salt Lake City: Deseret Book, 1989–). Still useful is the 1938 edition of Joseph Fielding Smith, ed., *Teachings of the Prophet Joseph Smith* (Salt Lake City: Deseret Book), which, in spite of recent textual and historical scholarship, remains the most cited work within the Church. A new edition has been published; it adds scriptural citations to the 1938 edition but does not incorporate any of the more recent textual work of Mormon scholars.

An excellent edition of the known texts of the Nauvoo discourses is Andrew F. Ehat and Lyndon W. Cook, comps. and eds., *The Words of Joseph Smith: The Contemporary Accounts of the Nauvoo Discourses of the Prophet Joseph* (Provo, Utah: Religious Studies Center, Brigham Young University, 1980). Truman G. Madsen has edited *The Concordance of the Doctrinal Statements of Joseph Smith* (Salt Lake City: I.E.S. Publishing, 1985). Information on the "Lectures on Faith," published in the Doctrine and Covenants from 1835 to 1921, is in Larry E. Dahl and Charles D. Tate Jr., eds., *The Lectures on Faith in Historical Perspective* (Provo, Utah: Religious Studies Center,

Brigham Young University, 1990). The important King Follett Discourse by Joseph Smith (June 7, 1844) is the subject of several essays in *BYU Studies* 18 (Winter 1978). The most cited summary of LDS beliefs is studied in David J. Whittaker, "The 'Articles of Faith' in Early Mormon Literature and Thought," in *New Views of Mormon History,* ed. Davis Bitton and Maureen Ursenbach Beecher (Salt Lake City: University of Utah Press, 1987), 63-92.

About one third of Brigham Young's known discourses are available in the *Journal of Discourses*. The rest have been assembled in Elden J. Watson, ed., *Brigham Young Addresses,* 6 vols. (Salt Lake City: By the compiler, 1979-1984). All the presidents of the LDS Church have had books compiled from their writings and sermons.

An important study which attempts an understanding of Mormon thought within the context of the western religious tradition is Sterling McMurrin, *The Theological Foundations of the Mormon Religion* (Salt Lake City: University of Utah Press, 1965). The serious student of Mormon thought will wish to study the writings of key thinkers who have tried to define and analyze various LDS doctrines. These include, among others, Parley P. Pratt, Orson Pratt, George Q. Cannon, B. H. Roberts, James E. Talmage, E. E. Erickson, John A. Widtsoe, Joseph Fielding Smith, J. Reuben Clark, Bruce R. McConkie, Leonard J. Arrington, and Hugh W. Nibley. A brief overview of LDS intellectual history is found in the *Encyclopedia of Mormonism* 2:685-91. See also Leonard J. Arrington, "The Intellectual Tradition of the Latter-day Saints," *Dialogue* 4 (Spring 1969): 13-26; Thomas G. Alexander, "The Reconstruction of Mormon Doctrine: From Joseph Smith to Progressive Theology," *Sunstone* 5 (July-August 1980): 24-33; and Robert L. Millet, "Joseph Smith and Modern Mormonism: Orthodoxy, Neoorthodoxy, Tension, and Tradition," *BYU Studies* 29 (Summer 1989): 49-68.

The first attempt to synthesize Mormon thought was Parley P. Pratt, *A Voice of Warning* (New York: Sanford, 1837). In 1855 he published *Key to the Science of Theology* (Liverpool: F. D. Richards, 1855). In 1899, James E. Talmage issued *A Study of the Articles of Faith . . .* (Salt Lake City: Deseret News, 1899), in many ways still a good introduction to Mormon beliefs. In 1915, John A. Widtsoe's *A Rational Theology* (Salt Lake City: The Church of Jesus Christ of Latter-day Saints for the use of the Melchizedek Priesthood, by the General Priesthood Committee, 1915) appeared, and other works have followed. One of the most ambitious attempts was written in the late 1920s, but was only recently published: B. H. Roberts, *The Truth, the Way, the Life: An Elementary Treatise on Theology* (Provo, Utah: BYU Studies, 1994).

A useful collection of personal reflections on faith by LDS scholars is Philip L. Barlow, comp. and ed., *A Thoughtful Faith: Essays on Belief by Mormon Scholars* (Centerville, Utah: Canon Press, 1986).

Mormon thought is best studied by examining specific areas. The most comprehensive bibliography on Mormons and science is by Robert Miller, "Science/Mormonism Bibliography" (unpublished MSS, January 1987). A useful introduction to the Mormon encounter with evolutionary thought is Duane E. Jeffrey, "Seers, Savants, and Evolution: The Uncomfortable Interface," *Dialogue* 8 (Autumn-Winter 1973): 41-75. Erich Robert Paul, *Science, Religion, and Mormon Cosmology* (Urbana: University of Illinois Press, 1992) places Mormon thought into the larger context of western culture. A useful anthology is Wilford M. Hess and others, *Science and Religion: Toward a More Useful Dialogue,* 2 vols. (Geneva, Ill.: Paladin, 1979). Ronald L. Numbers, *The Creationists: The Evolution of Scientific Creationism* (New York: Alfred A. Knopf, 1992), 308-14 suggests that the contemporary Mormon position is moving toward those of the Creationists, a view that seems incompatible with nineteenth-century Mormon thought.

Mormon attitudes toward the natural world are discussed in Gerald E. Jones, "Concern for Animals as Manifest in Five American Churches . . ." (Ph.D. diss., Brigham Young University, 1972); Jones, "The Gospel and Animals," *Ensign* 2 (August 1972): 62-65; Jones and Scott S. Smith, *Animals and the Gospel: A History of Latter-day Saint Doctrine on the Animal Kingdom* (Thousand Oaks, Calif.: Millennial Publications, 1980); Hugh W. Nibley, "Man's Dominion," *New Era* 2 (October 1972): 24-31; and Nibley, "Brigham Young on the Environment," in *To the Glory of God: Mormon Essays on Great Issues,* ed. Truman G. Madsen and Charles D. Tate Jr. (Salt Lake City: Deseret Book, 1972). See also Dan L. Flores, "Agriculture, Mountain Ecology, and the Land Ethic: Phases of the Environmental History of Utah," in *Working the Range: Essays on the History of Western Land Management and the Environment,* John R. Winder, ed., 157-86 (Westport, Conn.: Greenwood Press, 1985); and Thomas G. Alexander, "Stewardship and Enterprise: The LDS Church and the Wasatch Oasis Environment, 1847-1930," *Western Historical Quarterly* 25 (Autumn 1994): 341-64.

Mormon millennial thought is the subject of several studies by Grant Underwood: "Millenarianism and the Early Mormon Mind," *Journal of Mormon History* 9 (1982): 41-51; "Early Mormon Millenarianism: Another Look," *Church History* 54 (June 1985): 215-29; and, more fully, *The Millenarian World of Early Mormonism* (Urbana: University of Illinois Press, 1993).

The key role of temple building and worship in Mormon culture is seldom understood by outsiders. Basic introductions are James E.

Talmage, *The House of the Lord . . .*, rev. ed. (1912; reprint, Salt Lake City: Deseret Book, 1976); Boyd K. Packer, *The Holy Temple* (Salt Lake City: Bookcraft, 1980); and Richard O. Cowan, *Temples to Dot the Earth* (Salt Lake City: Bookcraft, 1989). See also David John Buerger, "The Development of the Mormon Temple Endowment Ceremony," *Dialogue* 20 (Winter 1987): 33–76. The unique doctrine/practice of ordinance work for deceased relatives is discussed in several articles in *Dialogue* 23 (Summer 1990). See also the essay by James B. Allen in *Mormon Americana.*

Education

A beginning point is with David J. Whittaker, "Bibliography: History [of the] Educational System of the LDS Church," *Mormon History Association Newsletter,* no. 68 (April 1988): 2–5. Selected works on key topics are Ernest L. Wilkinson and Leonard J. Arrington, eds., *Brigham Young University: The First One Hundred Years,* 4 vols. (Provo, Utah: Brigham Young University Press, 1975); Frederick S. Buchanan, "Education among the Mormons: Brigham Young and the Schools of Utah," *History of Education Quarterly* 22 (Winter 1982): 435–59; John Daniel Monnett, "The Mormon Church and Its Private School System in Utah: The Emergence of the Academies, 1880–1892" (Ph.D. diss., University of Utah, 1984); Leonard J. Arrington, "The Founding of the LDS Institutes of Religion," *Dialogue* 2 (Summer 1967): 137–47; and Gary James Bergera and Ronald Priddis, *Brigham Young University: A House of Faith* (Salt Lake City: Signature Books, 1985). A dissertation on more recent developments in the Church Educational System is John L. Fowles, "A Study concerning the Mission of the Weekday Religious Educational Programs of The Church of Jesus Christ of Latter-day Saints from 1890–1990: A Response to Secular Education" (Ph.D. diss., University of Missouri at Columbia, 1990). See also Charles S. Peterson, "The Limits of Learning in Pioneer Utah," *Journal of Mormon History* 10 (1983): 65–78; Joseph Heinerman, "Early Utah Pioneer Cultural Societies," *Utah Historical Quarterly* 47 (Winter 1979): 70–89; and Arthur R. Bassett, "Culture and the American Frontier in Mormon Utah, 1850–1896" (Ph.D. diss., Syracuse University, 1975).

Mormon Literature

From diaries and autobiographies to poetry, short stories, and fiction, a rich tradition of literary expression has developed in Mormonism. The best place to begin studying this topic is with Eugene England, "The Dawning of a Brighter Day: Mormon Literature After 150 Years," in *After*

150 Years: The Latter-day Saints in Sesquicentennial Perspective, ed. Thomas G. Alexander and Jessie L. Embry (Provo, Utah: Charles Redd Center for Western Studies, Brigham Young University, 1983), 95-146, or in a shorter version in *BYU Studies* 18 (1978): 131-60. See also Richard H. Cracroft, "Seeking 'the Good, the Pure, the Elevating': A Short History of Mormon Fiction," *Ensign* 11 (June 1981): 56-62, and 11 (July 1981): 56-61. Good compilations are Richard H. Cracroft and Neal E. Lambert, eds., *A Believing People: Literature of the Latter-day Saints* (Provo, Utah: Brigham Young University Press, 1974); Dennis Clark and Eugene England, eds., *Harvest: Contemporary Mormon Poems* (Salt Lake City: Signature Books, 1989). See more fully the essay by Eugene England on Mormon literature in *Mormon Americana.*

Ethnic Studies

An extensive introduction and historical survey of Mormon relationships with Native Americans is presented in David J. Whittaker, "Mormons and Native Americans: A Historical and Bibliographical Introduction," *Dialogue* 18 (Winter 1985): 33-64. An essay suggesting new perspectives is Ronald W. Walker, "Toward a Reconstruction of Mormon and Indian Relations, 1847-1877," *BYU Studies* 29 (Fall 1989): 23-42. The most comprehensive introduction (with bibliography) to Mormons and African-Americans is in Lester E. Bush Jr. and Armand L. Mauss, eds., *Neither White nor Black: Mormon Scholars Confront the Race Issue in a Universal Church* (Midvale, Utah: Signature Books, 1984). See especially Lester E. Bush Jr., "Mormonism's Negro Doctrine: An Historical Overview," *Dialogue* 8 (Spring 1973): 11-68; Armand L. Mauss, "The Fading of the Pharaoh's Curse: The Decline and Fall of the Priesthood Ban against Blacks in the Mormon Church," *Dialogue* 14 (Autumn 1981): 10-45; and Newell G. Bringhurst, *Saints, Slaves, and Blacks: The Changing Place of Black People within Mormonism* (Westport, Conn.: Greenwood Press, 1981). A recent study is Jessie L. Embry, *Black Saints in a White Church* (Salt Lake City: Signature Books, 1994). For the rich ethnic heritage of Utah see Helen Z. Papanikolas, ed., *The Peoples of Utah* (Salt Lake City: Utah State Historical Society, 1976). An insightful study of a neglected topic is Steven Epperson, *Mormons and Jews: Early Mormon Theologies of Israel* (Salt Lake City: Signature Books, 1992). See also Robert D. Bingham, "Swedish-Americans in Utah: A Bibliography," *Swedish Pioneer History Quarterly* 30 (July 1979): 205-10; Mark L. Grover, "The Mexican-American in Utah: A Bibliography," *Utah Libraries* 18 (Spring 1975): 34-38; William Mulder, "Utah's Ugly Ducklings: A Profile of the Scandinavian Immigrant," *Utah Historical Quarterly* 23 (July 1955):

233-59; and Mark L. Grover, "The Mormon Priesthood Revelation and the São Paulo, Brazil Temple," *Dialogue* 23 (Spring 1990): 39-53. On Mormonism in Africa, see Alexander B. Morrison, *The Dawning of a Brighter Day: The Church in Black Africa* (Salt Lake City: Deseret Book, 1990); and Newell G. Bringhurst, "Mormonism in Black Africa: Changing Attitudes and Practices, 1830-1981," *Sunstone* 6 (May-June 1981): 15-21.

The Book in Mormonism

The most complete guide to the first one hundred years of official and unofficial Mormon publications is Chad J. Flake, *A Mormon Bibliography, 1830-1930: Books, Pamphlets, Periodicals, and Broadsides Relating to the First Century of Mormonism* (Salt Lake City: University of Utah Press, 1978). A ten-year supplement appeared in 1989: Chad J. Flake and Larry W. Draper, *A Mormon Bibliography, 1830-1930: Ten Year Supplement* (Salt Lake City: University of Utah Press). A title index to both volumes was issued in 1992. The same authors are currently working on a bibliography of the periodical literature on Mormonism for the first one hundred years.

A useful guide to various reprint series of Mormon Americana is Gregory A. Prince, "Among the Mormons: A Bibliography of Mormon Reprints," *Dialogue* 11 (Autumn 1978): 120-24.

Other essential bibliographical guides to LDS publications include Peter Crawley, "A Bibliography of The Church of Jesus Christ of Latter-day Saints in New York, Ohio, and Missouri," *BYU Studies* 12 (Summer 1972): 465-537; David J. Whittaker, "Early Mormon Pamphleteering" (Ph.D. diss., Brigham Young University, 1982); L. R. Jacobs, *Mormon Non-English Scriptures, Hymnals, and Periodicals, 1830-1986: A Descriptive Bibliography* (Ithaca, New York: By the author, 1986); and Ronald D. Dennis, *Welsh Mormon Writings from 1844 to 1862: A Historical Bibliography,* Religious Studies Center Specialized Monograph Series, vol. 4, (Provo, Utah: Religious Studies Center, Brigham Young University, 1988).

Important studies of the Mormon scriptures have added insights to the historical and textual development of these works. On the Mormon use of the Bible see Philip L. Barlow, *Mormons and the Bible: The Place of the Latter-day Saints in American Religion* (New York: Oxford University Press, 1991); and Robert J. Matthews, *"A Plainer Translation": Joseph Smith's Translation of the Bible—a History and Commentary* (Provo, Utah: Brigham Young University Press, 1975). A comprehensive bibliography of published works on the Joseph Smith Translation of the Bible is Thomas E. Sherry, *Joseph*

Smith's Translation of the Bible: A Bibliography of Publications, 1847-1987, 3 vols. (Provo, Utah: By the author, 1988). Copies are available at the LDS Church Library, Salt Lake City; the Harold B. Lee Library, Brigham Young University, Provo, Utah; and the RLDS Library in Independence, Missouri.

On the Book of Mormon see Hugh G. Stocks, "The Book of Mormon, 1830-1879: A Publishing History" (master's thesis, UCLA, 1979); Stocks, "The Book of Mormon in English, 1870-1920: A Publishing History and Analytical Bibliography" (Ph.D. diss., UCLA, 1986); and on the current critical text project see Royal Skousen, "Towards a Critical Edition of the Book of Mormon," *BYU Studies* 30 (Winter 1990): 41-69. A good way to keep abreast with the scholarship on the Book of Mormon is by getting on the mailing list of Foundation for Ancient Research and Mormon Studies (F.A.R.M.S.). F.A.R.M.S. has issued a yearly volume entitled *Reviews of Books on the Book of Mormon.* In 1992 they issued the first volume of the *Journal of Book of Mormon Studies* and in 1987 published a bibliography on the Book of Mormon: John W. Welch, Gary Gillum, and DeeAnn Hofer, *Comprehensive Bibliography of the Book of Mormon (through December 1986): Arranged Alphabetically by Author* (Provo, Utah: F.A.R.M.S.).

On the Doctrine and Covenants see Robert J. Woodford, "The Historical Development of the Doctrine and Covenants," 3 vols. (Ph.D. diss., Brigham Young University, 1974); Richard P. Howard, *Restoration Scriptures: A Study of their Textual Development* (Independence, Mo.: Herald House, 1969); and Lyndon W. Cook, *The Revelations of the Prophet Joseph Smith: A Historical and Biographical Commentary of the Doctrine and Covenants* (1981; reprint, Salt Lake City: Deseret Book, 1985).

On the Pearl of Great Price, see James R. Clark, *The Story of the Pearl of Great Price* (Salt Lake City: Bookcraft, 1955); Clark, "Our Pearl of Great Price: From Mission Pamphlet to Standard Work," *Ensign* 6 (August 1976): 12-17; Hugh W. Nibley, "A New Look at the Pearl of Great Price," *Improvement Era* 71-73 (January 1968-May 1970); and Nibley, *The Message of the Joseph Smith Papyri: An Egyptian Endowment* (Salt Lake City: Deseret Book, 1975).

Mormon hymnals are studied in Helen Hanks Macaré, "The Singing Saints: A Study of the Mormon Hymnal, 1835-1950" (Ph.D. diss., UCLA, 1961); Michael Hicks, *Mormonism and Music: A History* (Urbana: University of Illinois Press, 1989); and Karen Lynn Davidson, *Our Latter-day Hymns: The Stories and the Messages* (Salt Lake City: Deseret Book, 1988).

The study of Mormon imprints has greatly benefited bibliographical studies. Among the more recent works see Peter Crawley, "Parley P. Pratt: Father of Mormon Pamphleteering," *Dialogue* 15 (Autumn 1982): 13-26; Crawley and David J. Whittaker, *Mormon Imprints in Great Britain and the Empire, 1836-1857* (Provo, Utah: Friends of the Brigham Young University Library, 1987); Whittaker, "Orson Pratt: Prolific Pamphleteer," *Dialogue* 15 (Autumn 1982): 27-41; Whittaker, "Almanacs in the New England Heritage of Mormonism," *BYU Studies* 29 (Fall 1989): 89-113; and "To 'Hurl Truth through the Land': Publications of the Twelve," in James B. Allen, Ronald K. Esplin, and David J. Whittaker, *Men with a Mission: The Quorum of the Twelve Apostles in the British Isles, 1837-1841* (Salt Lake City: Deseret Book, 1992), 236-66.

The study of Mormon newspapers is assisted by J. Cecil Alter, *Early Utah Journalism* (Salt Lake City: Utah State Historical Society, 1938); Wendell J. Ashton, *Voice in the West: Biography of a Pioneer Newspaper* (New York: Duell, Sloan and Pearce, 1950); Monte B. McLaws, *Spokesman for the Kingdom: Early Mormon Journalism and the Deseret News, 1830-1898* (Provo, Utah: Brigham Young University Press, 1977); and O. N. Malmquist, *The First 100 Years: A History of the Salt Lake Tribune, 1871-1971* (Salt Lake City: Utah State Historical Society, 1971). For the larger bibliography see Joseph Sudweeks, *Discontinued LDS Periodicals* (Provo, Utah: Brigham Young University Press, 1955). A recent history of Deseret Book, the Church-owned publishing concern, is Eleanor Knowles, *Deseret Book Company: 125 Years of Inspiration, Information, and Ideas* (Salt Lake City: Deseret Book, 1991).

RLDS Church

The second-largest group in the Latter-day Saint movement is the Reorganized Church of Jesus Christ of Latter Day Saints, with world headquarters in Independence, Missouri. Three essays by Roger D. Launius provide a comprehensive guide to the literature of the RLDS movement: "The Reorganized Church in the Nineteenth Century: A Bibliographical Review," in *Restoration Studies IV,* ed. Marjorie B. Troeh and Eileen M. Terril (Independence, Mo.: Herald Publishing House, 1988), 171-87; Roger D. Launius, "A New Historiographical Frontier: The Reorganized Church in the Twentieth Century," *John Whitmer Historical Association Journal* 6 (1986): 53-63; and Launius, "Whither Reorganization Historiography?" *John Whitmer Historical Association Journal* 10 (1990): 24-37. Recent overviews of the dissenting movements in the RLDS Church are William Dean Russell, "Defenders of the Faith: Varieties of RLDS Dissent," *Sunstone* 14 (June 1990): 14–19; and William Dean Russell, "The Fundamentalist Schism, 1958-Present," in *Let Contention Cease: The Dynamics of Dissent in the Reorganized Church of Jesus Christ of Latter Day Saints,* ed. Roger D. Launius and W. B. "Pat" Spillman (Independence, Mo.: Graceland/Park Press, 1991), 125–51. For recent histories of the RLDS movement see Paul M. Edwards, *Our Legacy of Faith: A Brief History of the Reorganized Church of Jesus Christ of Latter Day Saints* (Independence, Mo.: Herald Publishing House, 1991); and Richard P. Howard, *The Church through the Years,* 2 vols. (Independence, Mo.: Herald Publishing House, 1992–93).

Branches of the Restoration

There have been about one hundred and sixty organized breakoffs from the LDS Church, though most failed to survive their founders. The best place to begin studying this aspect of Restoration history is with three bibliographical essays by Dale L. Morgan: "A Bibliography of the Church of Jesus Christ, Organized at Green Oak, Pennsylvania, July, 1862," *Western Humanities Review* 4 (Winter 1949–50): 45–70; "A Bibliography of the Church of Jesus Christ of Latter Day Saints [Strangite]," *Western Humanities Review* 5 (Winter 1950–51): 43–114; and "A Bibliography of the Churches of the Dispersion," *Western Humanities Review* 7 (Summer 1953): 255–66. More recently see Steven L. Shields, *The Latter Day Saint Churches: An Annotated Bibliography* (New York: Garland Publishing, 1987); and for brief histories of most of the groups, Shields, *Divergent Paths of the Restoration: A History of the Latter-day Saint Movement,* 3d ed. (Bountiful, Utah: Restoration Research, 1982). Sociological studies of the "disaffection" of Mormons are Stan L. Albrecht, Marie Cornwall, and Perry H. Cunningham, "Religious Leave-Taking: Disengagement and Disaffection among Mormons," in *Falling from the Faith: Causes and Consequences of Religious Apostasy,* ed. David G. Bromley (Newbury Park, Calif.: Sage Publications, 1988), 62–80; Stan L. Albrecht, "The Consequential Dimension of Mormon Religiosity," *BYU Studies* 29 (Spring 1989): 57–108; and Howard M. Bahr and Stan Albrecht, "Strangers Once More: Patterns of Disaffection from Mormonism," *Journal of the Scientific Study of Religion* 28 (June 1989): 180–200.

Other more visible groups in LDS history are treated in the following works, each of which can lead the researcher into the larger literature: Milo M. Quaife, *The Kingdom of Saint James: A Narrative of the Mormons* (New Haven: Yale University Press, 1930); Roger Van Noord, *King of Beaver Island: The Life and Assassination of James Jesse Strang* (Urbana: University of Illinois Press, 1988); C. LeRoy Anderson, *For Christ Will Come Tomorrow: The Saga of the Morrisites* (Logan: Utah State University Press, 1981); Ronald W. Walker, "The Godbeite Protest in Making of Modern Utah," (Ph.D. diss., University of Utah, 1977); on Walter Murray Gibson compare Gwynn Barrett, "Walter Murray Gibson: The Shepherd Saint of Lanai Revisited," *Utah Historical Quarterly* 40 (Spring 1972): 142–62, with R. Lanier Britsch, "Another Visit with Walter Murray Gibson," *Utah Historical Quarterly* 46 (Winter 1978): 65–78; Hans A. Baer, *Recreating Utopia in the Desert: A Sectarian Challenge to Modern Mormonism* (Albany: State University of New York Press, 1988); and Roger D. Launius and Linda Thatcher, eds., *Differing Visions: Dissenters in Mormon History* (Urbana: University of Illinois Press, 1994). Steven L. Shields, *The Latter Day Saint Churches* (New York: Garland, 1987) provides an extended bibliographic guide to the larger literature on this topic.

Part II:

Special Collections in Utah and the West

Mormon Manuscripts in the Bancroft Library

Bonnie Hardwick

Hubert Howe Bancroft

In 1871, Hubert Howe Bancroft decided to move beyond the series of informational handbooks for the Pacific states issued by his San Francisco publishing house. Over the previous ten years he had amassed a surprisingly large collection of materials on California and western North America, from Panama to Alaska and east to the Rocky Mountain states. At more than ten thousand items, his library had overflowed the corner allotted to it in H. H. Bancroft & Co., Booksellers & Stationers, on Montgomery and Merchant streets, and had taken over the entire fifth floor of his new Bancroft Building, where it continued to grow until an entirely separate library structure became imperative.

Although he gathered materials with some abandon, Bancroft was not, as he noted in his autobiography, the kind of collector who when he "begins to accumulate books he ceases to make much use of them."[1] At the very least, he hoped to publish a bibliography based on his library. Then, at the urging of interested colleagues, he began to contemplate an encyclopedia of the Pacific states. A prospectus was printed, and letters were written to possible contributors. But whereas letters sufficed for the other areas, Bancroft personally visited Utah to enlist the support of the Mormons. "President Young and the leading elders entered heartily into my project, and a scheme was devised for obtaining information from every part of Utah," he reported.[2] Gradually, however, Bancroft abandoned the idea of a mere encyclopedia, turning instead to the grand project of writing a history of western North America. Nothing less would do, and in the end the project filled thirty-nine volumes.

True, Bancroft had wanted to turn his great library to good account. But it was also true that in writing the history of the West he was in a unique position of access to the first generation of history-makers. His were living sources, and he set out to gather their papers and record their reminiscences, arranging to have their life stories and accounts of major events either written for him or dictated to his agents.

Bancroft's *History of Utah*

In January of 1880, Bancroft was well into his series of histories when he again turned his attention to Utah, this time for volume twenty-six. Bancroft intended his history of Utah to be a truthful account—an impartial, critical analysis and accurate synthesis of all available evidence representing all points of view. For this he would need the active cooperation of the Mormon Church, both for access to the documentation preserved in the Church archives and for solicitation of the kind of contemporary accounts he had been able to gather in other parts of the West.

This time Bancroft first approached the Mormon leadership through an intermediary, a Salt Lake City bookseller named James Dwyer. When Dwyer reported back that Church Historian Orson Pratt would supply a complete history of Utah if Bancroft would print it "without mutilation," Bancroft responded with a long letter, dated January 12, 1880, in which he clearly laid out his methodology. He would use Pratt's account, but it would be but one of the many sources he hoped to draw upon in his "careful weighing of all gathered testimony." "What I should like from Utah," he wrote, "are narratives of early events, dictations, from different persons, of their several experiences, what they saw and did who made the history of the country," including an extensive account from Orson Pratt, which he outlined in detail. "This, then, is the point," he concluded: "Fair-minded men, who desire to see placed before the world a true history of Utah, cannot more directly or thoroughly accomplish the purpose, in this generation at least, than by placing within my reach the material necessary for the building of such a work."[3]

Dwyer took Bancroft's letter to John Taylor, president of the Mormon Church, who in turn presented the proposal to the Council of Twelve Apostles. Cooperation was assured, and Orson Pratt was delegated to the task. He became ill, however, and in July 1880 Franklin D. Richards, a member of the Quorum of the Twelve Apostles, was detailed to the work. He and his wife journeyed to San Francisco and spent two weeks there, most of the time as guests of the Bancrofts. Much of Richards's time was spent at Bancroft's library, where a staff member took down a 130-page dictation. Matilda Bancroft recorded her private conversations with Jane Richards about such topics as plural marriage and women in Mormon society, which were bound in a dictation titled "The Inner Facts of Social Life in Utah." At this time Richards also arranged for cases of books, newspapers, political and religious pamphlets, and other early printed materials to be sent from the Church Historian's Office to San Francisco for Bancroft's use.

After the Richardses returned home, they and the Church continued to exert themselves on Bancroft's behalf; the result was a flow of manuscripts and personal documents from Utah to the Bancroft Building between 1880 and 1883. During the first year alone, more than sixty individual manuscripts arrived. At Jane Richards's request, leading Mormon women penned autobiographies and reminiscences. Reports on Mormon institutions such as the Deseret Museum, Zion's Cooperative Mercantile Institution, Sunday Schools, the Salt Lake Street Railroad, and the Perpetual Emigrating Fund were sent. In addition, more than forty community and county histories were compiled by local bishops or pioneers who had participated in the founding of the settlements.

In the summer of 1884, Bancroft's son, Philip—not a robust child—developed a disturbing cough. Hoping for a beneficent effect from a drier climate and seizing an opportunity to fill in needed information for his histories, Bancroft took his family to Utah, Colorado, Wyoming, and New Mexico. The Bancrofts spent six weeks in Salt Lake City where, with some assistance from local stenographers, they took numerous dictations from principal men and women of the community.

Besides securing dictations, much of Bancroft's time was spent in close association with Mormon leaders, especially Wilford Woodruff, the newly appointed Church historian, and Franklin D. Richards, now assistant Church historian. Bancroft brought with him the manuscript history of Utah, as yet incomplete, which he presented to Woodruff and Richards for comment. Bancroft's methodology in the *History of Utah,* for the most part, was to present the Mormon point of view in the main text, with opposing accounts and opinions in the often extensive footnotes. He therefore gave the Mormon historians an opportunity to correct any mistakes in their side of the story. Bancroft continued to send proofs to Utah as the work progressed, and Richards provided corrections as well as answers to inquiries about specific topics, such as "Crime in Utah."

Bancroft's visit led to his receiving copies of other important items, chiefly through the Church Historian's Office, including three volumes of abstracts from the Manuscript History of Brigham Young, one of the most important collections in the LDS Archives. Additional personal accounts, as well as histories of pioneer settlements on the fringes of Mormon country, were obtained by the Church Historian's

Office, and copies were sent to Bancroft. Judging from the dates on forwarded materials, he acquired about fifty additional manuscript items as a result of his 1884 Salt Lake City visit. Of these manuscripts, approximately one-fourth were from prominent non-Mormons.

Bancroft's book agents, who fanned out through the West to sell subscriptions to the Bancroft Works, often wrote biographical sketches of prospective subscribers. Whether or not a person placed an order, the dictation was mailed to the business office. Most of these are only a page or two, but some also contain the agent's assessment of the narrator. Between 1884 and 1888, more than two hundred such statements were recorded and forwarded to the Bancroft Library at San Francisco by Bancroft's agents in Utah, L. H. Nichols and L. Leadbetter. Since most of these dictations were not available until the history was virtually complete, the history having been readied for printing in 1886, little use was made of them except as an occasional condensed biography belatedly attached to a footnote. Those collected in Utah come from more than fifty communities and are, for the most part, sketches of the children of first settlers—non-Mormon as well as Mormon—who in the 1880s were successful businessmen and prominent leaders in civic and ecclesiastical affairs. Collectively, these biographies are a rich source for demographic and business studies.

Bancroft added these sketches to the earlier manuscripts, to form part of the Bancroft Library. As he described in his 1880 letter to James Dwyer, the biographies were labeled with an appropriate title and the author's name, bound for preservation, assigned a number, and used as source material for his history. Each of Bancroft's histories includes a list of "Authorities Consulted"; in the *History of Utah, 1540-1886,* the list fills twenty-seven pages and includes more than a hundred named manuscripts, including original documents, copies of documents, and dictations.

The *History of Utah* was both applauded and condemned, just as Hubert Howe Bancroft anticipated when he wrote the preface to the volume: "If the writer . . . is wise and successful enough to find and follow the exact line of equity which should be drawn between the hotly contending factions . . . and speaks honestly and openly in the treatment of such a subject, he is pretty sure to offend, and bring upon himself condemnation from all parties."[4] He was satisfied, however, that the materials he had gathered and presented would

> constitute the foundation upon which future histories of western North America must forever be built. The reason is obvious. I take events from the men who made them. My facts, for the most part, are from original sources; and wherever the desired

> facts do not appear I tap the fountain for them. He who shall come after me will scarcely be able to undermine my work by laying another or a deeper foundation.[5]

Expansion of the Bancroft Collection

The many sources of documentation forming that foundation—the books, manuscripts, maps, newspapers, and other materials in the Bancroft Library—were purchased by the University of California at Berkeley in late 1905. Over the years since, the library's attention has not focused particularly on Mormon history. That is not to say, however, that the library has not added Mormon-related materials. One outstanding example of materials acquired since then is the Utah collection compiled by Hugh F. O'Neil, project editor and technical supervisor of the Historical Records Survey for Utah and of the state's Federal Writers' Project of the Works Progress Administration. Given to the Bancroft Library between 1942 and 1959, the collection includes about 350 original documents dating from 1851 to 1931 and copies of over fifty reports (over twelve hundred pages) made under the auspices of the Historical Records Survey and the Federal Writers' Project. Also included are copies of documents and Utah county histories. Some, but not all, of these materials are duplicates of the biographical sketches and pioneer interviews placed in the Library of Congress by the Historical Records Survey (and also available on microfilm at the Bancroft Library).

Any discussion of Mormon documentary sources at the Bancroft Library also needs to include the Dale L. Morgan Papers. During his intense career as researcher and historian, including the seventeen years of his association with the Bancroft Library from 1954 until his death in 1971, Dale Morgan amassed a tremendous amount of material. These papers, a bequest to the Bancroft Library, include materials relating to his work on the Utah Historical Records Survey, his research in connection with Hopi and Navajo land claims, transcripts of diaries and documents in many repositories, transcripts of articles from early newspapers, bibliographic notes, research notes, his book manuscripts and other writings, and a prodigious and valuable correspondence. Long unavailable to scholars, these papers have now been processed and microfilmed through a cooperative project with the Marriott Library, University of Utah.

Besides these important collections, the manuscripts catalog shows a number of letters, journals, reminiscences, and other papers relating to Mormons in California, Arizona, Illinois, Missouri, and Utah, which have been added over the years to Hubert Howe Bancroft's core collection. Many of these are originals; others, in the tradition of Bancroft's practice of copying what he could not obtain in the original, are microfilms, photocopies, or transcripts of manuscripts and documents in private hands or in other repositories such as the National Archives, the Library of Congress, or LDS Church archives. Information about individual items can be obtained from the library, but there are also several useful bibliographies relating to the collection.

Related Bibliographies

The first bibliography is, of course, Hubert Howe Bancroft's own "Authorities Consulted in the History of Utah," pp. xxi–xlvii of *History of Utah.* In compiling his own later bibliography, S. George Ellsworth termed Bancroft's list "indispensible as a bibliographic guide for the first forty years of Utah's history of settled occupation."[6] The "Authorities" list also illustrates the scope of nonmanuscript material included in Bancroft's library, with only a portion listed as being on loan from the Church archives.

Also very useful is Ellsworth's "A Guide to the Manuscripts in the Bancroft Library Relating to the *History of Utah.*"[7] This guide was compiled, however, at a time when the principal access to the manuscripts was the original geographic classification system used by Bancroft, wherein Utah manuscripts were filed sequentially under P-F (P for Pacific states, F for Utah). Related manuscripts in other states' classifications, such as Henry W. Bigler's "Diary of a Mormon in California," were made accessible more by staff memory than by a subject catalog. Ellsworth did, however, include some sources beyond the P-F materials and described later acquisitions (including the O'Neil gift) up to 1954.

The section "Utah and the Mormons" in *The Bancroft Library's Pacific and Western Manuscripts (except California)*[8] brings the bibliography up to 1962 and adds an extensive name and subject index.

Finally, like other major research libraries across the country, the Bancroft Library is devoting much energy to making its catalog records available on national bibliographic databases, both through current cataloging on automated systems and through retrospective conversion of existing records. Hubert Howe Bancroft had once tried to index his entire library as if it were a book. The time is not too distant when researchers across the country will have just that kind of instant online access to information about Mormon materials, both printed and manuscript, in the library he founded.

Bonnie Hardwick is Head of the Manuscripts Division, Bancroft Library, Berkeley, California.

NOTES

[1]*Literary Industries,* vol. 39 of *The Works of Hubert Howe Bancroft* (San Francisco: The History Company, 1890), 176.

[2]*Literary Industries,* 227.

[3]*Literary Industries,* 633–36.

[4]*History of Utah, 1540–1886,* vol. 26 of *The Works of Hubert Howe Bancroft* (San Francisco: The History Company, 1889), vi.

[5]Letter to James Dwyer, January 12, 1880, in *Literary Industries,* 635.

[6]"Hubert Howe Bancroft and the *History of Utah,*" *Utah Historical Quarterly* 22 (April 1954): 100.

[7]S. George Ellsworth, "A Guide to the Manuscripts in the Bancroft Library Relating to the *History of Utah,*" *Utah Historical Quarterly* 22 (July 1954): 196–247.

[8]Dale L. Morgan and George P. Hammond, eds., "Utah and the Mormons," in *The Bancroft Library's Pacific and Western Manuscripts (except California),* vol. 1 of *A Guide to the Manuscript Collections of the Bancroft Library* (Berkeley: University of California Press, 1963), 96–122.

Margaret Cannon Clayton, granddaughter of Mormon women's leader Emmeline B. Wells, shows the diaries of her grandmother to Donald K. Nelson, director of libraries at Brigham Young University. Mrs. Clayton donated the valuable collection to Brigham Young University in 1975. Courtesy University Archives, BYU.

The Archives of the Mormon Experience at Brigham Young University

David J. Whittaker

From humble beginnings in 1875, Brigham Young University has grown to become one of the largest private, religiously-owned and -operated universities in the United States. The growth of BYU's library mirrors this progress. In 1883 the library contained about 500 volumes and 2,082 periodicals. In 1884, however, a fire destroyed two-thirds of its holdings. From then until the 1920s the library's holdings increased slowly, but after 1920, especially through the efforts of individuals like Alice Louise Reynolds, the collections grew more rapidly. Especially valuable were such collections as the George H. Brimhall Theological Library, the John A. Widtsoe Library of Agriculture, the Charles W. Penrose Poetry Collection, the James E. Talmage Collection, and the Heber J. Grant Collection, to mention just a few of the more important gifts. By 1929 the library contained 35,000 volumes, and in October 1925, the Heber J. Grant Library building was dedicated. This growth surely helped BYU obtain accreditation in 1927.

By 1951 the library contained 170,000 volumes; twenty years later, it reached its first million. Such growth required a newer facility, and in 1961 the J. Reuben Clark Library building was dedicated. Additional growth brought a major addition to the structure in 1976, and the building was renamed the Harold B. Lee Library when the new law school on campus was named after Clark. At present the Lee Library contains about four million volumes, with another addition to the building being planned.

In the 1930s, BYU professor Wilford Poulson began to collect copies of various Mormon diaries for the library, adding material to the manuscript room organized in the Grant Library in 1925. Newburn I. Butt was also a key figure during these formative years. These efforts combined to create a "Mormon Americana" collection. But it was not until 1955 that the Archives Department was organized under the direction of S. Lyman Tyler, then director of the BYU library. Located

A hallmark of eighteenth-century printing, the Baskerville collection is of interest and value to library patrons studying the history and art of printing. Baskerville printed about 67 books of which BYU has acquired a representative collection. Displaying the Holy Bible is Chad Flake, curator of Special Collections, 1967. Courtesy University Archives, BYU.

in its early years in the Maeser Building, the Archives Department was moved into the first level of the new library building in 1961. That same year the manuscript collections were separated from Special Collections, with Ralph Hansen and Hollis Scott managing the former (including University Archives) and Chad Flake managing the latter.

The collecting activities, directed with vision by A. Dean Larsen, associate librarian, have broadened the Mormon and Western Americana areas of Special Collections. In 1976 the Archives moved to the fifth floor, where it will remain until a new facility is completed. Patrons access Archives manuscripts through the Pioneer Memorial Room on the fourth floor, where the main card catalog for the manuscripts is also located.

Various personal libraries and papers have come to BYU, including those of LeRoy Hafen in 1958, J. Reuben Clark Jr. in 1960, M. Wilford Poulsen in 1970, Dale Morgan in 1974, J. Earl Arrington in 1979, and Steven Christensen in 1992.

The 1974 appointment of Dennis Rowley as manuscript curator aided in the movement toward professionalization of the archival and manuscript collections and in a major broadening and deepening of the collecting efforts. The addition of professional curators to the department has aided in these areas as well. Combined with the work of Chad Flake and his staff who have collected printed material, the holdings of the University Archives and the Department of Special Collections and Manuscripts (created by recombining the two areas in 1990) make the BYU Library a significant center for Mormon studies.[1] Because another essay in *Mormon Americana* deals with the print materials, only the manuscript collections are considered here.

The manuscript collections consist of about six thousand collections and 1,300 oral histories, most of which have been transcribed. The manuscript collections are managed by full-time curators, with each major area identified as follows: Literary Arts and Communications, Photoarchives (containing over 500,000 images), Freedom Archives, Utah and the West, University Archives, and the Archives of the Mormon Experience.[2] Each area should have a separate essay devoted to its collections because each has Mormon content and thus overlaps with the others, but the focus of this essay will be on the Archives of the Mormon Experience.

Archives of the Mormon Experience

In its broadest sense, the Archives of the Mormon Experience seeks to document the Mormon experience in all its varied dimensions: personal and institutional, male and female, nineteenth and twentieth centuries. The collection focuses primarily on the American-Mormon experience. The greatest strengths of the collection are its breadth and depth. This essay can only suggest the richness of the holdings. Although somewhat dated, Davis Bitton's *Guide to Mormon Diaries and Autobiographies* (Provo: Brigham Young University Press, 1977), provides

J. Earl Arrington, 1979, donor of a 50,000-volume collection to Brigham Young University library. Courtesy University Archives, BYU.

the best published guide to BYU's collections of diaries and life histories and is the most convenient place for the researcher to begin. Since about 1984, the BYU library has been cataloging on RLIN (Research Libraries Information Network), a computerized database of over 100 libraries. Until a retroactive cataloging project is completed, however, researchers will also have to check the card catalog.

Useful are two out-of-print guides to the collections produced in-house over the years: Hyrum L. Andrus and Richard E. Bennett, comps. and eds., *Mormon Manuscripts to 1846: A Guide to the Holdings of the Harold B. Lee Library* (Provo, Utah: Archives and Manuscripts, Harold B. Lee Library, Brigham Young University, 1977); and [Dennis Rowley, comp.], "Women in History: A Guide to Selected Holdings of the Women's History Archives" (Special Collections and Manuscripts, Harold B. Lee Library, Brigham Young University [1976]). Detailed registers or guides to the more significant collections are available from the archives, including a recent guide to about 450 missionary journals and collections organized by country and mission: David J. Whittaker and Chris McClellan, *Mormon Missions and Missionaries: A Bibliographic Guide to Published and Manuscript Sources* (Provo, Utah: Special Collections and Manuscripts, Harold B. Lee Library, Brigham Young University, 1993).

One of the crown jewels of the Archives of the Mormon Experience is the Newell K. Whitney Collection, a treasure trove of early Latter-day Saint history. In addition to containing the earliest holographic copies of some of Joseph Smith's earliest revelations, it contains personal and institutional records of the first decades of the Church's history.[3] The recently acquired Hyrum Smith journals and papers add a significant dimension to BYU's early Mormon holdings. These documents include four Kirtland diaries, a book of records, a Liberty Jail letter, and various legal and property papers. Other early Mormon documents include the original bond signed by Joseph Smith and several others before Justice Austin King, August 1838; a collection of Mormon redress petitions for Mormon Missouri losses;[4] George Romney's Justice of the Peace Docket Book for Kirtland, Ohio (1841–43), the volume that follows chronologically the similar Oliver Cowdery volume owned by the Huntington Library; the Manchester, England, diary of William Clayton; the Nauvoo diary of Thomas Bullock, which contains a detailed account of the first fire in the Nauvoo Temple, as well as descriptions of the final months of the Mormon exodus from Nauvoo; the 1843–50 diary of Robert Lang Campbell; the Nauvoo-period diary of John D. Lee; and the Isaac Russell papers which contain the earliest known letters (August 1837) of the first Mormon mission to England.

The BYU archives also contains a collection of some 750 legal documents relating to the Hancock County Circuit Court, 1839-60. Significant collections of early notables such as Brigham Young, Orson Pratt, Parley Pratt, and Samuel Brannan are also important. The archives is also the repository of the Manuscript Retrieval Project, a BYU Religious Studies Center program, which with the assistance of the BYU Library, has supported faculty research and photocopying of various Mormon and Mormon-related manuscripts from various repositories in the midwest and eastern United States. These, combined with the archives' own gathering efforts have helped create a truly significant research basis for early Mormon studies.

Missionary work has been a core emphasis from the beginning of the LDS movement; thus missionary records continue to form a significant part of the manuscript heritage of the Church. Important in themselves for the record of spiritual events, educational experiences and important rites of passage for Church members, such records are also valuable for institutional and intellectual history as well as for the history of the areas where the missionaries served. A significant part of the manuscript collection is hundreds of these diaries. These significant records are represented by Robert Skelton's journal of his mission to India in the 1850s; the journals of California Mission president Ephraim Hesmer Nye, 1896-1901; the papers of William Hart Miles, president of the Eastern States Mission, 1865-69; the nineteen-volume journal of Canadian Mission president Charles H. Hart; the diaries of John Henry Gibbs, a missionary killed by the Ku Klux Klan in Tennessee in August, 1884, as well as the journals of Willis Eugene Robinson, the first Mormon missionary to arrive on the scene after the attack; the mission journal of Isaac A. Smoot, president of the Northern States Mission; the papers of Gustive O. Larson, president of the Swedish Mission, 1936-39; the eighteen journals (1885-1928) of Joseph Wilford Booth, who was both the Turkish Mission president and later the president of the Armenian Mission; the papers of South African Mission president Don McCarrol Dalton; the papers of Scandinavian Mission presidents John Van Cott, 1852-56, 1859-62, and Jesse N. Smith, 1862-64; the diaries of Swiss Mission president Daniel Tyler, 1853-55; the journals and papers of Harold Christensen, acting president of the New Zealand Mission; and the papers and photograph albums of Castle H. Murphy, president of the Hawaiian Mission. Representing almost all the countries where Mormon missionaries have traveled, these records provide an essential window into the heart of the LDS experience. As mentioned above, the archives has recently completed a bibliographical guide (70 pp.) to its significant holdings of missionary journals.

In addition to proselyting missions, Church members were also sent on colonizing missions, particularly during the second half of the nineteenth century. Records in the BYU archives of these missions are represented by such collections as the twenty-three journals of Charles Ora Card, the leader of the Mormon settlement of southern Alberta, Canada; and the recently acquired Abraham Owen Woodruff collection, which includes the papers for the Big Horn Basin Colonizing Co. in Northern Wyoming, the last effort of Mormon colonization in the nineteenth century. But scattered throughout the BYU collections are hundreds of items documenting many other Mormon colonization efforts in the American West, including, for example, the earliest records of the exploration of the Uintah Basin of northeastern Utah.

The BYU archives also contains, in addition to Mormon accounts, a significant number of overland journals and letters which document the larger context of the American westward movement and occasionally contain Mormon references. A guide to these collections (40 pp.) is available in the archives: David J. Whittaker and Chris McClellan, ***Bibliography of Western Americana, Emphasizing Non-Mormon Collections*** (Provo, Utah: Special Collections and Manuscripts, Harold B. Lee Library, Brigham Young University, 1993).

The Utah territorial period is represented by such collections as the extensive and significant Thomas L. Kane Collection, the Abraham H. Cannon papers, the L. John Nuttall papers, the Charles Ora Card Collection (in addition to Card's Canadian journals, BYU has about twenty volumes of his years as a leader in the Cache Valley area of northern Utah, including his years as stake president during the construction of the Logan Tabernacle and Temple), the Francis A. Hammond papers (stake president in the Moab area at the end of the nineteenth century), the William Farrar Collection, and the David John journals.

The BYU archives occasionally has collected records which document a significant episode or person in LDS history. For example, a collection which allows researchers to follow the events of the Mark Hofmann forgery and murder cases has been gathered both from public and private sources. Another example is the excellent collection of material relating to the Benjamin Cluff expedition to Central America in 1900–1902. Here the BYU archives contains the papers of John B. Fairbanks, Paul Henning, Chester Van Buren, Asa Solomon Kienke, Walter M. Wolfe, Walter S. Tolon, Heber Magelby, Royal Wooley, and Eugene L. Roberts. While the journals of Cluff are presumed lost for the period of the expedition, the archives holds his journals for the years before (including his time at the University of Michigan as a student) and after the journey (including his resignation as president of BYU and his subsequent move to Mexico, where he managed a banana plantation). We also have a newspaper clipping record of the accounts Cluff submitted to the *Deseret News* while on the expedition, often with accounts just copied out of his now missing journals. BYU Photoarchives also has about 200 photographs taken on the expedition.

Institutional records are also an important part of the archives. The United Order account books for Orderville, Utah Territory, 1877-95 (3 vols.); for Beaver, Utah, 1878-93 (1 vol.); and for Fillmore, Utah, 1869-72 (1 vol.) are good examples. But there are a variety of such records in the BYU collections: the Campaign Record of the Nauvoo Legion, Provo Command, to the San Pete and Paiute Military Districts, 1869; the ledger books of the Provo Tabernacle, 1882-93 (4 vols.); a Camp Floyd Day Book, Store Accounts, 1858-59; the sales ledger of Deseret Mills, Salt Lake City, 1870-72, said to be the first woolen mill in the Salt Lake Valley; the records of the Utah Territorial Insane Asylum, 1889-1900; and a large collection of the business and financial records of the Utah and Idaho Sugar Company. Also valuable for historians are the minutes of the Provo School of the Prophets, 1875; the Uintah Stake Academy records; the BYU Centennial History Collection; the records of Church meetings, Springville, Utah, 1860-61; the papers of William Dame, an important Mormon leader in southern Utah; and the papers of John Steele, also an important Mormon pioneer in southern Utah, which collection contains what is believed to be the oldest known Indian language dictionary (Paiute) prepared by the Mormons in the Great Basin, as well as some of the earliest known letters of the LDS Las Vegas Indian Mission in 1855. The BYU library also holds an 1868-70 journal of Jacob Hamblin, part of which details his mission to Moquis Indians in 1869.

Significant twentieth-century collections include: the extensive Thomas F. O'Dea papers, which include journals, research files, and correspondence of an important Catholic sociologist of religion and student of the Mormon experience; the papers of Utah politicians Joseph Howell, U.S. Congressman from Utah, 1903-8; Henry H. Dixon, U.S. Congressman from Utah in the 1950s; Arthur V. Watkins, the Senator who presided over the hearings on Joseph McCarthy; and Senator Wallace F. Bennett.

Personal records of individuals associated with Utah and Mormon history constitute a large number of items in the archives. A sampling will give the reader an idea of the richness of these collections: the Jack Anderson papers; a World War I diary of Nels Anderson; the diaries of George Washington Bean; the papers of Utah landscape artist George Beard; the papers of artist Mahonri M. Young; the diaries of Utah photographer Charles R. Savage; the Adam S. Bennion papers; the papers of Charles A. Callis; the eighteen journals of Abraham H. Cannon, 1879–95; three journals of Angus M. Cannon, 1885–86; the forty-four-volume journal of Charles Ora Card; the seventy-five journals of his son Joseph Y. Card; the extensive J. Reuben Clark papers; the Howard Coray family papers; the Matthew Cowley papers; the journals of Benjamin F. Cummings; the six journals of Winslow Farr, 1856–1910; the Thomas Ferguson papers; the papers of Utah artist John Hafen; the papers of LeRoy and Ann Hafen; the Andrew Jenson papers; the five-volume David John journal (1856–1908); the fourteen-volume journal of Francis W. Kirkham; the papers of Jesse Knight; the journals and papers of James E. Talmage; the journals (35 vols.) and papers of Utah Senator and Mormon Apostle Reed Smoot; the Gustive O. Larson papers; the papers of Richard R. Lyman; the papers of E. Cecil McGavin; the Thomas E. McKay papers; the papers of Lowry Nelson; the papers and journals of L. John Nuttall; the papers of M. Wilford Poulsen; misc. papers of Orson and Parley P. Pratt; misc. papers of George Reynolds, Franklin D. Richards, Franklin S. Richards, Sidney Rigdon, and B. H. Roberts; Vernon Romney papers; the Isaac and Samuel Russell collections; Abraham O. Smoot papers; Erastus Snow and Lorenzo Snow papers; the papers of Sidney B. Sperry; the Moses Whitaker Taylor papers; the six-volume Moses Thatcher journals (1866–81); letters of George D. Watt; a letter collection of John Willard Young; three volumes of the journals of Joseph Young; and misc. papers of Levi Edgar Young.

BYU archives holds a number of important collections relating to the Mormon settlements in Arizona. For example, the diaries and papers of Joseph Hill Richards covering 1876–1919; the papers of Jesse Nathaniel Smith, the president of the LDS Arizona Snowflake Stake; thirteen journals of Samuel Uriah Porter; and the extensive George S. Tanner Collection consisting of about 50 separate collections dealing with all aspects of the Mormon experience in Arizona.

While not as broadly representative as are the male collections, the Mormon women collections are a significant part of the archives. BYU has over three hundred women's collections, ranging from a single letter to those containing dozens of journals. Perhaps the single most important collection is the papers and forty-five-volume diary of Emmeline B. Wells, third general president of the Relief Society and editor of the important *Woman's Exponent.* But other collections add breadth to the women's archive: the Mary Fielding Smith collection; the Nauvoo letters of Jennetta Richards; the papers of Emma Lucy Gates Bowen; the Zina Young Williams Card collection; the autobiography of

Martha Cragun Cox; the papers of Ida Smoot Dusenberry; the journals of Lucy Hannah White Flake; the journals of Edna Coray Dyer; the papers of Mormon poet Emily Hill Woodmansee; the journals of Bernell E. Gardner; the papers of Susa Young Gates; the papers of Ann Hafen; the Hawaiian mission diary of Mary Jane Dilworth Hammond; the papers of Elizabeth A. Howard; the Mary Elizabeth Rollins Lightner papers; the eleven-volume journal of Mary Ann B. Freeze; the papers of Cornellia Sorenson Lund; the Amy Cassandra Brown Lyman collection; the papers of Utah opera-singer Viola Pratt Gillette McFarlane; the diary (1887-1902) of Emma Wartstill Mecham Nelson, the record of a polygamous wife in St. George, Utah, and New Mexico; the four-volume journal of Grace Greer Nuttall; the papers of Ann Pitchforth, a plural wife of John Taylor; misc. papers of Alice Louise Reynolds, a BYU professor and Friend of the BYU Library; the autobiography of Bathsheba Wilson Bigler Smith; the papers of Margaret Summerhays; the autobiography of Mary Jane Mount Tanner; the papers of Maurine Whipple; the papers of Ruth Partridge; the papers of Algie Ballif; the Helen Candland Stark Collection; and the journal and papers of Mary Ann Hoopes Yearsley. Useful guides to these collections are Dennis Rowley, "Women in the Archives," and Sunny McClellan, comp., "Selected Diaries and Autobiographies of Mormon Women in the Special Collections of the Harold B. Lee Libraries of Brigham Young University" (Special Collections and Manuscripts, Harold B. Lee Library, Brigham Young University).

Also important are the records of women's groups: the Record Book of the Female Relief Society, Salt Lake City, January to June, 1854 kept by Louisa R. Taylor; the papers of the Woman's Suffrage Association of Beaver County, 1892-95; and the papers of the Yesharah Society, a society for returned LDS women missionaries, which includes the minute books (1929-60) and account books (1935-51).

Collections which are not easily categorized but are important for a variety of topics and periods in Mormon history include the Lewis C. Bidamon collection of legal documents; the best single collection of material in existence relating to Etienne Cabet and the Icarian Community at Nauvoo following the exodus of the Mormons west; letters (1871-73) and overland diary (1868) of Vice President Schuyler Colfax; two volumes of the Hawaiian diaries of Walter Murray Gibson (1886-87); an original, unpublished book-length manuscript of a novel by John Hyde written in 1858; five diaries of Warren Post (1846-50); letters written to Samuel Powers, an early RLDS leader, 1852-70; the letters of George Rockwell, the postmaster of Warsaw, Illinois, 1838-46; letters of James J. Strang, 1846-56; the earliest known sketchbook of nineteenth-century artist Seth Eastman, which includes several views of the areas on the Mississippi River north and south of

Nauvoo; the scrapbook (1879-83) of Philip Taylor Van Zile, the U.S. District Attorney for Utah who was chiefly responsible for the prosecutions of polygamy cases; the papers of anti-Mormon lecturer Rose Glen Webster, 1897-1904; the oral history of Sandra Tanner, detailing the history and publishing activities of the anti-Mormon Modern Microfilm Company (now the Utah Lighthouse Ministry); and the later family correspondence of Benjamin Winchester, an early Church leader in the Philadelphia area.

These collections should give the researcher a general idea of the rich Mormon collection at Brigham Young University. Specific inquiries can be addressed to the Curator, Archives of the Mormon Experience, Special Collections and Manuscripts, Brigham Young University, P.O. Box 26877, Provo, UT 84602-6877.

NOTES

[1]The best sources on the history of the library are contained in various files in the University Archives. There are also scattered references in Ernest L. Wilkinson, Leonard J. Arrington, and Bruce C. Hafen, eds., *Brigham Young University: The First One Hundred Years,* 4 vols. (Provo, Utah: Brigham Young University Press, 1975-76).

[2]Other important collecting areas include Literary Manuscripts; Western Americana, much of which was acquired from Fred Rosenstock, the heart of which is some fifty non-Mormon overland diaries; and European Manuscripts, most of which are described in De Lamar Jensen, *Guide for Research in Early Modern European History at Brigham Young University* (Provo, Utah: n.p., 1988), especially pp. 83-214, which includes rare books and microfilm collections. The collections of Mormons in science are described in another essay in *Mormon Americana.*

[3]In addition to an extensive register to the collection, see the short description in Chad J. Flake, "The Newell K. Whitney Collection," *BYU Studies* 11 (Summer 1971): 322-28. This collection has recently been microfilmed and is available for purchase from the library.

[4]For a description of the BYU collection, see Paul C. Richards, "Missouri Persecutions: Petitions for Redress," *BYU Studies* 13 (Summer 1973): 520-43. More completely, see Clark V. Johnson, ed., *Mormon Redress Petitions: Documents of the 1833-1838 Missouri Conflict,* Religious Studies Center Monograph Series, vol. 16 (Provo, Utah: Religious Studies Center, Brigham Young University, 1992).

Charles Redd Center for Western Studies: The Oral History Program

Jessie L. Embry

Historical research has expanded with new technology. One of the most useful developments to the field was the tape recorder. Since 1938 when Columbia University history professor Allan Nevins published *The Gateway to History,*[1] scholars interested in the past have used tape-recorded memories as source material. The early oral historians conducted interviews with government and business leaders; a second generation of oral historians in the 1960s and 1970s saw taped interviews as a way to record the social history of the "ordinary people" and to "empower" scholars with an understanding of their past.[2]

History of the Redd Center Oral History Program

The oral history program at the Charles Redd Center for Western Studies began during the second generation of oral historians. In 1972 a donation from Charles and Annaley Redd to Brigham Young University led to the establishment of a center for studying the Intermountain West. Charles Redd's instructions were that the center should look honestly at those who settled the West. To help fulfill that dream, during the summer of 1973 the Charles Redd Center launched an oral history program dealing with Utah, Western America, and Mormons.

The center hired Gary L. Shumway, one of the prominent second-generation oral historians, to teach an oral history class. Graduate students and history faculty learned oral history techniques and conducted interviews which became the basis for the Redd Center's oral history program. In the fall the center's directors, Leonard J. Arrington and Thomas G. Alexander, hired John F. Bluth, the graduate assistant for Shumway's oral history class, to direct an oral history program. Bluth held that position until he took a post in the manuscript division at the Brigham Young University library; I was hired to replace him. I was also a member of the initial oral history class and continue to teach the oral history course for the history department and Independent Study at Brigham Young University.

In connection with the Utah State Historical Society, the first oral history class worked on community histories, especially those of

Monticello and American Fork, Utah. Most of the students participated in these projects and gathered information on all aspects of life in southeastern Utah and Utah County. However, one student, Richard Maher, struck out on his own and conducted interviews for his thesis on Mormon chaplains who served during World War II. Maher used the twenty-five interviews for his thesis and for his book *For God and Country.*[3] Another early project involved Charles Redd himself, who by 1973 had suffered a stroke and was unable to speak. In order to preserve Redd's personal history, Charles S. Peterson, a history professor at Utah State University and a former employee of Redd's, conducted fifty-five interviews with Redd's friends, relatives, and employees.

Since its beginning, the Redd Center oral history program has conducted oral history interviews on a variety of historical and contemporary issues. The center staff, with the assistance of an advisory board, selects topics where inadequate records exist and then finds individuals who can provide information. Some of the projects have been very small; for example, only a few interviews were conducted to supplement contract histories. Other projects were much larger, however, and have a history of their own.

In 1976 I was invited by John Bluth to become an interviewer/editor for the oral history program. At that time, the Redd Center was conducting interviews with Utahns involved in labor unions and industries. We started by talking with labor leaders in Salt Lake City, railroad workers in Utah County and Salt Lake County, and coal miners in Carbon County. This project was later expanded to include interviews with the residents of Castle Gate, Utah, before the community's original site was flooded; residents of Copperton, Utah; and union members working for Geneva Steel. Approximately sixty interviews were completed with these subjects.

We struggled to find labor union workers who were willing to talk to a female employee of a conservative Mormon university, and we were experiencing some discouragement when the Redd Center Council suggested another oral history project. The project concerned Maude Taylor Bentley, the third wife of Joseph C. Bentley. Maude died in 1976. She grew up in a polygamous family in Mexico and then married her father's partner as a plural wife when she was sixteen years old. Members of the Redd Center council pointed out that while Maude had written an autobiography, she had had many unrecorded experiences of what life was like in a Church-sanctioned polygamous marriage. Maude was one of the last surviving wives from the period when the Church allowed polygamy, so it would not be possible to interview many others who had actually married into the principle. Moreover, the children from these plural marriages were also advanced in age. Accordingly we transferred our emphasis from the Labor Oral History Project to a new project: the LDS Polygamy Oral History Project.

Identifying possible interviewees who had been raised in polygamous families required constant vigilance. We started with the Redd Center council suggestions and then followed up on all the leads we could develop. We talked about the project wherever we went. Once, for example, I traveled to Logan, Utah, for a six-month checkup with my family dentist. While Dr. Johnson was sticking his fingers into my mouth, I tried to answer his questions about our latest project. He explained that his mother came from a polygamous family and, while she had very few memories of her father because he died when she was young, Dr. Johnson's aunt and uncle had clear recollections. Both the aunt and uncle were interviewed.

After six months at the Redd Center, my term of employment ended and I left to look for other work. John Bluth continued the LDS Polygamy Oral History Project until I returned in 1979 to direct the program. With the financial assistance of the College of Family, Home, and Social Sciences, I hired interviewers to talk to the children of LDS polygamous families. The center conducted over 250 interviews for this project. We had limited travel funds, but we found children from polygamous families living along the Wasatch Front. We also received travel grants to go to the Mormon colonies in Mexico and the Mormon settlements in Alberta, Canada, as well as southern Utah, Nevada, and California.

As we began to examine the interviews, we wondered how polygamous families differed from monogamous families. In order to find out, we decided to start a new project: the LDS Family Life Oral History Project. In response to a newspaper article asking for people whose parents had been married prior to 1904, a number of potential interviewees volunteered to be part of the project. We adapted the outline from the LDS Polygamy Oral History Project and sent interviewers to talk to these volunteers. The center interviewed over 150 children from monogamous families. Most lived along the Wasatch Front, but we also received a travel grant to go to Arizona. I used the information from these two projects, along with archival materials, to write *Mormon Polygamous Families: Life in the Principle*.[4]

While I was writing *Mormon Polygamous Families,* we started looking for another oral history project. Alan Cherry, a black Latter-day Saint who joined the Church in 1969, lamented the fact that although African Americans have been members of the Mormon Church since the 1830s, we know very little about those early members. He added that unless some effort was made to preserve the stories of current LDS African Americans, future historians would face the same problem. Cherry convinced us that this was a worthwhile project. With the approval of Redd Center Director Thomas G. Alexander, Cherry was hired to work on the project.

From 1985 to 1989, Cherry conducted interviews with LDS African Americans. He tried to include people from all areas of the United States, all ages, and all walks of life. At first because of financial limitations, the interviews were conducted in Utah. It became quickly apparent, however, that while these interviewees had originally come from throughout the United States, life in predominately white Mormon Utah had greatly influenced them. Assistance from the College of Family, Home, and Social Sciences at Brigham Young University, the Silver Foundation, and some private donations allowed the Redd Center to expand the base.

Ultimately Cherry conducted interviews in Utah, elsewhere in the West (the Bay and Los Angeles areas in California and the Phoenix area in Arizona), North Carolina (from Asheville in the west to Greenville in the east), the Northeast (New York and Pennsylvania), the near South (Washington, D.C., area and Richmond, Virginia), the Deep South (Atlanta, Georgia; Birmingham, Alabama; Jackson, Mississippi; New Orleans and Baton Rouge, Louisiana; and Gulfport, Mississippi), the Midwest (Chicago, Illinois; Columbus, Ohio; and St. Louis, Missouri), and Hawaii. He interviewed a total of 224 black Latter-day Saints: single, married, divorced, and widowed people, some with doctoral degrees and others with only grade-school educations, ranging in age from a teenager to a great grandfather. Together these interviews constitute a significant body of information for students of the contemporary Church. I have published a book based on these interviews: *Black Saints in a White Church: Contemporary African American Mormons.*[5]

As Cherry conducted interviews with LDS African Americans, we realized that blacks were not the only American ethnic group whose history in the Church was inadequately documented. The Redd Center envisioned not just an LDS Afro-American Oral History Project but a larger umbrella project for Latter-day Saint ethnic groups. With continued funding from the College of Family, Home, and Social Sciences, the College of Religion, and private donations, the Redd Center has conducted interviews with Native, Hispanic, Asian, Tongan, and Samoan Americans. Whenever possible, we have hired interviewers from the ethnic group being targeted. These projects are ongoing.

All Redd Center interviews are tape-recorded and the original tapes are preserved, initially on reels and now on cassettes. Members of the Redd Center staff transcribe the tapes; the transcripts are then edited for clarity and grammar. Once the editing is completed, the transcript is returned to the interviewee, who is invited to make corrections. Approximately half of the interviews are returned, and the interviewees' changes can range from correcting the spelling of a name to completely rewriting the document. Most of the changes, however, are minor and clarify the information presented. If the interview is not returned, the transcript is finalized as it was edited. A preface is added to each interview which explains whether the interview was edited by the editor and interviewee or just the editor.

After the editor's or the interviewee's final corrections are made, copies of the transcript are bound. One copy is given to the interviewee as a courtesy for participating in the program; the other is placed in the manuscript division of the Harold B. Lee Library, Brigham Young University. Copies of the transcripts may be purchased through the Redd Center; the interviews can also be ordered through interlibrary loan.

Redd Center Oral History Projects[6]

The following descriptions present information about all the Redd Center's past and present projects.

American Fork, Utah. The Redd Center, in cooperation with the city of American Fork, Utah, and the American Fork City Library, sponsored this project. A group of American Fork citizens selected interviewees who were interviewed by BYU history students. Copies of tapes and transcripts are located at the American Fork City Library as well as at the Redd Center. Eleven interviews were conducted with people who helped develop the American Fork Hospital and who had lived in American Fork. Mary Pulley, a woman who claimed there was nothing to say about her history other than that she was "born, raised, and would die in American Fork," spoke for over eight hours about her life.

Bamberger Railroad. On the Bamberger project, the Redd Center worked with the Archives and Manuscripts Department, Harold B. Lee Library, to supplement information contained in its Bamberger Railroad Manuscript Collection, about an interurban railway which linked Ogden and Payson, Utah, by 1916. The four interviews give background information about the railroad and include anecdotes about its operations.

Brigham Young University. Miscellaneous interviews not created as a part of a specific project are classified as the BYU project. Some of these interviews were conducted by the Charles Redd Center for Western Studies; others were completed by Archives and Manuscripts.

Charles Redd. The Redd Center, along with the Ronald V. Jensen Living Historical Farm and Utah State University, has conducted interviews to document the life of Charles Redd. Copies of these interviews are located at Utah State University as well as at the Redd Center. Added to the Redd Project are interviews conducted by Karl Young, a Brigham Young University English professor and friend of Charles Redd. These interviews were conducted in preparation for a biography of Redd which was published as part of the Charles Redd Monographs in Western American History.[7] Leonard J. Arrington used these interviews in writing another biography of Charles Redd. There are approximately fifty interviews with members of Charles Redd's family, including those from his sons and wife, employees, and friends.

Forest Service. Thomas G. Alexander conducted oral histories as part of a contracted history of Region Four for the National Forest Service. These interviews were used in writing *The Rise of Multiple-Use Management in the Intermountain West: A History of Region 4 of the Forest Service*.[8]

Interstate Brick. Thomas G. Alexander also received a contract to write a history of Interstate Brick and supplemented his research with oral histories. Six interviews were completed for this project.

Labor. The Charles Redd Center for Western Studies and the Utah State Historical Society conducted interviews with labor leaders and workers for the labor project. In addition to those at the Redd Center, copies of the interviews are available in the Utah State Historical Society, Salt Lake City. The approximately sixty interviews include discussions about the company towns of Castle Gate and Copperton. There are also interviews with American Federation of Labor leaders in the state of Utah and with employees of Geneva Steel.

LDS Chaplains. Richard Maher conducted interviews of LDS chaplains for his BYU master's thesis.[9] The twenty-five interviews include a recording with Herbert Maw, who served during World War I.

LDS Afro-American. The Redd Center African American project consists of interviews conducted principally by Latter-day Saint black member Alan Cherry with other LDS African Americans. This project has already been described in detail.

LDS Asian American. The LDS Asian American project consists of interviews with mainly Southeast Asians who have immigrated to the United States. The interviewer was a Caucasian who had worked with an Asian branch. The interviews provide information about the social conditions of Asian members and their relationship to the Church and other members.

LDS Family Life. The Redd Center created its family life project as a companion to the LDS Polygamy Oral History Project. To create a set of interviews to serve as a control group, in the fall of 1981 the Redd Center began interviewing people who were reared in monogamous LDS families between 1890 and 1920. There are approximately 150 interviews in the project.

LDS Hispanic American. The Hispanic American project consists of interviews with Latinos from Mexico, Central America, and South America who were living in the United States. The interviewers were Hispanics from Mexico, Argentina, and Peru, and some of the interviews were conducted in Spanish. The interviews provide information about the social conditions of Hispanic members and their relationship to the Church and other members.

LDS Missionary. Created in cooperation with the Department of Sociology, the LDS missionary study looks at the experiences of Mormon missionaries who traveled without "purse or scrip." The project also contains interviews with women who served LDS missions. Some of the funding for the women interviews was furnished by the BYU Women's Research Institute. These interviews are in process.

LDS Native American. Interviews conducted with Mormon Native Americans by Brigham Young University students provide information about the social conditions of Native American members and their relationship to the Church and other members.

LDS Polygamy. These interviews examine life in LDS Church-sanctioned plural marriages. The first interviews were conducted in 1976. Most of the interviews were done by Brigham Young University students. There are approximately 250 interviews in this project.

LDS Polynesian American. The Polynesian American project is in process and will contain interviews with LDS Samoan Americans and LDS Tongan Americans. The histories will provide information about the social conditions of Polynesian members and their relationship to the Church and other members.

Posey War. Michael Hurst, a BYU English student and resident of Blanding, Utah, interviewed those still alive who were involved in what has been termed the last Indian War in the United States, namely the fight in the early 1920s between the people of Blanding, Utah, and a small band of Paiutes led by Posey. There are ten interviews in this project.

Provo City, Utah. Brigham Young University students interviewed mainly former Provo mayors or Latter-day Saint stake presidents. There are thirteen interviews in this project.

San Rafael Swell, Utah. Dee Anne Finken documented landform names and prepared a basic history for the Bureau of Land Management, Moab District Office. The interviews served as a basis for Finken's *A History of the San Rafael Swell.*[10] There are eleven interviews in this project.

Simpson Springs, Utah. John F. Bluth studied site restoration and stabilization of Pony Express and Overland Mail stations in Utah's West Desert for the Bureau of Land Management, Salt Lake City office. The ten interviews were utilized, in part, in Bluth's dissertation, "Confrontation with an Arid Land."[11]

Southeastern Utah. A project by the Redd Center; the Utah State Historical Society; and the city of Monticello, Utah, looked at life in southeastern Utah. Interviewees were selected in consultation with community leaders from Monticello. Copies of tapes and transcripts are located at the San Juan County Library, Monticello, Utah, and the Utah State Historical Society, Salt Lake City, as well as at the Redd Center. There are forty interviews in this project.

Utah Politics. J. Keith Melville, a political science professor, researched the role of Utah's first ladies, the wives of the governors of the state during the twentieth century. There are seven interviews in this project.

World War II Homefront. For the fiftieth anniversary of the U.S. entry into World War II, the Redd Center looked at the experiences of men, women, and children who stayed at home during World War II. There are approximately fifty interviews in this project.

As this essay has shown, the Redd Center's oral history program provides information on Western American and Mormon History that can be used to supplement "traditional" historical sources. The program opens a window into elements of the Mormon past which need to be studied in greater depth.

Jessie L. Embry is Oral History Program Director, Charles Redd Center for Western Studies, Brigham Young University.

NOTES

[1]Allan Nevins, *The Gateway to History* (1938; reprint, Chicago: Quadrangle Books, 1963), 440.

[2]David K. Dunaway and Willa K. Baum, eds., "Preface," *Oral History: An Interdisciplinary Anthology* (Nashville: American Association of State and Local History, 1984), xiii–xvii.

[3]Richard Maher, *For God and Country: Memorable Stories from the Lives of Mormon Chaplains* (Bountiful, Utah: Horizon Publishers, 1976).

[4]Jessie L. Embry, *Mormon Polygamous Families: Life in the Principle* (Salt Lake City: University of Utah Press, 1987).

[5]Jessie L. Embry, *Black Saints in a White Church: Contemporary African American Mormons* (Salt Lake City: Signature Books, 1994).

[6]The Redd Center's oral histories, along with other oral histories produced at Brigham Young University, are listed in published guides. There are four guides representing one thousand interviews: John F. Bluth, *Oral History Collection Guide, Archives and Manuscripts Department, Harold B. Lee Library, Brigham Young University, Interviews Numbered 1 to 250* (Provo, Utah: Department of Archives and Manuscripts, Harold B. Lee Library, 1981); John F. Bluth, *Oral History Collection Guide, Archives and Manuscripts Department, Harold B. Lee Library, Brigham Young University, Interviews Numbered 251-500* (Provo, Utah: Archives and Manuscripts, Harold B. Lee Library, 1983); LeGrand Baker and Kristen Goehring, *Oral History Collection Guide, Archives and Manuscripts Department, Harold B. Lee Library, Brigham Young University, Interviews Numbered 501-750* (Provo, Utah: Archives and Manuscripts, Harold B. Lee Library, 1990) [includes a cumulative index to interviews 1-750]; and Albert Winkler, *Oral History Collection Guide, Archives and Manuscripts Department, Harold B. Lee Library, Brigham Young University, Interviews Numbered 751-1000* (Provo, Utah: Archives and Manuscripts, Harold B. Lee Library, 1992) [includes an index for these interviews].

[7]Thomas G. Alexander, ed., *Essays on the American West, 1973-74,* Charles Redd Monograph in Western American History, vol. 5 (Provo, Utah: Brigham Young University Press, 1975).

[8]Thomas G. Alexander, *The Rise of Multiple-Use Management in the Intermountain West: A History of Region 4 of the Forest Service* (Washington, D.C.: U.S. Department of Agriculture Forest Service, 1987).

[9]Richard T. Maher, "LDS Military Chaplains Oral History Project: Tape and Transcript, 1973-1975" (master's thesis, Brigham Young University, 1975).

[10]Dee Anne Finken, *A History of the San Rafael Swell* (Boulder, Colo.: Western Interstate Commission for Higher Education, 1977).

[11]John F. Bluth, "Confrontation with an Arid Land: The Incursion of Gosiutes and Whites into Utah's Central West Desert, 1800-1978" (Ph.D. diss., Brigham Young University, 1978).

Harold B. Lee Library, Brigham Young University. BYU's extensive printed and archival materials on Mormonism have been housed in this library since its completion in 1962. Courtesy University Archives, BYU.

Printed Mormon Americana at Brigham Young University

Chad J. Flake and Larry W. Draper

During the 165 years since the publication of the Book of Mormon, interest in Mormon subjects—by antagonists as well as adherents—has never waned. Indeed, the astonishingly voluminous literature of Mormonism demonstrates that this interest has been intense, constant, and rigorously apologetic as well as vehemently polemic. This fervent interest has accelerated in the recent past to a near-feverish pace. More and more Mormons (and non-Mormons, for that matter) have applied university training in a variety of fields to the study of Mormonism. This increased scholarship and the increased number and variety of publications on Mormon topics require researchers to know the repositories that have the best resources for their particular topic. This essay identifies the collections at Brigham Young University as a central source of printed material for nearly any study of Mormonism. While Brigham Young University does have a substantial collection of manuscript sources relevant to Mormonism, we will primarily discuss published sources with only passing references to any manuscript collections.

Most printed sources on Mormon topics at BYU are housed in Special Collections, located on the fourth floor of the Harold B. Lee Library. Within this closed-stack environment is a large collection of books, pamphlets, broadsides, manuals, maps, and all manner of printed material relating to Mormonism. In fact, the size and diversity of BYU's collection is second only to that of the Church Historical Department. The BYU collection holds approximately 55 percent (sixty-six hundred items) of all pre-1930 publications and an even greater proportion of Church-produced literature,[1] identified in both volumes of *A Mormon Bibliography* edited by the authors.[2] BYU's collection of post-1930 Mormon printed material is equally impressive. Furthermore, beyond the large size of the Mormon collection, BYU holds many exceptional items which will be discussed in greater detail in the latter part of this essay.

Another area of collecting interest (which relates directly to the Mormon collection) is the collection of Western Americana. Because of

BYU's western location and the LDS Church's instrumental role in the early development of the Great Basin, it is not surprising that the university emphasizes collecting in this area. Special Collections boasts a particularly good collection of Utah imprints, the most complete set of Legislative Assembly of Utah Territory pamphlets known anywhere, a fine collection of material on Western exploration, travel literature of the western United States (including much material in foreign languages), and an extensive collection on Utah history.

History of Special Collections

Having generally enumerated the strong areas of BYU's collection of Mormon-related printed material, we will now discuss a small sample of items found in the several collections that make up Special Collections. In doing so, it will be helpful to briefly describe the evolution of Special Collections and list a few of the significant items acquired during its development.

The creation of a fine research library collection is by no means an accident of nature, nor does it happen overnight. Many years of effort and numerous employees of the university have contributed to the maturation of BYU's Mormon, Utah, and Western Americana collections. The collection of Mormon-related publications was created from several distinctive collections gathered over the years for the purpose of assisting scholars with special resource needs and preserving printed items that were particularly valuable monetarily as well as in terms of content. A researcher will find Mormon material at Special Collections in a number of separate collections, including the Vault, Mormon Americana, Clark, and Hafen collections.

Special Collections, as an area separate and distinct from the university's general library collection, was created in 1955 by library director S. Lyman Tyler. Before that time, the various printed collections which eventually became Special Collections were housed in diverse locations. The Locked Case collection, containing the library's most expensive books, was housed first in a locked bookcase located in the head librarian's office in the Heber J. Grant Building. Later it was moved to the west wall of the northeast corner of the Grant library—the area that would later become the Special Collection's book stacks.

Special Collections at that time was serviced by the Reserve Library personnel and consisted of the following collections which contained books on Mormonism: the Memorial Collection,[3] which contained books on various subjects donated to the library in memory of loved ones who had passed away; the George H. Brimhall Collection of Theology, created not by Brimhall but rather in his memory as late president of the university; the James E. Talmage Collection, donated in several pieces over a long period and eventually integrated into the Brimhall Collection; the Utah Collection, which included Utah documents secured through a depository agreement with the federal government; the Manuscript (Mss) Collection, comprised of typescripts of diaries loaned to the library and transcribed under the direction of N. I. Butt; and lastly, the library of Heber J. Grant, given to the university in 1952.

Over time, the makeup of these collections changed as Special Collections evolved. Some collections were disbanded and others retained (in whole or in part), while still others underwent a weeding process to eliminate material deemed unnecessary. This process resulted in the creation of the "Mormon Americana" Collection, which pooled items from all the collections. This collection included not only books about the Church, but also material about the various locales where the Church headquartered during its volatile history. These locales were New York, Ohio, Missouri, and Illinois, as well as New England, where many of the first converts to Mormonism had their early roots. The collection also included material on the Church's move to Utah, books on the exploration of the American West and the westward movement of many important groups, as well as the histories of the various western states that would eventually establish significant Mormon colonies.

Other Mormon-related subject areas emphasized in the Mormon Americana Collection included missionary work in most parts of the world, especially the south sea islands where proselyting activity was particularly fruitful, as well as archaeological material related to the traditional lands of the Book of Mormon. Additional subjects emphasized because of Mormon parallels included marriage customs, communal societies, health and dietary fields, and the Masonic movement. Also, theses and dissertations which fit any of the above categories (written either at BYU or elsewhere) were acquired whenever available.

Of all the collections that were drawn upon to create the Mormon Americana Collection, the Brimhall Collection of Theology had the richest cache of printed books on Mormon subjects. Among Mormon items found therein was a collection of books from Elder James E. Talmage's personal library.[4] The Talmage library included long runs of some principal Mormon periodicals such as the *Deseret Weekly, LDS Millennial Star, Improvement Era, Young Woman's Journal,* and *Relief Society Magazine,* as well as a large collection of Church auxiliary department manuals.[5] Three particularly interesting

Admiring the plaque of the Award for Distinguished Library Service are, left to right, the first four recipients, M. Wilford Poulsen, T. Earl Pardoe, Ann Hafen, and LeRoy Hafen, all outstanding supporters of the library at Brigham Young University, 1968. Courtesy University Archives, BYU.

books from the Talmage library include a "Committee copy" of the Book of Mormon[6] and two copies of the Pearl of Great Price used for Talmage's 1902 revision.[7]

As Special Collections grew and evolved in the Grant Building during the late 1950s, it became clear that space constraints were limiting the collection and that different facilities would soon be necessary. These problems were resolved in 1962 upon completion of the new Harold B. Lee Library. During relocation, portions of the Mormon Americana Collection were removed and placed in the Vault Collection that now had quarters of its own in a fourth-floor vault attached to Special Collections. Books from the Locked Case Collection that fit the Mormon Americana category and important books that had once been in the Brimhall/Talmage collections (including fairly complete runs of the many editions of the Book of Mormon, Doctrine and Covenants, and Pearl of Great Price) formed the nucleus of the new Vault Collection.

Post-1955 Acquisitions

Since 1955 other collections have been added to those already mentioned in order to enhance the Mormon holdings and ultimately make it one of the finest Mormon collections in existence. These include the personal libraries of LeRoy R. Hafen, J. Reuben Clark Jr., M. Wilford Poulsen, and Dale L. Morgan. These collections filled many gaps in the Mormon collection.

In 1958, the LeRoy R. Hafen personal library was acquired and placed in the Special Collections reading room (still in the Grant Building).[8] At the time, it was intended that this fine collection of books on the American West would eventually be integrated into the library's general collection, but the idea of breaking up the collection was an unpleasant one. Also, by the time any integration could be accomplished, the books had increased in value to the point that their permanent inclusion in the Mormon Americana Collection of Special Collections was assured.[9]

The next significant addition to the Mormon holdings in Special Collections was the J. Reuben Clark Jr., library donated by Clark in 1960.[10] This collection of books and pamphlets spans the years when Clark was involved in government service as well as his

Dr. Robert K. Thomas, left, academic vice-president, receives gifts of diaries of James E. Talmage from Talmage's son, John, and John's daughters, ca. 1975. Courtesy University Archives, BYU.

years as a General Authority in the Church. Consequently, this library is rich in material on U.S. law and foreign relations, as well as all areas of Mormonism. Several items dealing with the Church in Mexico are difficult to find elsewhere.[11] Clark's collection of Mormon books and pamphlets complemented those already found in the Mormon Americana Collection.[12]

The Newel K. Whitney Collection, a collection of major importance, was added to the Mormon holdings of Special Collections in 1969.[13] Although the collection was predominantly composed of manuscripts, including early manuscript copies of eighteen revelations published in the 1833 Book of Commandments,[14] there are several very important published items. For example, the collection includes a complete copy of the Church's monthly periodical *The Evening and the Morning Star*.[15] Also included are extremely rare copies of two broadsheets containing the first printed versions of three sections of the Doctrine and Covenants (Sections 101, 88:1–126, and 89 of the current edition).[16] Also acquired in the Whitney collection was a copy of the four-page "References to the Book of Mormon," a table of contents published for use with the first edition of the Book of Mormon printed in Kirtland before the appearance of the 1837 Kirtland edition,[17] and Whitney's copy of William Clayton's "Latter-day Saints Emigrants' Guide."[18]

The library of M. Wilford Poulsen, acquired from Poulsen's family in 1970, added greatly to BYU's sources on the early history of Mormonism. Poulsen, a faculty member in the psychology department for many years, was also an ardent collector of Mormon books and a book dealer. He was the first person to do any significant work in Mormon bibliography, but his area of greatest interest was the early history of Mormonism and events which may have influenced the early Church. Poulsen amassed a large collection of titles, copies of which existed in the Manchester (New York) Public Library when the Smith family lived in Palmyra. Although there is no evidence that Joseph Smith ever used the Manchester library, Poulsen's collection constitutes an interesting addition to the BYU collections. One item of special interest from Poulsen's collection is the only known copy of the 1844 periodical *The People's Organ*.[19]

Another private collection which added significant books of Western Americana (including related works on Mormonism) was the purchase of the Dale L. Morgan library in 1974. This collection added many titles previously unavailable to researchers at BYU. Furthermore, many of these volumes included Morgan's marginal notations where he indicated errors found in various publications and noted the locations of supplementary sources for other valuable information.

One person whose efforts played a significant role in the development of BYU's Western Americana and Mormon collections was Denver-based book dealer Fred Rosenstock. Rosenstock made several extremely important and generous donations to BYU's collection, as well as making many collections (both manuscript and printed) available to the library at reasonable prices. As a donor he contributed, among other things, a copy of the Book of Commandments, one of the most rare and valuable imprints in all of Mormondom, and the Warren Angus Ferris manuscript map of the West.[20] As a dealer Rosenstock became one of the library's chief selectors of newly published books of Western Americana. After selecting a group of titles, he would set them aside for the library's collection specialist, A. Dean Larsen, who would peruse the list and choose those titles the library should acquire. The long and warm association between Rosenstock and the library was eventually acknowledged in 1971 when the university awarded him an honorary doctorate in appreciation of his work.

Besides the foregoing collections, a number of monetary donations have allowed the library to continue collecting by purchasing many important items that relate to the study of Mormonism. With an endowment from Daniel C. Jackling, the library was able to acquire at the Thomas Streeter auction a copy of *The Reflector*[21] and Sidney Rigdon's Fourth of July [1838] "Oration."[22] Other important purchases made with Jackling's donation include the Missouri Fifth Circuit Court's "Document containing the correspondence, order, &c., in relation to the disturbances with the Mormons"[23] and two issues of James H. Carleton's *Report on the Subject of the Massacre at the Mountain Meadows.*[24]

Last, but certainly not least, are the contributors of single items or individuals who have made small or moderate monetary donations to the library's acquisitions fund. While these donors have contributed perhaps only moderate amounts individually, their aggregate donations are substantial and have allowed the library to add many significant and valuable Mormon items to the library's collections. Examples of Mormon items acquired through such funds include a particularly good collection of single issues of newspapers with articles on Mormonism and a superbly bound group of first editions of the Book of Mormon in foreign languages. Many of these books contain holograph presentation notes, and all are in mint-condition presentation bindings. A donation by the Franklin D. Richards family brought a rare copy of volume one of the *Deseret News* to the BYU collection.

One hundred and thirty-eight years of combined library service are shown in this 1943 photo. Left to right: Beth Richardson Webb, assistant, reserve, catalog, and subject librarian; Newburn I. Butt, library researcher, cataloger, and index specialist, 1922–1968; Anna Ollorton, assistant, acting and head librarian, 1912–1948; and Naomi Rich Earl, assistant, head librarian, and coordinator of Technical Services, 1937–1961. Courtesy University Archives, BYU.

These contributors, both large and small, have all played, in varying degrees, an important role in the development of one of the major academic resources on the subject of Mormonism. Brigham Young University is committed to future collecting in this area as well. One of the stated aims of the Lee Library's collection development policy is to continue providing materials for scholarly research in the area of Mormonism and related fields. Donors and dealers alike will continue to play a crucial role in the acquisitions of these important materials.

Chad J. Flake is Senior Librarian and Director of Special Collections at Brigham Young University, Provo, Utah. Larry W. Draper is Senior Librarian at the LDS Historical Department.

NOTES

[1]Chad J. Flake, ed., *A Mormon Bibliography, 1830-1930: Books, Pamphlets, Periodicals, and Broadsides Relating to the First Century of Mormonism* (Salt Lake City: University of Utah Press, 1978) (hereafter cited as Flake); and Chad J. Flake and Larry W. Draper, comps., *A Mormon Bibliography, 1830-1930: Ten Year Supplement* (Salt Lake City: University of Utah Press, 1989). These two volumes list over twelve thousand publications that either deal with the subject of Mormonism entirely or at least have some discussion of the Mormons or Mormonism. The figure of 55 percent is an estimate based upon counting a random sample of entries (from both of these volumes) that note BYU as holding a copy in its library. Also a record of items acquired by BYU since 1978 has been kept and incorporated into these figures. Of all other institutional libraries listed in the "holdings notes" of these two volumes, only the Church Historical Department shows a greater number than BYU.

[2]Nearly 11 percent of all items listed in both volumes of *A Mormon Bibliography* are cataloged under the corporate main entry "Church of Jesus Christ of Latter-day Saints." Imprints listed in this part of the bibliography were produced by the Church or by one of its auxiliary arms. As one might expect, BYU's holdings in this area are significantly higher (nearly 80 percent) than in the bibliography as a whole.

[3]This collection was the creation of the BYU Women's Organization.

[4]This material was donated from 1922 until Talmage's death in 1933. His family continued to donate material as late as 1936.

[5]An example of important manuals found in the Talmage Collection is B. H. Roberts's five-volume set, *The Seventy's Course in Theology,* published from 1907 to 1912 (Flake 7359, 7358, 7318, 7311, 7317).

[6]This book was used by a committee assigned to make revisions to the Book of Mormon. Changes were handwritten into this copy, with the revisions being published for the first time in the 1920 Salt Lake City edition (Flake 693). On the flyleaf of this copy, Talmage has written "Committee copy—containing all changes adopted by the Book of Mormon committee, Apr 1920." The copy was a 1911 large-type Chicago edition (Flake 673).

[7]These books were used by Talmage to make revisions to the Pearl of Great Price. The handwritten changes are made in two copies of the 1888 Salt Lake City edition (Flake 6170). The changes first appear in print in the 1902 Salt Lake City edition (Flake 6172).

[8]LeRoy R. Hafen was the former historian for the state of Colorado and published extensively on the history of the American West. He joined the history faculty at BYU in 1954. For biographical data on Hafen, a bibliography of Hafen's own writings, and a bibliographical listing of the Hafen Collection, see BYU Library, *LeRoy R. and Ann W. Hafen: Their Writings and Their Notable Collection of Americana Given to Brigham Young University Library* ([Provo, Utah]: Brigham Young University Library, 1962). See also Hollis J. Scott, "LeRoy R. Hafen, 47 Years as Chronicler of Western Americana," *Utah Historical Quarterly* 34 (Summer 1966): 243-54.

[9]This collection remains today as a separate collection in Special Collections.

[10]Joshua Reuben Clark Jr., born September 1, 1871, served in a number of prominent positions in the government of the United States, including a short stint as undersecretary of state, 1928–29, and as the American ambassador to Mexico, 1930–33. He served in the First Presidency of the Church from 1959 until his death on October 6, 1961.

[11]One example of a hard-to-find item from the Clark Collection is a government publication entitled "Disorders in Mexico," which discusses the condition of settlers in the Mormon colonies of northern Mexico. See Susan L. Fales and Chad J. Flake, comps., *Mormons and Mormonism in U.S. Government Documents: A Bibliography* (Salt Lake City: University of Utah Press, 1989), item 1368.

[12]The Clark library has also remained intact in Special Collections.

[13]Newel K. Whitney, born February 5, 1795, was Presiding Bishop of the Church from 1847 until his death on September 23, 1850. The bulk of this collection was acquired by donation, with a part being purchased.

[14]For a discussion of manuscript items from this collection see Chad J. Flake, "The Newel K. Whitney Collection," *BYU Studies* 11 (Summer 1971): 322–28.

[15]Flake 3272.

[16]Both of these broadsheets, "Verily, I say unto you, . . ." (Flake 2920a), and "Verily, thus saith the Lord unto you, . . ." (Flake 2916a) were published for the first time after the July 1833 printing of the Book of Commandments but before the publication of the 1835 edition of the Doctrine and Covenants. For a lengthy discussion of these items see Peter Crawley, "A Bibliography of the Church of Jesus Christ of Latter-day Saints in New York, Ohio, and Missouri," *BYU Studies* 12 (Summer 1972): 487–89.

[17]Flake 6841; and Crawley, "A Bibliography of the Church," 505.

[18]Flake 2424.

[19]Printed by A. J. Foster, only three numbers were issued: June 15, June 29, and July 14, 1844 (see Flake 6300).

[20]This extremely valuable manuscript map, known as The Northwest Fur Country, was drawn by Ferris in 1836. It sketches the region of the Great Basin, including Utah, and is the most detailed and accurate of any early map of the region.

[21]This periodical was published by Abner Cole under the pseudonym Obediah Dogberry in Palmyra, New York, from 1829 to 1831. In January 1830, before the first edition of the Book of Mormon was completed and made available for sale, the *Reflector* published portions of the Book of Mormon without Joseph Smith's consent (see Flake 6843). At the time BYU acquired this very important publication, it was the only known extant copy.

[22]This twelve-page pamphlet published in Far West, Missouri, only added to the existing enmity between Mormons and Missourians that eventually forced the Mormons to move out of the state altogether. See Flake 7284; and Peter Crawley and Chad J. Flake, *A Mormon Fifty: An Exhibition in the Harold B. Lee Library in Conjunction with the Annual Conference of the Mormon History Association* (Provo, Utah: Friends of the Brigham Young University Library, 1984), item 9. See also Peter Crawley, ed., "Two Rare Missouri Documents," *BYU Studies* 14 (Summer 1974): 502–27.

[23]Flake 5427.

[24]Flake 1189 and 1190. While Flake 1189 can be found in the holdings of half a dozen libraries and three other libraries have Flake 1190, BYU is the only repository that has both.

Resources at the Foundation for Ancient Research and Mormon Studies, Provo, Utah

Melvin J. Thorne

The library of the Foundation for Ancient Research and Mormon Studies (F.A.R.M.S.) has four main focuses: books and manuscripts on the Book of Mormon, books on other ancient scriptures, research papers (published and unpublished) on the Book of Mormon, and the collected papers of some important Latter-day Saint scholars.

The foundation is a nonprofit educational organization dedicated to the study of ancient scripture. It sponsors and facilitates research on ancient scripture, especially the Book of Mormon, and publishes and distributes the results of that research as a service to students and teachers of the scriptures. F.A.R.M.S. was founded in 1979 in California by John W. Welch, who saw a need for an organization that could make available to a wide audience the best of faithful and reliable scholarship on the Book of Mormon. One of its first operations, therefore, was to offer through the mail a selection of papers on the Book of Mormon that were reprinted from books and scholarly journals.

In 1980, Welch accepted a faculty position at the J. Reuben Clark Law School at Brigham Young University, and F.A.R.M.S. moved with him to Provo. There he was joined in his efforts in the foundation by John L. Sorenson and Kirk Magleby. They were further assisted by an advisory board that included scholars such as Hugh W. Nibley, Truman G. Madsen, Noel B. Reynolds, and Paul R. Cheesman. F.A.R.M.S. began publishing *Insights,* a newsletter (now issued six times a year), to keep subscribers current on new research, lectures, meetings, F.A.R.M.S. activities, and publications. Each newsletter features a one-page summary of recently completed or ongoing research on the Book of Mormon.

F.A.R.M.S. continues to make available reprints and original papers of Book of Mormon research, but its publishing efforts have expanded greatly to include an annual *Review of Books on the Book of Mormon,*[1] the *Journal of Book of Mormon Studies* (published twice each year),[2] and a series of scholarly and popular books of

In 1979, John W. Welch founded F.A.R.M.S. to distribute Book of Mormon scholarship. Photograph by John Snyder.

research on the Book of Mormon. New projects underway include the Ancient Texts and Mormon Studies series, which will publish ancient texts (and English translations) with commentary from a Latter-day Saint perspective, and an interdisciplinary *Journal of Temple Studies*. Perhaps the most ambitious publishing project is the *Collected Works of Hugh Nibley*,[3] which to date numbers thirteen volumes of reprinted and original writings of one of the foremost Latter-day Saint scholars. When completed, this series should contain twenty volumes.

F.A.R.M.S. also distributes information on compact discs and video and audio cassettes. The most prominent video products are an intellectual biography of Hugh Nibley titled *The Faith of an Observer*,[4] a two-year series of lectures delivered by Nibley to an honors Book of Mormon class at Brigham Young University, and a new video series, now in progress, that features fifty lectures on a wide variety of Book of Mormon topics by scholars and teachers from Brigham Young University and elsewhere.

Although the foundation provides some financial support to a limited number of research projects, it primarily assists Book of Mormon research in other ways. F.A.R.M.S. holds an annual lecture or symposium to help scholars share with each other and interested audiences their latest research. Periodically the foundation sponsors working groups that enable scholars pursuing similar lines of inquiry to collaborate and receive valuable feedback from their peers in an informal setting. Such working groups have completed projects on warfare in the Book of Mormon and on the olive tree allegory in Jacob 5 and in the world of the Bible. Every other week during the fall and winter semesters and spring term at Brigham Young University, F.A.R.M.S. holds a seminar at which faculty members and participants discuss their ongoing research. And in other less formal ways, the foundation works to put scholars in touch with each other so that they can assist each other.

The F.A.R.M.S. library began as a means of assisting working scholars. The collection of books, now numbering seventeen hundred, was begun to provide background materials for research. It also serves as a repository for all F.A.R.M.S. publications. More recently, the foundation has undertaken a bibliographic project to update its 1982 bibliography by identifying and annotating every book and article ever written about the Book of Mormon. The expanded bibliography should be published in 1995, and F.A.R.M.S. is now pursuing the acquisition of every obtainable item in the bibliography that would be of value to researchers. In addition to volumes on the Book of Mormon, the library contains Bible translations, commentaries, dictionaries, and concordances; works on the history of philosophy, Christianity, Judaism, and Islam; primary and secondary works on the apocrypha and pseudepigrapha; and a number of books on LDS history. A large number of the books have been donated to the foundation, and F.A.R.M.S. actively seeks such charitable donations.

Hugh Nibley served on F.A.R.M.S.' original advisory board. F.A.R.M.S. has since published many of Nibley's papers in the multivolume *Collected Works of Hugh Nibley*. Courtesy F.A.R.M.S.

The manuscript collection in the F.A.R.M.S. library grew out of the reprints that were originally gathered for possible mailing to interested F.A.R.M.S. subscribers. As the foundation grew, it also began to publish papers itself, which led to many submissions. Some of these were published; but even more papers, while not sufficiently developed to warrant publication, often contained valuable ideas that could help other researchers. Therefore the foundation began an archive to hold these materials to assist working scholars, and it continues to collect both published and unpublished materials. The largest and most significant portion of the manuscript collection is the Hugh Nibley archive, containing published and unpublished papers as well as several hundred audio and many video cassettes. Nearly all of these written materials will eventually be published in the *Collected Works of*

Hugh Nibley. Reprints of important Book of Mormon essays by Sidney B. Sperry and B. H. Roberts are also contained in the collection, and F.A.R.M.S. actively seeks the collected papers of other important Book of Mormon scholars.

All of the books in the F.A.R.M.S. library have been cataloged according to the Library of Congress system and have been entered into a computerized catalog. The same is being done for the manuscript collection. The library is open to the public during regular office hours. It is housed, along with the foundation offices, in Amanda Knight Hall. Brigham Young University generously provides this space to the foundation, although F.A.R.M.S. is independent of the university and all other organizations. Persons interested in learning more about using the materials in the library or about the other services of F.A.R.M.S. are welcome to call or write the foundation at 1-800-327-6715 or P.O. Box 7113, University Station, Provo, Utah 84602.

Melvin J. Thorne is Vice President of the Foundation for Ancient Research and Mormon Studies, Provo, Utah.

NOTES

[1]Daniel C. Peterson, ed., *Review of Books on the Book of Mormon* (Provo, Utah: F.A.R.M.S., 1989–).

[2]Stephen D. Ricks, ed., *Journal of Book of Mormon Studies* (Provo, Utah: F.A.R.M.S., 1992–).

[3]*Collected Works of Hugh Nibley* (Salt Lake City: Deseret Book; Provo, Utah: F.A.R.M.S., 1986–).

[4]*The Faith of an Observer: Conversations with Hugh Nibley* (Provo, Utah: Brigham Young University and F.A.R.M.S., 1985).

The LDS Family History Library, Salt Lake City

James B. Allen

The exceptional archive in Salt Lake City now known as the Family History Library of The Church of Jesus Christ of Latter-day Saints originated a century ago as the Church-sponsored Genealogical Society of Utah. It is currently the largest and best-known genealogical library in the world. The purpose of this essay is to summarize the origin, mission, and history of the Church's Family History Department and to provide a brief description of what its library offers to family history researchers. While this essay emphasizes the growth of the library's research and support facilities rather than administrative or theological matters, the library's major programs cannot be understood without some knowledge of the religious purpose for which they are intended. This religious purpose, therefore, constitutes a necessary background.[1]

Origin and Historical Overview

Latter-day Saints believe that their Church originated as a literal restoration of the ancient Church of Christ, which restoration includes Christ's priesthood, or the direct authority to act in the name of God. This priesthood includes the authority to perform certain "saving" ordinances such as baptism and the temple ordinances revealed to Joseph Smith in the 1840s.[2] Among the temple ordinances are the covenants known as the "endowment" and the "new and everlasting covenant" of marriage, whereby couples may be "sealed" for "time and all eternity." Children born to temple-married couples are considered to be "born in the covenant," meaning that they are automatically sealed to their parents in an eternal family unit.

The Saints believe, further, that the Old Testament prophecy concerning the return of the prophet Elijah has been literally fulfilled. As recorded by Malachi, the prophecy reads: "Behold, I will send you Elijah the prophet before the coming of the great and dreadful day of the Lord; and he shall turn the heart of the fathers to the children, and the heart of the children to the fathers, lest I come and smite the earth with a curse."[3] In April 1836, Elijah appeared in vision to Joseph Smith in the Kirtland, Ohio, Temple, and instilled within Joseph Smith and the Latter-day Saints in general the spirit and responsibility of seeking after their dead.

Before Joseph Smith's death in 1844 the Church began performing the saving ordinances in behalf of the dead, helping to inspire its members with a feeling of special responsibility to seek out their ancestors. From that time on, the "Spirit of Elijah" spread rapidly among the Mormons. Even though they did not form a genealogical society until 1894, the foundation was laid for an intensive genealogical program among them.

The validity of the principle that the dead would have a chance to hear and accept or reject the gospel in the spirit world was affirmed in 1918 in a vision given to President Joseph F. Smith. He saw the Savior visiting the spirits of the dead while his body lay in the tomb after his crucifixion. Christ organized missionary work among the dead, teaching them all the principles of the gospel essential to salvation, and teaching of the possibility of vicarious baptism and other saving ordinances in their behalf. "I beheld," President Smith reported, "that they were filled with joy and gladness, and were rejoicing together because the day of their deliverance was at hand."[4] It was a commitment to these principles that helped instill the "Spirit of Elijah" in the hearts of the Mormons and eventually led to the founding of their own genealogical society.

The Genealogical Society of Utah did not originate in a vacuum. By the end of the nineteenth century, a tidal wave of genealogical activity was sweeping the United States. This activity was not lost on the Mormons, many of whom took advantage of the opportunities being created. Mormon family groups promoted research, many individuals conducted prodigious personal research, and some became professional genealogists. The Church itself actively encouraged genealogical work through its publications both in America and Europe. It also encouraged missionaries to do research and tried in other ways to promote and support genealogical work. In addition, prominent Church leaders such as Parley P. Pratt, Orson Pratt, Wilford Woodruff, and Franklin D. Richards set worthy examples.

Franklin D. Richards, whose reputation extended far outside Utah, became the most well-known LDS genealogist of the nineteenth century. A member of the Council of the Twelve, he was also Church historian and general Church recorder from 1889 until his death in 1899. During those years, any official Church genealogical activity was conducted through the historian's office. Elder Richards's extensive personal library of genealogical publications became the foundation for the first

Church genealogical library when, in 1884, he turned it over to the historian's office. The Church paid him $527.89 for the collection.

Before 1894 there were several abortive attempts at some kind of Church-sponsored genealogical organization. A variety of problems intervened, however, including the preoccupation of many Church leaders with the intense difficulties between the Church and the national government in the 1870s and 1880s. By the early 1890s, however, these pressures were subsiding and Wilford Woodruff, one of the most avid genealogists among Church leaders, was President of the Church. In 1894, he received a special revelation affirming the importance of eternal family units and of "sealing" children to parents in the temple. The revelation also reemphasized the Saints' obligation to trace their ancestral roots as far back as possible. The time was ripe for a permanent, Church-sponsored organization.

President Woodruff and other Church leaders had, in fact, been considering such a plan for years. Various Mormon genealogists had also urged the matter in letters to the First Presidency. In July 1894, Elder Richards, along with John Jaques and A. Milton Musser, examined various versions of a proposal to establish a genealogical library corporation. Finally, on November 1, 1894, the First Presidency and the Council of the Twelve approved the articles of incorporation of the Genealogical Society of Utah. Elder Richards was appointed as the society's first president. At his invitation, the society was initially housed in a room in the Church historian's office, where it began to build upon the three-hundred-book nucleus already purchased from Elder Richards. By 1907, through donations of books and money from a variety of sources, the society boasted a collection of some eight hundred volumes.

As the society's resources improved and the Saints' genealogical impulse quickened, the need and desire for genealogical training became apparent. Here the women of the Church, and particularly Susa Young Gates, led out.[5] Gates, a daughter of Brigham Young, was a devout Latter-day Saint as well as a gifted and publicly active person. As a suffragist, writer, publisher, public speaker, educator, genealogist, and mother of thirteen children, she was respected both nationally and internationally. Amid all her activities she found time for Church activity, placing special emphasis on genealogical and temple work. Recognizing that it usually took women to goad the men into taking these responsibilities seriously, yet not wanting to push so hard as to unduly offend, she fondly quoted the motto of the women's auxiliary committee of the Genealogical Society of Utah: "Let us provoke the brethren to good works, yet not provoke the brethren."

In 1905, Gates was installed as president of the Daughters of Utah Pioneers (DUP), but only after the DUP agreed to support greater participation of women in temple work. As a result of Gates's leadership and the work of many other women, genealogical activity began to increase among the Mormons. In 1906, for example, the DUP began teaching the first genealogical classes among Mormons. Two years later, the Genealogical Society of Utah absorbed all the DUP genealogical programs.

The Genealogical Society came of age between 1907 and 1920, beginning publication of the *Utah Genealogical and Historical Magazine* in 1910 and increasing its library holdings. By 1919 the library held over five thousand volumes, including books from many parts of the United States and Europe.

During the 1920s and 1930s, the society's research facilities and general activities saw even more amazing growth. By the end of 1937, the library held over 19,200 books, including several thousand volumes from Scandinavia, Germany, and the British Isles. The society's library was by then the fifth largest genealogical library in the United States, with plans for spending twenty-five hundred dollars annually on new acquisitions.[6] The society also boasted an outstanding indexing system that one well-known Chicago genealogist described as the finest he had seen.

One of the most significant developments in this era was the Temple Index Bureau (TIB), which continued until the end of the 1980s as one of the society's most important research aids. Established in 1922 as a result of concerns over duplication of temple work for the dead, the TIB had a card index that acted as a clearinghouse for names submitted for temple work. In addition to the TIB, another important development of the time was the Genealogical Research Bureau (GRB), established in 1924 to assist library patrons in Salt Lake City. The GRB supervised all research work at the library, hired researchers to help patrons, made contacts with and transferred money to foreign researchers, conducted classes, helped obtain information not available in the library, and assisted in various other ways. Andrew K. Smith, who initially headed the GRB, wrote in 1928 that his department was capable of providing research help in several languages and that it would "undertake any kind of service connected with the searching and compiling of records."[7] The GRB had three major divisions: the research department, the instruction department, and the research clearinghouse. The latter helped avoid duplicate research and coordinated research for those who were interested in cooperating. It was later renamed the Church Genealogical Archives (CGA). In 1942, with two

The Family History Library houses the world's largest collection of genealogical records. More than 2,000 people come here daily to research their family histories. The five-floor library opened in Salt Lake City in 1985. Courtesy LDS Church Visual Resources Library.

million index cards in its files, the CGA was merged administratively with the TIB, which now boasted about ten million cards. The new unit became known as the Church Records Archives. The growth and administrative changes reflected in this move helped pave the way for the establishment of the present archives of the Family History Library.

During the 1940s, the legal nature of the Genealogical Society changed. Originally, it was a public corporation even though it operated under the auspices of the Church. In 1944, which was the year the society's original articles of incorporation expired, the society became a wholly Church-owned corporation. Annual memberships were dropped, and people who had signed up as life members received refunds of their fees. One reason for the legal change was the fact that the society housed certain personal, sensitive, and highly confidential records. As a Church entity, the society (now renamed the Genealogical Society of The Church of Jesus Christ of Latter-day Saints) could legally restrict access to such records more easily.

During the next three decades, the society went through many more major administrative changes. Indeed, the society was disincorporated and reincorporated several times, being disincorporated for the last time in 1975 and renamed the Genealogical Department of the Church. In 1987 the society received its present name, the Family History Department of the Church, and the library became known as the Family History Library.

Expanding Facilities and Branch Libraries

During the 1960s, 1970s, and 1980s, the society expanded its library facilities to improve its ability to help patrons' research. In 1965, for example, the stacks were opened so that patrons could find books for themselves. Access to the growing microfilm collection was still restricted until humidity control problems were resolved, but by the end of 1969 the microfilms were also open to the public. Only microfilms that contained sensitive material pertaining to certain temple ceremonies remained restricted.

Also in the 1960s, the society began to authorize branch libraries. In May 1964, the first official branch library was established at Brigham Young University as a pilot project to be evaluated before others were authorized. In June 1964, a second library was opened in Logan, Utah. Other branch libraries were soon established at various LDS meetinghouses. The branch library program worked well and expanded so rapidly that within four years the seventy-fifth such library was founded at Moses Lake, Washington.

Each branch library had a basic set of microfilms as well as books and other materials. Each library could also borrow additional microfilms from the society as needed. By 1968, between 170,000 and 200,000 patrons were using the branch libraries. By 1977 there were 235 branch libraries and the Genealogical Department received forty to fifty applications annually for new branches. It was estimated at the time that about fifty percent of all Genealogical Department patrons were using branch libraries.

The growth and research facilities of the Genealogical Society were dramatically highlighted in 1969, the society's seventy-fifth anniversary. In August, the society sponsored and hosted the first World Conference on Records, centered on the theme of "Records Protection in an Uncertain World." The society invited genealogists, archivists, librarians, historians, computer experts, microfilm technologists, civil leaders, and many other people from around the world. In all, over 6,000 people attended the conference, which provided extensive discussion about how to preserve and use records, as well as about genealogical methods and techniques. Another such conference was held in 1980.[8]

The constant growth of the Genealogical Department's work required continuing expansion of its physical facilities. In 1985, after numerous moves and leases of additional space, the Genealogical Department moved into its own magnificent new building on West Temple Street in Salt Lake City.

Multiple Use

By the mid-1970s, the Genealogical Department was becoming highly visible to non-Mormons with various research interests. The *Los Angeles Times* carried a highly laudatory article, describing the library collection as a "genealogical gold mine."[9] Academicians in a variety of fields found the library's data extremely useful in their research. Robert W. Fogel, for example, is a well-known American economic historian and recipient of the 1993 Nobel Prize in economics. In 1975, he reported how he suddenly discovered that the Mormons' collection would substantially enhance his exacting research in cliometrics (quantitative history):

> The biggest breakthrough in our effort to collect a representative sample took place in Atlanta. There we learnt that the court records of every county in Georgia were available on microfilms at the state archives. Upon examining some of the reels we made the further discovery that they had been donated by the

> Genealogical Society of the Church of Jesus Christ of Latter-Day Saints, which was engaged in a Southwide microfilming project. And so it was that we learnt that the Mormons, for religious reasons, had photographed and stored in their archives near Salt Lake City microfilms of the very records that were so critical to us. With the assistance of Larry Wimmer and Clayne Pope, two faculty members of the department of economics at Brigham Young University, we established a team of students that is still at work in Utah and which has been able to retrieve data for scores of counties throughout the South at quite moderate cost.[10]

That same year Latin American scholars told their colleagues about the society's vast holdings and explained how to do research in Salt Lake City or through the branch libraries.[11] So, likewise, did scholars interested in French studies, German studies, American studies, and economic and social history in general.[12] In 1978 Roger M. Haigh, a history professor at the University of Utah, received a $107,825 grant from the National Endowment for the Humanities to "facilitate and encourage research into the vast holdings of the Genealogical Society."[13] A year later the University of Utah Press published a preliminary survey of the Mexican material in the genealogical archives.[14] In addition, various scholars have used the facilities of the genealogical library for medical research relating to heredity and for the study of siblings, including a study of twins.[15]

The Genealogical Department's desire to cooperate with the government, other organizations, and responsible scholars was portrayed in a 1976 article by Ted F. Powell. Throughout the article, Powell referred to the department as the "Genealogical Society," for that term was generally more understandable and acceptable to the general public. Powell gave an excellent description of the society's process of collecting and preserving records and providing quality control. He also described the society's extensive microfilm holdings and demonstrated how valuable they were for people interested in a variety of important research topics:

> At present the society's collections are being used for study sponsored jointly by the American Cancer Society, the University of Utah, and the LDS Hospital endeavoring to determine whether cancer is hereditary and, if so, how we can predict it and warn living family members of the danger. The Yale University Medical School has spent many years in proving that twinning is based on heredity.
>
> The list of master's and doctor's candidates using our records for thesis preparation is too long to report. Their disciplines

> include anthropology, economic history, demography, population movement, and medieval family reconstitution. One scholar, who was trying to determine the economic status of typical English families during Shakespeare's time, was able to accomplish his task in less than a month in Salt Lake City, whereas it would have taken a year and a half to two years in England. The probates and wills are cataloged and readily available, without his having to wait or travel from shire to shire in order to gather information and records on his own.[16]

Powell concluded with a plea for continuing cooperation in the process of preserving the past: "We hope to continue to help archivists, government officials, and record custodians and preserve the irreplaceable records. . . . Through cooperation we can save the past for the future."[17]

The Microfilm Program and Granite Mountain Vault

Of all Genealogical Society activities, probably none captured the attention of people around the world as much as its immense microfilming program.[18] As the process of filming public, church, and other vital records extended throughout the world, the huge Granite Mountain vault near Salt Lake City became a priceless storehouse of family history. Like the library, the vault's resources were eventually used not only by genealogists and family historians but also by economists, demographers, statisticians, sociologists, medical history researchers, and scholars in a variety of other fields.

The microfilming program grew from small beginnings during the 1930s, when the need for a better way to acquire and store records became increasingly clear. Despite its relatively good library, the society's holdings left much to be desired. It did not have copies, for example, of many important genealogical books that were out of print. Furthermore, many government records throughout the world were never published; they existed only as manuscripts in government archives. As war threatened to engulf Europe, Church leaders became fearful that vital records would be destroyed. Therefore, in some countries such as the Netherlands, Church members began a laborious process of copying parish records by hand. These and other efforts to protect the records were obviously inefficient and loaded with possibilities for error.

Ernst Koehler, a German photographer who filmed some genealogical books before emigrating to the United States, is usually credited with planting the idea for the society's microfilm program. After he brought the possibilities to the society's attention, Koehler and James M.

Black were assigned to investigate equipment, conduct experiments, and make recommendations. One of their first discoveries was that existing genealogical materials on microfilm could be purchased from governments and other agencies. The society quickly raised money to purchase such films, especially in Europe, thus beginning a microfilm collection even before the society had a camera.

The society purchased its first microfilm camera in October 1938. The following month Ernst Koehler copied the first materials: LDS "sealing" indexes and records from Nauvoo, Illinois. By the end of the year, the society had twelve rolls of microfilm consisting of 9,913 pages in thirty-one volumes. This was a small beginning that mushroomed dramatically in a surprisingly short time.[19]

While fear of possible wartime loss of European records was a catalyst in establishing the microfilm program, most European filming had to wait until after the war. Meanwhile, a number of projects proceeded in the United States. These included filming county records in Tennessee, LDS Church records in Kentucky, records of the New York Genealogical and Biographical Society, collections of the North Carolina Historical Commission, and many important Hawaiian records.

The end of the war brought a rapid expansion of activity. In 1945 the society received sixty-nine rolls of film. Only three years later it received 10,012 rolls. A peak of 57,000 rolls was reached in 1959, and tens of thousands continued to arrive annually after that. Records were filmed throughout North America, in almost every country of Europe, and in many other locations as conditions permitted. The society was careful to obtain proper clearance before microfilming any records in the custody of governments, churches, or other groups. But the society usually received enthusiastic support, especially when it promised to provide a copy of the microfilm to the donating body. The advantages were obvious: not only would the custodian of the original records receive usable copies, thus helping preserve precious manuscript copies, but in case of disaster there would always be copies in Salt Lake City.

As might be expected, the microfilm program was not immune from problems. Quality control, for example, was a continual concern, which led to elaborate checking procedures. Costs grew as rapidly as the program itself, which led to discontinuing some projects, at least temporarily, and slowing down others. Nevertheless, the society achieved an enviable record. By the mid-1970s it had a total of 862,770 rolls of film. When some one-hundred-foot rolls were divided for cataloging purposes, the total exceeded one million. The films included records from every state in the United States and more than forty nations.

Perhaps the most well-known symbol of the society's achievement is the huge Granite Mountain vault. Just as World War II helped spur the microfilm program in the first place, the war was also a factor in the selection of a granite mountain southeast of Salt Lake City as a storage place. During and after the war, Church leaders held serious discussions about the possibility that Utah might come under air attack and that valuable records might be lost. Nothing was done at the time, but such discussions clearly contributed to the final decision to make the vault as impervious as possible to attack or to the forces of nature.

Early in 1954, the society announced that it was going to construct a "buried vault" where proper humidity and temperature conditions could be maintained and microfilm would last for "hundreds and hundreds of years." The society considered various sites, including caves and mines. The Granite Mountain site was finally announced in 1959. Located in Little Cottonwood Canyon, the site was near the quarry that had provided the granite for the Salt Lake Temple. Test drills demonstrated that the mountain was solid granite and that there would be no problems with excess moisture.

The vault was completed in 1964 at a cost exceeding two million dollars. But Church leaders were convinced that the expense was warranted, for the vault is a place where microfilm records can be stored

The Granite Mountain Records Vault, carved from solid rock in the Wasatch Mountains near Salt Lake City, Utah, is the repository of millions of feet of microfilmed genealogical records from around the world. Courtesy LDS Church Visual Resources Library.

in an ideal environment, fully protected from natural disasters. The completed vault consists of four huge tunnels, each measuring 190 feet long, 25 feet wide, and 15 feet high. The tunnels are connected at either end and through the middle by corridors. In the rear, behind the fourth tunnel, is a water reservoir. The front tunnel houses the office and laboratory area, while the other three, which lie under nearly 700 feet of granite, are the storage areas. The storage tunnels house not only microfilm but also certain valuable books and records belonging to the Historical Department of the Church. Heavy bank-vault doors at the front of each of the three storage tunnels protect the storage area. Temperature and humidity are ideal for film storage: a natural temperature of fifty-seven to fifty-eight degrees year round in the storage area and natural humidity of 40 to 50 percent. In addition, an elaborate circulation and filtering system was installed to keep fresh air, free from dust and chemicals, moving through the storage area. Unique spring-loaded fresh air valves above the entrances to the east and west passageways are designed to close automatically in case of a blast from the outside, making the interior airtight. The three storage tunnels are divided into six vault rooms. Total vault capacity can presently reach the equivalent of 25 million three-hundred-page books. The vault can also be expanded if necessary by further excavation.[20]

The Granite Mountain vault is indeed a fitting symbol of the activities of the Genealogical Society as it entered the age of modern technology. From 1963 to 1965, guided tours were offered. Since then, however, the vault has been closed to the public.

Automation[21]

In addition to the microfilm program, another significant development of the last three decades was the society's entry into the world of computers. In 1961, after months of discussion with Church members trained in computer technology, the First Presidency approved the use of electronic processing and authorized the society to employ some computer experts and to purchase a computer. At the same time, the society was developing a new Records Tabulation Program, generally referred to as R-TAB. With the ever-growing microfilming program providing the source material, R-TAB eventually developed into a huge program that went by the acronym GIANT—Genealogical Information and Name Tabulation. GIANT was introduced to the public in 1969.

The initial file for GIANT included six million names extracted through R-TAB. Among other things, it produced a microfiche output, originally called the Computer File Index but later identified as the International Genealogical Index (IGI). GIANT also provided the source for names submitted to the temples and a list of all extraction sources known as the Parish and Vital Records Listing. GIANT was progressively updated as improved computer technology became available. By 1992, however, GIANT became obsolete. The availability of the personal computer and compact-disc technology opened the door for dramatic new possibilities that facilitated both temple work and exciting new possibilities for family research.

Under GIANT, the process of clearing names for the temple involved two important checks. First the computer checked the names in GIANT to see if temple work had been done. This check was followed by a laborious manual check against the massive forty-year accumulation of TIB files. As Church membership grew and demand for name clearances increased, however, the burden of such a centralized clearance system became overwhelming. By 1988 the society began investigating the possibility of decentralizing the name clearance process. The First Presidency approved a new plan, soon to be labeled TempleReady, in May 1989.

TempleReady simplified the name clearance process and changed the nature of family history research in the Church. Computers placed in selected LDS meetinghouses allowed researchers to match names with the IGI, which had been made available on a compact disc. At the end of the matching process, researchers had a disk that could be submitted directly to the temple. Beginning in July 1990, TempleReady pilot programs were run in several stakes of the Church. In April 1991, the Family History Department replaced both GIANT and TIB with TempleReady. By November 1991, over two hundred stakes had requested that they be included in an expanded test of the program. Eventually all stakes in North America and Canada received the program. Likewise, TempleReady was shipped to all temples except those in Japan, Taiwan, and Korea (which still used manual name clearance based on non-Roman script).

The IGI is the heart of TempleReady. Originally available in an ever-growing microfiche edition, the IGI was first made available on compact disc in 1988. That year it contained 147 million names. The 1992 microfiche edition contained 187 million names. By the time the compact disc version became available in 1993, another 13 million names had been added, making a total of 200 million.

The IGI is a research tool with obvious value for many people, including non-Mormons. It is especially valuable for people interested in British research, since nearly 60 million of the 147 million names contained in the 1988 version are from British records. Since 1984 the IGI has been offered for sale to non-LDS groups and individuals.

Yet another powerful computer program designed to assist family history researchers is Ancestral File, installed in the main Family History Library in Salt Lake City in 1988. Ancestral File contains information from all family group sheets the library obtained as the result of a Churchwide program begun in the late 1970s, plus other data sources. In 1990, Ancestral File was released on compact disc. By 1993 the file contained 15 million names. Its value to anyone who wanted to compile and share family history information is obvious.

Another program, which stemmed from the development of Ancestral File, was the Personal Ancestral File (PAF), released initially in April 1984. Researchers could enter their own family history data in this program, share it with others, and receive input from computer disks sent to them. The 1988 version of PAF made it possible to transfer information to Ancestral File.

Another of the automated aids provided by the library is Family Registry, which helps researchers find others working on the same surname lines. Published quarterly on microfiche from 1984 to 1989 and annually thereafter, Family Registry will likely be merged with Ancestral File in the future.

While all these things were being developed, the society also automated its library catalog in Salt Lake City. Programming began in 1978 and computer terminals were installed in January 1979. The old card catalog was completely replaced in 1987. The new system produced a microfiche output that was not only available in the main library but also distributed to all the branch libraries as well as to public libraries and appropriate institutions.

In 1983 the Genealogical Department formally initiated what has become the umbrella for all its computer databases: the Genealogical Information System (GIS). First made available in 1986, GIS was released Churchwide in 1990. GIS includes the Automated Catalog, IGI, Ancestral File, Social Security Death Index, Military Index (U.S. military deaths in Vietnam and Korea), and TempleReady. When it first became available, GIS was cumbersome to use because several compact discs were needed to contain all the data. Hence, researchers had to do considerable "disc swapping" while using GIS on a personal computer. The "disc swapping" problem was solved at the main library and at the Brigham Young University branch library when a local area network (LAN) was installed. There has also been discussion about establishing national and international networks.

In 1992 GIS was made available not only to Church members but also to the public at large. Under a contract with the Church, Dynix (a non-Church corporation) distributes GIS to public libraries, archives, and genealogical and historical societies. Needless to say, GIS has met enthusiastic reception.[22]

The Library: Holdings and Services

The foregoing essay has been an attempt to provide a general view of the history of the Family History Library, including its response to the opportunities provided by modern technological advances. As the largest genealogical library in the world, its current holdings are too numerous to describe in detail here. A general view of these holdings, organized by regions around the world, is found in Johni Cerny and Wendy Elliott, *The Library: A Guide to the LDS Family History Library.* The interested reader is strongly encouraged to refer to this source.

A fact sheet published by the family history library at the end of 1992 provided the following information about its holdings and research area:

- The library holds 1.8 million reels of microfilmed genealogical records, equivalent to six million three-hundred-page volumes.
- The microfilms and books in the library contain nearly two billion names.
- The collection is growing at a rate of about five thousand rolls of film and one thousand books each month.
- The library includes family group records on eight million families.
- The IGI (which has about two hundred million names) is growing at a rate of seven million names each year.
- The collections in the library are protected from deterioration by specially designed humidity, temperature, and lighting control systems.
- The research area seats 963 people.
- Three thousand visitors come to the library each day.
- There are over eighteen hundred branch family history centers in fifty countries.
- Sixty thousand rolls of microfilm are circulated to the branch centers each month.[23]

The library offers abundant research opportunities for people interested in LDS Church history. Most important is the fact that the library contains some kind of record for virtually every LDS family, including records of family groups and ancestral information. The value of this data for biographers, especially, is inestimable. In addition, the library's bound volumes include hundreds of personal histories, family histories, state and local histories, biographies, and other material relating to Latter-day Saints and their communities. The library also has a magnificent collection of census materials, immigration data, and other public records.

While many of the library's bound volumes are available elsewhere, much of its material is not. In 1993 Kahlile Mehr prepared a list of sources for LDS biography and family history that were unique to the Family History Library. His listing follows:

- Early Church Information File, card file on seventy-five microfilm reels (1992 filming FHL 1750655-1750729). Name index to a wide range of LDS sources including early Church membership records and civil births, marriages, and deaths recorded in Utah and Idaho.
- Utah Pioneer Biographies, 1935–64, forty-four volumes also on microfilm (US/CANADA 979.2 D3u; FHL 982281-982305). Responses to questionnaires sent to various individuals by the Historical Records Survey in Utah; also miscellaneous items deposited by individuals in the library. First thirty volumes arranged alphabetically; rest have no arrangement. Indexed in Early Church Information File.
- Genealogical Survey of LDS Church Members, thirty-four volumes also on microfilm (US/CANADA 289.3 G286g; FHL 1059454-1059463). Forms containing genealogical and biographical information submitted by the members of the Genealogical Society during 1924–29 (the original four-generation program). Indexed in Early Church Information File.
- Genealogical Charts and Biographical Sketches of Members of the LDS Church, Ogden Stake, sixteen volumes also on microfilm (US/Canada 979.228 D2o; FHL 564276-564285). Material arranged by ward and then alphabetically. Indexed in Early Church Information File.
- Published family histories and genealogical papers. Many families who donate copies of their family histories to the Family History Library are not aware that the Historical Department library may be interested in those items with substantial biographical content.
- Microfilm copies of courthouse records, newspapers, etc., from localities where LDS members have lived.[24]

The Family History Library is designed to provide the best possible help for researchers who want to use its facilities.[25] Its microfilms are made available either at the library or through the branch libraries. Films are generally loaned to the branches for three weeks, though longer periods may be requested. Some films may not be circulated because of restrictions put on them as a condition of microfilming. Microfiche are also available either at the main library or at the branches.

The library has a well-trained staff to help its patrons find research materials, but it does not provide the services of researchers. The library does, however, accredit genealogical researchers in various areas of geographic specialties, as well as for specialties in American Indian research and in LDS Church records. Lists of those accredited researchers are available, though the library cannot guarantee their work.

The library provides photoduplication services (limited by copyright laws), genealogical forms and supplies, and various research guides and outlines. Information about these and other services may be obtained at the library, or by writing or calling.

On June 27, 1993, the newly-renovated Joseph Smith Memorial Building (formerly the Hotel Utah) in Salt Lake City was dedicated. In the refurbished structure are Church offices, meeting rooms, a chapel, a movie theater, two restaurants, and several rooms for banquets, business meetings, seminars, and similar activities. Symbolic of the extraordinary importance the LDS Church places on family history research is the fact that part of the main floor as well as floors three through six were given to the Family History Department of the Church. Particularly significant is the Family Search Center, located on the main level and fourth floor. Three rooms on the main floor contain 133 computers, each equipped with a laser printer and tied into the latest interactive software that will guide the visitor through all the research tools and databases available on computer. A staff of volunteers is available to help visitors, but the computer software itself makes research simpler and more productive than genealogical work has ever been. More computers on the fourth floor provide additional facilities specifically designed for group demonstrations. There could hardly be a greater tribute to the work of the Family History Department than these superb new facilities. But more important for anyone interested in family history research, there could hardly be a better place to begin.[26] The address of the Family History Library is 35 North West Temple, Salt Lake City, Utah, 84150. The current (1995) telephone number is 801-240-2331.

James B. Allen is Professor of History Emeritus at Brigham Young University.

NOTES

[1]This essay contains very few notes. It is based largely on James B. Allen, Jessie L. Embry, and Kahlile B. Mehr, *Hearts Turned to the Fathers: A History of the Genealogical Society of Utah, 1894-1994* (Provo, Utah: BYU Studies, 1995). This essay also draws from "Automating the Data," unpublished manuscript by Kahlile Mehr; and Johni Cerny and Wendy Elliott, eds., *Library: A Guide to the LDS Family History Library* (Salt Lake City: Ancestry Publishing, 1988). See also Kahlile Mehr, "International Activities and Services of the Genealogical Society of Utah," *Archivium* 37 (1992): 148-57. See also Merrill S. Lofthouse, "A History of the Genealogical Society of The Church of Jesus Christ of Latter-day Saints to 1970" (master's thesis, Brigham Young University, 1971).

[2]For authoritative discussions of the temple and its purposes, see James E. Talmage, *The House of the Lord* (Salt Lake City: Deseret News, 1912); and Boyd K. Packer, *The Holy Temple* (Salt Lake City: Bookcraft, 1980).

[3]Malachi 4:5-6.

[4]See Doctrine and Covenants, section 138.

[5]For details on the role of Susa Young Gates and the women of the Church in genealogical training, see James B. Allen and Jessie Embry, "'Provoking the Brethren to Good Works': Susa Young Gates, the Relief Society, and Genealogy Work," *BYU Studies* 31 (Spring 1991): 115-38; or Allen, Embry, and Mehr, *Hearts Turned to the Fathers,* index.

[6]The four larger collections were at the Library of Congress in Washington, the New England Historic and Genealogical Society Library in Boston, the Newberry Library in Chicago, and the New York Genealogical and Biographical Society Library in New York City.

[7]See Andrew K. Smith, "The Genealogical Research Bureau: Its Organization and How to Cooperate with It," *Utah Genealogical and Historical Magazine* 19 (July 1928): 114-32.

[8]For the proceedings of the 1980 conference, see *World Conference on Records: Preserving Our Heritage, August 12-15, 1980,* 13 vols. (Salt Lake City: The Church of Jesus Christ of Latter-day Saints, 1981).

[9]Charles Hillinger, "Cave Hides Genealogical Gold Mine," *Los Angeles Times,* September 29, 1976.

[10]Robert William Fogel, "From the Marxists to the Mormons," *Times Literary Supplement,* June 13, 1975, 669.

[11]Roger M. Haigh and Frank J. Sanders, "A Report on Some Latin American Materials in the Genealogical Library of The Church of Jesus Christ of the Latter Day Saints at Salt Lake City, Utah," *Latin American Research Review* 10 (1975): 193-96.

[12]Davis Bitton, "Research Materials in the Mormon Genealogical Society," *French Historical Studies* 8 (Spring 1973): 172-74; Ronald Smelzer, "Notes on the German Collection at the LDS Genealogical Society, Salt Lake City," *Central European History* 8 (December 1975): 375-76; Larry R. Gerlach and Michael L. Nicholls, "The Mormon Genealogical Society and Research Opportunities in Early American History," *William and Mary Quarterly* 32 (October 1975): 625-29; Larry T. Wimmer and Clayne L. Pope, "The Genealogical Society Library of Salt Lake City: A Source of Data for Economic and Social Historians," *Historical Methods Newsletter* 8 (March 1975): 51-55; and William Mulder, "Mormon

Sources for Immigration History," *Immigration History Newsletter* 10 (November 1978): 1-8.

[13]Note in *Genealogical Digest* (Fall 1978).

[14]*Salt Lake Tribune,* February 3, 1979.

[15]Colin White to George H. Fudge, June 24, 1966, in Genealogical Society Central File, CR 226 7 #6. Copies of several published articles based in part on such data are also in the file. See also "Genealogy Records May Help Doctors Prevent Diseases," *Church News,* November 26, 1977; "Genealogy May Aid Heart Screening," *Deseret News,* August 21, 1978.

[16]Ted F. Powell, "Saving the Past for the Future—Tales of International Search and Cooperation," *American Archivist* 39 (July 1976): 314.

[17]Powell, "Saving the Past for the Future," 317-18.

[18]For an excellent overview of the early years of microfilming, see Kahlile Mehr, "Preserving the Source: Early Microfilming Efforts of the Genealogical Society of Utah, 1938-1950" (master's thesis, Brigham Young University, 1985).

[19]See James B. Black, "Microfilm Experiences of James B. Black 1938-1972 in Service with the Genealogical Society," typewritten manuscript, Family History Library, Salt Lake City, for a very interesting and detailed personal view of early microfilming activities.

[20]See "Records Protection in an Uncertain World," pamphlet published by the Genealogical Society of the Church, 1975.

[21]Most of the material in this section is drawn from Kahlile B. Mehr's preliminary working paper, "Automating the Data" and from Allen, Embry, and Mehr, *Hearts Turned to the Fathers.*

[22]As Kahlile Mehr wrote: "The response to the system was enthusiastic. The system provided convenient and quick access to large amounts of information. The user could print out the information or transfer it to diskette for personal use. At a demonstration of the system at Stockholm in 1990, an archivist searched his own lines and found them extended back to the 12th century. He compared a published pedigree with the file and found no discrepancies, except that the file extended the line back further than the book. Many European archivists who saw the system demonstrated that year were visibly moved by its capabilities."

[23]The foregoing paraphrases "Fact Sheet," Family History Library of The Church of Jesus Christ of Latter-day Saints, Salt Lake City, dated December 1992. The fact sheet indicates that the IGI has over 187 million names. This has been updated to 200 million—as stated in this essay.

[24]Kahlile Mehr, "Sources for LDS Biography and Family History Unique to the Family History Library," handout dated February 11, 1993.

[25]For more information on these services, see Glade I. Nelson, "Services of the Family History Library," chapter 3 in Cerny and Elliott, *The Library.*

[26]See the various stories on the Joseph Smith Memorial Building in the *Church News,* June 26, 1993, 6-11.

Interior of Historical Department located in the east wing of the LDS Church Office Building, ca. 1990. Courtesy LDS Church Archives.

The Historical Department and Library of the LDS Church

Glenn N. Rowe

By scriptural mandate, The Church of Jesus Christ of Latter-day Saints has collected material about its history from its inception.[1] Much material from the early history of the Church survived the many persecutions and travels of the Saints and found a safe repository in the Historian's Office, predecessor of the current Historical Department. Church officials, employees, and members have added to the collection detailed records of their own lives, of the lives of other Church members, and of the important events that have occurred at both the general and local Church levels.[2] Throughout the history of the Church, members have generously and unselfishly donated family treasures as they have been moved by the Lord's request that a record be kept of the Church's activities.

The Church's efforts to preserve these materials have provided the Historical Department with one of the finest and richest collections dealing with the LDS Church. The collections span nearly the entire chronological, geographical, ethnic, linguistic, and organizational depth and breadth of the Church. Organizationally, they are divided between the Church Historical Library and the Church Archives. This article briefly discusses the collections of each of these units and suggests guidelines for their use. Because of the size of the department's collections and the public's general familiarity with many of the more famous collections, this article mentions only selected items which are historically valuable yet are less frequently publicized.

The Church Historical Library

The Church Historical Library, located in the east wing of the Church Office Building in Salt Lake City,[3] seeks to acquire a copy of every significant item published by or about the Church. Although statistics are not kept on the precise number of items in the library's collection, as of October 31, 1988, the library had assigned 220,881 call numbers to materials in its collection.[4] Of the nearly 12,000[5] separately identified items in Chad Flake's *A Mormon Bibliography, 1830–1930,*

Historian Office, 1865. Courtesy LDS Church Archives.

Historian Office staff, 1917. Photograph by Sainsbury-Siddoway. Courtesy LDS Church Archives.

approximately 70 percent can be found in the library's collection. The collection includes books, pamphlets, broadsides, periodicals, and audiovisual materials.

Books

Some idea of the depth and breadth of the library's collection of books can be gained by surveying its collection of LDS scriptures, hymnals, and class manuals.

LDS Scriptures. The library holds copies of every significant edition of scriptures published by the Church. For instance, the library has copies of each of the important English editions of the Book of Mormon, including the 1830 Palmyra edition, the 1837 Kirtland edition, the 1840 Nauvoo edition, the 1841 first European edition, the 1849 second European edition, the 1879 Liverpool edition, the 1920 Salt Lake City edition, and the 1981 Salt Lake City edition. Moreover, the library includes printed editions of the Book of Mormon in over thirty-eight languages, including Braille and the Deseret Alphabet, as well as editions of selections from the Book of Mormon in over fifty languages.

The library also owns copies of the extremely rare 1833 Book of Commandments, in both bordered and nonbordered title page variations. The collection also includes copies of each published edition of the Doctrine and Covenants in English as well as copies in over thirty other languages.

Finally, the library contains copies of all major English editions of the Pearl of Great Price, including the 1851 Liverpool edition; the 1878 Salt Lake City edition; the 1879 Liverpool edition; the 1888 Salt Lake City edition made from new plates; the 1902 Salt Lake City edition, which is divided into chapters and verses; the 1921 Salt Lake City edition, which has a double-column format; the 1976 Salt Lake City edition, which added two additional visions as revelation; and the 1982 Salt Lake City edition, which moved the two visions from the Pearl of Great Price to Doctrine and Covenants sections 137 and 138. As well, the library retains copies of the Pearl of Great Price in over thirty languages, including Braille.

Hymnbooks. In July 1830, Joseph Smith's wife, Emma, was told "to make a selection of sacred hymns, as it shall be given thee, which is pleasing unto me, to be had in my church."[6] Hymnbooks have played an important part in the Church ever since the publication of Emma Smith's hymnal in 1835. The library has copies of this 1835 edition, as well as other important editions that have been published subsequently, including the 1840 Manchester hymnal and the 1839 hymnal compiled by Benjamin C. Elsworth. The collection includes a variety of hymnbooks published in many languages by missions and by the Church.

Church Manuals and Handbooks. The library seeks to gather all of the manuals and handbooks published by the Church in all languages and editions. Important priesthood manuals found in the collection include B. H. Roberts's 1907 *Seventy's Course in Theology* and Orson F. Whitney's 1914 *Gospel Themes*. Some classic doctrinal books have also been printed in the past as Melchizedek Priesthood manuals; examples in the collection include *Jesus the Christ, Gospel Doctrine, Essentials in Church History, Discourses of Brigham Young, Priesthood and Church Government,* and *Teachings of the Prophet Joseph Smith.*

Other Books. The library houses many thousands of books besides those already named. While many of these may be found in other libraries as well, there are a few important books of which the library holds the only institutional copy known. One very rare publication is Orson Hyde's *Ein Ruf aus der Wüste . . . (A Cry out of the Wilderness),* published in Frankfurt, Germany, in 1842.[7] This booklet is the first Mormon imprint published in a foreign language and contains a unique description of Joseph Smith's First Vision. Another very rare book found in the library is Amalie Schoppe's 1846 novel *Der Prophet . . .*, which has been described as the earliest book of fiction about the Church.[8]

The library also contains a large collection of magazine articles, theses, and dissertations relating to the Church and written for historical, sociological, and scientific audiences.

Pamphlets

From early times, the Church's missionary endeavor has made use of pamphlets as a proselyting tool; the Church Historical Library therefore includes a large collection of them. While not the oldest item in the collection, *The Joseph Smith Story* is perhaps the most widely translated item; the library holds copies in over 130 languages. Several unique pamphlets found in the library include Hugh Findlay's *To the Marattas of Hindoostan,* printed in Bombay, India, describing the first principles of Mormonism in the Hindustani language,[9] as well as unique French,[10] Dutch,[11] and German[12] copies of Lorenzo Snow's very significant pamphlet *The Only Way to Be Saved.*

Another rare group of pamphlets in the collection begins with the 1844 Nauvoo imprint of *General Smith's Views of the Powers and*

Policy of the Government of the United States.[13] Although this item was reprinted at least eight times within four months of its first printing, it is now extremely rare; copies of two of those eight reprints can be found only in the Historical Department's collection.[14]

Broadsides

Broadsides are single-sheet publications printed on only one side of the sheet. They include things such as announcements, newspapers, and playbills. By design, broadsides are more ephemeral in nature than pamphlets. Pamphlets contain a greater amount of information, are physically easier to handle, and are more easily preserved than broadsides. Consequently, the likelihood of a pamphlet surviving a life of wear and tear is better than that of a broadside. Although significant pamphlets of the early Church may be found in many institutional repositories, most of the important broadsides are found in only one or just a few repositories.

One very rare broadside in the library is *Theology. Lecture First on the Doctrine of the Church of the Latter Day Saints[.] of Faith.*[15] Printed in Kirtland in 1835, this broadside is apparently a preliminary printing of the first of the seven "Lectures on Faith" which appeared in the early editions of the Doctrine and Covenants. Another rare broadside, *Behold, Blessed Saith the Lord, Are They . . .*, printed in Kirtland around 1834, contains the text of what later became Section 59 of the Doctrine and Covenants.[16] In addition to these unique items, the 1835[17] broadside *Extract from the New Translation of the Bible, It Being the 24th Chapter of Matthew . . .*,[18] is worthy of note. This broadside, found in the library's collection as well as at Brigham Young University and Yale University, is the first published portion of Joseph Smith's inspired revision of the Bible.

The early Church increased its publishing activities over time. Consequently, the number of imprints from the Nauvoo period is greater than that of either the Missouri or Kirtland periods.[19] The library's collection reflects this increase. A good example of the breadth of the library's pre-1930 collection is its collection of Nauvoo broadsides. Of thirty-seven broadsides attributed to Nauvoo presses during the years 1842–46, the library has thirty-five in its collection.[20]

Periodicals

Most major and minor LDS periodicals are available in their entirety in the Church Historical Library. Like a few other repositories, the library has complete runs of the most important Mormon periodicals such as the *Evening and the Morning Star,*[21] *Evening and Morning Star,*[22] *Latter Day Saint's Messenger and Advocate,*[23] *Elders' Journal of the Church of Jesus Christ of Latter Day [sic] Saints,*[24] the *Times and Seasons,*[25] the *Prophet,*[26] the *Latter-day Saint's Millennial Star,*[27] and the *Deseret Weekly,* also known as *Deseret News,*[28] as well as others. But only at the Church Historical Library will a researcher find obscure yet significant periodicals such as the *Gospel Light,*[29] published irregularly from 1843 to 1844 by John E. Page, or the *Latter-day Saints Millennial Star and Monthly Visitor,*[30] published in Madras, India, in 1854. The Church Historical Library also has the only known complete run of the original issues of the *Nauvoo Neighbor.* The library also collects non-English Church serial publications and has nearly complete runs of such magazines as *Der Stern, De Ster, Skandinaviens Stjerne, Nordstjernan, El Atalaya de Mexico, Liahona, El Mensajero Deseret, L'Etoile, Te Heheuraa Api,* and *Seito No Michi.* Several foreign-language newspapers were also published for the benefit of members of the Church in Salt Lake City and vicinity during the 1880s and 1890s. These include the *Utah Posten, Svenska Hardden, Mormon Zeitung, Bikuben, Valkyrien,* and others. Some of these did not last long and others continued for decades, but examples of them are preserved in the library.

The library houses complete sets of current periodicals, including the *Ensign* and its equivalent language edition in the unified magazines, the *New Era,* the *Friend,* and the *Church News.* The library also has complete runs of Church periodicals no longer in print, such as the *Contributor,* the *Young Woman's Journal,* and the *Improvement Era.*

Audiovisual Materials

Teaching Aids. The Church's annual distribution catalog includes hundreds of pictures, posters, charts, and maps for instructional use. While these current instructional materials are readily available, some of the older materials the Church has used may be very hard for researchers to locate. The library has regularly acquired these teachers' aids. The collection includes materials such as the "Be Honest with Yourself" series and George Reynolds's *Chronological Chart of Nephite and Lamanite History.*

Motion Pictures. The library collects a wide range of motion pictures produced by the Church, including videocassette and filmstrip formats. Films found in the collection include such titles as *It's about People,* a 1976 look at the Deseret Industries; *The Story of Mormon*

Temples, a 1954 film explaining the purpose of temples; *Johnny Lingo,* produced in 1969; and the "Church in Action" series produced for the Historical Department. The library has also acquired a few selected films produced by private film studios, such as Twentieth Century Fox's full-length film *Brigham Young.*

Audio Recordings. In addition to motion pictures, films, filmstrips, and videocassettes, the Church has also produced many audio recordings, such as the tapes of general conference sessions. The library collects not only what the Church has produced, but also what Church-sponsored groups have produced commercially, such as the many famous Tabernacle Choir records distributed under the Columbia label.

Guidelines for Use

To enter the Church Historical Library or the Church Archives, a researcher must sign in at the security desk on the first floor of the east wing of the Church Office Building (50 East North Temple St., Salt Lake City) and present picture identification. A core collection of publications is available on public shelving on the first floor. Other materials may be ordered by call slip from the closed stacks. Rare, valuable, or fragile materials, as well as printed materials retained as the Church's archival copy, must be used in the rare books reading area on the first floor. Some of these items may require special authorization due to their value and condition. Library materials do not circulate.

The Church Archives

The collections of the Church Archives are divided into manuscripts, Church records, local records, photographs, oral histories, audiovisual materials, architectural drawings, and microforms. Again because of the size of the collection this article will describe only a selection of the less widely publicized collections in each of the categories.

Manuscripts

The archives catalog includes records for approximately 12,000 manuscript call numbers. These include diaries, journals, letters, unpublished histories and articles, and other items. Holdings include materials written from before the Church was organized until the present. Individual collections range from a single piece of paper to over two hundred linear feet of material. Probably the most notable manuscript in the archives is the dictation manuscript of the Book of Mormon. There are about 148 pages of this manuscript of the Book of Mormon, mostly in the handwriting of Oliver Cowdery. There are also manuscripts of many of the revelations in the Doctrine and Covenants, as well as the remaining pieces of the papyri purchased by Joseph Smith while in Kirtland.

Autobiographical writings are a significant part of the archives' manuscript holdings, both in volume and value. About 3,200 cataloged collections contain autobiographical writings.[31] These materials include writings of both men and women and include diaries, correspondence, scrapbooks, personal histories, and financial records. Ever since the gift of William Appleby's journal to the Historian's Office, the acquisition of personal items or manuscripts has been important to the archives. Included in this group are the papers of many general Church leaders. Presently, the archives has hundreds of missionary diaries from all over the world and a large number of immigrant diaries. Selected examples of these follow.

Women's Collections. The Zina Card Brown Collection documents five generations of women, beginning with early nineteenth-century America: (1) letters of Dorcus Baker (a few as early as 1806); (2) letters from her daughter Zina Baker Huntington; (3) diaries, correspondence, and other items from her daughter Zina Diantha Huntington Young, who was one of President Brigham Young's wives and was acquainted with most prominent individuals in early Utah; (4) the journals, correspondence, and notebooks from her daughter, Zina Young Card, who settled Cardston, Alberta, with her husband, Charles O. Card; and (5) correspondence and a history by her daughter Zina Card Brown. Other notable women's collections in the archives include the papers of Mary Fielding, born in England in 1801; Jane Elizabeth Manning James, a black member;[32] and the journals of Olive Woolley Kimball, covering 1884 to 1903.

Other Members. One collection which documents an immigrant pioneer family is the Fluckiger family papers. Ulrich and Anna Kaser Fluckiger joined the Church in Switzerland and immigrated to the western United States where they settled in Star Valley, Wyoming. The correspondence, which is mostly in German, is from several members of their immediate family and those still in Switzerland who did not join the Church.

While members of the Mormon Battalion were on the march in 1846, many wrote to their families and friends who remained with the main body of the Church. Several of these letters were collected, probably within a few years after the famous trek, and preserved in the Historian's Office. Items in the Mormon Battalion Correspondence

Collection tell of conditions along the trail and include descriptions of Fort Leavenworth and Santa Fe. A number of the letters were written by persons who were detached to Fort Pueblo. There are also a few by women who accompanied the battalion.

Andrew Jenson, Assistant Church Historian, 1897–1941, was an indefatigable compiler and publisher of Church history. Courtesy LDS Church Archives.

Non-English Collections. Jens C. A. Weibye joined the Church in 1854 in his native Denmark. He wrote thirteen volumes of reminiscences and journals, giving a detailed account of his activities as a local missionary in Denmark, emigration to Utah in 1862, and subsequent activities in Manti and Richfield. Andrew Jenson credited Weibye with being "one of the best record keepers in the Church."[33] He wrote in beautiful script and indexed each of his journals except the last, having died before it was filled. The final volume was finished by someone else with an account of Jens's death and funeral in February 1893. His journals through 1865 have been translated from Danish to English.

Joseph H. Dean was born in 1855 and died on November 2, 1947. His journals, comprising seventy-six volumes, give a daily account of his activities for more than sixty-eight years, from 1876 to 1944, including service as a missionary in Hawaii and Samoa in 1877-81, 1887-90, and 1916-18.

Church Records

The Church Archives is the official repository for the records of the general Church offices. A Church records management program instituted for Church headquarters in 1965 has made it possible for old records in the general Church offices which have a continuing or historical value to be accessed by the Church Archives. These records are placed in the archives for official administrative uses. Because they were created for official uses, Church records are frequently confidential; however, to a limited degree this material is available to others for historical research.

Joseph Fielding Smith served as Apostle, Church Historian, and President of the Church. Courtesy LDS Church Archives.

Church records material dates mostly from about the turn of the century, with the majority being from the twentieth century and the bulk of that covering the period 1959 to the present. The records of the Presiding Bishopric, for example, show the development of that office. They are the largest collection in the Church records category.

Records of general interest include (1) patriarchal blessing records dating from the 1830s; (2) records of missionaries from 1860 to the present; (3) deceased member records, 1942 to the present; (4) Journal History of the Church, 1830 to the present (compiled by the Historian's Office); (5) Church census records; and (6) the Historian's Office Journal, 1844–1970.

Local Records

Local records consist of documents produced by Church missions, districts, stakes, wards, and branches. Primarily, they are composed of minutes of bishopric, high council, priesthood, sacrament, and auxiliary meetings. One very useful group of local records is the manuscript history collection. This collection includes for each unit of the Church a summary of historical events compiled by the Historian's Office, quarterly historical reports submitted to the department before 1977, annual historical records produced by each stake after 1977, and membership records. In addition to minutes, local records include meetinghouse dedication programs, newsletters, scrapbooks, correspondence, ecclesiastical corporation documents, and cooperative mercantile records.

The local records collection is invaluable in researching and writing local, ward, family, and community histories. These local ward and stake records cover almost every facet of Church life in the unit and document the participation of Church members. They include priesthood rolls and minute books, Young Men's and Young Women's Mutual

Improvement Association records, Relief Society records, Primary records, executive and general minutes, and some welfare and even home-teaching records.

The earliest local records in the collection date from 1832, although there are relatively few pre-Utah items. The majority of the nineteenth-century local records postdate 1850.

The Church was centered in the intermountain area until the mid-twentieth century. The local records collection, however, has a very respectable international dimension. Records from the British Isles, European countries, Society Islands, Japan, Hawaii, and many other countries comprise a significant portion of the local records. More recently, records have been added to the collection from Africa and other areas where the Church is expanding.

The history of the format of local records is varied. In the early years, the ward clerk always recorded his minutes on blank sheets of paper and thus was left to his own ingenuity as to what he would place on the paper. About 1912 the auxiliaries and priesthood minutes were printed on a form which had a fill-in-the-blank format for all the information with a short space at the bottom for additional information. The auxiliary and priesthood minutes after that date lost much of their usefulness to historians. Most of the ward priesthood and auxiliary minutes are available today only on microfilm. Records created by ward clerks, such as minutes of sacrament meetings, have been microfilmed and the original volumes have been preserved.

Photographs

The Church Archives catalog has approximately five thousand photograph collection call numbers. Photograph collections range from a single image to ten thousand photographs. The entire photograph collection is estimated to be over a hundred thousand items (positive images). The photographic images span from the Church's Nauvoo period in the early 1840s to the Mormon colonization of the West and include images documenting its present worldwide status.

Included in the photographic collections are images derived from the earliest photographic processes. Probably the earliest image is a daguerreotype of the Nauvoo Temple. Other items range from images produced on daguerreotypes, ambrotypes, tintypes, cyanotypes, albumen, and gelatin prints to modern slides and prints.

The archives includes several significant photograph collections. The Charles W. Carter Collection contains several hundred prints from glass negatives taken by this pioneer Utah photographer. This glass-plate negative collection contains scenes of early Salt Lake City, Native

Church Office Building, ca. 1972. The Church Historical Library and Archives are located in the east wing. Courtesy LDS Family History Library.

Americans in Utah, Church leaders, and many other places and people of Utah. The archives also has collections of early Utah photographers Charles R. Savage and George Edward Anderson. The latter collection contains several hundred prints and includes scenes of turn-of-the-century rural Utah, as well as views of Church historical sites in the East. One of the lesser-known collections is the George Lofstrom Strebel Collection. Strebel accompanied the Brigham Young University Art Caravan to Nauvoo and over the old Mormon Trail in 1936. He took numerous photographs of every significant site in Nauvoo and along the trail.

The Portrait Collection contains individual portraits from about 1860 to the present and includes those of many pioneers. The *Church News* Collection contains some of the photographs published in that section of the *Deseret News*. The Biographical Sketch Photograph Collection includes portraits and snapshots sent in by Church leaders with their biographical sketches. The archives also includes the portrait work of many other Utah photographers such as Charles R. Savage, Fox and Symons, and C. E. Johnson.

As the Church has grown and expanded beyond Salt Lake City and Utah, its members have documented their own experiences in writing and with photographs, many of which have been added to the Church's holdings. Of particular note are photograph albums and portrait collections put together by the Church's missionaries. These photographs, in combination with a growing "portrait" collection, are among the collections most frequently requested by patrons doing family research. These collections include portraits not only of fellow missionaries, but also families befriended and places visited.

Oral Histories

Since August 1972, the Historical Department has operated one of the larger oral history programs in the United States. The James Moyle Oral History Program (so named because of a generous grant from the James Moyle Genealogical and Historical Association to assist in covering program expenses) includes over 2,200 interviews with nearly 1,200 individuals, representing some 5,000 hours on tape. Interviews deal with all aspects of LDS life in the intermountain area and throughout the world.

The majority of the oral history collection has been transcribed. Completed oral histories generally include a preface describing the background of the interview and providing biographical information about the interviewee. Almost all finished oral histories also include fairly detailed tables of contents, as none of the transcripts are indexed.

Approximately 10 percent of the interviews are in a language other than English. Most of the non-English interviews have not been translated.

Audiovisual Materials

The audiovisual collections housed in the Church Archives include a variety of materials going back to the earliest days of recording history. The collections include early Edison wax-cylinder recordings, wire recordings, sixteen-inch glass phonograph record transcriptions, acetate and polyester audiotape recordings, video- and audiotape reels and cassettes, and transfers from nitrate film to motion picture safety film.

Representing the earliest item in the collections, the 1898 Wilford Woodruff testimony transcription has been taken from the original cylinder. Continuing chronologically, motion picture collections date from the early 1910s to the present and include the Clawson Film Company collection, which spans from 1911 to 1928. The bulk of the audio collection begins in 1936 with the recordings of Church general conference that were transferred from phonograph discs. The collection of videotape begins in the mid-1970s with general conference and regional representative seminar recordings.

Geographically, the major portion of the holdings reflect intermountain Church history, although the national and international history of the Church is partially represented. Collections which reflect the global nature of the Church include dedicatory services of chapels, temples, and other Church structures. Missionaries and members with home movie cameras and recorders have contributed significantly to the international content of the Church Archives audiovisual collections.

Architectural Drawings

The Historical Department's architectural collections consist of original drawings, blueprints, rough sketches, photographs, job files, art renderings, specifications, and some product samples. The collection includes several major collections, as well as hundreds of single or group collections of various architects contracted to design ward and stake meetinghouses, tabernacles, and temples.

Some of the major collections of architectural drawings include the Nauvoo Temple (William Weeks) Collection; the Truman Angell Collection (ca. 1851–70); the George Cannon Young Collection (1875–1985); the Don Carlos Young Collection (1885–1945); the Harold and

Douglas Burton Collection (1909-70); and the Cannon and Mullen, Architects, Collection (ca. 1937-75).

Microforms

Many of the Archives collections have been microfilmed. In order to preserve the originals, researchers today are required to use the microfilm copy. The archives has also acquired microforms of Mormon-related collections in other institutions.

Guidelines for Use

Some collections in the LDS Church Archives contain information which is confidential, private, or sacred.[34] Therefore, access to papers of living or recently deceased persons are sometimes restricted, as are those of a number of Church officials, although only about three percent of manuscript collections are restricted. Because of the current and confidential nature of materials in the Church records category, a larger percentage of those records is restricted. Permission to view restricted and uncataloged materials should be sought in writing. Letters should state what information is being sought and indicate the intended use.

Researchers register upon entering the Archives and Manuscripts Reading Room on the second floor. First-time users or researchers who have new research projects will interview with a reference archivist before proceeding. To use materials, patrons are asked to sign a standard researcher agreement.

Glenn N. Rowe was the Director of the Library-Archives Division of the Historical Department of The Church of Jesus Christ of Latter-day Saints from 1984 to 1989.
He would like to acknowledge the staff's contributions to this article.

NOTES

[1]Scriptures on keeping records, writing history, and collecting historical materials include Doctrine and Covenants 20:81-83; 21:1; 47:1-3; 69:3-4, 7-8; 72:5-6; 85; 93:53; 123; 127:9; and 128:2-7.

[2]Articles on the history of the Church Historical Department, The Church of Jesus Christ of Latter-day Saints, Salt Lake City, include Ronald K. Esplin and Max J. Evans, "Preserving Mormon Manuscripts: Historical Activities of the LDS Church," *Manuscripts* 27 (Summer 1975): 166-77; Max J. Evans and Ronald G. Watt, "Sources for Western History at The Church of Jesus Christ of Latter-day Saints," *Western Historical Quarterly* 8 (July 1977): 303-12; David M. Mayfield and

LaMond F. Beatty, "Libraries of The Church of Jesus Christ of Latter-day Saints," in *Church and Synagogue Libraries,* ed. John F. Harvey (Metuchen, N.J.: Scarecrow Press, 1980), 129–48; Donald T. Schmidt, "The Historical Department of The Church of Jesus Christ of Latter-day Saints," *Genealogical Journal* 2 (June 1973): 62–65; Ronald G. Watt, "Evolution of an Archives: From the Covered Wagon to SPINDEX II," *SPINDEX Users Conference, Proceedings, March 31–April 1, 1978,* ed. H. Thomas Hickerson (Ithaca: Cornell University Libraries, 1979), 1–5; Ronald G. Watt, "Genealogy and History at LDS Church Headquarters," *Genealogical Journal* 11 (Spring 1982): 3–13; Howard Clair Searle, "Early Mormon Historiography: Writing the History of the Mormons, 1830–1858" (Ph.D. diss., University of California at Los Angeles, 1979), 69–143; and Charles P. Adams and Gustive O. Larson, "A Study of the LDS Church Historian's Office, 1830-1900," *Utah Historical Quarterly* 40 (Fall 1972): 370–89.

[3]The Church Historical Library should not be confused with the Family History Library, located at 35 North West Temple, Salt Lake City.

[4]This number and other collection statistics mentioned here reflect only roughly the number of items as recorded in the department's computer catalog. Serials, for example, in the library figures are counted only once, but the number of volumes within that serial set may be quite large. Some monographs (such as encyclopedias) are also cataloged as a set and would only be counted once.

[5]Chad J. Flake, ed., *A Mormon Bibliography, 1830–1930* (Salt Lake City: University of Utah Press, 1978); (hereafter cited as Flake). This figure includes approximately 10,000 items in Flake's original bibliography, as well as over 1,800 additional items compiled since 1978. These additional items are listed in its ten-year supplement, Chad J. Flake and Larry W. Draper, comps., *Mormon Bibliography, 1830–1930: Ten Year Supplement* (Salt Lake City: University of Utah Press, 1989), (hereafter cited as Flake Supplement).

[6]Doctrine and Covenants 25:11.

[7]See Flake 4169.

[8]See Flake 7566.

[9]See Flake 3355.

[10]See Flake 8239a.

[11]See Flake 8239.

[12]See Flake 8239d. This pamphlet was published in several other languages, including Bengali. These editions can be found in other institutions besides the Church Historical Library.

[13]See Flake 7957.

[14]See Flake 7960 and Flake Supplement 7957a.

[15]See Flake 7285.

[16]See Flake 2914a.

[17]There is some debate as to the date of publication. See Peter Crawley, "A Bibliography of The Church of Jesus Christ of Latter-day Saints in New York, Ohio, and Missouri," *BYU Studies* 12 (Summer 1972): 505–7.

[18]See Flake 468.

[19]There are at least 110 imprints relevant to Mormonism published in the state of Illinois (most were published in Nauvoo, but some were published in other towns such as Warsaw, Quincy, and Carthage) between 1839 and 1846. See Cecil K. Byrd, *A Bibliography of Illinois Imprints, 1814–1858* (Chicago: University of Chicago Press, 1966); and Flake.

[20]Seventeen of these thirty-seven broadsides are either *Nauvoo Neighbor* extras or *Hancock Eagle* extras.

[21]See Flake 3272. Complete runs are extant only at the Church Historical Department and at the Huntington Library, San Marino, California.

[22]See Flake 3273.

[23]See Flake 4778.

[24]See Flake 3126.

[25]See Flake 8955.

[26]See Flake 6772.

[27]See Flake 4779.

[28]See Flake 2822.

[29]See Flake 3642. There are only three issues extant, all located in the Church Historical Department.

[30]See Flake 4784. This periodical consists of only seven issues. Several repositories have four of the seven, but only the Church Historical Department has all seven.

[31]Journals, diaries, reminiscences, and autobiographical sketches all fall under this classification. The genre tracing that the Church Archives uses to identify them in bibliographic records is *Journals*. Although incomplete and somewhat outdated, a useful guide is Davis Bitton, *Guide to Mormon Diaries and Autobiographies* (Provo, Utah: Brigham Young University Press, 1977).

[32]Jane Elizabeth Manning James, Autobiography (c. 1901), mss., LDS Church Archives.

[33]Andrew Jenson, *Latter-day Saint Biographical Encyclopedia,* 4 vols. (Salt Lake City: Andrew Jenson History, 1901–36), 1:818.

[34]This article has described materials held in the Historical Department. Records outside of this article's scope include those of many other Church departments and offices; these are not open to the public, typically in order to preserve confidential or personal information.

Henry Edwards Huntington (1850–1927), the developer and book collector who devoted much of the last years of his life to gathering and preserving an extensive collection of manuscripts and rare books emphasizing American history and English literature. In time his collection embraced Western Americana, which included Mormons in the West. To house these collections, he built and endowed the library that bears his name. Courtesy the Huntington Library.

Studying the Saints: Mormon Sources at the Huntington Library

Peter J. Blodgett

Beginnings and Early Acquisitions

When Henry Edwards Huntington retired in 1910 from a successful career in railroading and land development, he turned both his great fortune and his vast experience to the advancement of his fondest personal avocation, the collecting of rare books and manuscripts. Already well known for his accomplishments as a collector, he now applied himself with greater effort to this pursuit. By the time of his death in 1927, he had assembled one of the finest private holdings then in existence relating to Anglo-American history and literature. The research library established by Huntington on the foundation of that private collection has remained one of the preeminent resources for scholarship in America to this day. From the beginning, it has numbered significant documents of Mormon history among its many treasures.

The earliest Mormon acquisitions by Huntington resulted primarily from his enthusiasm for printed Americana and his decision to buy several large collections in their entirety. First and second editions of the Book of Mormon, for example, came to his library with the purchases of the E. Dwight Church and Augustin MacDonald collections in 1911 and 1916. The purchase in 1922 of Henry R. Wagner's magnificent library of Western Americana capped this trend, adding seventy-eight volumes concerning Mormonism alone, such as a first edition of William Clayton's renowned *The Latter-Day Saints' Emigrants' Guide.* By 1925, Huntington had already gathered a fine collection of printed Mormon titles, particularly focused upon the era of immigration to and settlement of Utah.

In subsequent years, that original collection of printed works grew enormously in breadth and depth, carefully nurtured by Leslie E. Bliss throughout his lengthy tenure as Huntington librarian. During the 1920s under Bliss's administration, the library began to expand into the field of unpublished Mormon materials. That pursuit of original sources reinforced Huntington's own interest in collecting the

The Henry E. Huntington Library, San Marino, California. Courtesy the Huntington Library.

"background materials" necessary for scholarly research, however pedestrian such materials might seem to rare-book collectors. The background materials obtained for the field of Western Americana included letters, diaries, journals, and reminiscences written by Latter-day Saints both famous and anonymous as well as by other observant commentators.

As early as 1929, the library added significant groups of Mormon manuscripts to its collections of original historical documents. Although not pursued initially with the vigor seen in later years, the acquisition of Mormon manuscripts began with several notable triumphs. In 1929, for instance, the Huntington obtained a series of six original diaries kept by John D. Lee, spanning a period from 1846 to 1876, as well as assorted Lee correspondence and an original diary from Rachel Woolsey Lee for the years 1856–60. The papers of Jacob S. Boreman, prominent opponent of the LDS Church and presiding judge at the two trials of John D. Lee, were acquired in 1934.[1] And in 1942, as the New Deal's Works Progress Administration was winding down its operations, the Huntington secured carbon copies of various pioneer reminiscences and histories as well as original historical ephemera brought together by Hugh O'Neil, an editor with the WPA Historic Records Survey in Utah.

Measured merely by these three acquisitions, the library had thus gathered a small but important collection of Mormon manuscripts that touched upon the end of the crucial Nauvoo period, the transcontinental flight to Utah, the colonization of the Great Basin, and the bitter conflict between Gentiles and Mormons in late nineteenth-century Utah.

Huntington Library and Juanita Brooks

By 1942, of course, the United States had joined World War II, and most of the nation's energies were absorbed by the escalating war effort. At the time, it must have seemed that the preservation of the past would have to give way to the urgent demands of the present. Yet, at that very moment, a series of coincidental events were about to occur that would thrust the Huntington Library into the forefront of those institutions collecting Mormon historical materials.

The first link in that chain of events was forged in 1943 when Robert Glass Cleland, professor of history at Occidental College, became affiliated with the Huntington's research staff. Cleland, a renowned expert in the history of California and the Southwest, sought ways to promote further research in Southwestern history at the library. Aware of the financial support being given to the study of regional history by the Rockefeller Foundation, Cleland prodded the library into applying for a foundation grant. The foundation's humanities program responded in August 1944 with the offer of an annual award of $10,000 a year for a five-year term to support fellowships, research grants, and the acquisition of both original documents and reproductions of those materials not available for purchase. Under the direction of an advisory committee headed by Cleland, a Southwest studies program took shape at the Huntington Library and began to attract a distinguished community of scholars to San Marino.

Cleland and the Rockefeller grant gave the library the impetus and the wherewithal to collect original source materials of Southwestern history. The Huntington's librarian, Leslie Bliss, faced the challenge of insuring that the funds devoted each year to acquisitions were well spent. Bliss himself had a well-deserved reputation as an able collector and an intelligent student of Western Americana, but collecting on the scale envisioned by the grant suggested the need for a full-time field representative. Thus the Rockefeller grant served its most important (if unintended) function by triggering the long and fruitful collaboration between the Huntington Library and Juanita Brooks.

Levi Peterson's recent biography of Juanita Brooks tells us much about this relationship.[2] The basic details, however, can be recounted quickly. Brooks had first come into contact with the Huntington Library in 1944, when she had learned of the library's John D. Lee diaries. She visited the library at the invitation of Robert Cleland to consult the diaries for her book on the Mountain Meadows Massacre. After the Huntington Library had received the Rockefeller grant, Brooks received one of the research fellowships in Southwestern history to continue her work. Apparently impressed with the caliber of her research and with her personal contacts in the Southwest, Bliss also hired her under the auspices of the grant as a field agent to collect manuscript material on the region's history. Through the remainder of the 1940s and into the 1950s, Brooks scoured Utah and northern Arizona for diaries, journals, letters, and reminiscences that would illuminate the settlement and the growth of the Great Basin area. In particular, she focused upon the southern portions of Utah known as Dixie and, during her labors, harvested an enormous crop of original records that were either acquired outright by the library or copied and then returned to the owners. The grant's renewal in 1951 and Brooks's personal friendship with Leslie Bliss kept her active as a field agent well into the 1950s.

Juanita Brooks (1898–1989), the diligent field agent for the Huntington Library during the 1940s and early 1950s. Brooks was instrumental in bringing many southern Utah and northern Arizona Mormon collections to the library. Courtesy Utah State Historical Society.

Acquisitions during the 1950s and 1960s

Juanita Brooks's notable success as a field agent made the postwar decade a golden era for the acquisition of Mormon historical documents at the Huntington. The accomplishments of the next two decades under Bliss's direction, although somewhat more modest in scope, maintained the momentum of previous years. Besides a continuing influx of diaries, journals, and autobiographies received from Brooks and other sources in Utah, several large and significant individual collections were added to the library's holdings. The 1959 acquisition of the papers of Frederic E. Lockley Jr., Oregon historian, editor, and rare-book dealer, included various letters written by his father, the editor of the *Salt Lake Tribune* from 1873 to 1875. The senior Lockley's correspondence commented on many aspects of Mormonism as well as on the 1875 trial of John D. Lee, which Lockley attended. In 1965 the Huntington Library received another collection dealing with a controversial phase of Mormon history when it obtained the original transcripts of Kimball Young's interviews for his examination of polygamy, *Isn't One Wife Enough?* A year later, the Huntington purchased a group of letters and documents concerning the business affairs of Lewis C. Bidamon, Illinois businessman and second husband of Emma Hale Smith, widow of the Mormon prophet Joseph Smith. Inspection of that collection revealed that it contained papers of Emma Smith Bidamon and her son Joseph Smith, eventual leader of the Reorganized Church of Jesus Christ of Latter Day Saints. Finally, in the field of printed matter, Bliss achieved his greatest coup with his successful pursuit of the Loughran Collection in 1962. These 15,000 books, pamphlets, and periodicals represented an enormous treasure trove of rare Mormon documents that vastly expanded the library's holdings.

As the 1960s closed, the Huntington could look back on three extraordinarily productive decades of collecting historical Mormon materials. Since then, the pace has slowed, but the library continues to make significant additions to both the printed and manuscript collections. The purchase or reproduction of Mormon family diaries and journals has continued, sometimes with the assistance of Brooks or other Mormon scholars, while fugitive copies of important printed texts have been tracked down through dealers and private collectors. In recent years, the library has acquired several valuable new pieces. A very rare 1845 broadside printed in Nauvoo announces the imminent departure of the Mormons from that beleaguered city. A run of *Zion's Watchman* (Sydney, Australia) from its inauguration in 1853 through May 1856 includes the announcement to the Australian Saints of the doctrine of plural marriage. And, from a later period of Mormon history, the manuscript autobiography of Almeda Perry Brown captures in detail the life story of a twentieth-century Mormon woman who overcame great obstacles to become a prominent member of Utah State University's faculty at an important stage in its development.

Contents of the Rare Books Department

Such a brief sketch can hardly do justice to the intricate history behind the Huntington Library's Mormon collection. It may convey, however, some sense of the great breadth of resources assembled over the last sixty years. But if the mere size of this collection commands our attention, do its contents merit the scholar's interest?

In the field of printed works alone, the library's accumulated holdings represent an exceptionally useful resource for scholars in many fields. Among the foundation texts of the Mormon faith, the Huntington's Rare Books Department possesses over 100 English-language editions of the Book of Mormon, another 40 editions in eighteen separate languages, and examples of editions produced by other groups such as the Brooksites and Whitmerites. Supplementing those many texts are first editions of the Doctrine and Covenants of The Church of Jesus Christ of Latter-day Saints (Kirtland, Ohio, 1835), the Pearl of Great Price (Liverpool, 1851), and Parley P. Pratt's *A Voice of Warning and Instruction to All People* (New York, 1837), as well as many subsequent printings in the United States and, in the case of *A Voice of Warning,* from overseas as well. Other volumes in the collection include most of the salient writings authored by early Church leaders.[3]

Over time, the library's collectors also brought together an extensive file of newspapers and periodicals documenting the Church's first half-century. Especially of note are complete runs of the *Evening and the Morning Star* in both its original publication between 1832 and 1834 and its 1835–36 Kirtland, Ohio, reissue; the *Latter-Day Saints' Messenger and Advocate* (Kirtland, Ohio, 1834–37); and the *Elders' Journal of The Church of Jesus Christ of Latter-day Saints* (Kirtland, Ohio, and Far West, Mo., 1837–38). Other publications inform readers about events during the Nauvoo years (*Times and Seasons,* vols. 1–6, 1839–46), about the course of the Church's foreign mission endeavors (*Latter-Day Saints' Millennial Star,* Liverpool, 1840–98), and about the initial settlement of the Great Basin (*Deseret News,* vols. 1–12, 1850–63 and scattered issues from later periods). The Huntington's microfilm collection reinforces our holdings of the *Deseret News* in particular with a copy of the weekly paper from 1850 through 1898 and the daily paper from volume 1, number 1 through volume 4, number 124 (November 21, 1867, through April 15, 1871).

Lastly, in its holdings the Huntington also numbers a great many of the major printed works about the Church. Since Huntington's time, the library has acquired a great assortment of volumes attacking, defending, or merely commenting upon Mormonism. Readers may discover the reminiscences of faithful Church members and bitter apostates, doctrinal works elaborating upon the structures of belief within the Church, the observations of such fascinated travelers as Sir Richard Burton, and the vast popular literature—including dramas and dime novels—that used Mormonism as the backdrop to adventure.

Equally close study of the Huntington's Mormon manuscript holdings reveals similarly impressive breadth and depth. The separate collections previously mentioned such as the Bidamon, the Boreman, and the Lee papers and such individual treasures as an 1834–38 Oliver Cowdery letterbook and two volumes of diaries kept by Eliza Roxcy Snow for the years 1846 to 1849 constitute by themselves a splendid array of original documents on the Mormon experience.

The Mormon File Manuscripts

The heart of the matter, however, remains the Mormon File, a synthetic arrangement of manuscripts containing approximately 120 reels of microfilm, 160 bound photostats and typescripts, and over 1200 discrete letters and documents, assembled in large part under the sponsorship of the Rockefeller Foundation forty years ago. Taken in toto, this file now encompasses every phase of Mormon history from the era of the Prophet, through the exodus and the gathering of Zion, to the colonization of the intermountain region and the evolution of modern Utah. While it would be impossible to comment here upon the contents of every manuscript, let me offer several examples of the collection's strengths. Mormonism's early evolution and the Church's combative relations with its gentile neighbors, for instance, especially in the state of Missouri, can be followed through a number of sources. Besides Oliver Cowdery's letterbook, the Huntington possesses original transcripts of the court suits filed in 1833 by Edward Partridge and William W. Phelps in Jackson County, Missouri, against the men who tarred and feathered Partridge and looted Phelps's home in Independence; a microfilm copy of David Lewis's account of the Haun's Mill massacre; and Reed Peck's 1839 manuscript sketch of Mormonism's Missouri period.

With the sesquicentennial of the British mission in mind, it should be noted that the Mormon File includes over thirty-five diaries and journals of Mormon missionaries in foreign lands. Most, of course, portray mission work in the British Isles or Scandinavia, but a few describe the search for converts in such distant locations as South Africa, India, New Zealand, Samoa, and the Sandwich Islands. Even those diaries kept by missionaries in the United Kingdom, although concentrating upon the same general subject, reproduce the experiences of many dedicated Saints over a five-decade span.

Other documents in the Mormon File capture all the steps in the process of gathering the faithful, including the drafts of converts raised by the foreign missions, and then dispersing them across the Great Basin Zion to hold it for God's chosen people. We can follow many emigrants through their diaries and autobiographies on their difficult passage from European ports or the Eastern states to Utah and realize that despite the helping hand extended by the Church through such mechanisms as the Perpetual Emigrating Fund (PEF), such a journey required great reserves of strength and courage. The papers of one PEF agent in Missouri, William Young Empey, outline the Fund's operations for the 1854 travel season, capturing with unintended pathos the tribulations that might befall the emigrants. In a letter dated April 24, 1854, written from the port of Liverpool, Samuel W. Richards, head of the British mission, chided Empey for failing to notify him of those emigrants in the parties Richards had sent out who had died in passage. The lack of news, he sternly reminded Empey, "leaves their friends in this country in terrible suspense." And among Empey's papers are several notebooks containing lists of PEF and 13£ Co. passengers with notations of those who succumbed.

At the end of that long voyage to the promised land, many of the Saints soon found themselves called upon to abandon their new homes and lay the cornerstones of new settlements in many different parts of the Great Basin. Within the Mormon File, researchers can find many diaries, journals, and other papers that picture the Mormon colonization of the Southwest. There are over twenty journals, diaries, and autobiographies, as well as several collections of personal papers, that describe colony building in Nevada, Arizona, and the southern reaches of Utah. The Edwin Bunker Collection includes many personal and business papers that highlight efforts to establish the United Order in Bunkerville, Nevada, between 1877 and 1879 as well as Bunker's many responsibilities as a Mormon bishop in Bunkerville in the 1880s, responsibilities which ranged from collecting tithes and making distributions to the poor to laying down rules that governed the conduct of dancing parties. The United Order is also the subject of Emma Seegmiller Higbee's account of life at Orderville, "Voices from Within." Efforts to advance the economic development of the region can be followed through the Huntington's Frederick Kesler Collection, which includes nearly sixty volumes of daybooks and account books discussing the various mills that Kesler, a skilled practical engineer, built or operated all over the territory between 1857 and 1894.

Other Collections

On these and many other topics, Mormon collections at the Huntington offer considerable scope for scholarly investigation. The complex phenomenon that is Mormonism, however, did not live in a vacuum and should not be studied in one. The Huntington also offers scholars access to a uniquely rich array of collateral materials that establishes the essential context of Mormonism's place in Western history. Among our extensive holdings on the nineteenth-century exploration of the trans-Mississippi West, for example, are the papers of John Williams Gunnison and Edward G. Beckwith. Gunnison's materials include letters written to his wife Martha during his travels in Utah with Stansbury's expedition during 1849–50 and his command of the ill-fated 35th Parallel Survey in 1953. Beckwith's collection contains the journals he kept as Gunnison's second-in-command as well as letters to his wife about the survey's progress and the disaster that befell it.

In addition to the Gunnison and Beckwith papers, the library's superb collection of overland journals furnishes a massive amount of information about the trans-Mississippi West and about westward migration, especially during the height of the California Gold Rush. Some of these manuscripts record the passage of their authors through the new Mormon commonwealth; as a group, they describe the hopes and aspirations of western immigrants as well as the experience of overland travel. The Huntington's recent acquisition of Professor Ralph P. Bieber's research archive deepens its resources concerning western movement and settlement. Bieber accumulated an enormous collection of newspaper transcriptions in the course of a long career spent studying the great rush to California in 1849–50 and the development of the American Southwest. Thousands of handwritten notecards or photostatic copies were made from hundreds of newspapers in every state and many territories, documenting the overland trek to California, the opening of the Santa Fe Trail, the Mexican War, the organization of the western range-cattle industry, and the establishment of overland trade and communications with California after statehood.

Another set of newspaper transcriptions compiled by another leading Western historian gathers together information on the topic "Mormons and the Far West." Dale Morgan drew upon newspapers in every state between 1809 and 1857 to reproduce hundreds of articles that might be useful to historians of Mormonism. His assiduous research, like that of Bieber, saved from near-permanent obscurity hundreds of sources residing in private hands or in anonymous local historical collections. Lastly, the Huntington has acquired for its reference collection hundreds of biographical dictionaries, state and county histories, city directories, and microfilm copies of territorial records from the federal government pertaining to Utah and several of its neighbors. These references help provide the substratum of facts necessary for much historical research.

Without attempting, therefore, to produce a detailed handlist that enumerates every item in the Huntington's collections, this essay has sought to describe the general contours of the collection and to highlight some of its particular strengths. The individual pieces and specific collections cited here represent only a small portion of the whole. Confronted by this vast assortment of materials, what can contemporary students of Mormonism and of Western American history learn from it as they conduct their research? And how can access to it at the Huntington be improved?

Diaries and Autobiographies

Clearly the importance of the Huntington's Mormon holdings, especially its numerous diaries, journals, and autobiographies, is as great, if not greater, to Western history than ever before. The growing sophistication of many regional historians, influenced by new techniques of social and cultural analysis, have encouraged a mounting interest in the documentary records kept by the relatively anonymous. Desirous of portraying society "from the bottom up," many historians now seek to understand how individuals shaped and in turn were shaped by the systems of belief or the social organizations of their times. For Mormon history, these manuscripts provide a great reservoir of details about all aspects of daily life in many Mormon communities from the perspectives of men and women, immigrants and old-stock Americans, farmers and town dwellers, recent converts and second-generation believers. For the social history of the American West, these manuscripts chronicle the settlement and development of a large portion of the Great Basin zone, often in minute detail. Scholars researching questions in these fields should find a number of productive sources at hand. They may even have the opportunity to delve into some of the diaries, journals, autobiographies, or life sketches that escaped inclusion in Davis Bitton's splendid *Guide to Mormon Diaries and Autobiographies*.

Bitton's guide remains an absolutely essential road map with which to plot the course of one's research in Mormon diaries and autobiographies. Over time, however, as cataloging of the Huntington's Mormon manuscripts has continued, a number of original and facsimile items not known to Bitton have surfaced. Among these manuscripts are various accounts of foreign missions, including the holograph missionary journals of Andrew Henry in Ireland during 1842 and 1843, Ira Hinckley in New Zealand during 1882 and 1883, and Edwin T. Wooley in England during 1884, as well as microfilm copies of William Fotheringham's mission journals from India, China, and South Africa in 1854-55 and 1861-62.

Other original or reproduced manuscripts that were not listed in Bitton include life sketches of Sariah Louisa Chamberlain, Margaret Miller Watson De Witt, Lorin Farr, George Elmer Gardner, Silas Harris, Heber Jarvis, Zadoc Judd, Mons Larson, James Richey, George Thomas Rogers, George H. Rothrock, August Maria Outzan Smith, Janet Mauretta Johnson Smith, and Barry Wride; autobiographies of Asahel Woodruff Burk, Joan Walker Fotheringham, John Addison Hunt, James W. Le Sueur, Sophrania Moore Martin, Samuel Miles, Lemuel Harrison Redd, and William Henry Streeper; and reminiscences of Thomas Day, Anna Maria Hafen, and Mary Minerva Judd.

Also worthy of note in the Mormon File are journals kept by Elias H. Blackburn (1904-5), Harriet Bunting (1885-90), Prime Thornton Coleman (1879-1930), Joab Collier (1874-75 and 1889),

William Farrer (1849-54), James Holt (1841-53), Sarah Sturdevant Leavitt (1874-75), Knud Swensen (1857-1902), Dana O. Walton (1890-1901), and Edwin Thomas Wooley (1884-86 and 1900-1906), as well as diaries written by James G. Bleak (1873), J. R. Bodham (1886), Orville S. Cox (1852-67), Moses H. Farnsworth (1862-64), Osmer Dennis Flake (1896-1938), A. H. Hill (1865), George W. McCune (1896-98), Emma W. Neilson (1887-1916), George Pectol (1871-98), Ethan Pettit (1855-91), John H. Richards (1876-92), and William Wride (1898-1901).

Filing Systems

Unfortunately, the substantial number of relatively untapped sources within our collection points up the existence of certain problems that have hampered efficient use of our Mormon manuscripts in the past, stemming in large part from the sheer bulk of the Mormon File and from the manner in which it was gathered. During the late 1940s and early 1950s, as original and facsimile copies of Mormon manuscripts poured into the library through the efforts of Juanita Brooks and others, the number of acquisitions taxed the resources of the institution to accession and organize them rapidly enough to remain current with new acquisitions at a time when large additions were being made to the holdings in other fields. Although no detailed records exist discussing the library's plans for the Mormon File, it seems likely that the file was created as a temporary expedient to absorb all the Mormon manuscripts in a common grouping.

The author card file established to inventory all these manuscripts served for a number of years with some success as the primary finding aid for the Mormon File. The card file's structure, however, has always imposed intractable limits upon its utility. The only bibliographic data common to each card has been the author's name. If the initial precataloging examination failed to reveal the inclusive dates or descriptive information about the subjects discussed in the manuscript, then such information was omitted, under the assumption that the collection would soon be receiving more systematic attention. For the same reason, almost no subject indexing was done on these texts. Many items were not even assigned call numbers since it was expected that the entire file would be reorganized. Today, the lack of call numbers slows down the process of locating and retrieving these manuscripts for readers and for photo reproduction orders. The lack of chronological detail and of subject indexing makes it very difficult for researchers to identify sources containing information on specific topics unless they have prepared a list of relevant individuals whose names can be cross-checked against our card index. Under some circumstances, therefore, the Mormon File can be a cumbersome tool to use.

Despite all these difficulties, many historians have drawn upon the rich resources of the Huntington's collections. We expect that this trend will only increase. Therefore, the library has embarked on a long-term project to remedy the existing problems with the Mormon File. An item-by-item review of its contents will produce necessary bibliographic information about each piece, including, in the case of reproductions, details about the original manuscript that will enable scholars, through comparison with guides such as Bitton's, to verify whether they are reading an exact copy of an original or a variation. Standardized cataloging will be accompanied by indexing of the most significant subjects in the card catalog under Library of Congress subject headings. Eventually, this review will result in a full, printed inventory of all Mormon items and, perhaps, a computerized data base for the Mormon File that could be updated routinely.

Conclusion

The Huntington's relationship with the history of Mormons and Mormonism has been a long and successful one. Since its founding, the library has assembled a collection of Mormon materials with few parallels outside of Utah. It has hosted several generations of scholars, who have authored many fine historical or biographical studies. The projected reorganization of the Mormon File, now in the preliminary stages, will enhance the file's accessibility to readers at the Huntington and improve the library's ability to assist serious advanced research in Mormon history for many years to come.

Researchers seeking more information about manuscripts mentioned in this essay or about other portions of the library's Mormon holdings are encouraged to inquire at the Department of Manuscripts, the Department of Rare Books, or the Reader Services Department, Huntington Library, 1151 Oxford Road, San Marino, California 91108.[4] Since the library is not a public institution, researchers should also contact the Department of Reader Services for further information about guidelines for admission and applications for reading privileges.

Peter J. Blodgett is Curator of Western Historical Manuscripts at the Henry E. Huntington Library.

NOTES

This article was originally published as "Studying the Saints: Resources for Research in Mormon History at the Huntington Library," *BYU Studies* 32 (Summer 1992): 71-86.

[1]Leonard J. Arrington, ed., "Crusade against Theocracy: The Reminiscences of Judge Jacob Smith Boreman of Utah, 1872-1877," *Huntington Library Quarterly* 24 (November 1960): 1-45.

[2]See Levi Peterson, *Juanita Brooks: Mormon Woman Historian* (Salt Lake City: University of Utah Press, 1988), esp. chapter 5. See also Juanita Brooks, "Jest a Copyin'—Word f'r Word," *Utah Historical Quarterly* 37 (Fall 1969): 375-95.

[3]See the brief sketch by Peter Crawley, "Mormon Americana at the Huntington Library," *Dialogue: A Journal of Mormon Thought* 6 (Autumn-Winter 1971): 138-40.

[4]For more information about the history of the library, see John E. Pomfret, *The Henry E. Huntington Library and Art Gallery: From Its Beginnings to 1969* (San Marino, Calif.: Huntington Library, 1969); *The Founding of the Henry E. Huntington Library and Art Gallery,* which was the August 1969 issue of *The Huntington Library Quarterly,* vol. 32, no. 4; and Selena A. Spurgeon, *Henry Edwards Huntington, His Life and His Collections, a Docent Guide* (San Marino, Calif.: Huntington Library, 1992), especially chapter 6, "The Library."

Mormon Sources in the Special Collections of the University of Utah Library

Gregory C. Thompson and Margery W. Ward

The University of Utah Library, one of the foremost research centers in the intermountain area, supports teaching and research in fifteen academic colleges and schools that grant graduate degrees in ninety-three disciplines. Within this system is the library's Special Collections Department, which is divided into five divisions—the Middle East Library, Rare Books Division, University Archives and Records Management, Western Americana, and Manuscripts.

Beginnings

The library probably had its beginning in 1850, when the University of Deseret was founded, although specific information is not available. However, sources indicate that in 1850 Utah received a $5,000 congressional appropriation to establish a territorial library. John M. Bernhisel, Utah delegate to Congress, received the appointment to purchase the library's books.[1] This library continued to grow and followed the territorial and later the state government as it moved from the Council House to the city hall, then to the city and county building, and finally to the new state capitol in 1916. During this time, however, the library was divided. The law books were retained in the territorial (later the state) law library, and some twenty-five hundred of the remaining books were transferred to the University of Deseret in 1891. Many are still in the University of Utah Library. Several of these books are in Special Collections, as are other books that came to the library in 1894 as a gift from longtime university president John R. Park.

When the university moved to its present location in 1899, the Liberal Arts Building (now the John A. Widtsoe Building), one of the three buildings on campus, was a library. In 1913 the library moved to the new John R. Park (Administration) Building, where it remained until 1935, when the George Thomas Library was finished.

Early Utah Room Collections

In this building, the library experienced real growth, including the inauguration of the Utah Room in the 1940s to provide space for the collection of university president John A. Widtsoe. This collection, consisting primarily of Utah and Mormon items, moved the library into the areas of rare books and specialized collecting. A compilation of the collection by the Special Collection staff in 1972 lists thirty-six copies of the Book of Mormon—most first editions—including an 1830 first edition that may be the Joseph Smith autographed copy. The 1972 list also includes twenty-eight copies of the Doctrine and Covenants, but not the first version. That version, known as the Book of Commandments, was obtained in the early 1970s from the John Mills Whitaker family.

John Mills Whitaker, a son-in-law of John Taylor, the third president of the Church, served as a scribe to his father-in-law and as a contact man while President Taylor was on the underground during the antipolygamy crusade. Whitaker's original Pittman shorthand notebooks are included in the Whitaker Collection. Whitaker later transcribed his shorthand notes and his diaries. Since their publication, they have been cited by many scholars writing on this period of Utah and Mormon history. In checking Whitaker's account of an event, LaJean Purcell Carruth, an expert in Pittman shorthand, found that the shorthand notes varied considerably from the published version. With this evidence, Special Collections undertook to transcribe the shorthand notes, but the project was only partially completed when the shorthand expert moved from the area.

The library also acquired the Judge Tillman D. Johnson Collection of Western Americana, which included a great deal of Native American material. With this collection, the Utah Room began to collect Western Americana, but the emphasis was still on Utah and the Latter-day Saints.

Also, limited purchases were made from the Herbert Auerbach Collection. Among these were *The Frontier Guardian,* a newspaper edited by Orson Hyde,[2] *The Book of the Law of the Lord* by James J. Strang,[3] and the *Deseret Almanac* by W. W. Phelps.[4]

Ann Widtsoe Wallace, daughter of John A. Widtsoe, presided over the Utah Room until 1961. Her replacement, Ruth Yeaman, supervised the functions of the Utah Room and the Treasure Room through 1968, after the library moved to its present building. In 1967 the name of the department was changed from the Utah and Rare Books Department to Western Americana, Rare Books, and University Archives, a more accurate description of the department's activities.

The J. Willard Marriott Library. Courtesy Special Collections, University of Utah Library.

Although many Utah and Mormon items were lost to libraries and collectors outside Utah over the years, the university library fortunately was able to purchase some valuable materials, and loyal alumni either sold or donated books and papers to the library.

Manuscript Collections

In 1969, Dr. Everett L. Cooley became director of the department. The Middle East Library was added to the department, which now consisted of Western Americana, Rare Books, University Archives,

Records Management, and Manuscripts. The budget was increased and full-time staff members were hired for Records Management and Manuscripts. In 1971 the Annie Clark Tanner Room became a study area for the patrons of Western Americana. The Western Americana stacks were closed to patrons except for those who met the criteria for research access, and the books in Western Americana became noncirculating. At this time the name of the department was changed from Western Americana to Special Collections. A policy was established in the Manuscripts Division to collect papers from Utahns, about Utahns, or by Utahns who had been successful, even if their success has been achieved outside of Utah.

The Manuscripts Division currently contains over a thousand collections, and of these over a third include or primarily consist of Mormon or Mormon-related materials, including one-of-a-kind items. The majority of the collections contain only a few items, such as diaries, typescripts, photocopies of life sketches, and journals. Obviously, space limitations preclude listing all the collections, but the following alphabetized list shows the rich diversity of the materials available in the Manuscripts Division of Special Collections. The list contains collections of women, authors, ordinary individuals, both early and contemporary individuals who have held positions in The Church of Jesus Christ of Latter-day Saints, and others.

Bennion Family Papers: John (polygamist and sheepman, 1820–77), Heber (polygamist, livestockman, bishop, and legislator, 1858–1932), and Mary Bennion Powell (1890–): journals and other papers.

M. Lynn Bennion Collection: Lynn (superintendent of Salt Lake City schools) and his father, Milton (dean of the University of Utah College of Education and director of the LDS Church institute associated with the university): papers.

Benson Stake Tabernacle Papers: account of materials, labor, etc. The tabernacle was demolished in 1962.

Philip Blair (descendant of the Young and Thatcher families): correspondence, documents, and memorabilia describing the social, religious, economic, and political development of Utah. Personal correspondence of Brigham Young to his wife Mary Ann Angell and his sons, and business correspondence, appointments, invitations, and land deeds. Materials of the families of Luna Young and her husband George Thatcher of Logan (mayor and active churchman), Nettie May Thatcher and her husband George Elias Blair (unsuccessful theatrical producer and actor), and Virginia Blair (bit actress in Hollywood).

Fawn McKay Brodie (author of *No Man Knows My History: The Biography of Joseph Smith, the Mormon Prophet*[5]): papers concerning all her books. Some records related to *No Man Knows My History* but no research material on the book.

George Brooks: account of the construction and dedication of the Manti Temple.

Fred Buchanan: material by and about early Scottish Mormons.

Albert Carrington (territorial civic leader, editor of *Deseret News* and LDS Apostle): diaries from 1849 to 1886 (with gaps) and correspondence with family members.

Hiram B. Clawson (business agent for Brigham Young and manager of the Salt Lake Theatre): family documents from 1847 to 1899. An interesting picture of polygamy.

Rudger Clawson (LDS Apostle and European Mission president from 1910 to 1913): diaries from 1887 to 1905.

Michael Q. Crofts: interviews with Utah politicians and their perception of Mormon influence in or on political events.

Dialogue: A Journal of Mormon Thought: original manuscripts, critiques, office files, and correspondence.

E. E. Ericksen (University of Utah philosophy professor): research materials on various Mormon themes.

John Fitzgerald (Mormon dissident): research materials on the Latter-day Saint doctrine toward the blacks.

Feramorz Young Fox: family papers and research files on Mormon land use and the United Order.

Isaac Chauncy Haight (prominent southern Utah churchman involved in the Mountain Meadows Massacre): journal (no mention of the Mountain Meadows Massacre).

Mervin B. Hogan (retired University of Utah professor): material on the Mormons and Freemasons.

Lester Hubbard (folklorist): materials on early Mormon folklore.

Edward Hunter (member of the LDS Church hierarchy): religious and personal papers, some of which concern the Perpetual Emigration Fund.

J. E. Johnson (newspaperman, printer, and horticulturist): writings, diaries, correspondence, photographs, and memorabilia of Johnson, his three wives, his children, his friends, and his business associates.

Sonia Johnson (Mormon activist): materials on the Equal Rights Amendment (ERA) and Johnson's conflict with the LDS Church.

Charles Kelly (author): published and unpublished manuscripts with accompanying research materials on Mormon subjects and short stories written by Kelly for his contemporary book "Young Pioneers."

Frederick Kesler (churchman and millwright): diaries, journals, and correspondence on the early trials of Mormons in the East, the exodus west, all types of mill construction in Utah, and life as a pioneer and polygamist. Collection also contains an original manuscript page from the Book of Mormon.

Joseph C. Kingsbury (grandfather of a president of the University of Utah): journals and correspondence.

A. C. Lambert (educator): materials on the doctrinal development of certain aspects of the LDS religion.

John D. Lee (only man executed for the Mountain Meadows Massacre): typescript of his journal, 1841–51.

Sterling McMurrin (United States Commissioner of Education and retired University of Utah philosophy professor): records of his administration as Commissioner of Education and teaching and administrative positions he held at the University of Utah.

Madeline McQuown: research material on Brigham Young and other Mormon subjects done primarily by Dale L. Morgan.

Dale L. Morgan (historian): papers found in other collections such as those of Fawn Brodie, Madeline McQuown, Gerald Bleak, and Everett L. Cooley. Research material is contained in the Dale Morgan Collection at Bancroft Library, a microfilm of which is available in Special Collections.

Mormon Historians and Historiographers: small collections, usually covering only one particular subject, on, about, by, or collected by questioning or disaffected Mormons.

Mormon Settlements in Arizona: copies of account books, diaries, journals, autobiographies, biographies, correspondence, and histories covering the period from the earliest settlements of 1876 to 1974. Settlements represented are Joseph City, Maricopa, Moenkopi, St. John's, Snowflake, Sunset, Taylor, Tuba City, Winslow, Woodruff, Eastern Arizona and Snowflake stakes, and Little Colorado Stake.

Lowry Nelson (sociologist): research materials on or about Mormon subjects, including priesthood for the blacks.

Linda King Newell (author): research files for her book *Mormon Enigma: Emma Hale Smith, Prophet's Wife, "Elect Lady," Polygamy's Foe, 1804–1879.*[6]

Matthew and Clair Noall (educator and author, respectively): material on early Mormon activities, particularly those of Willard Richards (an ancestor of Clair Noall) about whom Clair wrote the book *Intimate Disciple: A Portrait of Willard Richards, Apostle to Joseph Smith, Cousin of Brigham Young.*[7]

George D. Pyper (actor and manager of Salt Lake Theatre): material on the early Salt Lake Theatre.

Alice Louise Reynolds Forum (Mormon women's group): records of women's group in the Provo, Utah, area formed to discuss various issues facing women in the Church during the 1970s.

B. H. Roberts (Mormon historian and theologian): personal and other papers. Of note are his files on his 1922 studies of the Book of Mormon.

Ellis Reynolds Shipp (early Mormon physician and polygamist wife of Milford Bard Shipp): material about and by her, including *The Autobiography and Diary of Ellis Reynolds Shipp, M.D.,*[8] compiled and edited by her daughter Ellis Shipp Musser.

Linda Sillitoe (author): material on the Equal Rights Amendment (ERA) and Sonia Johnson, Mormon dissident.

William H. Smart (stake president, Uintah Basin): records of his life and mission, 1898–1937.

George A. Smith Family: personal papers, correspondence, journals, family records, church records, and legal documents of George A. Smith (first counselor to Brigham Young), Elias Smith (president of high priests quorum in Salt Lake Stake and probate judge), John Henry Smith (Apostle), George Albert Smith (eighth president of The Church of Jesus Christ of Latter-day Saints), Lucy Emily Woodruff Smith (wife of George Albert Smith), and Emily Smith Stewart (daughter of George Albert and Lucy Emily Woodruff Smith).

Sunstone: office files, correspondence, and articles submitted for publication.

George S. Tanner (author): biographies, journals, and manuscripts about or by members of the John Tanner family, who were early converts to Mormonism and early pioneers in Utah and adjoining territories.

John Taylor Family (son of John Taylor, LDS Church president and apostle, excommunicated for the practice of plural marriage): materials on, by, and about John Taylor. Papers of his son Samuel W., author of *Family Kingdom, Nightfall at Nauvoo,* and *I Have Six Wives.*[9] Papers of his son Raymond W., author of *Uranium Fever.*[10] The brothers collaborated on a biography of their father titled *The John Taylor Papers: Records of the Last Utah Pioneer.*[11] Research materials on these books and other Mormon subjects are in the collection.

Paul Thatcher and Family (prominent family of Logan, Utah): records of the Thatcher and Smoot families of Provo, Utah, and material about and by Mormon women in the nineteenth century.

Utah Humanities Research Foundation: cultural materials collected and preserved in Utah and neighboring regions. Materials include diaries, biographies, autobiographies, histories, poetry, music, folklore, correspondence, and printed material. Also records, correspondence, and articles of *The Utah Humanities Review,* later *The Western Humanities Review.*

Helen Clawson Wells (descendant of Young and Clawson families): records of this socially prominent Mormon woman and her mother, Clara Clawson, and early Brigham Young family material.

Western Americana Collections

The boundaries for collecting Western Americana publications are not as confining as those established for collecting manuscripts. The Western Americana division collects all types of printed materials on the eight intermountain states—Utah, Idaho, Wyoming, Montana, Colorado, Nevada, Arizona, and New Mexico. The greatest emphasis is given to Utah and the Mormons. At times these boundaries were expanded—for example, in regard to overland travel, Native Americans, or irrigation. A good deal of Western Americana's collecting activities have been focused on items listed in Wagner-Camp,[12] and a fair number of these deal with Mormons and Mormonism, such as publications on overland travel.

The library has not attempted to collect all materials published by the LDS Church because these items can be found in those institutions connected with the Church. However, the works by authors dealing with Mormon subjects, both fiction and historical, have been collected. These include Wallace Stegner, Paul Bailey, Charles Kelly, Dale Morgan, Samuel Taylor, Zane Grey, William Mulder, and Juanita Brooks. In many cases, the private papers of these individuals are also held.

Efforts have been made to collect local community histories. Other aids of unique value are the Newspaper Clip File and Vertical File, which contain information on countless Mormon subjects. These files are constantly expanded and updated.

The Everett L. Cooley Oral History Program is collecting interviews of individuals concerned with many facets of Utah's history. Most of the histories are connected with the LDS Church in some way. For example, the administrators and staff of the Church-owned radio station (KSL) and television station (KSL-TV) have been interviewed by individuals collecting information on broadcasting. Others have been interviewed about their perception of LDS Church influence on politics, education, and other facets of Utah life.

Space limitations preclude a detailed list of materials and publications on Mormons and Mormonism. Special Collections in the University of Utah Library has registers and additional finding aids to help researchers. In addition, there is a photograph section to supplement the written materials. Hours vary because of the time school is in session. Researchers are advised to check the schedule prior to visiting the area. The address is Special Collections, Marriott Library, University of Utah, Salt Lake City, Utah 84112. The general library phone number is (801) 581-6273.

Gregory C. Thompson is Assistant Director of Special Collections, University of Utah Library. Margery W. Ward is General Editor of the series Utah, the Mormons, and the West. The authors thank the following individuals who have been of inestimable help in preparing this article: Dr. Everett L. Cooley, author of "History of Special Collections, University of Utah," 1986; Ruth Yeaman, Rare Books Librarian; and Nancy Young, Manuscripts Librarian; and Young's staff.

NOTES

[1]Everett L. Cooley, "History of Special Collections, University of Utah Library" (Enlarged version of an address given to the Utah Library Association, Park City, Utah, April 9, 1986).

[2]Published in Kanesville, Iowa.

[3]James J. Strang, *The Book of the Law of the Lord: Consisting of an Inspired Translation of Some of the Most Important Parts of the Law Given to Moses, and Very Few Additional Commandments, with Notes and References* (Saint James, A.R.I.: Royal Press, 1852).

[4]W. W. Phelps, *Deseret Almanac* (Great Salt Lake City, Utah Territory: W. Richards, 1852).

[5]Fawn M. Brodie, *No Man Knows My History: The Biography of Joseph Smith, the Mormon Prophet* (New York: Alfred A. Knopf, 1945).

[6]Linda King Newell and Valeen Tippetts Avery, *Mormon Enigma: Emma Hale Smith, Prophet's Wife, "Elect Lady," Polygamy's Foe, 1804-1879* (New York: Doubleday, 1984).

[7]Clair Noall, *Intimate Disciple: A Portrait of Willard Richards, Apostle to Joseph Smith, Cousin of Brigham Young* (Salt Lake City: University of Utah Press, 1957).

[8]Ellis Shipp Musser, ed., *The Autobiography and Diary of Ellis Reynolds Shipp, M.D.* (Salt Lake City: Deseret News Press, 1962).

[9]Samuel W. Taylor, *Family Kingdom* (London: Stoughton, 1951); Taylor, *Nightfall at Nauvoo* (New York: Macmillan, 1971); Taylor, *I Have Six Wives* (New York: Greenbay, 1956).

[10]Raymond W. Taylor, *Uranium Fever: Or, No Talk under $1 Million* (New York: Macmillan, 1970).

[11]Samuel W. Taylor and Raymond W. Taylor, *The John Taylor Papers: Records of the Last Utah Pioneer* (Redwood City, Calif.: Taylor Trust, 1984).

[12]Henry R. Wagner and Charles L. Camp, *The Plains and the Rockies: A Critical Bibliography of Exploration, Adventure and Travel in the American West, 1800-1865,* ed. Robert H. Becker, 4th ed., rev. and enl. (San Francisco: John Howell-Books, 1982).

Utah State Archives, Archives Building, Salt Lake City, Utah. Courtesy Utah State Archives.

Introduction to the Utah State Archives and Record Services

Jeffery Ogden Johnson

Beginnings

The Utah State Archives was created to help state agencies and local governments manage their records as well as to care for government documents with historical value. The archives holds records from Utah's earliest territorial days to current records created by modern government agencies. Both state and local government records, along with records of special districts, are stored in the state archives. While the care of public records was an issue during Utah's territorial and early statehood period, it was not until 1917 that an official agency was created to collect those records.

In 1917 the Utah Legislature passed a law that recognized the Historical Society of Utah as a state institution. The law stated that the society "is hereby made custodian of all records, documents, relics and other material of historic value, which are now or hereafter may be in charge of any State, county, or other official." This law allowed the society to take into its custody state government records, including records of local governments.[1] However, because of a small budget and staff, the depositing of public records was haphazard during this period.

The Historical Records Survey

In March 1936, the Historical Records Survey, a nationwide undertaking, was initiated in Utah as part of the Federal Writers' Project of the Works Progress Administration. The survey was undertaken to provide useful employment to needy, unemployed historians, lawyers, teachers, researchers, and clerical workers, with the object of surveying and publishing inventories of the records of federal, state, county, city, or other governmental units. This survey stimulated interest in Utah's governmental records.

In 1939 the survey came under the sponsorship of the Utah State Historical Society. At that time, the survey had several very capable directors, including Utah historian Dale L. Morgan.[2] The information about most of the counties and some of the cities was published by the survey in several inventories. The survey closed down early in 1943, and the files, including unfinished and unpublished drafts of inventories, were turned over to the society.[3]

The Office of State Archivist

While working with the survey, William R. Palmer realized a need to collect and care for the records of local governmental units. As a member of the Board of State History, he expressed this need in the meeting of that board on April 3, 1937: "They need safety, if we are ready for them."[4] Ten years later the board acted and appointed Palmer to serve as state archivist.

In June 1947, Palmer began his official activities. He spent a year visiting ten counties in southern Utah, copying some records, and beginning a microfilming program, but his activity was halted on the advice of Utah's attorney general, who recommended that legislation be obtained to clarify the society's authority. In a bill passed by the legislature on March 3, 1951, the State Board of History was directed to appoint a state archivist, who would be legal custodian of the official records of the state and local government agencies, but once again Palmer was stymied: there were no funds to hire him. Joel E. Ricks, president of the historical society, explained in a report sent to Governor J. Bracken Lee, "Several state and county agencies have already approached the Historical Society looking toward the implementation of this bill, but hampered by insufficient funds and inadequate quarters, the society has been unable to carry forward its archival program."[5] Finally, in 1954, the historical society obtained enough money to hire Everett L. Cooley as the first official state archivist. During the next few years Cooley devised a master plan for the archives, obtained further clarifying legislation from the 1957 legislature, and engaged a small staff of assistants.

The transfer of the military records section from the National Guard in 1957 increased the responsibilities of the archives division of the society, but the continued lack of personnel and a shortage of storage space dictated a low-key program. The records were being stored in the basement of the Thomas Kearns mansion, where the historical society was housed. The archives staff planned to build an archives building on the grounds of the mansion but postponed the idea when Cooley resigned as state archivist in 1960 to accept a teaching position at Utah State University. In 1961, however, Cooley returned as director of the society, and he appointed T. Harold Jacobsen to be state archivist in 1963. The position had been vacant since Cooley's resignation in 1960. Jacobsen had served as director of the microfilm and records divisions of The Church of Jesus Christ of Latter-day Saints' Genealogical Society and had authored several articles and books on microfilming public records. He assumed his new position upon completion of a specialized study in archives administration at the National Archives in Washington, D.C.[6] Jacobsen was designated state records administrator within the historical society. That same year, a new state records management act was passed.

The Utah State Archives

In 1966, Governor Calvin L. Rampton commissioned a study of the organization of state government. This commission was soon called the Little Hoover Commission after the earlier commission headed by former President Hebert Hoover that looked at the organization of the federal government. The commission proposed the consolidation and coordination of several functions of state government and recommended that the archives program be moved from the historical society into a department for general services. Later, in 1969, the archives became a part of the Department of Finance.[7]

File cabinets at the Utah State Archives hold many territorial, state, and county records. Courtesy Utah State Archives.

While in the Department of Finance, the archives developed a strong microfilming program and extended its records management activities. The Information Practices Act Administration was transferred to the archives in 1979. In 1981 the Legislature approved the establishment of the Department of Administrative Services, with the archives as a division.[8] The archives, having run out of room in the basement of the state capitol, moved some its records to a warehouse in the Decker Lake area in Salt Lake City. In 1983, Liisa Fagerlund was appointed as state archivist. Under Fagerlund's supervision, a new direction of archival activity begin in state government. Records analysts were hired to teach records management and work with agencies to schedule and transfer records to the archives. An expanded records center for temporary records was created, as well as an expanded cataloging effort for historical records. The archives offices were moved out of the basement of the state capitol into a former agriculture building on Capitol Hill. The new Archives Building had room for an expanded public research room.[9]

Present-Day Services

Today the staff of the state archives works with records officers in each state and local government agency to assure correct management and preservation. Schedules are created to facilitate the orderly transfer to the archives of those records which have long-term value. The schedules take into consideration the administrative, fiscal, legal, and historical value of the records. The staff also prepares general schedules which cover records created by both state and local governments and can be used for the retention and disposal of commonly held records. Before these schedules come into force they are approved by the State Records Committee, composed of the director of the Division of State History, the state auditor, a citizen member, the governor or the governor's designee, a records manager from the private sector, an elected official representing political subdivisions, and an individual representing the news media. The committee meets quarterly to consider these schedules.

The state archives also runs a record center which provides low-cost storage for those records that have not met their schedules. After these schedules are met, the Records Services Section will destroy the records or transfer those that have historical value to archival storage. The state archives oversees the microfilming of all government agency records. Records that are old and fragile are microfilmed at the archives, but other records are often filmed by the agency that holds them. The film is processed by the archives so that the quality and the processing standards will remain high. Master films are stored by the archives in special environmentally controlled vaults.

Professional archivists arrange and catalog records which have high research value and descriptions of these records are entered into the Research Library Information Network, a national database that can be accessed in research libraries all over North America. The archives research center is used by scholars, family historians, genealogists, local historians, and government agency employees to access records held by the archives. Staff members answer mail and phone requests for information concerning these records.

Holdings

The state archives holds some very interesting and important records from the nineteenth century. The records of the territorial secretary begin in November 1850 and end in 1896 when Utah became a state. These records were transferred from the Secretary of State's office in 1957. This series documents the supervision of the militia, appointment of officials, regulation of the court system, pardoning and extradition of criminals, supervision of Indian affairs, regulation of liquor, and the supervision of the executive departments of the territorial government. The archives also holds election papers from 1851, including reports from local election officials that document the election process.

The records of the state auditor start in 1852 and continue through the territorial period. The auditor was responsible for the fiscal concerns of the territory and examining county collection and remittance of taxes and their disbursement. These activities are documented with correspondence, reports, accounts, warrants, and receipts.

The prison commitment registers contain admission data for men and women who were committed to the prison after 1875. Data include basic social information about the prisoners; additionally, the registers contain photographs after 1889. These records, along with the territorial court records, record the interesting story of crime in Utah.

Records of the territorial legislature include the council journals from 1858 to 1882, house journals from 1858 to 1878, and legislative laws from 1851.

The Utah Commission was created in 1882 under the Edmunds Law, an act by the United States Congress to punish polygamy in the Utah Territory. Disqualifying polygamists from voting and from holding office were among the penalties of the law. This commission took charge of Utah's elections; their records include election registers, accounts, letterbooks, and minute books from 1882 to 1896. Also included are records of the Women's Christian Industrial Home Association, which the commission created to help polygamous wives leave their husbands.

In July 1894, Congress enacted a law to enable the Territory of Utah to be admitted into the Union as a state. The act spelled out the calling of a convention to meet beginning in March 1895 to draw up a state constitution. The archives contains records of that convention, including transcripts, published and unpublished, of the proceedings; files of proposals, petitions, and other recommendations for inclusion in the state constitution; and a limited number of committee reports, minutes, and notes.

After statehood, the records of state agencies document changes dealing with the modernization of Utah. For example, the Secretary of State records include motor vehicle registers from 1909 to 1919 which list each automobile registered with the state. Information concerning the state's early health programs are included in the Health Department records. Records of the Utah Arts Council, which was the nation's first state-funded arts program, are also in the archives. The National Guard records, among others, document the state's reaction to the Carbon County coal strikes of 1903 and 1909.

One of the most interesting modern record collections is that of the MX Coordination Office, which lasted from 1979 to 1981. These records detail the office's effort to keep abreast of the developments relating to the federal placing of the MX missiles in Utah. The agency vigorously pursued its main function, which was to provide state-level coordination and planning with respect to possible community impacts of the MX program.

The state archives also holds records created by local governments, including town council minutes for many rural communities. For example, the archives has the city council minutes of Corrine, the center of non-Mormon Utah in the 1870s, from 1870 to 1938. The most complete record for a local government are the minutes of the Salt Lake County Commission from 1852. The commission controlled timber and water privileges and granted mill sites. It created election precincts, road districts, and school districts, and appointed superintendents of such districts. It also provided for the maintenance of the poor, mentally disabled, and orphaned, and levied property taxes. All these activities are noted in the minutes. Information concerning the laying out of roads and irrigation canals is also included.

District court records, from 1852, document the daily court proceedings of the territory. Cases include murder, larceny, robbery, burglary, theft, embezzlement, assault, riot, polygamy, gambling, liquor law violations, prostitution, and other crimes. Also included are cases involving property claims, debt, repossession, foreclosure, receivership, dissolution of corporations, divorces, and commitments to reform school. Most are exercises of original jurisdiction but do include appeals from probate, county, and justice of the peace courts. Notable cases include the divorce and alimony case between Ann Eliza Webb and Brigham Young, spanning several years in the mid-1870s, and several cases revolving around the settlement of Brigham Young's will from 1879 to 1883. Bigamy, polygamy, and cohabitation cases peak after 1874 and particularly in the mid- to late 1880s. Mining claim disputes are common in the 1870s and 1880s, as are land disputes with the railroads to the end of the territorial period. These records also contains certificates of citizenship, declarations of intention, and naturalization papers from 1869 which document the movement of immigrants into American society.

The state archives holds the records of the state's governors, many of which are fascinating. For example, the archives holds the records of Governor William Spry relating to the Joe Hill case. Joe Hill was an important labor leader who was convicted of murder and executed in Utah on November 19, 1915. These records include the letters and petitions Spry received from all over the world asking for a pardon for Hill.

The foregoing has presented only a sample of the rich and interesting records held by the state archives. These records are vital to understanding Mormonism because much of Mormonism's history in the nineteenth century and early twentieth century is intertwined with Utah's history. Utah's political history affected policies and actions of the Church, while the drive for Utah's statehood changed Mormonism's plural marriage system. For these reasons, Utah's governmental records are important to understanding the relationships between Utah's Mormon and non-Mormon communities.

The Utah State Archives and Records Service is located in the Archives Building near the Utah State Capital. The address is Archives Building, State Capitol, Salt Lake City, Utah 84114. The telephone number is (801) 538-3013 and the FAX number is (801) 538-3354. The Research Center is open 8:00 A.M. to 4:30 P.M., Monday through Friday. It is closed on state holidays.

Jeffery Ogden Johnson is State Archivist at the Utah State Archives.

NOTES

[1]*Compiled Laws of Utah,* title 100, ch. 8 (1917).

[2]Charles S. Peterson, "Dale Morgan, Writer's Project, and Mormon History as a Regional Study," *Dialogue* 24 (Summer 1991): 47-64; and Juanita Brooks, "Just a Copyin'—Word F'r Word," *Utah Historical Quarterly* 37 (Fall 1969): 396-408.

[3]The files are at the Utah State Historical Society, Salt Lake City, Utah.

[4]Utah State Historical Society, "Minutes" (April 3, 1937): 4.

[5]Joel E. Ricks to the Honorable J. Bracken Lee, published in *Utah Public Documents,* 1952.

[6]"State Chooses Archivist after 3 Years," *Salt Lake Tribune,* June 29, 1963.

[7]*Utah Code,* title 63, ch. 2 (1969). For a brief summary of the major record groups in the Utah State Archives in 1972, see T. Harold Jacobson "The Utah State Archives," *Genealogical Journal* 1 (June 1972): 31-34.

[8]*Utah Code,* title 63, ch. 2 (1981).

[9]Liisa Fagerlund, Oral History, 1987, Utah State Archives, Salt Lake City.

Mormon Manuscripts at the Utah State Historical Society

Gary Topping

In comparison with sister institutions in other states, the Utah State Historical Society, located in Salt Lake City, is in some ways uniquely fortunate. For one thing, the existence a few blocks away of the remarkable Family History Library, the greatest genealogical collection in the world, absolves the society from needing to provide services to genealogists, who comprise one of the largest blocks of patrons for most state historical societies. The society, of course, welcomes genealogists, but maintaining large name indexes and collections of primarily genealogical value has never been a central part of its operation.

Likewise, the society has never felt the necessity of collecting material primarily documenting the activities of The Church of Jesus Christ of Latter-day Saints, even though a very large portion of Utah history has also been Mormon history. The excellent archival and manuscript holdings at the library and archives of the Church and at Brigham Young University have largely preempted the need for other institutions to collect Church records. Thus, with three other institutions doing what would otherwise be the society's job, the society has felt largely free to focus on collecting the rest of Utah history.

Of course things are by no means that simple and clear-cut. Genealogists and family historians, who tend to be tenacious researchers, may spend most of their time at the Family History Library but certainly do not neglect the society, and in fact they account for a large percentage of our patrons. Similarly, it is impossible to identify a Utah history that is completely divorced from Mormon history except in very limited aspects; thus, in its mission to collect the history of the state, the society inevitably collects substantial amounts of Mormon history as well.

The Society's Early History

The society began to seriously collect manuscripts only recently. Founded in 1897 in a burst of pride spilling over from the recent achievement of statehood and the fiftieth anniversary of the arrival of the Mormon pioneers, the Utah State Historical Society quickly diminished to little more than a paper organization for many years. Though an annual meeting was held, the society's program consisted of little else; and the amount of serious Utah history the society collected, published, and otherwise promoted was minimal. Inauguration of the *Utah Historical Quarterly* in 1928 was a major step in the society's development because the *Quarterly* required a consistent budget, a staff, an office (a modest two-room suite in the basement of the state capitol building), and—most germane to the subject of this article—a rudimentary library.[1]

In the beginning, the library contained no manuscripts; it was a modest reference collection devoted as much to general Western history as to the history of Utah (the literature of Utah history at that time was nearly nonexistent). The first manuscripts that the society obtained were the records of the Historical Records Survey and the Writers Project of the Works Progress Administration (WPA), donated when the New Deal agency was disbanded in 1942. The pioneer diaries, autobiographies, and questionnaires collected by the WPA were individually cataloged for public use, and other collections soon followed. Acquisition during the 1950s of what was then regarded as capacious quarters in the Kearns mansion on South Temple Street encouraged further manuscript collecting. Since that time, largely through the efforts of staff members such as John James, Everett Cooley, and Jay Haymond, the society's holdings in manuscripts and photographs have grown to occupy several thousand linear feet.

It is difficult to draw a defensible line between the "Mormon" portion of the society's holdings and the "non-Mormon" portion, so extensively have the two been interrelated. The Mormon religion's pragmatic application of religious ideas further compounds the problem. When one finds the minutes of the Manti Ward in 1855 primarily devoted to a discussion of irrigation problems, is that a religious or a secular record? My principle of selection in this essay—which may be inconsistently applied in certain cases and which I do not expect to be universally approved—leans toward records of Mormons acting in behalf of the Church or interpreting Mormon history and culture. The simple fact that the creator of a collection of papers was or was not a Mormon is not enough to justify inclusion or exclusion; the documentation of the history of the LDS Church is the criterion.

In a description of the Mormon manuscripts at the society, it seems appropriate to begin where the collection itself began: with the records collected by the WPA. The Historical Records Survey (HRS), among other things, attempted to borrow diaries and autobiographies bearing upon Utah history for the purpose of preparing typescript copies. The originals were in most cases then returned to the donor, though some have since found their way into various repositories. Also, HRS staff members interviewed many pioneers by means of a procrustean questionnaire that often either delights or frustrates modern researchers. Few interviewers were flexible and imaginative enough to probe for elaboration of cryptic answers or to supplement the questionnaire with queries of their own in following up on unforeseen answers. The questionnaire was actually quite good, given the assumption that one list of questions could serve all cases, but untrained interviewers too often had such a literal conception of their responsibility that the questionnaires often serve the historian's needs poorly.

In cavalier, but perhaps defensible, disregard for archival procedures, the catalogers of the WPA collection separated it and cataloged each diary, each autobiography, and each interview, with few exceptions, as a separate collection, though fortunately they kept a note on the card indicating its provenance within the WPA records. Thus the collection is easy to use, as each manuscript has its own cataloging apparatus and a researcher does not need to cope with a lengthy register in order to find a single item. (There is a WPA Register, but it covers the remainder of the collection, primarily the inventories of county archives and the Writers Project; the "Mormon" material is largely cataloged individually.)[2]

Current site of Utah State Historical Society, 300 Rio Grande, Salt Lake City, Utah. Built in 1910, this structure was the Denver and Rio Grande Railroad Depot. Courtesy Division of State History, Utah State Historical Society.

Manuscript Collections

Among its major manuscript collections, the society has personal papers of several General Authorities of The Church of Jesus Christ of Latter-day Saints, including John A. Widtsoe, John T. Caine, Anthony W. Ivins, Charles W. Penrose, and Erastus Snow. In richness of historical detail and variety of material, the best of those collections are probably the Widtsoe and Ivins papers.

Widtsoe Papers. John A. Widtsoe (1872–1965) was a many-faceted man: an agricultural scientist and chemist of national reputation, president of both Utah State University and the University of Utah, and an Apostle of the LDS Church. The Widtsoe papers held by the society concentrate heavily on his activities in the latter capacity. Of the six boxes (three linear feet) of his personal papers, two contain biographical material and correspondence, while the rest are devoted to manuscripts, lecture notes, and other papers bearing on Mormon history and doctrine.

Ivins Papers. Anthony W. Ivins (1852–1934) was an important figure in the colonization of St. George, a prosperous cattleman on the Arizona Strip, and leader of the Mormon colonists in Mexico. Most research to date in the Ivins collection has slighted the first two enterprises in favor of the third, and the collection is, to be sure, a major source on the Mexican colonies and Mormon plural marriage, both before and after the Manifesto. One might hope, though, that future researchers would direct their attention to the other, relatively untapped, riches of this collection.

The Ivins collection, which comprises eighteen boxes in extent (nine linear feet), includes his diaries and journals for the years 1875 to 1932 filling six of the boxes. The diaries are the daily record of Ivins's life, and their entries naturally vary in extent and depth. The journals are a more polished autobiographical account based on the diaries and cover the years 1852–1900. There are also more than two boxes of correspondence which supplement the diaries.

Charles W. Penrose Papers. The other General Authorities' papers in the society's holdings are less extensive and offer perhaps less general research appeal than those of Widtsoe and Ivins. A possible exception is the papers of Charles W. Penrose (1832–1925), which consist of diaries covering the period 1854 to 1911. (Through the kindness of the Church Historical Department, a Penrose diary in their possession was microfilmed with the society's diaries, thus making all extant Penrose diaries available at both institutions.) Although William C. Seifrit has published those Penrose diaries recounting a secret mission to bribe Utah's way into the Union in 1885,[3] the remainder of Penrose's life—his missions to England and Europe, his career as editor of the *Millennial Star* and *Deseret News,* and his activities as an Apostle—remains largely unknown. Since Penrose was a man of considerable culture and a figure of importance at the highest level of the Church during a critical period in its history, this omission is regrettable.

Erastus Snow and John T. Caine Letters. The several dozen Erastus Snow letters in the society's possession are primarily addressed to his wife Elizabeth R. Ashby during the period 1851 to 1887, though the collection also contains correspondence with Brigham Young, Anthony W. Ivins, and others. The letters, of considerable importance, are well known to scholars through various sources, especially Andrew Karl Larson's exhaustive biography.[4] The John T. Caine papers consist only of some twenty letters and various publications and ephemera, much of which document his terms in Congress (1882–93) and efforts to obtain statehood for Utah.

The society also holds the papers of several people who might be called the "foot soldiers of Zion"—that multitude of everyday Church members whose participation, prayers, and tithing make the Church work at the grassroots level. Among those that one could include are Hosea Stout, Elias Hicks Blackburn, and Volney King. These are all primarily collections of daily diaries created in fortunate obedience to the Church's desire that all members should keep such a record. They are often illiterate, sometimes humorous, and frequently insignificant, but at their best they give intimate views of the daily, mundane creation of Zion and the little tragedies and glories that accompany such an ambitious enterprise.

Hosea Stout Diaries. The Stout diaries are one of the inescapable foundations of Mormon history during the Nauvoo and pioneer Utah periods. As one of Joseph Smith's, and later Brigham Young's, strong-arm men, Stout was an intimate associate of these and other leaders of the Church. He saw much and recorded much, not all of which vindicates the sunny vision of official Mormon historiography. Vitally important as those diaries are, though, they are probably of little use in their original form after the appearance of Juanita Brooks's two-volume published version, truly one of the monuments of Mormon scholarship.[5]

Elias Hicks Blackburn and Volney King Diaries. The diaries of Blackburn, an early bishop in Provo, and of Volney King, who founded the United Order settlement of Kingston, are of a different order of importance, since they document few of the events that concerned Stout in the power center of Mormondom and focus instead on the daily tribulations of making Mormon principles work in the hinterland. Here, instead, are the skirmishes with the natives, the capricious weather, the perceived insensitivity of remote Church leadership, and the occasional gaps between Mormon ideals and frontier realities that characterized life in rural Utah for the vast majority. We turn to Penrose for accounts of performances of prominent players at the Salt Lake Theater; in Volney King we read how, late in life and suffering from failing eyesight, he mistakenly hoed up his newly germinated cucumbers instead of the weeds he thought he was getting. Mormon historians have been criticized for being too enamored with the supposed uniqueness of their overall story and thus neglecting comparative approaches on a more fundamental level that could pay large dividends in broadened insights. Whatever the merits of that criticism, such studies based on the writings of "common folk" Mormons, have a great deal to offer.

Musser Family Collection. Closed until 1993, the papers of various Musser family members have not been exploited by Mormon historians. Approximately nineteen linear feet in extent, the collection's primary value is its focus on post-Manifesto polygamy through the papers of Saint Joseph White Musser and his wife Ellis Shipp Musser. A register and microform edition are being prepared at this writing.

Women's Studies. In the currently popular area of women's studies, Utah historiography is much more up to date than in other fields. In support of that new historiography, several institutions in the state, including the Utah State Historical Society, have identified women's history as a major collecting area. In 1985 the society published Linda Thatcher's "Guide to the Women's History Holdings at the Utah State Historical Society Library," a seventy-five-page annotated listing of all unpublished material on women. Although now scheduled for major revision, a limited quantity of the first edition is still available free of charge from Ms. Thatcher.

Leah Dunford Widtsoe Papers. Mormon women are, of course, prominent among those whose papers are included in the collection. One might begin with the papers of Leah Dunford Widtsoe, a daughter of Susa Young Gates and wife of John A. Widtsoe. Like her mother, Leah Widtsoe was an aggressive advocate of women's rights and an author of various publications on issues of interest and importance to women, including health and nutrition and the role of women in the LDS Church.

Susa Young Gates Papers and Emma Lucy Gates Bowen Papers. Considered together, the papers of Susa Young Gates and those of her daughter, opera singer Emma Lucy Gates Bowen, constitute an important body of source material for Mormon women. It is difficult to describe briefly the career and influence of Susa Young Gates

(1856–1933) because her importance as a role model and activist for Mormon women's interests went far beyond the mere list of her accomplishments as writer, editor, lecturer, and suffragist. Her status as a daughter of Brigham Young was clearly no hindrance to her rise to prominence, but her imposing personal presence and persuasive prose would likely have brought her to public attention in any event.

The Susa Young Gates papers cover eleven linear feet and include a wide variety of material. While each researcher will discover his or her own treasures in the collection, perhaps the items of greatest general interest are early drafts of two book-length histories: her biography of her father, and her history of Utah women. While the former was published in an edited (some would say bowdlerized) version by her daughter Leah, the early drafts include details about her father and his family that do not appear in the book and are well worth examining as firsthand recollections of Brigham Young.[6] Her history of women was never published as a whole and unfortunately has been lightly utilized by historians. Though it is in rough literary condition, it contains much detail on individual women, now almost forgotten by history, and themes of considerable interest.

The papers of Emma Lucy Gates Bowen (1880–1951) are of much less general interest, but they are important as documentation of music history and musical culture within the LDS Church. Trained as a child in piano performance, Bowen as a youth decided later to devote her major efforts to voice training and became a locally important singer and eventually a figure of some national importance as well. Her papers consist largely of concert programs and clippings regarding her career.

Ellis Reynolds Shipp Papers. The papers of Dr. Ellis Reynolds Shipp (1847–1939) are one of the society's best known and most frequently used collections. As one of Utah's first women physicians and a plural wife, her career holds a great deal of human interest—an interest solidly sustained by her articulate pen, from which we have one of Utah's autobiographical classics.[7] Her papers cover over five linear feet and contain a great deal of information on medicine, polygamy, and related subjects, as well as a considerable amount of poetry.

Oral History Collections. Two large oral history collections bring the story of women in Utah into modern times and document much of the newly found freedom and turmoil of the 1960s and 1970s. These collections are interviews done by JoAnn Freed in connection with the 1977 International Women's Year conference in Salt Lake City and by Marilyn Warenski on the status of women in Mormon culture in connection with her book *Patriarchs and Politics.*[8] One of the main sources of interest in the Warenski interviews is the fact that many of them were done after the appearance of her book and thus contain information on her theme that has not been previously published.

Utah Historiography

Juanita Brooks Papers. Utah historiography has long been a major collecting area of the society, and the papers of several Utah historians are among the society's finest collections. The papers of Juanita Brooks, for example, which comprise almost thirty linear feet, document every conceivable aspect of the personal and professional life of the woman who became in some ways Utah's finest historian. Born in 1898 in exceedingly modest circumstances in Bunkerville, Nevada, possessed of limited formal education, widowed at an early age, and forced to write history under some of the most discouraging conditions, Juanita Brooks nevertheless produced many fine articles, reviews, and several large and impressively researched volumes of Utah history that have attained the status of classics.[9] Although Levi S. Peterson has completed an exhaustive biography based on them,[10] the papers of Juanita Brooks will remain an immense gold mine for historians of this state—particularly those interested in southwestern Utah, the Muddy Mission, and the Arizona Strip—for generations to come. In addition to extensive diaries and correspondence that give an intimate glimpse of the unfolding of her intellectual and professional life, her papers contain copious unused research notes, biographical sketches of pioneers, unpublished essays on a wide variety of historical topics, and copies of primary sources. Although Brooks is best known for her studies of colorful and controversial topics such as John D. Lee and the Mountain Meadows Massacre, her papers exhibit a much broader interest in all aspects of southern Utah history, including the most mundane and inconspicuous.

Andrew Karl Larson Papers. Some of the same ground is covered by the papers of Andrew Karl Larson (1899–1983), Brooks's St. George neighbor, friend, and colleague. The seven linear feet of Larson's papers contain research notes and correspondence relating to his books on the history of Utah's Dixie and his long career as a professor at Dixie College. Larson himself was a figure of considerable importance in the cultural life of southern Utah, not only as a historian and teacher but also as a musician and poet.[11] His papers contain information on all these aspects of his life.

Stanley S. Ivins Correspondence Files. Stanley S. Ivins (1891–1967), a son of Anthony W. Ivins and donor of his father's papers to the society, was one of Utah's least-known historians, but among his fellow scholars he was known as one of the most tireless and careful researchers in his chosen field of the history of Mormon polygamy. Ivins's reputation was limited by the unfortunate fact that he published very little.[12] Possessed of a comfortable living through the Ivins Investment Company, Ivins, a lifelong bachelor, devoted his time and resources to historical research, compiling an impressive library and file of research notes. His friendship with Juanita Brooks, Dale Morgan, and staff members of the Utah State Historical Society is exhibited in correspondence files regarding matters of mutual historical interest, but the main interest in the eight linear feet of his papers is his research notes, his transcripts of newspaper articles of historical interest, and his unpublished essays on polygamy, Utah political history, and other topics.

Samuel W. Taylor Collection and Paul Bailey Collection. Juanita Brooks and Stanley Ivins are only two of many examples of scholars lacking professional degrees in history who have contributed outstanding riches to Utah and Mormon historiography. In compiling such a list, one would need to mention the names of two popular writers, Samuel W. Taylor and Paul Bailey, whose many works of fiction and nonfiction include substantial contributions to the literature. The papers of both writers are at the Utah State Historical Society. The Taylor collection is some nineteen linear feet in extent and includes extensive correspondence; research notes; manuscripts of stories, plays, and other works; and, most germane to this article, copies of primary sources of Mormon history, including the correspondence of President John Taylor as transcribed by Raymond Taylor. The Bailey collection of over sixteen linear feet consists primarily of correspondence and drafts of manuscripts. The correspondence and an unpublished autobiography go far toward documenting the struggles of a creative mind attempting to make a successful writing career based on his attempts at an honest appraisal of Mormon history in the face of unsympathetic Mormon readers and critics.

LeRoy Hafen Papers. Papers of academic historians of Mormonism are also found in the society's collection. The papers of LeRoy Hafen, for example, constitute a large supplement to the Hafen material at Brigham Young University. Mostly correspondence, the ten linear feet of Hafen papers include early personal letters during his student years, an extensive file of correspondence with his publisher Arthur H. Clark, and many financial records.

David E. Miller Papers. The seventeen linear feet of papers of David E. Miller, who spent his professional career at the University of Utah, document a number of important episodes in Mormon history.

Miller's interests embraced a number of historical fields, including the fur trade, Western trails, the Great Salt Lake, and several Mormon subjects. Among his Mormon interests were the Hole-in-the-Rock mission of (1879–80) and the Nauvoo period of Mormon history. His book on the Hole-in-the-Rock expedition is a standard work of Utah and Mormon history,[13] and his papers include research notes and early drafts of that manuscript. Miller also contracted with Nauvoo Restoration to prepare a thorough history of the Latter-day Saints at Nauvoo, and his notes and a copy of that report are in the collection. Miller's writing and teaching featured a strong geographic emphasis; he thought it important to retrace trails and examine historic sites for physical evidence that would help interpret the written record. Thus it is not surprising that his papers include a large collection of black-and-white photographs and color slides that effectively supplement his written narratives.

Mormon History Association Collection and Association for Mormon Letters Collection. The society also has the archives of two Mormon associations of likely interest to readers of this article. The first is the Mormon History Association, whose records at this writing measure seven linear feet in extent and date from 1965. It is an ongoing collection, the completeness of which at any given time is dependent upon submissions from outgoing officers of records of their tenure. Likewise, processing of the records is always incomplete, and researchers are warned to be patient. The other Mormon organization is the Association for Mormon Letters, whose records were recently donated by Lavina Fielding Anderson. Formed to encourage both creative writing on Mormon themes and dialogue among those engaged in such writing, the association has existed since 1975. The society's records extend to 1983 and fill one-half linear foot.

Guide to Archives and Manuscript Collections in Selected Utah Repositories. Although the society's manuscript holdings are included in the RLIN automated database, RLIN searching is restricted to trained librarians at affiliated institutions. A more convenient means of access for anyone with a DOS-based computer and at least seven megabytes of hard disk capacity is the "Guide to Archives and Manuscript Collections in Selected Utah Repositories," which is available on floppy disks from the society for twenty-five dollars. Full-text searches are possible by following the instructions included with the package. A further advantage is access to manuscript and archives catalogs at nine Utah institutions besides the society, including Brigham Young University, the University of Utah, the Utah State Archives, and Utah State University. Researchers can contact the society at 300 Rio Grande, Salt Lake City, Utah 84101-1182. The telephone number is (801) 533-3536.

Gary Topping was Curator of Manuscripts for the Utah State Historical Society (Salt Lake City) from 1979 to 1991. He is currently a History Instructor at Salt Lake City Community College.

NOTES

[1]On the history of the Utah State Historical Society, see "Utah State Historical Society: Sixty Years of Organized History," *Utah Historical Quarterly* 25 (July 1957): 190–220; and Glen M. Leonard, "The Utah State Historical Society, 1897–1972," *Utah Historical Quarterly* 40 (Fall 1972): 300–334.

[2]See Dale L. Morgan's description of the WPA collection, now incorporated in the "Register of the WPA Collection" at the society.

[3]William C. Seifrit, ed., "'To Get U[tah] in U[nion]': Diary of a Failed Mission," *Utah Historical Quarterly* 51 (Fall 1983): 358–81.

[4]Andrew Karl Larson, *Erastus Snow: The Life of a Missionary and Pioneer for the Early Mormon Church* (Salt Lake City: University of Utah Press, 1971).

[5]Juanita Brooks, *On the Mormon Frontier: The Diary of Hosea Stout*, 2 vols. (Salt Lake City: University of Utah Press, 1964).

[6]Susa Young Gates (in collaboration with Leah D. Widtsoe), *The Life Story of Brigham Young* (New York: Macmillan, 1931).

[7]Ellis Shipp Musser, ed., *The Early Autobiography and Diary of Ellis Reynolds Shipp, M.D.* (Salt Lake City: Deseret News Press, 1962).

[8]Marilyn Warenski, *Patriarchs and Politics: The Plight of the Mormon Woman* (New York: McGraw-Hill, 1978).

[9]In addition to the Hosea Stout diary cited earlier, Brooks's best-known works are *The Mountain Meadows Massacre* (Palo Alto, Calif.: Stanford University Press, 1950); and *John Doyle Lee: Zealot-Pioneer Builder-Scapegoat* (Glendale, Calif.: Arthur H. Clark, 1973). A bibliography of her writings is included with Davis Bitton and Maureen Ursenbach, "Riding Herd: A Conversation with Juanita Brooks," *Dialogue* 9 (Spring 1974): 11–33. Her early life and intellectual background are detailed in Juanita Brooks, *Quicksand and Cactus: A Memoir of the Southern Mormon Frontier* (Salt Lake City: Howe Brothers, 1982).

[10]Levi S. Peterson, *Juanita Brooks: Mormon Woman Historian* (Salt Lake City: University of Utah Press, 1988).

[11]In addition to his biography of Erastus Snow cited earlier, Larson's best-known book is *I Was Called to Dixie* (Salt Lake City: Deseret News Press, 1961). His intellectual background and contributions (other than historical) to the cultural life of southern Utah are detailed in his *The Education of a Second Generation Swede: An Autobiography* (Salt Lake City: Deseret News Press, 1979).

[12]See "Tribute to Stanley S. Ivins," *Utah Historical Quarterly* 35 (Fall 1967): 307–9, which includes a bibliography of his publications and reprints his best-known one, "Notes on Mormon Polygamy."

[13]David E. Miller, *Hole-in-the-Rock: An Epic in the Colonization of the Great American West* (Salt Lake City: University of Utah Press, 1959).

Exterior, Merrill Library, Utah State University. Courtesy A. J. Simmonds.

Mormon Americana in the Utah State University Special Collections Library

Kenneth W. Godfrey

The Mormon Collection in the Merrill Library at Utah State University in Logan, Utah, according to A. J. Simmonds, associate director and curator, is one of the largest repositories of materials pertaining to the Mormon faith—surpassed only by the Salt Lake City library-archives of The Church of Jesus Christ of Latter-day Saints and the collection housed at Brigham Young University.[1] However, only the most serious students of Mormonism are aware of the Merrill Library's vast collection containing primary sources, original manuscripts, and diaries—many of which are of unusual historical value. This essay presents a brief history of this repository and focuses on some of the most important collections housed within it.

Historical Highlights

President E. G. Peterson purchased the first Utah State University Mormon collection from Mormon bibliophile Eli H. Peirce in 1916.[2] The rarest of the 680 volumes relating to the history of Utah, the western United States, and the Mormons were stored in a vault, together with other important documents subsequently purchased. When the collection quickly outgrew the vault, a section of the main stacks was secured by chicken wire (still visible today) and used to house as well as segregate the books. Many of the collections are currently stamped "cage," indicating that they were once located behind the chicken-wire fence.[3]

After receiving a sizable endowment from Mr. and Mrs. L. Boyd Hatch in the 1950s, the "rare book reading room" expanded to include the department of special collections. With the erection of a new library in the 1960s, the special collections staff spent three years carefully searching the university's library in quest of valuable rare books still on the shelves. Among other literary treasures, they found a first English translation of the Russian poet Pushkin. A. J. Simmonds also surveyed the 2,204 books and periodicals pertaining to the LDS Church already housed in the library and began a systematic quest to "fill the gaps." In addition, he surveyed the library holdings of personal papers of Latter-day Saints, as well as the broadsides, rare books, and materials pertaining to groups that had splintered from the main Mormon faith. Then Simmonds, with the help of several assistants, began to search out rare books, diaries, and financial papers pertaining to the Latter-day Saints, even to the extent of combing attics. Simmonds's success is demonstrated by the numerous valuable holdings in the library today. What follows is a brief survey of the more significant documents. Where relevant, the list is alphabetized by the surname associated with the collection.

Important Mormon Manuscript Collections at Utah State University

Leonard J. Arrington Collection. Early in the 1990s, one of Mormonism's most respected historians, most prolific writers, and perhaps its most honored Western scholar, Leonard J. Arrington, donated his diaries, papers, and manuscripts to Utah State University. This vast collection, some of which is restricted to researchers for twenty-five years, contains the important documents of a scholar who served a decade as Latter-day Saint Church historian. The acquisition of these papers greatly enhances both the size and the importance of Utah State's Mormon and Western History collection.

Edgar Brossard Collection. The manuscripts and published works of Edgar Brossard were donated to the university. Brossard was a thirty-four-year member of the United States Tariff Commission and a college professor who served once as an LDS branch president, twice as a bishop, once as president of the Washington D.C. Stake, and three times as a mission president. The list of items in this valuable collection is almost thirty pages long.

General John K. Cannon Collection. Air Force general John K. Cannon, a Mormon and a 1917 graduate of Utah State University, deposited his papers, consisting of biographical materials and numerous letters to World War II generals, at the library. Of particular interest and importance are a series of reports concerning interrogations of German prisoners captured shortly after the Allied invasion of Italy and a letter from Charles Lindbergh thanking Cannon for teaching him to fly.[4]

Daryl Chase Presidential Papers. Former institute director and Utah State University president Daryl Chase's papers represent one of the more complex record series in the university's archives. The Chase papers are collected and indexed in thirty boxes and include hundreds of memos from Academic Vice President Milton R. Merrill to

President Chase. Thus, they are an important resource in recounting the history of Utah State University during an era of unprecedented growth. They provide a source for some Latter-day Saint history as well.

Bernard DeVoto Papers. In 1979 the university purchased the papers of the Ogden-born writer Bernard DeVoto. This collection includes correspondence between DeVoto and Madeline Reeder Thurston McQuown, Robert Hillyer, and others regarding writing projects. Also included are the drafts of some of DeVoto's works in progress, as well as letters to poet Robert Frost.

Virginia Hansen Diaries. Former Cache County librarian, cultural catalyst, and devout Mormon, Virginia Hansen kept diaries covering the years 1933 to 1978. Those wanting to study Church history in rural Utah will find a rich resource in the Hansen volumes. She is also a valuable source for those studying movie history, sports in Cache Valley, and the culture of the Far West. While her diary entries are neither long nor self-revealing, they are witty, provocative, and helpful in understanding life in a community of less than three hundred people and in a valley housing both a university and a temple.

Gunn McKay Papers. The library collection holds the papers of former congressman and LDS stake president Gunn McKay. McKay, a nephew of Church president David O. McKay, gave his extensive papers to the university in 1980. The papers were acquired largely through the efforts of his administrative assistant, attorney Herman Olsen.

Joel E. Ricks Collection. Still another very important collection is that of Joel E. Ricks, which pertains to the early history of Cache Valley. Ricks, a Utah State University professor of history for four decades, collected hundreds of valuable documents in preparing his history of Cache Valley. This collection includes notes, transcriptions, and copies of historical essays and remembrances regarding Cache Valley's beginnings. Working notes from Ricks's lectures, his *History of Utah State Agricultural College: The First Fifty Years,* and his book *The History of a Valley: Cache Valley, Utah—Idaho* are a part of this collection.[5] They were given to the university by S. George Ellsworth.[6]

George Schweick Materials. Other documents of interest to students of Mormonism include the George Schweick letters and his annotations on the margins of the David Whitmer pamphlet, *An Address to All Believers in Christ.*[7] Schweick, the grandson of Whitmer, had possession of the printer's manuscript of the Book of Mormon for a time. His letters detail the history of the manuscript after he acquired it and before it passed into the keeping of the Reorganized LDS Church. The extensively annotated pamphlet provides additional information about the beginnings of the LDS Church and the translation of the Book of Mormon.

Heber C. Snell Collection. The papers of institute teacher Heber C. Snell include his journals, diaries, and class notes, as well as a draft of his important, though argumentative, book titled *Ancient Israel: Its Story and Meaning,* the writing of which occupied most of his academic career. Also essential to this collection are several boxes of correspondence, including an account of the LDS Church court trial of former seminary teacher John W. Fitzgerald, who was an opponent of the Church's former position on priesthood and the blacks.

Thatcher Family Papers. The Thatcher family papers are an important collection containing the mission diaries of Apostle Moses Thatcher, several letter books, scrapbooks, newspaper clippings, and a steel-plate engraved portrait of the Mormon leader. Records of the Thatcher Brothers Banking Company, as well as the George W. Thatcher Sr., family papers and the diaries of Moses Thatcher Jr. comprise the remainder of this collection. Anyone doing serious research regarding the Mexican mission, Mormon colonization of Mexico, the financial history of Logan, or missionary life in England during the 1860s should examine the primary sources described above.

In addition to the information concerning business and ecclesiastical history, the Thatcher family papers provide personal history. We learn, for example, that George W. Thatcher was not only an extraordinary businessman but also an excellent sprinter. After a plea from his friends, he agreed to race a man named George Adams, who at that time held the world record for the hundred-yard dash. Even though Thatcher had just returned from an extended Indian campaign, he easily beat Adams. Such incidents make the Thatcher family papers an entertaining as well as valuable Mormon historical source.

Mary Lucetta Shumway Thompson Diaries. Late in the 1970s, the family of Mary Lucetta Shumway Thompson donated approximately twenty volumes of her diaries, covering the period 1930 to 1970. Thompson, a lifelong resident of Garland, Utah, daily chronicled her activities as a wife, mother, and church worker.

Roy B. West Collection. An important collection pertaining to Western literature is the papers of Roy B. West. West, as editor of the *Rocky Mountain Review* and later the *Western Review,* was an important figure in solidifying a Western literary tradition. Bradford Cole states that "the correspondence files in the [West] collection read like a Who's Who of American 20th century authors."[8]

Whitney Collection. Recently a register of the correspondence of Apostle Orson F. Whitney was published by Special Collections archivists. The bulk of the more than twenty-four hundred letters comprising this collection are to and from Zine Beal Smoot, Whitney's wife.

The Whitney collection also contains letters from Provo mayor Abraham O. Smoot, Susa Young Gates, Emmeline B. Wells, and Whitney's mother, Helen Mar Kimball Whitney. That Orson F. Whitney was not only an Apostle but also the author of an enormous four-volume *History of Utah,* as well as numerous other books and a large body of poetry, makes this large collection of his correspondence of more than passing interest.

Augmenting its Whitney holdings, in November 1992 Utah State University acquired from D. Whitney and Alice Smith other documents relative to the Whitney family, including the diaries of Helen Mar Kimball and Charles S. Whitney. There are, furthermore, numerous letters written by Vilate Kimball while she resided in Nauvoo in 1841 and Winter Quarters in 1847, as well as Horace K. Whitney's letters written while he traversed America's great plains with Brigham Young and the 1847 pioneer company. Later, when he remained in Salt Lake City while most of the Saints moved south to Provo in the spring of 1858, Whitney wrote an important letter just twenty-four hours before Johnston's Army arrived in the Salt Lake Valley. Still other missives he authored include some written in 1855, while he served a mission in England; one from Parley's Park penned in 1862; and an 1871 letter he composed while staying in Kirtland, Ohio. His 1870 diary is also included in this collection.

Helen Mar Kimball's diaries are detailed, reflective, and literary pearls. One November 1886 entry perhaps illustrates the historical trove found within the leather covers of these volumes. After visiting the Logan Temple, she wrote,

> I was first baptized for my health, then for Elizabeth Ford Sikes Whitney and Lucy Blackson Kimball Whitney, then was washed and anointed by Sisters Richards and Clark. The latter afterwards addressing me and Lucy Walker Kimball who were standing there as "the wives of a God," meaning the Prophet and a number of things she said by the power of the spirit that were calculated to make us feel the greatness of the responsibility resting on us to carry ourselves streight in this life to be worthy of that which is awaiting us.[9]

John A. Widtsoe Collection. For many years, John A. Widtsoe, former Utah State University president, world-renowned professor of chemistry, and Mormon Apostle, was the most prolific writer in the Church. A large collection of his correspondence and presidential papers was donated to Utah State University. Widtsoe, after leaving Utah State, became president of the University of Utah and is arguably one of Utah's premier educators, scholars, and theologians. Scholars doing serious Widtsoe work will find the holdings at Utah State helpful, if not invaluable.

Brigham Young Financial Records. The acquisition of the financial records of LDS Church president Brigham Young is considered by curator Simmonds to be his most important purchase. In essence these volumes are the financial records of the LDS Church from 1859 to 1877. Ledger C of this collection is, oddly enough, written in the Deseret Alphabet. These papers include a series of receipt books showing expenses for the Gardo House in 1882. The collection consists of thirty manuscript volumes.[10]

Morrisite Papers. In 1987 archivists acquired virtually the complete extant records of the Church of the Firstborn (Morrisites). The Morrisite papers, library officials assert, "are almost certainly the only surviving archive of a nineteenth century Mormon schismatic group that were still in private hands."[11]

Other Cache Valley History Materials. More than twenty years of historical newsletters published by Preston, Idaho, editor Newell Hart are housed in the archives. These newsletters contain letters and histories of communities and their clubs and guilds, and they provide important source material for fleshing out information relative to many of Cache Valley's Mormon communities. The library also has the local history material on Cache Valley gathered years ago by S. George Ellsworth.

***Mutual Improvement Association Journal* Manuscripts.** Manuscripts of the Hyrum, Utah, Young Men's and Young Ladies' Mutual Improvement Association journal provide the historian with an important offering of essays on moral guidance and religious anecdotes covering the years 1884–93. These "newsletters" provided source material for an essay by Leonard Arrington that appeared in *This People* magazine.[12]

Papers of Mormon Authors. The papers of Rodello Hunter as well as drafts of novels by Virginia Sorenson and the sealed papers of poet-novelist David Lane Wright[13] are housed in Special Collections. Scholars working on the two popular women writers would be well advised to consult the manuscripts located in this collection.

Papers of Mormon Common Folk. During the past decade, historians have been turning their attention more and more to a study of the common folk, and Mormon historians are no exception. Special Collections holds a large number of diaries, journals, and letters written by rank-and-file Latter-day Saints, including those of Matthew P. Fifield, whose history covers the years 1843–1920. Fifield discusses many of the events in early Mormon history, as well as his difficulties with various Mormon officials. Other important diaries include those of Howard Egan, Nathaniel Vary Jones, Levi Riter, Elizabeth W. Pugmire, Christian Christiansen Binorup, and Thomas Steed. Thus, the archives at Utah State are an unusually rich source of primary materials pertaining to all aspects of Mormon history.

Photograph Collection. Historians from as far away as Belgium have accessed the massive photograph collection now numbering more than 400,000 prints. Not only does this unique archive have thousands of pictures regarding daily life in rural Utah, but it also houses a large railroad collection especially focused on American trains from 1860 to 1900; much early Utah history involving many Latter-day Saints has to do with the construction of railroads. The collection includes more than 150 photos on the construction of the transcontinental railroad and more than 300 pictures from the C. R. Savage photo studio. The photographs of General John K. Cannon represent a superb collection of aerial warfare in the Mediterranean area during World War II. The 500 excellent photographs of George H. Warren, a Utah and Idaho surveyor, depict all phases of life in Utah and Idaho during the period 1908 to 1927 while emphasizing electric power generation and transmission of the time.[14] Logan's daily newspaper, *The Herald Journal,* also donates its old photographs to the library.

Rare Documents. Copies of several rare documents have been procured by university archivists. Examples include John McCutchen Conyers's 1882 "Handbook on Mormonism"; a copy of a John Taylor discourse delivered in the Salt Lake Tabernacle, February 1, 1885; and a first edition of Edward Bonney's *The Bandetti of the Prairies*. Other valuable published works include Lorenzo Snow's "The Only Way to Be Saved" and Orson Pratt's 1857 work, "Universal Apostasy or the Seventeen Centuries of Darkness," as well as his "Necessity for Miracles." A volume of Logan Temple lectures, as well as a first edition of James H. Hunt's 1844 book *Mormonism: Embracing the Origin, Rise and Progress of the Sect* are also important acquisitions.

Other items of historical importance include a first edition of Frank J. Cannon's *Under the Prophet in Utah,* as well as a copy of John E. Page's 1866 *The Spaulding Story concerning the Book of Mormon.*

Conclusion

While many libraries now require historians and other scholars to work mostly from microfilm, the Utah State Special Collections Library, more often than not, provides the original document. The library has also worked to acquire all of the theses and dissertations pertaining to the Latter-day Saints or the American West written in graduate schools around the world. Through hard work and vision, Utah State University has compiled one of the best collections of Mormon material to be found anywhere.

Kenneth W. Godfrey is Director of the LDS Institute of Religion, Logan, Utah.

NOTES

[1]Ingrid Ricks, "USU Special Collections Offers Glimpse at History," *The Herald Journal,* August 15, 1991, 3; see also interview with A. J. Simmonds, by Kenneth W. Godfrey, August 19, 1991.

[2]Ann Buttars, "The Peirce Mormon Bibliography at Utah State University," *BYU Studies* 32 (Winter 1992): 159-69; reprinted in this volume.

[3]Annual Report of the Department of Special Collections and Archives, 1978-1979, Utah State University Special Collections Library, Logan, Utah.

[4]Bradford R. Cole, "Important Manuscript Collections at Utah State University," paper presented at the American Historical Association Pacific Coast Branch Meeting at the University of Utah, n.d., copy in Utah State University Special Collections, 3.

[5]Joel Edward Ricks, *The Utah State Agricultural College: A History of Fifty Years, 1888-1938* (Salt Lake City: Deseret News Press, 1938); and Joel E. Ricks, *The History of a Valley: Cache Valley, Utah—Idaho* (Logan, Utah: Cache Valley Centennial Commission, 1956).

[6]Annual Report of the Department of Special Collections and Archives, 1980, 3, copy in Utah State University Special Collections.

[7]David Whitmer, *An Address to All Believers in Christ by a Witness to the Devine [sic] Authenticity of the Book of Mormon* (Richmond, Mo.: By the author, 1887).

[8]Cole, "Important Manuscript Collections," 11.

[9]Diary of Helen Mar Kimball, November 16, 1886, Utah State University Special Collections.

[10]Twenty-four in original holograph and six photocopies.

[11]Report to the Trustees of the Marie Eccles Caine Foundation, 1989, copy in Utah State University Special Collections.

[12]Leonard J. Arrington, "Zion's Manuscript Newspapers," *This People* 10 (Holiday 1989): 63.

[13]Bruce W. Jorgensen, "The Vocation of David Wright: An Essay in Analytic Biography," *Dialogue: A Journal of Mormon Thought* 11 (Summer 1978): 38-52.

[14]Annual Report of Special Collections and Archives for the Academic Year 1976-77, 78, copy in Utah State University Special Collections.

The Peirce Mormon Collection at Utah State University

Ann Buttars

Purchase of the Eli H. Peirce Library

In 1916 the Board of Trustees of the Agricultural College of Utah in Logan purchased the Eli H. Peirce library, a collection of books dealing with Mormon and Utah history. This purchase generated a fair amount of concern and a number of problems. However, it also provided a solid foundation upon which to build the special collections of Utah State University and one of Utah's most robust Mormon collections.

The biennial report of the board of trustees for the years 1915–16 reported the purchase this way:

> The Pierce [*sic*] Library of Utah History was purchased by the Board of this Institution. The books have been classified and cataloged with other books of the Library, but shelved as a special collection. This Pierce Library consists of 680 volumes relating to the history of Utah and Western United States. The collection includes also many of the publications of the Latter-day Saints, and much of the vast literature which has been written on Mormonism, pro and con.
>
> Many of the volumes are very rare and the entire collection is a valuable and desirable addition to the library.[1]

This statement, though short, is an accurate description of the books the library had just acquired and to which Peirce had dedicated a major portion of his life. However, this purchase had been neither approved nor appreciated by the library staff.

On July 5, 1916, Elizabeth Church Smith, librarian at the Agricultural College, wrote an irate letter to Dr. E. G. Peterson, newly appointed president of the college, questioning the appropriation of library funds for this purchase and saying that "the requisition for the purchase of the Pierce [*sic*] collection of Utah History books amounting to $1299 is to be taken from the 1916 library fund of $1900" which would leave "practically nothing . . . for the purchase of any new books for the departments and none for magazines."[2] She was extremely concerned because no new books had been ordered for the coming school year and the majority of the library budget had been spent. Later that month, she again wrote to Peterson reemphasizing her concern and frustration while acknowledging the inherent value of the collection:

> I wish that I might say to you unofficially that the Pierce [*sic*] Library was not a library buy. It was done entirely by the Board and I feel that they should arrange in someway by special appropriation to pay for it as it was fully expected would be done. To be sure it is a splendid collection.[3]

Smith had apparently not been included in making the arrangements for the purchase of the Peirce Library. Although she had called it "a splendid collection," she, being a devout Episcopalian, probably did not entirely approve of the acquisition of a Mormon collection of books, let alone its consuming almost the entire library budget.

After voicing her opinion in several letters on the handling of this purchase, Smith left the matter in the hands of President Peterson in hopes that he would do something about this situation. On September 8, 1916, Smith received a letter from the secretary to the president informing her that an order for new library books had been sent off and an additional appropriation had been made to cover all other requests.[4] With her budgeting problems taken care of, Smith finally accepted the purchase of Eli Peirce's library and began making preparations for its arrival in Logan.

Peirce's Life and Collecting

Eli Harvey Peirce was born in Salt Lake City, February 27, 1850. He received his early education in the Salt Lake City public schools and later graduated with honors from Deseret University, now the University of Utah. In addition, he graduated as a telegraph operator from a school organized by President Brigham Young in 1870 for the benefit of the Utah Northern Railroad.[5] After completing his training, he worked in Brigham City for eighteen years as an agent for the Utah and Northern branch of the Union Pacific Railroad Company, as an agent for the Pacific Express Company, as a coal agent, and finally as manager of the Western Union and Deseret Telegraph offices.[6] During Peirce's tenure with the Union Pacific Railroad Company in Brigham City, historian Edward W. Tullidge aptly described him as

> a young man of as much business capacity and push as any young man in our Territory. . . . We should offer him to those who would investigate the meaning of young Utah as one of the best specimens of that class, concerning whom even our Gentile brethren are prophetic with great promises of the

> future. Doubtless it is the type of Mormon origin, like Eli H. Peirce, that has suggested to the Gentiles this idea of young Utah. Expounded, the class signifies a host of young men who have received a better education than their fathers, consequently are men of more culture, yet who have sprang from that hardy, indomitable race of pioneers who have peopled and subdued this mountainous country.[7]

While in Brigham City, Peirce displayed his flair for culture by organizing the Brigham Dramatic Association, where he developed a great appreciation for various literary and historical works. There seemed to be nothing that could stop him in his endeavors. He was indeed a very ambitious man and continued to be so throughout his entire life.

Upon leaving Brigham City, Peirce moved to Salt Lake City, where he became associated in the insurance business with Heber J. Grant, future President of the LDS Church, and later operated his own prosperous insurance business with offices in the Templeton Building. During this time, he was an active member of the Mormon Tabernacle Choir, for which he also served as business manager. He played a prominent part in planning and organizing some of the earliest trips taken by the choir.[8] While living in Salt Lake City, he became well known as a singer, actor, and lover of rare books.[9]

Throughout his active business career, Peirce found time to collect what was reputed to be "the most complete library of books written for and against 'Mormonism' ever brought together."[10] This library was built painstakingly over many years despite Peirce's modest means and large family.[11] Most of his book purchases were handled through the Shepard Book Company on South State Street in Salt Lake City.[12] The company published, imported, bought, and sold old, rare, and new books. It advertised:

> We carry the largest stock of MORMON and ANTI-MORMON BOOKS in the world. If you are interested in this subject, write or call on us and we will quote you prices on any book on Mormonism in or out of print.[13]

This company was later responsible for buying and selling many of Peirce's books. Through a 1911 Shepard Book Company advertisement offering a major collection of books on Mormonism for sale, Harvard University became interested in Peirce and his Mormon library. News of Harvard's intent to buy the collection was leaked to the *Salt Lake City Herald,* and Peirce received extensive criticism from friends and neighbors, the community, the governor, and the University of Utah. It was even rumored that General Authorities of The Church of Jesus Christ of Latter-day Saints strongly disapproved of the sale and offered to purchase five hundred of the most outspoken anti-Mormon books to prevent their leaving the state. It was not until three years later that Harvard actually purchased 2,653 books and pamphlets from Peirce. The *Harvard Alumni Bulletin* announced the news of the purchase and proudly listed its contents.[14]

Shortly after the sale, Peirce began collecting another, essentially duplicate, library beginning with a few copies of works he had left from the Harvard sale. He was no longer working as an insurance agent and had more time for book collecting. He spent the rest of his life reading and studying these books, making notations inside each volume which listed the page numbers where there was a reference to Mormons. In 1914, just a few months prior to his death, he used a number of these books to write a series of three articles in the *Deseret Evening News* arguing that the Garden of Eden was located in the region of the country that now borders Utah, Wyoming, and Colorado.[15] At the time of his death, on February 9, 1915, Peirce owned approximately seven hundred volumes mentioning Mormons.

Content of the Collection

These volumes were the library that the Agricultural College of Utah purchased from Mrs. Peirce during the spring of 1916. When the purchase was completed, the books were moved to Logan and deposited in the library. Elizabeth Church Smith shortly thereafter began processing them for patron use. She registered the books in the accession records, giving a complete description of each and assigning it an accession number as well as a call number.[16] Under the assumption that these Mormon books were not that significant, she classified them according to the ninth edition of the *Dewey Decimal Classification,* which placed books about Mormons with non-Christian religious groups (#289.9).[17] The books were put there whether Mormons considered themselves Christian or not. The rest of the books were classified and placed in whatever category they corresponded to in the Dewey Decimal system, despite Peirce's notations about mentions of Mormons. The books apparently were never shelved in a separate, special collection; rather they were scattered throughout the stacks of the entire library. Furthermore, there were never any book plates made to identify the books as belonging to the Eli H. Peirce library. The only thing that identified the books as part of the Peirce library was the accession number stamped inside each volume. When it came to the cataloging of the Peirce books, Smith did an exceptional job of descriptive cataloging, but she did not take the time nor feel it appropriate to put Mormon subject headings on all of the books.

The original shelflist cards reveal that many of them were cataloged under author and title only.

The Peirce library also included a large collection of pamphlets, but these were never fully processed because the policy of the library at that time was not to process such items. They were simply laid on shelves in the back of the library with the myriad of other too-small-to-catalog items waiting to be taken care of later or bound in buckram as a book that could be processed. There is no way of knowing how many pamphlets were in the Peirce library, but apparently there were quite a few; many pamphlets with notations about Mormon material and in the same handwriting as that in the Peirce books have been transferred over the years to the Special Collections Department from other areas of the library.

Little did Elizabeth Smith know that the Peirce library would be not only the beginning of a Mormon collection at Utah State University, but also the foundation of the Special Collections Department of the Utah State University Merrill Library. Although the 1915–16 Biennial Report of the Board of Trustees stated that the Peirce Library would be shelved as a special collection, a department for doing so was not established at Utah State University until January 1965. In announcing the creation of the Merrill Library's Special Collections Department, Dr. Milton C. Abrams, university librarian, indicated that books "acquired over a period of years by purchase, gift and university publication" would be used as the foundation for the new department.[18] Some of the books he referred to were those of the Peirce library.

Though many of the books from the Peirce library were placed in the newly established Special Collections Department, they were not gathered into the originally promised Peirce special collection until 1971. Under the direction of A. J. Simmonds, curator of special collections at Utah State University, and with the aid of the library accession records for 1916, the stacks of the Merrill Library were searched to find the remaining books of the Peirce library. At last, the Peirce books were gathered together and placed in the Special Collections Department as Book Collection 13.

This time the actual content and value of the Peirce library was finally realized. The books range in date from 1830 to 1914, with volume one of *The Millennial Harbinger* being the earliest published volume in the collection. The books span the history of the LDS Church from its organization through 1914, the year prior to Peirce's death. They include everything from fact to fiction on such subjects as history, geography, sociology, anthropology, archaeology, geology, and, of course, religion. Even such general titles as *Travels around the World*, *Men and Manners in America,* and *Story of the Wild West* are found in the library. At first glance, such books do not appear to be overly concerned with Mormons and Mormonism. However, Peirce's notations concerning Mormon content inside each volume make it quite evident that the entire collection is indeed relevant to the study of Mormonism.

Interestingly, when Dale Morgan visited the Agricultural College Library in 1948 in a search for books to include in his Mormon collection, he did not find a substantial number of books on that subject.[19] He was unable to locate many titles because the Peirce books did not have the subject headings under which he looked to identify the books for his collection. Had Morgan been able to find and identify all of the books in the Peirce library, he would have found a gold mine of Mormon sources and probably would not have thought Utah to be quite as "bibliographically naive" as he indicated in the introduction to *A Mormon Bibliography, 1830–1930*.[20] Because of the Peirce Library at the Agricultural College of Utah, Utah was not the "bibliographic desert" that Bernard DeVoto is thought to have judged it to be.

The Peirce library consists of numerous significant titles. Morgan included such titles as E. D. Howe's *History of Mormonism* and Frederick Piercy's *Route from Liverpool to Great Salt Lake.* Other titles such as *The Latter Day Saint's Messenger and Advocate* and *Voree Herald* are included in his collection but are not shown as holdings of Utah State University. Some hard-to-find titles in his collection that are also in the Peirce library include *The Olive Branch* and Lucy Mack Smith's *Biographical Sketches of Joseph Smith.* There are a few titles such as Francis Gladden Bishop's *Zion's Messenger* that are part of the Peirce Library but are not listed in Morgan's bibliography.

The purchase of the Peirce library brought a wealth of Mormon sources to the Agricultural College of Utah (later called Utah State University). In 1916 the board of trustees paid $1,299 for the Peirce library, making the average price per volume $1.98 (a slightly better price than Harvard had been given). Today this collection is virtually irreplaceable. Numerous articles, theses, dissertations, and books concerning "Utah and Mormons" (as Peirce would have annotated them)[21] have been written using the library. What was a rather insignificant and troublesome purchase of library books for Elizabeth Church Smith is today one of Utah State University's most cherished and valuable library possessions, as cherished as it once was by Eli H. Peirce.

Ann Buttars is Assistant Curator of the Special Collections and Archives Department at Utah State University. This article is a modified version of a paper presented at the Mormon History Association's Twenty-third Annual Conference, May 7, 1988, in Logan, Utah.

NOTES

This article was originally published, with additional illustrations, in *BYU Studies* 32 (Fall 1992): 159-69.

[1]Biennial Report of the Board of Trustees of the Agricultural College of Utah for the years 1915-1916 (Salt Lake City, 1917), 161.

[2]Elizabeth C. Smith to E. G. Peterson, July 5, 1916, E. G. Peterson Papers, Box 3, Folder S-1916, Utah State University, Special Collections and Archives.

[3]Elizabeth C. Smith to E. G. Peterson, July 28, 1916, E. G. Peterson Papers, Box 3, Folder S-1916, Special Collections and Archives, Utah State University.

[4]Secretary to the President, Utah Agricultural College to Elizabeth C. Smith, September 8, 1916, E. G. Peterson Papers, Box 3, Folder S-1916, Special Collections and Archives, Utah State University.

[5]Andrew Jenson, Journal History of the Church (Salt Lake City: Andrew Jenson History Co., 1901-36), February 9, 1915, 3, LDS Church Archives.

[6]*Tullidge's Quarterly Magazine* 2, no. 1 (April 1882): 412.

[7]*Tullidge's Quarterly Magazine,* 411-12.

[8]*Salt Lake Tribune,* February 10, 1915, 14.

[9]Jenson, Journal History, February 9, 1915, 3.

[10]*Deseret Evening News,* February 10, 1915, 2.

[11]Ray Allen Billington, "The Origins of Harvard's Mormon Collection," *Arizona and the West* 10, no. 3 (Autumn 1968), 216.

[12]The sign from the Shepard Book Company now hangs over the rare book room in the Special Collections Department, Marriott Library, University of Utah, Salt Lake City.

[13]The Shepard Book Company advertisement was found on the back cover of William A. Hickman, *Brigham's Destroying Angel* (Salt Lake City: Shepard Book, 1904).

[14]Billington, "Harvard's Mormon Collection," 211-22.

[15]Jenson, Journal History, November 14, 1914, 4; November 28, 1914, 4-5.

[16]Library Accession Ledgers of the Agricultural College of Utah, vol. 6, 1913-16, nos. 29001-29656, Library Archives, Special Collections and Archives, Utah State University.

[17]Melvil Dewey, *Decimal Classification and Relative Index for Libraries, Clippings, Notes,* 9th rev. (Lake Placid Club, N.Y.: Forest Press, 1915).

[18]*The Herald Journal,* January 22, 1965, 6. The announcement of the new department was also published in Student Life, February 1, 1965, 2.

[19]Dale L. Morgan to Fawn Brodie, April 20, 1948. *Dale Morgan on Early Mormonism* (Salt Lake City: Signature Books, 1986), 154-55.

[20]Dale L. Morgan, Introduction to *A Mormon Bibliography, 1830-1930* (Salt Lake City: University of Utah Press, 1978), 2.

[21]"Utah and Mormons" is the most common reference to Mormons used by Peirce in his handwritten notations.

Fawn McKay Brodie as a student at Weber College's Acorn Ball, 1931.
Courtesy Weber State University Archives.

Mormon Archival and Manuscript Holdings at Weber State University

John Sillito

Weber State University in Ogden, Utah, was organized in late 1888 as Weber Stake Academy, and its first classes were held on January 7, 1889. The school was established as part of The Church of Jesus Christ of Latter-day Saints' academy system, which was begun in the 1870s and expanded in the next decade as Church leaders sought to provide schools "where the Bible, the Book of Mormon and the . . . Doctrine and Covenants can be used as textbooks, and where the principles of our religion may form a part of the teachings of our schools."[1] The academies were established under the direction of a stake board of education, which was in turn supervised by the Church's General Board of Education.

From 1889, when Louis F. Moench was selected as principal, until 1933, when Aaron W. Tracy served as president, Weber was administered by the Church. During that period it was known by several names, including Weber Stake Academy, Weber Normal School, Weber Junior College, and finally Weber College. In the spring of 1933, the Utah State Legislature provided for the transfer of Weber (and other Church-owned colleges in Utah) to the state. During that forty-seven-year period, Weber had been closely associated with developments in the Church, and a number of prominent Latter-day Saints had taught at or attended the school, including David O. McKay, Thomas E. McKay, Ernest L. Wilkinson, Lydia H. Tanner, J. Willard Marriott, and David M. Kennedy.[2]

Because of the close ties between Weber College and the LDS Church, the Weber State University Archives contains several records of interest to students of Mormonism. Among these are the files of the registrar's office, which include both general information on curriculum and individual student records. These archival records would be of interest to scholars researching the development of curriculum and pedagogy in Church schools. Also within the record of the registrar's office are commencement files from 1895 to the present. A second major record group is the Centennial History Project, a compilation of various record series containing materials accumulated in preparation for writing a centennial history of the school. These include Devotional Minutes 1911–12, 1924–30; Board of Directors' Minutes, 1888–93; Board of Education Minutes, 1888–1933; and other compilations which bring together information on Weber during the period it was a Church school.

In addition, the archives holds collections of papers of several individual faculty members associated with developments in Mormon history and literature. These include the papers of Gene Sessions pertaining to his book *Mormon Thunder: A Documentary History of Jedediah Morgan Grant*;[3] the files of Leland H. Monson, a member of the Church Board of Education and the author of several Sunday School manuals; and a major collection of manuscripts and correspondence of Levi S. Peterson, which trace the development of his work and include files on his novel *The Backslider*[4] and his biography, *Juanita Brooks*.[5] The papers of Donald Moorman, a deceased history faculty member at Weber State, are also housed in the archives. His collection—which includes research files on various topics of Mormon history, especially regarding Brigham Young—was opened in late 1989.

In addition to these collections, the archives has photographic holdings and a number of printed works—including student newspapers, annuals, and literary magazines—which would be helpful in studying aspects of life at a Church school in the early twentieth century. Moreover, the archives maintains a small oral history program, and many of the transcribed interviews are related to Mormon history. Among these are interviews with Elder Joseph Anderson recalling his days at Weber as a student in 1905 and several interviews which focus on the proposed 1950s transfer of Weber back to the LDS Church.

Other holdings of interest to students of Mormon history and literature can be found in the Weber State University Special Collections/Howell Library department, which is also housed in the Stewart Library. Among the major holdings are the papers of Mark Evans Austad, which document his career in broadcasting and his service as ambassador to Finland (1971–77) and Norway (1981–84); the Laurence J. Burton collection, which documents his ten-year term as a member of Congress from Utah's First Congressional District; the Arvil B. Harris collection, which has material concerning Martin Harris and his family; the Chester "Chet" Olsen collection, which includes material dealing with Bernard DeVoto; the Roland Parry collection, which includes information on the composer and his major works (*A Child Is Born* and *All Faces West*[6]); and the Hyrum Wheelwright collection, which includes, among other things, Wheelwright's journal of his mission to the southern states (1912–17).

Roland Parry at work in his Ogden Canyon home. Courtesy Weber State University Archives.

A number of collections—including the papers of Richard Richards, Myrene Brewer, and Elizabeth Vance—have value to students of Utah politics in the post-World War II period, and several other collections deal with contemporary social and civic issues in Ogden. Finally, the department contains a number of small collections primarily concerning Mormon and Utah authors, including Juanita Brooks, Vardis

Fisher, Rodello Hunter, Clinton F. Larson, and Lydia Holmgren Tanner. These collections supplement more extensive holdings elsewhere.

The Weber State University Archives in Ogden, Utah, is open Monday through Friday from 9:00 A.M. to 4:30 P.M. Special Collections is open Monday through Friday from 7:30 A.M. to 12:00 noon and 1:00 to 4:30 P.M. Both the archives and special collections provide various finding aids, including published registers and container lists. Both are open to researchers, though restrictions may apply to some collections. Photocopying facilities are also available.

John Sillito is Archivist at Weber State University in Ogden, Utah.

NOTES

[1]James R. Clark, *Messages of the First Presidency*, 6 vols. (Salt Lake City: Bookcraft, 1965–75), 3:168.

[2]Richard W. Sadler, ed., *Weber State College: A Centennial History* (Ogden, Utah: Weber State College, 1989).

[3]Gene Sessions, *Mormon Thunder: A Documentary History of Jedediah Morgan Grant* (Urbana: University of Illinois Press, 1982).

[4]Levi S. Peterson, *The Backslider* (Salt Lake City: Signature Books, 1986).

[5]Levi S. Peterson, *Juanita Brooks* (Salt Lake City: University of Utah Press, 1988).

[6]Roland Parry, *A Child Is Born* (Ogden, Utah: By the author, 1967); Parry, *All Faces West* (Ogden, Utah: By the author, 1948).

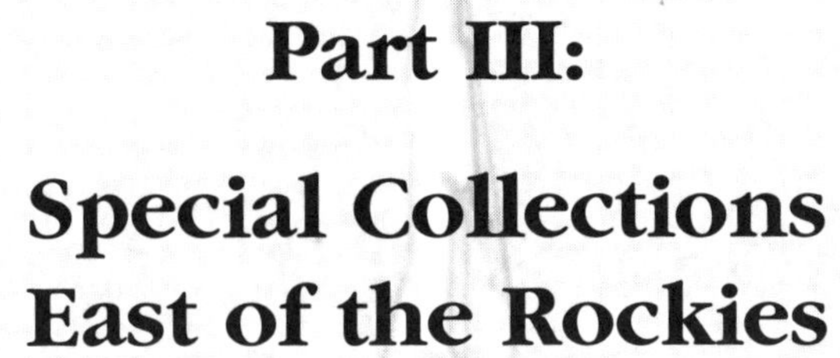

Part III:

Special Collections East of the Rockies

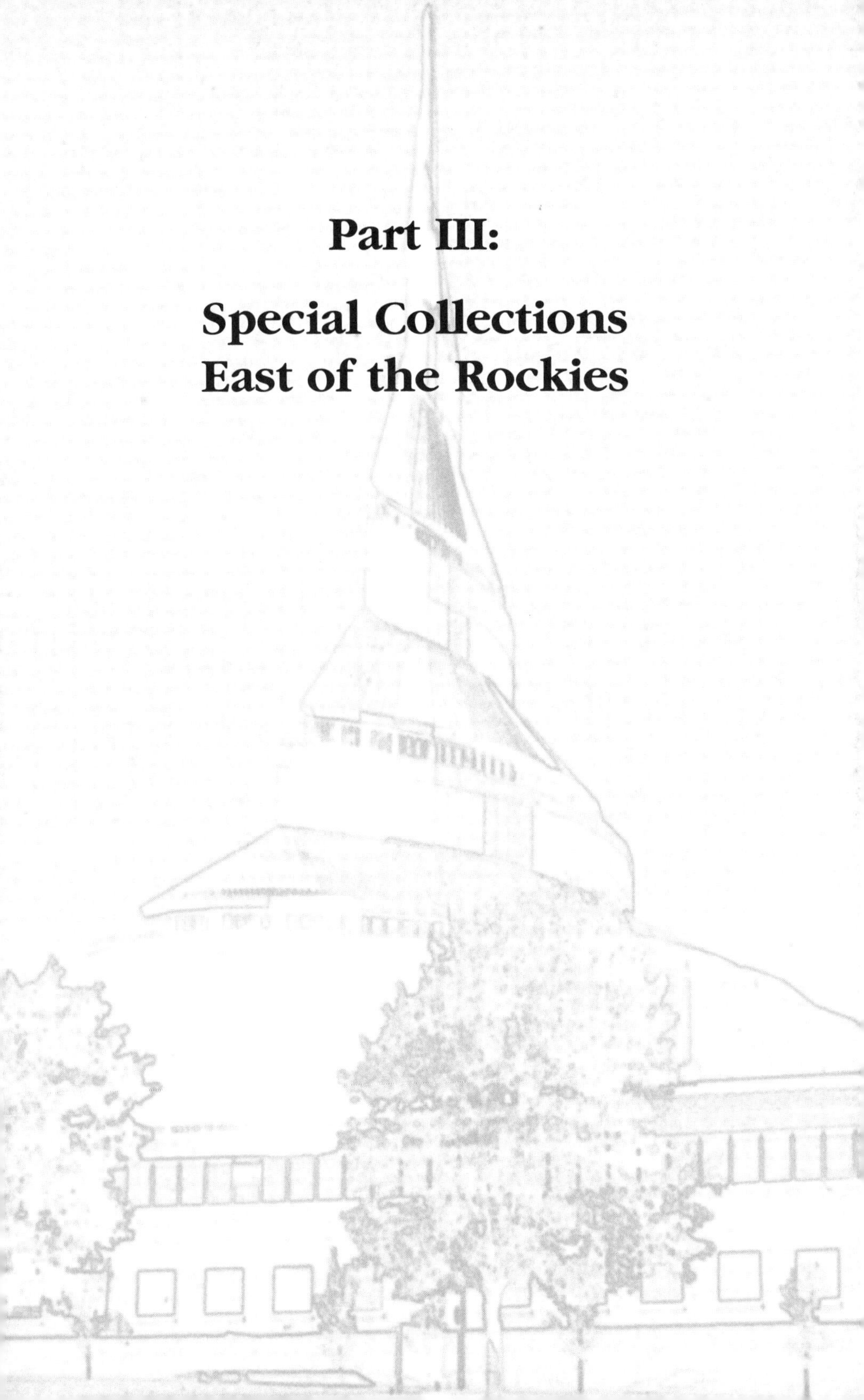

The Eli H. Peirce Collection of Mormon Americana at Harvard University

Alan K. Parrish

Some of the controversial saga surrounding Harvard's acquisition of the heart of its Mormon collection has been published; however, no attempt has been made to evaluate the content and significance of the materials Harvard acquired.[1] Likewise, no attempt has been made to answer some of the unresolved questions concerning the collector, Eli H. Peirce, and certain details of the negotiations. This article endeavors to resolve some of those controversies about Peirce and to provide some analysis of the large collection Harvard purchased from him in 1914.

Born in Salt Lake City on September 27, 1850, Eli Harvey Peirce Jr. was the son of Utah pioneers who had fled the East and crossed the plains to escape religious persecution from Eastern neighbors who would not tolerate a belief in Joseph Smith, the religious ideas he taught, or the devoted life required by his teachings. His father was bishop of the Brigham City Ward and was sent on a Church mission while Eli was just a boy. The elder Peirce died from an illness he contracted on that mission. Many years later Eli served a similar mission, a mission that altered the course of his life. His adherence to the Church developed as a result of that service. Following his mission, Eli became an ardent defender of the faith and began to collect books and pamphlets about The Church of Jesus Christ of Latter-day Saints and its people.

From its earliest days, much had been written for and against the Church. Nine months prior to his own sudden illness and death, on February 10, 1915, Eli sold his valuable collection to Harvard University. Some of Harvard's top officials were drawn into the purchase negotiations by the renowned historian of the American West, Frederick Jackson Turner, whose driving interest set the whole effort in motion. Turner considered the collection a vital library resource to support the program of studies on the American West he was developing.

Eli Harvey Peirce (1850–1915), avid collector of early printed materials about the Mormons. Courtesy Lydia Peirce, Salt Lake City.

Life Story of the Collector

Though born of Mormon pioneer stock and raised in protected Mormon communities, Eli grew up quite outside the religious life one would expect. His assessment of his first twenty-six years, to the time of his first mission call, indicates his lack of devotion:

> My mind to that time had been entirely given up to temporalities. I had never read to exceed a dozen chapters of the Bible in my life, and little more than that from either the Book of Mormon or Doctrine and Covenants, and concerning Church history was entirely ignorant. Had never made but one attempt to address a public audience, large or small, and that effort was no credit to me. Had been engaged in the railroad business for a number of years, and this occupation would have deprived me of meetings and religious services even had my inclinations led in that direction, which I frankly confess they did not. I had become almost an inveterate smoker, and bought cigars by the wholesale, a thousand at a time. Was addicted to the use of language which, if not profane, was at least vulgar and reprehensible. Frequently visited saloons, but was not a habitual drinker. Was not proficient in billiards, but squandered considerable money in acquiring what little knowledge I possessed of the game; and pool frequently cost me more for drinks than my board bill came to. Though these indiscretions were common and frequent, thanks to a mother's sagacious training, they never led to grosser or more alluring ones.
>
> Nature never endowed me with a superabundance of religious sentiment or veneration; my region of spirituality is not high, but below the average. A phrenologist once said to me: "You are too level-headed to ever make a sanctimonious church member." With this list of disqualifications, which serious reflection helped to magnify, is it surprising that I marveled and wondered if the Church were not running short of missionary material.[2]

Eli served in the Eastern States Mission from November 1875 to September 1876. On his return, he passed through Council Bluffs, Iowa, where he received another call to serve in Iowa with Elder James A. Little. In April 1877, Eli was given a second honorable release. Three days after returning home, Eli was called by President Brigham Young, speaking from the pulpit during general conference, to accompany Young's son and Eli's cousin, B. Morris Young, on another mission, this time to Iowa, Washington, D.C., and Pennsylvania. His departure was delayed four months, but this mission lasted from August 1877 through August 1878. He calculated the financial burden of his missions at $1,320 and three years of lost wages, but, he declared, "I have never for one moment regretted the sacrifice; the experience gained more than compensated for time, labor and means; while the knowledge acquired, of the things of God and the testimony of Jesus, I hold as invaluable."[3] His was a productive mission. He became a preacher of note, succeeded in baptizing 108 people, and he had many unusual experiences with healing the sick.

In 1882, Eli married Lydia Snow, daughter of Mary Elizabeth Houtz and Lorenzo Snow. In 1888 he followed Church teachings and entered polygamy by marrying Henrietta "Etta" Madsen. Eli and Lydia had four children before Lydia's death in 1898. Eli and Etta also had four children. The families resided in Brigham City, where he was a telegrapher for eighteen years. During these years, he was a fully participating church member. His ecclesiastical responsibilities as an active member of the Fifty-ninth Quorum of the Seventy included presiding over the seventies in the town of Mantua. He was also a successful local stage actor and is credited with organizing the Brigham Dramatic Association. He was also a prominent speaker and a popular figure.

In 1890, Eli began to devote his talents to the Mormon Tabernacle Choir. At this time, the family moved to Salt Lake City, making their permanent residence at 161 C Street. Eli's church activity during the major period of his life centered around the Tabernacle Choir. In addition to singing in the choir, he served as its business manager for a considerable time. Beyond his regular administrative duties, he compiled and published a volume containing printed news coverage of six choir excursions between 1893 and 1909.[4]

In 1911 a lengthy letter from Eli defending certain actions of the Tabernacle Choir was carried in the *Deseret News.*[5] Newspaper accounts record Eli's defense of Church members in Brigham City against charges from Reverend R. G. McNiece[6] of Ogden, who, in addressing the citizens of Brigham City, challenged anyone to debate him on the issues he raised in criticizing LDS beliefs. On at least two occasions, Eli defended the faith in major addresses from the pulpit in the Salt Lake Tabernacle.[7]

Eli worked in the insurance business for many years, first with the Heber J. Grant Company and later as a general agent with his own office. Large advertisements for Peirce Independent Underwriters appeared regularly in the Salt Lake City directories from 1900–10. He sold his business a few years before his death. The hard economic times of the 1890s forced Eli to enter into bankruptcy proceedings in 1899. Several personal items, including his books, were listed in Etta's name. Lewis B. McCornick, a 1902 Harvard graduate and a Salt Lake City banker who assisted Harvard in negotiations with Eli, wrote,

"It appears that Peirce was discharged from the bankruptcy court sometime ago and prior to that time had made over into his wife's name a part of the library."[8] The collection survived the claims of creditors and its value became a vital part of the family's financial security. Naturally, the Harvard sale was a matter of great importance to Etta and the family.

Harvard's efforts to purchase the collection faltered in 1911 but were renewed in 1914. Key figures involved in the acquisition seemed less than enthusiastic about spending much money on "Mormon" materials and were determined to pay the bare minimum to acquire the Peirce collection. These same officials made considerable efforts to avoid paying commissions to the Torch Press Book Store and the Shepard Book Company, with whom they had corresponded in discovering the collection. They even sent their own agent to Salt Lake City to deal directly with Eli, though to have a staff examination of such a large purchase may have been standard procedure. Roger Pierce replaced E. H. Wells as Secretary of the Harvard Alumni Association and the Harvard Commission of Western History and thus became Harvard's major representative in acquiring the collection. Assisting Roger Pierce with the final arrangements were David Heald, a member of the library staff, and Lewis B. McCornick.

Despite their own shrewd behavior and subsequent refusals to pay the commissions, Harvard negotiators criticized the business behavior and moral character of Eli, Joseph Smith, and the people of Utah. After reading the accounts of his emissaries in the final negotiations, Roger Pierce wrote the following to McCornick:

> I might have known that he was shifty on his feet from the indignation he worked up at my request that there should be something written in the option. Evidently there is considerable in the religion of the Latter Day Saints not found in the "Book of the Mormon." I should say that Joseph Smith had very little on him. I suppose that this is nothing new, however, to you who live in the atmosphere all the time.[9]

Published accounts of Harvard's negotiations with Eli raised questions about his church standing and marriage.[10] McCornick sent word east that if Eli sold the collection to "Gentiles" at Harvard, there would be Church disciplinary action leading to his excommunication. Heald reported that Etta Peirce insisted on receiving half of the proceeds from the sale while Eli attempted to make private arrangements to prevent it. Careful study of his life has failed to yield any evidence to support these assertions. Available information indicates that his was a happy marriage and that he was highly regarded by neighbors, business associates, and Church leaders.

Less than nine months after the sale to Harvard, Eli H. Peirce died. A paragraph from one of the obituaries reads:

> Eli Harvey Peirce, actor of note during the early days of Utah, collector of rare volumes and singer of ability, who had been associated with the Salt Lake tabernacle choir for years as business manager and successful insurance man, died at L.D.S. hospital at 2:40 o'clock yesterday afternoon. Peritonitis was the cause of death, which came after but four days of illness. He was 64 years of age.[11]

Probate records list among his assets, a "library of 1500 volumes." The records further indicate receipts for $2,250 from the sale of approximately twelve hundred of these volumes.[12]

Funeral services for Eli H. Peirce Jr. were held on February 12, 1915, in the LDS Salt Lake Eighteenth Ward chapel. The services began with prayer offered by his longtime friend, Charles W. Nibley, the Presiding Bishop of the Church. A special chorus of forty members from the Tabernacle Choir performed several selections in memory of their friend and colleague. Rudger Clawson and Orson F. Whitney, members of the Quorum of the Twelve Apostles, spoke. Both had been associated with Eli for the twenty-five years he had lived in Salt Lake City, and Elder Whitney had been his bishop. They commended Eli's exemplary role of devotion and church activity. Elder Clawson said he could unhesitatingly place Eli Peirce in the First Resurrection among those faithful to gospel principles. They both spoke highly of his integrity "in every capacity."[13]

Harvard's Quest for the Peirce Collection

Frederick Jackson Turner's arrival at Harvard in the autumn of 1910 drew the attention of Alice Forbes Perkins Hooper. She was interested in creating a memorial in honor of her father, Charles Eliot Perkins, who had been instrumental in establishing railroads in the western United States while residing most of the time in Burlington, Iowa. She expressed her desire to E. H. Wells, secretary of the Harvard Alumni Association. Shortly thereafter he presented her with a recommendation that she

> lend a hand in assisting the Harvard Library to build up a collection on the history of the West which would enable Professor Turner to carry on his historical work more easily. As you probably know, Professor Turner had at his command at Madison

in the library of the State Historical Society the most complete collection on the history and development of the West that has ever been brought together.[14]

Frederick Jackson Turner, a key player in Harvard University's acquisition of the Peirce collection of Mormon Americana. Courtesy Henry E. Huntington Library.

Alice Hooper became an ardent supporter of Turner's efforts to establish a strong program of study on the American West and agreed to contribute a thousand dollars a year as a memorial foundation in her father's name to build a library collection of valuable items according to the judgment of Professor Turner.[15] On November 8, 1910, Hooper sent to the president and fellows of Harvard, her written answer which in part stated:

> In talking with Mr. Turner, lately called to the Chair of History, at Harvard University, I find that the collection of material bearing on the history & development of that part of America which lies beyond the Alleghanies, is incomplete and I write to offer to the Harvard College Library the sum of one thousand dollars a year, as long as I am able to give it, for the purchase of books and material for the above collection.[16]

Turner, who had been accustomed to the splendid collections at the University of Wisconsin, had been invited to Harvard to establish a similar program. Following a brief acquaintance with and limited discussion of Hooper's interests, Turner wrote her an expression of his gratitude:

> I am sure that it is possible to make your gift in honor of your father, the means of making Harvard a unique center, in important respects, for understanding how the West was built up. Students of later generations—not only those of the present—will appreciate it, and will be obliged, I hope, to come to Harvard for important sources of their country's history.[17]

Through the Harvard Library, the Harvard Commission on Western History, and the alumni offices, a campaign to collect library material was launched. On February 2, 1911, Alfred C. Potter, assistant librarian of Harvard University, requested information on a Mormon library offered for sale by the Shepard Book Company of Salt Lake City. In their response, the Shepard Book Company described the collection:

> It consists of about 1400 volumes—All books abtainable [*sic*] pro and con on the subject of Utah and Mormonism. Many of the pamphlets on the subject have been bound up in volumes [47] of say 500 to 600 pages each yet when bound are counted as one volume. . . . There are only five collections of Mormonism in this country—viz., the one in Congressional Library, one (the Berrian Collection) in N.Y. Public Library, one in Wisconsin Library at Madison, The Church (Mormon) Library here, and the one we offer for sale. . . .
>
> . . . We can assure you that its like cannot at this day be duplicated at all, while many of the volumes could be, yet there are many rare ones that can not be at all procured.[18]

The cost of the collection, $6,000, was far in excess of the funds Mrs. Hooper had offered, yet when no other sources were forthcoming, Turner attempted to convince her to make the purchase anyway. Enclosing a copy of the Shepard letter, Turner described to her the value of Mormon material to a library on the American West.

> Mormonism touches not only Utah but the characteristics of a vast area about Utah where Mormons are living, and it touches some pretty important matters of national legislation as well—so such a library has a value beyond local history. Perhaps in the long run its greatest value will lie, however in the field of the history of religions. Here was a native growth under the eyes of the American of the nineteenth century, of a religion that colonized an area equal to that of a great European nation, and built up an industrial empire at the same time. I wish we could get a donor, and I am sending you the letter remembering your desire to know when such things appeared.[19]

Hooper's response may have reflected the national view of the Church in 1911. That year *Cosmopolitan Magazine*, a popular family magazine, ran a series of strongly critical articles about the Church that gave the impression that it was made up of strange notions and strange people. Her answer to Turner stated:

> Of course I'm too poor to give this particular collection on Mormonism and while it must be of value have we not other things now which we need more than this kind of a collection? There can be no doubt about the Mormons' part in our western country from Nauvoo on, and if we were very rich it

> would seem a pity to allow this to get away from us—but I don't know of anyone whom I could induce to bury $4500 with the Mormons![20]

Efforts to acquire the collection, having failed for want of capital, remained dormant for three years until notice of a larger collection was announced by the Torch Press Book Shop. Investigations soon revealed that this was in fact the same collection, though substantially larger through Eli's continuous collecting efforts. Greater efforts were made this time by Harvard alumni officials, library staff, Professor Turner, and even Harvard president, Charles W. Eliot. Ultimately, Harvard bypassed both the Torch Press Book Shop and the Shepard Book Company and dealt directly with Eli in arranging the purchase. On March 3, 1914, a document labeled "classified schedule, Mormon library of E. H. Peirce" became the basis of a thirty-day option to purchase which was granted to Harvard. Handwritten on the face of this document, over the signatures of E. H. Peirce and Roger Pierce, is the statement, "This option to hold good for thirty days after submission of complete schedule."[21] As soon as the complete schedule arrived, university officials assiduously sought to determine the value of the collection and the extent of duplication in their current holdings.

Noteworthy opinions of the Peirce collection are contained in the correspondence file of the Harvard Commission on Western History. Roger Pierce recorded:

> the History Department at the University is of the opinion, from information which they have at hand, that this is an exceedingly valuable collection and that future investigation will prove that it would be a great addition to the Harvard University Library.[22]

Lewis B. McCornick had been asked to check into the value of the collection. He reported:

> There is no question about this library being complete and valuable, but that value can be best determined by the need of the University. It is perfectly safe to say that no such library could be again accumulated for thrice the asked price.[23]

Worthington C. Ford of the Massachusetts Historical Society wrote Professor Turner:

> The newspapers, pamphlets and books of local (Utah) imprint would by themselves be worth four or five thousand dollars, and in the auction room might bring more. Assuming them worth that much in money, they are worth more to the Harvard Library, where the possible utility of the material must count,

Houghton Library, Harvard University, where the Eli H. Peirce collection is housed. This exterior view was photographed about 1942. Courtesy Harvard University Archives.

> rather than the money value. It is an unusual opportunity, and all the more unusual as representing so remote a region, for few (if any) Eastern collections would give attention to the subject. Taking the list as it stands, and the little prospect of having as good an opportunity to obtain what the College Library needs, I consider the price not only fair, but on the whole moderate. What is difficult to obtain in the collection is worth to the Library what must be paid for the whole collection. The sale of duplicates will be so much gain.[24]

In a letter to his distinguished grandfather, Charles W. Eliot, former president of Harvard, Roger Pierce stated that:

> From such expert opinion as I obtained there [Salt Lake City] and have since obtained, it is the second most valuable collection of Mormon material in existence; the most valuable one is in the possession of the Mormon Church.
>
> The History Department is extremely desirous of obtaining this for the Harvard Library.[25]

President Eliot's response, as an assessment of Mormonism, is of interest and significance to the Church because Eliot, in his day, was the foremost citizen of the country in many peoples' estimation and certainly the foremost educator.

> I cannot think at this moment of any person who would be likely to give the money to obtain that Mormon collection. Nevertheless, I very much hope that you will ultimately succeed in buying it; for thirty years hence it may be possible for some impartial scholar to write a very interesting account of the whole Mormon movement. It had many quite extraordinary merits in the way of exploration, pioneering, colonizing, and cooperation in fundamental industries.[26]

David Heald, the Harvard librarian who went to Salt Lake City to finalize the purchase, examined and packed each volume in the collection, arranged for the shipping and insurance, and supervised loading the cartons on the train. By the time he left Salt Lake City, he had developed considerable competence on Mormon library materials. In a letter from Roger Pierce to Mrs. Hooper is the following important evaluation of Eli's collection: "Mr. Heald, on his return trip visited the University of Wisconsin, and saw the collection of Mormon material which they have. In his estimation it is not nearly so valuable or complete as ours."[27]

After Roger Pierce obtained for Harvard a thirty-day option to purchase the collection, news of the transaction leaked to the press and the *Salt Lake Herald* published an announcement. From information in letters from Lewis B. McCornick to Roger Pierce, it appears that the

University of Utah, the Governor of Utah, and the Church were quite opposed to the sale and that serious efforts to prevent it would be made. McCornick even suggested that Eli Peirce's actions would likely result in his excommunication from the Church:

> From the beginning I have suspected Mr. Pierce's [*sic*] intentions in this sale, as he is directly under the influence of the Mormon Church, and the church has often forbidden him to sell the collection. The church exercises such an influence by giving counsel, and this mild form of threatened excommunication is seldom broken.[28]

David Heald indicated to Alfred Potter, assistant librarian over the Purchasing Department, that Eli had received "a letter from the Prophet urging him not to sell, saying that would be a sin for the library to get into the hands of the enemies of the faith."[29]

Eli's letters imply that someone from the Church had been in contact with him, because he indicated to Harvard that the Church was interested in purchasing approximately five hundred items from the collection. McCornick became alarmed, and Turner and the others at Harvard sent David Heald to Salt Lake City to oversee the exchange and prevent Church, state, or university officials from interfering with the acquisition or commandeering the collection. While Eli may have wished to duck out of the sale to Harvard in favor of an arrangement with the Church or another purchaser, such a conclusion finds no support in the available records.

In the final negotiations in Salt Lake City, the Shepard Book Company insisted on its commission. Eli agreed they were entitled to it even though their contract had expired. Heald refused and tempers flared. Finally, it was agreed that Eli would pay seventy-five percent and Harvard twenty-five percent of the commission. On May 18, 1914, Heald wrote to Potter with a sense of relief:

> I lived up to my telegram of yesterday and shipped the books early this afternoon by freight. They are in twenty-six cases—total weight upwards of 5,200 pounds, and at three dollars and some odd cents per hundred weight, the freight charges come to the tidy sum of $161. I have sent you by registered mail the following documents—
>
> (1) Receipt for $6,562.50, payment in full signed by both the Peirces
>
> (2) Receipt for $100 from Shepard Book Co.
>
> (3) Bill of lading for books
>
> (4) Insurance policy [$25] for shipment.[30]

Harvard's total costs, exclusive of Heald's personal expenses, were $6,848.50. Having been persuaded by Turner, Alice Hooper agreed to pay $6,000; the remainder came from Harvard Library funds. Hooper's enthusiasm over the purchase had grown through the period of negotiations as indicated in a letter to Roger Pierce:

> My dear fellow, far from thinking you pressuring I like your keen interest & the expression of it= If we catch those Mormons I shall be glad of it= paying the piper is a good deal more than I can do without some sacrifice but so thoroughly do I believe in the gamble of the thing as an important asset for our purpose that I undertake to finance the venture= In so doing I am pleasing myself & it therefore seems to me as being hardly a matter for praise= but pleasure & satisfaction on the part of man making for nice collection of American Hist. is certainly legitimate. . . . I am but a passenger paying my fare & being carried along by those in command who know far more than I may ever dream of knowing.[31]

A few days later Alice Hooper again wrote Roger Pierce expressing her pleasure in the acquisition and significant praise for the efforts of those involved in carrying out the plan:

> I have read the enclosed letters in regard to the purchase of the Mormons with a real thrill. You Mr. Turner & Mr Coolidge showed great wisdom in speeding Mr. Heald to Salt Lake when you did & I owe you each & all a debt of gratitude certainly because my satisfaction is great in this acquisition & I feel sure this collection adds a value & an importance to the Charles Elliot Perkins Collection which will mean something for always.[32]

On June 12, 1914, the day the shipment arrived at Harvard, Hooper sent Roger Pierce a long-awaited letter: "I think your plans for the Mormons excellent & herewith enclose my checque [*sic*] for six thousand dollars. The cost of the Mormon Library belonging to your Utah namesake. I hoped to be able to supply an extra five hundred at some future date."[33]

The Peirce Collection

After many failed attempts to find it, the detailed schedule Eli submitted to Harvard officials listing the actual contents of his collection finally surfaced. In the Library Order Department records for the relevant years was a large, crumbling, gray envelope labeled "Mormon Library." On fifty-one single-spaced typed pages, is a list of the volumes in the collection, including the name of the publication, the number of volumes, the author or publisher, the place of publication, year of publication, approximate value, and notes. In the margins are numerous notations in Eli's familiar handwriting. Also in the envelope were four half-sized pages of blue Hotel Utah stationery. On two of these, Heald had begun letters to Potter, dated May 17, 1914. On the back of these pages is a list from 1 to 51 and a number matching the number of volumes listed at the bottom of each of those fifty-one pages. The total for the fifty-one pages and the purchase price shown is 2,612 "@ $2.50 per vol. = $6,530." On the last page, centered at the top appears the following note, "E. H. Peirce Library, Count of sheets by bound vols."[34] A legal-sized sheet at the back, apparently made up after the books were sorted and packed, showed unlisted and missing volumes which changed the total to 2,622 volumes and the price to $6,562.50.

A review of the inventory of the Peirce library shows that Eli was a thorough collector. The very detail with which the list is made out is an indication of the meticulous attention he gave to such things. As the whole collection is best measured by the sum of its many parts, a brief review of those major parts will help determine the contribution the collection makes to the Harvard library.

LDS Church Periodicals

The first eight pages in the schedule list the Church periodicals that were included. They are listed chronologically by date of publication. (See table 1.)

LDS Church Scriptures

The LDS scriptures in the collection included twenty copies of the Book of Mormon. Among them were copies of the first, second, and third American editions; the first, second, third, and fourth European editions; a Deseret alphabet edition; a copy of an edition published in Chicago by the Northern States Mission in 1907; an early, bound, triple combination volume of the Book of Mormon, Doctrine and Covenants, and Pearl of Great Price; and a copy of early editions in ten foreign languages. There were seven copies of the Doctrine and Covenants, including the first, second, third, and fourth American editions; the first European edition; one bound in the triple combination volume; and two foreign language editions. There was also an 1888 Salt Lake City edition of the Pearl of Great Price.

Pamphlets

Perhaps the most unique part of the Peirce collection is the pamphlet collection. The pamphlets were bound into 47 volumes of about 800 pages each. Eli Peirce prepared a directory of all of the pamphlets

Table 1: Peirce Collection Periodicals

Periodical	Years	Vols.
Evening and Morning Star	1832-33	2
Messenger and Advocate	1834-35	2
Elders' Journal	1837-38	1
Times and Seasons	1839-46	6
Millennial Star	1840-1913	75
Gospel Reflector	1841	1
The Prophet	1844	1
Frontier Guardian	1849-51	3
Guardian and Sentinel	1852	1
Udgorn Seion (Welsh)	1849-55	8
Deseret News	1850-63	13
Etoile du deseret (French)	1851	1
The Seer	1853-54	2
Zion's Watchman	1843-44, 1855-56	2
Skandinaviens Stjerne (Danish)	1853-89	33
Le Réflecteur (French)	1853	1
Journal of Discourses	1854-86	26
The Mormon	1855-57	3
Der Darsteller (German)	1855-57	3
The Western Standard	1856	1
Die Reform (German)	1862	1
Woman's Exponent	1872-1905	34
Juvenile Instructor	1866-1906	41
Nordstjernan (Swedish)	1877-80	4
Ungdommens Raadgiver (Danish)	1880-86	4
The Contributor	1880-96	17
Morgenstjernen (Danish) & Historical Record	1882-90	9
Deseret Home	1882-83	2
Deseret Weekly	1888-92	8
Zion's Home Monthly Magazine	1888-94	3
Der Stern (German)	1894	1
De Ster (Dutch)	1896-1904	9
Improvement Era	1897-1908	11
The Children's Friend	1902-13	10
Young Woman's Journal	1889-1910	21
Elder's Journal	1903-7	4
Liahona	1906-8	2
Utah Genealogical & Historical Magazine	1910-12	3
Southern Star	1899-1900	2
Conference Reports	1897-1912	8

arranged in alphabetical order by titles, including authors, dates of publication, total pages, and estimated values. The number of pages listed in the directory is 37,846 from a total of 1,016 individual publications. Harvard has made microfilm copies of this collection for research and for purchase by other libraries.

The pamphlets were organized by Peirce into twelve classifications and were cut and bound together in an attractive binding with a red and black spine. The bindings have deteriorated badly, and Harvard has wisely placed restrictions on their use. It appears that the pages, however, are in excellent condition. They had been cut for uniform binding, excepting those of smaller size, and the edges have been painted to give them a green and white finished appearance. All forty-seven volumes would occupy approximately fourteen feet of bookshelf space.

The description at the top of the index, written in Eli's handwriting, reads: "A collection of pamphlets for and against the Church of Jesus Christ of Latter-day Saints." Almost a hundred items in the pamphlet collection exceed 100 pages in length and several exceed 200 pages. The pamphlets cover numerous topics of historical interest about the Church, its people and practices, the railroad, legislative and legal topics, Indians, the University of Utah, Church manuals, and much more. There are numerous items listed as "Reorganite," "Josephite," "Strangite," the "Mission Tract Society," the "Tribune," and the "Utah Gospel Mission." It is evident that Eli sought everything he could obtain about the LDS Church, both pro and con. This breadth made his collection more valuable.

The pamphlets span nine decades, from the 1820s through 1912. No date is given for many of them, but table 2 shows the distribution by decade of those that are dated. Of the 83 pamphlets from the 1830s–1840s, many are by prominent Church leaders as indicated in table 3. The pamphlets are bound and categorized by topic, and each is identified by a label printed on its spine, as shown in table 4.

A Mormon Bibliography, 1830–1930, edited by Chad J. Flake of the Harold B. Lee Library at Brigham Young University, is the authoritative bibliographical listing of publications on Mormonism in its first century. Considerable efforts were made to locate in Flake's bibliography each pamphlet named in the Peirce index, but about 250 items were not found. Evidently Peirce had a wider focus than that covered in the bibliography.

Mormon Magazine Miscellany

A unique part of the collection is a set of fifteen volumes labeled "Mormon Magazine Miscellany" and listed as "magazine articles for &

Table 2: Chronological Distribution of 1830–1840 Documents

Decade	No. of Pamphlets
1820s	1
1830s	8
1840s	75
1850s	83
1860s	19
1870s	76
1880s	200
1890s	117
1900s	106

Table 3: Distribution by Author

Authors	No. of Pamphlets
Parley P. Pratt	6
John Taylor	5
Orson Hyde	3
Joseph Smith	2
Orson Spencer	2
Brigham Young	1
John P. Greene	1
Thomas Ward	1
John E. Page	1
Lorenzo Snow	1
Benjamin Winchester	1

Table 4: Topical Breakdown

Labels	Volumes
Doctrinal	1-3
Historical	4-6
Ecclesiastical	7
Biographical	8
Constitutional	9
Governmental	10
Poetical	11
Educational	12
Statistical	13
Apostatical	14
Antagonistical	15
Supplemental	16-47

against" the Church. Above the listing, in Eli's handwriting, is the notation, "Chiefly Anti-Mormon." The inventory list indicates that these fifteen volumes contain 350 articles spread across a total of 6,052 pages.

Legal and Legislative

In the collection is a substantial legal and legislative section with a nearly complete set of the acts, resolutions, and laws from the Utah territorial and state legislative sessions beginning in 1855 and running through 1909. There are also numerous copies of the House and Senate journals of the State of Utah, a copy of the proceedings of the Utah State Constitutional Convention, dated 1898, and the charter relating to the early organization of Salt Lake City. Another volume contains the proceedings of the State Bar Association for 1894-1905. Sixteen volumes of the Utah Reports contain the Territorial Supreme Court cases for 1872-91.

Church History and Teachings

The collection appears to be substantially complete in books on the doctrinal teachings and Church history written mostly by LDS authors and used widely within the Church in its first century. There are also copies of numerous hymnals used over many years in Church worship services.

Publications of Dissenting Factions

A section labeled "Publications of Dissenting Factions" is made up primarily of material from the Reorganized Church of Jesus Christ of Latter Day Saints (RLDS). There are copies of an 1858 and 1874 edition of the Book of Mormon published by the RLDS Church and copies of their first, second, and third editions of the Doctrine and Covenants. There is a copy of the 1867 edition of the RLDS "Retranslation Scriptures," the first published edition of the Joseph Smith Translation of the Bible. There are approximately thirty other volumes on miscellaneous subjects.

Assorted Publications

Mormon publications in foreign languages consist of about 35 volumes. Almost 20 volumes are about Utah history before the arrival of the Mormon pioneers. Another section of about 150 volumes is labeled, "Antiquitie-Indian Tradition Etc. Confirming Book of Mormon History." More than 100 volumes are listed under the label "Other Sects, Creeds and Denominations."

Utah Publications and Authors

A large section (about 225 volumes) under the label "Utah Publications & Utah Authors" includes a wide assortment of local histories and literary expressions about Utah, the life of its people, its geology, fauna, flora, mining, agriculture, locally produced magazines, business and university directories, volumes of the proceedings of local lodges of the Masons and other fraternal orders, and publications of various local clubs.

Anti-Mormon Publications

There is a large section of anti-Mormon publications of local, national, and international origin. Under a separate heading, yet also largely anti-Mormon, is a 75-volume section labeled, "Doctrinal—published outside the Church." These volumes and the large numbers of anti-Mormon publications in both the pamphlet and magazine article collection gave rise to the rumors that the Church opposed the sale to Harvard. Some have wondered if its existence indicated that Eli Peirce himself was skeptical about the Church. As noted above, such conclusions are not founded in fact, and Eli's faithfulness is a matter of record.

Mormon Americana

Further evidence that Eli was an avid collector of anything relating to Utah or Mormonism is seen in the Americana section, the largest single part of his collection. This section lists approximately nine hundred volumes in seventeen pages of inventory and is arranged alphabetically by author. Justification for the volumes in this large collection is given in his handwriting as part of the heading preceding this section, "Americana. . . Treating of Utah and (or) the Mormons Incidentally."

Conclusion

This paper does not attempt to assess Harvard's total holdings on Mormonism. Harvard had gathered many materials before it acquired the Peirce collection, and it has since added many more including some unique items. For example, between 1948 and 1955, the Laboratory of Social Relations at Harvard, supported by the Rockefeller Foundation, sponsored the "Comparative Study of Values in Five Cultures" in the Rimrock Area of western New Mexico. "Mormons" was one of the five cultures studied. Many notable social scientists participated in this study and files of their research notes and field diaries are on file at Harvard.

In the single purchase of the Eli H. Peirce Collection, however, Harvard acquired one of the best collections of printed Mormon Americana of the time. It was acquired from a practicing and believing Mormon who was also a conscientious collector. The collection included all items obtainable for and against the Mormons and their beliefs. The most significant features of the collection are the pamphlets and magazine materials purporting to deal with the subject or people associated with Mormonism. The collection supports the kind of scholarly research that Frederick Jackson Turner envisioned as part of his academic program on the history of the American West. Through it, Harvard can boast of having one of the finest collections of early printed materials treating the broad subjects of Mormonism and Utah.

Alan K. Parrish is Associate Professor of Ancient Scriptures at Brigham Young University.

NOTES

A version of this article was originally published in *BYU Studies* 32 (Fall 1992): 137-58.

[1]Ray Allen Billington, "The Origins of Harvard's Mormon Collection," *Arizona and the West* (Fall 1968): 211-24.

[2]Eliza R. Snow, *Biography and Family History of Lorenzo Snow* (Salt Lake City: Deseret News, 1884), 407-8.

[3]Snow, *Biography,* 421.

[4]Eli H. Peirce Jr., *Mormon Tabernacle Choir, Being a Collection of Newspaper Criticisms and Cullings from Metropolitan Magazines and Musical Journals Covering Six Excursions, from the World's Fair in 1893 to the Seattle Exposition in 1909* (Salt Lake City: E. H. Peirce, 1910).

[5]*Deseret News,* February 22, 1911, 4.

[6]*Salt Lake Herald,* September 5, 1886.

[7]*Deseret Evening News,* September 12, 1892, and October 22, 1894, 2.

[8]Lewis B. McCornick to Roger Pierce, May 19, 1914, the Harvard Commission on Western History, Correspondence Box L*O, "Mormon Collection," UA III.50.29.12.2.5, Harvard University Archives, Pusey Library, Harvard University (hereafter cited as Harvard Archives).

[9]Roger Pierce to Lewis B. McCornick, May 25, 1914, Harvard Archives.

[10]Billington, "The Origins of Harvard's Mormon Collection," 211-24. See also, Ray Allen Billington, *Dear Lady* (San Marino, Calif.: Huntington Library, 1970), 34-37.

[11]*Herald-Republican,* February 10, 1915.

[12]Petition for Sale of Personal Property, Third District Court, Salt Lake County, Utah. Regarding the estate of Eli H. Peirce, August 14, 1915.

[13]"Last Rites for Eli H. Peirce," *Deseret Evening News,* February 12, 1915, 9.

[14]E. H. Wells to Alice Forbes Perkins Hooper, August 26, 1910, Box: UA III.50.29.12.2.7, Harvard Archives.

[15]An extensive record of the friendship and association of Turner and Hooper, documenting their efforts to raise a substantial collection of Western American materials is recorded in Billington, *Dear Lady.*

[16]Alice Forbes Perkins Hooper to the President and Fellows of Harvard University, November 8, 1910, Box: UA III.50.8.11.1, Harvard Archives.

[17]Billington, *Dear Lady,* 89.

[18]Shepard Book Company to Alfred C. Potter, February 6, 1911, Harvard Archives.

[19]Billington, *Dear Lady,* 94.

[20]Billington, *Dear Lady,* 95.

[21]Classified Schedule, Mormon Library of E. H. Peirce, Harvard Archives.

[22]Roger Pierce to L. B. McCornick, March 20, 1914, HCWH.

[23]Lewis B. McCornick to Roger Pierce, March 30, 1914, Harvard Archives.

[24]Worthington C. Ford to Frederick Jackson Turner, May 10, 1914, Harvard Archives.

[25]Roger Pierce to President Charles W. Eliot, May 4, 1914, Harvard Archives.

[26]President Charles W. Eliot to Roger Pierce, May 7, 1914, Harvard Archives.

[27]Roger Pierce to Alice Hooper, June 10, 1914, Box: UA III.50.29.12.2.7, Harvard Archives.

[28]Lewis B. McCornick to Roger Pierce, April 14, 1914, Harvard Archives.

[29]David Heald to Alfred C. Potter, May 17, 1914, Harvard Archives.

[30]David Heald to Alfred Potter, May 18, 1914, Harvard Archives.

[31]Alice Hooper to Roger Pierce, May 14, 1914, Box: UA III.50.29.12.2.5, Harvard Archives.

[32]Alice Hooper to Roger Pierce, May 29, 1914, Miscellaneous Correspondence, "Mrs. Hooper," Box: UA III.50.29.12.2.7, Harvard Archives.

[33] Alice Hooper to Roger Pierce, June 12, 1914, Box: UA III.50.29.12.2.7, Harvard Archives.

[34]In Box, U.A. III.50.8.116, "Library-Order Dept.," Harvard Archives.

Theodore Schroeder, who dedicated his life to writing and collecting materials to defame Mormonism. Courtesy Special Collections, Morris Library, Southern Illinois University at Carbondale.

The Theodore Schroeder Collection in the New York Public Library

A. Burt Horsley

The *New York Times* of February 12, 1953, carried the following obituary for Theodore Schroeder,[1] who had died two days before on his farm in Cos Cob, Connecticut:

> Theodore Albert Schroeder of Valley Road, lawyer, author and a leading authority on the legal aspects of freedom, died last night of a coronary thrombosis at his home. His age was 88.
>
> Mr. Schroeder, who was known as the Sage of Cos Cob, was the author of several books and many essays. While some of his works became standard college texts, he prided himself that "no one in America has published so much controversial literature."
>
> At his death he was engaged in editing a definitive collection of his writings, which were said to total twenty volumes. . . . He advocated the psychoanalysis of judges and teachers to free them of prejudices.
>
> He was a founder with Lincoln Steffens, author, and Brant Whitlock, former Ambassador to Belgium, of the Free Speech League of New York. Born in Wisconsin, he received a law degree from the University of Wisconsin and later entered the field of psychology. He was a specialist in evolutionary psychology and psychoanalysis.

This rather innocuous account makes no reference to the fact that Schroeder (1864–1953) spent the greater part of his lifetime writing against Mormonism and collecting everything he could find that would help to expose and destroy it, a fact that might have remained obscure had several of his papers not been purchased by the New York Public Library in 1966 from a dealer in Cos Cob. Other Schroeder papers are found in the Wisconsin State Historical Library[2] and at the Southern Illinois University Library. This article describes the highlights of the Schroeder collection in the New York Public Library.[3]

Schroeder's Life and Works

In a letter dated December 3, 1979, Paul R. Rugen, keeper of manuscripts at the New York Public Library, wrote the following about the

Schroeder collection: "We know nothing of the provenance of these papers beyond the fact that Schroeder was a resident of Cos Cob, Connecticut, at the time of his death in 1953." Much information about Schroeder's life and works is available, however, from David Brudnoy's 1971 dissertation at Brandeis University, entitled "Liberty's Bugler: The Seven Ages of Theodore Schroeder," and from a small work by Lesley Kuhn, director of Psychological Library Publishers, entitled *Theodore Schroeder's Last Will* (1958).

As a boy, Schroeder came under the influence of Robert Ingersoll's skepticism (Ingersoll, 1833–99, was a famous agnostic orator and pamphleteer); by age thirteen Schroeder was earning his own living[4] and viewing the world through less than rose-tinted glasses. He took work as a store clerk[5] and a railroad laborer[6] and saw quite a bit of the world before he graduated with a law degree from the University of Wisconsin. According to the Reverend Ilesley Boone, "when [Schroeder's] wanderlust ended, he revisited Utah, determined to settle down. At twenty-five years of age he established himself in Salt Lake City as a lawyer. This choice of location was also expressive of his unusual curiosity. He wanted to see and study a new religious establishment in the making."[7]

Schroeder practiced law in Salt Lake City from 1889 until the turn of the century, and during those years he was repeatedly embroiled with the LDS Church. He criticized what he called "the secularist government of the Mormons," gaining many supporters among the "Gentile" population.[8] He resisted the annual $3 poll tax on constitutional grounds,[9] and he prosecuted the case against B. H. Roberts that excluded Roberts from Congress.[10] The New York Public Library collection includes the typescript of Schroeder's article on the Roberts case, "The Mormon Breach of Faith, Polygamy in Congress," and a typescript of his "Response to Roberts' Defense," as well as several articles and letters on the Reed Smoot case published a few years later.

In June 1898, Schroeder founded a periodical, *Lucifer's Lantern,* to publicize his views on Mormon issues;[11] there are several copies of *Lucifer's Lantern* in the collection. Schroeder was also involved in making the *Salt Lake Herald* "the official organ of the Democratic Party." (He was one of the party's forty charter organizers in Utah.)[12] The collection contains many Mormon-related news clippings from Salt Lake papers.

During his years in Utah, Schroeder befriended Sarah Pratt, a dissident Mormon and widow of Orson Pratt, and James Thornton Cobb, a Gentile with a Mormon wife and family. They funneled to Schroeder much of the "inside" information he used to sweeten his concoctions of exposé.

In 1900, disenchanted with his Utah experience, Schroeder moved to New York City to practice law. However, after about a year, he gave up his legal practice. Schroeder spent the rest of his life as a maverick psychologist, studying and writing about the amatory, erotic dimensions of life, particularly with reference to religion and religious behavior. His prime target was Mormonism. He later wrote, "Years ago I intended writing a book about Mormonism. While thus studying the literature of the Mormons, I saw that all the peculiarities of their theology had a sexual reason for existence," that in fact there is an "erotic origin of all religions."[13]

Schroeder developed his own brand of evolutionary psychology. His writings and the items he collected reveal his preoccupation—indeed his obsession—with the connection he saw between religion and sexuality. The collection also contains ample evidence of Schroeder's lifelong involvement with free speech, anticensorship, and civil liberties movements.

Schroeder left his estate to two friends, Lesley Kuhn and Ethel Clyde, with explicit directions that it "be expended in the collection and arrangement and publication of my writing."[14] Two cousins—whom Schroeder had not included in his will—contested the bequest, insisting that Schroeder's writings were not worth republishing and that it would be "not only a waste of the residuary estate, but contrary to public policy."[15] After several years of litigation, the Supreme Court of Connecticut ruled in favor of the cousins. Superior Court Judge Covello held that "an examination of the writings of the deceased indicates that there is no social improvement to be had from their publication or that they will produce even a slight advantage. On the contrary, they offend religion and extol anti-social ideas." He concluded that Schroeder had been mainly preoccupied with fighting the Mormon Church and with "a desire to perpetuate his name rather than to provide something which would be for the general public good."[16] Supreme Court Justice O'Sullivan affirmed: "The law will not declare a trust valid when the object of the trust, as the finding discloses, is to distribute articles which reek of the sewer."[17] A brief description of the Schroeder Collection in the New York Public Library may help us decide whether we agree with the court's decision.

Republication of Schroeder's writings would have been an enormous project. The first bibliography of Schroeder's works, completed thirty years before his death, included psychological, philosophical, sociological, and legal articles in nearly two hundred professional and scholarly publications; some of his work had already been translated into six languages. What did he write about? According to Justice

O'Sullivan, "the very enumeration of some of the titles which Schroeder selected for his writings brands them indelibly": "Polygamy and Inspired Lies," "The Sex-Determinant in Mormon Theology," "Mormonism and Prostitution," and "Sadism in Mormonism."[18]

Over a period of about two weeks I examined more than 150 folders in the Schroeder collection, each containing from one to several items. One folder contains a bibliography of Schroeder's extensive writings on Mormonism. I have classified Schroeder's anti-Mormon works into three categories: those directed against the Church as an institution, against its leaders, and against the Book of Mormon.

Works Directed against the LDS Church

A selection of titles in the first category shows that Schroeder was indeed obsessed with what he called "the sexual determinant in Mormon theology."[19] The collection includes typescripts for undated articles entitled "Sexual Theology in Mormonism," "Mormonism and Erotogenesis of Religion," and "The Endowment Ceremony" (making claims about alleged debaucheries and immoralities). Other titles include "Polygamy and the Constitution" (1906) and "Mormonism and the New Polygamy" (1910). Schroeder's "Incest in Mormonism" appeared in *The American Journal of Urology and Sexology* (no date), and the *Journal of Religious Psychology* published his "Outline for a Study of the Erotogenesis of Religion" (1912). The New York Public Library collection contains these and many similar articles and pamphlets by Schroeder.

Works against Church Leaders

Schroeder also attacked particular Mormon leaders. Not satisfied with the efforts of earlier anti-Mormon writers, Schroeder ferreted out every tidbit he could find that might support his conclusions that Joseph Smith's character was spurious. Some of Schroeder's claims anticipate those made later by anti-Mormons. For example, Schroeder argued that Joseph Smith was not only a liar in general but an incestuous man, prostitute in his sexual activities,[20] who supposedly encouraged abortion among those whom he had defiled[21] and who was given to drunkenness on occasion.[22]

Schroeder did not like Brigham Young much, either—he seems to have spent years in research and correspondence accumulating personal letters to, from, and about Brigham in a debunking crusade against this stalwart. Although Schroeder had no less contempt for the leaders of the Reorganized Church of Jesus Christ of Latter Day Saints, he sought critical statements from them about Brigham. He rejoiced when he could extract criticisms from President Young's former associates among the Utah dissidents. Of particular interest to Schroeder were letters written by Augusta Adams Cobb, one of Brigham's wives, to Brigham complaining of neglect or mistreatment.

Works against the Book of Mormon

Schroeder's collection also includes letters and other items first acquired by James Cobb, who came to Utah in 1858 and married Camille Meith, the Mormon sister-in-law of Karl G. Maeser. Cobb was connected with the *Salt Lake Tribune* for many years and maintained a running correspondence with people everywhere in his desire to obtain evidence that would discredit the founders of Mormonism and the origins of the Book of Mormon. Schroeder's interest in the anti-Mormon crusade and his method of collecting materials were likely influenced by his association with Cobb.

Schroeder collected Cobb's correspondence about the origin of the Book of Mormon, which includes letters to Cobb from T. H. Gregg of Hamilton, Illinois (1892), and from William E. McLellin of Independence, Missouri (1880), concerning Sidney Rigdon and the Spaulding manuscript. Two letters to Cobb, dated February and March 1874, are from John H. Gilbert, who set type for the Book of Mormon in Grandin's printing office in Palmyra, New York. In these Gilbert makes disparaging remarks about Joseph Smith, Oliver Cowdery, Martin Harris, and Sidney Rigdon.

Schroeder also clearly sought to discredit the Three Witnesses. He put together evidence calculated to disqualify Oliver Cowdery and Martin Harris on grounds of incompetence and gullibility, but he concentrated special attention on David Whitmer and the Whitmers in general, apparently with character assassination as the objective. The following excerpt from a letter dated June 25, 1884, from Richmond, Missouri, purports to be the words of a member of the Whitmer family:

> I have drank with David Whitmer. If I have seen him seen him [*sic*] drunk once, I have an hundred times. All the Whitmers know that he drinks. They have all seen him drunk. I never saw him down, but drunk enough for his tongue to be loose at both ends. When he is drunk he is more apt to talk about religion than at any other time. I never heard him speak in tongues only when he was drunk. I have heard him speak in tongues two or three times. John Whitmer has talked to me about uncle Dave's drinking and asked what we should do about it. George Seveitch and I have talked about it. George said to me: "I told grandpa to keep out of the saloons, and I would take his

> whiskey home to him." And George did carry it home to the old man, to keep him from going to the saloons and getting drunk before the world. . . . It runs in the Whitmer blood to be libidinous. Whitmer's livery stable used to be a resort for prostitutes and drunkards. Little Dave [son of David the witness] is a constitutional liar, a shylock and miser. . . . He used to be known as about the worst libertine in town. If he has had "private disease" once, he has had it not less than a half dozen times. He is superstitious and ignorant.

When he moved from Salt Lake City to New York, Schroeder apparently shifted his attention to the origin and authorship of the Book of Mormon. He accepted the Spaulding theory about the origins of the Book of Mormon and from that erroneous theory willingly drew this conclusion:

> So far as I know Mormonism (The Church of Jesus Christ of Latter-day Saints) is the only religious sect that was ever established on a one-hundred percent, conscious fraud in its founder. The Book of Mormon is a clumsily patched plagiarism from an unpublished manuscript of Solomon Spaulding.[23]

As might be expected, Schroeder's collection includes letters solicited from members of the Solomon Spaulding family and from associates and neighbors who might be able to shed additional light on the Spaulding manuscript theory. Much of this material would whet the appetite of the iconoclast, but it was never conclusive enough to satisfy Schroeder.

Cobb's correspondence with ex-Apostle William E. McLellin and others on the subject sometimes backfired, producing materials to defame some of the early Church leaders but simultaneously thwarting his attempts to get at the Book of Mormon. For example, Cobb and Schroeder must have been frustrated by this admonition from apostate McLellin:

> I dont know that I am surprised at a thinking man for rejecting L.D.S.ism as its now developed, in any and all branches of what is called Mormonism. But when a man goes at the Book of M. he touches the apple of my eye. He fights against truth—against purity—against light—against the purest, or one of the truest, purest books on earth. I have more confidence in the Book of Mormon than any book of this wide earth! And its not because I dont know its contents, for I probably have read it through 20 times. I have read it carefully three times within a year and made many notes on it. It must be that a man does not love purity when he finds falt [*sic*] with the Book of Mormon!![24]

Works about Religious and Social Customs

Schroeder's later writings, such as "Some Difficulties of the Psychologists of Religion" (1922), "Sex and Psychoanalysis" (1926), and "Sex and Censorship—the Eternal Conflict" (1927), seem directed away from Mormonism in particular and toward religious and social customs in general. The collection includes many of these articles championing free speech and psychoanalysis and decrying censorship. Such writings make up more than half of the materials in the New York Public Library's Schroeder collection.

Conclusion

In a summary glance at the materials in box #3, I noticed a previously passed-over item, a clipping of a magazine advertisement:

> THE MORMON ELDER'S DAMIANA WAFERS FOR NERVOUS DEBILITY, A POSITIVE CURE FOR IMPOTENCY, NO MATTER OF HOW LONG STANDING, SPERMATORRHAEA, NON-RETENTION OF URINE, LUCORRHEA, DIABETES, OVERWORK OF THE BRAIN, DYSPEPSIA, AND GENERAL BREAKING DOWN OF THE NERVOUS SYSTEM. THE WELL-KNOWN AND GENERAL USE OF DAMIANA AMONG THE MORMONS FOR THE PAST FIFTY YEARS IS THE MOST WE CAN SAY FOR THE EFFICASY OF THE DRUG.

Knowing Schroeder's obsession for objective and scientific consideration, I doubt he took seriously the claims of the Mormon Elder's Damiana Wafers. But—who knows?—maybe he should have tried them.

A. Burt Horsley is Emeritus Professor of Religion, Brigham Young University.

NOTES

[1]Schroeder was born Albert Theodore Schroeder. When his father died, he dropped the Albert and became Theodore Schroeder or Theodore A. Schroeder. David Barry Brudnoy, "Liberty's Bugler: The Seven Ages of Theodore Schroeder" (Ph.D. diss., Brandeis University, 1971), 139.

[2]Richard H. Cracroft and Thomas D. Schwartz, "The Schroeder Mormon Collection at the Wisconsin State Historical Library," *Dialogue: A Journal of Mormon Thought* 2 (Autumn 1967): 154–58. See also Brudnoy, "Liberty's Bugler"; Brudnoy, "A Decade in Zion: Theodore Schroeder's Initial Assault on the Mormons," *The Historian* 37 (February 1975): 241–56; and Brudnoy, "Of Sinners and Saints: Theodore Schroeder, Brigham Roberts and Reed Smoot," *Journal of Church and State* 14 (Spring 1972): 261–78. A listing of Schroeder's writings is Ralph Edward McCoy, comp., *Theodore Schroeder, a Cold Enthusiast; a Bibliography* (Carbondale: Libraries of Southern Illinois University, 1973). See also the essay by Michael Edmunds and Lian Partlow in this volume.

[3]In addition to its Theodore Schroeder collection, the New York Public Library also houses the William C. Berrian Collection, donated in 1899, which includes 451 books, 325 pamphlets, 52 volumes of newspapers, and over 500

individual unbound newspapers relevant to Mormon studies ("Introduction to Research in Mormon History," New York Public Library Research Guide no. 10, 1). The Berrian Collection was donated in 1899 (The William Berrian collection is described in Berrian, *Catalogue of Books, Early Newspapers and Pamphlets on Mormonism* [New York, 1898]. This collection was presented to the New York Public Library in December 1899 by Helen Miller Gould. For a complete description of the library's collections in 1909, see "Lists of Works in the New York Public Library Relating to Mormons," *Bulletin of the New York Public Library* 13 [March 1909]: 183-239). The library holds other Mormon materials, including early editions of the Book of Mormon and one of the nine known copies of the Book of Commandments. The Manuscripts Division of the library houses several Mormon documents. Most of these (thirty-seven letters) are in the Schroeder collection, but the Charles L. Woodward scrapbooks also contain six letters; other files include correspondence from Joseph Smith, Orson Hyde, Sidney Rigdon, and Willard Richards. The library has one of the diaries of Brigham Young Jr. ("Introduction to Research in Mormon History," 1).

[4]Brudnoy, "Liberty's Bugler," 9.

[5]Brudnoy, "Liberty's Bugler," 9.

[6]Brudnoy, "Liberty's Bugler," 12.

[7]Ilesley Boone, "He Became an Evolutionary Psychologist," in *Evolutionary Psychology,* ed. Ilesley Boone (Stanford, Conn.: Next Century Fund, 1949).

[8]Lesley Kuhn, ed., *Theodore Schroeder's Last Will* (New York: Psychological Library Publishers, 1958), 7.

[9]Brudnoy, "Liberty's Bugler," 41.

[10]Brudnoy, "Liberty's Bugler," 90-94.

[11]Brudnoy, "Liberty's Bugler," 62.

[12]Brudnoy, "Liberty's Bugler," 41.

[13]Theodore Schroeder, "Outline for a Study of the Erotogenesis of Religion," *Journal of Religious Psychology* 5 (October 1912): 394-401.

[14]Kuhn, *Theodore Schroeder's Last Will.* The opinion is reported as *In re Estate of Theodore Schroeder*, sub nom. *Fidelity Title and Trust Company v. Clyde,* 143 Conn. 247, 121 A.2d 625 (1956).

[15]Kuhn, *Theodore Schroeder's Last Will.*

[16]Kuhn, *Theodore Schroeder's Last Will.*

[17]Kuhn, *Theodore Schroeder's Last Will,* citing *Fidelity Title and Trust,* 629.

[18]Kuhn, *Theodore Schroeder's Last Will,* citing *Fidelity Title and Trust,* 627, 629.

[19]Theodore Schroeder, "Some Difficulties of the Psychologists of Religion," reprint from the *Truth Seeker* (1922).

[20]Theodore Schroeder, "Mormonism and Prostitution," *The Medical Council* (May 1909): 171-72.

[21]Theodore Schroeder, "Joseph Smith—a Polygamist and Abortionist," typescript.

[22]Theodore Schroeder, "Mormonism and Intoxicants," *American Historical Magazine* 3 (May 1908): 241-47.

[23]Theodore Schroeder, "Sexual Theology in Mormonism," unpublished typescript. The New York Public Library also holds Schroeder's article, "The Origin of the *Book of Mormon* (continued): From Rigdon to Smith via P. P. Pratt," *American Historical Magazine* (January 1907), and B. H. Roberts's response, "The

Origin of the *Book of Mormon* (A Reply to Mr. Theodore Schroeder)," from the November 1908 issue of the same magazine. Roberts was invited by the editor of the *American Historical Magazine* to write a history of the LDS Church. What Roberts produced became the basis for his *A Comprehensive History of the Church, Century One,* 6 vols. (Salt Lake City: Deseret News Press, 1930). See especially vol. 1, preface, iii–v. On the history of the Spaulding theory of the origins of the Book of Mormon, see Lester E. Bush Jr., "The Spalding Theory Then and Now," *Dialogue* 10 (Autumn 1977): 40–69.

[24]Letter from W. E. McLellan to Mr. J. T. Cobb, dated Independence, Mo., Aug 14th, 1880 (see *Church News,* December 8, 1985, 6, 10); see also letters from J. L. Traughber to Schroeder which discuss Traughber's William E. McLellin collection of Mormon Americana. These letters played a role in the Mark Hofmann murder and forgery case. See Richard E. Turley Jr., *Victims: The LDS Church and the Mark Hofmann Case* (Urbana and Chicago: University of Illinois Press, 1992), 112–14.

RLDS Temple, south side. The library and archives is now located in this building. Courtesy Library-Archives, Reorganized Church of Jesus Christ of Latter Day Saints.

The Archives of the Reorganized Church of Jesus Christ of Latter Day Saints

Sara Hallier Nyman and L. Madelon Brunson

At the April 1865 annual conference held at Plano, Illinois, the newly established Reorganized Church first publicly noted the need for a church library. In his speech of April 6, 1865, President Joseph Smith III "recommended that a library should be established for the benefit of the church."[1] Two months later the Reorganization's First Presidency and Quorum of Twelve Apostles appointed Isaac Sheen as librarian, giving him approval to collect money and books.[2] Sheen had been the first editor of the official RLDS periodical, the *True Latter-Day Saints' Herald* (later known as *The Saints' Herald*); thus his appointment linked Herald Publishing House to the library, a union which lasted until the early 1920s. As a result, the initial function of the library was to serve primarily as a resource for the publishing and literary concerns of the RLDS Church.

History of the Library and Archives

Early library development came slowly. Although a small budget was provided at times, volumes were acquired primarily by donation. The collection development was unsystematic and the contents were largely unclassified. The RLDS Church owned few of the church archival records and documents for 1830 to 1844, these having been retained by Brigham Young and his followers. However, over the library's early years, the Reorganized Church attempted to acquire and preserve some of the published works of that period.

By the end of the nineteenth century, the Reorganized Church began to develop a sense of its own history, and the library became a primary way to collect and preserve that history. The purposes of the library began to be better defined when Frederick M. Smith, strong advocate of the library and later President of the RLDS Church, assumed the duties of librarian in 1896, after having served as church historian for a short time.

Joseph Smith III. Courtesy Library-Archives, Reorganized Church of Jesus Christ of Latter Day Saints.

Out of a professional concern and a respect for historical materials, Smith commented on the "deplorable condition" of the library:

> Many of our most valuable books, historically valuable at least, have been badly used and shamefully mistreated by borrowers, proofreaders, typos, copy preparers, and others proverbially hard on books. Your present librarian has seen whole pages of such books as volumes of the *Times and Seasons, Millennial Star, Messenger and Advocate,* and others, disfigured by marks of blue, red, and black pencils, and even ink had been used to mark, underscore, strike out, and punctuate matter in them. . . . If a library is worth keeping at all, it is worthy of decent, thoughtful treatment.[3]

During Frederick Smith's service as librarian, Heman C. Smith, church historian, proved to be a valuable library advocate. He participated in secular historical societies and preserved the documentation needed in his work. He was instrumental in publishing *The Journal of History,* which disseminated and thus preserved some of the church members' diaries and journals as well as providing an outlet for the publication of local Reorganized Church history. His sense of historiography, although developed to help prove that the church was true, provided a focus for accumulating the historical collection.

With more emphasis on acquisition efforts, the library needed strong administrative direction. To improve the library's service, Heman C. Smith introduced the Dewey Decimal classification system. He also defined the purpose of the library: to provide "information upon any subject beneficial to the church."[4] This broad goal was to be met with a budget that represented 0.23 percent of the Reorganized Church's expenses.[5]

On January 5, 1907, a disastrous fire destroyed the Herald Publishing House in Lamoni, Iowa, site of RLDS Church headquarters since 1881. The fire destroyed the historian's office and most of the library's holdings, including some of the RLDS Church's own growing collection of archival materials. A well-known example of the loss is the Lyman Wight journal. The fire was a major setback for the library and archives.

A few months later, the leadership and the general conference supported efforts to administer the recovering library more professionally and in 1907 appointed a library commission.[6] This group was composed of representatives from the RLDS General Sunday School Association, Zion's Religio-Literary Society, the First Presidency, the Presiding Bishopric, and one member at large. The commission's duties were to administer the Reorganization's library, appoint the librarian, and select and purchase books.[7] This was a concentrated effort to reinforce the library endeavors and accelerate accumulation of books and materials after the tragic losses. As part of that effort, the commission supported the library's acquisition of historically significant materials. One of the commission's early reports stated that "the general library shall have the preference of all rare books, especially such as deal with church history and American archeology."[8] This mention of rare books instituted a more intentional approach to growth.

Another development that demonstrated church support of the library was the establishment of a special column entitled "The Library Department" in the General Sunday School Association's magazine, the *Sunday School Exponent*. This column became a forum not only for local library development, but also for encouraging library use in the community by making RLDS Church members aware of the library's existence and resources.

A third major contribution to the library's development occurred as space became increasingly tight at the rebuilt Herald Publishing House, where the collection had started accumulating after the 1907 fire. The Library Commission, with Fred M. Smith's support, advocated that the various extant book collections in offices and in the RLDS Church's still young library be relocated at Graceland College in Lamoni, Iowa. Although this plan did not entirely come to fruition, it made the library an entity independent from Herald House and thus made the library's holdings more accessible. Apparently by 1918 part of the books were consolidated at Graceland. But the rare books and historical materials undoubtedly moved with the church historian to Independence, Missouri, when headquarters moved there in 1921.

In spite of the setbacks, the early years of the twentieth century proved to be a time which brought significant overall growth for the library. The Reorganized Church's publishing efforts—which continually added to the library—were well established by this time, offering a wealth of "good" reading material including books, tracts, and periodicals. A national trend toward greater literacy during these years encouraged people, especially the youth, to read the "right" type of literature. Accordingly, branch or local libraries started to grow throughout the church.

By 1922 collections were consolidated in Independence, Missouri. The historian's collection, the remaining part of the general Reorganized Church library, the Independence Stake Library, and the library of the Institute of Arts and Sciences came together under one roof. The new collection was named the Emma Hale Smith Memorial Library.

The Institute of Arts and Sciences had been developed so that working persons could complete their high school education. The library was open to the community, thereby reinforcing its focus as an education center. RLDS Church departments began to form and grow, and book collections increased to meet their needs, with close to fifteen thousand volumes available for use, including a number of children's books. The demand for increased library services was met by hiring a full-time librarian, Blanche Farrar.

Samuel A. Burgess, church historian from 1923 to 1942, described three aspects of the library's work at this time: to encourage reading of the best literature, to maintain books of reference in local and departmental libraries, and to collect books of historical interest, including publications for and against the church.[9] However, just when the library was beginning to expand and become more accessible to users, the Great Depression brought growth to a halt.

Notwithstanding limited economic support during the 1930s, the library focused on meeting the needs of scholars who used the collection. In 1932, church historian Burgess reported to a general conference of the Reorganized Church that

> an important development is the number of students who are doing research work in the University of Iowa, University of Chicago, and other colleges, who have found it advisable to come here and consult our historical collection. Our collection is not a very large one compared with some others, but it does comprise a few thousand items, including early publications and manuscripts, early periodicals, and a few photostats. This is becoming in fact a very large part of our work. We regret that we have not been able to have this collection fully accessioned and indexed, but this latter would require a cross-indexing of items, not simply of the books.[10]

During the next twenty years, the library was merely maintained. WPA workers provided some help by doing research, answering questions, and identifying materials to be filed in the Library of Congress. (However, it is not known that any items were ever filed there.) Still, the library lacked professional guidance and proper security. The succeeding few years saw some progress in these areas. A move toward improved security for library holdings came in 1952 when a closed-access research library was established on the top floor of the Auditorium. These quarters, with high ceilings and soundproof walls, were originally designed to be a radio room, although it is doubtful they were used much for that purpose. A second major step toward professionalism was the installation of a microfilm camera in 1959. With the camera, important, fragile, and rare documents could be preserved on film.

In 1965, Richard Howard assumed office as RLDS Church historian. Under Howard's guidance in instituting professional practices, the collection grew. Through the next several years, the library and archives became much better prepared to meet the research needs of a renewed interest in well-documented, objective writing of the Reorganization's history. One of these preparations was the establishment of an archive for rare books and manuscripts which was to be separate from the rest of the library.

In a sense, the history of the archives goes back only to 1973. Manuscript materials and some rare books accumulated under the historians' purview in a rather disorderly fashion until the 1960s. However, church historians since at least 1965 have made efforts to preserve documents of historical value. Even earlier than this, accession registers and card catalogs for quick retrieval gave some shape

The Auditorium, Independence, Missouri, ca. 1985. The Auditorium was the RLDS World Church Headquarters for many years. Courtesy Library-Archives, Reorganized Church of Jesus Christ of Latter Day Saints.

and coherence to the existing materials. In addition, librarians and historians attempted to preserve materials more professionally in environments conducive to document protection. The first archivist was named in 1973 and the first full-time archivist in 1976. With the full-time archivist, accessioning became more deliberate, a system of classification and description was developed, and use of the archives and library increased.

Accessioning was assisted by a directive from the First Presidency in September 1978 that encouraged all offices to transfer their pre-1930 records to the archives. A records management program was implemented in 1980 and continues to develop. This program has begun to assure a more systematic transfer of records with historical value into the archives. These programs have increased the 6.5 linear feet of cataloged manuscripts which were available in 1976 to approximately 540 linear feet of papers and records to date.

Library Collections

Today, the Library and Archives continues to develop its collections through selective acquisition and cataloging. The library's collection development currently involves the following areas: all Herald House and in-house headquarters publications; the broad field of LDS history, including scholarly works in RLDS history, as well as selected publications from other branches of Mormonism; religion and theology; pastoral concerns; and peace studies. The last area is now emphasized because of its connection with the new RLDS Temple.

Titles on religion and theology make up the majority of the book holdings. Acquisitions have increased in Old and New Testament studies and in the history of Christian thought. Formats of the collected materials on theology vary. These include books (20,000 volumes) classified according to the Library of Congress system; pamphlets (3,500), primarily LDS related; periodicals (145 current subscriptions), plus numerous bound volumes of back issues; unpublished works (700) which include primarily theses, dissertations, and RLDS Church reports; newspapers, selected issues as well as clipping collections which contain articles concerning the LDS churches; cassette tapes (250) comprising a select set of Herald House produced tapes; and vertical files (800) containing miscellaneous materials kept in subject and biographical folders.

The library currently maintains several special historical collections. For example, the Herald House book imprints are compiled in order to preserve all the known editions and printings of books published by Herald House. Another special collection is an antiquarian book group comprised of mostly nineteenth-century copyright dates and dealing with the general subjects of religion and archaeology. Many of these titles formed the nucleus of the earlier library's holdings and have now been retired to closed stacks. Another small collection is one of state histories, many published in the late nineteenth century. The histories primarily concern the states where the church was located. Foreign language publications make up another special collection. These have been written or translated by the RLDS Church as well as The Church of Jesus Christ of Latter-day Saints and LDS factional groups.

Housed in the vault is the library's rare-book collection with copyright dates up to 1915. Some items of interest in this group are first editions of the Book of Mormon and Doctrine and Covenants, the Book of Commandments, and Bibles, including the earliest edition of the Inspired Version, as well as the marked Bible belonging to Joseph Smith Jr. and David Whitmer's family Bible. Also included in the rare books are some titles that appear to have belonged to Joseph Smith Jr. as well as contemporaneous books which may have influenced his thought. Titles include books written both for and against LDS factions. Early periodicals, hymnals, and pamphlets make up the rest of the vault holdings.

Indexing, a library priority for the last several years, is now complete for most of the RLDS-produced magazines. Obituaries that appear in the *Saints' Herald* have been indexed by name from 1860–1944. This index is particularly helpful for those doing genealogical research. A complete reindexing of the *Saints' Herald* is finished up to 1891.

Archive Collections

The archive's collections focus mainly on materials relating to the formation and development of Mormonism, its post-1844 dispersion, and the subsequent organization and growth of the RLDS Church. The materials include the official records of the Reorganized Church of Jesus Christ of Latter Day Saints headquarters.

Some of the most significant documents in the RLDS archives are in the small collections of Joseph Smith papers and Emma Smith papers. These manuscripts each fill less than one document box. The Early Reorganization Minutes (1852–71) are frequently referenced as are some eighty linear feet of early branch records. Other early originals are the "John Whitmer History, Kept by Commandment," the "Record of the First Quorum of Elders of Geauga County," the Book of Mormon printers' manuscript, and the Inspired Version of the Bible manuscript.

Another source of important documents is the "Miscellaneous Letters and Papers." This collection was an early attempt to catalog and store items in acid-neutral folders. As important documents were found in the holdings, they were cataloged and placed in chronological order along with correspondence or other items from the presidency and other RLDS Church offices. While the folders provide physical protection to each of these papers, they ignore the archival principle of provenance or origin. "Miscellaneous Letters and Papers" became a separate collection in 1976 and has not been added to since.

The William H. Kelley papers (1863–1914) are contained in forty-seven document boxes and cover a significant period of history in the RLDS Church. Kelley became a member of the Council of Twelve in 1873 and served as president of the council from 1897 to 1913. Approximately this same time period is also covered in the ten Letterpress Copy Books of Joseph Smith III, President of the Church from 1860 to 1914.

Another prominent acquisition is the L. F. P. Curry papers, which cover the period from 1900 to 1977. Curry became the Presiding Bishop in 1931 and counselor to the President of the Church in 1938, serving in that capacity until 1946, when President Frederick M. Smith died. Curry played a major role during the depression years, countering the church's indebtedness and placing the Reorganization on a more solid financial footing.

In the early 1980s, the archives received records from the RLDS administrative offices—those of the First Presidency, the Council of Twelve, the Presiding Bishop, and the Presidents of the Seventy. These records are accessible to researchers, including minutes and correspondence which help fill historical gaps in the early development of the church.

Users

The collections in the Library and Archives serve various needs. Users of the facility include RLDS Church headquarters personnel, Park College graduate students, Temple School students, researchers in LDS history, RLDS Church members, and the general public. According to 1992 statistics, 7,043 patrons used the Library and Archives.

Since 1984 the library has been the main research facility for the Park College Masters in Religion program. The Reorganized Church's newly appointed, full-time ministers are expected to complete this program.

Genealogists heavily use the early membership records for information about people who were members of the RLDS Church.

Many callers are referred to the more comprehensive genealogy services of The Church of Jesus Christ of Latter-day Saints, which has an office in Independence.

Facilities

The Library and Archives of the Reorganized Church of Jesus Christ of Latter Day Saints moved to the new RLDS Temple in July 1992 and is within one block of the Auditorium. The two buildings are connected by an underground walkway. The spacious quarters represent an increase of 357 percent more than the room allotted in the Auditorium. It is comfortable and conducive to research.

Library and Archives Administration and Services

The services that the Library and Archives offer are meant to assist the researcher. Photocopying (excluding archival material) is available for a fee. Interlibrary loan is provided for circulating materials as well as microfilm. The circulating collection was opened to the general public after 1976. Archival and published materials became, and still are, available to the public with virtually no restrictions. Microfilms of manuscripts are available through interlibrary loan, but the films must be used in the local library and cannot be photocopied.

Currently, twenty major bibliographies are available at no cost. These include archival holdings, Herald House books, total periodical holdings, RLDS periodicals, theses and dissertations on LDS history, and books recommended for the beginning researcher in LDS history. Short bibliographies are compiled upon request for given subjects. Quick reference work is provided for users by phone and letter. The Library and Archives newsletter is printed nine to ten times a year, giving news as well as listings of the latest new books and processed archives.

The Library and Archives is administered by the director of Temple School Division. Staff currently includes one professional librarian, one professional archivist, and two assistants. Approximately twenty volunteers provide valuable service in maintaining the Library and Archives. The facility is open from 8:00 A.M. to 5:00 P.M. weekdays and from 9:00 A.M. to 1:00 P.M. on Saturday, excluding holiday weekends. More information can be obtained by writing RLDS Temple, River and Walnut, Box 1059, Independence, Missouri 64051 or by calling (816) 833-1000 extension 2400.

Sara Hallier Nyman and L. Madelon Brunson are former administrators of the RLDS Library and Archives.

NOTES

[1]"Annual Conference," *True Latter Day Saints' Herald* 7 (April 15, 1865): 124.

[2]"Council," *True Latter Day Saints' Herald* 7 (June 1, 1865): 163.

[3]*General Conference Minutes* (May 12, 1897), 15.

[4]*Minutes of General Conference* (April 6, 1906), 857.

[5]Mary Lou Goodyear, "A History of the General Church Library of the Reorganized Church of Jesus Christ of Latter Day Saints" (master's thesis, University of Missouri, 1975), 15.

[6]*Minutes of General Conference* (April 3, 1907), 964.

[7]"Of General Interest," *Saints Herald* 55 (February 5, 1908): 132.

[8]"Of General Interest," 133.

[9]S. A. Burgess, "The Church Library," *Saints Herald* 73 (October 13, 1926): 977.

[10]"A Conference Day," *Saints Herald,* Conference Daily Edition no. 4 (April 9, 1932): 74.

Mormon Americana at Princeton University

Alfred Bush

The largest collection of printed works concerning The Church of Jesus Christ of Latter-day Saints, outside Utah libraries, is in the Princeton University Library in Princeton, New Jersey.[1] The Princeton Collections of Western Americana include substantial portions of the surviving imprints from Mormonism's first century. Princeton's collection of Utah territorial imprints rivals even those of Utah repositories. These printed holdings are supplemented by growing collections of manuscripts and graphic materials, which include unusually rich accumulations of nineteenth-century prints and photographs of Mormon and Utah subjects. Books and journals in the Princeton University Library's open stacks and microfilms of newspapers and unpublished materials in the microform collections support these rarities in such a comprehensive way that, given the demands on these materials in Utah repositories, Princeton may well be the most convenient place in the country at the moment to pursue studies in Mormon history and culture.

Setting Acquisition Directions

Since Princeton's founding in the 1740s, its humanities library has consistently been one of the nation's largest. The natural accretion of a university library the size and age of Princeton's makes it inevitable that collections on innumerable subjects—particularly American ones—would grow over the centuries into an almost accidental distinction. Inevitably there was a considerable amassing of Mormon books.

But in 1947, when Philip Ashton Rollins of the Princeton class of 1889 presented his distinguished collection of Western Americana to Princeton, the library's foci of special interests were expanded to further the strengths of his collection. Because one of these strengths was the history of the Rocky Mountain states, Utah and its attendant Mormon past became one of the new special interests.

Independent research is the goal of much of the undergraduate curriculum at Princeton, and original research is required for junior papers and senior theses. Consequently, a collection of enough depth and comprehension for research is necessary. Recognizing how extensively Mormonism spanned the American past chronologically, geographically, and ideologically, numerous students have conducted research for American studies conferences and classes and, most frequently, for anthropology seminars. Because of this emphasis on original research based on primary materials, rare documents of the Mormon past without a larger context of printed materials clearly would not be useful to this community. Thus, equally essential are the complete runs of journals, newspapers on microfilm, and copies of unpublished journals.

Harvey S. Firestone Memorial Library, Princeton University. Photograph by Samuel Chamberlain.

There were times when student demands surprised even the curator, who thought he was collecting comprehensively enough to make possible most excursions into Mormon history and culture. When anthropologists began asking for Sunday School manuals and Primary education guides—primary documents on the process of socializing the young—it was clear that some materials deliberately excluded from the collecting policy of the department could, in fact, be the most useful to contemporary scholars.

Assessing acquisition directions in 1965, the first curator of the Princeton Collections of Western Americana, which includes the Philip Rollins collection, recognized that with Yale's rich collection of early Mormon rarities close by, Princeton could set its sights on the strengths of Rollins's collection: the less-collected later material of Utah's territorial period that seldom found its way into Eastern libraries. One could find the great rarities of the first decades of Mormonism in many libraries east of the Mississippi at the time, but few held runs of, for instance, the basic organs of institutional Mormonism, like the *Latter-day*

Saints' Millennial Star; the *Contributor;* or the Lamoni, Iowa, *Journal of History*. To the student making his or her way into Mormon history and culture for the first time, the latter would be the most useful route to the Mormon past. So Princeton determined not only to gather as many of the primary sources as possible about the Mormons during the Utah territorial period (1849–96), but also to place these primary materials into a context of periodicals, journals, microfilms of newspapers, dissertations, and monographs which would make it possible to pursue Mormon and Utah studies at Princeton without recourse to other libraries.

Another direction was adopted to counter one of the unconscious prejudices of curators of Mormon holdings in Eastern collections: their natural leaning toward materials documenting the Salt Lake City church rather than the numerous smaller organizations that trace their origins to the Book of Mormon. A deliberate effort was begun at Princeton to bring in nets filled with all kinds of Latter-day Saints. One of the results is the most comprehensive gathering of works on the Reorganized Church of Jesus Christ of Latter Day Saints and, in Dale Morgan's phrase, "the lesser Churches of the Dispersion," to be found outside Independence, Salt Lake City, and Provo.

Building the Collections

Once the parameters of the Mormon past appropriate to Princeton were assessed, the collecting began. Fortunately, these decisions were made early enough in the 1960s that quantities of out-of-print works on the Mormons were available inexpensively—the following decade's private collecting rage rapidly erased most of these opportunities. In those days, the curator could acquire the contents of whole bookcases from such accumulators as M. Wilfred Poulsen, annually set aside boxes of nineteenth-century books at Sam Weller's Zion Bookstore and Johann Becker's various Salt Lake City houses, and packets from Jacob Heinerman's Cottage Bookstore in Provo—all for a minuscule outlay of acquisition

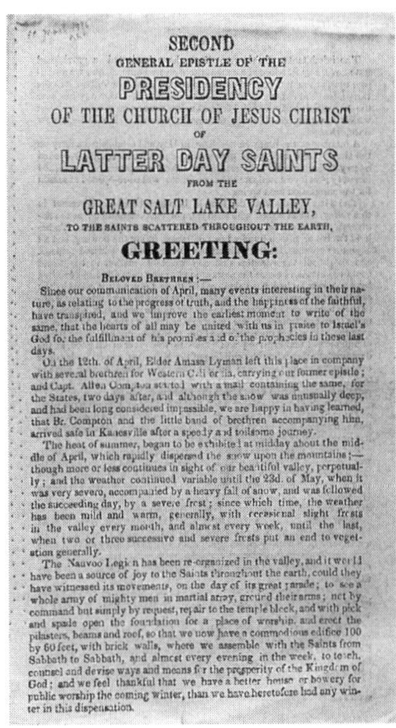

SECOND
GENERAL EPISTLE OF THE
PRESIDENCY
OF THE CHURCH OF JESUS CHRIST
OF
LATTER DAY SAINTS
FROM THE
GREAT SALT LAKE VALLEY,
TO THE SAINTS SCATTERED THROUGHOUT THE EARTH,
GREETING:

Beloved Brethren:—

Since our communication of April, many events interesting in their nature, as relating to the progress of truth, and the happiness of the faithful, have transpired, and we improve the earliest moment to write of the same, that the hearts of all may be united with us in praise to Israel's God for the fulfillment of his promises and of the prophecies in these last days.

On the 12th. of April, Elder Amasa Lyman left this place in company with several brethren for Western California, carrying our former epistle; and Capt. Allen Compton started with a mail containing the same, for the States, two days after, and although the snow was unusually deep, and had been long considered impassible, we are happy in having learned, that Br. Compton and the little band of brethren accompanying him, arrived safe in Kanesville after a speedy and toilsome journey.

The heat of summer, began to be exhibited at midday about the middle of April, which rapidly dispersed the snow upon the mountains;—though more or less continues in sight of our beautiful valley, perpetually; and the weather continued variable until the 23d. of May, when it was very severe, accompanied by a heavy fall of snow, and was followed the succeeding day, by a severe frost; since which time, the weather has been mild and warm, generally, with occasional slight frosts in the valley every month, and almost every week, until the last, when two or three successive and severe frosts put an end to vegetation generally.

The Nauvoo Legion has been re-organized in the valley, and it would have been a source of joy to the Saints throughout the earth, could they have witnessed its movements, on the day of its great parade; to see a whole army of mighty men in martial array, ground their arms; not by command but simply by request, repair to the temple block, and with pick and spade open the foundation for a place of worship, and erect the pilasters, beams and roof, so that we now have a commodious edifice 100 by 60 feet, with brick walls, where we assemble with the Saints from Sabbath to Sabbath, and almost every evening in the week, to teach, counsel and devise ways and means for the prosperity of the Kingdom of God; and we feel thankful that we have a better house or bowery for public worship the coming winter, than we have heretofore had any winter in this dispensation.

"Second General Epistle," 1849. Courtesy Princeton University Library.

funds. Nyal Anderson's Beehive Antique Shop invariably provided rare, sometimes even unique, examples of Utah territorial imprints. Fred Rosenstock in Denver could always be counted on to chink many important gaps in the collection for reasonable prices.

Exchange programs of duplicate books with the Brigham Young University Library and the Historian's Office at the Reorganized Church of Jesus Christ of Latter Day Saints brought large quantities of missing titles to the Princeton shelves for little effort and no money. Nineteenth-century photographs were found in stores of second-hand "junk" in towns across the state for prices that must have been less than the original expense of creating them. Friendships were formed or furthered that motivated gifts to Princeton which helped push the effort toward distinction.

Once the collection began to reach imposing quantity, it demanded quality. The Utah territorial imprints were given a solid foundation when, at the sale of the collections of Thomas W. Streeter in New York City in 1968, Princeton purchased such high points of the Utah territorial press as the *Second General Epistle of the Presidency of the Church* . . . (Great Salt Lake City: Brigham H. Young, 1849) and the *Minutes of the General Conference, Held at Great Salt Lake City, Deseret, April 6, 1850*. Added to the Deseret currency already in the collection, the acquisition of the *Second General Epistle* gave Princeton both the complete output of the territorial press's first year of production and an ambition to pursue the products of the Utah territorial presses in subsequent years. Following soon after were such rarities as the Deseret brand book of 1850, the *William Clayton Recorder,* the 1850 *Address* by Willard Richards, the 1855 *Rule for Conducting Business in the House of Representatives of the Territory of Utah,* and the 1857 broadside announcing the coming of Johnson's army—*Citizens of Utah We Are Invaded by a Hostile Force*. The pursuit of everything printed in the territory pulled in Native American vocabularies, the deliberations of governmental bodies, local election tickets, army orders printed on itinerant camp presses, and doggerel both satirizing and apotheosizing the peculiarly Utah institution of polygamy.

Once the solidity of the collection was apparent, attracting gifts became easier. J. Lionberger Davis of the Princeton class of 1900 provided funds for additions to the territorial imprint collections. Dr. J. Monroe Thorington (class of 1915), whose family connections reached back to Kit Carson and Mexican New Mexico, contributed to the collection's overland narratives, many of them involving Utah and the Mormons. LaMar Peterson gathered a large collection of mostly twentieth-century Mormon pamphlets which now rests in Princeton.

LIST OF RECORDED BRANDS.

Brand	Length of Letter (Inches)	Breadth of Brand (Inches)	Place of Brand	Date of Record	Owner's Name	Place of Residence	Ward	Lot	Block
W R	7-8	1 1-2	Left Horn	1849 Dec. 29	Willard Richards	G. S. L. CITY	14	7	76
W	3 1-4	4 1-2	Horses Hoof Left Hip	Do	do	do	"	"	"
S	3 1-2	"	Right Hip	Do	Daniel Spencer	do	13	1	57
•S	3 1-2	"	Left Hip	Do	Orson Spencer	do	"	2	57
A P R	1-2	1 1-2	Left Horn	Do	A. P. Rockwood	do	"	6	75
H	3 1-4	2 3-4	Left Hip	Do	Heber C. Kimball	do	18	3	93
W S	2 1-4	5	Left Shoulder	Do	Willard Snow	do	13	1	71
D J	7-8	"	Left Horn	Dec. 31	Dan Jones	do	14	4	69
J	3 3-4	"	Left Hip	Do	do	do	"	"	"
N K W	1-2	2 1-4	Left Horn	Do	Newel K. Whitney	do	18	5	88
W	3 3-4	3 1-4	Left Shoulder	Do	do	do	"	"	"
W C	2 3-4	4 1-2	Do	Do	William Clayton	do	17	1	95
P	3 1-2	"	Both Hips	Do	David Peters	do	15	7	48
J R	5-8	"	Left Horn	1850 Jan. 2	John Robinson	West of Jordan up the River.			
J D	3	"	Right Hip	Jan. 3	James Davis	G. S. L. CITY	19	4	117
T	3 1-2	"	Left Hip	Do	Thomas Jeremy	do	16	4	60
D	3 3-4	"	Do	Do	Daniel Daniels	do	"	5	60
Y	4 1-8	3 1-8	Do	Do	Brigham Young	do	18	2	89
L	3 1-4	2 1-8	Do	Jan. 4	Elizabeth Lewis	do	13	3	70
C F	3 1-2	5	Do	Jan. 5	Charles A. Foster	do	16	2	100
F	3	2	Left Shoulder	Do	Loren Farr	do	17	8	95
F	3 1-2	1 1-2	Left Hip	Do	Aaron F. Farr	do	"	7	93
M	2 3-8	2 3-4	Left Shoulder	Do	Thomas Moore	do	2	2	19
P N	2 1-8	5 1-2	Do	Do	Peter Nebeker	do	19	5	116

Deseret brand book, 1850. Courtesy Princeton University Library.

William H. Scheide of Princeton's class of 1936—the last private owner of a Gutenberg Bible—made it possible to acquire the equivalent capstone to any Mormon collection, the 1833 *Book of Commandments*.[2] This legendary Mormon rarity escaped a mob attack on the press that produced it and survives in nine known copies made up from sheets rescued from the ruins of the printing cabin.

David N. Pierce of the class of 1967 added significantly to the collections shortly after leaving Princeton. With bibliophilic sleight-of-hand, he managed to uncover nineteenth-century Utah and Mormon imprints while piloting U.S. Air Force planes during the Vietnam War. He and his siblings later presented the papers of their father, Norman C. Pierce, an insistent Mormon millennialist, to the collection. For a decade, the Pierces even put into the collection for safekeeping a stellar Mormon artifact: a seer stone with a provenance that traces it back to Joseph Smith through the man who made the death masks of the Mormon prophet and his brother after their deaths in Carthage, Illinois, in 1844.

The most recent addition of significance to the Mormon holdings is Jørgen W. Schmidt's collection of Danish imprints.[3] Schmidt assiduously sought every mention in the Danish press of the Mormons from the 1850s to the present day. As a result, Princeton's Mormon holdings in Danish are the most comprehensive to be found anywhere.

The manuscript element of the collection is composed largely of transcripts and photocopies of the nineteenth-century journals, most notably those in the Herbert S. Auerbach collection of transcripts of Utah and Mormon manuscripts. However, original material can also be found at Princeton, ranging from an extraordinary 1846 letter in Brigham Young's hand, written from the "Camp of Israel" and chastising one of his wives for her attempt to abandon him and the exodus,[4] to the minutes of the Ephraim North Ward Sunday School, 1879–86.

In between these are original letters from Mormon figures such as John M. Bernhisel, H. R. Clawson, Benjamin Cluff, Lorenzo Snow, and G. W. Thatcher. Juanita Brooks gathered manuscript patriarchal blessings, which are also now in the collection.

An awareness of the importance of visual materials documenting the perception of Utah and the Mormons has led to an extensive collection of nineteenth-century photographs and prints, with a special interest in those that helped form the popular image of the Mormons over the years.

These diverse collections provide the many-sided evidences of Mormon life and culture that make study at Princeton fruitful and fascinating.

Alfred Bush is Curator of Princeton Collections of Western Americana, Princeton University, New Jersey.

NOTES

[1]Alfred L. Bush, "The Princeton Collections of Western Americana," *The Princeton University Library Chronicle* 33 (Autumn 1971): 1-17.

[2]Peter Crawley, "Joseph Smith and *A Book of Commandments*," *The Princeton University Library Chronicle* 42 (Autumn 1980): 18-32.

[3]William Mulder, "Denmark and the Mormons: The Jørgen W. Schmidt Collection," *The Princeton University Library Chronicle* 52 (Spring 1991): 331-57.

[4]Fawn M. Brodie, "A Letter from the Camp of Israel, 1846," *The Princeton University Library Chronicle* 33 (Autumn 1971): 67-70.

Mormon Americana at the State Historical Society of Wisconsin

Michael Edmonds and Lian Partlow

Wisconsin? Hardly the first place most people associate with The Church of Jesus Christ of Latter-day Saints. Far from the sites where Mormonism originated or flowered, off the beaten track of the historic migrations west, at first glance Wisconsin seems barren ground for researchers in Mormon history. Yet through a peculiar combination of odd personalities and bizarre events, the State Historical Society of Wisconsin, in Madison, owns a small but rich collection of Mormon Americana. Though modest in size (several thousand printed works and a few linear feet of manuscripts), the collection is particularly strong in nineteenth-century pamphlets and ephemeral materials.

The existence of such a collection in Madison is not as unusual as it might appear at first glance. The State Historical Society of Wisconsin began collecting materials on American history in the mid-nineteenth century, under a mandate to gather the historical record of life in the entire United States, not simply local history. Today the society's research collections include 2.2 million printed items in its library and 80,000 cubic feet of manuscripts and public records in its archives, as well as thousands of historical maps, photographs, prints, and the like. Other society divisions operate six historic sites, a historical museum, and a statewide historic preservation program.

Although twenty-five Mormon items are listed in the library's 1872 printed catalog, the bulk of our Mormon Americana began to flow into Madison only at the turn of the century. It came in two streams: one originated in the state's own fascinating Mormon history, and the other resulted from the aggressive private collection activities of a native son who moved to Salt Lake City in 1889. This article summarizes the society's holdings of books, pamphlets, newspapers, periodicals, manuscripts, and ephemera that came from these and other sources.

The Legacy of James J. Strang

It all began when backwoods lawyer James J. Strang settled into his chair at a Mormon proselyting meeting in Burlington, Wisconsin, in the winter of 1843–44, thereby setting off one of the most peculiar episodes in American religious history. Strang was baptized by Joseph Smith a few months before the Prophet's assassination, and after the subsequent power struggle Strang founded a Mormon community (called "Voree") on the rolling prairies between Milwaukee and Chicago. Confronted by hostile Gentiles outside and apostate members within, Strang moved his community between 1847 and 1850 to Beaver Island at the head of Lake Michigan, where he proclaimed himself king. Although his empire peaked at about thirty-five hundred followers in the mid-fifties, legal problems, internal dissent, and outside hostility ultimately led to its downfall. In June 1856, Strang was shot by disgruntled converts and died a few weeks later. After his death, an armed mob forcibly evicted his followers and dispersed them to a variety of Great Lakes ports.[1]

Although most of Strang's manuscripts are at Yale University's Beinecke Library, the State Historical Society of Wisconsin possesses a variety of essential primary sources. These include Strang's memoirs of his childhood, copied by Charles Strang in 1897 for historian Henry E. Legler (1861–1917) and preserved among Legler's papers. The Legler papers also include nineteenth-century newspaper clippings, letters from Strang's family, and research notes; they have been microfilmed and may be borrowed through interlibrary loan.

State Historical Society of Wisconsin. Courtesy State Historical Society of Wisconsin.

Quasi-official records of the Strangite communities exist in the "Chronicles of Voree" and "Minutes of the Conferences of the Beaver Island Church," both of which were photostatted years ago by the State Historical Society of Wisconsin from originals in private hands. The "Chronicles of Voree . . . made by the Scribes appointed to that office" cover the years 1845 to 1849 and detail the founding of the colony, relations between Nauvoo and Voree, Strang's claim to be Joseph Smith's true heir, and various religious records.[2] The "Minutes . . . of the Beaver Island

Church" describe Strang's mystical revelations, legal matters, and selected religious affairs from 1847 to 1855.[3] Although unavailable for interlibrary loan, these two manuscripts can be copied for a small fee.

Strang was an accomplished propagandist and operated a newspaper in both communities. The *Voree Herald,* whose name changed first to *Zion's Reveille* and then to the *Gospel Herald . . . for the Church of Jesus Christ of Latter-day Saints,* was published from 1846 to 1850 (Flake 3641[4]); it was succeeded by the *Northern Islander,* issued at Beaver Island from 1850 until Strang's death in 1856 (Flake 5868). Both runs of these papers are complete, although they are in composite form (some issues being originals, some photostats, some on microfilm). Other printed Strangite materials include *A Collection of Sacred Hymns* (Voree, 1850; Flake 2365), G. J. Adams's *A True History of the Rise of the Church of Jesus Christ of Latter Day Saints . . .* (Baltimore, 1849[?]; Flake 21),[5] and the later writings of Wingfield Watson (Flake 9645–57), Elizabeth Whitney Williams (Flake 9873), and other true believers who outlived their spiritual master.

Many photographs of Strang, his family, and sites at Voree and Beaver Island are preserved in the Visual and Sound Archives; the best are reproduced in Lewis, "'For Life, the Resurrection, and the Life Everlasting,'" and copies can be provided upon application.

Finally, the autobiography of James O. McNutt (1849–1931), who was raised on Beaver Island and lived among the surviving Strangites for decades after, forms an epilogue to the Strang story. The McNutt memoirs total nearly two hundred pages and were microfilmed from an original in private hands in 1966; they are available through interlibrary loan.

The Theodore Albert Schroeder Collection

About the time that Strang's memory was fading into obscurity, Theodore Albert Schroeder (1864–1953) was born on a farm near the headwaters of Wisconsin's Rock River.[6] Like many other farm boys, he migrated to the big city to attend college, graduating from the University of Wisconsin with a B.S. in 1886 and an LL.B. in 1889.[7] In August of that year, he opened a law practice in Salt Lake City, where he specialized in debt collection and land claims.[8]

As a freethinker, Schroeder was fascinated by Mormon society and soon began to collect all the books and manuscripts he could lay his hands on relating to Utah and the Mormons. As his collection grew, he distributed large numbers of an eight-page brochure headed, "I want all books on the subject of MORMONISM of which I do not already own a copy . . . ." The brochure listed more than one hundred desiderata.

About the same time, his law practice and political activities brought him into close contact with community and Church leaders such as B. H. Roberts,[9] Moses Thatcher,[10] and Joseph F. Smith.[11] He strenuously opposed theocracy, and his work to keep church and state apart led to a job offer from the League for Social Service in New York. Although he did not take the job, he did move to New York in June of 1900.[12] From that date on, Schroeder largely abandoned his collecting of Mormon materials to become increasingly involved in civil libertarian issues and the psychology of religion.[13] He joined the bar in New York,[14] helped to found the Free Speech League in 1902 (incorporated in 1911),[15] became an associate of Emma Goldman,[16] and studied evolutionary sexual psychology until his death in 1953.[17]

In the autumn of 1901, Schroeder shipped nineteen crates containing almost thirteen hundred books, pamphlets, newspapers, and bound manuscripts on Mormonism to Madison. He made very few later additions to this initial shipment, commenting in a letter to the society in 1915, "For fully 10 years I have been trying to forget Mormonism—I spent more time & money on the subject than it was worth—Though of course as the years roll on the relative scarcity & importance of the subject may change this aspect of things." He was right, of course. While Schroeder argued for complete freedom of speech and investigated phallic worship or the "erotogenesis of religion" (and collected hundreds of volumes on these subjects), the relative scarcity and value of his Mormon materials continued to rise. When his five hundred pamphlets were entered into the Online Computer Library Center (OCLC) in 1984, 81 percent were unique to the database (which contains eighteen million records contributed by eight thousand libraries nationwide). Today, scholars from around the country and abroad make regular use of the Schroeder Collection.

To characterize his materials is difficult. When attempting to describe any collection of artifacts, one must steer between empty generalization and mere inventory. In the paragraphs that follow, we hope to achieve this by first highlighting selected books, pamphlets, newspapers, periodicals, and manuscripts and then offering an overview that compensates for the inevitable omissions.

Like most collectors, Schroeder eagerly sought early and rare materials on his chosen subject. The collection contains editions of the Book of Mormon published at Palmyra, New York, in 1830 (Flake 595, the first edition), Liverpool in 1841 (Flake 598, the first English [European] edition), and Nauvoo in 1842 (Flake 599, the latter printed by Joseph Smith and thought to be scarcer than copies of the first edition). The earliest example of controversial literature in the Schroeder collection is E. D. Howe's *Mormonism Unvailed [*sic*]* . . . (Flake 4104), issued at Painesville, Ohio, in 1834. Schroeder was especially interested in periodical literature and succeeded in obtaining copies of the *Elders' Journal of the Church of Latter Day Saints* (Kirtland, Ohio, and Far West, Missouri, 1837–38; Flake 3126) and the *Times and Seasons* (Nauvoo, 1839–1846; Flake 8955). The former title unfortunately contains dog-eared copies of only numbers one through three, but the latter is clean and complete.

The Schroeder Collection contains two early manuscripts of interest. The first is the "Patriarchal Blessings Book," which contains copies of 122 blessings given by William Smith, brother of Joseph Smith, at Nauvoo in 1845 and 1846. Also included are copies of two blessings given in 1841 by Hyrum Smith and another given by Joseph Smith Sr., the Prophet's father, in 1838. Enclosed in the book is an open letter dated April 1, 1849, in which William Smith asserts his claim to be Joseph's successor. The second manuscript item is the Cobb Family Papers, collected by James T. Cobb of Salt Lake City in the 1880s. These include letters of Augusta Adams Cobb (divorced by her husband in 1846 for "the crime of adultery with one Brigham Young") and her family, as well as those addressed to her during her move from Massachusetts to Utah. They include many copies of letters from Mrs. Cobb to Young, in which she laments her state of affairs, begs for favors, and reproaches him for unfair treatment.

Materials from the third quarter of the nineteenth century are more numerous than those listed above, and space permits the mention of only a few. Early and contemporary editions of the works of the Pratt family are well-represented, including Parley Parker Pratt's *A Dialogue between Josh. Smith and the Devil* (Liverpool[?], 1846[?]; Flake 6569), Belinda Marden Pratt's *Defence of Polygamy, by a Lady of Utah* . . . (Salt Lake City, 1854[?]; Flake 6441) and the *History of Orson Pratt (Written by Himself, March, 1858),* a nine-page pamphlet without imprint and not recorded in Flake. Other early or rare printed works from this middle period include Willard Richards's *Address . . . to the Chancellor and Regents* . . . (Salt Lake City, 1850[?]; Flake 7255) and Brigham Young's *A Series of Instructions and Remarks . . . at a Special Council* . . . (Salt Lake City, 1858; Flake 10,066). Schroeder also picked up Strang's *The Book of the Law of the Lord* in the scarce 1856 edition, "Printed by Command of the King. At the Royal Press, St. James" (Flake 8498).

Schroeder's most important manuscript from the period 1850 to 1880 is the "Major General's Record Book" and related correspondence kept at Salt Lake City (1852–66). It documents military preparedness and organization and reports on Indian activity and related concerns of the Great Salt Lake District of the Nauvoo Legion. Schroeder also acquired a collection of mounted clippings and copies of legal documents relating to Brigham Young's will and the trial, imprisonment, and release of his estate's executors (1877–79).

An interesting group of foreign evangelical materials in the Schroeder Collection also dates from the middle of the century. The earliest is an 1841 edition of Parley Parker Pratt's *A Voice of Warning,* issued at Manchester, England (Flake 6629), followed by the anonymous supplement, *Address to the Saints,* issued in Liverpool by the *Millennial Star* in 1844 (Flake 4780) and the *Proclamation of the Twelve Apostles,* issued at Liverpool in 1845 (Flake 1512). The earliest bibliographical work in the Schroeder collection is a four-page *Catalogue of Works Published by the Church of Jesus Christ of Latter Day Saints* that was issued by Orson Pratt in Liverpool in 1856(?) (Flake 1886). An early anti-Mormon pamphlet from England is Richard Livesey's *An Exposure of Mormonism . . .* published at Manchester, England, in 1840 (Flake and Draper 4963a).[18] After the 1840s, the number of evangelical works in the Schroeder collection increases substantially; more interesting than the printed materials is the George F. Gibbs Letterbook (1871–73), which details the missionary activities of Brigham Young's secretary in England as he worked to facilitate emigration to Utah.

In terms of sheer quantity, the bulk of the Schroeder Collection dates from the last two decades of the nineteenth century. As might be expected, much of this material is not especially rare; but since most of it was printed on very poor paper, it is likely to grow scarcer as the decades pass. In an attempt to ensure future access, the pamphlets and other ephemeral material in the Schroeder Collection have all been cleaned, housed in acid-free file folders, and microfilmed.

The most interesting materials from the end of the century are the manuscripts and "near-print" items which Schroeder assembled. These include the record of his law practice and his activities in local politics from 1889 to 1901; taken together, his legal, financial, and personal papers reveal much about Salt Lake City public life at the end of the last century. Several bound volumes are of particular interest in this regard: "Printed Circulars, Leaflets, Notices and Petitions" deals primarily with polygamy and Utah statehood, while "Mounted Clippings and Clipping Scrapbooks" relates to Church history and Utah politics from 1854 to 1899. The clippings were taken from the *Deseret News,* the *Salt Lake Tribune,* the *Salt Lake Democrat,* and the *Salt Lake Herald,* in rough chronological order, and serve as an *ad hoc* subject collection on the topics most interesting to Schroeder.

Obviously, a few paragraphs can do no more than whet one's appetite for the contents of those nineteen crates that arrived on our loading dock in 1901. Manuscripts fill two archive boxes and seven bound volumes and have been microfilmed onto eight reels of 35mm film which can be borrowed on interlibrary loan. The five hundred pamphlets fill fifteen archives boxes, have not yet been microfilmed, and are perhaps the most interesting and valuable portion of the collection. A systematic sample of the pamphlet catalog revealed that 93 percent were listed in Chad Flake's bibliography, suggesting that as many as forty items are not recorded there. (Unfortunately the pamphlets had not been processed at the time that Flake edited his landmark bibliography, and the State Historical Society of Wisconsin is not shown as a location for most of the 93 percent that do appear in Flake.) All the Schroeder pamphlets, however, have been entered into OCLC and the University of Wisconsin's on-line Network Library System. The newspapers and periodicals in the collection were printed in dozens of cities around the country, and partial runs of several foreign Mormon newspapers are also present; most newspapers have been microfilmed and entered into OCLC.

Other Collections

Not all of our Mormon Americana came through Schroeder or derived from Strang's experiments; a small collection was developed by the society's founding officers in the nineteenth century. They shrewdly acquired a selection of controversial literature that includes Alexander Campbell's *Delusions: An Analysis of the Book of Mormon* . . . (Boston, 1832; Flake 1107) and Origen Bacheler's *Mormonism Exposed, Internally and Externally* (New York, 1838; Flake 242), as well as the only recorded copy of *A Supplement to Mormon, Containing the Book of Anak,* by Bukki, a satire on the Book of Mormon issued at Cooperstown, New York, in 1851 (Flake 1003). They also acquired selected rare Mormon periodicals such as *The Olive Branch* . . . (Kirtland, Ohio, and Springfield, Illinois, 1848–1852[?]; Flake 5987), *Étoile de déseret* . . . (Paris, 1851–52; Flake 3185), and *Le Réflecteur* (Geneva, 1853; Flake 6842), and collected the second and third editions of the Book of Mormon (Kirtland, 1837; Flake 596) (Nauvoo, 1840; Flake 597). There are, finally, a handful of brief manuscript accounts of nineteenth-century Mormon life in the society archives. These include letters of C. W. Brewer and Lucien Hanks from the 1860s referring to travels through Salt Lake City; a letter of Winslow Blake recounting his 1852 overland trip to California; and a diary in which E. Kitchell records impressions during a similar trip in 1852–53, including six pages on Salt Lake City and Kitchell's meeting with Orson Pratt.

The State Historical Society of Wisconsin has long been committed to providing the broadest possible access to its materials, and we make no exception in the case of Mormon Americana. Most printed works, including virtually all of the Schroeder Collection, can be searched on OCLC or through dialing the University of Wisconsin's Network Library System (608-262-8670) via a personal computer and modem. Unless they are too fragile, most items described in this article can be photocopied for ten cents per page; those that have been microfilmed can be borrowed through interlibrary loan. Inquiries about books and pamphlets should be addressed to the reference librarian, and those about manuscripts and ephemeral material should be sent to the reference archivist, State Historical Society of Wisconsin, 816 State Street, Madison, Wisconsin 53706; 608-262-9590.

Michael Edmonds is Supervisor of Public Services at the State Historical Society of Wisconsin library, and Lian Partlow is a graduate student in American history at the University of Wisconsin, Madison.

NOTES

[1]The best short account of Strang's experiment is Robert P. Weeks, "A Utopian Kingdom in the American Grain," *Wisconsin Magazine of History* 61 (Autumn 1977): 3–20. See also David Rich Lewis, "'For Life, the Resurrection, and the Life Everlasting': James J. Strang and Strangite Mormon Polygamy, 1849–1856," *Wisconsin Magazine of History* 66 (Summer 1983): 274–91.

[2]John J. Hajicek, ed., *The Chronicles of Voree (1844–1849)* (Burlington, Wisc.: John J. Hajicek, 1991), photostated by State Historical Society of Wisconsin.

[3]"Minutes of the Beaver Island Church," same library as *The Chronicles of Voree.*

[4]Chad J. Flake, *A Mormon Bibliography, 1830–1930* (Salt Lake City: University of Utah Press, 1978).

[5]Long titles of nineteenth-century works have been shortened.

[6]David Barry Brudnoy, "Liberty's Bugler: The Seven Ages of Theodore Schroeder" (Ph.D. diss., Brandeis University, 1971; reprint, Ann Arbor, Mich.: University Microfilms, 1972), 1–2. Our account of Schroeder is heavily indebted to research done in 1984–85 by Geoffrey Wexler, now with the special collections department of the University of California Library at San Diego. See also Richard H. Cracroft and Thomas D. Schwartz, "The Schroeder Mormon Collection at the Wisconsin State Historical Library," *Dialogue: A Journal of Mormon Thought* 2 (Autumn 1967): 154–58; and Brudnoy, "Liberty's Bugler."

[7]Brudnoy, "Liberty's Bugler," 13, 25.

[8]Brudnoy, "Liberty's Bugler," 37.

[9]Brudnoy, "Liberty's Bugler," 82, 94.

[10]Brudnoy, "Liberty's Bugler," 81.

[11]Brudnoy, "Liberty's Bugler," 45.

[12]Brudnoy, "Liberty's Bugler," 95-97.

[13]Brudnoy, "Liberty's Bugler," 97.

[14]Brudnoy, "Liberty's Bugler," 139.

[15]Brudnoy, "Liberty's Bugler," 144.

[16]Brudnoy, "Liberty's Bugler," 142.

[17]Brudnoy, "Liberty's Bugler," 274.

[18]Chad J. Flake and Larry W. Draper, comps., *A Mormon Bibliography, 1830-1930: Ten Year Supplement* (Salt Lake City: University of Utah Press, 1989).

The Beinecke Library at Yale University. The Yale Graduate School appears in the distance. Courtesy David J. Whittaker.

Mormon Americana at Yale University

George Miles

The William Robertson Coe Collection

Yale's interest in Mormon Americana began in 1942 when William Robertson Coe presented the university with his personal collection of Western Americana. Between 1942 and 1949, Coe gave the Sterling Memorial Library over seven thousand items concerning the exploration, settlement, and development of the American West. Among the books, pamphlets, broadsides, manuscripts, and art in Coe's collection were more than nine hundred pieces concerning the early history of the Latter-day Saints. Since 1949 the Yale Collection of Western benefactors has built an extensive collection documenting the origins and growth of Mormonism in the nineteenth century.

Yale's collection of Mormon Americana has grown rapidly since Coe's gift, but a discussion of his collection as a means of introducing Yale's seems appropriate for several reasons. Its creation represents a major chapter in the history of America's social and cultural response to Mormonism; that Coe and other collectors of his generation who were not members of the LDS Church found the documents and papers of early Mormonism interesting is, in itself, significant. Second, the recent profusion of forgeries and facsimile reproductions not only in Mormon Americana but also Texana and Early Americana, demonstrates the value of establishing the provenance of rare documents, even well-known ones. Finally, although Coe imposed no restrictions on Yale's future acquisitions of Mormon Americana, the composition of his collection has exerted important influences on them.

Coe began to collect Western Americana after his purchase in 1910 of William "Buffalo Bill" Cody's Wyoming ranch. From the early 1920s through the 1930s, he relied heavily upon the assistance of noted New York City antiquarian bookman Edward Eberstadt to build his collection. The origins of Western communities and institutions, the first exploration of an area, its initial settlement, and its earliest imprints intrigued Coe. He had less interest in tracking the development of frontier regions and none in documenting the post-frontier era. Consequently, his Mormon collection focused almost exclusively on the years between 1830 and 1870, from Joseph Smith's organization of The Church of Jesus Christ of Latter-day Saints through the "Utah War" and its aftermath.

Coe's collection is especially distinguished in its coverage of Mormon history before the Saints' immigration to Utah. The collection contains first and later editions of major doctrinal works including the Book of Commandments (Independence, Mo., 1833), and the Doctrine and Covenants of the Church of Latter-Day Saints (Kirtland, Ohio, 1835) as well as numerous editions of the Book of Mormon. Also well represented are pro- and anti-Mormon polemical writings, including Alexander Campbell's *Delusions: An Analysis of the Book of Mormon* (Boston, 1832), Charles Thompson's *Evidences in Proof of the Book of Mormon* (Batavia, 1841), and Oliver Cowdery's *Letters on the Origin of the Book of Mormon* (Liverpool, 1844).

Missouri and Illinois Manuscripts. Mormon efforts to establish a settlement in Missouri and the resistance Mormons encountered are thoroughly documented. William S. West's *A Few Interesting Facts Respecting the Rise and Pretensions of the Mormons* (Warren, 1837), Parley P. Pratt's *A Voice of Warning and Instruction* (New York, 1837; Nauvoo, 1844), John Greene's *Expulsion of the Mormons from the State of Missouri* (Cincinnati, 1839), John Corrill's *A Brief History of the Church of Christ of Latter-Day Saints* (Saint Louis, 1839), and Heber C. Kimball's *Journal* (Nauvoo, 1840) are a few of the many contemporaneous accounts in the collection. They are well complemented by lengthy runs of such important Mormon periodicals as the *Evening and the Morning Star* (Independence, Mo., 1832–33, and Kirtland, Ohio, 1834–35), the *Latter-Day Saints' Messenger and Advocate* (Kirtland, 1834–37), and the *Elders' Journal of the Church of Latter-Day Saints* (Kirtland, Ohio, and Far West, Mo., 1837–38).

As the preceding discussion suggests, Coe was especially interested in printed accounts of Mormon history, but his collection also includes several valuable manuscripts describing Mormon life in Missouri and Illinois. Charles Coulson Rich's daybook describes his journey from Tazewell County, Illinois, to Mormon Camp at Salt River, Missouri, in June 1834. William Law's daybook records his business accounts in Nauvoo in 1841 and 1842. James Monroe's diary and journal describe his conversion to Mormonism and his service as tutor to the children of Joseph Smith and Brigham Young in 1845. The collection's most extensive manuscripts concerning Nauvoo are the Oliver Olney papers. Olney became a Mormon in 1831 but was denounced by Joseph Smith in 1842. After the denunciation, from April 6, 1842, through January 23, 1843, Olney kept a virtual chronicle of life in

Nauvoo. The perspective of a gentile trader familiar with Nauvoo is provided in James M. Sharpe's journal, written principally in 1843 and in September and October 1844.

Nauvoo and the Exodus. The dramatic rise and fall of the Mormon community at Nauvoo is thoroughly recounted in complete sets of the *Times and Seasons* (Commerce and Nauvoo, Ill., 1839–46) and of the *Latter-Day Saints' Millennial Star* (Manchester and Liverpool, 1841–1905). Numerous contemporary accounts document the assassination of Joseph and Hyrum Smith as well as the tumult which ensued between the Mormons and their neighbors. Newspapers like the *Nauvoo Neighbor* (Nauvoo, Ill., 1843–44), the *Prophet* (New York, 1844–45) and the *Messenger* (New York, 1845) provide valuable coverage of the events which by the spring of 1845 convinced Brigham Young and the Church elders to abandon Nauvoo. In the Coe collection is a manuscript letter dated April 25, 1845, written by "a Committee in behalf of the Church of Jesus Christ of Latter-Day Saints" to Massachusetts Governor George Briggs, which appeals for help and protection against the abuses the Mormons had suffered in Missouri and Illinois and for assistance in establishing an unmolested asylum in the far West. The letter, copies of which were simultaneously sent to the president and to the governors of every state except Missouri and Illinois, was the first public declaration of the Mormon hierarchy's intention to relocate beyond the settled regions of the United States.

The initial exodus of Mormons from Nauvoo to Winter Quarters (now Florence, Nebraska) and then to Salt Lake City is recorded in Howard Egan's journals. A major in the Nauvoo Legion and captain of the ninth group of ten during the trip from Winter Quarters to Salt Lake City in 1847, Egan returned east to repeat the trip with his family in 1848. His first journal covers the period from April 8 to July 27, 1847, when Brigham Young led the so-called pioneer band from Winter Quarters to the Great Salt Lake. Egan describes the trip in detail, lists the members of the party, quotes Brigham Young's sermons, gives an inventory of provisions and provides a table of distances. Egan's second journal describes life at Salt Lake from July 28 through August 26 and then recounts his return journey to Winter Quarters as far as Pacific Springs. Egan's later journals as well as considerable material written by his son William Monroe Egan are also part of Coe's collection.

Salt Lake City and Utah. On December 23, 1847, after completing the initial trip to Salt Lake, Brigham Young released the first *General Epistle from the Council of the Twelve Apostles to The Church of Jesus Christ of Latter-Day Saints throughout the Earth,* in which he described the enlistment of the Mormon Battalion, the establishment of Winter Quarters, the experiences of the pioneer band, and the founding of Salt Lake City. Coe was fortunate to acquire both the Saint Louis and Liverpool editions of this pivotal document of Mormon history as well as copies of William Clayton's *The Latter-Day Saints' Emigrants' Guide; Being a Table of Distances . . . from Council Bluffs to the Valley of the Great Salt Lake* (St. Louis, 1848). The collection also features a complete set of Orson Hyde's *Frontier Guardian* (Kanesville, Iowa [now Council Bluffs], 1849–52). Published at an important jumping-off site on the overland trail, the paper was filled with information for and about Mormon emigrants.

Coe's collection documents in detail the early history of the Salt Lake community. *The Constitution of the State of Deseret* was printed in Kanesville as no local press suitable for the job had been established. On October 20, 1849, however, the first major publication from a press in Utah was issued. Brigham Young's *Second General Epistle of the Presidency of The Church of Jesus Christ of Latter-Day Saints from the Great Salt Lake Valley to the Saints Scattered throughout the Earth* marked the inauguration of full-scale printing within the new settlement. Coe's collection features forty-five of the territory's earliest imprints including the *Ordinances Passed by the Legislative Council of Great Salt Lake City* (Great Salt Lake City, 1850), Brigham Young's *Third General Epistle . . .* (Great Salt Lake City, April 12, 1850), the *Governor's Message to the Senators and Representatives of the State of Deseret* (Great Salt Lake City, 1850), and the *First Annual Message of the Governor to the Legislative Assembly of Utah Territory* (Great Salt Lake City, 1851). Although government-related printing predominated through the early 1850s, Utah presses soon began publishing on a broader range of topics. Brigham Young's *A Revelation on Celestial Marriage* (Great Salt Lake City, 1852), a series of issues of W. W. Phelps's *Deseret Almanac* beginning with 1852, and Belinda Pratt's *Defense of Polygamy* (Salt Lake City, 1854) are examples found in Coe's collection. In addition to Utah imprints and other materials published by the Mormons themselves,[1] Coe's collection contains numerous diaries, guide books, and memoirs by men and women who traveled through Salt Lake City on their way to Oregon, California, or other western destinations. Their observations provide important information not only about the social and economic development of Utah, but also about the continuing tension between the Latter-day Saints and other Americans.

Even as Mormon leaders struggled to establish a stable, permanent community in the United States, they began an aggressive, foreign missionary campaign. The worldwide scope of their efforts is reflected in Coe's collection in such pieces as Parley P. Pratt's *Proclamation!*

To the People of the Coasts and Islands of the Pacific (Sydney, New South Wales, ca. 1851), his *Proclamation Extraordinary! To the Spanish Americans* (San Francisco, 1852), and Lorenzo Snow's *The Voice of Joseph* (Malta, 1852), as well as numerous nineteenth-century translations of the Book of Mormon. On a more prosaic level, the collection features an extensive set of Liverpool Mission imprints. Among the most spectacular is James Linforth and Frederick Piercy's pictorial work, *Route from Liverpool to Great Salt Lake Valley* (Liverpool, 1855).

Missionary Manuscripts. The Mormons enjoyed great success in attracting converts, but the Church itself was rent by various schisms. Some dissenters split from Joseph Smith before his assassination, but after his death arguments about who should succeed to the leadership of the Church created further divisions. James Brewster's *The Words of Righteousness* (Springfield, Ill., 1845), *A Warning to the Latter-Day Saints* (Springfield, Ill., 1842), and *An Address to the Church of Latter-Day Saints* (Springfield, Ill., 1848), as well as Sidney Rigdon's *Disunion and Disfellowship with the Adherents of the Twelve* (Nauvoo, Ill., 1844) and Jason Brigg's *A Word of Consolation to the Scattered Saints* (Janesville, Wis., 1853), are among the important schismatic tracts in Coe's collection. One of the most charismatic and outspoken of Brigham Young's opponents was James Jesse Strang, who claimed to have received a secret appointment by Joseph Smith as his successor. Coe acquired copies of most of Strang's published works as well as some two thousand pages of his correspondence and diaries, including the purported "letter of appointment" on which Strang based his claim.

The Utah War. Brigham Young had hoped to establish the Mormon Zion in an area sufficiently isolated from the principal settlements of the United States to insure its domestic tranquility. The discovery of gold in California shattered those hopes. By the mid-1850s, disputes between Mormon and gentile residents of Utah and between the Mormon hierarchy and the federal government escalated to the brink of war. As for the various topics discussed above, Coe's collection is replete with printed documents and accounts of the test of wills between President Buchanan and Governor Young. Present are Brigham Young's *Proclamation by the Governor* (Great Salt Lake City, September 15, 1857) declaring martial law, his *Governor's Message to the Legislative Assembly . . . December 15, 1857* (Great Salt Lake City), and one of the only two known copies of his *A Series of Instructions and Remarks at Special Council* (Great Salt Lake City, 1858), in which he suggests that the Saints prepare to flee rather than conduct open war against the federal government. Documenting the federal side are a complete file of the "War Department's General Orders of the Army"

(New York, 1856–58), "General Orders of the Department of Utah" (Fort Leavenworth, Camp Scott, and Camp Floyd, 1857–59), and a series of pamphlets concerning overland freighting service supplied to the army by the firm of Majors, Russell, and Waddell.

Printed sources about the Utah War are complemented by several important manuscripts. Mormon preparations for war are described in "The Record of Orders, Returns, & Courts Martial &c. of 2nd Brigade, 1st Division, Nauvoo Legion." Joseph Heger's portfolio of original pencil sketches of scenes in Utah provides a pictorial record of one federal cavalryman's experiences in the campaign. Most important, however, are Thomas L. Kane's papers and correspondence. Colonel Kane had become acquainted with Mormon leaders as early as 1846. In 1858, President Buchanan sent Kane to Utah as his special representative; Kane mediated a compromise between Presidents Buchanan and Young and helped prevent a major war. His papers provide an invaluable perspective on the crisis and the Mormons' response to it.

Coe had relatively little interest in Mormon history after the Utah War. He did, however, acquire two important manuscript collections which document Mormon affairs in the 1860s. William Clayton's "Letter Press Copy Book" for February 1860 through April 1869 contains documents he executed as notary public of Great Salt Lake County, auditor of public accounts, and territorial recorder of marks and brands. One of the premier items in Coe's entire collection is a file of sixty letters from Brigham Young to William Hooper, Utah's territorial delegate to Congress. The letters, written between November 1859 and January 1869, describe events and conditions in Salt Lake City, gentile attitudes towards Utah, gold discoveries, and Indian affairs, as well as give family and Church news. In addition to the Clayton book and the Young letters, Coe's collection includes numerous Mormon periodicals from around the world and a complete file of the first twenty-six volumes of the *Deseret News* (Great Salt Lake City, 1850–76).

Recent Additions

Since 1949, Yale has added significantly to Coe's collection. Sterling Memorial Library, the university's central research collection, has assumed responsibility for acquiring modern scholarly studies, documentary editions, and other secondary material; the Collection of Western Americana, housed in the Beinecke Rare Book and Manuscript Library, acquires primary sources in their original format. In its acquisitions, the Western Americana collection has followed Coe's general interests, building upon the strengths of his gift. As did Coe, it has emphasized printed works rather than manuscripts; it has, however, broadened the chronological range of interest to include events and imprints of the late nineteenth and early twentieth century. Thus acquisitions reflect Yale's continuing interest in early Mormon imprints from Ohio, Missouri, Illinois, and Utah; in the social and economic development of Utah; in doctrinal developments; in missionary activity in Britain, Scandinavia, and the Far East; and in the literature of the various schismatic sects. The collection has also continued to collect Mormon and anti-Mormon polemical tracts and periodical literature. In forty years, it has acquired more than fifteen hundred additional titles on virtually every aspect of early Mormon history.

To complement Coe's initial collection, Yale has sought to identify and acquire printed material concerning the doctrine, practice, and controversy of polygamy, as well as to develop holdings of privately printed reminiscences, memoirs, and local histories. Yale has been fortunate to acquire some great rarities in all areas, but its principal concern has been to build a comprehensive research collection in which scholars can investigate nearly any aspect of the Mormon experience in the nineteenth and early twentieth centuries. To this end, considerable attention has been devoted to adding important albeit commonplace works.

For more information about Yale's collection of Mormon Americana, readers may consult Mary Withington, *A Catalog of Manuscripts in the Collection of Western Americana Formed by William Robertson Coe: Yale University Library* (New Haven, 1952); Edward Eberstadt, *The William Robertson Coe Collection of Western Americana* (New Haven, 1948); or the G. K. Hall Company's reproduction of the collection's catalog (Boston, 1974). Since 1981 additions to the collection have been cataloged on the Research Libraries Information Network (RLIN). Inquiries about the collection, its hours, and photoduplication policies may be directed to The Yale Collection of Western Americana, Box 1603A Yale Station, New Haven, Connecticut 06520-1603.

George Miles is the William Robertson Coe Curator of Western Americana, Beinecke Library, Yale University.

NOTES

The article was originally published in *BYU Studies* 32 (Summer 1992): 61–69.

[1]See the brief sketch by Jeffrey R. Holland, "A Note on Mormon Americana at Yale," *BYU Studies* 10 (Spring 1970): 386–88.

Part IV:

Special Topics in Mormon Americana

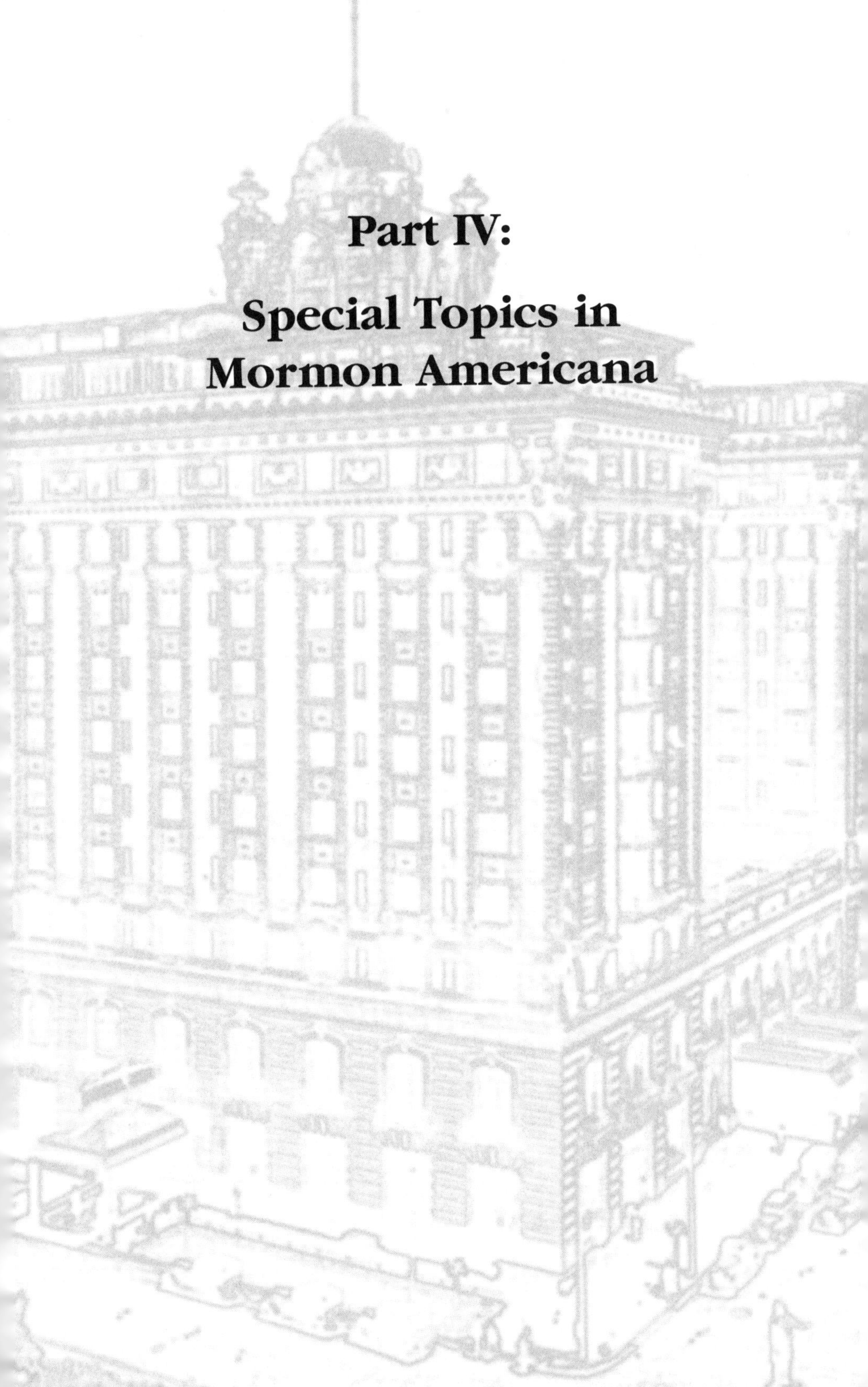

The "Utah Stone" by William Ward, the State of Utah's contribution to the Washington Monument in Washington, D.C., ca. 1851–53. Courtesy LDS Church Archives.

Woodcarved toys by Orson Pratt Lee, Monroe, Utah, ca. 1900. Courtesy Utah Arts Council.

Material Culture: An Introduction and Guide to Mormon Vernacular

Carol A. Edison

A number of traditional resources are available to historians, anthropologists, and other students of culture in their attempts to understand life during earlier times. While written materials have long provided the most common sources of information, contemporary scholars are more frequently turning to an equally eloquent—though nonverbal—resource as they expand and refine the story of the past. Material culture (literally, the material manifestations of a culture) is the collective term for the everyday objects that are part of people's lives.[1] Students of Mormon history and culture are among those discovering that the study of material culture can add new dimensions and valuable insights to their work.

Perhaps the first mention of "Mormon material culture" was in an article written by Utah folklorist Austin Fife in 1957.[2] In that article, Fife stated that many objects of material culture are products of folk (nonprofessional) technology. Such technology results from the combination of knowledge passed down from antiquity with people's innate ingenuity. Fife further noted that all items of folk culture are worthy of investigation and then described those "lines of investigation which might be followed in order to assess their importance in the formation of the heritage of the American West."[3] Among the subjects Fife deemed integral to an understanding of the Mormon frontier experience were the following: the layout of frontier towns; the designs and materials used in building houses; the construction and spatial relationships of domestic buildings; the production of furniture and other home furnishings; the production of clothing, tools, and occupational gear; the ornamentation of both interior and exterior spaces; and the construction of cemeteries and gravemarkers. Fife's inventory of objects—their production, placement, and use on the landscape and within the community—provided a blueprint for investigation that still directs studies of Mormon material culture today.[4]

Patterns of Settlement and Land Use: The Creation of Community

Mormon towns in the western United States look and feel different from non-Mormon towns. During the last forty years, several scholars have attempted to define the characteristics that contribute to this difference. Of particular importance are Lowry Nelson's 1920s field study and 1952 book about the Mormon village,[5] Donald W. Meinig's 1965 delineation of the Mormon cultural region,[6] and Richard Francaviglia's 1970s analysis of Mormon landscape.[7]

Lowry Nelson's 1952 study was one of the first to analyze the small communities of rural Utah and adjacent states in an attempt to define what makes them distinct from other western settlements. Nelson identified the village settlement pattern—in which homes and yards are clustered together and fields are located on the outside edge of the village—as the defining characteristic of Mormon villages.[8]

In the Mormon village, farm structures such as barns and pig pens were typically built on town lots adjacent to the house. Family orchards, vegetable and flower gardens, and even small pastures were also just outside the door. A stackhouse (for storing feed) and, possibly, a corral were the only structures built in the outlying fields. Although this is an ancient and common pattern in agricultural societies throughout the world,[9] it is a very unusual pattern in the United States where, aside from the Mormon West, it is only seen in parts of New England and in the Hispanic Southwest.[10] In contrast, most nineteenth-century American frontier settlements consisted of widely scattered homesteads or farms in which settlers worked and lived on the same property.

Climate, geography, demographics, and religious beliefs all contributed to the success of this Mormon settlement plan—a plan which might not have worked so well for other frontier settlers. The arid climate meant sites for Mormon villages were typically chosen at the mouths of canyons, where mountain streams provided water that could be dammed and diverted through irrigation ditches to dry fields and thirsty livestock. Given these limited water resources, the numbers of families and livestock and the size of a settled area were necessarily small. As a result, the distances between homes and fields were easily traveled.

Each settlement was part of a systematic plan to establish Mormon communities throughout the territory. Therefore, the settlers often included people selected to supply the variety of skills needed to build a self-sufficient community. Settling as a group also allowed a division of labor that encouraged workers to trade or barter their specialized skills. Furthermore, living in close proximity stimulated the development and growth of group institutions like churches and schools, as well as group social activities like dances, concerts, and dramatic productions. And although Mormon settlers were not always from the same ethnic heritage, their religious homogeneity undoubtedly contributed to the success of these early communities. For Mormons, who were building a new, communitarian society in an isolated environment, the village settlement pattern was the perfect choice.[11]

In addition to the village settlement pattern, other distinguishing elements of the Mormon environment were identified in Richard Francaviglia's 1978 study. Francaviglia compiled a list of characteristics frequently found in towns of Mormon origin and population. Those elements are: (1) wide streets with deep shoulders—often without sidewalks; (2) a grid system of roads, oriented to the cardinal points of the compass, that intersect at right angles to create ten-acre blocks divided into four residential lots; (3) a system of roadside irrigation ditches; (4) unpainted barns and outbuildings adjacent to homes on town lots; (5) open fields, sometimes with corrals or stackyards, but without windmills, barns, or farmsteads; (6) a high percentage of adobe or fired-brick homes, usually in earth colors, and a high percentage of homes with central-hall floor plans, often with Greek Revival elements; (7) Mormon hay derricks, Mormon fences (built from scrap pickets or from cedar posts and barbed wire), and inside-out granaries (built with strong and smooth inside walls to facilitate grain storage and retrieval); (8) the use of fast-growing Lombardy poplars or cottonwoods along ditch banks to provide windbreaks either in town or bordering fields; (9) the pasturing of cattle and sheep in the same field; and (10) a public square in the center of town with church buildings and sometimes a school or city park.

According to Francaviglia, "the Mormon landscape contains three main types of elements: those that had been present in the areas from which the Mormons had come; those that came west with them as concepts; and those that are unique to the semi-arid West either by invention or by the introduction of other peoples."[12] Among those elements transplanted from previous areas of residence were the house types built by early settlers (specifically the central hall and variations of this plan), the widespread use of Greek Revival ornamentation, and a grid system of wide roads are among those elements transplanted from previous areas of residence.[13] The road system is generally thought to have originated within Joseph Smith's ideal city plan, but such systems are a common feature of eastern and midwestern cities built during the seventeenth and early eighteenth centuries. Landscape concepts that the Saints brought west were often part of Brigham Young's ambitious system of village-based colonization. Two concepts became strategies for building group solidarity and self-sufficiency: (1) the placement of gardens and outbuildings on city lots and (2) the calculated selection of settlers with complementary skills.

As for Francaviglia's third category—elements unique to the semi-arid West—the following are included among those elements introduced to or invented by the Mormons because of the West's unique climate and geography: the placement of towns at the mouths of canyons near water sources; the use of irrigation ditches; the use of unfired brick or adobe in building construction; and the development of the "Mormon" hay derrick.[14] Using Francaviglia's scenario, perhaps a fourth category should be added to this list—a category of elements inspired by the isolation of early Mormon settlements. In this category, the planting of home gardens and orchards,[15] the penning of sheep and cattle in the same pasture, and the saving of used machinery and scrap materials to build or mend fences and other structures suggest both a common-sense approach to the realities of frontier life and a desire for self-sufficiency—two ideas that characterized the Mormon settlement experience.

As Elaine Thatcher has noted, "Every object created or modified by members of a group is part of that group's material culture. LDS material culture encompasses a particular constellation of objects, only a few of which are unique. But, taken together, they create what can be identified as a Mormon environment."[16] What can these objects or these patterns for arranging objects tell us about the daily life and culture of the people who built and used them? What can they tell us about the Mormon experience, aside from its communitarian base? Perhaps these questions can be answered by exploring how Mormon patterns of settlement and land use provided a framework wherein houses, outbuildings, home furnishings, and ultimately most other items of material culture fit. By looking at these everyday objects, some insight into the needs, concerns, and motivations of earlier generations and a better understanding of the Mormon legacy in the Intermountain West can be gained.

Vernacular Architecture: An Expression of Cultural Roots

Months of living outdoors made finding permanent shelter a priority for Mormon pioneers when they reached Utah. Just a few days after their arrival in 1847, the first pioneers used mud and clay to build a fortlike "stockade of adobe homes."[17] Caves, dugouts, and crude log structures provided the earliest shelter for many others, but most wanted to build more substantial structures and were soon trading skills and labor to construct more comfortable homes.[18] A limited supply of lumber led many pioneers to build homes out of adobe bricks. Clay, often dug on site, was mixed with water and straw, then packed into simple wooden frames and sun-dried. Constructed from bricks measuring roughly 5" x 11" each,[19] adobe houses were usually finished with a layer of plaster to protect the adobe from moisture.[20]

Even though lumber was not plentiful, pioneers often found a wealth of building stone in nearby mountains. In some areas, lumber was used primarily for foundations; in other areas, entire houses were fashioned using local granite, sandstone, limestone, or basalt. As Austin Fife pointed out in a 1971 study of houses in northern Utah, "the stone was quarried locally, and in each of the communities there is a visible kinship between the stone of the houses; of a few of the older business establishments; of churches, temples and tabernacles; and of the adjacent fields and mountains."[21]

Though the choice of building materials was often defined by available resources, design and style were another matter. Many scholars have studied Mormon vernacular architecture, describing and analyzing the various single- and double-cell, hall-parlor or central

One-and-a-half-story Gothic Revival house in Midway, Utah, built by Irish convert John Watkins, ca. 1875. Courtesy Utah Arts Council.

passage, and cross-wing T or L plans. These scholars have further noted that most folk houses are symmetrical, with windows, doors, and chimneys placed in balanced opposition to each other in apparent deference to Georgian ideals of the nineteenth century.[22] The use of decorative elements commonly found on gables, eaves, dormers, and entrances, inspired by popular Federal, Greek Revival, and Gothic Revival styles, has also been studied.[23] Likewise, researchers have documented the Mormon inclination to cover log structures with plaster or lumber siding; to cover adobe structures with plaster, often scored and painted to resemble brick; or to build stone structures with rocks dressed to convey the smoothness and regularity of man-made bricks.[24] As Francaviglia asserted, these characteristics suggest that Mormon builders were influenced by the housing stock they knew from other locations.[25] These characteristics also imply that the Mormons had an understanding of popular nineteenth-century architectural styling and that, like most Americans, they preferred manufactured over organic building materials, reflecting their desire to subdue and dominate nature.[26]

In an attempt to better understand nineteenth-century Mormon housing, some have suggested that certain homes throughout the Mormon cultural region exhibit ethnic-based design and construction. For example, Linda Bonar's research has shown that stonework techniques used in Beaver, Utah, reflect the Scottish origins of two of the town's builders: Thomas Frazier and Alexander "Scotty" Boyter.[27] Both builders added prestige and style to homes by using techniques employed in Scotland to make homes appear more expensive.[28] Thomas Carter's field research in central Utah's Sanpete County has also documented multiple structures in which ethnic architectural traditions are evident. Among the traditions he identified is the Anglo-Germanic tradition of log construction, characterized by gaped, horizontal logs with chinking and dovetailed notches at the corners.[29] He also identified the Scandinavian log tradition, featuring horizontal logs trimmed so they fit together tightly with a full dovetail notch at the corners,[30] as well as an English/New English frame construction tradition known as box-framing.[31] Carter further documented several Scandinavian house types and construction techniques in Sanpete Valley that were part of nineteenth-century Danish tradition, concluding that Mormon immigrants built "houses and barns which recalled the traditions of their previous homelands rather than those they encountered in Zion."[32]

Folk builders in Utah, whether originally from the British Isles, Scandinavia, or states other than Utah, were interested in building substantial, permanent housing as soon as possible. Using locally available materials, builders constructed homes and outbuildings to shelter their families and livestock. In doing so, builders employed floorplans, construction techniques, and facades that were familiar to them. As Carter concluded, "since there was no officially prescribed or sanctioned building policy, the Saints merely built strong and attractive houses according to the fashion of the times. Efforts toward creating visible symbols of specifically Mormon values were channeled instead toward group-oriented projects. . . . Appropriately, it is the nucleated town settlement pattern and its monumental religious architecture, not the houses, that distinguish the Mormon West from its neighboring regions."[33]

The Material Culture of Occupation: Evidence of an Agrarian Lifestyle

Developing a reliable food source was essential for early Mormon settlers in Utah. Two major activities—the growing of fruit, vegetables, and grain and raising livestock—resulted in the development of many structures that reflect this agriculturally based economy. Today, pioneer-era hay derricks, barns, granaries, root cellars, and outbuildings that served farming activities, as well as the fences, corrals, cowsheds, roundup pens, and loading chutes associated with livestock, still dot the landscape throughout the Mormon cultural region.

Hay Derricks. Described by Richard Francaviglia as "a curious pole-like element in a farmyard scene already cluttered with posts, sticks and poles,"[34] a hay derrick is a homemade device that was commonly used to load or stack hay throughout the Intermountain West during the late nineteenth and early twentieth centuries. A derrick consists of a wooden stand or base with a mobile arm-like boom, rigged with ropes, that can be manipulated to pick up and move loose or bailed hay. Great Basin farmers, having discovered that the region's cold and dry winters allowed them to store alfalfa safely in the open, used derricks to transfer cut alfalfa from wagon beds and stack it into piles that repelled most moisture, sacrificing only the top layer to the elements. Initially, most farmers grew just enough alfalfa to feed the livestock that supplied the needs of a single family, so stationary derricks were sufficient. But as herds multiplied and fields expanded, farmers had to either build additional derricks or make existing derricks mobile, leading to several modifications and variations on the original design. The vernacular nature and widespread use of hay derricks was carefully described in a 1948 study coauthored by Austin Fife and James Fife. Driving northward from Bunkerville, Nevada, approximately

Built of wood and rigged with ropes, hay derricks were used during the late nineteenth and early twentieth centuries to load and stack hay. Today they provide an eloquent statement about the region's agrarian past and cultural boundaries. Courtesy The Church of Jesus Christ of Latter-day Saints.

one thousand miles across the Mormon region to Yellowstone National Park, the Fifes counted nearly fifteen hundred homemade hay derricks.[35]

Today, hay derricks remain an important component of the manufactured landscape of the Mormon cultural region. In many western states, derricks are even referred to as "Mormon hay derricks" or "Mormon stackers"—an interesting acknowledgment of the derricks' identification with and widespread use in Mormon communities.[36] In some small villages of central Utah, derricks are still rigged with ropes and are regularly used. Many more derricks throughout the region, however, are idle, their angular frames rising from the edges of fields or towering over barnyard sheds. Though not functional, they are allowed to remain—icons to the past that, like many of the items comprising our material inheritance, provide an eloquent reminder of an occupational heritage grounded in agrarian self-sufficiency.

Straw-Thatched Cowsheds. During the 1970s, folklorists Hector Lee and David Lee studied another material marker on the Mormon landscape: open-sided animal shelters with thatched roofs made from twigs or straw. The Lees identified hundreds of such structures and studied nearly sixty in some detail. Typically constructed from juniper posts with crossbeams of fir or pine, the sheds were covered with moisture-resistant "thatching" built from a bed of twigs or willow, often with several feet of straw piled on top.[37] Dating before the 1930s, when grain was threshed in the stackyard and the leftover straw could be easily added to the roof, these sheds provided shelter for milk cows, work horses, pigs, and lambs.

The cowshed has been used by many cultures and could have been transplanted from Europe or the eastern United States, or it might be a version of the open-air shelters used by both Hispanics and Native Americans in the Southwest. Yet, "the large number of [cowsheds] which have survived into the 1970s and 80s suggests that they must have been accepted more completely and for a longer period of time among the Mormons than among any other group."[38] Like hay derricks, these characteristically open-sided structures are well-suited to the arid valleys of the Mormon cultural region.

Another benefit of the thatched cowshed was that "many were used as an emergency supply of feed during bad winters. Mendon, in northern Utah's Cache Valley, . . . was one community where the entire straw thatching was fed to cattle on at least two occasions during the nineteenth century."[39] This suggests that the popularity and widespread use of thatched-roof cowsheds might also reflect their contribution to the self-sufficient lifestyle of the region.

Today, though the number of thatched-roof cowsheds grows smaller every year, their successors—sheds topped with tangles of left-over baling twine and wire—continue to provide shelter for farm animals. Like the straw that provided emergency feed when needed, these newer roofs provide a repository for useful materials that may have future use in a society that still values economy.[40]

Fences and Pens. Other farm structures, such as handmade fences, corrals, roundup pens, and loading chutes, silently testify to the economic and occupational history of the Mormon region. These structures were originally constructed from readily available materials—split or whole logs, cut timber, woven willow, or stacked stone—with barbed or netted wire added later. Some fence types have been categorized and studied, including the common jack fence;[41] but aside from a study of ranching structures in northwestern Utah's village of Grouse Creek, where Mormon traditions meet buckaroo traditions from Nevada,[42] there has been little intensive study of these ranching structures.

The ubiquitous roundup pens, often in disrepair and seemingly abandoned, are scattered throughout the Mormon region. They are built with angles or curves in a configuration often defined by topography. Most roundup pens have two openings to aid in the gathering and loading of livestock: one at ground level and another that is elevated.

The large number of pens still in existence can be attributed to the region's ranching history, which is characterized by a climate and topography that limit available feed and water, a community tradition of relatively small herds, and an abundance of publicly owned lands. These factors created a biannual pattern of gathering small herds into a larger community-owned group and then either driving or transporting them to alternate feeding ranges. This twice-yearly trek between summertime mountain pastures on federal lands to wintertime feed lots in town or on public lands in the desert has continued for more than a century. As a result, many of the holding pens and loading chutes built by earlier generations are still in use today.

As Francaviglia wrote, "an important part of the rustic, rural feeling of the Mormon village is a result of the farmyard settings right in town. The large and solid houses; the barns and granaries; the hay derricks, gardens, orchards and sheds all conspire to bring the farm right to the city center."[43] Indeed, "the impression is almost one of a series of small farms pieced together to form a town."[44] Even today, the rural villages of the Mormon region provide visual reminders of their agricultural past as "thousands of Utahns tend vegetable and flower gardens, gather harvest from grapevines and fruit trees, and decorate their yards and homes with wagon wheels and old farm implements."[45]

Domestic Material Culture

Physical isolation forced the earliest Mormon settlers to produce at home whatever they needed to feed, clothe, and shelter their families. In addition, the settlers' desire to remain apart from the temptations of the world led them to value items made "in Zion" over those made in "Babylon" even after the railroad supplied goods from the east. This emphasis on local production resulted in a rich array of domestic material culture.

Besides making furniture from locally available pine, the settlers used pottery, wood, iron, and tin to make dishes, storage containers, and utensils. They also produced carpets, drapes, quilts, and household linens from recycled materials or from locally produced textiles. Hats, shoes, clothing, and accessories were also produced at home from natural fibers or from the hides and coats of homegrown cattle and sheep.

Though they once existed in great numbers, domestic articles from earlier generations are by nature more ephemeral than buildings or other elements in the built environment. Typically, most were used until worn out, perhaps recycled, and ultimately discarded. Despite this problem, a number of items of Mormon domestic material culture from the nineteenth century still exist, and they provide one of the best opportunities for gaining insight and understanding into the daily life of generations past.

Mormon Pine Furniture. Aside from the common storage chest or steamer trunk and the occasional piano or organ, Mormon pioneers did not typically bring furniture with them on their trek across the plains. What they did bring were the tools and skills needed to craft furniture from whatever materials they might find in their new western home.

In the early years, chests and trunks often doubled as tables. Beds were frequently constructed by suspending ropes or strips of rawhide from corner walls to an interior post and then covering the ropes with a straw-filled mattress. Settlements generally counted carpenters (woodworkers) and often cabinetmakers (furniture specialists) in their population and, as was the case with other pioneer artisans, many had been trained in formal apprenticeships in Britain or Scandinavia.[46] Within a few years, Mormon artisans were making fan-back Windsor chairs or ladder-back chairs (often with rush or rawhide seats), rocking chairs, tables, baby cradles, flour bins, bedsteads, cupboards, and lounges to supply the growing needs of the pioneer population.

Although some furniture was produced in professional workshops, most pieces were the products of individual artisans meeting the needs of individual customers. Influenced by what was used in their previous homes, customers ordered furniture that sometimes reflected their ethnic backgrounds or local taste.[47] While most forms and styles were similar to those in the eastern United States or in Europe, at least one type of furniture became associated with Mormon culture. According to Elaine Thatcher, "Lounges, made and used throughout the country, were so common in Utah that they have become widely known as Mormon lounges."[48] The lounge was a wooden sofa that could seat several people or accommodate one person lying down. Some were constructed with a double frame on the bottom made of alternating slats—one stationary and the other movable—so one frame could slide out to form a double bed. Connie Morningstar notes that "in some areas, these were called Bishop's couches—ready on short notice to accommodate an extra guest or two overnight."[49] Given the ever-growing needs for sleeping space in most Mormon families, the popularity of the lounge is understandable.

Accustomed to working with hard woods, Mormon artisans were limited to available soft woods, which are "referred to in the historical accounts as pine, cedar, and quaking aspen (*Populus tremuloides*). The term *pine* often referred to a variety of different woods, including lodgepole pine (*Pinus contorta*), Englemann spruce [or red pine]

Glazed earthenware, ca. 1880. Left and right, work of Danish potter James J. Hansen of Hyrum, Utah; middle, work of English potter Thomas Davenport of Parowan, Utah. Courtesy Utah Arts Council.

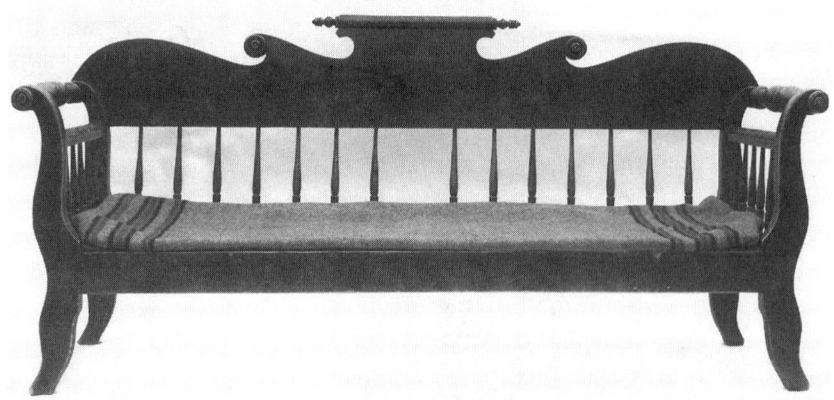

This softwood "Mormon lounge," attributed to Ole Swenson of Manti, Utah, was painted and grained to simulate mahogany. Altering softwood to look like hardwood was a common practice during pioneer times, suggesting the Mormons' desire to produce and own finely crafted possessions despite their frontier location. Courtesy Utah Arts Council.

(*Picea engelmannii*), and Douglas fir (*Pseudotsuga menziesii*). . . . The cedar mentioned in local records was actually Rocky Mountain juniper (*Juniperus scopulorum*)."[50] Since most furniture was crafted in the Empire or Sheraton styles popular at midcentury in the eastern United States, use of these softer woods resulted in simplified versions of those styles, often with somewhat larger proportions.[51]

A common practice that resulted from the use of soft woods was the manipulation of surface stains and paints to visually reproduce hardwood grains. After applying either oil-based stains, lard colored with red earth, or paint made from a mixture of buttermilk and animal blood,[52] artisans dragged combs, sticks, or other objects through the wet surface, "graining" the furniture and making it look like hardwood. Like scoring and plastering adobe to look like fired brick, this interest in making frontier-produced furniture look like furniture from the East makes a strong statement about the desire of early settlers to build and furnish their homes in compliance with contemporary standards and conventions.

Utah Pottery. Throughout pioneer Utah, potters, trained in England or Denmark, produced household containers. According to Kirk Henrichsen's 1988 study of nineteenth-century pottery making, storage jars were the most common forms of earthenware produced.[53] Wide-mouth storage jars were typically used for pickling or for protecting dry goods from vermin or rodents, while narrower jars were used to store and preserve fruit. Also commonly produced was "a large, flat-bottomed bowl commonly referred to as a milk pan or basin"[54] because it allowed milk to cool quickly and made the process of skimming off cream easy. Bowls of this type were also used as mixing bowls or wash basins. Pitchers, jugs, and churns were also commonly made, although very few still exist, while specialty items (butter molds, umbrella stands, and foot warmers, for example) are even more rare.[55]

By the late 1800s, many factors contributed to the decline of Mormon pottery making. A reduction in immigration to the region, growing concern with the danger of lead-glazed pottery, and the availability of less expensive metal crockery were all factors, but "the innovation that finally spelled doom for kitchen crockery was the [glass] canning jar."[56] These see-through fruit storage jars, which became widely available after the invention of a semiautomatic glass-blowing machine, were understandably popular in a region where food preservation was an integral part of life. Both the storage jars, handcrafted by Utah potters, and the imported glass jars tell the same story of home production and self-sufficiency in the Mormon cultural region.

Wool Textiles and Mormon Quilts. Although the clothing and linens carried across the plains were repeatedly recycled into children's clothing, rag rugs, and patchwork quilts, ultimately Mormon settlers had to produce their own cloth. Attempts to cultivate cotton and flax for linen were both short-lived,[57] as was a major Church-sponsored effort at raising silkworms to produce silk that never quite met expectations.[58] Ultimately, the widely produced wool yarn and wool cloth became the mainstay of Mormon textile manufacturing.

Wool production required a lengthy process involving shearing the sheep, cleaning the wool, carding it, spinning it, and finally dyeing it with vegetable dyes or soil pigments.[59] Only then could the yarn be knitted or crocheted into stockings, sweaters, or baby clothing. Additional steps were required to weave the yarn into wool blankets or bedspreads, drapes, table coverings, or carpeting, or to turn finer woolen yarn into fabric suitable for clothing. Tufts of wool, sometimes gathered from bushes or fences, also provided the batting for thousands of scrapbag quilts—one of the most common nineteenth-century textiles. Backed with bleached muslin retrieved from flour sacks and fronted with patchwork designs painstakingly created from leftover bits of clothing, quilts were used to divide rooms, cover doorways, and provide warmth in wagons and beds.

Quilts, perhaps more than any other material expression, have come to symbolize Mormon culture. "Quilts entered the valley with the first pioneers. Pianos and fine china often had to be left to that easier life . . . but the quilt, in its functional nature, was folded and packed for a journey that held room only for necessities of survival. For the pioneer woman, the fact that the quilt was beautiful could be her secret comfort—the fact that it kept her family warm was its justification for those precious few inches of space."[60] Instead of playing the piano or displaying fine china, many nineteenth-century Mormon women directed their creative talents toward one of their domestic chores: quilting. Through quilting, as functional as it was beautiful, Mormon women created a legacy that was passed along to subsequent generations.

For the most part, Mormon quilts of any time period have always looked like those made in other parts of the country—with patterns and colors that blend traditional design with contemporary taste. But unlike other cultural groups, Mormons continued to make many quilts long after quilting went out of vogue elsewhere. The Relief Society's mission to provide for the poor certainly contributed to the perpetuation of Mormon quilting.[61] Furthermore, the custom of making quilts to commemorate special junctures in life contributed to their continued importance in Mormon society. Life's rites of passage, like birth or marriage, as well as rites distinctively Mormon, such as successfully completed missions or church leadership positions, provided occasions for special quilts to be made.[62]

Straw Hats. Providing clothing—not just everyday wear and clothes for church, but ritual clothing for blessings, weddings, funerals, and temple wear—was a major responsibility for every pioneer family.[63] Even hats, a customary and popular part of nineteenth-century American fashion, were not forgotten. Made of beaver, otter, or velvet for winter wear or from silk or straw for the summer, hats were made and worn by people of all ages and were considered a necessary item of clothing by Mormons living on the frontier. "After the harvest time was over, the women went into the fields and gleaned straw for making hats. They were careful not to waste the heads. Instead they added them to the stacks to be threshed. The finer [straws] were used for the nicer hats. The coarser ones for work hats."[64] Some women even raised special patches of wheat specifically for straw hats, and for the best hats they bleached the straw and added horse hair, dyed straw, or dried flowers for decoration.[65]

By the turn of the century, millinery shops were found in many Mormon communities, and Mormons valued the specialized skills of those who could successfully braid straw and weave it into hats. Hatmaking, and especially the making of finely crafted and decorated straw hats, once again reminds us that although early Mormons were physically isolated, they were aware of popular fashion.

Decorative Needlework, Woodwork, and Toys. As they create their material surroundings, many people have an underlying need to move "beyond necessity" by crafting things that are not only useful, but also beautiful.[66] Many of the everyday objects that have survived from the nineteenth-century Mormon West demonstrate this desire to move beyond necessity. Nowhere was this more evident than in the domestic arena, where utilitarian objects were customarily embellished with decoration and where some objects were crafted for the pure joy of creation.

Pioneer women were grounded in the needle arts—a necessity for those with the responsibility of clothing their families and furnishing their homes. Not only were spinning, weaving, knitting and crocheting common skills, but so were netting, tatting, hardanger, needlepoint, cross-stitch, and embroidery. As Shirley Paxman noted in her study of pioneer-era domestic skills, "Sheets, pillowcases, pillow shams, table covers, towels, napkins, blankets, petticoats, dresses, hats, scarves, quilts, baby clothes, shawls, Bible covers, pin cushions, suspenders, watch holders, purses and bags, chair seats, diaper bags, bell pulls, samplers, nightgowns and caps—all were created or embellished with needlework."[67]

Another material expression that had widespread popularity during the nineteenth century was the arrangement of fruit or flowers for domestic display. "One of the cherished decorations in the parlor of the pioneer home was the glass globe, underneath which reposed in colorful splendor, waxed fruit, flowers made from wool, cloth, and silk. Sometimes natural flowers were used, and treated for preservation. These globes usually were placed in the center of the table." [68] Because excess fabric, wax, or other materials could not often be spared for purely decorative projects, pioneer folk artists looked for frontier replacements. As a result, many flower arrangements were painstakingly made from the abundant supply of human hair. Framed under glass, these hair flowers and wreaths are preserved in collections throughout the region—evidence of individual creativity and the need for beauty.

Things made from scraps of wood—whittled chains or balls-in-a-cage, or carved miniature animals, wagons, or people—are among the many items that were produced for the pleasure they brought to both the maker and the owner. Many creations were toys painstakingly crafted by loving parents and grandparents. "Carefully constructed dolls, doll furniture, horses, animals, pull toys, [and] spinning tops" are among those items that have survived.[69] Additional items include wooden game boards used for checkers, tic-tac-toe, Nine Men's Moves (like Chinese checkers) or Fox and Geese; clay marbles; and dolls made from wood, nuts, corncobs, rags, or clay.[70] Although most objects of this type were probably loved to death, the handful that survive provide evidence of the human need to be creative and to add visual pleasure to everyday life.

Cemeteries and Gravestones

Just as Mormon pioneers combined their previous knowledge with local resources to provide life's necessities, in confronting death they also turned for guidance to the customs, ideas, and material expressions from their past experience. As a result, early Mormon cemeteries and the gravemarkers placed within them are among those material expressions that provide important insights into the values of nineteenth-century Mormon culture.

The Mormon West was settled several decades after the rural cemetery movement was firmly in place in the eastern United States. This movement promoted the creation of peaceful, parklike cemeteries as an alternative to traditional burial grounds that were dark and foreboding.[71] Even though the very first graves in Mormon communities were often hastily placed on private lots in town,[72] the pioneers pursued the goals of the rural cemetery movement, locating their cemeteries in picturesque areas on the edges of towns and often near the mountains. More than a century passed before water and greenery could be brought to some of these cemeteries,[73] but a border of trees—often evergreens—eventually marked many locations.

Although the first Mormon graves were likely marked with fieldstones or simple wooden markers, permanent markers carved from locally quarried stone soon appeared—from a surprisingly early date—as part of the pioneers' conscious effort to build a permanent community in their new frontier home.[74] The majority of the stonecutters came from England, while a few were from Danish or Yankee backgrounds. Even though they used carving styles transplanted from their homelands, the stonecutters' repertoire of traditional Christian symbols gave their work meaning for their new Mormon neighbors.[75]

Gravestones and their symbols provide one of the most eloquent statements of a culture's values, concerns, and beliefs. The widespread use of the handclasp motif visually proclaims the Mormon belief in life and reunion after death. Courtesy Utah Arts Council.

The completion of the railroad and the availability of stone from eastern quarries resulted in the appearance of marble markers in Mormon cemeteries. Like their predecessors of local sandstone, these marble gravestones typically used biblical imagery. Doves (representing the soul, Holy Ghost, or good tidings), the lamb (Christ, meekness and obedience, innocence), the rose (love, life), and the clasped hands were among the most commonly used symbols.[76]

The image of clasped hands, a Masonic symbol used on gravestones throughout America, was enthusiastically adopted and widely used by Mormons. As Richard Poulsen noted, "the most ubiquitous burial symbol in the Mormon cemeteries of the West is the Handclasp motif . . . [It] represents the Mormon burial in much the same way the winged death's-head connotes Puritan burial . . . [through] a symbol of transformation—of transcendence."[77] Though the handclasp symbol has a multiplicity of religious meanings, it most simply signifies reunion after death. Other symbols adopted by the Mormons, such as the beehive or the All-Seeing Eye, were evidently not as popular or as meaningful; today, they are found on only a handful of nineteenth-century markers. The symbolism of clasped hands, however, continued into the twentieth century through the image of the Mormon temple—another symbol of reunion after death.[78]

"Through their design, imagery and text—made available by carvers and chosen by family or friends—gravestones can make an eloquent statement of both individual and community beliefs about life, death and the afterlife. Gravestones function as important intermediaries between the temporal and the spiritual worlds. They can show how individuals and society reconcile themselves to the inevitability of death. And they can reassure those who mourn, whose time will eventually come, of the truth of their beliefs."[79] Nineteenth-century Mormon gravestones, like the many other items that comprise Mormon material culture, provide an essential and exceptional historical resource. By examining the material record, researchers can uncover new dimensions and valuable insights about the Mormon past.

A Guide to Mormon Material Culture

As scholars investigate the Mormon past, they should be careful to review the results of material culture studies and incorporate those studies into their work. As an aid to that work, major material culture collections and scholarly sources are listed below.

Archival Collections

Fife Folklore Archive, Utah State University (Logan, Utah)

Index of American Design, National Gallery of Art (Washington, D.C.)

Utah State Folklife Archive, Chase Home Museum of Utah Folk Art (Salt Lake City, Utah)

Church History Sites

Beehive and Lion Houses (Salt Lake City, Utah)
Brigham Young Winter Home (St. George, Utah)
Cove Fort (Cove Fort, Utah)
Jacob Hamblin Home (Santa Clara, Utah)

Displays/Events

Festival of the American West (Logan, Utah)
Harvest Homecoming Days in Capitol Reef (Fruita, Utah)
Springville Quilt Show (Springville, Utah)
Utah State Fair (Salt Lake City, Utah)
County fairs throughout Utah

Living History Facilities

Ronald V. Jensen Historical Farm (Wellsville, Utah)
Old Deseret, Pioneer Trail State Park (Salt Lake City, Utah)

Museums

Chase Home Museum of Utah Folk Art, Liberty Park (Salt Lake City, Utah)
Daughters of Utah Pioneer Museums (Salt Lake City, Utah, and in towns throughout Utah)
LDS Museum of Church History and Art (Salt Lake City, Utah)
Utah State Historical Society Museum (Salt Lake City, Utah)

National Monuments, State Parks, and Other Sites

Iron Mission State Park Museum (Cedar City, Utah)
Territorial Statehouse and Daughters of Utah Pioneers Museum (Fillmore, Utah)
Pipe Springs National Monument (Moccasin, Arizona)
Pioneer Village at Lagoon (Farmington, Utah)

Organizations and Associations

Utah Arts Council Folk Arts Program (Salt Lake City, Utah)
Folklore Society of Utah (Salt Lake City, Utah)
Western Folklife Center (Elko, Nevada)

Recommendations

1. *Best areas to see vernacular architecture*
   Northern Utah: Willard, Mendon, Randolph, Midway. Central Utah: Spring City, Manti. Southern Utah: Beaver, Virgin, Toquerville. Snowflake, Arizona; Chesterfield and Paris, Idaho; Manassa, Colorado; Panaca, Nevada
2. *Best areas for derricks, thatched sheds, and other farm structures*
   Central Utah, particularly Scipio and Paragonah

3. *Best collections of Mormon pine furniture*
   LDS Church Collection; Pioneer Trail State Park Collection
4. *Best collections of historic Mormon quilts*
   Daughters of Utah Pioneers Collection, Salt Lake City; LDS Church Collection
5. *Cemeteries with interesting nineteenth-century Mormon gravestones*
   Salt Lake City Cemetery. Northern Utah: North Ogden, Willard, and Wellsville. Central Utah: Kanosh, Fillmore, Holden, Oak City, Manti, Ephraim (abandoned), and Fairview. Southern Utah: Panguitch, Beaver, Parowan, Cedar City, Leeds, and Santa Clara. Panaca, Nevada.
6. *The only two places to see actual sunstones from the Nauvoo Temple*
   National Museum of American History, Smithsonian Institution, Washington, D.C.; Nauvoo Temple site, Nauvoo, Illinois

Additional References

Patterns of Settlement and Land Use

Anderson, Paul L. "An Idaho Variation on the City of Zion." In *Chesterfield: Mormon Outpost in Idaho,* ed. by Lavina Fielding Anderson, 71-78. Bancroft, Idaho: The Chesterfield Foundation, 1982.

Francaviglia, Richard V. "The Passing Mormon Village." *Landscape* 22 (Spring 1978): 40-47.

Jackson, Richard H. "Religion and Landscape in the Mormon Cultural Region." In *Dimensions of Human Geography,* ed. by Karl W. Butzer. Chicago: University of Chicago, Department of Geography, 1978.

Jackson, Richard, and Robert L. Layton. "The Mormon Village: Analysis of a Settlement Type." *The Professional Geographer* 28 (1976): 136-41.

Leone, Mark P. "Archeology as the Science of Technology: Mormon Town Plans and Fences." In *Research and Theory in Current Archeology,* ed. by Charles L. Redman, 125-50. New York: John Wiley and Sons, 1973.

Peterson, Charles S. "A Mormon Town: One Man's West." *Journal of Mormon History* 3 (1976): 3-12.

Reps, John W. *Cities of the American West: A History of Frontier Urban Planning.* Princeton, N.J.: Princeton University Press, 1979.

———. *Town Planning in Frontier America.* Rev. ed. Columbia, Mo.: University of Missouri Press, 1980.

Spencer, Joseph Earle. "The Development of Agricultural Villages in Southern Utah." *Agricultural History* 14 (October 1940): 181-89.

Stewart, George, and John A. Widtsoe. "Contribution of Forest Land Resources to the Settlement and Development of the Mormon Occupied West." *Journal of Forestry* 41 (September 1943): 633–40.

Wahlquist, Wayne L. "Review of Mormon Settlement Literature." *Utah Historical Quarterly* 45 (Winter 1977): 4–21.

"Wheels of Pioneer Progress." In *Treasures of Pioneer History,* comp. by Kate B. Carter, 285–344. Vol. 2. Salt Lake City: Daughters of Utah Pioneers, 1953.

Architecture

Bennett, Keith, and Thomas Carter. "Houses with Two Fronts: The Evolution of Domestic Architecture Design in a Mormon Community." *Journal of Mormon History* 15 (1989): 47–58.

Brunvand, Jan H. "Architecture in Zion: Early Mormon Houses." *American West* 13 (March/April 1976): 28–35.

———. "A Survey of Mormon Housing Traditions in Utah." *Revue roumaine d'histoire de l'art* 11 (1974): 111–35.

Cannon, Georgius Young. "Early Domestic Architecture in and near Salt Lake City." *The American Architect and the Architectural Review* 125 (May 21, 1924): 473–76.

Carter, Thomas. "'The Best of Its Kind and Grade': Rebuilding the Sanpete Valley." *Utah Historical Quarterly* 54 (Winter 1986): 88–112.

———. "North European Horizontal Log Construction in the Sanpete-Sevier Valleys." *Utah Historical Quarterly* 52 (Winter 1984): 50–71.

———. "Studies in Utah Vernacular Architecture: An Overview." *Utah Folklife Newsletter* 24 (Spring 1990): 2–4.

———. "Traditional Design in an Industrial Age: Vernacular Architecture in Victorian Utah." *Journal of American Folklore* 104 (Fall 1991): 419–42.

Carter, Thomas, and Peter Goss. *Utah's Historic Architecture, 1847–1940.* Salt Lake City: University of Utah Press, 1988.

Fairbanks, Jonathon. "Adobe Housing in Nineteenth Century Utah." In *Frontier America: The Far West,* 197–212. Boston: Museum of Fine Arts, [1975].

Francaviglia, Richard V. "Mormon Central Hall Houses in the American West." *Annals of the Association of American Geographers* 61 (March 1971): 65–71.

Goeldner, Paul. *Utah Catalog, Historic American Buildings Survey.* Salt Lake City: Utah Heritage Foundation, 1969.

Griffith, Teddy. "A Heritage of Stone in Willard." *Utah Historical Quarterly* 43 (Summer 1975): 286-300.

Hayden, Dolores. "Eden versus Jerusalem." In *Seven American Utopias: The Architecture of Communitarian Socialism, 1790-1975,* 104-47. Cambridge, Mass.: MIT Press, 1976.

Markham, Fred. "Typical Houses of Provo." In *Provo Patriotic Reader,* ed. by Gail W. Bell, 96-147. Provo, Utah: Provo City Corporation and Press Publishing, 1976.

Noble, Allen. "Building Mormon Houses: A Preliminary Typology." *Pioneer America: The Journal of Historic American Material Culture* 15 (July 1983): 55-66.

"Old Homes and Buildings." In *An Enduring Legacy,* comp. by The Lesson Committee, 217-64. Vol. 2. Salt Lake City: Daughters of Utah Pioneers, 1978.

"Pioneer Houses and Enclosures." In *Our Pioneer Heritage,* comp. by Kate B. Carter, 117-88. Vol. 1. Salt Lake City: Daughters of Utah Pioneers, 1958.

Poulsen, Richard C. "Stone Buildings of Beaver City." *Utah Historical Quarterly* 43 (Summer 1975): 278-85.

Rice, Cindy. "Spring City: A Look at a Nineteenth Century Mormon Village." *Utah Historical Quarterly* 43 (Summer 1975): 260-77.

Spencer, Joseph. "House Types of Southern Utah." *Geographical Review* 35 (1945): 444-57.

Winter, Robert. "Architecture on the Frontier: The Mormon Experience." *Pacific Historical Review* 43 (February 1974): 50-60.

Furniture

Bates, Elizabeth Bidwell, and Jonathon L. Fairbanks. *American Furniture: 1620 to the Present.* New York: Richard Marek, 1981.

Carter, Thomas. "Traditional Design in an Industrial Age: Vernacular Architecture in Victorian Utah." *Journal of American Folklore* 104 (Fall 1991): 419-42.

Hatch, Ann F. "The Beehive Buffet." *Western Folklore* 50 (October 1991): 421-30.

"Pioneer Furniture." In *Heart Throbs of the West,* comp. by Kate B. Carter, 357-404. Vol. 12. Salt Lake City: Daughters of Utah Pioneers, 1951.

Thatcher, Elaine. "Nineteenth Century Furniture in Cache Valley, Utah: Form and Function." Master's thesis, Utah State University, 1983.

"Trunks, Chests and Boxes." In *Our Pioneer Heritage* 19:437-88.

Industries

Arrington, Leonard J. "The Deseret Agricultural and Manufacturing Society in Pioneer Utah." *Utah Historical Quarterly* 24 (April 1956): 165-70.

"Pioneer Gunsmiths and Guns." In *An Enduring Legacy* 3:377-424.

"Pioneer Mills and Milling." In *An Enduring Legacy* 7:85-136.

"Pioneer Undertakers, Sextons and Cemeteries." In *Heart Throbs of the West* 6:313-52.

"Pioneer Vocations." In *An Enduring Legacy* 8:213-64.

"Shops and Factories." In *Heart Throbs of the West* 3:201-40.

Clothing and Furnishings

"Historic Costumes and the Slough House Pioneer Cemetery." In *An Enduring Legacy* 1:302-72.

Lamprecit, Helen. "Textile Arts of the Mormon Pioneers from 1847-1900." Master's thesis, Oregon State University, 1963.

Lavitt, Wendy. "Children's Clothing on the Utah Frontier." *Beehive History* 15 (1989): 27-30.

"Museum Artifacts." In *An Enduring Legacy* 3:329-76.

"Old Samplers." In *An Enduring Legacy* 2:89-128.

Paxman, Shirley. "Pioneer Family Life and Home Production." In *One Hundred & Fifty Years: Sesquicentennial Lectures on Mormon Arts, Letters and Science,* comp. by the Harold B. Lee Library Forum Committee, 35-51. Provo, Utah: Harold B. Lee Library Forum Committee and Friends of the Library, Brigham Young University, 1980.

"Pioneer Artisans and Artifacts." In *An Enduring Legacy* 5:41-92.

"Pioneer Fashions." In *Heart Throbs of the West* 8:1-44.

"Pioneer Fashions." In *An Enduring Legacy* 8:265-308.

Gravestones

Cunningham, Keith. "Navajo, Mormon, Zuni Graves: Navajo, Mormon, Zuni Ways." In *Cemeteries and Gravemarkers: Voices of American Culture,* ed. by Richard E. Meyer, 197-215. Ann Arbor, Mich.: UMI Research, 1989.

Edison, Carol A. "The Gravestones of Parowan." *Utah Folklife Newsletter* 17 (Winter 1983): 2-3.

———. "Motorcycles, Guitars and Bucking Broncs: Twentieth-Century Gravestones in Southeastern Idaho." In *Idaho Folklife Reader: Homesteads to Headstones,* ed. by Louie W. Attebery, 184-89. Salt Lake City: University of Utah Press, 1985.

Grant, Helen R., comp. "Graves along the Pioneer Trail." In *An Enduring Legacy* 12:305–52.
"Graves along the Trail." In *Our Pioneer Heritage* 16:421–76.
Haseltine, Maury. "A Progress Report on the Pictorial Documentation of Early Utah Gravestones (Abstract)." In *Forms upon the Frontier: Folklife and Folk Arts in the United States,* ed. by Austin Fife, Alta Fife, and Henry Glassie, 79–88. Logan, Utah: Utah State University Press, 1969.
"Old Cemeteries." In *An Enduring Legacy* 20:133–84.
Poulsen, Richard C. "Polynesians in the Desert: A Look at the Graves of Iosepa." *AFF Word* [Arizona Friends of Folklore] 3 (April 1973): 2–15.
Schoemaker, George H. "Symbolic Consideration in Nineteenth Century Tombstone Art in Utah." *Material Culture* 20 (Summer/Fall 1988): 19–26.
———. "The Shift from Artist to Consumer: Changes in Mormon Tombstone Art in Utah." In *The Old Traditional Way of Life: Essays in Honor of Warren E. Roberts,* ed. by Robert E. Walls and George H. Schoemaker, 130–45. Bloomington, Ind.: Trickster, Indiana University Folklore Institute, 1989.

Symbols and Material Culture

Cannon, Hal. *The Grand Beehive.* Salt Lake City: University of Utah Press, 1980.
Hamilton, C. Mark. "The Salt Lake Temple: A Symbolic Statement of Mormon Doctrine." In *The Mormon People: Their Character and Tradition,* ed. by Thomas G. Alexander, 103–27. Charles Redd Monographs in Western History, no.10. Provo, Utah: Brigham Young University Press, 1980.
Oman, Richard, and Susan Staker Oman. "Mormon Iconography." In *Utah Folk Art: A Catalogue of Material Culture,* ed. by Hal Cannon, 109- 25. Provo, Utah: Brigham Young University Press, 1980.
Poulsen, Richard C. *The Pure Experience of Order: Essays on the Symbolic in the Folk Material Culture of Western America.* Albuquerque: University of New Mexico Press, 1982.
Roberts, Allen D. "Where Are the All-Seeing Eyes? The Origins, Use and Decline of Early Mormon Symbolism." *Sunstone* 4 (May/June 1979): 22–37.

Miscellaneous References

Brunvand, Jan H. *A Guide for Collectors of Folklore in Utah,* 100–116. Salt Lake City: University of Utah Press, 1971.

Carter, Thomas R. "Studies in Mormon Culture." *Utah Historical Quarterly* 56 (Fall 1988): 307-9.

Edison, Carol A. "Material Culture Studies in Utah: A Survey." *Utah Folklife Newsletter* 23 (Spring 1989): 4-5.

Fife, Austin, and Alta Fife. *Saints of Sage and Saddle: Folklore among the Mormons.* Bloomington: Indiana University Press, 1956. Reprint. Salt Lake City: University of Utah Press, 1980.

Wilson, William A. "A Bibliography of Studies in Mormon Folklore." *Utah Historical Quarterly* 44 (Fall 1976): 389-94.

Carol A. Edison is Coordinator of the Folk Arts Program, Utah Arts Council, Salt Lake City, Utah.

NOTES

[1]Introductions to the study of material culture are found in Jules David Prown, "Mind in Matter: An Introduction to Material Culture Theory and Method," *Winterthur Portfolio* 17 (Spring 1982): 1-20; Thomas J. Schlereth, ed., *Material Culture: A Research Guide* (Lawrence: University of Kansas Press, 1985); and Robert Blair St. George, ed., *Material Life in America, 1600-1860* (Boston: Northeastern University Press, 1987). For a discussion of the advantages and limitations of material culture research, see Cary Carson, "Doing History with Material Culture," in *Material Culture and the Study of American Life,* ed. Ian M. G. Quimby (New York: W. W. Norton, 1978), 41-64.

[2]Austin E. Fife, "Folklore of Material Culture on the Rocky Mountain Frontier," in *Exploring Western Americana,* ed. Alta Fife (Ann Arbor, Mich.: UMI Research Press, 1988), 133-40.

[3]Fife, "Folklore of Material Culture," 134.

[4]The discussion of Mormon material culture in this paper is limited to the Mormon cultural region of the Intermountain West and is primarily centered on historical expressions of the nineteenth century.

[5]Lowry Nelson, *The Mormon Village: A Pattern and Technique of Land Settlement* (Salt Lake City: University of Utah Press, 1952).

[6]D. W. Meinig, "The Mormon Culture Region: Strategies and Patterns in the Geography of the American West, 1847-1964," *Annals of the Association of American Geographers* 55 (June 1965): 191-220. See also Meinig's "American Wests: Preface to a Geographical Interpretation," *Annals of the Association of American Geographers* 62 (June 1972): 159-84.

[7]Richard V. Francaviglia, *The Mormon Landscape: Existence, Creation and Perception of a Unique Image in the American West* (New York: AMS, 1978). For a summary of Francaviglia's earlier work, see "The City of Zion in the Mountain West," *Improvement Era* 72 (December 1969): 10-17.

[8]Nelson, *Mormon Village,* 25.

[9]Nelson, *Mormon Village,* 3.

[10]Nelson, *Mormon Village,* 3.

[11]Dean L. May, "The Making of Saints: The Mormon Town as a Setting for the Study of Cultural Change," *Utah Historical Quarterly* 45 (Winter 1977): 75-92.

[12]Francaviglia, *Mormon Landscape,* 71.

[13]Richard H. Jackson, "The Mormon Village: Genesis and Articulation of the City of Zion Plan," *BYU Studies* 17 (Winter 1977): 223-40.

[14]Hay derricks are described later in this essay.

[15]According to Esther Truitt, in pre-railroad Salt Lake City "water flowed down almost every street and in front of every door, irrigating gardens and orchards heavy with fruit and flowers . . . [making it] a garden-plot city in the tradition of medieval Europe, having a commercial character but growing much of its food in the city" (352-53). For a thorough discussion of urban gardening, fencing, and landscaping traditions in early Salt Lake City, see Esther Ruth Truitt's "Enclosing a World," *Utah Historical Quarterly* 56 (Fall 1988): 352-59.

[16]Elaine Thatcher, "Material Culture," in *Encyclopedia of Mormonism,* ed. Daniel H. Ludlow, 5 vols. (New York: Macmillan, 1992), 2:864.

[17]"Pioneer Homes and Houses," in *Heart Throbs of the West,* comp. Kate B. Carter, 12 vols. (Salt Lake City: Daughters of Utah Pioneers, 1939-51), 3:38-39.

[18]"Pioneer Homes and Houses" 3:46-47.

[19]Leon Sidney Pitman, "A Survey of Nineteenth Century Folk Housing in the Mormon Cultural Region" (Ph.D diss., Louisiana State University, 1973), 30. See also Thomas Robert Carter, "Building Zion: Folk Architecture in the Mormon Settlements of Utah's Sanpete Valley, 1850-1890" (Ph.D diss., Indiana University, 1984), 252. Carter notes that the fired or burned bricks used somewhat later were typically smaller (4" x 8") than the earlier adobe bricks.

[20]Some researchers have suggested that the techniques of adobe construction were introduced to members of the Mormon Battalion as they traveled through the Southwest. Battalion members were among the first pioneers to enter Salt Lake Valley. See Richard H. Jackson, "The Use of Adobe in the Mormon Cultural Region," *Journal of Cultural Geography* 1 (Fall/Winter 1980): 82-95.

[21]Austin Fife, "Stone Houses of Northern Utah," *Utah Historical Quarterly* 40 (Winter 1972): 7. (This article also appears in *Exploring Western Americana,* 167-94.)

[22]Pitman, "Nineteenth Century Folk Housing," 191-97.

[23]Peter L. Goss, "The Architectural History of Utah," *Utah Historical Quarterly* 43 (Summer 1975): 208-39.

[24]Thomas Carter, "Folk Design in Utah Architecture: 1849-90," in *Utah Folk Art: A Catalog of Material Culture,* ed. Hal Cannon (Provo, Utah: Brigham Young University Press, 1980), 41-42. See also Thomas Carter, "Cultural Veneer: Decorative Plastering in Utah's Sanpete Valley," *Utah Historical Quarterly* 49 (Winter 1981): 68-77.

[25]Francaviglia, *Mormon Landscape,* 70.

[26]"While the settlers were forced by necessity in the first years to hovel in dugouts, the experience only intensified their antipathy to nature. . . . Logs for dwellings were usually sawed or hewn square and were thus deprived of their identity as round trees. Often the logs were further disguised by the application of lumber siding or plaster." Carter, "Folk Design in Utah Architecture," 41.

[27]Linda L. Bonar, "Historic Houses in Beaver: An Introduction to Materials, Styles and Craftsmen," *Utah Historical Quarterly* 51 (Summer 1983): 219-24.

[28]The ideal was to build with perfectly rectangular stones and lay them in perfectly lined up courses. To achieve this effect with irregular stones, extra mortar—slightly raised and squared (a beaded mortar joint)—was sometimes used; and to cut back on labor costs but retain the effect, this special treatment was sometimes used only on the front facade or the surface layers. In addition to this style, two other styles were used: the first, Aberdeen bond, placed a large stone next to three small stacked stones; the second, an imitation of Aberdeen bond, used small pebbles pressed into extra-wide strips of mortar. See Linda L. Bonar, "The Influence of the Scots Stonemasons in Beaver, Utah," *Utah Preservation/ Restoration* 3 (1981): 54-60.

[29]"Building Zion," 260-64.

[30]"Building Zion," 264-69.

[31]"Building Zion," 269-70.

[32]"Building Zion," 10.

[33]"Building Zion," 294.

[34]Francaviglia, "The City of Zion in the Mountain West," 16.

[35]Austin E. Fife and James M. Fife, "Hay Derricks of the Great Basin and Upper Snake River Valley," *Western Folklore* 7 (1948): 224-39. (This article is also found in *Idaho Folklife: Homesteads to Headstones,* ed. Louie Attebery [Salt Lake City: University of Utah Press, 1985], 2-11; and in *Exploring Western Americana,* 141-57.)

[36]Francaviglia, *Mormon Landscape,* 51, 57, 152-53.

[37]David R. Lee and Hector H. Lee, "Thatched Cowsheds of the Mormon Country," *Western Folklore* 40 (April 1981): 174.

[38]Lee and Lee, "Thatched Cowsheds," 180.

[39]Charles S. Peterson, "Winter Feed, Summer Shelter, Tabernacles, and Genealogy: Reflections on Straw-Thatched Cowsheds," *Western Folklore* 41 (April 1982): 146. Peterson also points out the similarity in design between these thatched-roof cowsheds and "the pioneer Bowery—a sprawling, open-sided, willow-and-brush-covered structure into which 3,000 saints could move quickly and freely." Peterson, "Winter Feed, Summer Shelter," 145.

[40]Peterson, "Winter Feed, Summer Shelter," 147.

[41]Austin E. Fife, "Jack Fences of the Intermountain West," in *Exploring Western Americana,* 159-66.

[42]Thomas Carter and Carl Fleischhauer, *Grouse Creek Cultural Survey: Integrating Folklife and Historic Preservation Field Research* (Washington, D.C.: Library of Congress, 1988).

[43]Francaviglia, *Mormon Landscape,* 29.

[44]Francaviglia, *Mormon Landscape,* 8.

[45]David H. Stanley, "Folklore," in *Utah History Encyclopedia,* ed. Allan Kent Powell (Salt Lake City: University of Utah Press, 1994), 192-95.

[46]English-trained woodworker Ralph Ramsay, known for the carved wooden eagle that topped the original Eagle Gate in Salt Lake City, was among those artisans who produced furniture during the early days of Mormon settlement in the West. See *Heart Throbs of the West* 2:489-90.

[47]Thomas Carter, "Spindles and Spoon Racks: Local Style in Nineteenth-Century Mormon Furniture," in *The Old Traditional Way of Life: Essays in Honor of Warren E. Roberts,* ed. Robert E. Walls and George H. Schoemaker (Bloomington, Ind.: Trickster, 1989), 40-47.

[48]Elaine Thatcher, "'Some Chairs for My Family': Furniture in Nineteenth-Century Cache Valley," *Utah Historical Quarterly* 56 (Fall 1988): 344.

[49]Connie Morningstar, *Early Utah Furniture* (Logan, Utah: Utah State University Press, 1976), 3.

[50]Thatcher, "Some Chairs for My Family," 333.

[51]For another discussion of Mormon pine furniture, see Richard Oman's article on Mormon visual art in this volume.

[52]Morningstar, *Early Utah Furniture,* 6.

[53]Kirk Henrichsen, "Pioneer Pottery of Utah and E.C. Henrichsen's Provo Pottery Company," *Utah Historical Quarterly* 56 (Fall 1988): 395.

[54]Henrichsen, "Pioneer Pottery," 395.

[55]Henrichsen, "Pioneer Pottery," 395.

[56]Henrichsen, "Pioneer Pottery," 392.

[57]Shirley B. Paxman, *Homespun: Domestic Arts and Crafts of Mormon Pioneers* (Salt Lake City: Deseret Book, 1976), 75-76.

[58]For description and analysis of the Mormon venture into silk production, see Chris Rigby Arrington, "The Finest of Fabrics: Mormon Women and the Silk Industry in Early Utah," *Utah Historical Quarterly* 46 (Fall 1978): 376-96; or "Silk Industry in Utah," in *Heart Throbs of the West* 11:53-92.

[59]"Color might have been added as a variation to the natural gray or white, but it would also be by her own hand—blue from large pots of indigo and aniline, wild greasewood for a yellow dye or to mix with indigo for a green, logwood for black, brown made from madder set with copperas and a red from madder and sour bran-water set with lye made of ashes." Sandi Fox, *Quilts in Utah: A Reflection of the Western Experience* (Salt Lake City: Salt Lake Art Center, 1981), 12.

[60]Fox, *Quilts in Utah,* 6.

[61]Martha Sonntag Bradley, "Folk Art," in *Encyclopedia of Mormonism,* ed. Daniel H. Ludlow, 5 vols. (New York: Macmillan, 1992), 2:517.

[62]For another discussion about Mormon quilts, see Richard Oman's essay in this volume.

[63]For a discussion of nineteenth-century clothing, see Carma de Jong Anderson's "A Historical Overview of Mormons and Their Clothing, 1840-50" (Ph.D. diss., Brigham Young University, 1992). Anderson notes that nineteenth-century seamstresses commonly sewed fifteen to twenty stitches per inch compared to the six stitches per inch generally seen today! Sheridan R. Sheffield, "From Hand-Me-Downs to History, Clothing Is a Marvel for Her," in *Church News* (May 15, 1993), 11.

[64]"Early Arts and Crafts of the West," in *Heart Throbs of the West* 2:476.

[65]"Early Arts and Crafts of the West," 476-77.

[66]This phrase, often used to describe the art that goes into the production of everyday items, was generated by committee to title a seminar and catalog sponsored by thc Winterthur Museum. Personal communication with the author, Kenneth L. Ames, *Beyond Necessity: Art in the Folk Tradition* (New York: W. W. Norton for the Winthur Museum, 1977).

[67]Paxman, *Homespun,* 35.

[68]*Heart Throbs of the West* 2:473.

[69]Paxman, *Homespun,* 116.

[70]Paxman, *Homespun,* 115-29.

[71]Austin Fife and Alta Fife, "Gravestone Imagery," in *Utah Folk Art: A Catalog of Material Culture,* 138. (Another version of this article appears in *Exploring Western Americana,* 195-213.)

[72]In some settlements, like Spring City and Scipio in central Utah, there are two community cemeteries—the first one on a town lot and the second and larger one on the edge of town.

[73]Fife and Fife, "Gravestone Imagery," 138.

[74]Carol Edison, "Custom-Made Gravestones in Early Salt Lake: The Work of Four English Stonecarvers," *Utah Historical Quarterly* 56 (Fall 1988): 329.

[75]Edison, "Custom-Made Gravestones," 330.

[76]Carol Edison, "Motorcycles, Guitars and Bucking Broncs: Twentieth-Century Gravestones in Southeastern Idaho," in *Idaho Folklife Reader: Homesteads to Headstones,* ed. Louie W. Attebury (Salt Lake City: University of Utah Press, 1985), 184–89.

[77]Richard C. Poulsen, "Folk Material Culture of the Sanpete-Sevier Area: Today's Reflections of a Region Past," *Utah Historical Quarterly* 47 (Spring 1979): 135–36. See also Richard C. Poulsen, "The Handclasp Motif in Mormon Folk Burial," in *The Pure Experience of Order: Essays on the Symbolic in the Folk Material Culture of Western America* (Albuquerque: University of New Mexico Press, 1982), 45–55; and Poulsen, "Folk Material Culture of the Sanpete-Sevier Area," in *The Pure Experience of Order,* 70–94.

[78]Carol Edison, "Mormon Gravestones: A Folk Expression of Identity and Belief," *Dialogue: A Journal of Mormon Thought* 22 (Winter 1989): 88–94.

[79]Edison, "Custom-Made Gravestones," 311–12.

Perspective of the Nauvoo Temple, published ca. 1885. The original caption printed below this illustration reads in part: "The temple was built of light gray limestone; it was 128 ft. long, 88 ft. broad, 60 ft. high and to the top of the tower 200 ft. The whole cost of the building was $1,000,000. . . . Corner stone laid, April 6, 1841. Burned October 8–9, 1848. Joseph Smith killed at Carthage, June 27, 1844" (Benedict & Co., lithographers; Baumert Brothers, printers and publishers of the *Nauvoo Independent;* Ida Blum Collection, BYU Photoarchives). Photograph courtesy BYU Photoarchives.

Mormon Architectural Records

Brad Westwood

Introduction

I am inclined to define architecture, and specifically Mormon architecture, very liberally. Traditional architectural thinking would use the term *architecture* sparingly. Indeed, until recently, only the finest and most elaborate expressions of Mormon culture would have qualified as architecture. Most Mormon temples, tabernacles, and meetinghouses would with some reluctance be considered architecture by the keepers of such thinking, but not much more due to the generally utilitarian aspirations in Mormon architecture.

Some of this traditional thinking still lingers. Fortunately, however, architectural history has become much more democratic, much more interested in what architecture can reveal about a society instead of how much it qualifies as artistic expression—although that, too, remains important. As Louis Sullivan aptly stated, "The critical study of architecture becomes, not the study of art—for that is but a minor phase of a great phenomenon—but in reality a study of the social conditions producing it."[1]

In addition to the term *architecture,* I use the phrase *the built environment* to draw my circle wider, to include all building expression. Mormon architecture subsumes not just ecclesiastical edifices, but the entire built environment constructed under the influence of Mormonism. This subsumption does not suggest the existence of one continuous and distinctive Mormon building tradition or way of designing. Yet since its beginning, Mormon society has taken inspiration from both the familiar (often conventional) and the unusual (often obscure and cryptic) to produce something different, something peculiar enough to be identified as "Mormon."

With the exception of some scattered pieces, the large picture puzzle called "Mormon architecture" has yet to be assembled and interpreted. Even the major patterns and figures in the picture have yet to be understood or connected, and there is no box cover to study. At best, I hope to separate some of the pieces and shed a little more light on the puzzle.

In the past, architectural history has generally been guided by a well-defined and, at times, restrictive series of methodologies that evolved from the fields of art history and criticism, archaeology, and history. The locus of traditional architectural history has been analyzing the antecedents of what critics and historians have considered innovative, aesthetically or politically influential, and well articulated. In sweeping strokes, surveyors of American architecture have stated, or at least implied by the absence of its treatment, that much of the Mormon built environment is derivative and prosaic. Until recently, the few published writings on Mormon architectural history have followed this tradition and have been confined primarily to (1) the finer examples of ecclesiastical buildings, large meeting halls, and spaces of ritual service (particularly temples) designed and built by Mormons; (2) a select group of residences, haunts, and workplaces used by esteemed early Church leaders and members; and (3) Church historic sites.

Local historians and antiquarians have surveyed the entire Mormon landscape (mostly community-by-community) for a long time, but only relatively recently has academia taken a serious look. Generally, those who have found significance in the seemingly common landscape of Mormon culture have not been traditional architectural historians. Rather, they have been cultural geographers, folklorists, anthropologists, historical archaeologists, and scholars of religion. Also part of this modern movement are the fields of the ever-mutating twentieth-century "new history," such as American studies, social history, urban history, and environmental history.

These new approaches have opened the whole historical physical world for examination. In Mormon architecture, that world includes all expressions in building, from the highly complex, aesthetically pleasing, and informed to the simplest and most pragmatic—from the highest expression of a society to the most idiosyncratic idioms or incidental constructions. These expressions include the built environments produced by the mainline as well as the schismatic churches tethered to the teachings of the first Mormon, Joseph Smith Jr.

All buildings can be tendered as meaningful documents and expressions of culture. Individuals and groups ascribe or invest, consciously or subconsciously, symbolic meaning to their architecture, revealing personal and cultural values. As one architectural historian has aptly stated, "If properly understood, [a building or series of buildings] can serve as an environmental diary."[2] Material things, when systematically and methodically studied and compared, can offer a variety of evidence, a language that self- and culture-conscious communications (both oral and written) rarely, if ever, speak. Furthermore, nothing is so abundant and so accessible to study in a culture than its built environment. Hence, Mormon architecture and the Mormon built environment have much to tell.

Ideally, with the foregoing comprehensive approach to the built environment, this essay should include allied subjects such as landscape history, city and regional planning, historic archaeology, engineering history, industrial archeology, building materials and technology, decorative arts, interior design, material culture, and historic preservation. Obviously, all these topics cannot be discussed here. Some sources on these subject areas will be included in this essay, some will be addressed elsewhere in this volume, and others will, of necessity, be excluded here.

Architectural Records, Mormon and Otherwise, and Where They Can Be Found

Typically, architectural records are defined as sketched or drafted materials. They are created by professional design practitioners (architects, artists, delineators, engineers, interior designers, historical surveyors and preservationists), tradespeople (carpenters, housewrights, and masons), building contractors, and the occasional and one-time building designer—all of whom have prepared a graphic or textural means to express a building concept either before or after construction.

In addition to the foregoing documents, other relevant—and often equally significant—records exist. These records include written instructions (especially for buildings schemed without graphic representation); building specifications (often bidding documents); builders' journals; clerks, captains of the works, supervising architects' records; business or office files (of the architects, builders, and subcontractors); photographic documentation (site, construction, post-construction, and historical documentation); building samples (test walls, building units, samples of finish work, and fabric swatches); and various governmental records (recorders, probate, and assessor). Further important historical records include professional and trade books, periodicals, portfolios, and pamphlets, such as carpenter guides and architectural pattern books; traveler's accounts, descriptions, commentaries, and guide publications; farm and horticultural publications and periodicals (grange publications, land-grant studies, and agrarian or mechanical college studies); trade or manufacturers' literature and catalogs; and in the twentieth century, technical-historical surveys such as the Historic American Building Survey (HABS) and Historic

American Engineering Register (HAER) and documentation produced by other federal programs.

The architectural records are diverse; for both the novice and the expert researcher, they are frequently difficult to find. Still, such sources are surprisingly plentiful, although less so for specifically Mormon-generated materials. Notwithstanding the abundance of sources, researchers should avoid the erroneous assumption that a particular source is not worth investigating simply because it is not conspicuously Mormon-related. Mormon architecture must be understood through careful study of both the narrower and the broader strains in the Mormon and American experiences.

One problem that makes sources difficult to find is the way that repositories classify architectural materials. Common classifications, such as *primary* or *secondary, published* or *unpublished,* and *artwork* or *artifact,* are often inapplicable, misleading, or difficult to ascertain. In other words, architectural materials do not fit handily into well-established collection categories. Hence, researchers should not assume that all primary documentation can be found in an archives or manuscript collection, that all published architectural materials can be found in a library, or that museum collections include only fine art and artifacts while omitting textural, graphic, and photographic materials.

In summary, researchers must look for all clues. The absence of conspicuous architectural listings in a repository's catalog, such as a design practitioner's name, architectural subject headings *(architecture* or *building),* or applicable genre headings *(architectural drawings),* should not deter researchers from searching a particular repository. Most architectural materials in historical repositories are either woefully undercataloged or not cataloged at all. In libraries, some oversize architectural and engineering treatises are cataloged and stored in cartography (map) collections, while the cataloging of significant architectural books often neglects provenance.

Besides the libraries and archives listed below, Mormon-related architectural materials are held by numerous government entities, private societies, and museums. These repositories offer museum, library, and manuscript collections wrapped en masse and stored so as to be obscure even to the most seasoned architectural researchers. These collections often hold unexpected caches of architectural materials, including historical photographs of local building stock, building sketches and drawings, local builders' journals, builders' tools, architectural artifacts, fixtures, and building hardware. Although such small historical organizations abound throughout the United States, Utah—with numerous chapters of Daughters of Utah

Pioneers and Sons of Utah Pioneers—is of particular interest to the researcher of Mormon architecture.

This essay outlines Mormon architectural sources in the following segments: (1) published sources, including national surveys and anthological works that offer the broader American context; (2) published Mormon sources as of 1993; and (3) books and periodicals used as primary sources for Mormon architectural design. The essay concludes by listing repositories with primary and secondary Mormon architectural sources, national and regional libraries and archives, and pertinent organizations and projects.

Published Sources—American Architectural Surveys and Anthologies

Several general survey publications on architecture and the built environment will profit a student of Mormon architecture. I have selected only a handful of eligible titles. I stress the term *general* because hundreds of applicable titles deal specifically with historical periods, styles and modes, typology, building materials, and biographies that have not been included.

These published works are divided into three categories: (1) traditional art history, (2) anthropological approaches, and (3) hybrids of traditional art history and anthropological fields. Some address religious architecture, although most address the built environment in more general terms.

Traditional Perspective. The most comprehensive, although very dated, survey of American architecture under the matrix of traditional architectural history is the Doubleday (Garden City, New York) series *American Buildings and Their Architects,* which is the work of architectural historians William H. Pierson Jr. and William H. Jordy. Series titles include *The Colonial and Neoclassical Styles* (ca. 1700–1820), *Technology and the Picturesque, the Corporate and the Early Gothic Styles* (ca. 1800–1860), *Progressive and Academic Ideals at the Turn of the Twentieth Century* (ca. 1890–1920), and *The Impact of European Modernism in the Mid-Twentieth Century* (ca. 1920–60). These works are relatively traditional and speak of high-art architecture, major trends, and early and introductory examples. Alan Gowans addresses both the high-art examples and popular cultural expressions in *Images of American Living: Four Centuries of Architecture and Furniture as Cultural Expression* (Philadelphia: J. B. Lippincott, 1964). Although recommended, Gowans's book needs to be updated and revised. Other titles written by Gowans should be mentioned:

The Comfortable House: North American Suburban Architecture 1890–1930 (Cambridge, Mass.: MIT Press, 1986); and *Styles and Types of North American Architecture: Social Function and Cultural Expression,* 2d ed. (New York: Icon Editions, 1993).

The writings of former Yale University architectural historian Vincent Scully give an invigorating, richly complex, and readable look at both the American and the international built environment. A "continuing dialogue between generations which create an environment across time" is how Scully defines architecture, and his writings indulge in scanning and comparing across time. Scully's *American Architecture and Urbanism,* rev. ed. (New York: Henry Holt, 1988) briskly surveys American architecture and city planning. Another of his books, *New World Vision of Household Gods and Sacred Places: American Art and the Metropolitan Museum of Art, 1650–1914* (Boston: Little, Brown, 1988), which is based on a PBS television series, describes the American traditions of realism and classicism, including painting, sculpture, decorative arts, architecture, and urban planning.

James F. O'Gorman's *Three American Architects: Richardson, Sullivan, and Wright (1865–1915)* (Chicago: University of Chicago Press, 1991) chronicles three of the United States' modern axial architects and taste makers. *Three American Architects* gives insightful general context and is a good example of readable architectural biography.

The published works of Henry-Russell Hitchcock, the father of modern American architectural history, are classic reference works in the field. So far as general architectural surveys of the modern era are concerned, Hitchcock's *Architecture: Nineteenth and Twentieth Centuries* (New York: Penguin Books, 1977) should be studied carefully.

The *Macmillan Encyclopedia of Architects,* ed. Adolf K. Placzek (New York: Free Press, 1982) offers insightful biographies about the world's most significant designers of the built environment (and their surrounding historical context); it contains essays by many of the most respected researchers of architectural biography and history.

For more annotated bibliographies on American architecture, see chapter three of Frederick L. Rath Jr. and Merrilyn Rogers O'Connell, eds., *Research: A Bibliography on Historical Organization Practices,* vol. 6 of *A Bibliography on Historical Organization Practices* (Nashville: American Association for State and Local History, 1984); Jack Salzman, ed., *American Studies: An Annotated Bibliography,* 3 vols. (London and New York: Cambridge University Press, 1986), 1:109–236; and Richard Guy Wilson, "Popular Architecture," in *American Popular Culture,* ed. M. Thomas Inge, 3 vols. (Westport, Conn.: Greenwood Press, 1980), 2:265–85.

Anthropological Perspective. Dell Upton, ed., *America's Architectural Roots: Ethnic Groups That Built America* (Washington, D.C.: Preservation Press, 1986) contains short, concise articles about the contributions of the United States' major ethnic groups to the diverse vernacular built environment. Upton's background in traditional architectural history is supplemented by his expertise in American civilization and social history. This combination has allowed him to produce some of the best contemporary writing on American architecture.

Several volumes offer the interdisciplinary work of the new architectural history, which includes folklore, American civilization, historical archaeology, cultural history, and geography.[3] For example, *Perspectives in Vernacular Architecture* vols. 1–2, ed. Camille Wells, and vols. 3–4, ed. Thomas Carter and Bernard L. Herman (Columbia: University of Missouri Press, 1986, 1987, 1989, and 1991), offer a Whitman Sampler-like exposure to contemporary subjects and methodologies. All of the articles in these volumes were papers presented at the annual conferences of the Vernacular Architecture Forum. These books, in addition to Dell Upton and John Michael Vlach's *Common Places: Readings in American Vernacular Architecture* (Athens: University of Georgia Press, 1986), offer the latest in American vernacular architectural studies—from roadside architecture (neon-light motels and golden arches) to the dawn of the New England built environment and back to twentieth-century commercial architecture.

Regarding the broader patterns of the common American landscape, see John Brinckerhoff Jackson's *Discovering the Vernacular Landscape* (New Haven: Yale University Press, 1984) and John Stilgoe's *Common Landscape of America, 1580–1845* (New Haven: Yale University Press, 1982). The greater part of these works has been written with broad brushstrokes as only historical and cultural geographers can do. Stilgoe's work addresses the manufactured environment preceding the advent of Mormonism.

Hybrids. Students of Mormon architecture (ecclesiastical, domestic, and otherwise) will see much in Spiro Kostof's books. Kostof has been characterized as one who skillfully combines the canonical goals and subjects of art history with newer themes and ideologies. As one eulogist stated, Kostof's "particular skill was to shake the interpretation of architecture out of aesthetic and ideological prejudices."[4] The study of Kostof's energetic and insightful interdisciplinary approach will aid students who wish to apply this thinking to the Mormon built environment. Two of Kostof's books, *A History of Architecture: Settings and Rituals* (New York and Oxford: Oxford University Press, 1985) and *America by Design* (New York and Oxford: Oxford

University Press, 1987), are especially good. *America by Design* is intended for nonacademic readers and provides ample material in a survey format.

Published Sources—Mormon

Throughout the remainder of this essay, the *Improvement Era* will be cited as *"IE," Utah Historical Quarterly* as "*UHQ*," and *Utah Preservation/Restoration* as *"UP/R."* References to Nauvoo Restoration Incorporated will hereafter be cited as "NRI," Brigham Young University as "BYU," the University of Utah as "U of U," and Utah State University as "USU."

The only readily accessible bibliography on Mormon architecture is Donald H. Dyal, comp., *Mormon Architecture: A Bibliography* (Monticello, Ill.: Vance Bibliographies, 1981). Many available sources were overlooked when this bibliography was compiled and an update is now needed.

Many college and university papers, theses, and dissertations address Mormon architecture and designed environments. Some of these materials study Mormon city planning, while a few provide historic structure reports and many others outline individual building histories (temples, tabernacles, Church-owned academies and schools, and a few other building types). Only a few of these studies will be discussed here. Researchers should consult the catalogs of libraries with major Mormon collections for more information. Studies of Mormon historic sites are discussed in Steven Olsen's essay in this volume.

General LDS Church—Surveys. Richard W. Jackson, former architect with the LDS Church Building and Engineering Department, has written an unpublished manuscript entitled "Meeting Places of the Latter-day Saints, 1820–1980 [1995]." The manuscript includes over four hundred pages of text and appendices; it is the most systematic and encyclopedic effort to survey the architects, buildings, major trends, and periods of LDS chapels, tabernacles, and temples. This huge effort, which Jackson began over twenty years ago, surveys Church architecture in ten- or twenty-year increments. Furthermore, it includes over a dozen appendices listing building patterns, architects who worked for the LDS Church and the buildings they designed, and "standard plans" from the mid-1950s to the 1980s.[5] Unfortunately, Jackson's work does not discuss the extensive international building program instigated in the mid-twentieth century. Those wishing to study the manuscript may do so at the LDS Church Archives.

For a postage-stamp treatment of Mormon architecture, see Franklin T. Ferguson's "Architecture" and Paul L. Anderson and Richard W.

Jackson's "Building Program" in the *Encyclopedia of Mormonism,* ed. Daniel H. Ludlow, 5 vols. (New York: Macmillan, 1992), 1:63–65 and 1:236–38. These pieces are brief and, in the case of the Ferguson entry, much too simple.[6]

BYU architectural and art historian C. Mark Hamilton is completing a monograph for Oxford University Press tentatively entitled *Nineteenth Century Mormon Architecture*. Beginning with his master's thesis (U of U, 1972) and his doctoral dissertation (University of Ohio, 1978), Hamilton has explored the history and architectural influences of the Salt Lake Temple. *Nineteenth Century Mormon Architecture* clarifies and continues this work, examining the ecclesiastical architecture of greater Mormon society. When it appears, the book will be the first published survey on Mormon architecture written for the broader architectural history community.

New York to Nauvoo. Talbot Hamlin, *Greek Revival Architecture in America* (1944; reprint, New York City: Dover Publications, 1964) briefly describes the Mormon architecture that came under the sway of Greek Revival style (1820–60). This very popular style pervaded American culture (politics, art, architecture, and literature) and had a strong residual effect on common Mormon building almost to the end of the nineteenth century.[7] Rexford Newcomb's *Architecture of the Old Northwest Territory* (Chicago: University of Chicago Press, 1950) discusses in very general terms the architecture context of Kirtland, Ohio, although the book is outdated. Frontier cultural geographer Fred Kniffen's study "Folk Housing: Key to Diffusion," *Annals of the Association of American Geographers* 55 (December 1965): 549–77 also gives insight about the antecedents of Kirtland and Nauvoo's built environment. Urban planning professor Dolores Hayden's *Seven American Utopias: The Architecture of Communitarian Socialism, 1790–1975* (Cambridge, Mass.: MIT Press, 1976) discusses early Mormon communitarian city planning, architecture, and spatial schemes. Walter C. Kidney's *Historic Buildings of Ohio* (Pittsburgh, Penn.: Ober Park Associations, 1972); Robert M. Lillibridge's "Architectural Currents on the Mississippi River Frontier: Nauvoo, Illinois," *Journal of the Society of Architectural Historians* 19 (October 1960): 109–15; and Frederick Koeper's *Illinois Architecture from Territorial Times to the Present: A Selective Guide* (Chicago: University of Chicago Press, 1968) give detailed—although dated—analyses of Mormon architecture and that of the Mormons' Ohio and Illinois neighbors.[8]

Temples. Richard O. Cowan, "History of the Latter-day Saint Temples from 1831–1990," in *Encyclopedia of Mormonism,* ed. Daniel H. Ludlow, 5 vols. (New York: Macmillan, 1992), 4:1450–55, provides a succinct and general discussion on Mormon temple history and design.

Other entries in the *Encyclopedia of Mormonism,* particularly those that address the meaning and function of LDS temples, are also interesting.[9]

Although much has been written on the subject of LDS temple architecture, treatment of the topic, with some exceptions, remains unsatisfactory.[10] An exception to this problem is Kent State University architectural historian Elwin C. Robinson's research on the Kirtland Temple. Robinson's "English Precedent in the Design of the Kirtland Temple" (unpublished, in the possession of the author) and his architectural study for the RLDS Church's Restoration Trails Foundation warrant attention and emulation. Robinson is completing a book on the Kirtland Temple's architectural history that should be available soon. RLDS historian Roger D. Launius's *The Kirtland Temple: A Historical Narrative* (Independence, Mo.: Herald Publishing House, 1986) discusses the development of the temple concept, tells the construction history, and describes the temple's uses as a facility owned by the RLDS Church.[11]

Regarding the Independence Temple (originally described as the "House of the Lord"), the antecedent and prototype of the Kirtland Temple, see the following articles by Ronald E. Romig and John H. Siebert: "Jackson County, 1831-1833: A Look at the Development of Zion," in *Restoration Studies III,* ed. Maurice L. Draper (Independence, Mo.: Herald Publishing House, 1986), 286-304; "The Genesis of Zion and Kirtland and the Concept of Temples," in *Restoration Studies IV,* ed. Marjorie B. Troeh (Independence, Mo.: Herald Publishing House, 1988), 99-123; and "Historic Views of the Temple Lot," *John Whitmer Historical Association Journal* 8 (1987): 21-27.[12]

The Nauvoo Temple's design has yet to be addressed capably, and the Utah temples—while treated extensively—require more in-depth treatments in light of recent scholarship and the ever expanding pool of primary sources. Here are the principal sources about the Nauvoo Temple: Don F. Colvin, "A Historical Study of the Mormon Temple in Nauvoo, Illinois" (master's thesis, BYU, 1962), which describes the basic building history; Stanley B. Kimball's 1962 NRI report "The Nauvoo Temple: An Essay on its History, Architecture, and Destruction" (LDS Church Archives), and his articles "Nauvoo," "The Nauvoo Temple," and "Nauvoo as Seen by Artists and Travelers," *IE* 65 (July 1962): 512-17, 66 (November 1962): 974-82, and 69 (January 1966): 38-43; and Lisle G. Brown's carefully crafted "The Sacred Departments for Temple Work in Nauvoo: The Assembly Room and the Council Chamber," *BYU Studies* 19 (Spring 1979): 361-74, which is a study of the interior architecture and function of the Nauvoo Temple's upper floors. An important and extensive, if somewhat unorganized, study of the Nauvoo Temple by J. Earl Arrington is in his papers at BYU. It remains unpublished.

The first full-scale, academic, and critical treatments of Mormon temples were by David S. Andrew and Laurel B. Andrew, "The Four Mormon Temples in Utah," *Journal of the Society of Architectural Historians* 30 (March 1971): 51-65, and Laurel Blank [Andrew], "Nineteenth-Century Temple Architecture of the Latter-day Saints" (Ph.D. diss., University of Michigan, 1973). Andrew's dissertation, later revised and published as *The Early Temples of the Mormons: The Architecture of the Millennial Kingdom in the American West* (Albany: State University of New York Press, 1978), attempted to integrate architectural analysis with Mormon social and cultural history.[13]

Regarding the Salt Lake Temple and earlier temples, C. Mark Hamilton has produced several works. These include "Authorship and Architectural Influences on the Salt Lake Temple" (master's thesis, U of U, 1972); "The Salt Lake Temple: An Architectural Monograph" (Ph.D. diss., University of Ohio, 1978); "The Salt Lake Temple: A Symbolic Statement of Mormon Doctrine," in *The Mormon People: Their Character and Traditions,* ed. Thomas G. Alexander (Provo, Utah: BYU Press, 1980), 103-27; and "The Salt Lake Temple—a Monument to a People," in *UP/R* 3 (1981): 2-3, 6-19.

Hamilton and University Service's beautifully illustrated *The Salt Lake Temple: A Monument to a People* (1983; reprint, Salt Lake City: University Services, 1992) includes an excellent assortment of historical photographs and architectural drawings. The book is wanting, however, because Hamilton's purposes were only partially fulfilled. Originally intended as a condensed version of Hamilton's dissertation with expanded illustrations, the text was severely trimmed after a conflict arose between the author and the publisher. Hence, the illustrations often are not described, the building's symbolism is unappraised, and the architectural history goes untold. Nevertheless, the book is a wonderful archive of images. Had it been produced as intended, it would have been as much a scholarly treatise as it is a beautifully illustrated book.[14]

Concerning twentieth-century temples, the most thorough and erudite writings are those of Paul L. Anderson, a former LDS Church Museum of History and Art administrator and currently a curator at BYU's new art museum. See, for example, Anderson's "First of the Modern Temples," *Ensign* 7 (July 1977): 6-11; "The Early Twentieth Century Temples," *Dialogue: A Journal of Mormon Thought* 14 (Spring 1981): 8-19; and "Mormon Moderne: Latter-day Saints Architecture, 1925-1945," *Journal of Mormon History* 9 (1982): 70-84.[15] See also Nelson B. Wadsworth, *Set in Stone, Fixed in Glass: The Great Mormon Temple and Its Photographers* (Salt Lake City: Signature Books, 1992).

The function and design of the newly completed RLDS Temple, designed by the St. Louis architectural firm of Hellmuth, Obata and Kassabaum, is discussed in "RLDS Choose Temple Architect," *Restoration: The Journal of Latter Day Saint History* 7 (April 1988): 5-6 and in Richard A. Brown, "What Will We Do with the Temple?" *Saints' Herald* 136, no. 4 (April 1989): 9-10, 12. *Preparing for the Temple: A Selection of Herald Articles* (Independence, Mo.: Herald Publishing House, 1989) offers a series of articles originally published in the *Saints' Herald* that address events leading to the Temple's construction. Concerning the function of the new RLDS Temple, see Richard A. Brown, *Temple Foundations: Essays on an Emerging Concept* (Independence, Mo.: Herald Publishing House, 1991). Concerning the history and meaning of the RLDS Temple, see "RLDS Church Plans Temple in Jackson County," *Sunstone* 11 (November 1987): 40, 43.

Tabernacles. Mormons' use of the term *tabernacles* is a biblical allusion to, among various Old Testament references, Isaiah's prophecy that tabernacles will be a part of Zion and its establishment before Christ's second coming (Isaiah. 33:20). During Mormonism's first 120 years, tabernacles were second only to the temple in the hierarchy of Mormon ecclesiastical architecture. That hierarchy exists today in communities where a tabernacle still stands, although a newer building type, the stake center, has supplanted the tabernacles' original function in Mormon stakes (dioceses).

Tabernacles first acted as community-wide meetinghouses. Later, as wards (congregations) were created, each ward built separate smaller meetinghouses. Tabernacles then became assembly halls built to accommodate members of a stake. Eventually, due to urban growth and expanding Church programs, the tabernacles' role as single large meeting spaces became obsolete. Beginning earnestly in the 1920s, tabernacles evolved into multipurpose buildings that were part school (multiple classrooms), part local leadership offices (multiple office suites), part recreation facility (gymnasiums and outdoor playing fields), and part cultural social center (stage areas and kitchen facilities). Eventually, the tabernacles were transformed and renamed "stake buildings" or "stake centers." Those tabernacles that remain continue to function as large assembly halls, usually for a number of stakes in a given area.

The dome-shaped Salt Lake Tabernacle (1863-67), second only to the Salt Lake Temple for international recognition so far as Mormon edifices are concerned, has been the subject of a number of academic studies. Stewart L. Grow's *A Tabernacle in the Desert* (Salt Lake City: Deseret Book, 1958) tells the story of the Tabernacle's construction and testifies to the innovative engineering performed by bridge builder Henry Grow

Truman O. Angell, 1890. Photograph by E. G. Williams and Brothers. Courtesy LDS Church Archives.

(the author's ancestor). Under the supervision of Brigham Young, Church architect William H. Folsom drafted the Tabernacle plans. Former (and later) Church architect Truman O. Angell designed much of the exterior detail and interior woodwork. A brief but exacting history of the Tabernacle, Paul L. Anderson's "Tabernacle, Salt Lake City," can be found in the *Encyclopedia of Mormonism* 4:1433-34. Anderson has also presented at least two papers (unpublished, in the possession of the author) regarding the evolution and the place tabernacles have had in Mormon society. See also the appendix "Tabernacles" in Richard W. Jackson's previously mentioned manuscript "Meeting Places of the Latter-day Saints, 1820-1980 [1995]." The appendix surveys the development of the Salt Lake Tabernacle and lists all other tabernacles, including those later structures that might be considered proto-stake centers. The Daughters of Utah Pioneers has also published a lesson on the tabernacle, Kate B. Carter, comp., *The Great Mormon Tabernacle* (Salt Lake City: DUP, 1967).

Provo's two tabernacles—the first completed in 1867 and the second first used in 1884-85 and completed in 1893—are the topics of former newspaper editor N. LaVerl Christensen's *Provo's Two Tabernacles and the People Who Built Them* (Provo, Utah: Provo Utah East Stake, 1983). I have also presented an unpublished paper on the architecture, design, and history of the first Provo tabernacle.

Dozens of other published and unpublished treatises on Mormon tabernacles can be found in the on-line and card catalogs of BYU, the UofU, and LDS Church libraries (researchers should search under the specific tabernacle name and also under specific community names). For example, a researcher who looks up Richmond, Utah, can find *The History of Richmond, Utah* (Richmond, Utah: Richmond Bicentennial Committee, 1976), which contains a brief history of local Church buildings, including the long-since razed Benson Stake Tabernacle (1904-63).

Reorganized Church of Jesus Christ of Latter Day Saints (RLDS). The RLDS Church has had its headquarters in several places: Plano, Illinois (ca. 1870–76); Lamoni, Iowa (ca. 1876–1920s); and Independence, Missouri (1920s–present). Since the mid-1980s, the RLDS Herald Publishing Company (Independence, Mo.) has produced a series of illustrated histories. The histories contain some architectural history and descriptions of various buildings and historic sites that served as pulpit to the Reorganization. Among these histories are Roger Launius, *An Illustrated History of the Kirtland Temple* (1986); Richard A. Brown, *An Illustrated History of the Stone Church* [in Independence, Mo.] (1988); Barbara J. Higdon, ed., *An Illustrated History of Graceland College* [Lamoni, Iowa] (1989); and Steven L. Shields, *An Illustrated History of Nauvoo* (1992).[16]

Latter-day Saints in Utah: Surveys and Works of General Value (1847–Present). Alice Merrill Horne's *Devotees and Their Shrines* (Salt Lake City: Deseret News, 1914) includes a hurried and precious survey of the great ages of architecture and a selective look at local architecture that Utahns should appreciate. Horne's work, however, has more value as a period piece than as a scholarly source for architecture research. Mary Henderson, *History of Utah: Historic Sites and Landmarks,* 3 vols. (privately published, n.d. [ca. 1940s]) gives a survey-like description with brief histories of existing historic sites in each Utah community and county. The survey includes much of the remaining nineteenth-century Mormon landscape (meetinghouses, schools, granaries, and mills) as it appeared before the post–World War II economic and population growth.

A near-exhaustive look at both surviving and destroyed LDS Church buildings in Utah (meetinghouses, tabernacles, tithing offices, Relief Society halls, and granaries) can be found in Allen D. Roberts's Utah-wide reconnaissance survey, "Historic Architecture of the Church of Jesus Christ of Latter-day Saints: A Survey of L.D.S. Architecture in Utah, 1847–1930" (privately printed, 1974). This is the first systematic register, architectural report, and analysis of Mormon Church buildings in Utah. Roberts's effort was funded jointly by the LDS Historical Department, the Utah State Division of State History, and the now-vanished LDS historic preservation group Cornerstone, an organization that is needed now more than ever. Sadly, many of the buildings Roberts describes as standing no longer exist.

Karl T. Haglund and Philip F. Notarianni's *The Avenues of Salt Lake City* (Salt Lake City: Utah State Historical Society, 1980) offers a brief urban and city planning history, architectural history, local history, and a smattering of biographical information on local architects who practiced in Salt Lake City and designed residences in the downtown

Hotel Utah, 1936. After extensive renovation by the Church following its closure as a hotel, the Hotel Utah was renamed the Joseph Smith Memorial Building and reopened in 1993. Photograph by David F. Davis. Courtesy LDS Church Archives.

avenues (ca. 1870–1950). The balance of the book offers a stylistic breakdown of the foregoing survey. John S. McCormick's *The Historic Buildings of Downtown Salt Lake City* (Salt Lake City, Utah: Utah State Historical Society, 1982) surveys Salt Lake City's commercial building stock and offers short building histories that include information on many Utah architects, building owners, and some business history.

The most authoritative guidebook to Utah's architecture is Thomas Carter and Peter L. Goss's *Utah's Historic Architecture, 1847–1940* (Salt Lake City: U of U Press, 1988). This book categorizes Utah's architecture stylistically and typologically; it includes a handy Utah-based glossary and a very good bibliography. Researchers touring Utah and Utah-Mormon architecture in hopes of identifying major architectural trends and types should not leave without this book.[17] Mormon ecclesiastical structures are sparingly included and only if they are good examples of a particular style or plan type. *Utah's Historic Architecture* was not intended to be a guide to Utah's religious architecture. Such a book is now needed.

General LDS Church—Articles. Much of the Mormon architectural history written in the 1960s and 1970s closely followed the traditional art history model of identifying architecture based on stylistic features (which is actually an arduous and complex task). In other cases, authors were simply attempting to get the word out that Mormons had landmarks of value—if not whole man-made environments—worthy of study and preservation. As the national historic preservation movement blossomed during the 1960s and 1970s, so also did the interest in Mormon architectural history and preservation. NRI, which was inspired by the reconstructions of colonial Williamsburg, Virginia, was established in 1962. In 1966, Utah's statewide historic preservation organization, the Utah Heritage Foundation, was established. Later, during the mid 1970s, the Mormon historic preservation organization Cornerstone was organized.

California architect Georgius Y. Cannon, who was a son of George Q. Cannon and a grandson of Brigham Young, wrote two articles. His first article, published in *American Architecture and Architectural Review* (May 21, 1924), gives a brief, chatty, yet surprisingly detailed avant view of Utah's early domestic architecture. When Mormon arbiters of taste were appealing for modernization and "beautification" (which often meant dismantling early buildings and landscapes), Cannon offered to his national readers early Mormon domestic architecture—including barns—as admirable and educational. As a practicing modern architect, Cannon was no doubt influenced by the early twentieth-century European modernist movement and its admiration of vernacular architecture. Cannon gives specific examples with builder's names and their national origins, thus describing accurately the multicultural composition of Utah's early built environment, something that was not widely appreciated until the 1970s. Cannon's second article, "Architecture and Building" in *The Arts of Utah* (Salt Lake City: Utah Arts Council, 1968), 50–51, written forty years later, offered more sympathetic commentary for a national audience. The second article reflects Cannon's enduring appreciation for pioneer architecture as well as his notions about what is fitting architecture. In 1937 Cannon received national industry attention for his Mormon meetinghouse in Glendale, California, which was published in *Architectural Forum.*[18]

In his "Architecture on the Frontier: The Mormon Experiment," *Pacific Historical Review* 43 (February 1974): 50–60, cultural and architectural historian Robert Winter asked whether unconventional or unique elements in Mormon architecture represented a break from Eastern customs. Winter answered that loaded question with the hyperbole one would expect:

> Always the tendency of the Mormon pioneer was, like the Angel Moroni on his temples, to face the East whence came his culture. He was constantly measuring himself and his art against the eastern models. (59)

Winter is more incorrect than correct because the issue is far too complex for such a pat answer. Mormons, by and large, did look east, but their hearts looked elsewhere. Mormons looked from whence they came (the cultural conventions they brought with them) to where they wanted to go (transformation via religious experience), and, finally, to where they were (the limitations and advantages of the landscape).

In the summer of 1975, the *UHQ* (volume 43) dedicated an entire issue to Utah and Utah-Mormon architectural history. The articles included U of U architectural historian Peter L. Goss's "The Architectural History of Utah" (208–39),[19] Utah State architectural historian Allen D. Roberts's "Religious Architecture of the LDS Church: Influences and Changes since 1847" (301–27), and LDS Church arts and sites curator Paul L. Anderson's biography of nineteenth-century Mormon architect William Harrison Folsom (see the biography section in this essay). This *UHQ* issue, like no other publication thus far, announced that the architectural past of Utah and the Mormons was worthy of study and appreciation.[20]

Biographies. While scores of early Utah and Mormon building designers need to be profiled and put into their historical context, only a few have received such attention. J. Earl Arrington, whose vast library of early Mormon bibliography and personal papers is housed in BYU's Special Collections, authored the article "William Weeks, Architect of the Nauvoo Temple," *BYU Studies* 19 (Spring 1979): 337–59. Arrington's article is the only published biographical writing on Weeks, a most enigmatic early Mormon architect who deserves further attention. Allen D. Roberts's likable biographical vignettes, "Utah's

Unknown Pioneer Architects: Their Lives and Works," *Sunstone* 1 (Spring 1976): 67-85; and "More of Utah's Unknown Pioneer Architects," *Sunstone* 1 (Winter 1976): 42-56, need to be duplicated. Paul L. Anderson's "William Harrison Folsom: Pioneer Architect," *UHQ* 43 (Summer 1975): 240-59;[21] and "Truman O. Angell: Architect and Saint," in *Supporting Saints: Life Stories of Nineteenth-Century Mormons*, ed. Donald Q. Cannon and David J. Whittaker (Provo: Religious Studies Center, BYU, 1985), 133-73, are good models for short biography. Both are examples of Anderson's keen analysis, understanding of the greater American architectural context, and his literary writing style.

Through over a decade of class instruction, undergraduate and graduate advising, successful architecture preservation advocacy, and scholarly writing, U of U professor Peter L. Goss has introduced and shaped much of the scholarly writing on Mormon and Utah architectural history since the early 1970s. His "William Allen, Architect-Builder, and His Contribution to the Built Environment of Davis County," *UHQ* 54 (Winter 1986): 52-73, provides a sample of Goss's scholarly output. In addition, Goss has supervised numerous other scholars' work. Here is a selection of biographical works Goss has guided: Linda L. Bonar, "Thomas Frazer: Vernacular Architect in Pioneer Beaver, Utah" (master's thesis, U of U, 1980); Craig Lewis Bybee, "Richard Karl August Kletting, Dean of Utah Architects, 1858-1943" (master's thesis, U of U, 1980); and Judith Brunvand's thesis and same-subject article "Frederic Albert Hale, Architect," *UHQ* 54 (Winter 1986): 5-30.

The three foregoing works address important subjects. Thomas Frazer was one of the master masons and building designers who brought European masonry and design techniques to pioneer Utah. Richard Kletting was a German émigré, a polytechnically trained architect and a Lutheran, yet he was one of the most influential architects in late nineteenth- and early twentieth-century Utah. Frederic Hales was also an influential non-Mormon architect; he designed for the growing wealthy class of non-Mormon businesspeople. Judith Brunvand's thesis about Hales aptly describes the general milieu of professional architects in Salt Lake City before the turn of the century. Scores of research papers—many of them biographical works—by Peter Goss and Thomas Carter's architectural history students are maintained at the U of U's Special Collection Department. Since 1987, Goss has piloted the "Biographical Dictionary of Utah Architects and Building Designers, 1847-1947" project, which is intended to include the biographies of all who took part in the design of Utah's built environment from 1847 to 1947.

My biographical writings include "The Early Life and Careers of Joseph Don Carlos Young (1855-1938), Utah's First Academically

Joseph Don Carlos Young, Albany, New York, 1879. Courtesy LDS Church Archives.

Trained Architect (1855-1884)" (master's thesis, University of Pennsylvania, 1994). This work describes the life, historical and architectural context, and early commissions (including the Brigham Young Academy building, designed in 1884 and completed in 1892) of one of Brigham Young's most artistically gifted children. My "Account of Professional Life," in *Joseph Nelson, Architect: A Biography by His Family* (Provo, Utah: privately published, 1986), 45-62, concerns the life of Joseph Nelson (1876-1952). Nelson studied at the University of Pennsylvania under the French transplant and beaux-art architect Paul P. Cret (1876-1945). Nelson was one of several Utah-Mormon architects who studied under or were influenced by this most famous twentieth-century neoclassicist.

Vernacular, Typological, Building Materials, and Geographical Studies. At any given time, although most certainly before 1870, ninety percent of Mormon architecture could be characterized as vernacular. Long held—and differing—construction and design conventions of LDS converts from New England, the Mid-Atlantic, and the South in the United States, from the British Isles, Scandinavia, and Western Europe influenced the built environment of Mormon Ohio, Illinois, and Missouri, and especially in Utah. This vernacular tradition has continued; indeed, arguments can be made that much of the Mormon built environment—even up to the present—is vernacular.

Some of the early studies of the Mormon-vernacular built environment were conducted by geographers. These studies include Joel Edward Ricks's *Forms and Methods of Early Mormon Settlement in Utah and the Surrounding Region, 1847-1877* (Logan, Utah: USU Press, 1964); D. W. Meinig, "The Mormon Culture Region: Strategies and Patterns in the Geography of the American West, 1847-1964," *Annals of the Association of American Geographers* 55 (June 1965): 191-220; several works by Richard V. Francaviglia, including "The City of Zion in the Mountain West," *IE* 72 (December 1969):10-11, 14-17; "The Mormon

Landscape: Definition of an Image in the American West," *Proceedings of the Association of American Geographers* 2 (1970): 59–61; "The Passing Mormon Village," *Landscape* 22 (Spring 1978): 40–47; and the published version of Francaviglia's dissertation, *The Mormon Landscape: Existence, Creation, and Perception of a Unique Image in the American West* (New York: AMS Press, 1978). Care should be taken with Francaviglia's studies. While they offer an exhilarating bird's-eye view, the broad summarizing, outlining of features, and generalizing of design attribution are now considered somewhat misleading.

Geographer/photographer Gary B. Peterson and Humbolt University geographer Lowell C. Bennion's richly illustrated *Sanpete Scenes: A Guide to Utah's Heart* (Eureka, Utah: Basin Plateau Press, 1987) contains an enormous amount of easy-to-read cultural geography. It includes natural history and geology as well as topographical, geopolitical, historical, ethnocultural, and architectural analysis. *Sanpete Scenes* presents an eclectic but exacting view that gives short, in-depth, and concise descriptions of the evolving Mormon landscape in Utah's Sanpete Valley (1850–1980).

For over fifteen years, U of U professor (and former Utah State architectural historian) Thomas Carter has carefully and systematically documented the nineteenth-century Utah-Mormon vernacular built environment. A nationally recognized folklorist and architectural historian, Carter has produced some of the best vernacular architecture studies in the United States. All of Carter's works on Mormon architecture should be carefully studied, including "Folk Design in Utah Architecture," in *Utah Folk Art: A Catalog of Material Culture,* ed. Hal Cannon (Provo, Utah: BYU Press, 1980), 34–59; "A Hierarchy of Architectural Values," in *The Other Forty-Niners: A Topical History of Sanpete County, 1849–1983,* ed. Albert C. T. Antrei (Salt Lake City: Western Epics, 1982), 457–88; "'The Best of Its Kind and Grade': Rebuilding the Sanpete Valley, 1890–1910," *UHQ* 54 (Winter 1986): 88–112; "Danes," in *America's Architectural Roots: Ethnic Groups That Built America,* ed. Dell Upton (Washington, D.C.: Preservation Press, 1986), 118–23; "Traditional Design in an Industrial Age: Vernacular Domestic Architecture in Victorian Utah," *Journal of American Folklore* 104 (Fall 1991): 419–42; "Building Zion: Folk Architecture in the Mormon Settlements of Utah's Sanpete Valley, 1850–1890" (Ph.D. diss., Indiana University at Bloomington, 1984, now being revised for publication); and, with Carl Fleischhauer, *The Grouse Creek Cultural Survey: Integrating Folklife and Historic Preservation Field Research,* American Folklife Center, no. 13 (Washington, D.C.: Library of Congress, 1988).

Other articles addressing Mormon vernacular architecture include Jan Harold Brunvand's "The Architecture of Zion," *The American West* 13 (March-April 1976): 28-35; and "A Survey of Mormon Housing Traditions in Utah," *Revue roumaine d'histoire de l'art* 11 (1974): 111-35. See also Cindy Rice, "Spring City: A Look at a Nineteenth Century Mormon Village," *UHQ* 43 (Summer 1975): 260-77; and Richard C. Poulsen, "Folk Material Culture of the Sanpete-Sevier Area: Today's Reflections of a Region Past," *UHQ* 47 (Spring 1979): 130-47.

Typology. Typology goes beyond analysis of stylistic references and surface treatments; it studies the architecture and the built environment via types. Such types include floor plans (individual types such as hall parlor and central hall, or basic unit types that are varied and enlarged based on ratios derived from multiplication or division of the original base units) and types that combine floor plans with exterior form, such as "Salt Box." Regarding typological approaches to Mormon architecture and building, see Joseph E. Spencer, "House Types of Southern Utah," *The Geographical Review* 35 (1945): 444-57; Henry H. Glassie, "The Impact of the Georgian House Form on American Folk Housing (abstract)," in Austin Fife and Alta Fife, eds., *Forms upon the Frontier: Folklife and Folk Arts in the United States* (Logan, Utah: USU Press, 1969), 16:23-25; and Richard V. Francaviglia's "Mormon Central-Hall Houses in the American West," *Annals of the Association of American Geographers* 61 (March 1971): 65-71. The most comprehensive and accurate guide to Mormon building types based on floor plan is Gross and Carter's previously mentioned *Utah's Historic Architecture, 1847-1940* (Salt Lake City: U of U Press, 1988). See also Carter's doctoral dissertation, which gives the most scholarly analysis of regional Mormon housing stock (more specifically Sanpete Valley, Utah).[22] Some of these articles are comparatively old. There are errors of both attribution and the issue of cultural transfer in some of them.

Building Materials. The earliest academic study on building materials in Mormon Utah is David Winburn's "The Early Homes of Utah: A Study of Techniques and Materials" (bachelor's thesis, U of U, 1952). Nationally recognized folklorist Austin E. Fife's "Stone Houses of Northern Utah," *UHQ* 40 (Winter 1972): 6-23, suggested the need for systematic study and surveying of Utah stone houses. Mormon communities with an abundance of stone construction were studied thereafter. See Richard C. Poulsen, "Stone Building of Beaver City," *UHQ* 43 (Summer 1975): 278-85; Teddy Griffith, "A Heritage of Stone in Willard," *UHQ* 43 (Summer 1975): 286-300; Linda L. Bonar, "Historic

Houses in Beaver: An Introduction to Materials, Styles, and Craftsmen," *UHQ* 51 (Summer 1983): 212-28; and Bonar, "The Influence of the Scots Stonemasons in Beaver, Utah," *UP/R* 3 (1981): 54-62.

Leon Sidney Pitman's "A Survey of Nineteenth-Century Folk Housing in the Mormon Culture Region" (Ph.D. diss., Louisiana State University, 1973), a cultural geography-anthropology analysis, has been a vital reference to researchers studying the introduction and geographical patterns of particular building materials in nineteenth-century Utah (adobe, kiln-dried brick, timber, and so forth). Also, Thomas Carter's "Cultural Veneer: Decorative Plastering in Utah's Sanpete Valley," *UHQ* 49 (Winter 1981): 68-77, demonstrated that despite humble means, Utah's early Mormon settlers did not abandon a desire for gentility and decoration. Jonathan L. Fairbanks, "Shelter on the Frontier: Adobe Housing in Nineteenth Century Utah," in his *Frontier America: The Far West* (Boston: Museum of Fine Arts, 1975), 197-212, is the most readable and insightful scholarly work on the introduction of adobe building into the Mormon cultural region. Regarding Mormon log construction, see Thomas Carter's "North European Horizontal Log Construction in the Sanpete-Sevier Valleys," *UHQ* 52 (Winter 1984): 50-71. Regarding art and stained glass, see Allen D. Roberts, "Art Glass Windows in Mormon Architecture," *Sunstone* 1 (Winter 1975): 8-13; Joyce Athay Janetski, "A History, Analysis and Registry of Mormon Architectural Art Glass in Utah" (master's thesis, U of U, 1981); Janetski, "The First Vision and Mormon Stained Glass," *Stained Glass Quarterly* 75 (Spring 1980): 47-50; and Janetski, "Louis Comfort Tiffany: Stained Glass in Utah," *UP/R* 3 (1981): 20-25. Polygamy's effect on the design of domestic architecture is the topic of Paul Goeldner's "The Architecture of Equal Comforts: Polygamists in Utah," *Historic Preservation* 24 (Jan/Mar. 1972): 14-17; and in Rickey Lynn Hendricks, "Landmark Architecture for a Polygamous Family: The Brigham Young Domicile, Salt Lake City, Utah," *The Public Historian* 11 (Winter 1989): 25-47. Thomas Carter treats this subject in the forthcoming *The Material Culture of Gender*, edited by Kenneth L. Ames.

Iconography, Semiology, and Symbolism.[23] Allen D. Roberts, Utah's first state architectural historian (mid-1970s), has made enormous contributions to Mormon architectural history and historic preservation. His award-winning (best article of 1979 by a junior historian, *MHA Newsletter* [June 1980], 4) "Where Are the All-Seeing Eyes?: The Origin, Use, and Decline of Early Mormon Symbolism," *Sunstone* 4 (May/June 1979): 22-37, later published again in *Sunstone* 10 (May 1985): 36-48, gives an insightful analysis of the pervasive use of symbols in nineteenth-century Mormon Utah and the gradual decline of such use in the twentieth century. Other sources that should be consulted include the following by Steven L. Olsen: "Zion: The Structure of a Theological Revolution," *Sunstone* 6 (November/December 1981): 21–26; and "The Mormon Ideology of Place: Cosmic Symbolism of the City of Zion, 1830–46," (Ph.D. diss., University of Chicago, 1985). Additional sources include Peggy Fletcher, "About the Sunstone," *Sunstone* 1 (Summer 1976): 10–13; and Richard C. Poulsen, *The Pure Experience of Order: Essays on the Symbolic in the Folk Material Culture of Western America* (Albuquerque: University of New Mexico Press, 1982).[24]

Regarding the symbolism of the Salt Lake Temple, see James H. Anderson, "The Salt Lake Temple," *Contributor* 14 (April 1893): 241–303; C. Mark Hamilton, "The Salt Lake Temple: A Symbolic Statement of Mormon Doctrine," in *The Mormon People: Their Character and Traditions*, ed. Thomas G. Alexander (Provo, Utah: BYU Press, 1980), 103–27; and Matthew Heiss, "The Salt Lake Temple and the Metaphors of Transformation" (master's thesis, University of Virginia, 1986). Folklorist George H. Schoemaker's "Acculturation and Transformation of Salt Lake Temple Symbols in Mormon Tombstone Art," in *Markers IX, Journal of the Association for Gravestone Studies,* ed. Theodore Chase (Worcester, Mass.: 1992), 197–215, briefly describes the evolving use and function of symbols in Mormon ideology. The article also suggests possible sources of symbolism and outlines the effect that the Salt Lake Temple iconographic scheme had on gravestones in the Mormon cultural region. Schoemaker's endnotes list numerous related articles that will be of interest to the student of Mormon iconography.

Historical Archeological Studies. NRI was a major catalyst behind many of the historical archeological studies conducted over the last thirty years. In the early 1960s, NRI contracted with many nationally recognized specialists in historic archaeology, sites management, American history, and other supporting specialties to assist in the gradual and selective (and, unfortunately, at times misleading) reconstruction of Mormon Nauvoo, Illinois. Experts with experience in the National Parks Service, colonial Williamsburg, and institutions across the country, formed a team that trained and inspired many managers of Mormon historic sites, historians, and archaeologists. Most of the quasi-published reports produced in Nauvoo for NRI are available in the NRI Archives, which is, at least for the time being, maintained by the LDS Historical Department. Other Mormon-related archeological studies can be found in the Anthropological Library in the Museum of People and Cultures at BYU, the LDS Historical Library (Salt Lake City) and the library of the Church Museum of History and Art (Salt Lake City).

The best-known investigation conducted in Nauvoo was on the Nauvoo Temple site. See Virginia S. Harrington and J. C. Harrington's *Rediscovery of the Nauvoo Temple* (Salt Lake City: NRI, 1971) as well as various other unpublished Nauvoo Temple site reports preserved in the NRI Archive. See also Donald L. Enders, "Platting the City Beautiful: A Historical and Archeological Glimpse of Nauvoo Streets," *BYU Studies* 19 (Spring 1979): 409–15.

Since the early NRI experience, numerous other Mormon historic sites have been investigated. For example, Dale L. Berge, "Archaeological Work at the Smith Log House," *Ensign* 15 (August 1985): 24–26, studied the Joseph Smith Sr. log home in Farmington (later Manchester) County, New York. In addition, Dale L. Berge, Donald L. Enders, and T. Michael Smith, "A Preliminary Architectural and Archaeological Study of the Newel K. Whitney Store" investigates the Whitney Store in Kirtland, Ohio.[25] Regarding an archaeological investigation of the E. B. Grandin Building in Palmyra, New York, see T. Michael Smith and Don Enders, "Architectural and Archaeological Investigation of the E. B. Grandin Building, 1980," housed at the library of the LDS Museum of Church History and Art in Salt Lake City.[26]

The most recent reports worthy of mention are Dale L. Berge, "Lower Goshen: Archaeology of a Mormon Pioneer Town," *BYU Studies* 30 (Spring 1990): 67–89; and Donald Southworth and others, *A Final Report of the Archaeological Investigations at Cove Fort, Millard County, Utah* (Provo, Utah: Museum of Peoples and Cultures, 1990), 90–93. A copy of the latter is housed at the LDS Museum of Church History and Art. Numerous other historical archaeology reports analyze sites throughout Utah; these can be found in the repositories mentioned above, with the exception of the NRI Archive. Furthermore, the RLDS Church's numerous architectural and archeological studies in Nauvoo and in Kirtland are available in the RLDS offices in Nauvoo.

Travel Accounts. Numerous nineteenth-century travel accounts by easterners and foreigners offer a contemporary glimpse into the appearance of Mormon communities, often including detailed descriptions of specific communities and buildings. Charles Lanman, for example, who visited the Nauvoo Temple in 1846, provided detailed descriptions of the temple's interior features that proved most useful to NRI archaeologists and historians.[27] In 1860, Sir Richard F. Burton described the Mormons' use of adobe brick, which he said was "common to all parts of the Eastern World." To Burton, the "dull leaded blue" of the brick, which was "deepened by the atmosphere to a grey" hue, made the Mormons' fledgling "holy city" somewhat oriental in appearance.[28]

Another early account of Salt Lake City and environs is William Chandless's *Visit to Salt Lake; Being A Journey across the Plains and a Residence in the Mormon Settlements at Utah* (London: Smith, Elder, and Co., 1857).

In 1872, Elizabeth (Sarah) Wood Kane accompanied her husband, Colonel Thomas L. Kane, who was a friend and defender of the Mormons, on an extensive visit to Utah. Mrs. Kane describes her impressions of Mormon community and home life in *Twelve Mormon Homes Visited in Succession on a Journey through Utah to Arizona* (1874; reprint, Salt Lake City: Tanner Trust Fund, 1974). At one point, Mrs. Kane introduces her visit to a Mormon residence in Provo as follows: "we entered the grounds of . . . a villa built in that American-Italian style which [architectural tastemaker Andrew J.] Downing characterizes as indicating 'varied enjoyments, and a life of refined leisure.'"[29] In this book, Kane attempted to convince the American public that Mormons are people very much like the rest of the nation, possibly even cultivated and refined. Two decades later, Florence Augusta Merriam Bailey recounted her experiences in Utah in *My Summer in a Mormon Village* (Boston and New York City: Houghton Mifflin, 1894).

Many of the travel accounts that describe early Mormon settlements have been briefly outlined in Howard Clair Searle's "Early Mormon Historiography: Writing the History of the Mormons, 1830–1858" (Ph.D. diss., University of California–Los Angeles, 1979). The subheading "Mormon Curiosa and Travel Chronicles of the Period" in chapter one contains Searle's outline. William Mulder and A. Russell Mortensen's *Among the Mormons: Historic Accounts by Contemporary Observers* (New York: Alfred A. Knopf, 1958; Lincoln: University of Nebraska, 1973) includes excerpts and historical notes for scores of published accounts. To date, however, so far as can be determined, no exhaustive bibliography lists travel accounts reporting conditions in nineteenth-century Mormon settlements. Such a bibliography would be a worthy undertaking.

Researchers interested in travel literature may want to study Mormon bibliography in Chad Flake's *A Mormon Bibliography, 1830–1930: Books, Pamphlets, Periodicals, and Broadsides Relating to the First Century of Mormonism* (Salt Lake City: U of U Press, 1978); the supplement by Flake and Larry W. Draper, *A Mormon Bibliography, 1830–1930: Ten Year Supplement* (Salt Lake City: U of U, 1989); Merrill J. Mattes, *The Great Platte River Road: The Covered Wagon Mainline via Fort Kearny to Fort Laramie*, 2d ed. (Lincoln: University of Nebraska Press, 1987), offering overland narratives; and Lannon W. Mintz, *The Trail: A Bibliography of the Travelers on the Overland Trail to*

California, Oregon, Salt Lake City, and Montana during the Years 1841-1864 (Albuquerque: University of New Mexico Press, 1987). Besides Flake and Draper's bibliographies, the researcher should consult Edwina Jo Snow, "Singular Saints: The Image of the Mormons in Book-Length Travel Accounts, 1847-1857" (master's thesis, George Washington University, 1972); Snow, "William Chandless: British Overlander, Mormon Observer, Amazon Explorer," *UHQ* 54 (Spring 1986): 116-36; Snow, "British Travelers View the Saints, 1847-1877," *BYU Studies* 31 (Spring 1991): 63-81; and Fawn M. Brodie, "Sir Richard F. Burton: Exceptional Observer of the Mormon Scene," *UHQ* 38 (Fall 1970): 295-311.

Twentieth Century. Many conspicuous gaps exist—chronologically, stylistically, and otherwise—in the treatment of early twentieth-century Mormon architecture. Two elements, however, have been discussed in great detail. These are prairie-style architecture (in LDS Church buildings, 1908-22) and the modernist modes (Art Moderne, Art Deco, and International, 1925-45).

In the 1970s, U of U professor Peter L. Goss, who specializes in Frank Lloyd Wright and his contemporaries, wrote about Wright and the architectural philosophy he spawned—the Prairie school (1905-20)—as an influence on Utah and LDS Church architecture (1908-22). The late nineteenth- and early twentieth-century arts and crafts movement, from which the Prairie school architecture sprang, has enjoyed sustained interest from academia and the public for over twenty years. Goss's articles that encouraged local interest are: "The Prairie School Influence in Utah," *Prairie School Review* 12 (1975): 5-22; "Utah's Architectural Heritage: Park Stake First Ward—Pope and Burton, Architects," *Utah Architect* 56 (Summer 1974): 14-16; and "A Tour of Prairie School Architecture in Salt Lake," *UP/R* 2 (1980): 60-65. Paul L. Anderson discusses the LDS Church's use of modernist architectural modes between World War I and II in "Mormon Moderne: Latter-day Saint Architecture, 1925-1945," *Journal of Mormon History* 9 (1982): 71-84.

Due to many Mormons' migration from Utah to the West and East Coasts during the Great Depression and World War II, a number of Church buildings were lavishly designed and built to accommodate growing populations as well as to provide high-profile buildings that demonstrated the stability and growth of Mormonism beyond Utah. Three of these flagship buildings were the Hollywood Stake Tabernacle (Harold Burton, architect, 1929), the Oahu Stake Tabernacle (Harold Burton, 1937), and the Washington, D.C., Chapel (Young and Hansen, 1933). No expense was spared in the design or construction of these extraordinary Church buildings. Regarding the Washington, D.C., Chapel, see Sue A. Kohler and Jeffery R. Carson, "2810 Sixteenth Street, N.W., the Unification Church (formerly Washington Chapel, Church of Jesus Christ of Latter-Day Saints)," in *Sixteenth Street Architecture,* 4 vols. (Washington, D.C.: U.S. Government Printing Office, 1988), 2:520–43.

Stephen Allan Hales, "The Effect of the Rivalry between Jesse Knight and Thomas Nicholls Taylor on Architecture in Provo, Utah: 1896–1915" (master's thesis, BYU, 1991) gives an insightful look at how local Mormon politics affected and reflected local architecture, city planning, and commercial development. In *Mormon Country* (New York City: Duell, Slone, and Pearce, 1942), famous author and Utah native Wallace Stegner fondly describes the peculiar features of rural and suburban Utah, including the then-ubiquitous basement houses (full- and half-basements topped with a temporary roof awaiting the completion of the entire house), a once common feature of post–World War II Utah.

Several articles explain the Church's move to standard-plan architecture. Martha Sonntag Bradley's "The Church and Colonel Sanders: Mormon Standard Plan Architecture" (master's thesis, BYU, 1981) seeks to explain why and how the Church slowly adopted standard-plan architecture and why, in turn, such architecture is disagreeable to so many. These issues are also discussed in Bradley, "The Cloning of Mormon Architecture," *Dialogue* 14 (Spring 1981): 20–31. An informal group discussion between four young LDS architects about modern (1970s) Mormon architecture is the model for former U of U architectural historian Donald J. Bergsma's "Mormon Architecture Today," *Dialogue* 3 (Spring 1968): 17–28. In this piece, Bergsma uses John Ruskin's *Seven Lamps of Architecture* (1849) as the model for and as a test of Mormon ecclesiastical architecture. The discussion focuses on Church architect Emil Fetzer's near-identical temple designs for Provo and Ogden, Utah.

In "Sunset Ward," *Dialogue* 22 (Summer 1989): 119–30, Claudia L. Bushman offers a brief history of the planning and construction of San Francisco's Sunset Ward Meetinghouse, which was dedicated in 1941. The article includes a series of personal remembrances about the building and a description of the difficulties that Sunset Ward leaders encountered with the fledgling Church bureaucracy. In "Battling the Bureaucracy: Building a Mormon Chapel," *Dialogue* 15 (Winter 1982): 69–78, Dennis L. Lythgoe shares his Don Quixote–like experience as a bishop negotiating with the Building and Engineering Division of the Church Physical Facilities Department after asking for changes to a standard-plan meetinghouse. Researchers can find a more sympathetic insider's look at complexities the Church has encountered in shepherding the construction of hundreds of Church buildings each year in the later chapters (and appendices) of Richard W. Jackson's unpublished manuscript "Meetinghouses of the Church of Jesus Christ of Latter-day Saints" (located in the LDS Church Archives). Jackson was employed by the Church Building Committee and Building Department three times in his career: first in the early 1940s, again in the early 1960s, and finally during the 1970s and 1980s.

Architectural Books and Periodicals as Sources for Mormon Architectural Design and Building

For many nineteenth- and early twentieth-century Mormon building designers, the instructions found in handbooks offered practical and artistic assistance. These manuals include carpenters' and builders' handbooks (technical and stylistic information for tradespeople) or their eventual replacements, the copiously illustrated and much more broadly marketed architectural pattern books. In addition, for the designer in need or for the informed and insistent client, such books offered the opportunity to pilfer an entire design. The survival of these nineteenth-century architectural books and periodicals used by Mormon designers should summon further careful research into these often overlooked primary sources that influenced the Mormon built environment.

During the second half of the nineteenth century, and to a lesser extent into the twentieth century, a flood of illustrated architectural reference works inundated the United States. These works exercised a pervasive national influence and Mormon building designers likely came under that influence.[30] The traffic and use of published sources in the Mormon and Utah environs appears to have been quite extensive, although more systematic research is needed to conclusively link specific architectural bibliography to Mormon architects and architectural designs.[31]

When searching for possible published sources used by an architectural designer, researchers should first consult Henry-Russell Hitchcock, *American Architectural Books, a List of Books, Portfolios, and Pamphlets on Architecture and Related Subjects Published in America before 1895*, new expanded edition (1946; New York City: Da Capo Press, 1976). With a specific title and book number from Hitchcock's list, researchers can examine a reproduction of the book in Research Publications' *American Architectural Books* on microfilm. Research Publications has microfilmed nearly every book listed in *American Architectural Books* (1962 edition).[32] A copy of Research Publication's film is in the micrographic section of the Marriott Library, U of U.

Many major Utah libraries hold nineteenth- and early twentieth-century architectural sources that were originally owned and used by Mormon building designers. These libraries are also committed to maintaining contemporary architecture and architectural history collections. Included among these libraries are the Marriott Library (U of U), where researchers can use the general stacks, the Art and Architecture Reference (includes locked cases), and the Special Collections Department, which includes a regional architecture drawings and manuscripts collection; the Harold B. Lee Library (BYU), which has architecture sources in the general stacks (Dewey and Library of Congress call number sections) and in Special Collections (Rare, Americana, and Victorian collections); the LDS Historical Department (Salt Lake City), which has general and reserved library collections; and the Utah State Historical Society's library (Salt Lake City).

When searching the card and automated catalogs in the foregoing institutions for period architectural bibliography, researchers should look under the obvious headings. Such headings include *architecture* and *building* and headings from the building trades (*carpentry* and *masonry,* for example). For those researching nineteenth-century guides and description books (described earlier in this essay), the best way to find such works is to look under a particular state or city name with the subdivision *Description and Travel.*

Like building designers before and throughout much of nineteenth-century America, early Mormon building designers were first masons, carpenters, or mechanics (early engineers); they obtained training from their parents or through apprenticeship-like experiences. With skills and ample on-the-job experience, many tradespeople became contractors for large private and civic organizations.[33] Sometimes with and sometimes without the skill of drafting, these builder-architects understood architectural planning, scale, proportion, and composition. Furthermore, they were often proficient in both practical and aesthetical conventions of building.

Truman O. Angell Sr., a joiner carpenter turned architect, is an excellent example of these builder-architects. Called into service as architect of public works for the infant Salt Lake City, Angell augmented his practical training by studying a work by English architect and mathematician Peter Nicholson.[34] This instance was likely not the first time Angell consulted an architectural book, nor was it likely the last. With the assignment to design, as Angell later recounted, "buildings of almost every description throughout the territory," he apparently turned to a number of architectural references for assistance.[35] One likely place Angell (or any other early Utah Mormon building designer) studied would be the *Architecture and Engineering* section in the Utah Territorial Library (Salt Lake City). Angell may have also secured various titles from other carpenters, masons, and early engineers.

In 1852, territorial librarian William C. Staines listed the contents of the territorial library in the *Catalogue of the Utah Territory Library* (Salt Lake City: Brigham H. Young, 1852). The catalog lists numerous design and technical titles that were available primarily through the late 1860s, although the library's potential use extended into the 1880s. A few of the treatises available in the library include: Peter Nicholson, *Principles of Architecture* (1836); Asher Benjamin, *Practical House Carpenter* (1850), authored by the man who wrote the first domestically published architectural book in the United States;[36] three works by Andrew Jackson Downing, including *Hints to Young Architects* (1847), *A Treatise on the Theory and Practice of Landscape Gardening with Remarks on Rural Architecture* (1847), and *The Architecture of Country Houses* (1850);[37] Minard Lafever, *The Beauties of Modern Architecture* (1849);[38] and William H. Ranlett, *The Architect,* 2 vols. (1849).[39] A number of these books, such as those by Nicholson, Benjamin, and Downing, were late editions of long-standing, influential works. Indeed, some of Downing's works remained popular and in print until the mid-1880s.[40] In addition to the foregoing, the library contained treatises that were more practical. These treatises include William Johnston, *Carpenter's New Guide* (14th ed., 1850); Thomas Tredgold, *Elementary Principles of Carpentry* (1837); and Louis Joseph Vicat, *A Practical and Scientific Treatise on Calcareous Mortars and Cements, Artificial and Natural* (1837).

The library also provided numerous farm and horticulture books and one farm journal, nearly all of them containing some description and/or illustration of farm plans, farmhouses, barns, and other agrarian buildings and land improvements. These sources included both foreign and domestic works that promoted the most recent, the most reliable, and the most scientific means of improving life and labor at home, on the farm, or on the ranch. Examples of these works include *Essays on Practical Agriculture* (1844); Henry Coleman, *European Agriculture and Rural Economy* (1850); and nine volumes of *The American Agriculturist,* a farm journal.[41]

Although the extent to which farm publications affected the evolving Mormon landscape has yet to be studied, evidence supports the fact that such publications had some impact. Learned Mormons interested in the development of agriculture as the Mormon commonwealth's fundamental industry subscribed to illustrated farm and scientific journals. Albert Carrington, for example, who was an advisor to Brigham Young and an earnest horticulturist, subscribed to numerous farm periodicals in the 1860s, including *The Country Gentleman, The American Agriculturist, The Cultivator,* and *Rural Affairs*.[42] Many of these journals contained—often as a monthly feature—arguments for and descriptions of nearly every conceivable farm or ranch building or improvement. The models offered were both domestic and foreign, and many of the designs were touted as the latest in economic betterment and scientific planning.

The Utah Territorial Library was open to all interested parties, from the well-trained design practitioner to the mechanic or agriculturist. The Library's architectural books and periodicals represented architectonic thought (from relatively high cultural expression to the common day-to-day building environment) that reached back into the late-eighteenth century and progressed to the latest building and design conventions of the day. Many of the library's sources influenced (directly or representationally) the Mormon built environment to the cusp of the twentieth century. Over the course of the library's lifetime, other architectural books were acquired and made available. At the library's closure in the 1880s, its contents were transferred to the University of Deseret (predecessor of the UofU).

The architectural books available in the territorial library were by no means the only published sources used by nineteenth-century Mormon designers. While the library probably contributed the largest corpus of architectural sources in early Utah, those were not the only sources available. Many books and periodicals (directly or indirectly architectural) were privately shipped or mailed. Fortunately, a number of private architectural and architectural-related libraries—originally created and owned by Mormon leaders, architects, and builders—have found their way into the present pool of Utah libraries.

The following are a few examples of Mormon architects who found instruction and design ideas "by the book": James Snyder (1820–1906), a Philadelphia builder and Mormon convert, came to Utah and settled in Provo in 1861. Snyder owned and used a copy of William H. Ranlett's *The Architect,* vol. 1, an illustrated pattern book that contained floor plans, elevations, detail drawings, rendered perspectives, and specifications for "domestic and ornamental villas and landscapes."[43] Snyder added marginalia and sketches to his copy, including, in one case, a client's name beneath a design: "H. H. [Harvey Harris] Cluff." Cluff was a Provo rancher and prominent local Church leader. Snyder took inspiration from Ranlett's plates in preparing his design for Cluff's house, which Snyder built after the latter's return from a mission in the mid-1870s.[44]

In 1879, aspiring Mormon architect Samuel C. Dallas purchased by mail order a copy of Amos Bicknell's *Detail, Cottage and Constructive Architecture* (1873). Just a few years after his purchase, Dallas formed a partnership with railroad engineer William S. Hedges to form Dallas & Hedges, a popular architectural firm that was active until shortly after the first decade of the twentieth century.[45] A comparative study between the early work of Dallas & Hedges with Bicknell's book, and others owned by the firm (specifically the firm's Queen Anne-inspired residences) may turn up some surprising similarities.

Other treatises offered architectural theory and history that interested only the most earnest of architects. One such architect was John H. Burton (1857–87), son of noted Mormon soldier, pioneer, and Church leader Robert Taylor Burton (1821–1907). John Burton, whose training and background still needs investigation, accumulated a small but useful library that suggests serious interest in the subtle locutions of architectural practice. Included in this young architect's library was volume one of Boston architect and critic Henry Van Brunt's translation of Eugene-Emmanuel Viollet-le-Duc's *Discourses on Architecture,* 2 vols. (1875). Viollet-le-Duc was possibly the most important theorist of architecture in the Modern era. Van Brunt's translation was the first English translation, first published in Paris in 1863, of Viollet-le-Duc's atelier lectures on architectural theory. Burton's library also included the two-volume set of British architect Joseph Gwilt's *Encyclopedia of Architecture* (1871).[46]

Architectural periodicals made their debut in the United States in the mid-nineteenth century. The *American Architect and Building News* (AABN), first published in Boston in 1876, was the first American architectural periodical that had, as one historian described it, "a future."[47] Architectural periodicals did not appear in Utah until the advent of the AABN.[48] Sporadic runs of this journal and various others, including Denver's *Western Architect,* San Francisco's *Western Architect and Building News,* and Chicago's *The Inland Architect and News Record* can be found in the UofU and BYU libraries.[49]

The professional library of William W. Fife (b. 1856) is one example of the influence of professional periodical literature on Mormon and Utah architecture in the late nineteenth century. At the age of thirteen, Fife began his professional training under his father, William N. Fife (b. 1831, Scotland), one of the most successful builder-architects in Ogden, Utah. Fife's training included instruction in carpentry, masonry, building supervision, and drafting. At fifteen, Fife became clerk of the works; at seventeen, chief of the "draughting department;" and at eighteen (following his father's retirement), operator of the business. Fife acted as both a builder and an architect until 1886, when, at age thirty, he devoted himself exclusively to the gentlemanly profession of architecture. Fife's knowledge of the profession was acquired, as he would later describe, "in the best school of learning, viz.; practical experience." And like many other late nineteenth-century American architects who advanced through the building trades and the contracting business, Fife (according to his promotional press) buttressed the practical by

> studying hard and earnestly to perfect himself in the details of architecture, and in order to keep abreast of the times and give his patrons the benefit of the latest and most approved productions of recognized authority and eminent draftsmen and designers, *subscribes to, and keeps constantly on file, the very best works and periodicals on architecture published in the United States,* and is in communications with publishers in different parts of Europe to bring to his aid and to use in his work the finest and most magnificent and substantial class of work in planning and construction of building.[50]

In surprisingly candid terms, Fife announced that inspiration for his designs came from published works that offered "the latest and most approved productions." The latest sources, as Fife's promotional press went on to report, included *American Architect and Building News* (international editions), *Inland Architect, Scientific American* (architects' and builders' edition), and *Architect and Builder.* All of these outlined architectural trends of which fashion-conscious Utahns would have wanted to be apprised.[51] To his readers this was to say he was informed unlike the hundreds of uninformed tradesmen-architects. For Fife, having and using such periodicals was a mark of a well-advised practitioner.

Repositories with Architectural Sources (Primary and Secondary)

The LDS Historical Department

The largest cache of Mormon-related architectural materials is located in the LDS Historical Department in Salt Lake City. The immense size of the collection, which contains hundreds of linear feet of materials concerning the building history of the Church and its people, dictates that any attempt at description be accompanied by two caveats: (1) researchers must carefully search for sources themselves; and (2) the sources described in this essay are merely samples and do not necessarily represent the depth and breadth of the collection.

Indeed, the materials mentioned here are primarily large collections, overtly Mormon and predominately institutional. The Historical Department holds thousands of institutional and private records regarding thousands of individual Church members, congregations, events, and locales that document the building of the Mormon landscape. As mentioned in the introduction, architectural and building information is not always labeled as such. Therefore, a carefully planned research strategy, developed with the assistance of Historical Department staff, will offer the best results.

The Historical Department has well-defined policies regulating access to and use of materials—particularly manuscript materials, including photographs and architectural drawings. Access to manuscript items may be partially or completely restricted for six reasons: (1) manuscripts may be considered sacred and not for general consumption; (2) they may encroach upon the privacy of or be libelous to someone, whether living or dead; (3) they may be confidential records, such as minutes of Church leaders' meetings; (4) they may be active corporate records used in the day-to-day operations of the Church; (5) they may pose a security risk to the Church if released; or (6) they may not be cataloged to department standards.

To gain access to restricted materials, a researcher must have an interview with a staff member and may also have to write a letter of request. Researchers who cannot gain personal access should ask a staff member to search in their stead.

A hierarchy of materials exists so far as access restrictions are concerned. The likelihood of receiving access to restricted materials increases when a petition is exact and informed. Before drafting a petition, researchers should carefully study non-restricted documents and collections. After deducing specific descriptions of restricted documents or collections they wish to examine, researchers should ask for access or, even better, go one step further and describe exactly the kind of information they wish to extract. The petition for access should specify exact or circa dates (for example, between 1913 and 1915), names (with letters, researchers should note both the writer's and receiver's names), and the subject matter (for example, directions given to John Doe from Jane Doe).

Church Department Records. Many of the First Presidency's records include materials relevant to Church architecture and building. The largest and best example is the voluminous Brigham Young Papers, which documents nearly every aspect of early Utah's architectural and building issues. The correspondence section (letterpress books) includes letters between Young and local Church leaders, builders, and others regarding numerous subjects: town planning and fortification;

the dispersement, purchase, and sale of real estate; and the locale, materials, and construction of ward buildings, tabernacles, temples, and numerous other building types in the Mormon built environment. While the collection was reorganized and divided into name and subject files sometime after Young's death, over the last decade the Church Archives has attempted to reconstitute the collection to its original condition.

Other collections that may include architectural information include the Historian's Office Journal (1844–1994), and the Historian's Office Letterpress Books. The best parts of these indexed series are the early records made while George A. Smith was Church historian (ca. 1854–86). As with many LDS Church collections, researchers should approach these records only after having completed substantial research in determining the specific material they require.

Subset groups of First Presidency records relate to architecture and building in the twentieth century, such as the Ward and Stake Building Files (1917–40). These include correspondence, memoranda, and other materials to and from local Church leaders regarding local buildings.

The constant evolution and growth of the corporate Church makes finding specific corporate architectural records a complex, if not daunting, task. As the various Church agencies expanded and divided, previous agency records were either turned over to successor agencies, divided among newly constituted agencies, or benignly neglected and allowed to fall into a ruinous state or even destruction. Hence, when an agency's records finally reached the Historical Department, they often included records of various antecedent agencies, sometimes separately maintained and sometimes consolidated.

The Public Works records (1847–60s), which are well indexed, detail many specifics of the Utah Church's early building and improvements campaigns (for example, the council house, Church leaders' houses, Temple Square, roads, ditches, and other Salt Lake City projects). The collection includes records addressing the production of building material (adobe, rough and milled timber) and labor records of workers, tradespeople, and mechanics (adobe brick makers, masons, carpenters, tinsmiths, blacksmiths), which describe workers' time and daily worth compared to other labor classes, with labor exchanged for credits for foodstuffs and dry goods from the church's tithing yard.

The Law Department records (1870–1964) and the Financial Department records (1848–1969) suffer from the agencies' complex origins as described earlier. The records include materials of the Church's Trustee-in-Trust and the Corporation of the President, two legal entities under the control of the Church's First Presidency. The financial record series also includes materials generated while both departments were under the supervision of the Presiding Bishopric. In each of these cases, records addressing Church property and building campaigns are included. In addition, architectural or architecture-related records of the Presiding Bishopric Office (PBO) are available. These records include property files from the Church's nonecclesiastical property arm, Zion's Securities Corporation, as well as those from the Building Facilities Department (1921–43); the PBO's Architectural Department (1919–38); and the Building Committee and Building Department (1938–72), the latter including architectural records that document the gradual development and application of the standard plan designing that commenced in the mid-1950s.

Like the First Presidency records, many subset record groups under the heading of the Presiding Bishopric Office exist. Many of these groups have registers and inventories placed in binders and arranged in numeric order; they are located in the Historical Department's reading room. In addition to the PBO's General Office files (correspondence, 1897–1948), researchers should search under general office files: (1) PBO subject files, (1899–1956, headings such as Bldg. Committee, Bldg., Committee *Bulletin*); (2) materials relating to the First Presidency regarding Church buildings, (1908–37); (3) PBO Building and Remodeling files; and (4) inventories of furnishings, equipment, and so forth. Researchers can also look in the PBO record series under separate subset titles to find the following: the Architectural Department files (1921–45), the Building Facilities files (1921–29), the Improvement and Beautification Committee general files (1920–49), the Deleted Building files (1933–65), and the Board of Temple Architects (1934–44; the board designed the Idaho Falls Temple and an unexecuted design for the Los Angeles Temple).

The Physical Facilities Department's photographic collection (ca. 1870–1994) includes views of buildings built, purchased, or rented by the Church, whether designed, remodeled, maintained, or sold. The collection primarily documents properties in the United States, although international properties are included. This collection, which was formed by the gathering and extraction of photographic and graphic materials from the department's obsolete files, includes materials from the Real Estate Division, the Architectural and Engineering Division, and numerous area offices formed and re-formed during the last three decades. Some of this material was transferred to the Historical Department as early as the 1930s; hence, documents from the 1870s to the present are available.

During 1988 and 1989, after the Church decided to microfilm and destroy all the obsolete Real Estate Division Records (encompassing hundreds of linear feet of files), the Historical Department chose to extract from these records all graphic materials, including photographs, plat maps, brochures, and sketches. Unlike the textual materials, these graphic materials could not be suitably studied or reproduced from microfilm. In addition to the foregoing, the Historical Department also took possession of many pre-1930 files that were interspersed throughout the file series. Much of this material was produced to document sites, pre-purchase or pre-construction conditions (exterior and interior), and surrounding physical contexts. Hence, while valuable, the photography is not the most flattering or artistically pleasing.

In the late 1980s, the Historical Department acquired the entire Physical Facilities Department's (PFD) architectural drawing archive (through 1970), on 105 millimeter microfiche. Before the mid-1960s the PFD had maintained blueprint copies or original drawings for a vast number of Church buildings. In an effort to reduce volume and to make this growing body of material more accessible, the Church placed the entire collection on 110 mm microfiche and—by way of "blow-back" reproductions—made copies available for in-house use. Later, in the mid-1970s, the Church updated this storage and retrieval technology by transferring all but the obsolete ("deleted") property records (properties sold or razed) to a 35 mm microfilm. These transferred images were then cut and affixed to aperture cards for easy handling and copying. Eventually, the PFD transferred the obsolete 105 mm collection to the Historical Department.

Unfortunately, the enlarging equipment used to "blow back" the 105 mm micro images became outmoded. The 105 mm format is making something of a commercial comeback, however, because the copy prints (made from a format larger than 35 mm) are often more to scale than those made from the 35 mm format. For the present time, however, making copies from the 105 mm format entails sending the microfiche to a costly reproduction service. Regardless of this handicap, the micro images' ability to present thousands of Church architectural drawings spanning the entire history of the Church in Utah is remarkable. Had the Church not transferred these unstable blueprints to a micro format, many of them would likely have deteriorated with constant use.

In addition to the 105 mm collection, the PFD's obsolete 35 mm property records (including some properties that were included in the 105 mm collection) are periodically culled from the PFD's working 35 mm library. The culled records are transferred to the

Historical Department when a building is razed or sold. These 35 mm records can be easily enlarged and copied by the Historical Department for a reasonable reproduction fee.

All of the foregoing collections, including the photograph files, the Real Estate Division records, and the architectural drawings (on both the 105 mm and 35 mm microforms) are indexed by a property number. Such a number is given to each piece of real estate owned or rented by the Church. This number follows a property from purchase, to building construction, and throughout its use, until the property's "deletion" if that occurs. The property number is cross-referenced by current property name, properties under a particular stake (Mormon diocese), and by geopolitical setting (state and city) on microfiche. The property index is updated quarterly and can only be accessed with the assistance of Historical Department staff. As properties are sold or buildings razed, both the buildings and the property numbers are deleted. The numbers are deleted with each updated microfiche index, making the obsolete property number indexes invaluable to researchers.

Nauvoo Restoration Incorporated (NRI) Records. In 1988 the entire research archive of the Church-owned NRI was placed in the Historical Department in Salt Lake City. NRI's objectives, according to its 1962 articles of incorporation, were:

> To acquire, restore, protect, and preserve, for the education and benefit of its members and the public, all or a part of the old city of Nauvoo in Illinois and the surrounding area, in order to provide an historically authentic physical environment for awakening a public interest in and an understanding and appreciation of, the story of Nauvoo and the mass migration of its people to the Valley of the Great Salt Lake.[52]

In concert with these objectives, the organization gathered every imaginable type of artifact and record relating to Nauvoo (copy and original, primary and secondary) that could aid in the reconstruction and understanding of the pre-Utah Mormon experience. The collection represents over thirty years of sporadic data and document gathering and document producing (reports, studies, and so forth) related to the construction of this park-like historical community.

Consisting of hundreds of linear feet of historical material, the NRI collection includes original and reproduced manuscripts, photographic materials, maps, graphic materials, and NRI research data, much of which is indexed on note cards. The collection documents Mormon social history, material culture, architecture and building, archeological investigations, historic preservation policy and technique, and the construction and use of reconstructed Nauvoo. At this writing, the NRI collection is not fully cataloged and its permanent repository is yet to be decided. The collection is not currently accessible to the public. However, patrons at the Church Archives, can study a separately cataloged microfilm copy (sixteen rolls) of the NRI card index.

Local Records. The Local Records (LR) collection consists of individual branch, ward, stake, and mission records of the Church. Many of the earliest pre-Utah local unit records are not cataloged as LR. Rather, such records are cataloged as noninstitutional manuscripts (Mss.). Hence, local unit records may be on two different catalogs. Each local unit potentially has over a dozen different record series. These records may include Church leaders' minutes (stake and ward), council minutes (stake and ward), Relief Society minutes, Primary minutes, and other auxiliary minutes. Many of the stake and ward leadership minutes describe aspects of building campaigns, such as acquiring land, acquiring the services of an architect and builders, and calculating costs. In addition to these locally produced records, the Historian's Office began producing its own histories of local units around the turn of the twentieth century. These histories, labeled *manuscript histories,* are often rich in building data.

Manuscript Collection. The earliest known Church architectural drawings are the "Plan of the House of the Lord for the Presidency, 1833," and selected study drawings of the Nauvoo Temple by William Weeks (1813–1900), the first historically recognized Church architect. Although these original drawings are not available for study, researchers can obtain photographic and microform copies. Other valuable drawings are the extant drawings of New York- and Rhode Island-trained Truman O. Angell Sr. (1810–87). Those drawings depict the State House in Fillmore, Utah, and numerous buildings in Salt Lake City, including the old and new Temple Square tabernacles, the residences of Brigham Young and other Church leaders, and the Endowment House.

The Church Architect's Office (1842–93) collected selected study and progress drawings (interior and exterior) and stonemasons' diagrams and schedules, for the quarry and the building site of the Salt Lake Temple. These drawings and schedules were produced by various Church architects: Truman O. Angell Sr., William W. Ward (1827–93), Truman O. Angell Jr. (1852–1933), William H. Folsom (1815–1901), and Joseph Don Carlos Young (1855–1938). Other architectural drawing collections, including collections for the St. George and Logan Temples are stored and described separately. The few extant drawings of the Manti Temple are included in the George Cannon Young Collection.

The Nina Folsom Moss Collection contains material related to Moss's father, William H. Folsom, who was both an assistant Church architect and Church architect. The collection contains papers and scrapbook material related to the Manti Temple and tabernacle, the Salt Lake Theater, the second tabernacle on Temple Square, the Salt Lake City Hall, and the ZCMI buildings in Salt Lake City.

The George Cannon Young Collection (ca. 1850–1980) and the Don Carlos Young Collection (ca. 1870–1965) contain the professional records of three generations of Mormon architects: Church architect Joseph Don Carlos Young, son of Brigham Young; Joseph's sons Don Carlos Young Jr. (1882–1960), George Cannon Young (1891–1981), and Edward Partridge Young (b. 1903); and Joseph H. Young and Richard W. Young (b. 1931). Also included in these two collections are professional papers of the firms of Young and Son(s), Young and Hansen, Deseret Architects & Engineers, and selected materials from the Church Architect's Office, among others. These collections represent over one hundred years of architectural design on behalf of the Church and nearly every imaginable building type associated with Church architecture, including temples (Salt Lake, Manti, and Arizona), tabernacles, Relief Society halls, visitors' centers, and ward houses. Also included are the architectural drawings and records for the Church Administration Building (designed by Young and Son, completed in 1917) and the Church Office Building (designed by George Cannon Young & Associates, completed in 1974).

The Douglas W. Burton Collection includes the architectural drawings and records of Harold W. Burton (1887–1969), Church supervising architect from 1955 through 1965. The collection also includes the papers and drawings of his son, Douglas W. Burton (1908–82). In addition, the collection contains selected works of the firms of Pope & Burton, Alexander & Burton, Burton & Burton; selected works of architect Francis D. Rutherford (1883?–1933); and works from the Church Building Committee, which later became the Building Department then Physical Facilities Department. Some of the noteworthy drawings of Church buildings included in this collection depict the Alberta Temple, the Hawaii Temple, the Honolulu Hawaii Stake Tabernacle, the Church College in Hawaii (now BYU—Hawaii), the Polynesian Cultural Center, the Hollywood Stake Tabernacle, and the Oakland Temple. Finally, the collection includes all specifications, photographs, and correspondence files of Burton Sr. and Jr.

The Cannon and Mullen Collection includes the architectural drawings and records of architect Howell Quayle Cannon (b. 1908) and the firms of Cannon & Fetzer, Fetzer & Fetzer, Cannon & Mullen,

Pope & Burton, and numerous other early- to mid-twentieth-century Mormon architects. This collection includes numerous designs from the South Seas region, designs used in the worldwide Building Missionary Program, and materials that document the gradual adoption of standard planning. The collection also documents the influence of modern-school designs on meetinghouses.

The William F. Thomas Collection (1923–65) includes the Church-related professional work of Thomas (1911–87) and mid-twentieth century designs for various Church functions worldwide. The Louis A. Thomas Collection consists of the office records of Louis A. Thomas (1885–1955), the firm of Pope & Thomas, and numerous other individual architects. The Fetzer and Fetzer Collection (1920–77) includes working drawings and some specifications for thirty meetinghouses. It details the work of the architectural firms of Fetzer & Fetzer, made up of Henry P. Fetzer (1906–90), John B. Fetzer (b. 1911) and Emil B. Fetzer (b. 1916), the latter being Church architect from 1964 through 1985; Cannon & Fetzer (the predecessor firm of Fetzer & Fetzer and Cannon & Mullen, both of Salt Lake City), and Woolley & Evans (also of Salt Lake City). Many of the renderings included in this collection express the very modern and artistic mind of Beaux-art trained Henry P. Fetzer. Fetzer was the oldest son of Mormon convert and German immigrant John Fetzer, likewise an architect, originally of Cannon & Fetzer. Henry P. Fetzer was one of the Church's most gifted architectural designers of the twentieth century, responsible for some of Mormondom's most innovative and modern architectural designs.

The firm of Evans & Allred (Salt Lake City), consisting of Dal C. Allred and Clifford Evans, worked closely with the Church's building department over a thirty-year period. The firm enlarged and remodeled dozens of pioneer meetinghouses throughout rural Utah and the Salt Lake Valley. In addition, the firm documented much of its Church work with before-and-after photographs of their commissions. These photographs are now included in the Dal C. Allred Photograph Album Collection. As was thought needed at the time, Evans & Allred radically altered and modernized many nineteenth-century meetinghouses, sometimes beyond recognition.

The Church Archives also has reference copies of measured drawings and photographs of selected Mormon or related properties produced by the Historic American Building Survey (HABS, original materials housed in the Library of Congress, Washington, D.C.). A sample of the properties represented are: the Kirtland Temple; the Salt Lake Tabernacle; the George Mason granary in Willard, Box Elder

County, Utah; the house of LDS Church President Lorenzo Snow (1814–1901) in Brigham City, Box Elder County; and the Bishop's Storehouse in Panguitch, Garfield County, Utah. The reference collection is selective and the list of all Utah HABS and HAER (Historic American Engineering Record) documents, as well as the information needed to purchase copies, can be found at both the LDS Church Archive and the library of the Utah State Historical Society.

Photograph Collections. Perhaps the largest and most diverse type of architecture record in this repository is the photograph collection. Considered the largest and most significant (and by far the best cataloged and preserved) Mormon-related photograph collection in the world, the collection encompasses hundreds of locations, thousands of different creators, subjects, and events, covering nearly every major locale Mormons have traveled, proselyted, and lived. The collection also documents nearly every major photographic process and format employed since the advent of photography. Despite these grand circumstances, the process of finding specific buildings, structures, and sites—save the most well known and significant—takes patience and careful planning.

The cross-referencing of photographic documents does not always include every possible feature in a view; even seemingly major features or aspects are often overlooked. A good reason supports this organizational scheme: over-cataloged collections can lead researchers down the path of someone else's thinking and into a false assumption that everything can be found by reviewing a catalog or index. Not even the most seasoned archivist can anticipate every possible research use to be had from a document; this is particularly true of photographic documentation. Catalogs such as that in the LDS Church Archives offer general geopolitical locations, creator's names (authors, photographers, and architects), and very general subject matter. The rest is up to the researcher.

The Archives has several major photograph collections that are rich in Mormon architectural and material culture. The Charles W. Carter Collection, for example, contains many views of nineteenth-century Salt Lake City and environs. The individually cataloged photographs of Charles R. Savage are also valuable, although nearly all of Savage's pre-1880s negatives were destroyed in a studio fire. Hundreds of views of newly constructed buildings, streetscapes, and bird's-eye views—once owned by Savage's clients—are available. These photographs were taken predominately throughout Utah, although some were taken throughout the western states and territories, selectively east, and across the Mormon trail. The George Edward Anderson

Collection is jointly held by BYU and the Church Archives. Conspicuous LDS subjects are in LDS Church Archives; all else is at BYU. This collection includes some of the most artistically composed views of natural and manufactured environments in Mormondom, including views from central and northern Utah (1880–1926) and from sites in the Midwest and New England associated with the impetuses of Mormonism (1907–8). Anderson captured both the principal and ambient material features of the late nineteenth- and early twentieth-century Mormon experience. Architecture, the built environment—particularly the vernacular—and the transformed Mormon landscape abound in nearly all of Anderson's out-of-studio views. A register is available for the Church Archives portion of the collection, while catalog cards (based on geopolitical and general subjects) and reference photocopies are available for the BYU collection.

The works of other Mormon photographers abound in the LDS Church Archives: Salt Lake City photographer Edward Martin; Charles E. Johnson; the Shipler photography family (James, Harry, and their progeny), representing three generations of professional work in the Salt Lake Valley, commencing in the 1890s; the partnership of Fox and Symons; and scores of others. Regarding meetinghouses in the Salt Lake Valley as of 1915, see the photographic collection "Salt Lake Valley meetinghouses, circa 1915," which includes nearly eighty photographs of the then-extant meetinghouses.

Local record photograph collections, once known as P-2000 collections, contain views of the buildings that once housed Sunday schools, branches, wards, stakes, and missions. This collection is slowly being dismantled for separate cataloging.

Oral History Program. The James Moyle Oral History Program has a small but significant number of oral histories that document architecture in the twentieth-century Church. Paul L. Anderson, LDS Church architectural historian and former curator for the LDS Church Museum of History and Art, conducted most of these interviews in the mid-1970s. The interviews include the following: (1) California architect Georgius Young Cannon (1892–1987), son of LDS Church leader George Q. Cannon and Brigham Young's daughter Caroline Partridge Young (Croxall) Cannon; (2) Edward O. Anderson (1891–1977), Church Supervising Architect (1945–55); and (3) architect George Cannon Young (1898–1981). Another oral history was conducted by Edward O. Anderson's daughters-in-law about Anderson. In addition, the collection contains an interview of Arnold Ehlers, who was Church Supervising Architect from 1953 to 1955—produced by the author with retired architect Richard W. Jackson. Finally, the collection contains oral histories of Physical Facility Department employees as well as leaders and missionaries in the Church's Building Missionary Program (1955–65).

Library Division. This division includes nearly all the runs, historical and contemporary, of central and local Church-published periodicals. Many of these journals, magazines, and quarterlies, describe building purchases and building campaigns. One outstanding example of such periodicals is the *Millennial Star,* which was published in the British Isles for British members. As a regular feature, the monthly published newsy correspondences from missionaries and local leaders that often described the whereabouts, appearances, and conditions of rented halls or locally owned meetinghouses. The *Star* also frequently described major construction projects and public improvements in Utah. Two additional journals that described Church facilities in the twentieth century are the *Elder's Journal* (Atlanta, Ga.; 1903–7) and its successor publication *Liahona: The Elders' Journal* (Independence, Mo.; 1907–45). The journals' intended audience was predominately missionaries and members from the eastern United States, encompassing the southern, central, and eastern states missions. The journals frequently included articles—often illustrated with photographs—describing newly acquired or built meetinghouses, mission homes and other Church buildings.

Beginning in the 1880s, Church periodicals sporadically featured articles on the building program, past and present. These articles often included counsel and direction for the construction and maintenance of Church buildings, or, after Church design and construction became centralized, how and why the Church designed the way it did. Articles were also written to offer advice about the construction, care, and improvement of members' homes and farms. The following describes some of these articles.

William S. Hedges, "Architecture of Common Houses," *The Contributor* 5 (July 1884): 373–78, (August 1884): 428–30, and (September 1884): 451–56, offered what Hedges—a recent Indiana transplant, aspiring young railroad engineer and architect—considered necessary in a comfortable house. In these vaguely self-promoting writings, Hedges described what to consider when buying a home, what to consider when building, and how to properly ventilate, decorate, and furnish a house. At the time he wrote this article, Hedges was a partner with Salt Lake City native Samuel C. Dallas in the architectural firm of Dallas & Hedges.

The *IE* 17 (June 1914) contained—along with a series of articles about Church architecture—a substantial number of photographs of Church buildings ranging from the pioneer era to the second decade of the twentieth century. In this issue, architect Lewis T. Cannon's

"Architecture of Church Buildings" (793-801) briefly described the characteristics of early twentieth-century Mormon architecture. Cannon stated that for his time, Mormon "buildings are not those developed solely from within" and that Mormons' "contact[s] generally with their fellow men are assimilated and sooner or later find expression in [Mormon] accomplishments." Cannon also described what makes "a successful ward house."[53]

L. S. Morris's "Home Beautification," *IE* 32 (April 1929): 460-65 described how old and dilapidated property could, with some attention, gain a fresh and becoming appearance. This article was written during the Great Depression, a time when Church and community

Church Beautifying Echoes Into the Home

Before

After

When you dignify and beautify the church you instill a desire to improve and beautify the home. *BELIEVE IT OR NOT*, these two photo's taken in Salt Lake City are of the same home. *A SHED TRANSFORMED INTO A BEAUTIFUL HOME.*

FORMULA

"Before" + Vision and Family Teamwork = "After"

"For Zion must increase in beauty, and in holiness; her borders must be enlarged; her Stakes must be strengthened; yea, verily I say unto you, Zion must arise and put on her beautiful garments."—*Doc. & Cov., Sec.* 82, *Verse* 14.

"Our Churches and Homes Shall Be Beautiful"

A before and after illustration and message from an LDS pamphlet entitled "Our Churches Shall Be Beautiful," published by the Improvement and Beautification Committee, Church Security Program, The Church of Jesus Christ of Latter-day Saints, January 1938. Distributed Churchwide, this pamphlet urged Church members to improve and beautify church, home, and all that surrounded them. Here a humble laborer's house or "shed," as the pamphlet describes it, is transformed into a respectable cottage. Courtesy LDS Church Archives.

leaders concerned themselves with the need for respectability, perhaps even refinement, by urging the improvement and updating of Mormon communities, homes, and farms. This effort was directed by the Improvement and Beautification Committee, Church Security Program, Presiding Bishopric Office. The campaign urged the removal or modernization of many nineteenth-century buildings and landscape features, which were thought to be dilapidated and even gauche in comparison to the new and modern American homes and farms that Mormons frequently saw in newspapers and home magazines.

During a ten-year period (1955–65), the Church's building program exploded with new construction campaigns throughout the world. This explosive growth led to a deficit spending policy that abruptly came to an end with a building moratorium that began in 1965 and continued for over two years. The Church's earlier enthusiasm for growth and its bullish development campaign was exhibited in Church supervising architect Harold W. Burton's "Our Church Architectural Development," *IE* 62 (April 1959): 252–65.

A series of articles under the byline "Latter-day Saint Settlements of the West" appeared in the *Ensign* 10 (February 1980): 18–49. These articles included dozens of photographs of Utah-Mormon architecture. These articles offered a story of Church history and a subtle sub-text expressing a growing interest in the preservation of historic Church buildings. Researchers should check the Church's periodical indexes for other articles relating to Church architecture and building. Researchers should also look under specific geographical areas such as California (extensive building campaigns began in the 1920s); major eastern and southern cities (throughout the twentieth century); and, after World War II, international locations.

Microfilm copies of newspapers, available both in the Church Archives library and nearly any other, contain information about local architecture. Some of the larger newspapers also provide a glimpse into national building and architectural trends. One example of the latter is the American Press Association's 1892 series—published in the Salt Lake *Deseret Evening News*—about domestic and farm buildings. Elevations and floor plans were included with a description and a discussion as to why and for whom the building was most suited, such as a laborer's cottage (cost: $500), a suburban house for a genteel family (cost: $1,500), or a barn for the farmer who wanted a more pleasing exterior. The series also included discussions about practical matters such as property insurance, plumbing, and how best to furnish a home.[54]

Over the years, the library has extracted and cataloged numerous articles from local and national publications that address Mormon topics, some of which include architectural topics. In addition thousands of small leaflet, booklet, and souvenir publications of Church dedications for nearly every conceivable building type can be found in the department's computer catalog. Lately, many of these locally produced publications have been placed in the Church Archives under the label of "Local Records"; they are not necessarily described on a department computer catalog. The same is true for the collection of stake and ward histories, which includes photos of buildings. Hence, the researcher must inquire about these local Church publications.

Historic Sites Collection. The Historic Sites Collection, collected by the Curator Division (the predecessor division to the Church Museum of History and Art), is a large series (roughly fifty linear feet) of research files organized in alphabetical order; it contains research notes, bibliography, and photocopies of historic sites. The term "historic sites" has been generously defined in this collection to include town sites, Mormon trail sites, Church buildings, and even historic markers from across the United States and beyond. The collection can be accessed only with the assistance of the library staff; patrons may copy only staff-selected items.

The Journal History. The Journal History was started in 1900 and has been described, somewhat accurately, as a giant scrapbook for the LDS Church. The history is a massive aggregation consisting of Historian's Office news accounts (from numerous official sources) and press clippings. The compilers attempted to gather documentation about the nineteenth-century Church as well as current affairs. With varying degrees of success, the compilers attempted to make the collection a continuous encyclopedic registry of what they perceived as the Church's progress toward the Millennium.

This chronicling effort was greatly concerned with the physical building of the Church. Therefore, the Journal History documents building campaigns for Salt Lake City, throughout the Mormon cultural region, and beyond. Salt Lake City and Wasatch Front articles that mention pre-1970 Church buildings and the people associated with them have been clipped out and indexed for the Journal History. Although the Church's building campaigns are not necessarily a major focus of recent compilers, accounts of Church buildings are still included in the Journal History. As of this writing, the Journal History is maintained current through the five years preceding the current date.

In the Historical Department, the Journal History can be accessed by the original subject index cards and by a microfilmed copy of the index cards. The Journal History can be viewed only by microfilm copy. At BYU and the Family History Library (Salt Lake City), the Journal History can be accessed through microfilm copies of both the index and volumes.

In addition to the Journal History, the library also has a large collection of published biographical materials. This collection includes the valuable Obituary File, produced by the Church Historian's Office, which is an indexed collection of Salt Lake City and Wasatch Front newspaper clippings reporting Church members' obituaries (1850–1970).

The Open and Reserve Stacks. The stacks at the Historical Department contain an eclectic collection of published works. Many of these works focus on the Mormon experience. The collection also represents the evolving interests of Church leaders and employees over the library's near one hundred and fifty years of existence. The library's primary purpose is to provide a reference service to the General Authorities of the Church. To a limited degree, the library's holdings reflect this fundamental purpose. Architecture per se has not been an area of interest for Church leaders and bureaucrats, while the worlds of the Old Testament, the primitive Christian Church, and pre-Columbian America have. The sources for these topics, however, have often included discussions on architecture. Mormon leaders and policy makers (or their architects) have studied these sources, have been inspired by them, and have in some cases imitated the architecture described therein.

The library's architectural holdings seldom bare a banner announcing "architectural information here." Here is another example. The rapidly diversifying economy (from agrarian to a mixed economy) of early twentieth-century Utah prompted Church leaders to explore ways of aiding young Mormon men to prepare for new career opportunities. Taking a popular progressive step into social assistance, the Church's General Board of the Young Men's Mutual Improvement Association (YMMIA) created the Vocational Guidance Committee. In 1917 this committee published Claude Richards's *The Man of Tomorrow.* Although applicable to any reader, this book was intended for Church youth and their leaders. Careers in the building industry were prominently profiled, including the building trades and the professions of architecture and engineering. Richards's book offers numerous insights relating to architecture, building, and the changing twentieth-century Mormon society.

As with the Church in general, employees in the Historian's Office (later the Historical Department) believed that Mormon settlements were always progressing, always offering evidence of the Church's inspired mission. Therefore the settlements needed to be measured and documented. A major part of the settlement's progress included the Mormon's ever-changing building stock, land improvements, industry, and material culture. Much of this Historian's Office collection, can be found in geopolitical (city, county, state) and ecclesiastical (ward, stake, and mission) histories located in the library's open and reserve stacks.

Reorganized Church of Jesus Christ of Latter Day Saints (Independence, Missouri)

The RLDS Church's Presiding Bishopric Office (PBO) maintains all past and current property records, including titles and other financial and legal records. These files are not accessible to the general public, although specific records can be accessed through the Legal Department of the RLDS Church. The RLDS archives has not actively collected architectural materials. Instead, much of the information that would be of interest to researchers of RLDS architecture is held by individual congregations. The Restoration Trails Foundation (RTF) of the RLDS Church is responsible for various historic sites, including the Kirtland Temple and various buildings in Nauvoo, and all the historic properties owned by the RLDS Church. The records of the RTF are not currently available to the public.

University of Utah (Salt Lake City)

Over the last fifteen years, the Special Collections Department at the U of U's Marriott Library has aggressively collected architectural materials documenting Salt Lake City, the Mormon cultural region, Utah, and the interior western states. Most of the materials date after the 1880s; they represent some of the state's most significant architectural collections.

In 1990, the Manuscript Division of the Special Collections Department published the *Guide to the Architectural Collections at the U of U Marriott Library Manuscripts Division.* This small guide created by former archivist, Elizabeth Perkes, describes the University's major architectural collections and includes a Salt Lake City alphabetic address index, an architect index, and a building/owner's name index. This guide is available in every major Utah library. The following describes several of the U of U's architectural collections; Perkes's guide should be consulted for a more detailed listing.

One of the valuable collections is the William Allen (1849–1928) papers, which document the career of William Allen, a cabinet maker, builder, and eventual builder-architect. Allen influenced much of the late nineteenth-century architectural design of Utah's Davis County (directly north of Salt Lake City).

Another important collection is a select group of papers and drawings of Lorenzo S. "Bing" Young (1894–1978), grandson of Brigham Young. Bing Young studied and graduated from the Pratt Institute in Brooklyn, New York, and later studied at Columbia University and the University of Pennsylvania. Young worked for the Church Architectural Department, Young & Hansen (Salt Lake City). He also worked as a partner with Edward O. Anderson and later Arnold Ehlers, both of whom became supervising architects for the Church.

The select drawings and papers of Georgius Y. Cannon (1892–1987) are likewise valuable. Cannon, as mentioned previously, was the grandson of Brigham Young and the son of Apostle and First Presidency counselor George Q. Cannon. Cannon was a 1918 graduate of the Massachusetts Institute of Technology's (MIT) architectural program and practiced mainly in California.

The Taylor Woolley (1884–1965) Collection includes architectural drawings by Woolley, his Salt Lake City partners Miles E. Miller and Clifford Evans, American architectural icon Frank Lloyd Wright (1869–1957), and contemporaries. After working for the Salt Lake City firm of Ware & Treganza, Woolley traveled to Chicago, where he secured employment with Wright and thereafter other Chicago architects. Woolley traveled to Italy in 1909 as did Wright's son Lloyd Wright, to make the final preparation of Wright's Wasmuth Portfolio (*Ausgefuhrte bauten und entwurfe von Frank Lloyd Wright*). This publication introduced Wright's work to Europe and inspired a modern movement that aspired to take in Wright's principles of *architettura organica.* In the 1986 reproduction of the Wasmuth folio, Vincent Scully described it as one of the three most influential architectural treatises of the twentieth century.[55] After working on the Wasmuth folio, Taylor Woolley eventually returned to Utah, where he practiced architecture and raised a family. Woolley's son Nathan also practiced architecture in Utah and in New Jersey; some of his papers and architectural materials are also included in this collection. The senior Woolley's collection is only available on microfilm.

The R. Lloyd Snedaker (b. 1905) Collection includes Snedaker's student work for the U of U (undergraduate studies, 1923–25), University of Michigan (architectural engineering, 1925–28), and Harvard University (masters of architecture, 1928–31). In addition, the collection contains the professional papers of this most qualified and skillful Mormon architect. The collection includes a near-complete corpus of pedagogical materials (graphic and otherwise) that exemplify the final glory of beaux-art architectural education in America. Snedaker's professional work reflects the manner of beaux-art training and the early-twentieth-century modernist vocabulary.

The Montmorency, Hayes, and Talbot Collection is the largest in Special Collections and represents over seventy years of architectural practice in Salt Lake City beginning with the predecessor arm of Ashton and Evans in the 1920s. Commissions are throughout Utah and treat nearly every possible building type.

Other valuable collections in the library include selected drawings and papers of various Utah architects. Those architects are Richard K. A. Kletting, Richard Calvin Watkins, A. Frederic Hale, Lewis T. Cannon, John B. Fetzer, Dan A. Weggeland, Miles Miller, Frank Winder Moore, Francis D. Rutherford, Alberto O. Treganza, Clifford Percy Evans, Slack W. Winburn, and many others.

During the late 1980s, in a joint effort between the Church Archives and the U of U, two large Utah architectural collections were jointly acquired and preserved. Records of buildings built by the Church were placed in the Church Archives; most of the other material—representing the vast majority of all materials required—was placed in the University's Special Collections Department. Normally, dividing manuscript collections between institutions is against professional archival principles. The Church's restricted collection policy, however, made such an arrangement necessary. The joint collection of the Church Archives and the U of U collection includes the Don Carlos Young Jr. Collection and the Richard W. Young Collection. Combined, these two collections represent Mormon architecture from the 1870s to the middle of the twentieth century; they include the papers and drawings of Joseph Don Carlos Young (LDS Church Architect, 1887–93; Supervising Architect, 1923–ca. 1933), Don Carlos Young (1882–1960), George Cannon Young (1891–1981), and a half-dozen other noted Mormon architects and firms. Fortunately, both halves of these collections are located in the same city and the two institutions have cataloged the collections in such a way as to make cross referencing possible. The two institutions have also correlated conservation measures. From 1988 to 1993, the Marriott Library's conservation laboratory has established a state-of-the-art preservation and conservation treatment approach for both collections.

As mentioned previously, the Special Collections Department has copies of most, if not all, papers relating to Utah and Mormon architecture produced by university students of architectural historians Peter Goss and Thomas Carter. These papers span from the beginning of Utah-Mormon history to the middle of the twentieth century.

The Special Collections Department also has a selected collection of Historic American Building Survey (HABS) drawings of Utah and Mormon structures and a Utah fire insurance map collection produced by the Sanborn Perris Map Company. The map collection was transferred to the university from the Library of Congress. This collection contains detailed, large scale, plat-like maps of Utah's cities (population of three thousand or more) dating from the mid-1880s to the late 1930s.[56] In the preface of *Fire Insurance Maps in the Library of Congress* (1981), the library describes the original intent and the type of information offered on these maps.

> The maps were designed to assist fire insurance agents in determining the degree of hazard associated with a particular property and therefore show the size, shape, and construction of dwellings, commercial buildings, and factories as well as fire walls, locations of windows and doors, sprinkler systems, and types of roofs. The maps also indicate widths and names of streets, property boundaries, building use, and house and block numbers. They show the locations of water mains, giving their dimensions, and of fire alarm boxes and hydrants. Sanborn maps are thus an unrivaled source of information about the structure and use of buildings in American cities. (xiii)

Besides the U of U's collection, the Utah State Historical Society also has a select group of original insurance maps. And as may be expected, the Library of Congress has the most complete run of Utah insurance maps.[57] The U of U also has a very impressive photographic archive, including the collections of numerous Mormon architects, Utah photographers who served the architectural community, and many private collections that document the Mormon cultural region. This photographic collection has no guide.

Utah State Historical Society (Salt Lake City)

The Utah State Historical Society (USHS) is located in the restored Rio Grande Railroad Station in Salt Lake City. Like the LDS Church Archives and the U of U Special Collections, USHS actively collects Mormon architectural materials. Unlike the other two repositories, however, USHS also creates architectural records by way of historic preservation surveys, reports, and nominations to the National Register of Historic Places. The Preservation Offices of the USHS contain over twenty years of architectural documentation for every county and nearly every community in Utah. The files are available to the public. Arranged geopolitically, material is categorized first by county, then community or city, and finally by street address. The files also contain a duplicate file of each Utah nomination to the National Register of Historic Places.

The Utah Architect File (1847–1940) is one of USHS's important collections. The file, which was initiated in the early 1970s by Allen Roberts, describes hundreds of architects who practiced in Utah. The materials frequently include building lists, bibliography, photocopies of published and unpublished materials, and numerous other bits of professional or biographical information.

The USHS library's published holdings on Utah architecture are respectable and—unlike the holdings of large university libraries—are relatively easy to access through the card catalog and by browsing. The library has a complete microfilm set of the Sanborn Perris Insurance Company's maps of Utah (ca. 1880s–1950s). Unfortunately, the microfilm copy is in black and white, which prevents the user from reading the color coding that describes building materials.

The USHS Library has a half-dozen major Utah-Mormon architectural drawing collections. These collections represent the work of building designers and organizations that influenced Salt Lake City and other Mormon communities. One of those collections contains the architectural drawings and scrapbooks of Denver and Salt Lake City architect Walter E. Ware (1861–1951). Ware, who was not a Mormon, and his partner Alberto O. Treganza designed for a number of prominent Mormons and for the LDS Church. The firm designed, for example, Salt Lake City's Seventeenth Ward chapel; a Manti, Utah, ward meetinghouse; the 1908 home of eventual Church Architectural Department Director Colonel Willard Young (a son of Brigham Young, Army West Point Academy graduate, and nationally recognized engineer); and the Maeser Memorial Building on the upper campus of BYU (ca. 1908–11). A register for the Ware Collection can be found in the library and under the heading "Walter E. Ware" in the Preservation Office's Utah Architects file. Ware materials can also be found at the U of U (sixty-six folders, including many ink-on-linen drawings) and the University Archives of BYU (in the Maeser memorial building's time capsule materials).

The Howell Q. Cannon Collection (ca. 1900–1950), which contains selected files of the Salt Lake City (and Mormon) firms of Cannon & Fetzer, Cannon & Mullen and all preceding and succeeding offices and firms, is another valuable collection. Cannon was the son of Mormon architect Lewis T. Cannon. The Church-related files and drawings from this collection are housed in the Church Archives.

Other collections worthy of note include a collection based on style; the Frederic A. Hales (a noted non-Mormon Salt Lake City architect) architectural drawing collection; and the Georgius Y. Cannon

Collection, a previously mentioned California architect and son of nineteenth-century Church leader George Q. Cannon. Another important collection is the Salt Lake City Engineer Collection (1900–1925), which contains important materials developed by a city agency. Materials from this agency can also be found at the U of U Special Collections Department.

Major photograph collections that document Utah and Mormon architecture include: the Photograph Reference Collection (ca. 1860s–1960s), the Shipler Commercial Photograph Collection (1890–1980), the Richard Kletting Collection, and the Hal Rumel Collection. The Photograph Reference Collection—the most accessible photograph collection in Utah—contains hundreds of donated collections organized and divided by subject. Scores of Utah communities are documented here. The massive Shipler Collection encompasses the professional work of three generations of photographers in Salt Lake City. During the 1890s and the early decades of the twentieth century, Shipler was a favorite commercial photography company. Hence, the collection includes commissioned photographs of numerous Salt Lake City buildings shortly after construction. Unfortunately, this collection is not yet fully processed and cataloged, no complete description or index exists, and access is limited. The Richard Kletting Collection was originally extracted from the architectural drawings collection of noted Salt Lake City architect Richard Kletting. These photographs, which document much of Kletting's executed designs, were integrated into the library's large photographic reference collection more than twenty years ago. Sadly, most of the original Kletting drawings were stolen from the society.

Utah State Archives (Salt Lake City)

The Utah State Archives collects all state agency records and any local records where no local government records program exists. This repository holds a number of territory-turned-state and municipal records series rich in architectural and building information. These records include tax assessment documents, tax ledgers, and deeds for Salt Lake City and later Salt Lake County from the 1850s to the mid-1970s; Salt Lake City building permit records from the 1890s to the 1950s; and minutes from the Salt Lake City Council's meetings in the nineteenth century.

Different search approaches must be taken for the foregoing records. The tax and property records, for example, can only be accessed through a chronological search. The same is true for the City Council Minutes. The Salt Lake City building permits, on the other hand, can be accessed through a master address index. Records from other Utah counties and municipalities are also housed here. Researchers should consult with the Archives Research Room staff to make specific inquiries.

Territorial and state building activity (buildings, roads, and land management construction) can be studied initially through state agencies' annual reports. Many of these early reports offer a surprising amount of textural description about state-sponsored construction activities. With each successive year, however, the reports offer less textural description and more statistical information, making individual project research a more complex task. Two of the agencies that researchers should consider are the Division of Facility Construction and Management and the Department of Transportation (UDOT). The archives has some administration histories for these agencies and their predecessor agencies. By consulting these histories, researchers may be able to determine what record group to search.

Utah State University (Logan, Utah), Merrill Library, Special Collections and Archives

Since the mid-1970s, USU has been one of the most active collecting institutions on the Wasatch Front and has maintained one of the most accessible collections about the Mormon experience. USU holds many materials dealing with Mormon architecture from central Utah to southern Idaho. The Photograph Reference Collection contains thousands of indexed photographs, many of which document the built environment and material culture from the 1860s to the mid-twentieth century. This artificially assembled collection can be accessed by geographical names, general subjects, and in many cases by specific building names. USU has also maintained the Cache County Tax Assessor's files, which include photographs of all taxed real properties in the county from 1934 to 1970.

The Compton photograph collection was produced by three generations (Alma W., Matthew, and Glen Compton) of photographers from Brigham City, Utah. It includes thousands of photographs of townscapes, special events, and gatherings that document Mormon architecture of Northern Utah, mainly in Box Elder County, from 1890 to 1965. Curiously, USU holds the entire Compton Studio negative collection (glass plate and nitrate), while U of U Special Collections holds the Compton original print collection.

The Heber Thomas photograph collection—so far as the library staff has been able to ascertain—contains mainly portraiture, with some views of Ogden architecture from the 1910s and 1920s. In addition to these two USU holdings, BYU has an original Heber Thomas collection, which includes Ogden views prior to the turn of the century.

USU has the extant architectural drawings of the university (formerly Utah Agricultural College) from 1890 to the present. USU also holds the drawings for the Church-owned Brigham Young College of Logan (ca. 1883–1926), including the designs of architects Joseph Don Carlos Young and Richard Kletting. Perhaps USU's largest and most historically rich collection is the Smith Brothers' Lumber Company (Logan) Collection, which contains material from 1890 to approximately 1970. This massive collection includes over two hundred drawings and blueprints—principally of Logan buildings—produced for lumber company clients. This collection includes, so far as can be determined, the only known library of building trade catalogs (building construction and artisan industry mail-order catalogs) used by late nineteenth- and early twentieth-century Utah and Mormon builders. In addition, the collection includes the lumber company's complete business archive.

As to documenting early-twentieth-century Utah, USU holds the Fred S. Hodgson architectural drawing collection (ca. 1917–30). This collection contains drawings of Ogden City residences and commercial and public buildings.

USU holds hundreds of linear feet of agriculture-related publications dating back to the 1890s and earlier. These publications include treatises on farm technology, building and planning; riparian management and engineering; and site and road engineering. The Merrill Library also has almost every extension service bulletin produced by the college and experiment stations. These bulletins are individually cataloged with the subject indexes. By studying the catalog and consulting with staff, researchers can find dozens of different agrarian building designs offered free-of-charge to Utah's agrarian industry from the late 1880s to the present. The library's Special Collections department has a number of small "working men's and farmer's" libraries that contain mechanics' and builders' manuals intended for self-education and practical application.

Archives and Manuscripts, Brigham Young University (Provo, Utah)

BYU, although indisputably rich in Mormon manuscripts, has not actively collected architectural records. Nevertheless, the BYU Photoarchives contains many collections relating to architecture and the Mormon built environment. Collections of interest include photographs of Kirtland, Ohio (part of the Kirtland, Ohio Collection) and Nauvoo, Illinois (in the Ida Blum Collection). BYU's most noted photograph collection, the George Edward Anderson Collection, includes hundreds of human landscape photographs that Anderson took from about 1880 to approximately 1925. Besides taking thousands of views documenting Mormon country and its people from southern Idaho to southern Utah, Anderson also composed some of the most historically and artistically rich images ever taken of Mormon landscapes and sites. When he was called to England to serve a proselyting mission, for example, Anderson delayed his oceanic voyage for over a year to satisfy his personal historical and artistic "mission" to photograph the abandoned Mormon sites and landscapes of New England and the Midwest.

The Huntington-Bagley Collection (ca. 1905–36) represents the work of deaf female photographer Effie Huntington (1868–1949). The collection, which is unprocessed, contains various views of central Utah. These views include the human landscape, the built environment, and some candid snapshots of turn-of-the-century residential interiors. The Charles Ellis Johnson Collection (ca. late 1880s–1917) includes views of Salt Lake Valley that offer evidence of rapid changes before and after the turn of the century. Johnson (1857–1926) was at one time the best-known and patronized photographer in Salt Lake City. The Heber Thomas Collection (ca. 1900) also includes views of architecture. The James E. Talmage photograph collection contains, among Talmage's personal and scientific photographs, the 1911 Savage & Company photographs of the Salt Lake Temple's interior (Ralph Savage, son of Charles R. Savage, had a studio in Salt Lake City). These photographs were taken specifically for inclusion in Talmage's book *The House of the Lord* (1912; reprint, Salt Lake City: Bookcraft, 1962). Many of these views have been recently republished in *The Salt Lake Temple: A Monument to a People* (Salt Lake City: University Services Corp., 1983). These interior photographs are generally restricted.

In addition to the foregoing, the archives collections include the work of many other fine nineteenth- and early twentieth-century photographers. Unfortunately, this remarkably rich archive is under-cataloged, relatively inaccessible, and consequently under-used. Aside from some card indexing (based on geographical locations and limited subjects) and some selective general collection descriptions in the university's catalog system and RLIN, the BYU Photoarchives has little to offer in finding aids. The archives does contain photocopy indexes (photocopies of the actual photographs); these yield much but are time consuming. The university's corporate photographic archives maintains the historical photography of the school's architecture (1875 to the present). BYU's Physical Facilities Division has retained control of the architectural records of the University. The University Archives does house photographs documenting the construction of many BYU buildings.

Weber State University (Ogden, Utah)

The Weber State Special Collections has two architectural drawing collections that selectively document twentieth-century Ogden. They are the Thomas J. Moore/Carolyn R. Nebeker Collection and the Lawrence Olpin Collection. The first collection documents architect-designed residences and commercial buildings architecture (ca. 1910–20). The other collection chiefly contains institutional designs of the 1960s (including Weber State University). Both collections include LDS chapels in the Ogden area from the 1910s and 1960s, respectively. With the exception of one box of manuscript material, the Moore/Nebeker collection is comprised of the architectural drawings of Ogden architect Leslie S. Hodgson. This repository also has numerous photographic collections that document Ogden architecture from 1890 and thereafter.

Daughters of Utah Pioneers (Salt Lake City)

The Daughters of Utah Pioneers has collected and published hundreds of Utah- and Mormon-related documents for the DUP's unified lesson program. This program, introduced in 1930, is produced for use by a network of local chapters or camps. The lessons are distributed as pamphlets and several series of books that abound in stories of community settlement, building, industry, and material culture. They also include numerous journal entries, personal recollections of Utah-Mormon building designers and construction tradesmen, and personal home builders' descriptions of the building process. Here are the series, each of which has been indexed: Kate B. Carter, comp., *Our Pioneer Heritage,* 20 vols. (Salt Lake City: Daughters of Utah Pioneers, 1958–77); Kate B. Carter, comp. *Heart Throbs of the West,* 12 vols. (Salt Lake City: Daughters of Utah Pioneers, 1939–51); Kate B. Carter, comp., *Treasures of Pioneer History,* 6 vols. (Salt Lake City: Daughters of Utah Pioneers, 1952–57); The Lesson Committee, comp., *An Enduring Legacy,* 12 vols. (Salt Lake City: Daughters of Utah Pioneers, 1977–89); and The Lesson Committee, comp., *Chronicles of Courage,* 4 vols. (Salt Lake City: Daughters of Utah Pioneers, 1990–93, ongoing series).

The following are some examples of articles from the above publications and another document that relate to Mormon architecture and the built environment: "Pioneer Homes and Houses," in *Heart Throbs of the West* 3:37–72; "Pioneer Houses and Enclosures," in *Our Pioneer Heritage* 1:117–87; "Old Homes and Buildings," in *An Enduring Legacy* 2:217–64; and Kate B. Carter, comp. and ed., *The Mormon Village* (Salt Lake City: Daughters of Utah Pioneers, 1954), which is also found in *Treasures of Pioneer History* 4:133–88. For the centennial year (1947) commemorating the Mormon pioneers' 1847 arrival in Utah, the Daughters of Utah Pioneers prepared county histories throughout Utah. Nearly all of these publications include a wealth of information about Mormon architecture, building, and land planning. One example is Alice Paxman McCune, *History of Juab County: A History Prepared for the Centennial of the Coming of the Pioneers to Utah, 1847–1947* (Springville, Utah: Art City Publishing, 1947).

Over the last decade, the LDS Church Archives has worked closely with the Daughters of Utah Pioneers museum (Salt Lake City) staff to microfilm hundreds of Mormon and early Utah manuscripts. A copy of this microfilm and an inventory of its contents are available at the Church Archives. In addition to the microfilm, the museum has a collection of building- and architectural-related artifacts. The many Daughters of Utah Pioneers Museums across Utah also hold a surprising amount of building-related documents and artifacts. Unfortunately, no organization-wide registry of holdings for these small repositories exists.[58]

National and Regional Research Libraries and Archives

Researchers in Mormon architecture will likely not find large quantities of materials specifically relating to Mormonism in the major architectural libraries and archives mentioned below. Nevertheless, information about national and regional contexts abounds. Examples of sources include architectural and building documentation of non-Mormon nineteenth-century American religious groups and institutions; the papers of architects, pedagogues, taste-makers and others that may have influenced Mormon architecture indirectly; regional sources, such as building traditions of New England and the Mid-Atlantic states conveyed by Mormon converts; ethnographic materials, such as design works of nineteenth-century German emigrant architects and Scandinavian builders; and works that represent overlapping social and aesthetic milieus.

Until recently, collecting policies of many libraries and archives have focused on the unique, the nationally or regionally well-known, and trend-setting architecture and architects. These policies are slowly changing, and many repositories now cast their acquisition nets farther out to gather documentation of more common American landscapes.

Several architectural research libraries hold regionally significant collections that will not be mentioned here. Many of these research libraries and archives have ties with schools of architecture and other allied disciplines.

New York City. The Avery Architectural and Fine Arts Library, Columbia University, New York City (Broadway & 116th St., 10027) is the most well-known and respected architectural repository in the United States. The architectural library is the most accessible and possibly the largest in the world. The Avery has three publications of broad national interest. The first is the *Catalog of the Avery Memorial Architectural Library, Columbia University,* 2d ed. (Boston: G. K. Hall, 1968). This catalog contains descriptions of the Avery's collections; it is a multivolume catalog with five supplements, the fifth of which was published in 1982. After 1982, all bibliographic descriptions of library holdings were entered on RLIN, a database that can be accessed at numerous university and research libraries across the United States. The second Avery publication is the *Avery Index to Architectural Periodicals,* 2d ed. (Boston: G. K. Hall, 1973), which has been successively updated to the present. This multivolume work gives full bibliographic information on architecture-related articles and includes brief abstracts. The index is also available with day-to-day updates through the RLIN computer database. In addition, the index is available through the commercial database *Dialogue* (updated every six to twelve months) and will soon be available on CD ROM. The third Avery publication is the *Avery Obituary Index of Architects,* 2d ed. (Boston: G. K. Hall, 1980). The index contains obituary information about American and international architects before 1978; obituaries after 1978 have been placed on RLIN. In addition to Avery, another New York City repository holding materials of national significance is the Cooper-Hewitt Museum, National Museum of Design (2 East 91st St., New York, N.Y., 10128), which is a bureau of the Smithsonian Institution.

Washington, D.C. Various divisions in the Library of Congress (Washington, D.C., 20540) include architectural records and related materials from across the United States. The largest collection of photographs relating to American architecture is contained in the Prints and Photographs Division. This division also has architectural drawing collections of national significance, including the HABS and HAER collections. The Smithsonian Institute's Archives of American Art and the National Anthropological Archives in the Museum of Nature History also have architectural records. Primary source materials are described on the RLIN database as well as a Smithsonian database system.

The library of the American Institute of Architects (1735 New York Ave., N.W., 20006) has both a library and archives. The focus of the library collection is professional architectural practice. The manuscript collection contains professional papers of noted American architects (including drawings and photographs). The AIA library has just recently produced the on-line computer database system *Vitruvius, AIA On-Line,* which includes bibliographic information on the library's holdings. Manuscript collections will be included in that system sometime in the future.

New England Region. The American Antiquarian Society (185 Salisbury St., Worcester, Mass., 01609) and the Society for the Preservation of New England Antiquities Library (141 Cambridge St., Boston, Mass., 02114) contain important architectural materials. The collections of the former are described in two publications: *The Collections and Programs of the American Antiquarian Society: A 175th Anniversary Guide* (1987) and the recently updated version titled *Under Its Generous Dome: The Programs and Collections of the American Antiquarian Society* (1992). AAS's books and series are also described in RLIN.

Mid-Atlantic Region. The Athenaeum of Philadelphia (219 So., 6th St., 19106), has both an architectural library and archives collection. The library's focus is American architecture and building technology, while the archives focuses on architecture in the Delaware Valley and the Mid-Atlantic region. The library's holdings are cataloged on the Library of Congress's book cataloging system, *OCLC,* and will eventually also be included on RLIN. The architectural drawings are described in the *Catalog of Architectural Drawings, the Athenaeum of Philadelphia* (Boston: G. K. Hall, 1986), compiled by Bruce Laverty, curator.

The Henry Francis de Pont Winterthur Museum (Winterthur, Delaware, 19735) has both a library and manuscript department that would be of interest to a student of American architecture and decorative arts. The Winterthur's Library collection of trade catalogs, much of them supporting the building industry, are described in *Trade Catalogs at Winterthur* (1984) and *Trade Catalogs at the Winterthur Museum* (1989). All of the catalogs described in these two publications are available on microfiche. Winterthur also has a collection of architectural treatises that were not included in Hitchcock's *American Architectural Books;* these center around construction and building practices more than architectural design. The Winterthur Manuscripts Division actively collects late eighteenth- to twentieth-century architectural drawing collections, many of them described on RLIN.

Canada. The Canadien Centre d'Architecture (1920 Baile St., Montreal, Quebec H3H2S6), which was formally established in 1979, is quickly becoming one of the most significant architectural repositories in the world. The Centre's collection parameters are global; the focus, however, is the western architectural tradition and all influences that have converged with it. In 1989, the Centre moved into a custom-designed facility that houses four major collection areas. These collections are: (1) the library, which includes treatises addressing and chronologically spanning much of the western architectural tradition; (2) the Photograph Collection, which includes the photographic works of the noted and obscure, documenting architecture from 1840 to the present; (3) prints and drawings, including engravings, sketches, lithographs, and freehand sketches; and (4) the Archival Collection, which includes professional papers, office files, and manuscripts of architects and designers primarily from North America.

The Centre's published works have been described in RLIN, and many of the archival (or nonpublished) materials have also been described there. The archival materials, however, have only been described at an acquisition level, which means that only a minimal amount of information has been included. On-line catalog access is forthcoming, but all inquiries regarding nonpublished materials should be addressed directly to the institution.

Midwestern Region. The Ryerson and Burnham Libraries of Art and Architecture, Art Institute of Chicago (111 South Michigan Ave., Chicago, Ill. 60603), contain works about Chicago and the Midwest. Bibliographic information on published materials can be found in the RLIN database. Bibliographic information on archival collections, at the present time, can only be searched in-house.[59] The Northwest Architectural Archives and the Architectural Library at the University of Minneapolis (826 Berry St., St. Paul, Minn. 55114) collects architectural materials relating to Minnesota and surrounding states. The Archives is preparing a collection guide to be published in the near future.

California. The Getty Center for the History of Art and the Humanities (401 Wilshire Blvd., Suite 700, Santa Monica, Calif. 90401) does not actively collect original American architectural records. Getty has chosen not to compete with other institutions that collect in this area. Instead, Getty's focus is broad, concentrating on the art and architecture of the Western European tradition. All of Getty's architectural materials are cataloged and described on RLIN. In addition to Getty, other California architectural libraries and archives include the Library of Environmental Design at the University of California at Berkeley and the library of the University of California at Santa Barbara.

Organizations. At the present time, no organization is chartered to encourage the preservation and specific study of Mormon architecture. Two national organizations do exist, however, that aid in the preservation and promotion of architectural and landscape records. These two organizations are COPAR (Cooperative Preservation of Architectural Records), which is located in the Prints and Photographs Division of the Library of Congress (Washington, D.C.), and Wave Hill (675 West 252nd St., Bronx, New York, 19476), which holds a catalog of landscape records. Utah has an organization called Utah COPAR (Cooperative Organization for the Preservation of Architectural Records, a slightly different use of the COPAR acronym), which is an inter-institutional organization established in 1985 to seek out, identify, and encourage the preservation of Utah's historical architectural drawings and records. Utah COPAR is based in the U of U's Special Collections Department.

Project of Interest Relating to Mormon Architecture

In 1992, the U of U Graduate School of Architecture, Utah's Foundation for Architecture and the Built Environment (UFABE), the Utah Society of the American Institute of Architects (Utah AIA), Utah COPAR, and the Utah State Historical Society joined forces to seek funding and produce a reference work entitled *The Bibliographical Dictionary of Utah Architects and Building Designers, 1847-1947,* with Brad Westwood as project director. Initiated in 1987 by now-deceased Salt Lake City architect Lloyd Snedaker, with the assistance of Peter Goss, the dictionary project has been partially funded by the supporting organizations; additional federal and private funding is now being sought. The purpose of the dictionary is to encourage further research into Utah's diverse architectural past and to create a comprehensive work of essential biographical information about Utah's architects and building designers from 1847 (when Utah was first inhabited by Mormon settlers) to 1947, the year that Utah reached its centennial year of settlement.

Brad Westwood lives in Provo, Utah, with his wife Virlie Vincent Westwood and their two sons, Ryan and Isaac. He is a graduate of BYU in American Studies (B.A., 1985) and the University of Pennsylvania in Historic Preservation (M.S., 1994). He is an archivist at the LDS Historical Department. When writing this essay Brad was working as a private consultant in historic preservation and archival administration. He has also been employed by the Architectural Archive of the University of Pennsylvania, the Athenaeum of Philadelphia (a regional research center for architectural history and the decorative arts) and for the LDS Historical Department as an archivist of architectural and photographic materials.

NOTES

[1]Quoted by Bruce Thomas, Review of *War Memorials as Political Landscape* by James M. Mayo (Praeger, 1988) and *America's Armories: Architecture, Society, and Public Order* by Robert M. Fogelson (Harvard University Press, 1989) in *Design Book Review* 21 (Summer 1991): 34.

[2]Richard Guy Wilson, "Popular Architecture," in *Handbook of American Popular Culture,* ed. M. Thomas Inge, 3 vols. (Westport, Connecticut: Greenwood Press, 1978-), 2:265.

[3]Another collection of articles worth mentioning but more to do with material culture than the built environment is Robert Blair St. George's *Material Life in America 1600-1860* (Boston: Northeastern University Press, 1988).

[4]Richard Ingersoll, "The Death of Architectural History" [Eulogy for Spiro Kostof], *Design Book Review* 23 (Winter 1992): 4.

[5]The book is divided into twelve chapters: (1) "The Beginning, 1820-1838"; (2) "In and Out of Nauvoo and to Salt Lake City, 1836-1846"; (3) "Settlements of the Valley of the Great Salt Lake, 1847-1859"; (4) "Growth and Expansion, 1860-1877"; (5) "Local Autonomy in Construction, 1878-1899"; (6) "Growth and Embellishment, 1900-1919"; (7) "The Church Furnishes Free Plans, 1920-1933"; (8) "Building to Match Programs, 1934-1950;" (9) "The World-Wide Program, 1951-1959"; (10) "The Building Missionary Program, 1960-1964"; (11) "Contract Construction, 1965-1972"; and (12) "World-Wide Expansion, 1973-1980."

[6]For a much more detailed description of the LDS Church's major building stock see "Temples and Churches," in *Utah Gazetteer and Directory of Logan, Ogden, Provo and Salt Lake Cities for 1884,* ed. and comp. Robert W. Sloan (Salt Lake City: Herald Printing and Publishing, 1884), 195-204.

[7]Of Hamlin's book, see pages 259, 269, 287, and 306-307 regarding Mormon examples of Greek Revival.

[8]Ohio State Preservation Officer W. Ray Luce's short piece "Building the Kingdom of God: Mormon Architecture before 1847," *BYU Studies* 30 (Spring 1990): 33-45, asks many essential questions and describes some subtle political and Church organizational conditions that are integral to understanding the period's architecture. Luce also offers an intriguing analysis of the parallelism between the interior architecture of the Kirtland and Nauvoo Temples and Joseph Smith's 1833 "City of Zion" plan.

[9]See also *Temples of The Church of Jesus Christ of Latter-day Saints* (Salt Lake City: Corporation of the President, LDS Church, ca. 1979) and the Deseret News's *Church Almanac* for basic information (locations, dates, architects, building materials, dimensions) on each Mormon temple. Not everything in the latter is perfectly accurate.

[10]See also *Utah Gazetteer and Directory.* Regarding the history of the primary internal functions of the temples, see James E. Talmage, *The House of the Lord* (Salt Lake City: Bookcraft, 1962); and David J. Buerger, "The Development of the Mormon Temple Endowment Ceremony," *Dialogue* 20 (Winter 1987): 33-76.

[11]See also, Launius, *An Illustrated History of the Kirtland Temple* (Independence, Mo.: Herald Publishing House, 1986); Clarence L. Fields, "History of the Kirtland Temple" (master's thesis, BYU, 1963); Thomas E. O'Donnell, "The First Mormon Temple at Kirtland, Ohio," *Architecture* 24 (August 1924): 265-69;

and Lauritz G. Petersen, "The Kirtland Temple," *BYU Studies* 12 (Summer 1972): 400-409.

[12]See also C. Mark Hamilton, "The Salt Lake Temple: An Architectural Monograph" (Ph.D. diss., University of Ohio, 1978); and Joseph Smith Jr., *The History of the Church of Jesus Christ of Latter-day Saints,* ed. B. H. Roberts, 2d ed. rev., 6 vols. (Salt Lake City: Deseret Book, 1973), 1:357-365. Regarding the Mormon doctrine that twelve temples will be constructed in Independence, see Julius C. Billeter, *The Temple of Promise, Jackson County, Missouri* (Independence, Mo.: Zion's Printing and Publishing Company, 1946); Roy W. Doxey, *Zion in the Last Days* (Salt Lake City: Olympus and Bookcraft, 1965), 61-69; and Gerald N. Lund, *The Coming of the Lord* (Salt Lake City: Bookcraft, 1971), index. Regarding the proposed Independence and Far West Temples, see N. B. Lundwall, *Temples of the Most High* (Salt Lake City: Bookcraft, 1956), 248-68.

[13]See also Richard O. Cowan, *Temple Building Ancient and Modern* (Provo, Utah: BYU Press, 1971); and Cowan, *Temples to Dot the Earth* (Salt Lake City: Bookcraft, 1989). See also Richard O. Cowan and Frank Alan Bruno, *Bibliography on Temples and Temple Work* (Provo, Utah: Religious Instruction, BYU, 1982).

[14]Other sources worth mentioning include: Wallace A. Raynor, "History of the Construction of the Salt Lake Temple" (master's thesis, BYU, 1961); Leonard J. Arrington and Melvin A. Larkin, "The Logan Tabernacle and Temple," *UHQ* 41 (Summer 1973): 301-14; and Melvin A. Larkin, "The History of the L.D.S. Temple in Logan, Utah" (master's thesis, USU, 1954). Building histories, such as this one, have been written for every nineteenth-century temple (sometimes two or three times over) and some twentieth-century temples.

[15]For an anthropological perspective and commentary, see also Mark P. Leone, "The New Mormon Temple in Washington, D.C.," *The Society for Historical Archeology,* Special Publication Series, no. 2 (1977), 43-61. Concerning the Washington Temple, see Keith W. Wilcox, *A Personal Testimony concerning the Washington Temple* (N.p., [1979]). Wilcox was one of four LDS architects asked by the Church to collaborate in designing this temple.

[16]I am indebted to RLDS Church archivist Ron Romig for this list of publications.

[17]See also Paul Goeldner, ed., *Utah Catalog: Historic American Building Survey* (Salt Lake City: Utah Heritage Foundation, 1969).

[18]See Paul L. Anderson, "Mormon Moderne: Latter-day Saint Architecture, 1925-1945," *Journal of Mormon History* 9 (1982): 71-84.

[19]See also Peter L. Goss, "Utah's Architectural Heritage: An Overview," *Utah Architect* no. 52 (1973).

[20]Under the auspices of the Utah Heritage Foundation, photographer Douglas Hill produced "Early Mormon Churches in Utah: A Photographic Essay," *Dialogue* 1 (Autumn 1966): 13-22. An original copy of Hill's work was placed in the LDS Church Archives.

[21]See also Nina Folsom, "History of William Harrison Folsom (1815-1901)," unpublished manuscript, n.d.

[22]Thomas Robert Carter, "Building Zion: Folk Architecture in the Mormon Settlements of Utah's Sanpete Valley, 1850-1890" (Ph.D. diss., Indiana University, 1984).

[23]For a selective and annotated bibliography in the broader American context, see William R. Gwin and Mary M. Gwin, *Semiology, Symbolism, and Architecture: A Selected and Partially Annotated Bibliography* (Monticello, Illinois: Vance Bibliographies, 1985).

[24]See also Allen H. Barber, *Celestial Symbols: Symbolism in Doctrine, Religious Traditions and Temple Architecture* (Bountiful, Utah: Horizon Publication and Distributors, 1989).

[25]The final evaluation and report of the Newel K. Whitney Store by the same authors is forthcoming.

[26]See also Berge's "Archaeology at the Peter Whitmer Farm, Seneca County, New York," *BYU Studies* 13 (Winter 1973): 172; and "The Jonathan Browning Site: An Example of Archaeology for Restoration in Nauvoo, Illinois," *BYU Studies* 19 (Winter 1979): 201-29.

[27]See Charles Lanman, *A Summer in the Wilderness, Adventures in the Wilds of the United States and British American Provinces* (1856), vol. 1. Lanman's description is included in NRI's final archaeological report on the Nauvoo Temple. See Virginia S. Harrington and J. C. Harrington, *Rediscovery of the Nauvoo Temple, Report on Archaeological Excavations* (Salt Lake City: NRI, 1971), 5, 17, 25, and 28.

[28]Richard F. Burton, *The City of the Saints and across the Rocky Mountains to California* (New York: Harper and Brothers, 1862), 196-97. See also Richard F. Burton, *The City of the Saints and across the Rocky Mountains to California,* ed. Fawn M. Brodie (New York: Alfred A. Knopf, 1963); and William Mulder and A. Russell Mortensen, *Among the Mormons: Historic Accounts by Contemporary Observers* (New York: Alfred A. Knopf, 1958), 328-30.

[29]Mulder and Mortensen, *Among the Mormons,* 399.

[30]See Frank J. Roos, *Writings on Early American Architecture* (Columbus: Ohio State University, 1943), revised as *Bibliography of Early American Architecture: Writings on Architecture Constructed before 1860 in Eastern and Central United States* (Urbana: University of Illinois Press, 1968).

[31]Over the last decade, the author has surveyed the holdings of Utah's largest and oldest libraries (including the U of U's Marriott Library, BYU's Lee Library, USU's Merrill Library, and the LDS Historical Department) for nineteenth-century architectural and building sources. In these random expeditions, the author searched for inscriptions, signatures, book vendor notes, and marginalia that might suggest original ownership or sequence of ownership. This research demonstrated that a good number of these works were originally owned by identifiable Utah architects and builders. Unfortunately, library cataloging—with the exception of rare book cataloging—does not always include recording or cross-referencing a publication's provenance. Further systematic surveys of library holdings are needed to extract more accurate information regarding provenance of such works in Utah and in past and current Mormon locales.

[32]See Julie K. Ellison, comp., *American Architectural Books* (New Haven, Conn.: Research Publications, 1973), a microfilm edition based on the Henry-Russell Hitchcock bibliography of the same title and Helen Park's "A List of Architectural Books Available in America before the Revolution." There is an index to this microfilm collection.

[33]See Joan Draper, "The Ecole des Beaux-Arts and the Architectural Profession in the United States: The Case of John Galen Howard," in *The Architect:*

Chapters in the History of the Profession, ed. Spiro Kostof (New York: Oxford University Press, 1977), 215.

[34]Truman O. Angell, Journal (1854–56), 24, LDS Church Archives, Salt Lake City. Angell did not indicate which of Nicholson's books he was studying.

[35]Kate B. Carter, ed., *Our Pioneer Heritage,* 20 vols. (Salt Lake City: Daughters of Utah Pioneers, 1958–77), 10:201; and Paul L. Anderson, "Truman O. Angell: Architect and Saint," in *Supporting Saints: Life Stories of Nineteenth-Century Mormons,* ed. Donald Q. Cannon and David J. Whittaker (Provo, Utah: BYU, 1985), 147.

[36]Staines described this book as "ARCHITECT or practical house carpenter. A. Benjamin, Boston, 1850." The complete citation is *The Practical House Carpenter . . .* (Boston: Benjamin B. Mussey, 1850) as recorded in Henry-Russell Hitchcock, *American Architectural Books* (New York City: Da Capo Press, 1976), 12 (book no. 129). The 1976 edition of *American Architectural Books* is the latest edition of that monumental listing of architectural works in the United States. Regarding Benjamin as the author of the first American architectural book, see *American Architectural Books,* vii.

[37]Staines described the first title mentioned here as "ARCHITECTS, hints to young A. J. Downing. N.Y., 1847." The book was actually authored by A. J. Downing and George Wightwick. The full citation is: George Wightwick, *Hints to Young Architects Calculated to Facilitate Their Practical Operations . . . With Additional Notes and Hints to Persons about Building in this Country by A. J. Downing* (New York and London: Wiley and Putnam, 1847) as recorded in Henry-Russell Hitchcock, *American Architectural Books,* 116 (book no. 1404).

Staines described the second Downing title mentioned here as "COTTAGE residences, adapted to N. America 3d ed., A. J. Downing, New York, 1847." If Staines correctly recorded the publication information, this edition is indeed rare because as of 1976, no institution held a copy. Henry-Russell Hitchcock, *American Architectural Books,* 33 (book no. 357).

The full citation of the third Downing title is *The Architecture of Country Houses: Including Designs for Cottages, Farm Houses and Villas . . .* (New York: D. Appleton & Co.; Philadelphia: G. S. Appleton, 1850) as recorded in Henry-Russell Hitchcock, *American Architectural Books,* 31 (book no. 325).

[38]Staines recorded this title as "ARCHITECTURE modern, Beauties of M. Lafeore [*sic*] New York, 1849." The complete citation is: *The Beauties of Modern Architecture . . .* (New York: D. Appleton & Co., 1849) as recorded in Henry-Russell Hitchcock, *American Architectural Books,* 58 (book no. 690).

[39]Staines recorded this title as "ARCHITECT, original designs and landscape gardening 2 v., W. H. Ranlett. New York, 1849." The complete citation is: *The Architect, a Series of Original Designs for Domestic and Ornamental Villas, Connected with Landscape Gardening . . .* (New York: William H. Graham, 1847–1849) as recorded in Henry-Russell Hitchcock, *American Architectural Books,* 80 (book no. 971).

[40]See Mary Woods, "The First American Architectural Journals: The Profession's Voice," *The Journal of the Society of Architectural Historians* 48 (June 1989): 117–38; and Dell Upton, "Pattern Books and Professionalism: Aspects of the Transformation of Domestic Architecture in America, 1880–1860," *Winterthur Portfolio* 19 (Summer–Autumn 1984): 107–50.

[41]*Catalogue of the Utah Territorial Library,* 25–26.

[42]*The Country Gentleman: A Journal for the Farm, the Garden, and the Fireside* (December 27, 1860); *The American Agriculturist, Adapted to the Farm, Garden, and Household* (all issues for 1860); *The Cultivator: A Monthly Journal for the Farm and the Garden, Designed to Improve the Soil and the Mind* (all issues for 1862–63); and *Illustrated Annual Register of Rural Affairs* (all issues for 1860). See the Richard Wright Young Papers, Special Collections Department, Marriott Library, U of U, Salt Lake City, (hereafter cited as Special Collections, U of U).

[43]Ranlett, *The Architect,* title page.

[44]A photocopy of James Snyder's copy of William H. Ranlett's *The Architect,* vol. 1, is in the possession of the author. Snyder's original is in the possession of one of his descendants. Frank Esshom, *Pioneer and Prominent Men of Utah* (Salt Lake City: Utah Pioneer, 1913), 1174.

[45]Upon receiving his copy of Bicknell's publication, Dallas inscribed "Samuel Dallas, Salt Lake City, December 27 1879" on the title page. The book is available in the Locked Case, Art Reference, Marriott Library, U of U. The full citation is *Detail, Cottage, and Constructive Architecture Showing a Great Variety of Designs* . . . (New York: A. J. Bicknell, 1873) as recorded in Henry-Russell Hitchcock, *American Architectural Books,* 15 (book no. 164). In the early 1880s, Dallas formed a partnership with William S. Hedges, a former railroad engineer from Indiana who eventually married a daughter of LDS Church leader Daniel H. Wells. LDS Church Obituary File, "Death of W. S. Hedges, Well-Known Architect," *Deseret News,* February 25, 1914, 6.

[46]Eugene Emmanual Viollet-le-Duc, *Discourses on Architecture,* trans. Henry Van Brunt (Boston: James R. Osgood, 1875); M[illard] F[illmore] Hearn, *The Architectural Theory of Viollet-le-Duc* (Cambridge, Mass.: Massachusetts Institute of Technology, 1990), 2, 17; and Joseph Gwilt, *Encyclopedia of Architecture* (London: Longmans, Green, 1871). Burton's widow gave both the Van Brunt and Gwilt titles, which contain evidentiary inscriptions, to Joseph Don Carlos Young, another Mormon architect. See boxes 77 and 83 of the Richard Wright Young Papers, Special Collections, U of U. Burton designed the first wing of the Territorial Insane Asylum (1883–85, Provo) and was the second and principal architect of the University of Deseret building (1883–87, Salt Lake City).

An ambitious and well-connected young Mormon architect, Burton was senselessly gunned downed in the prime of life. The events surrounding Burton's death are described in Janet Burton Seegmiller, *"Be Kind to the Poor," the Life Story of Robert Taylor Burton* (Salt Lake City: privately published, 1988), 381–82. A brief discussion regarding Burton's major architectural commissions is included in P. Bradford Westwood, "The Early Life and Career of Joseph Don Carlos Young (1855–1938), Utah's First Academically Trained Architect (1855–1884)" (master's thesis, University of Pennsylvania, 1994).

[47]Mary Woods, "The First American Architectural Journals," 117–18.

[48]The earliest journals that I have been able to trace to a Mormon architect practicing in Utah were those subscribed to by Joseph Don Carlos Young (1855–1938). Clippings from the British *Architect* (London), *American Architect and Building News* (Boston), the *Inland Architect* (Chicago), and others dating from 1879 (AABN), are included in Young's papers. These can be found in two

manuscript collections: the Richard Wright Young Papers and the Don Carlos Young Papers, Special Collections, U of U.

[49]Original copies of *AABN* can be found in the Harold B. Lee Library (BYU) for the years 1881-82, 1886-90, 1891-95, 1900-1918, and 1933-38; copies of *The Inland Architect and News Record* for the years 1891-93 are available as well. The U of U holds the following: *AABN* from 1876-1908 (microfilm) and 1906-38 (originals), *The Western Architect and Building News* for 1910-17 (originals), and the *Inland Architect* from 1883-87 (microfilm) and 1887-1908 (originals). Researchers should consult the periodical divisions of these and other Utah libraries for various twentieth century architecture and engineering periodicals.

[50]Manly and Litteral, *Utah, Her Cities, Towns, and Resources* . . . (Chicago: Manly and Litteral, 1891), 170-73, emphasis added.

[51]Manly and Litteral, *Utah, Her Cities, Towns, and Resources,* 170-73.

[52]*What is Nauvoo Restoration Incorporated?* (Salt Lake City: Church of Jesus Christ of Latter-day Saints, 1970); this pamphlet is in the author's possession. See also Janath R. Cannon, *Nauvoo Panorama, Views of Nauvoo before, during, and after Its Rise, Fall and Restoration* (Nauvoo, Ill.: NRI, 1991).

[53]Lewis Telle Cannon, "Architecture of Church Buildings," *IE* 17 (June 1914): 793-801.

[54]The series I was able to study ran sporadically in *Deseret Evening News* from January 27, 1892, to April 9, 1892.

[55]Vincent Scully, foreword to *Studies and Executed Buildings by Frank Lloyd Wright,* by Frank Lloyd Wright (New York City: Rizzoli, 1986), 5.

[56]After cataloging the Sanborn Map Company Collection, the Library of Congress divided the surplus maps by state and offered them to a repository in each state. See *Fire Insurance Maps in the Library of Congress* (Washington, D.C.: Library of Congress, 1981), xiii.

[57]*Fire Insurance Maps in the Library of Congress,* ix, first column. A listing of extant insurance maps of Utah in the Library of Congress can be found in *Fire Insurance Maps,* 629-32. See also Riley M. Moffat, *Maps of Utah to 1900* (Santa Cruz, Calif.: Western Association of Map Libraries, 1981), 18-22.

[58]There has been a desperate need for an organization-wide registry and a collection control policy for these small repositories. With a declining membership base, many Daughters of Utah Pioneers museums have become understaffed or have closed, leaving many collections wanting for basic care.

[59]The Institute's ten-volume set, *Burnham Index to Architectural Literature, 1919-1934* (New York: Garland Publications, 1989), should also be consulted.

Wagons, Echo Canyon, ca. 1868. Courtesy LDS Church Archives.

Mormon Emigration Trails

Stanley B. Kimball

Introduction

We are in the midst of an American western trails renaissance. Interest in historic trails has never been higher. There is an annual, quarterly, almost monthly increase in the number of books, guides, bibliographies, articles, associations, societies, conferences, symposia, centers, museums, exhibits, maps, dramatic presentations, videos, festivals, field trips, trail-side markers and monuments, grave sites, trail signing, and other ventures devoted to our western trail heritage.[1]

In 1968, Congress passed the National Trails System Act and in 1978 added National Historic Trail designations. Since 1971 at least fifteen major federal studies of the Mormon Trail have been made.[2] So much is going on that at least half a dozen newsletters must be published to keep trail buffs properly informed. Almost every newsletter records the discovery of new trail ruts and artifacts—for example, the recent discovery of some ruts on the Woodbury Oxbow-Mormon Trail in Butler County, Nebraska, and new excavations regarding the Mormon occupation of Fort Bridger.

Hundreds of trail markers with text, many referring to the Mormons, line the western trails. These markers have been placed by many federal, state, county, municipal, and private associations, including the Bureau of Land Management; Daughters of the American Revolution; Daughters of Utah Pioneers (who alone have placed more than 465 historical markers); Sons of Utah Pioneers; Utah Pioneer Trails and Landmarks; the Boy Scouts; the Illinois, Iowa, Nebraska, Wyoming, Kansas, New Mexico, Arizona, California, and Utah state historical societies; and many county historical societies. Major sources for these trail markers appear in this essay's lists and bibliography. See, for example, the works of Lida L. Green, Aubrey L. Hains, Gregory Franzwa, Mary B. Gamble, Jane Mallison, Bruce J. Noble Jr., the Missouri Daughters of the American Revolution, and Stanley B. Kimball.

Some of the newer trail-related ventures are the Rails to Trails aficionados (tens of thousands of Mormons used rail to reach their wagon route) and the American Greenway movement. The latter association is developing "verdant corridors"—old trail routes carefully worked into greenways—in urban areas. These verdant corridors seek to restore in part, or at least to memory, the many miles of the trail heritage that have been obliterated by urban sprawl.

In addition to the 1993 commemoration of the Oregon Trail's sesquicentennial, several other anniversaries related to the Mormon trek will soon be celebrated. These include the sesquicentennial of Iowa statehood (1996); the centennial of Utah statehood (1996); and the sesquicentennial of the Mormon Trail (1996-97). These events will, no doubt, generate many items that will subsequently be archived and used by future researchers. See, for example, Oregon Trail Coordinating Council, *Sesquicentennial Report* (Portland, Ore.: Oregon Trail Coordinating Council, 1994).

Numerous "Mormon" trails exist. In addition to variants of *the* Mormon Trail (Nauvoo to Salt Lake City), Mormons used other trails, such as the Oregon, Santa Fe, Dragoon, Golden Road, Oxbow, Nebraska City Cutoff, Overland, and Trappers. [3] Notwithstanding that variety, this essay focuses on the Mormon Pioneer National Historic Trail, the 1846-47 route between Nauvoo, Illinois, and Salt Lake City, Utah. Because hundreds of miles of the Oregon, California, and Pony Express trails are nearly identical to the Mormon Trail, because many Mormons used the Oregon Trail, and because the Mormon Battalion walked the entire Santa Fe Trail, selected studies of those trails are also listed in the general sections of this essay. Other trails are addressed in a separate section.[4] As a final note, readers should understand that this essay makes a careful distinction between emigrant trails to Utah and colonizing trails originating in Utah—the latter are excluded. Also excluded are exploration, military, and transit trails in and across Utah.[5]

Archives, Libraries, and Historical Societies

The most important archival collections concerning Mormon trails are held by the Historical Department of The Church of Jesus Christ of Latter-day Saints ("LDS Church"); Brigham Young University; the Utah State Historical Society; the University of Utah; the Iowa, Nebraska, Wyoming, and Kansas state historical societies; and the Santa Fe Trail centers in Larned, Kansas, and in the National Frontier Trails Center (NFTC) at Independence, Missouri, especially in the Merrill J. Mattes Research Collection housed there.

The library of the University of Wyoming at Laramie holds most of the papers, maps, slides, and copies of overland diaries that belonged to the late Paul Henderson. Henderson, a retired railroad man, was one of the earliest and best students of the Oregon/California

Trail. His maps are among the best. In 1993 some of his materials were donated to the Mattes Library in the NFTC.

Trail students should also be aware of the Mormon Pioneer Trail Foundation archives. This foundation was an early (1969) attempt "to foster research, encourage development and preservation of significant historic sites, and [provide] information concerning the Mormon Pioneer Trail."[6] The archives are housed at Southern Illinois University, Edwardsville, Illinois, c/o Stanley B. Kimball. Kimball also has extensive files from 1971 of Mormon trail-related correspondence with and documents of the Bureau of Outdoor Recreation (BOR), Heritage Conservation and Recreational Service (HCRS), and the National Park Service. The Service superseded both the BOR and the HCRS in managing the Mormon Pioneer National Historic Trail.[7]

The Daughters of Utah Pioneers have extensive archives pertaining to Mormon trail matters and, to a lesser degree, so do the Sons of Utah Pioneers. The Mormon Trails Association (founded 1991 in Salt Lake City) is currently generating its own collection of pertinent documents. The records of the old Pioneer Trails and Landmarks Association of the 1930s have yet to be located. The only item that has surfaced is a booklet, *Charting and Marking Pioneer Trails and Landmarks,*[8] which is available in the Utah State Historical Society.

The Archives of the Union Pacific Railroad at the Nebraska State Historical Society in Lincoln holds some late trail-related documents. Many counties through which the Mormon Trail passes also have local historical societies, such as the Iowa counties of Lee, Wayne (with its special "Come, Come, Ye Saints" exhibit), Clark, Union, Adair, and Pottawattamie; the Nebraska counties of Dodge, Nance, Dawson, Lincoln, Hall, and Keith; and the Wyoming counties of Fremont and Sweetwater. There are also some special historical associations, including the North Platte Valley Historical Association in Gering, Nebraska, and the Fort Bridger (Wyoming) Historical Association.[9]

Maps

Excellent maps of all the Mormon emigration trails may be found in each of the appropriate state historical societies and archives. Among the most important are the Federal General Land Office's surveyor maps and notes. These documents are indispensable; they represent the earliest detailed maps of the trans-Mississippi west. (The original GLO surveyors did not prepare the final maps; these were done by others from the surveyor's notes and sketches. Furthermore, the surveyors walked only section lines; the course of old trails between section lines is largely conjecture.)

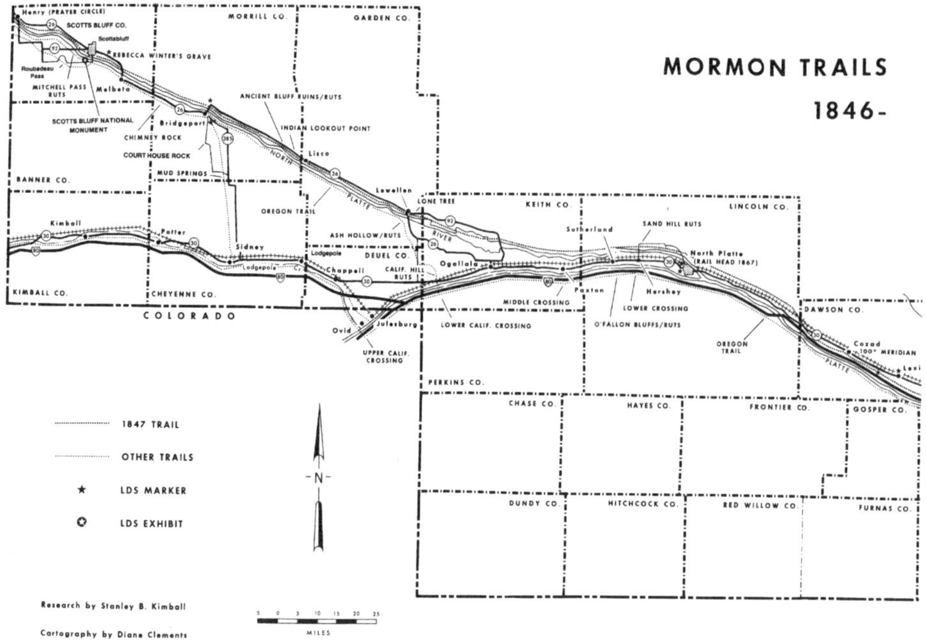

In addition to the GLO maps, other important maps include manuscripts from various sources and historic maps. Most useful in the field are the county maps (one-half-inch-to-the-mile; scale 1:126,720), the newer United States Geologic Survey (USGS) topographic maps (five-eighths-inch-to-the-mile; scale 1:100,000), and the splendid USGS 7.5-minute topographic quads (two-and-five-eighths-inches-to-the-mile; scale 1:24,000)—the most accurate map series covering almost the entire United States. Some prefer to work with the topographic maps (one-quarter-inch-to-the-mile; scale 1:250,000) from the USGS. For further information, researchers should contact the U.S. Geological Survey (Denver) and request its *Index to Topographic and Other Map Coverage* and *Catalog of Topographic and Other Published Maps*.

The Bureau of Land Management (BLM) publishes full-color maps (one-half-inch-to-the-mile; scale 1:126,720) for lands it manages. These color quads are not published county by county. Rather, one must consult a "Quad Index Map" to secure the quad wanted—in much the same way one has to consult an index to the USGS 7.5-minute quads. The BLM maps are especially useful because they show land ownership and use by color and include many other details not shown on other maps.

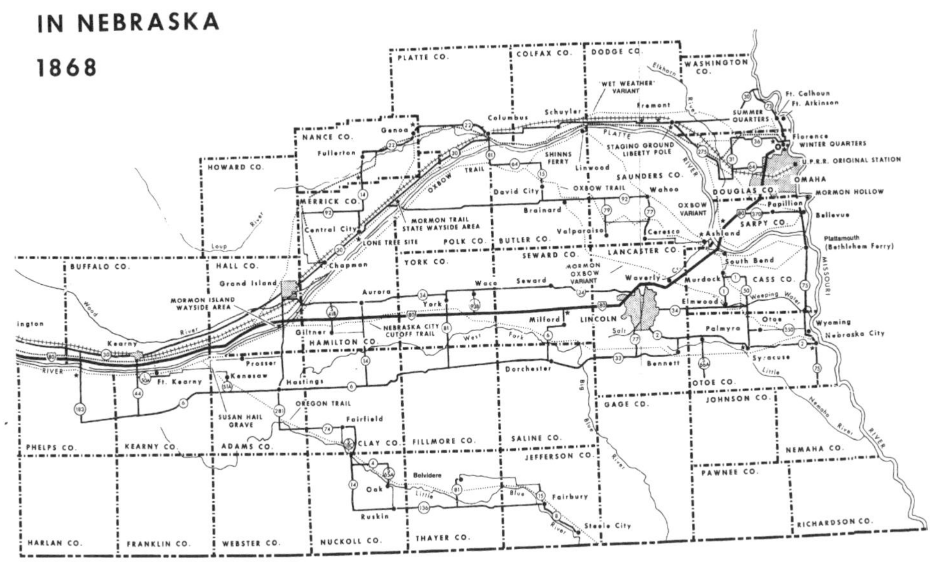

The National Park Service (NPS) recently published the *National Trails System Map and Guide,* which shows, in color, nineteen national scenic and historic trails totaling over thirty thousand miles. A brief description of each trail and the address of each trail manager is included. The NPS has also published useful foldout maps of the Oregon Trail and the Mormon Trail. In addition, the Oregon-California Trails Association (OCTA) sponsors the Mapping Emigrant Trails (MET) program. This is a systematic and exhaustive effort to verify and map the vast emigrant trail network—including the Mormon trails.[10]

Almost all counties have plat books showing property ownership by township (one-quarter-inch-to-the-mile). Most trail researchers will eventually use these plat books.

In addition to maps, most states and many counties have published useful atlases. Good atlases for trail researchers include, for example, M. Huebinger, *Atlas of the State of Iowa* (Davenport: Iowa Publishing, 1904); Wayne L. Wahlquist and others, eds., *Atlas of Utah* (Ogden, Utah: Weber State College, 1981); and Homer E. Socolofsky and Huber Self, *Historical Atlas of Kansas* (Norman: University of Oklahoma Press, 1972). The previously mentioned Mapping Emigrant Trails program of OCTA also publishes atlases. Finally, the University of

Oklahoma Press has published historical atlases of Arizona, California, Kansas, Missouri, New Mexico, and Oklahoma. Additional sources are listed under the subheading *Maps and Atlases* below.

Photographs—Land and Aerial

Between 1935 and 1944, the Department of Agriculture took aerial (medium-level, vertical, black-and-white) photographs covering approximately 85 percent of the contiguous land area of the United States. Subsequently, from about 1940 to 1960, the military similarly photographed most of the continental United States. These photographs can be very useful for trail research and are available from the Cartographic and Architectural Branch of the National Archives (Washington, D.C., or Alexandria, Va.). The aerial photographs are usually nine inches square (scale 1:20,000). These old aerials, especially when viewed in stereo, can reveal fifty-year-old clues as to the location of old trails. This information is especially valuable since many sections of the old trails have been obliterated within the past half century. Trail researchers should order the National Archives's booklet *Cartographic and Architectural Records in the National Archives,* no. 2 (1986) for more information about these aerials.

The Bureau of Land Management has stereo aerial photographs of most of the lands for which it is responsible. Viewing these aerials is almost like taking a helicopter ride over the old trails. Other federal agencies, such as the Army Corps of Engineers, also generate their own aerials, some of which pertain to Mormon trails. In addition to these federal agencies, most counties west of the Mississippi River can provide aerial photographic plats (scales vary from one-hundred-feet-to-the-inch to four-hundred-feet-to-the-inch) and the older quarter-section plats which show ownership.

State-of-the-art LANDSAT satellite images might help some researchers. For interested researchers, the EOSAT (Earth Observation Satellite) Company, c/o EROS Data System (Sioux Falls, S.Dak.), markets LANDSAT images. In addition, a French satellite system known as SPOT (*Le Systeme pour l'observation de la terre*) produces LANDSAT-type images but with greater resolution. The U.S. office is SPOT Image Corporation (Reston, Va.).

Of more use to trail students than LANDSAT images is the satellite Global Positional System (GPS). GPS is a navigation and coordinate recording system which receives radio signals from space into a hand-held unit carried by the trail researcher traveling by foot, horseback, or a vehicle. The data can be entered into a computer that prints out the information on 7.5 minute USGS quad maps showing the movements of the receiver. This system plots trails to an accuracy of about twelve meters—that is, to an accuracy of the forty-foot intervals used to show contour.

For more information on LANDSAT, GPS, and SPOT, as well as other state-of-the-art satellite imaging, researchers should contact the EROS Data Center (Sioux Falls, S.D.), which archives and sells all kinds of aerial photographs and maps. In addition, researchers should contact GPS World (Eugene, Ore.). Environmental Research Institute Michigan (Ann Arbor, Mich.) is a good source on remote sensing. Trail historians would also do well to consult with university colleagues who teach various geographic information system classes.

Most state and county historical societies, museums, and trail centers have trail-related photographs. OCTA, as previously noted, has a photographic committee collecting trail photos. The LDS Church maintains large photographic collections on all phases of Mormon history, including the emigrant trails. These photo collections are housed in the LDS Historical Department and the Visual Resource Library (Salt Lake City). The photo collection of the Union Pacific Railroad Museum (Omaha, Nebr.) is useful for study of trails in the late 1860s. In addition to these institutional collections, some individuals have extensive collections of photographs, including aerials, of Mormon trails. These individual collectors include Greg Franzwa, Tucson, Arizona; LaMar Berrett, Orem, Utah; and Stanley B. Kimball, Edwardsville, Illinois.

Lists and Select Bibliography

The following section outlines the organizations and publications of which trail researchers should be aware. Organizations are listed according to category along with brief descriptions. Publications are likewise listed by category. The bibliography begins with general categories and becomes more specific.

The secondary literature is enormous. Indeed, the standard trail bibliographies probably list only about half of what exists. This essay's bibliography, therefore, is a highly selective list of the most important items. Readers will note that the bibliography contains several references to rail and water travel. These references reflect two facts. First, approximately half of Mormon immigrants traveled the railroads to reach their waiting wagons by the Missouri River. Second, more than ninety percent of Mormon immigrants also traveled by water, to a greater or lesser degree, to reach those same wagons.

Because the number of known trail journals and accounts runs into the thousands, with more being discovered all the time, only a few are listed here. For access to these accounts, see works listed under the subheading *Guides to Trail Journals*.

Some books and articles treat more than one trail and need to be listed in more than one category. There is, therefore, some duplication in the bibliography. Furthermore, some disappointing publications are listed—mainly as a warning to avoid them. As a final note, some trail material makes great reading. See, for example, the works of David Lavender and Wallace Stegner, and especially Francis Parkman's *The Oregon Trail* (1849), Mark Twain's classic *Roughing It* (1872), and Sir Richard Burton's *The City of the Saints* (1862).

Trail Centers, Museums, and Visitors' Centers

Ash Hollow State Historic Park, Box A, Lewellen, Nebr. 69147.

Bent's Old Fort, La Junta, Colo. 81050.

Chimney Rock Visitors Center, planned by the Nebraska State Historical Society.

Echo Canyon Visitors' Center, off I-80 at the mouth of Echo Canyon, Utah (just east of Salt Lake City).

Fort Bridger State Historic Site, Fort Bridger, Wyo. 82933.

Fort Caspar Museum, 4001 Fort Caspar Rd., Casper, Wyo. 82604.

Fort Kearney State Historic Park, Rt. 4, Fort Kearney, Nebr. 68847.

Fort Laramie National Historic Site, P.O. Box 218, Fort Laramie, Wyo. 82212.

Fort Larned National Historic Site, Rt. 3, Larned, Kans. 67550.

Fort Union National Monument, Rt. 477, Watrous, N.Mex. 87753.

Mormon Battalion Memorial Visitors' Center, 2510 Juan St., San Diego, Calif. 92110.

Mormon Visitors' Center, 3215 State St., (North) Omaha, Nebr. 68112.

Museum of Church History and Art, 45 North West Temple St., Salt Lake City, Utah 84150.

National Frontier Trails Center, 318 West Pacific, Independence, Mo. 64050.

National Historic Trails Interpretive Center, Casper, Wyo. Under consideration; write OCTA for more information (see under "Trail Associations").

Nauvoo Restoration Inc. Visitors' Center, Nauvoo, Ill. 62354.

Nebraska National Trails Museum, P.O. Box 268, Ogallala, Nebr. 69153. Under development.

Pecos National Monument, Pecos, N.Mex. 87552.

Pioneer Memorial Museum, Daughters of Utah Pioneers, 300 North Main St., Salt Lake City, Utah 84103.

Pioneer Trail State Park, 2601 Sunnyside Ave., Salt Lake City, Utah 84108.

Pony Express Museum, Marysville, Kans. 66508.

Rock Creek Station, Rt. 4, Fairbury, Nebr. 68352.

Santa Fe Trail Center, Rt. 3, Larned, Kans. 67550.

Scotts Bluff National Monument, P.O. Box 427, Gering, Nebr. 69341.

Western Historic Trails Center, 110 South Main St., P.O. Box 1565, Council Bluffs, Iowa 51502. Under development.

Trail-Related Organizations

American Hiking Society, 1015 31st St. NW, Washington, D.C. 20007. Good on trail politics and policy; has little to do with historic trails.

American Greenways, 1800 North Kent St., Arlington, Va. 22209.

American Trails, 1400 16th St. NW, 3d floor, Washington, D.C. 20036.

Bureau of Land Management, P.O. Box 1828, Cheyenne, Wyo. 82003.

Daughters of Utah Pioneers, 300 North Main St., Salt Lake City, Utah 84103.

Iowa Mormon Trail Association, c/o Garden Grove Historical Society, P.O. Box 22, Garden Grove, Iowa 50103. A new, developing association.

Mormon Battalion, Inc., c/o Sons of Utah Pioneers, 3301 East 2920 South, Salt Lake City, Utah 84109.

Mormon Church Historic Sites Committee, c/o Glen Leonard, Director, Museum of Church History and Art, 45 North West Temple St., Salt Lake City, Utah 84150.

The Mormon History Association, P.O. Box 7010, University Station, Provo, Utah 84602.

Mormon Pioneer Trail Foundation, c/o C. Booth Wallentine, 5300 South 360 West, Salt Lake City, Utah 84105. An early (1969) trail organization.

Mormon Trails Association, 300 Rio Grande St., Salt Lake City, Utah 84101. A relatively new association devoted to Mormon trails. Works closely with the National Park Service in Denver, Colorado.

National Historic Trails Coordinating Committee, 3 Drum Hill Rd., Summit, N.J. 07901.

National Park Service, Rocky Mountain Regional Office, P.O. Box 25287, c/o Mike Duwe, Denver, Colo. 25287. Administers the Mormon Pioneer National Historic Trail for the federal government.

National Park Service, Southwest Regional Office, David Gaines, Santa Fe Trail National Historic Trail, P.O. Box 728, Santa Fe, N.Mex. 87504-0728. The Santa Fe National Historic Trail is also known as the Mormon Battalion Trail. The advisory council to the Santa Fe office of the National Park Service has several subcommittees: awards, resource protection, visitors' centers/interpretation, history/resource/mapping, landowner needs, fundraising/logo, and cooperative agreements/certification.

National Pony Express Association, 1002 Jenkins, Marysville, Kans. 66508.

National Scenic and National Historic Trails Council, c/o Steven Elkinton, National Park Service, P.O. Box 37127, Washington, D.C. 20013-7127.

Oregon-California Trails Association (OCTA), 524 South Osage St., P.O. Box 1019, Independence, Mo. 64051-0519. Leading trail association with many chapters organized along the Oregon, California, and Mormon trails. Has many programs and committees working to research, preserve, and foster overland trails. Committees and programs include the Census of Overland Emigrant Documents (COED), which gathers information from the overland documents, mainly 1840s through 1860s, and records the information in a computer database for the use of historians, genealogists, and trail buffs; the Mapping Emigrant Trails (MET) program, which accurately maps historic western trails; the Archaeology Committee, which presents workshops at OCTA's annual meetings; the Graves and Sites Project, which researches and authenticates graves on the overland emigrant trails; the Trail Marking Project, which marks the historic overland trails properly with route, informational, and interpretive signs; the Historical Preservation Fund, which is used to preserve overland trails and associated sites; and the Photographic Committee, which maintains an inventory of trail photographs for use in publications, trail promotion, and public relations.

Rails-to-Trails Conservancy, 1400 16th St. NW, 3d floor, Washington, D.C. 20036.

Sons of Utah Pioneers, 3301 East 2920 South, Salt Lake City, Utah 84109.

Utah Historic Trails Consortium, Utah Historical Socieity, 300 Rio Grande St., Salt Lake City, Utah 84101. Organized in 1991 to promote Utah trails, especially in connection with the Utah Centennial of 1996. Their motto is "This is still the right place."

Historical Society Periodicals

In addition to the periodicals listed below, periodicals that often publish trail-related articles include *BYU Studies, Dialogue: A Journal of Mormon Thought, Journal of Mormon History,* and *Overland Journal.*

Annals of Iowa
Annals of Wyoming

Colorado Heritage
Journal of the West
Kansas History
Missouri Historical Review
Montana: The Magazine of Western History
Nebraska History
Utah Historical Quarterly
Western Historical Quarterly

Newsletters and Publications

Centennial Star, Utah Statehood Centennial [1996] Commission, 300 Rio Grande St., Salt Lake City, Utah 84101. Forthcoming; will contain reference material.

Crossroads, Utah Crossroads Quarterly Newsletter, 1451 Kensington, Salt Lake City, Utah 84105. Crossroads is a chapter of OCTA.

Folio: The Newsletter of the Patrice Press, 1810 West Grant Rd., Suite 108, Tucson, Ariz. 85745. Much more than a blurb; full of trail lore not found in other newsletters.

Iowa, Iowa Mormon Trail Association, Inc., Newsletter, 500 East Taylor, Creston, Iowa 50801.

Mormon History Association Newsletter, 2470 North 1000 West, Layton, Utah 84041. Devoted to Mormon history, including, somewhat tangentially, Mormon trails. Published by the same entity that produces the *Journal of Mormon History.*

Mormon Pioneer National Historic Trail Newsletter, c/o Mike Duwe, National Park Service, P.O. Box 25287, Denver, Colo. 80225. An occasional publication largely devoted to Park Service activities concerning the MPNHT.

News from the Plains, Oregon-California Trails Association, Box 1019, Independence, Mo. 64051-0519. Oregon-California Trails Association's quarterly newsletter. Chronicles miscellaneous activities, especially the doings of the various chapters of OCTA.

Overland Journal, Oregon-California Trails Association, P.O. Box 1019, Independence, Mo. 64051-0519. The quarterly journal of OCTA devoted to the Oregon, California, and related trails, book reviews.

Pathways across America: A Newsletter for National Scenic and Historic Trails, American Hiking Society, 1015 31st St. NW, Washington, D.C. 20007. Largely devoted to scenic trails.

The Pioneer, National Society of Sons of Utah Pioneers, 3301 East 2920 South, Salt Lake City, Utah 84109. Bimonthly. Publishes occasional articles and notices on the Mormon trail.

Santa Fe National Historic Trail, National Park Service, P.O. Box 728 Santa Fe, N.Mex. 87504-0728. A trail newsletter for the NPS.

Trail Tracks: The Trails Information Exchange Newsletter, American Trails, 1400 16th St. NW, Washington, D.C. 20036. Excellent for trail politics and policy.

Trailletter. A one-sheet newsletter of the short-lived (1967-74) Mormon Trails Association. James D. Cannon of Salt Lake City, editor.

Wagon Tracks: Santa Fe Trail Association Quarterly, Rt. 1, Box 31, Woodston, Kans. 67675. Quarterly. Perhaps the best of all the several newsletters.

General Trail Studies (Mormon, Oregon, California, and Santa Fe)

Atwood, Harriet T. "The Mormon Migration and Adaption to Geography." *Vassar Journal of Undergraduate Studies* 4 (1929): 137-58. Fine in its day, but now superseded.

Bennett, Richard E. "Eastward to Eden: The Nauvoo Rescue Missions." *Dialogue* 19 (Winter 1986): 100-108.

———. "Finalizing Plans for the Trek West: Deliberations at Winter Quarters, 1846-1847." *BYU Studies* 24 (Summer 1984): 301-20.

Boyack, Hazel Noble. "Wyoming: Pathway of the Mormon Pioneers to Utah." *Improvement Era* 50 (June 1947): 374-75, 408-9, 413.

Brown, Joseph E. *The Mormon Trek West*. Garden City, New York: Doubleday, 1980. An interesting study for armchair travelers. Illustrated, excellent photographs.

Cannon, D. James, ed. *Centennial Caravan: Story of the 1947 Centennial Reenactment of the Mormon Trail.* Salt Lake City: Sons of Utah Pioneers, 1948. Illustrations.

Carter, John E. "Photographing across the Plains: Charles R. Savage in 1866." *Nebraska History* 71 (Summer 1990): 58-63.

Christansen, Lawrence. "The Story of the Mormon Battalion." Kernersville, N.C. An unpublished, eleven-hundred page definitive study of the Mormon Battalion.

Creer, Leland H. "Lansford W. Hastings and the Discovery of the Old Mormon Trail." *Western Humanities Review* 3 (July 1949): 175-86.

Daughters of Utah Pioneers. *They Came in [various years].* Salt Lake City, 21 vols. to date. An annual devoted to Mormon pioneers.

Deseret News . . . Church Almanac. Salt Lake City: Deseret News, 1973 and later editions. Useful for a variety of reasons, especially the list of Mormon pioneer companies.

Duehlmeier, Fred D. "The 1847 Mormon Migration." Master's thesis, University of Utah, 1977. General.

Durham, Michael S. "'This Is the Place': Retracing the Pioneer Trail in Mormon Utah." *American Heritage* 44, no. 2 (April 1993): 65-82.

Franzwa, Gregory M. *Images of the Santa Fe Trail*. St. Louis, Mo.: Patrice Press, 1988. A splendid photographic essay.

Gentry, Leland H. "The Mormon Way Stations: Garden Grove and Mt. Pisgah." *BYU Studies* 21 (Fall 1981): 445-61. Excellent.

Gibbons, Boyd. "The Itch to Move West" *National Geographic* 170 (August 1986): 147-77. Great reading and great photos.

Golder, Frank Alfred. *The March of the Mormon Battalion from Council Bluffs to California: Taken from the Journal of Henry Standage*. New York: Century, 1928. One of the best Mormon accounts of this march.

Graham, Bruce L. "The Mormon Crossing of Iowa in 1846." Parts 1-3. *Restoration Trail Forum* 7 (August 1981): 1, 3-4; (November 1981): 3, 7; 8 (February 1982): 4, 6; and (May 1982): 6-8. A short, basic treatment.

Greene, Lida L. "Markers for Remembrance: The Mormon Trail." *Annals of Iowa* 40 (Winter 1970): 190-93. A very brief discussion.

Hafen, LeRoy R., and Ann W. Hafen, eds. *The Utah Expedition, 1857-58*. Glendale, Calif.: Arthur H. Clark, 1982. Perhaps the best account of this military venture along the Mormon Trail during the "Utah War."

Hartley, William G. "The Great Florence Fitout of 1861." *BYU Studies* 24 (Summer 1984): 341-71. The best on this topic.

Holmes, Gail G. "The LDS Legacy in Southwestern Iowa." *Ensign* 18 (August 1988): 54-57. Holmes is the expert on this subject. Maps.

Homer, Michael W. "After Winter Quarters and Council Bluffs: The Mormons in Nebraska Territory, 1854-1867." *Nebraska History* 65 (Winter 1984): 467-83. A good study of a neglected topic.

Jackson, Richard H., ed. *The Mormon Role in the Settlement of the West*. Provo, Utah: Brigham Young University Press, 1978. A collection of articles, one of which (by Jackson, a geographer) is based entirely on primary sources and titled "The Overland Journey to Zion."

Jenson, Andrew. "Church Emigration." Parts 1-22. *The Contributor* 12-13 (1891-92). A series of detailed articles on emigration or immigration.

———. "Utah Pioneer Companies." *Utah Genealogical and Historical Magazine* 8 (January 1917): 1-6. Dated.

Kimball, Stanley B. "The Captivity Narrative on Mormon Trails, 1846-65." *Dialogue* 18 (Winter 1985): 81-88.

Kimball, Stanley B. "The Dark Side of Heroism on Mormon Trails: A New Look at the Mythic Pioneers." Paper presented at the Mormon History Association, Kansas City, Mo., May 1985.

———. "Disease, Trauma, and Medicine of Mormon Trails, 1831-68." Paper presented at the Western History Conference, Wichita, Kans., October 1988.

———. "Love, Marriage, Romance, and Sex on Mormon Trails, 1831-68." Paper presented at the Mormon History Association, Salt Lake City, Utah, May 1986.

———. "Mormon Pioneer Trail." In *Encyclopedia of Mormonism,* ed. by Daniel H. Ludlow, 942-46. Vol. 2. New York: Macmillan, 1992.

———. "Route from Nauvoo to Council Bluffs." In *Historical Atlas of Mormonism,* ed. by S. Kent Brown, Donald Q. Cannon, and Richard H. Jackson, 70-71. New York: Simon and Schuster, 1994.

———. "The Unusual and *Outre* on Mormon Trails." Paper presented at the Mormon History Conference, Logan, Utah, May 1988.

———. "Women, Children, and Family Life on Pioneer Trails." Paper presented at the National Convention of the Daughters of Utah Pioneers, Salt Lake City, Utah, October 1980.

Lavender, David. *Westward Vision: The Story of the Oregon Trail.* 1963. Reprint, University of Nebraska Press, 1985. A literary history.

Little, James A. *From Kirtland to Salt Lake City*. Salt Lake City: By the author, 1890. Based on Little's personal journal account of immigrating to Utah in 1849.

Lyon, T. Edgar. "Some Uncommon Aspects of the Mormon Migration." *Improvement Era* 71 (September 1969): 33-40. Insightful.

Madsen, Brigham D. *Gold Rush Sojourners in Great Salt Lake City: 1849 and 1850*. Salt Lake City: University of Utah Press, 1983. One excellent chapter on the use of the Mormon Trail by gold rushers.

Murdock, Steve. "Mormon Trails in the Midwest." *Travel* 137 (January 1972): 58-63, 68. Popular.

Neff, Andrew L. "The Mormon Migration to Utah, 1830-47." Ph.D. diss., University of California-Berkeley, 1918. Out of date.

Nibley, Preston. *Exodus to Greatness: The Story of the Mormon Migration.* Salt Lake City: Deseret News Press, 1947. An old, orthodox, but still useful interpretation of westerning Mormons.

Parkman, Francis. *The Oregon Trail*. 1849. Many printings and editions. A classic; great literature.

Petersen, Bryan L. "A Geographic Study of the Mormon Migration from Nauvoo, Illinois, to the Great Salt Lake Valley (1846-47)." Master's thesis, University of California at Los Angeles, 1941. General.

Peterson, William J. "Mormon Trails in Iowa." *The Palimpsest* 47 (1966): 353-84. An Iowan's interpretation.

Piercy, Frederick H. *Route from Liverpool to the Great Salt Lake Valley.* Ed. by Fawn Brodie. Cambridge, Mass.: Harvard University Press, 1962. A firsthand account from the year 1853. Illustrations.

Richards, Aurelia P. *The Mormon Trail (in Story Form).* Salt Lake City: Hawkes, 1980. General.

Richmond, Robert W. "Developments along the Overland Trail from the Missouri River to Fort Laramie before 1854." *Nebraska History* 33 (December 1952): 237–47.

Stegner, Wallace. *The Gathering of Zion: The Story of the Mormon Trail.* Salt Lake City: Westwater Press, 1981. The most readable book on the topic.

Taylor, Philip A. M. "The Mormon Crossing of the United States, 1840–1870." *Utah Historical Quarterly* 25 (October 1957): 319–37. General, out of date.

Tyler, Daniel. *A Concise History of the Mormon Battalion in the Mexican War: 1846–1847*. 1881. Reprint, Chicago: Rio Grande, 1964. One of the best accounts of this march.

Unruh, John D., Jr. *The Plains Across: The Overland Emigrants and the Trans-Mississippi West, 1840–60.* Urbana: University of Illinois Press, 1979. The most comprehensive study to date.

Van der Zee, Jacob. "Mormon Trails in Iowa." *The Iowa Journal of History and Politics* 12 (January 1914): 3–16. Now completely outdated.

White, Hiram F. "The Mormon Road." *Washington Historical Quarterly* 6 (October 1915): 243–50. Out of date.

Guides to Trail Journals[11]

Andrus, Hyrum L., and Richard E. Bennett, comps. *Mormon Manuscripts to 1846: A Guide to the Holdings of the Harold B. Lee Library.* Provo: Brigham Young University Library, 1977. The most extensive guide to manuscripts in the Harold B. Lee Library.

Bashore, Melvin, and Linda Haslam. *The Mormon Pioneer Companies Crossing the Plains (1847–1868) Narratives*. 3d. ed. rev. Salt Lake City: The Church of Jesus Christ of Latter-day Saints, 1990. Lists firsthand accounts by year and name of company. A must.

Bitton, Davis. *Guide to Mormon Diaries and Autobiographies*. Provo, Utah: Brigham Young University Press, 1977. Incomplete but invaluable; lists and describes 2,894 items in fourteen repositories. Indexed.

Mattes, Merrill J. *Platte River Road Narratives: A Descriptive Bibliography of Travel over the Great Central Overland Route to Oregon, California, Utah, Colorado, Montana, and Other Western States and Territories, 1812-1866.* Urbana: University of Illinois Press, 1988. Monumental. A must. Lists and describes 2,082 items located in ninety-seven repositories. Mattes carefully selected some 216 Mormon narratives.

Utah State Historical Society (USHS). "Utah Historical Society Corrections to Davis Bitton's Guide to Mormon Diaries and Autobiographies." 1978. A thirty-page typescript detailing additional items held by the USHS.

Trail Guides

Anderson, William C., and Eloise R. Anderson. *Guide to Mormon History Travel.* American Fork, Utah.: By the authors, 1991. A useful guide for the traveler.

Berrett, Lamar C. *The Mormon Trail: Fort Bridger to Salt Lake Valley.* Salt Lake City: Utah Crossroads Oregon-California Trails Association, 1993.

Boye, Alan. *The Complete Roadside Guide to Nebraska*. St. Johnsbury, Vt.: Saltillo Press, 1989. A useful guide to have in the glove compartment of a car. Maps, illustrations.

Burton, Alma P. *Mormon Trail from Vermont to Utah: A Guide to Historic Places of The Church of Jesus Christ of Latter-day Saints.* Provo, Utah: Brigham Young University Press, 1952. An early, quick guide to the Mormon Trail. Of little use today.

Carley, Maurine. "Emigrant Trail Trek No. 10." *Annals of Wyoming* 32 (April 1960): 102–23; and (October 1960): 218–38. Treks 4-9 are in vols. 29–31. An account of an Oregon Trail trek by automobile. Not recommended. Maps.

Charting and Marking Pioneer Trails and Landmarks. Salt Lake City: Utah Pioneer Trails and Landmarks Association, 1931. An eight-page pamphlet.

Clayton, William. *The Latter-Day Saints' Emigrants' Guide*. . . . St. Louis: Missouri Steam Powered Press, 1848. The famous guidebook.

Daughters of the American Revolution (Missouri). *Milestones in Missouri's Past.* N.p., 1976. Simple but good description of the little-known Boone's Lick Trail, which the Mormons used from 1831 to 1839.

Driggs, Howard R. *Mormon Trail, Pathway of Pioneers Who Made the Desert Bloom*. New York: American Pioneer Trails Association,

1947. An early booklet describing the Mormon westward movement from Vermont to Utah. Of little value today.

Franzwa, Gregory M. *The Oregon Trail Revisited*. 4th ed. St. Louis, Mo.: Patrice Press, 1988. Essential, journalistic, and detailed. Maps, illustrations.

———. *The Santa Fe Trail Revisited*. St. Louis, Mo.: Patrice Press, 1989. A must. Illustrated.

Gamble, Mary B., and Leo E. Gamble. *Santa Fe Trail Markers in Colorado*. Spearville, Kans.: Spearville News, 1987. Many Mormons used this trail.

Haines, Aubrey L. *Historic Sites along the Oregon Trail*. 2d ed. Gerald, Mo.: Patrice Press, 1981. Definitive, a must. Maps, illustrations.

Harlan, Edgar R. *The Location and Name of the Mormon Trail*. Knoxville, Tenn.: Express, 1914. Outdated.

Harvey, R. E. "The Mormon Trek across Iowa Territory." *Annals of Iowa* 10 (July 1946): 36–60. Good, but barely adequate.

Hastings, Lansford W. *The Emigrants' Guide to Oregon and California*. Cincinnati: George Conclin, 1845. Of historical value only.

Henderson, Paul C. *Landmarks on the Oregon Trail*. New York: Westerners, 1953. Paul was the dean of Oregon Trail students. Map and many illustrations.

Jenson, Andrew. *Day by Day with the Utah Pioneers, 1847*. Salt Lake City: Salt Lake Tribune, 1934. Based on a series of newspaper articles. Good reading, many biographical sketches.

Kasparek, Bob. "A Tour of the Mormon Pioneer Trail." *Overland Journal* 5 (Spring 1987): 35–40. A general account based on an automobile tour. Illustrated.

Kimball, Stanley B. *Discovering Mormon Trails*. Salt Lake City: Deseret Book, 1979. An early study of the Mormon use of eight other trails. Largely a reprint of articles that appeared in the *Ensign*.

———. "The Fort Leavenworth Branch of the Santa Fe Trail in 1846: An Annotated Map." In *Adventure on the Santa Fe Trail,* ed. by Leo Oliva, 97–106. Topeka: Kansas State Historical Society, 1988.

———. *Historic Sites and Markers along the Mormon and Other Great Western Trails*. Urbana: University of Illinois Press, 1988. The best of its kind. Definitive. Maps, illustrations.

———. "The Iowa Trek of 1846: The Brigham Young Route from Nauvoo to Winter Quarters." *Ensign* 2 (June 1972): 36–45. Map. A good early study.

———. "The Mormon Trail in Utah." In *Utah History Encyclopedia,* ed. by Allan Kent Powell, 380–81. Salt Lake City: University of Utah Press, 1994.

Kimball, Stanley B. "The Mormon Trail Network in Iowa, 1838-63." *BYU Studies* 21 (Fall 1981): 417-30. Definitive. Map.

———. "Mormon Trail Network in Nebraska, 1846-68: A New Look." *BYU Studies* 24 (Summer 1984): 321-36. Definitive. Maps.

———. *Mormon Trail, Voyage of Discovery: The Story behind the Scenery*. Las Vegas: KC Publications, forthcoming.

———. "Rediscovering the Fort Leavenworth Military Branch of the Santa Fe Trail." In *The Mexican Road: Trade, Travel, and Confrontation on the Santa Fe Trail,* ed. by Mark Gardner, 59-68. Manhattan, Kans.: Sunflower University Press, 1989.

———. "Rediscovering the Fort Leavenworth Military Branch of the Santa Fe Trail." *Journal of the West* 28 (April 1989): 59-68. Maps.

Kimball, Stanley B., and James B. Allen, eds. *William Clayton's The Latter-Day Saints' Emigrants' Guide.* Gerald, Mo.: Patrice Press, 1983. The best edition to date. Maps, illustrations.

Knight, Hal, and Stanley B. Kimball. *111 Days to Zion*. Salt Lake City: Deseret Press, 1978. A compilation of newspaper stories. Maps.

Korns, J. Roderic, ed. "West from Fort Bridger: The Pioneering of the Immigrant Trails across Utah, 1846-1850." *Utah Historical Quarterly* 19 (1951). The whole issue of *UHQ* is devoted to this topic.

Lambourne, Alfred. *The Pioneer Trail*. Salt Lake City: Deseret News, 1913. An old but good account of the 1846 Mormon overland expedition.

Langley, Harold D., ed. *To Utah with the Dragoons . . . 1858-59*. Salt Lake City: University of Utah Press, 1974. A fine firsthand account of the Mormon Trail during the "Utah War" period.

Long, Margaret. *The Oregon Trail: Following the Old Historic Pioneer Trails on Modern Highways.* Denver: W. H. Kistler Stationery, 1954. A classic.

Mallison, Jane. "DAR Markers on the Santa Fe Trail." Parts 1 and 2, *Wagon Tracks: Santa Fe Trail Association Quarterly* 5 (February 1991): 8-9; (August 1991): 14-16; Part 3, *Wagon Tracks* 7 (February 1993): 10-11. Handy.

Martin, Charles W., and Dorothy Devereux Dustin. "The Omaha-Council Bluffs Area and the Westward Trails." *Overland Journal* 7, no. 4 (1989): 2-11. Map, illustrations.

Mattes, Merrill J. "The Council Bluffs Road: A New Perspective on the Northern Branch of the Great Platte River Road." *Nebraska History* 65 (Summer 1984): 179-94. The Mormon Trail is sometimes called the Northern Branch of the Oregon Trail, which in fact it was. A very good study. Excellent maps.

———. *The Great Platte River Road: The Covered Wagon Mainline via Fort Kearny to Fort Laramie.* 1969. Reprint, Lincoln: University of Nebraska Press, 1987. A classic study. Maps, illustrations.

———. "The Northern Route of the Non-Mormons: Rediscovery of Nebraska's Forgotten Historic Trail." *Overland Journal* 8, no. 2 (1990): 2–14. Maps. Illustrations.

Mormon Guide . . . from Omaha to Salt Lake City. N.p.: Farmer's Oracle, 1864. Of historical value only.

Mormon Way-Bill to the Gold Mines from the Pacific Springs. Salt Lake City: W. Richards, 1851. Of historic value only.

Murphy, Dan. *Oregon Trail: Voyage of Discovery.* Las Vegas: KC Publications, 1991. Popular; excellent photographs.

Noble, Bruce J., Jr. "Marking Wyoming's Oregon Trail." *Overland Journal* 4 (Summer 1986): 19–31. An excellent study of the history of trail marking in Wyoming and a county-by-county listing of sixty-five Oregon Trail markers in that state. Illustrated.

Oscarson, R. Don, and Stanley B. Kimball. *The Travelers' Guide to Historic Mormon America.* 20th ed. Salt Lake City: Bookcraft, 1994. A simple, up-to-date, useful, basic guide. Maps, illustrations. Good to have in a glove compartment.

Paden, Irene D. *The Wake of the Prairie Schooner.* New York: Macmillan, 1944. A classic.

Peterson, Charles S., and others. *Mormon Battalion Trail Guide.* Salt Lake City: Utah State Historical Society, 1972. Excellent in its day, now outdated. Maps.

Pratt, Orson, and Millroy and Hayes. *Guide to the Route Map of the Mormon Pioneers from Nauvoo to Great Salt Lake, 1846–47.* Salt Lake City: Millroy and Hayes, 1899. Of historical value only.

Simmons, Marc. *Following the Santa Fe Trail.* 2d ed. Santa Fe: Ancient City Press, 1986. The best. Illustrations, maps.

Smart, William B. *Exploring the Pioneer Trail.* Salt Lake City: Young Men's Mutual Improvement Association, 1962. General, out of date.

Steele, Olga Sharp. "The Geography of the Mormon Trail across Nebraska." Master's thesis, University of Nebraska, 1933. Old, but still the single best study of the subject. Maps.

Talbot, Dan. *A Historical Guide to the Mormon Battalion and Butterfield Trail.* Tucson, Ariz.: Westernlore Press, 1992.

Wilcox, Wayne. "Thirty-Six Miles of History." *Utah Historical Quarterly* 23 (October 1955): 363–67. Brief, outdated study of the trans-Wasatch route.

Multiple Trails

Bailey, Paul. *The Armies of God*. Garden City, N.Y.: Doubleday, 1968. An account of the Mormons' use of several western trails, including the Mormon Trail, for military purposes.

Dunlop, Richard. *Great Trails of the West*. Nashville, Tenn.: Abingdon, 1971. General, popular.

Goetzmann, William H. *Army Exploration in the American West: 1803–1863*. Lincoln: University of Nebraska Press, 1979. Essential.

Jackson, W. Turrentine. *Wagon Roads West: A Study of Federal Surveys and Construction in the Trans-Mississippi West, 1846–1869.* Lincoln: University of Nebraska Press, 1979. Essential. Excellent bibliography.

Kimball, Stanley B. *Historic Sites and Markers along the Mormon and Other Great Western Trails*. Urbana: University of Illinois Press, 1988. Photos, maps. A detailed study of twenty-one trails in sixteen states.

Marcy, Randolph B. *The Prairie Traveler.* 1859. Reprint, Cambridge: Applewood Books, 1988. Offers an unusual appendix on several western trails.

Morgan, Dale. *Utah's Historic Trails*. Salt Lake City: Utah Tourist and Publicity Council, 1960. Touristy.

Smart, William B. *Old Utah Trails*. Salt Lake City: Utah Geographic Series, 1988. Popular, current, excellent; by a first-rate journalist. Beautiful photos, maps, illustrations.

Trails West. Washington, D.C.: National Geographic Society, 1979. A typical National Geographic publication of six important western trails, including the Mormon Trail. Maps, illustrations.

Winther, Oscar Osburn. *The Transportation Frontier: Trans-Mississippi West, 1865–1890*. Albuquerque: University of New Mexico Press, 1974. The best study of this subject. Maps.

Worcester, Don, ed. *Pioneer Trails West*. Caldwell, Idaho: Caxton Printers, 1985. A popular study; the chapter on the Mormon Trail (166–83) is by a recognized scholar, S. George Ellsworth. Map.

Other Trails Used by the Mormons[12]

Burton, Sir Richard F. *The City of the Saints and across the Rocky Mountains to California.* 1862. Reprint, Niwot: University of Colorado Press, 1990. A classic account of the trail west from St. Joseph, Missouri, to Salt Lake City. One of the best dealing with this variant of the Oregon Trail. Great literature.

Hill, William E. *The California Trail Yesterday and Today.* Boulder, Colo.: Pruett, 1986. An amateur's collection of maps, guides, diaries, illustrations, and photographs. Interesting.

Jennings, Warren A. "The Army of Israel Marches into Missouri." *Missouri Historical Review* 62 (Winter 1968): 107–35. An excellent article on the Zion's Camp march.

Jenson, Andrew. "Latter-Day Saints Emigration from Wyoming, Nebraska: 1864–66." *Nebraska History Magazine* 27 (1936): 113–27. The best on this topic, the Nebraska City Cutoff trail.

Kimball, Stanley B. "Another Route to Zion: Rediscovering the Overland Trail." *Ensign* 14 (June 1984): 34–45. One of the best studies of this trail. Maps, illustrations.

———. "The Golden Road." *The Pioneer* 27 (November, December 1980): 11, 15, 17, 20. Map.

Korns, J. Roderic. "The Golden Pass Road, 1848–50." *Utah Historical Quarterly* 19 (October 1951): 224–47. General.

Lass, William E. *From the Missouri to the Great Salt Lake: An Account of Overland Freighting.* Lincoln: Nebraska State Historical Society, 1972. A first-rate study of freighting through the Platte Valley with brief references to the Mormon Trail. Maps.

Launius, Roger D. *Zion's Camp: Expedition to Missouri.* Independence, Mo.: Herald Publishing House, 1984. The best study of this topic.

Lee, Wayne C., and Howard C. Raynesford. *Trails of the Smoky Hill.* Caldwell, Idaho: Caxton Printers, 1980. Maps, illustrations. A few Mormons, including Brigham Young Jr., traveled the routes described in this book.

Lewin, Jacqueline A., and Marilyn S. Taylor. *The St. Joe Road.* St. Joseph, Mo.: St. Joseph Museum, 1992. Maps, illustrations.

Mattes, Merrill J. "The Northern Route of the Non-Mormons: Rediscovery of Nebraska's Forgotten Historic Trail." *Overland Journal* 8, no. 2 (1990): 2–14. An update of his argument in *Great Platte River Road.* Maps.

———. "The South Platte Trail: Colorado Cutoff of the Oregon-California Trail." *Overland Journal* 10, no. 3 (1992): 2–16. The best study I know of regarding the trail.

Rieck, Richard L. "Geography of the California Trails: Part I." *Overland Journal* 11 (Winter 1993): 12–22.

Stewart, George R. *California Trail: An Epic with Many Heroes.* Lincoln: University of Nebraska Press, 1962. A scholarly account; includes a discussion about the relationship of the Mormon Trail to the California Trail.

Topping, Gary. "Overland Emigration, the California Trail, and the Hastings Cutoff." *Utah Historical Quarterly* 56 (Spring 1988): 109–27.

Twain, Mark. *Roughing It.* 1872. Exists in many printings and editions. A classic account of going west from St. Joseph, Missouri, to Salt Lake City. Great literature.

Williams, Helen Roberta. "Old Wyoming." *Nebraska History Magazine* 27 (1936): 79–90. Excellent.

Handcart, Wagon Train, Railroad, and Water Routes

Agnew, Dwight. "Iowa's First Railroad." *Iowa Journal of History* 48 (January 1950): 1–26. An excellent study, helpful in understanding the handcarters and the Chicago and Rock Island Railroad into Iowa.

Ames, Charles Edgar. *Pioneering the Union Pacific: A Reappraisal of the Builders of the Railroad.* New York: Appleton-Century-Crofts, 1969. An excellent introduction of the subject.

Bartholemew, Rebecca, and Leonard J. Arrington. *Rescue of the 1856 Handcart Companies.* Provo, Utah: Charles Redd Center for Western Studies, Brigham Young University, 1982. An interesting booklet.

Chisum, Emmett D. "Boom Towns on the Union Pacific: Laramie, Benton, and Bear River City." *Annals of Wyoming* 53 (Spring 1981): 2–13. As good a study as there is for general purposes.

Clements, Donald. "Saints and Railroads: Immigration Transportation in Transition." Unpublished manuscript, 1984.

Clevenger, Homer. "The Building of the Hannibal and St. Joseph Railroad." *Missouri Historical Review* 36 (October 1941): 32–47. An excellent study showing how the Mormons could have used this railroad in their immigrating.

Galloway, Andrew. "First Mormon Handcart Trip across Iowa." *Annals of Iowa* 20 (October 1936): 444–49. Outdated.

Hafen, LeRoy, and Ann W. Hafen. *Handcarts to Zion: 1856-60.* Glendale, Calif.: Arthur H. Clark, 1960. The best there is on this topic. Only one map.

Hartley, William G. "'Down and Back' Wagon Trains: Bringing the Saints to Utah in 1861." *Ensign* 15 (September 1985): 26–31. An excellent general account of the wagon trains.

———. "Down and Back Wagon Trains: Travelers on the Mormon Trail in 1861." *Overland Journal* 11 (Winter 1993): 23–34.

Hulmston, John K. "Mormon Immigration in the 1860s: The Story of the Church Trains." *Utah Historical Quarterly* 58 (Winter 1990): 32–48. The latest and best study of this subject.

———. "Transplain Migration: The Church Trains in Mormon Immigration, 1861-68." Master's thesis, Utah State University, 1985. The thesis from which his article was taken.

Jensen, Richard L. "Steaming Through: Arrangements for Mormon Emigration from Europe, 1869-1887." *Journal of Mormon History* 9 (1982): 3-23. An excellent account of railroad immigrants after 1868.

Kimball, Stanley B. "Eastern Ends of the Trail West." *Ensign* 10 (January 1980): 30-33.

———. "Rail/Trail Pioneers to Zion, 1855-69: A Preliminary Study." Paper presented at the annual meeting of the Mormon History Association, St. George, Utah, May 1992.

———. "Sail and Rail Pioneers before 1869." *BYU Studies* 35 (1995): forthcoming.

———. "Wakes to Trails: Mormon Water Pioneers, 1831-66." Paper presented at the annual meeting of the Mormon History Association, Lamoni, Iowa, May 1993.

———. "Water and Rail Routes Routes Used by Mormons, 1831-69." In *Historical Atlas of Mormonism,* ed. by S. Kent Brown, Donald Q. Cannon, and Richard H. Jackson, 72-73. New York: Simon and Schuster, 1994.

———. "The Way It Looks Today: Sites on the Trail West." *Ensign* 10 (January 1980): 34-47. Contains thirty-seven beautiful photographs, including aerials, of the Mormon Trail.

Larson, Gustive O. *Mormon Handcart Story.* Salt Lake City: Deseret Book, 1956. A popular general study.

Monaghan, Jay. "Handcarts on the Overland Trail." *Nebraska History* 30 (March 1949): 3-18. Good study of the carts themselves.

Sonne, Conway B. *Saints on the Seas: A Maritime History of Mormon Migration, 1830-90.* Salt Lake City: University of Utah Press, 1983. The best study of its kind. Illustrated.

———. *Ships, Saints, and Mariners: A Maritime Encyclopedia of Mormon Migration, 1830-1890.* Salt Lake City: University of Utah Press, 1987.

Starr, John W. *One Hundred Years of American Railroading.* New York: Dodd, Mead, 1928. An old but useful general history.

Stover, John F. *Iron Road to the West: American Railroads in the 1850s.* New York: Columbia University Press, 1978. By far the best study of railroads for this period of the Mormon immigration.

Wakefield, Eliza M. *The Handcart Trail.* Mesa, Ariz.: Sun Valley Shopper, 1949. Basically a slight editing of the 1856 diary of Twiss Bermingham.

Atlases and Maps

Most states and many counties have published useful atlases, for example, M. Huebinger, *Atlas of the State of Iowa* (Davenport: Iowa Publishing, 1904); Wayne L. Wahlquist and others, eds., *Atlas of Utah* (Ogden, Utah: Weber State College, 1981); and Homer E. Socolofsky and Huber Self, *Historical Atlas of Kansas* (Norman: University of Oklahoma Press, 1972). See also the previously mentioned Mapping Emigrant Trails program of OCTA. The University of Oklahoma Press has published historical atlases of Arizona, California, Kansas, Missouri, New Mexico, and Oklahoma. The following lists several other useful sources:

Baughman, Robert W. *Kansas in Maps*. Topeka: Kansas State Historical Society, 1961.

Beck, Warren A., and Ynez D. Haase. *Historical Atlas of the American West*. Norman: University of Oklahoma Press, 1989. A good, but not excellent, atlas of limited use to trail students. Its extensive bibliography, however, should be noted.

Brown, S. Kent, Donald Q. Cannon, and Richard H. Jackson, eds. *Historical Atlas of Mormonism*. New York: Simon and Schuster, 1994.

Franzwa, Gregory M. *Maps of the Oregon Trail*. Gerald, Mo.: Patrice Press, 1982. Excellent and useful; the best book of maps on this trail.

———. *Maps of the Santa Fe Trail*. St. Louis, Mo.: Patrice Press, 1989. As good as the maps of the Oregon Trail.

List of Selected Maps of States and Territories. Special List No. 29. Washington, D.C.: The National Archives, 1971.

Miller, David, comp. *Utah History Atlas*. N.p.: David E. Miller. 1964. A very general, but useful, tool. Mimeographed.

Morgan, Dale L. *Utah Historical Trails Map*. Utah State Department of Publicity and Industrial Development, 1948. Reprint, Salt Lake City: Utah State Historical Society, n.d.

Sale, Randall D., and Edwin D. Karn. *American Expansion: A Book of Maps*. Lincoln: University of Nebraska Press, 1962. Basic, but very useful.

Wheat, Carl I. *Mapping the Transmississippi West, 1540-1861*. 5 vols. San Francisco: Institute of Historical Cartography, 1957-63. Essential.

Government Publications: 1963 to the Present

Brown, William E. "The Santa Fe Trail." National Park Service, 1963. Reprint, St. Louis, Mo.: Patrice Press, 1988. A National Survey of Historic Sites and Buildings study. Maps, illustrations.

"The California and Pony Express Trails: Eligibility/Feasibility Study and Environmental Assessment for National Trail Authorization." Washington, D. C.: National Park Service, 1987. Maps.

Corps of Engineers. "Little Dell Lake Project." Salt Lake City: Timpanogos Research Associates, 1993. A study of the Mormon trail in the Mount Dell area of Utah. Maps, illustrations.

"Fort Laramie Draft Development Concept Plan." Denver, Colo.: National Park Service, 1981.

Frémont, John C. *A Report on an Exploration of the Country Lying between the Missouri River and the Rocky Mountains on the Line of the Kansas and Great Platte Rivers*. Washington, D.C.: Government Printing Office, 1843. A classic account by the putative "Pathfinder."

"Independence and the Three Trails." Paper prepared by the City of Independence Task Force on the Three [Oregon-California-Santa Fe] Trails, City of Independence, Missouri, 1984.

James, Edwin, comp. *Account of an Expedition from Pittsburgh to the Rocky Mountains.* 1823. Official report of Major Stephen H. Long's western expedition of 1820; prepared by Long's physician. The best early account of what later became the Mormon Trail.

Jones, Carl Hugh, and Paul Riley. *The Mormon Pioneer National Historic Trail Study*. Bureau of Outdoor Recreation, 1974. Prepared by the Nebraska State Historical Society.

Kimball, Stanley B. *Historic Resource Study: Mormon Pioneer National Historic Trail*. Denver, Colo.: National Park Service, 1991. Maps, illustrations.

———. *Inventory of Historic Sites along the Mormon Trail*. Denver, Colo.: Bureau of Outdoor Recreation, 1974. Simple but useful.

———. *Threatened Sites Study of the Mormon Pioneer National Historic Trail*. Denver, Colo.: National Park Service, 1989.

———. *Trailside Federal, State, and Local Information Sources on the Mormon Pioneer National Historic Trail*. Denver, Colo.: National Park Service, 1990.

Mattes, Merrill J. "State of Nebraska Historic Resource Management Plan." Lincoln, 1975. Mimeographed, Maps.

"Mormon Battalion Trail Study: Santa Fe to San Diego." [Santa Fe, N.Mex.]: Bureau of Outdoor Recreation, 1974.

"The Mormon Emigration Trail, Utah Portion." San Francisco: Bureau of Outdoor Recreation, 1971. One of the earliest of recent Mormon Trail studies.

"The Mormon Pioneer National Historic Trail: Comprehensive Plan." Denver, Colo.: National Park Service, 1981. Maps.

"The Mormon Pioneer National Historic Trail Study." Lincoln, Nebr.: Bureau of Outdoor Recreation, 1974. Prepared by the Nebraska State Historical Society. Maps.

"The Mormon Trail." Denver, Colo.: Bureau of Outdoor Recreation, 1974. A public information brochure.

"The Mormon Trail: A Study Report." Washington, D.C.: Heritage Conservation and Recreation Service and National Park Service, 1978. Maps.

National Park Service. *The Overland Migrations: Handbook 105*. Washington, D.C.: National Park Service, 1980. An excellent but small guidebook.

National Register Bulletin, No. 16. Washington, D.C.: National Park Service, 1986.

National Trails Assessment. Washington, D.C.: National Park Service, 1986.

"Old Pioneer Wagon Road." Salt Lake City: U.S. Forest Services, n.d. Maps.

"Oregon, California, Santa Fe Trails Interpretation Center." Independence: City of Independence, Missouri, 1984.

"Oregon/Mormon Pioneer National Historic Trails Management Plan." Washington, D.C.: Wyoming Bureau of Land Management, 1986. Maps.

"Oregon National Historic Trail Management Plan." Washington, D.C.: National Park Service, 1981. Maps.

"The Oregon Trail." Lincoln: Nebraska Game and Park Commission, 1985.

"Oregon Trail Cultural Resource Study." Cheyenne: Wyoming Bureau of Land Management, 1981. Maps.

The Pony Express Stations of Utah in Historical Perspective. Washington, D.C.: Utah Bureau of Land Management, 1979. Maps.

"Preliminary Reconnaissance Report—Mormon Trail Route in Iowa." Ann Arbor, Mich.: Bureau of Outdoor Recreation, 1971. Another early Mormon Trail study.

"Santa Fe National Historic Trail: Comprehensive Management and Use Plan." Washington, D.C.: National Park Service, 1990. Maps.

Stansbury, Howard. *Exploration and Survey of the Valley of the Great Salt Lake of Utah Including a Reconnaissance [*sic*] of the New*

Route through the Rocky Mountains. Philadelphia: Lippincott, Grambo, 1852. An account of some early exploring and surveying along the Mormon Trail. Maps.

"Wyoming Historic Trails Management Plan: Significant Trail Resource Management Recommendations." Cheyenne: Wyoming Recreation Commission, 1984. Maps.

Varia

In addition to the sources listed below, some old Mormon newspapers are rich sources for trail study. See, for example, *The Frontier Guardian* [Kanesville, Iowa], 1849–52; the English *Millennial Star*, 1840–49 and beyond; and the *Deseret News* [Salt Lake City], 1850–present.

Carter, Kate B. *The Story of the Telegraph*. Salt Lake City: Utah Printing, 1961. A good short study.

Christian, Lewis Clark. "A Study of Mormon Knowledge of the American Far West prior to the Exodus." Master's thesis, Brigham Young University, 1972. The best study to date.

———. "A Study of the Mormon Westward Migration between February 1846 and July 1847 with Emphasis on and Evaluation of the Factors that Led to the Mormons' Choice of Salt Lake Valley as the Site of Their Initial Colony." Ph.D. diss., Brigham Young University, 1976.

———. "Mormon Foreknowledge of the West." *BYU Studies* 21 (Fall 1981): 403–415. An excellent short study. Compare article by Esplin in this bibliography.

Grove, Noel. "Greenways: Paths to the Future." *National Geographic* 177 (June 1990): 76–99.

Jackson, Clarence S. *Picture Maker of the Old West: William H. Jackson*. New York: Charles Scribner's Sons, 1947. An excellent pictorial account of the photographs and paintings of William H. Jackson, "dean of American photographers."

Jackson, Richard H. "Myth and Reality: Environmental Perception of the Mormons, 1840–65: An Historical Geosophy." Ph.D. diss., Clark University, 1970.

Makower, Joel, ed. *The American History Sourcebook*. New York: Prentice-Hall, 1988.

Mormon Trail Relay Run. Salt Lake City: Deseret News, 1979. A brief account of a 1979 relay run from Nauvoo to Salt Lake City.

Tompkins, Harland G. "Early Trail Explorers Had Stars in Their Eyes." *Overland Journal* 8, no. 4 (1990): 28–34. A useful introduction to determining longitude and latitude on the old trails.

Wheeler, Mary Bray, ed. *Directory of Historical Organizations in the U.S. and Canada*. 14th ed. Nashville: American Association for State and Local History, 1990.

Bibliographies

In addition to the bibliographies listed below, outstanding bibliographies have appeared annually in *BYU Studies* since 1962 (1962–77 by Chad J. Flake, 1980–90 by Scott H. Duval, and 1991 to the present by Ellen M. Copley). A cumulative index (1959–91) to *BYU Studies* was published as volume 31, number 4 (Fall 1991). In addition, dozens of equally definitive, specialized bibliographies have appeared in *Dialogue* since 1966. See Gary Gillum, comp., and Daniel Maryon, ed., *Dialogue: A Journal of Mormon Thought, Index to Volumes 1-20, 1966-87* (Logan, Utah: Dialogue Foundation, 1989), 15–16.

Andrews, Thomas F. "'Ho! For Oregon and California!': An Annotated Bibliography of Published Advice to the Emigrant, 1841–47." *Princeton University Library Chronicle* 33 (Autumn 1971): 41–64.

Flake, Chad. *A Mormon Bibliography, 1830–1930*. Salt Lake City: University of Utah Press, 1978. Definitive.

Flake, Chad, and Larry Draper. *A Mormon Bibliography, 1830–1930: Ten Year Supplement*. Salt Lake City: University of Utah Press, 1989. Excellent. A title index to both volumes was published in 1992. See Chad Flake and Larry Draper, *A Mormon Bibliography, 1830–1930: Indexes to* A Mormon Bibliography *and* Ten Year Supplement (Salt Lake City: University of Utah Press, 1992).

Kimball, Stanley B. *Historic Resource Study: Mormon Pioneer National Historic Trail*, 205–26. National Park Service, 1991. Fairly extensive. Illustrated.

Krol, Helen B. "The Books That Enlightened the Emigrants." *Oregon Historical Quarterly* 45 (June 1944): 103–23. An essential bibliography of the Oregon Trail.

Malone, Michael P., ed. *Historians and the American West*. Lincoln: University of Nebraska Press, 1983. An excellent bibliographic study, especially the chapters on the Mormons and on transportation.

Mintz, Lannon W. *The Trail: A Bibliography of the Travelers on the Overland Trail to California, Oregon, Salt Lake City, and Montana during the Years 1841–1864*. Albuquerque: University of New Mexico Press, 1987. An excellent work devoted largely to "collectible" primary accounts for the benefit of book dealers and collectors. Of limited use for Mormon trails.

Rittenhouse, Jack D. *The Santa Fe Trail: A Historical Bibliography*. Albuquerque: University of New Mexico Press, 1971. Best to date.

Townley, John M. *The Trail West: A Bibliography—Index to Western American Trails, 1841-1869*. Reno, Nev.: Jamison Station Press, 1988. Useful. Five-star, excellent all around, especially on the Mormons.

Stanley B. Kimball is Professor of Historical Studies at Southern Illinois University at Edwardsville.

NOTES

[1]That heritage, however, remains vulnerable to people's carelessness. Indeed, stories frequently appear regarding the destruction of yet another piece of our trail legacy.

[2]See the subheading *Government Publications: 1963 to the Present* in the bibliography section of this article. The designations of *Mormon Trail* and *Mormon Pioneer National Historic Trail* require some comment. The former is the almost universally used name for the 1846–47 Mormon route from Nauvoo, Illinois, to Salt Lake City, Utah. The latter is the formal name assigned to the same trail by the National Trails Systems Act.

The Mormons blazed very little of the trail that bears their name. Nevertheless, as Wallace Stegner points out in *The Gathering of Zion: The Story of the Mormon Trail* (New York: McGraw-Hill, 1964), "by the improvements they [the Mormons] made in it, they earned the right to put their name on the trail they used" (12). One vigorous, dissenting voice to Stegner's position is that of Merrill J. Mattes, who favors the term Great Platte River Road. For Mattes's arguments, see his publications referenced in this article's bibliography.

[3]For a detailed study of trails used by the Mormons, see Stanley B. Kimball, *Historic Sites and Markers along the Mormon and Other Great Western Trails* (Urbana: University of Illinois Press, 1988). This book details more than 550 historic sites and markers along ten thousand miles of trails used by the Mormons (twenty-one trails in sixteen states).

[4]Also, since the Mormons followed the year-old Reed-Donner track from Ft. Bridger to Donner Hill just east of Salt Lake City, some reference to this trail is appropriate. See, for example, Eliza Houghton, *The Expedition of the Donner Party* (Chicago: A. C. McClurg, 1911); C. F. McGlashan, *History of the Donner Party* (San Francisco: T. C. Wohlbruck, 1934), with bibliography; and George R. Stewart, *Ordeal by Hunger: The Story of the Donner Party* (New York: H. Holt, 1936), the classic study.

[5]This article does not treat at least twenty-nine historic Utah trails. These excluded trails include famous routes ranging from the trail of Father Silvestre Vele

de Escalante in 1776 through the Pony Express Trail of 1860–61. Time and space prohibited inclusion of information about these trails. For more information about these, see the Dale Morgan map under the subheading *Atlases and Maps* in this article. See also Peter H. DeLafosse, ed., *Trailing the Pioneers: A Guide to Utah's Emigrant Trails, 1829–1869* (Salt Lake City: University of Utah Press and Utah Crossroads Oregon-California Trails Association, 1994).

[6]Articles of Incorporation for the Mormon Pioneer Trail Foundation, State of Iowa, 1969.

[7]Kimball also has many records of the Mormon Pioneer National Historic Trail Advisory Council that advised the National Park Service for the years 1980–84 and similar records for the Santa Fe National Historic Trail Advisory Council to the National Parks Service for the years 1988 to the present. The National Park Service doubtless has these records in its Denver and Santa Fe offices.

[8]*Charting and Marking Pioneer Trails and Landmarks* (Salt Lake City: Utah Pioneer Trails and Landmarks Association, 1931). This is an eight-page pamphlet published for association members.

[9]See Mary Bray Wheeler, *Directory of Historical Organizations in the United States and Canada,* 14th ed. (Nashville: AASLHS Press, 1990).

[10]*Mapping Emigrant Trails* (Independence, Mo: Oregon-California Trails Association, 1992). This publication was privately printed for association members.

[11]Serious trail students should consult the Early Church Information File (ECIF) of the LDS Church, especially the "Guide to Mormon Diaries and Autobiographies." The ECIF consists of seventy-five rolls of microfilm containing approximately 1.5 million entries from more than one thousand sources. Write to Family History Department, 50 East North Temple Street, Salt Lake City, Utah 84150.

[12]For background on these other trails, see Kimball, *Historic Sites and Markers.*

Mormon Folklore

William A. Wilson

One of the few characteristics all human beings hold in common is the propensity to reduce their lives, and what is most important in those lives, to stories. We are, all of us, inveterate storytellers. We talk about our jobs, our hobbies, our successes and failures, our courtships and marriages, our children, and our religious beliefs and experiences. We do so because in order to communicate effectively to others what is in our hearts and minds we must make the abstract concrete—we must transform experience and belief into narrative. It would follow, then, that to know each others' hearts and minds, we must know each others' stories. Certainly this principle holds true in our study of Mormons and their folklore.

This essay describes the archives that make Mormon folklore available for research. Experience has taught me, however, that unless I first say something about the nature of folklore and about the contribution it can make to the study and interpretation of Mormon life, some scholars will not pay serious attention to a subject they have too often deemed frivolous.[1]

The Church is awash with stories. Members talk constantly of hardships faithfully endured by pioneer ancestors, of present-day persecutions, of missions, of conversions, of God's interventions in individual lives, of admiration for and sometimes frustration with Church authorities, of acts of sacrifice and kindness performed by charitable Church members, and of the day-to-day delights and sorrows of Church membership.

Because these stories are cut from the marrow of everyday experience and reflect the hopes, fears, joys, and anxieties of common Church members, they bring us about as close as we are likely to get to Mormon hearts and minds and to an understanding, from the lay membership's point of view, of what it really means to be Mormon. Yet these stories have been largely ignored by interpreters of the Mormon experience—partly because they are "just stories" and partly because until the 1980s they have not been adequately collected, archived, and made available to researchers.

Consider the following two accounts detailing events from the pioneer trek west and from the settlement of central Utah:

> The McDonalds were among the several thousand Mormons who lost all their worldly possessions in the tragic mid-winter exodus from their beloved homes in Nauvoo. With little food and scant protection from the elements, they suffered greatly from hunger and disease at Winter Quarters and during their long migration to Salt Lake City. Yet on reaching the Platte River crossing, they were still in sufficiently good condition to kneel together and thank the Lord for getting them through the worst part of the journey.
>
> During the river crossing cholera broke out among the members of the company. The terrible disease raged throughout the camp. Dozens died. It was necessary for James McDonald to assist in digging graves for the victims. James was a willing worker and finished three graves that October morning, even though he began to feel a little ill as he started the third. A short time after the last grave was completed, James was dead from the effects of cholera. His young daughters Elizabeth and Jane helped their mother wrap him in an old blanket, place him in the grave, and cover him with the dirt he had spaded up two hours earlier.[2]

....

> After the Indians and the white people had become a little friendly, they didn't go to the fort quite as often. This one day there was this girl down in town and she was washing. They lived quite close to the hills and Indians were camped quite close in the foothills. This girl was washing; she had a washing machine that was an old wooden one that had a wheel that would turn. This Indian brave came down and he had long braids. He came down and he started acting smart to her and talking smart to her and she couldn't understand him. He wanted different things that she had at her home; she wouldn't give them to him. When she wouldn't give them to him, he grabbed her and started throwing her around. She grabbed one lock of his hair, his braid, and hurried and put it into the wringer [of the washing machine] and wound it up tight and fixed it so it couldn't run back, and then she turned and fled while he was tied to the wringer.[3]

The teller of the first story, the great-great-grandson of one of the little girls who helped bury her father, will not easily turn from the faith his ancestor died for. But the story is more than just a family narrative. It, as well as countless stories like it, stands as a metaphor for the entire migration experience and for the faith and courage of the pioneers who endured these hardships that life might be better for those who would follow them. The view of the past reflected in such stories may or may not square with historical reality, but to the investigator trying to fathom the religious commitment of those who have told and listened to the stories, historical veracity may prove less significant than the fact that these people have generally believed the stories and have therefore been motivated by them to honor their ancestors and remain faithful to their church.[4]

The second story might easily be dismissed as an engaging piece of local color interesting to the amateur history buff yet of little consequence to serious scholars. But to the careful researcher, the narrative recounts a paradoxical tale: It mirrors a time when Mormon settlers and local Indians lived on the fringes of open hostility toward each other. It captures a continuing Mormon fascination with that time. And it draws in heroic lines a portrait of a typical pioneer woman who bravely and resourcefully faced down marauding Indians and whose courage can inspire contemporary women facing a new set of dangers in today's society. But, in an age when we supposedly value cultural diversity and practice ethnic tolerance, the narrative also reflects and perpetuates an uncomplimentary and dehumanizing picture of Native Americans. Probably the Native Americans, whose valleys the early Saints moved into, would tell quite different stories of the pioneer settlement. The story serves, therefore, as an unsettling reminder that we have failed to reach our stated ideals (we do not usually ridicule those we consider our equals) and that we have some distance to travel before we overcome old animosities.

Both these stories, then, can enhance our understanding of crucial Mormon beliefs and attitudes that lie behind Mormon actions. Both are part of that ocean of story we call Mormon folklore. To the uninitiated, folklore may seem not unlike that other important ocean of story we call oral history. Though the line between the two is sometimes blurred, folklore differs from oral history in at least one significant way. Oral histories are first-person accounts told by individuals who witnessed or participated in the events they describe. Folk narratives, on the other hand, are third-person accounts narrated by individuals who have heard about the events they describe from others.[5]

Neither the oral history nor the folk narrative will ever fully capture the truth of "what really happened," but the oral history will come closer to that end than will the folk narrative. Folk narratives will yield a different, but equally important, kind of truth. Kept alive by the spoken word as they are passed from person to person through time and space, folk narratives will be formularized by the storytellers, usually unconsciously, to make them more aesthetically appealing and persuasive; and they will be reshaped, again unconsciously, to reflect not so much the events recounted, but rather the storytellers' attitudes and beliefs toward these events. In other words, some of these narratives comprise what we might call a "folk," or "people's," history—that is, a history generated by the folk (in this case the Mormons), circulated orally by them, constantly re-created in the process in response to their current needs and concerns, and reflective of what is most important to them. In our attempts to deepen our understanding of Mormon life, we ignore such stories at our peril.

Because the stories given above describe the pioneer era, they may strengthen a common misperception about folklore—that it is always tied to the past. Folklore will, to be sure, tell us something of the past, but, as we shall see, it will usually tell us much more of the present. Folklore provides keys to understanding contemporary culture for the simple reason that people keep alive those practices and tell those stories that interest them most. Once people lose interest in particular practices or stories, these will disappear. The folklore current at any given time will therefore serve as an excellent barometer, helping us plumb the beliefs and emotions of the people who possess the lore. The following narrative, known widely in Mormon country, is a good example of a story born in recent times and reflective of current needs and interests:

> A dear L.D.S. lady left her small family in Phoenix to go to the temple in Mesa. While she was in the middle of a session, she got a strong feeling that she should go home—that something was terribly wrong. The feeling wouldn't go away, so she told the temple president and asked him what she should do. He said, "Have no fear. You are doing the right thing by being here. All is well at home." So she continued the session. She hurried home when she was through and found her six-year-old daughter in bed. She asked her daughter if something was wrong. She told her mother that she had left the house while the baby sitter was busy with the other children and had gone out by the canal near their house. While she was playing, she slipped on some grass and fell in. She couldn't swim, and the canal is deep. Many people drown this way. But a lady all dressed in white came along just then and got her just before she would have drowned. The lady set her on the bank and made sure she was okay. The little girl asked the lady who she was because she knew that the lady didn't live near by. So, the lady told her what her name was. The lady who saved the little girl was the lady whom the mother had done work for in the temple that day.[6]

To believing Mormons, this story speaks many messages. It encourages them to persist in the search for their ancestral roots; it testifies to the validity of temple ordinances; it suggests that God is a caring God who will protect them in time of need; it stresses the importance of the family and strengthens family ties; and it gives them hope that these ties will continue beyond this life. These messages are brought forcefully home by an artistic performance designed to move listeners to action and are made all the more powerful by the narrative symmetry in which two lives are saved at the same moment—the physical life of the young girl and the eternal life of the rescuer, the mother serving as the link between the two. It is, therefore, an important artifact for anyone interested not just in the Mormon past, but also in Mormon social organization, Mormon belief, and Mormon creative expression.

Because the materials of folklore are traditional—existing among the people only in the spoken word or in customary practices—many of the stories recounted by earlier generations of Mormons and applied to the circumstances of their lives have been irretrievably lost. A few of these stories did make their way into early Church publications, albeit without the social contexts necessary to give them life. The bulk of them, however, were not preserved for the simple reason that no one was there to record them. Fortunately, as scholars have gradually become aware of the wealth of intellectual history embodied in folklore, they have begun redressing past neglect and, in order to enhance their understanding of Mormon life, have turned to stories once ignored.[7]

Because the materials of folklore reside not on library shelves, but in the minds of people, informed study and interpretation of Mormon folklore must always be preceded by three steps: collecting, archiving, and indexing.

Collecting

Fieldwork in Mormon folklore commenced in earnest in the 1930s and 1940s. Thomas E. Cheney and Lester A. Hubbard began collecting Mormon folksongs. Hector Lee gathered stories of the Three Nephites—ancient American disciples of

William A. Wilson and Austin Fife at the annual Fife Folklore Conference at Utah State University, August 1978. Together with his wife, Alta, Austin published *Saints of Sage and Saddle: Folklore among the Mormons* (Indiana University Press, 1956).

Christ allowed, according to the Book of Mormon, to "tarry in the flesh" until the second coming of the Savior. Austin E. and Alta S. Fife crisscrossed the highways and byways of the Mormon cultural region, recording a full range of Mormon expressive forms and, in the process, bringing together one of the most important personal collections of folklore in the United States.[8]

Beginning in the 1960s and inspired by the work of their predecessors, a second generation of folklorists began to break new ground: William A. Wilson and Richard C. Poulsen at Brigham Young University; Jan H. Brunvand and Margaret Brady at the University of Utah; Barre Toelken, Steven Siporin, Barbara Walker, and Jay Anderson at Utah State University; Ed Reber and Joe Peterson at Dixie College; Thomas Carter, formerly at the Utah Historical Society and now at the University of Utah; David Stanley at Westminster College; Carol Edison, Craig Miller, and Annie Hatch at the Utah Arts Council's Folk Arts Program; and Hal Cannon at the Western Folklife Center.[9]

Not only have these scholars collected a considerable body of folklore themselves, but also those teaching at universities have for three decades sent scores of students armed with notepads, tape recorders, and cameras into the field to collect folklore. Under the direction of their professors, these students have brought together a massive body of material, much of it dealing with Mormons. Some of these student collections are understandably weak, but many are first-rate and, taken together, provide a depth and range of topics earlier collectors, working alone or in pairs, could not hope to reach. To demonstrate the nature and use of folklore archives, I have focused in this essay on one of the dominant forms of Mormon folklore, the legend—a story generally told as true. In fact, the archives contain a broad range of Mormon folk materials: verbal lore (songs, jokes, sayings, as well as legends);[10] descriptions of customs (medicinal practices, courtship and marriage practices, and family and community traditions and celebrations);[11] and slides and photographs of material objects (handicrafts, gravestone markers, and architecture).[12]

The first generation of collectors, like their contemporaries, tended to be item oriented. This orientation meant they would collect a song or story, give the place and date of the collection, and record minimal biographical information about the informant. They provided little data, however, on the social context of the item collected—the situation in which it was performed or practiced, the use made of it, the makeup of the audience for whom it was performed, its impact on the audience. In recent years, folklorists have shifted away from the study of items to the analysis of process—from the story told to the "telling" of the story. This shift has required a corresponding change in what is collected. Folklorists, including our student collectors, still collect folklore items, but they now surround those items with as much social and cultural context as possible in order to give a fuller, more dynamic picture of the lore in actual life.

Archiving

For many years, the materials brought in by this second wave of collectors, by both professors and students, were stuffed into boxes and filing cabinets in the professors' offices—the result being that, even though an adequate Mormon folklore data base was coming into being, it was still not available for scholarly analysis. General readers may find it interesting to know how this circumstance has gradually changed.

When I left Brigham Young University in 1978 to direct the folklore program at Utah State University, I offered to give the BYU library copies of the student collections in my office if the library would do the photocopying. The library accepted my offer; I took the originals to Utah State University and left the copies behind. At Utah State University, I discovered that the magnificent Fife collections—manuscripts, audio recordings, and color slides—resulting from more than forty years of field research were housed in the university library but were not generally available to researchers. We managed to secure a special room in the library, name it the Fife Folklore Archive, house both the Fifes' personal collections and the student-based collections there, and for the first time open both for public use. Under the able direction of Barbara Walker, the archive has continued to develop into one of the best in the country.[13]

As I prepared to return to Brigham Young University in 1984, I once again began photocopying, this time the student collections that had been submitted during my years at Utah State University. The process lasted nearly a year. Upon arriving at BYU, I retrieved the earlier student collections from the corner of the library where they had been gathering dust in my absence, combined them with the photocopied Utah State University collections I had brought with me, secured a library room, and made these collections available for scholarly use. Thus the student collections on file at both the USU and BYU archives contain identical materials to 1984; since then, each archive has developed in its own direction. During these same years, Jan Brunvand and Margaret Brady at the University of Utah turned the student collections crowding their offices over to their university library. As a result of these efforts, three research archives now exist in Utah: the Fife Folklore Archive, located in the Merrill Library at Utah

State University; the University of Utah Folklore Archive, located in the Marriott Library; and the Brigham Young University Folklore Archive, located in the Lee Library. All three of these archives contain significant amounts of Mormon materials.

William A. Wilson delivering the Honor Lecture at the annual Fife Folklore Conference, Utah State University, June 1985. Photograph by Carol Edison. Courtesy Utah Arts Council.

An additional archive, the Utah Folk Arts Program Folklore Archive, is located at the Chase Home in Salt Lake City's Liberty Park. The Folk Arts Program, following its public-service mandate, brings together materials more for exhibits and performances than for scholarly analysis. However, since good public presentations must be based on equally good documentation and field research, the Folk Arts Program has collected considerable data useful to the scholar. For example, its impressive color-slide collection of Utah gravestone art will provide valuable insights into Mormon cultural and spiritual values.

Elsewhere, a smattering of Mormon folklore has made its way into archives all across the country, as university students have collected from Mormons they have encountered in the field. The best collection outside Utah is located at the Folklore and Mythology Center at the University of California at Los Angeles. The past director of the center, Wayland D. Hand, now deceased, was also a strong supporter of Mormon folklore collection and study in Utah.

Potential folklore archive users should be aware of how these repositories are like and unlike other archives containing Mormon materials. The special features of folklore archives grow out of the characteristics of folklore discussed above. These need further elaboration here.

First, like archives in general, folklore archives provide space where materials can accumulate until a sufficient data base is available to warrant sound generalizations. The archives thus provide an effective countermeasure against those who would jump to quick and easy conclusions on the basis of only a few texts. One occurrence of the story of the child saved from an irrigation canal cannot guide us to safe conclusions about its importance as a mirror of Mormon spiritual values; but the numerous versions of the story in various archives, attached to different temples and existing over a period of years, can help us better understand the importance of temple activity in Mormon life. Similarly, one or two stories describing relations between Mormon settlers and the original occupants of the land, though possibly striking accounts valuable for their own sakes, will teach us little about Mormon attitudes toward Native Americans and will scarcely prove or disprove generalizations like those drawn above; but a thousand such accounts available to the scholar in archives will make defensible conclusions possible. Also, good contextual background data accompanying these accounts will make the conclusions still more convincing.

Second, like other archives, the folklore archives contain a wealth of material describing the pioneer past. Unlike these other repositories, however, the folklore archives will not greatly increase our understanding of that past. This is so for two reasons already discussed above. Stories generated and circulated about past events such as the practice of polygamy were not collected during the time the events were taking place. In addition, because people tell stories about the past in terms meaningful to them in the present, stories that did originate during the pioneer era and have remained in circulation through our day will have been reshaped during the frequent tellings and retellings to reflect the attitudes and meet the needs of the present tellers. Though describing pioneer happenings, the stories will speak to us most clearly of the contemporary Mormon world.

As we study stories that have been born in the past but live in the present, we may occasionally pick up a thin residue of truth about that past. But, of first importance, we will discover how contemporary Mormons have, through their stories, constructed the past in order to negotiate their way through the present. Consider the following polygamy story:

> This is just a story I heard once about three wives who were helping their husband push a new piano up the hill. They stopped to rest for a moment at the top of the hill and the husband said, "You know, this piano will belong to Martha." "What about us?" the other two said. "No," said the husband, "it's for Martha alone." So the two wives jumped up, pushed the piano down the hill, and watched it bust into a thousand pieces.[14]

Many contemporary Mormon women, almost always the narrators of such stories, identify with the piano-busters in this account and cheer their victory over the crass and unfeeling husband. Whatever the practice of polygamy was actually like, few Mormon women today contemplate its practice with pleasure. Though humorous on the surface, this story captures some of the pain of these modern storytellers and, at least vicariously, satisfies their need for justice. When I asked one woman why she liked the story, she replied, "Because they [the husband and the favored wife] got what they deserved."

Other narratives cast polygamy in a more favorable light and reflect a more positive attitude toward it. The point to remember is that the picture of polygamy, or of any other historical event emerging from the narratives in the archives, will be a picture drawn by contemporary Mormons. Because people are motivated not by what actually happened in the past, but by what they believe happened, learning what contemporary Mormons believe about events in Church history will help us better understand the forces that move them to action.

In addition to making available the data that will help us understand these motivating forces, the folklore archives will provide future scholars an opportunity denied us in our study of the Mormon past: the archives will preserve the folk narratives circulating today and will thus help future scholars understand our time from the perspective of stories told during our time.

Third, unlike other repositories of unpublished data, folklore archives seldom contain completed or closed collections. If a traditional research archive receives the papers of a prominent figure or the diaries and letters of an ordinary individual, once those papers have been indexed they are closed—new material is not usually added to them. Folklore collections, on the other hand, are open-ended—and this is their strength. As new variants of the irrigation-canal story are recorded or new accounts of appearances of the Three Nephites are collected, they are added to the existing files, expanding all the while our understanding of the stories and of the Mormon life they reflect. Examining the ever-changing nature of the folklore collections, therefore, is an excellent means of keeping a finger on the Mormon pulse.

Further, folklore archives help us measure that pulse across time. For instance, tracing changes in the Nephite stories over the fifty-year period they have been collected will help us understand changes taking place in the Church during that same period.[15] An extended example from the folklore of Mormon missionaries[16] will help illustrate this point.

Most of the stories told of divine intervention in the lives of missionaries have to do with supernatural assistance in preaching the gospel or supernatural protection from physical harm. The following story, known worldwide, illustrates the supernatural protection:

> This story happened when two missionaries were in a tough neighborhood somewhere in Australia. They came out of the apartment in the rough part of town, and there were at least thirty-five people standing around their car with chains, clubs, and knives. The missionaries looked at each other and asked if they should go inside and call the police, go outside and handle the crowd, or just fake it and just walk right in and hope nothing happens. [In many versions the missionaries pray for help.]
>
> Well, they decided on the latter, and so they walked right through the crowd and opened the car door. They started up the car and drove away. When the car started, the crowd jumped back and scratched their heads. The missionaries drove away and didn't understand what had happened.
>
> They drove some twenty miles, checked in with some missionaries for the evening and returned to their car a few moments later and found it would not start. On opening the hood, they found that there was no battery. The battery was back with the mob which had apparently removed it to keep the missionaries from leaving. No wonder they jumped back when the car started.[17]

Given the fact that missionaries face constant danger, they quite naturally tell stories like this one to reassure themselves that divine help is available in times of need. Such stories are legion. In the past, almost all these have been told about male missionaries, the elders. In recent years, however, a new story has emerged and swept the mission fields:

> These two sister missionaries were out tracting [going from door to door] one day, and they came onto this deserted house, and they didn't know this but the guy living in there had escaped from prison. He was in prison for killing women, and the women he had killed were right there in the 21–23 age group. Well, they knocked and he wasn't interested, so they went on their way.
>
> Well, they saw a flyer or something that showed his picture and said that he was wanted, so they turned him in and identified him. And when he was taken into the police department they asked him why he hadn't killed those two girls that had come tracting, because they were just the age group that he was always killing.
>
> And he said that there was no way that he was going to even touch those girls because they had three big guys with swords standing behind them. So he just wanted to get rid of them as quickly as possible because those three big guys with swords would have killed him if he had touched the girls.[18]

The sisters' protectors, whom they never see themselves, are generally thought to be the Three Nephites, though sometimes they are simply called angels or divine personages. Of the thirty-seven versions of this story in the Brigham Young University Folklore Archive, the earliest was collected in 1985. In none of the accounts was the action described thought to have occurred before 1980. What we have here is a good example of narratives mirroring changes occurring in the surrounding society—as more and more women have entered the mission field, they, quite naturally, have become subjects of missionary lore.

But the lore does more than simply catalog the fact that the number of sister missionaries is increasing. Since far more elders than sisters still serve missions, one would expect more of the collected versions of this story to have come from males. Instead, twenty-four of the thirty-seven accounts were collected from women, suggesting that this is a narrative especially meaningful to them. Sister missionaries know that because they cannot hold the priesthood held by the male elders and because they have not been encouraged to serve missions as strongly as the elders have, they will sometimes be scorned and held in less regard as missionaries than are the elders. When elders do tell this story, they again stress the possibility of divine protection in the face of danger. Sisters stress the same possibility, but some of them also see in the story a validation of their roles as missionaries. One of them said, "Since it specifically concerned sisters, [it] helped calm some of my fears. The fact that the story was about sisters instead of elders showed me that the Lord was just as concerned about the few as the many."[19] Another said that the mission president's wife had told her the story to remind her "that God protects sisters, as well as the elders."[20] If sisters and elders were held in equal regard, such a reminder would, of course, not be necessary.

As the story has moved from the sisters' to the elders' domain, the Nephite warriors have disappeared:

> There were two missionaries tracting one day. They knocked on the door of one gentleman's house who appeared to be interested and invited them in. The man was very hospitable and asked the two elders to sit down for a moment while he fetched them a glass of milk. The man served the milk and one elder attempted to take a drink. The elder felt some sort of distinct restraining force, like an invisible hand, holding back the glass of milk so that he could not bring it to his lips. The elder was quite alarmed and felt very strongly they should leave. Though they felt awkward, the two missionaries politely excused themselves and left. The man looked perplexed but made no objection. Later that day the missionaries happened to pass the police station and were shocked to see the picture of the same man on a "wanted" poster. The poster claimed that the man was being sought for repeated murders which he had committed by giving people poisoned milk.[21]

Hector Lee at the annual Fife Folklore Conference, Utah State University, August 1978. Lee authored the first book-length study of Mormon folklore: *The Three Nephites: Substance and Significance of the Legend in Folklore* (University of New Mexico Press, 1949).

The elders in this account are saved by divine intervention. Still, they tend to rely on inner strength and inspiration rather than on external beings, as the sisters do. Indeed, as I spoke to a class on this topic recently, one young man, a former missionary, said that the elders in his mission told the story of the sister missionaries derisively—to make fun of sisters for not being able to take care of themselves without Nephites coming to their aid.

Hopefully this is an isolated response. Whatever the case, the story emerging here, as new material is constantly added to the open-ended missionary collection, is typical of stories emerging in folklore archives across the full spectrum of Mormon cultural life. As changes in the missionary system continue to occur, influencing gender roles and sometimes inspiring gender conflicts, missionary lore accumulating in folklore archives will remain a sensitive indicator of missionary attitudes and beliefs, helping us take the pulse of missionary life. Similarly, as changes occur in the larger Church, the full range of Mormon folklore accumulating in folklore archives will help us keep our fingers on the pulse of Mormon life.

Indexing

One of the most difficult tasks in making Mormon folklore available for research is to develop indexing systems that will make open-ended archive collections accessible. For several years, Barbara Walker of the Fife Folklore Archive and I have been working on such a system. Ann Reichman at the Marriott Library has begun applying the same system to materials in the University of Utah Folklore Archive. Our hope is to enable a researcher to find the same set of data at all three of our archives with relative ease. To achieve this end, we have developed a hierarchical system that simply divides data into smaller and smaller thematic units and then moves to individual stories within these units—the irrigation-canal story, for example—and finally to variants of that story.

A brief look at our large legend collections will illustrate the method. We have broken data contained in many volumes of legends into the following thematic divisions: (1) Supernatural Religious, (2) Supernatural Non-Religious (ghost stories), (3) Human Conditions, (4) Character, (5) Etiological, and (6) Urban. Most Mormon legends occur in division 1, stories of divine intercession in human affairs; division 3, stories of recurring human situations such as migration (for example, the trek West) or marriage (for example, polygamy); division 4, stories of extraordinary characters in Church history; and division 5, Mormon place-name stories.

Let us trace our irrigation-canal story through the system. The story clearly falls into the first thematic division, "Supernatural Religious" legends. That division, in turn, can be subdivided into further thematic divisions:

1. Appearances or manifestations of supernatural beings
2. Unsolicited divine intervention
3. Solicited divine intervention

   Plus nine further divisions.

Our story falls under "Appearances or manifestations of supernatural beings," which can be further subdivided:

1. Deity, dead prophets, saints, prominent figures
2. Dead family members or friends
3. Unknown beings
4. Malevolent beings

The woman who saves the child in the story is unknown to the family, so the story falls under the third category, "Unknown beings," which can again be subdivided, this time according to reasons for the appearance:

1. Comfort
2. Protect or aid
3. Urge or cause change in behavior

   Plus seven further divisions.

Because the woman saves the child from drowning, the story falls under the second division, "Protect or aid"; it is the second of twenty-four separate stories in the division, and the version given at the beginning of this paper is the fourteenth variant. Charted, it would appear this way:

1. Supernatural Religious Legends
    1. Appearances or manifestations of supernatural beings
        3. Unknown beings
            2. Protect or aid
                2. Child saved from drowning by person for whom parent has performed temple work
                    14. variant number

The index number for the story would thus be 1.1.3.2.2.14. This number is derived from these categories:

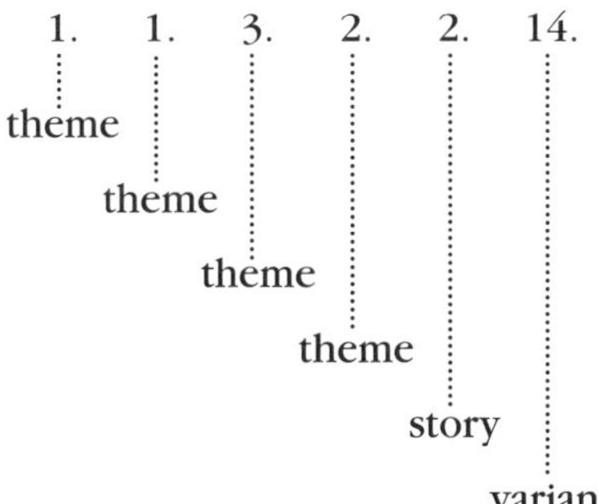

The benefit of this system is its open-endedness—new material can be worked in constantly without restructuring the basic index. The

335th variant of the irrigation-canal story submitted to the archive would simply be placed in the proper file following the 334th. Should so many variants be collected that they begin to break into subtypes, the thematic division to which the stories belong would be further subdivided without affecting the rest of the index. The index can thus be infinitely expanded to accommodate and manage an ever-growing body of Mormon folklore.

In the final analysis, a good index is much more than just an information retrieval system. By identifying major themes in Mormon folklore and by including under these themes stories that are similar to each other and by excluding those that are not, the archivist identifies corresponding themes and emphases in Mormon cultural life and moves the researcher a step closer to interpretation.

Such study and interpretation should make clear that Mormon folklore not only expresses the needs and aspirations of Mormons, it also reveals their essential humanity and, properly understood, can help us better understand both Mormon and universal human strivings. The folklore archives provide a record of those strivings.

Editor's note: These collections are accessible to interested and qualified readers at the libraries that house them. Knowing how these collections are organized and indexed will hopefully help readers understand how to access these resources. These archives are constantly expanding. People all over the world are invited to submit stories that have become meaningful parts of their experiences as Latter-day Saints. A submission form for use in adding stories to the Brigham Young University Folklore Archives is available at 4069 HBLL, Provo, Utah 84602.

William A. Wilson is Humanities Professor of Literature and Folklore and Director of the Charles Redd Center for Western Studies at Brigham Young University.

NOTES

This article was originally published as "Mormon Folklore: Cut from the Marrow of Everyday Experience," *BYU Studies* 33, no. 3 (1993): 521–40.

[1]For general introductions to folklore, see Jan Harold Brunvand, *The Study of American Folklore: An Introduction,* 3d ed. (New York: W. W. Norton, 1986); Barre Toelken, *The Dynamics of Folklore* (Boston: Houghton Mifflin, 1979); and Elliott Oring, *Folk Groups and Folklore Genres: An Introduction* (Logan: Utah State University Press, 1986).

[2]Collected by Steven C. Walker in 1964. Brigham Young University Folklore Archive [hereafter BYUFA]: L3.5.2.2.6.1.

[3]Collected by Susan Christensen and Doris Blackham in 1971. BYUFA: L3.2.1.5.2.2.1.

[4]For more on the relation of folklore to history, see Brynjulf Alver, "Historical Legends and Historical Truth," in *Nordic Folklore: Recent Studies,* ed. Reimund Kvideland and Henning K. Sehmsdorf (Bloomington: Indiana University Press, 1989), 137–49; Seppo Knuuttila, "What the People of Sivakka Tell about Themselves: A Research Experiment in Folk History," in *Studies in Oral Narrative,* ed. Anna-Leena Siikala, *Studia Fennica* 33 (1989): 111–26; and William A. Wilson, "Folklore and History: Fact amid the Legends," *Utah Historical Quarterly* 41 (Winter 1973): 40–58.

[5]See Jessie L. Embry's "Charles Redd Center for Western Studies: The Oral History Program" in this volume. For more on the distinction between folklore and oral history, see William A. Wilson, "Mormon Folklore and History: Implications for Canadian Research," in *The Mormon Presence in Canada,* ed. Brigham Y. Card and others (Edmonton: University of Alberta Press; Logan: Utah State University Press, 1990), 150–66.

[6]Collected by Kathryn Wright in 1975. BYUFA: L1.1.3.2.2.17.

[7]For an overview of the development of Mormon folklore study, see William A. Wilson, "The Study of Mormon Folklore," *Utah Historical Quarterly* 44 (Fall 1976): 317–28.

[8]For the results of these efforts, see Lester A. Hubbard, *Ballads and Songs from Utah* (Salt Lake City: University of Utah Press, 1961); Thomas E. Cheney, *Mormon Songs from the Rocky Mountains: A Compilation of Mormon Folksong,* American Folklore Society, Memoir Series, vol. 53 (Austin: University of Texas Press, 1968); Hector Lee, *The Three Nephites: The Substance and Significance of the Legend in Folklore,* University of New Mexico Publications in Language and Literature, no. 2 (Albuquerque: University of New Mexico Press, 1949); and Austin E. and Alta S. Fife, *Saints of Sage and Saddle: Folklore among the Mormons* (Bloomington: Indiana University Press, 1956).

[9]For examples of changed emphases in the works of these and other contemporary scholars, see William A. Wilson, "The Paradox of Mormon Folklore," *BYU Studies* 17 (Autumn 1976): 40–58; Wilson, "Mormon Folklore," in *Handbook of American Folklore,* ed. Richard M. Dorson (Bloomington: Indiana University Press, 1983), 155–61; Wilson, "The Study of Mormon Folklore: An Uncertain Mirror for Truth," *Dialogue: A Journal of Mormon Thought* 22 (Winter 1989): 95–110; George H. Schoemaker, "Made in Heaven: Marriage Confirmation Narratives among Mormons," *Northwest Folklore* 7, no. 2 (Spring 1989): 38–53; Margaret K. Brady, "Transformations of Power: Mormon Women's Visionary Narratives," *Journal of American Folklore* 100 (October–December 1987): 461–68; Carolyn Flatley Gilkey, "Mormon Testimony Meeting: Some Aspects of a Narrating Event," *Southwest Folklore* 3 (Fall 1979): 45–59; Clifton Holt Jolley, "The Martyrdom of Joseph Smith: An Archetypal Study," *Utah Historical Quarterly* 44 (Fall 1976): 329–50; Ellen E. McHale, "'Witnessing for Christ': The Hill Cumorah Pageant of Palmyra, New York," *Western Folklore* 44 (January 1985): 34–40; Susan Peterson, "The Great and Dreadful Day: Mormon Folklore of the Apocalypse," *Utah Historical Quarterly* 44 (Fall 1976): 365–78; Richard C. Poulsen, "Fate and the Persecutors of Joseph Smith: Transmutations of an American Myth," *Dialogue* 11 (Winter 1978): 63–70; Wayland D. Hand, "Magic and the Supernatural in Utah Folklore," *Dialogue* 16 (Winter 1983): 51–64; and Barre Toelken, "Traditional Water Narratives in Utah," *Western Folklore* 50 (April 1991): 191–200.

These and all other citations in this essay are representative only; for fuller bibliographical references to the full range of Mormon folklore study, see William A. Wilson, "A Bibliography of Studies in Mormon Folklore," *Utah Historical Quarterly* 44 (Fall 1976): 389-94; and Jill Terry, "Exploring Belief and Custom: The Study of Mormon Folklore," *Utah Folklife Newsletter* 23 (Winter 1989): 2-5.

[10]See William I. Kaufman, with Thomas E. Cheney and Richard P. Condie, *The Mormon Pioneer Songbook* (Bryn Mawr, Penn.: Theodore Presser, 1980); Jan Harold Brunvand, "As the Saints Go Marching By: Modern Jokelore concerning Mormons," *Journal of American Folklore* 83 (January-March 1970): 53-60; Thomas E. Cheney, *The Golden Legacy: A Folk History of J. Golden Kimball* (Salt Lake City: Peregrine-Smith, 1973); William A. Wilson, "The Seriousness of Mormon Humor," *Sunstone* 10, no. 1 (1985): 6-13; Barbara Bosen, "Danish Stories from Ephraim," *AFF word* 2 (Fall 1972): 24-34; and William A. Wilson and John B. Harris, "And They Spake with a New Tongue (On Missionary Slang)," in *Conference on the Language of Mormons,* ed. Harold S. Madsen and John L. Sorenson (Provo, Utah: Brigham Young University Language Research Center, 1974), 46-48.

[11]See Davis Bitton, "The Ritualization of Mormon History," *Utah Historical Quarterly* 43 (Winter 1975): 67-85; Wayland D. Hand and Jeannine E. Talley, eds., *Popular Beliefs and Superstitions from Utah,* collected by Anthon S. Cannon and others (Salt Lake City: University of Utah Press, 1984); and Suzanne Volmar Riches, "Threads through a Patchwork Quilt: The Wedding Shower as a Communication Ritual and Rite of Passage for the Mormon Woman" (Ph.D. diss., University of Utah, 1987).

[12]See Austin E. Fife, "Stone Houses of Northern Utah," *Utah Historical Quarterly* 40 (Winter 1972): 6-23; Ann Hitchock, "Gods, Graves, and Historical Archaeologists: A Study of a Mormon Cemetery in Tucson," *AFF word* 1 (January 1972): 11-16; Jan Harold Brunvand, "The Architecture of Zion," *The American West* 13 (March-April 1976): 28-35; Hal Cannon, ed., *Utah Folk Art: A Catalog of Material Culture* (Provo: Brigham Young University Press, 1980); Hal Cannon, *The Grand Beehive* (Salt Lake City: University of Utah Press, 1980); Thomas Carter, "Building Zion: Folk Architecture in the Mormon Settlements of Utah's Sanpete Valley, 1849-1890" (Ph.D. diss., Indiana University, 1984); and Richard C. Poulsen, *The Pure Experience of Order: Essays on the Symbolic in the Folk Culture of Western America* (Albuquerque: University of New Mexico Press, 1982).

[13]See William A. Wilson, "USU Fife Folklore Archive," *Folklore Society of Utah Newsletter* 17 (Autumn 1983): 2-3.

[14]Collected by Peggy Hansen in 1971. BYUFA: Collection #253, no. 26.

[15]See, for example, William A. Wilson, "Freeways, Parking Lots and Ice Cream Stands: The Three Nephites in Contemporary Mormon Culture," *Dialogue* 21 (Autumn 1988): 13-26.

[16]For an overview of Mormon missionary folklore, see William A. Wilson, *On Being Human: The Folklore of Mormon Missionaries,* Utah State University Faculty Honor Lecture (Logan: Utah State University Press, 1981).

[17]Collected by Tiare Fullmer in 1981. BYUFA: HWC5.2.3.5.12.

[18]Collected by Jane England in 1990. BYUFA: HWC5.2.3.12.2.

[19]Collected by Laura Andersen in 1990. BYUFA: HWC5.2.3.12.18.

[20]Collected by Rhonda Jones in 1992. BYUFA: HWC5.2.3.12.14.

[21]Collected by Joshua D. Heiner in 1992. BYUFA: HWC5.2.8.1.4.

Mormon Literature: Progress and Prospects

Eugene England

Expectations

Mormonism has been called a "new religious tradition," in some respects as different from traditional Christianity as the religion of Jesus was from traditional Judaism.[1] Its beginnings in appearances by God, Jesus Christ, and ancient prophets to Joseph Smith and in the recovery of lost scriptures and the revelation of new ones; its dramatic history of persecution, a literal exodus to a promised land, and the building of an impressive "empire" in the Great Basin desert—all this has combined to make Mormons in some ways an ethnic people as well as a religious community. Mormon faith is grounded in literal theophanies, concrete historical experience, and tangible artifacts (including the Book of Mormon, the irrigated fields of the Wasatch front, and the great stone pioneer temples of Utah) in certain ways that make Mormons more like ancient Jews and early Christians and Muslims than, say, Baptists or Lutherans.

Mormonism is also growing rapidly, with the highest convert rate in the United States among religious groups larger than one million, and now has over four million members in the United States.[2] Harold Bloom, the distinguished literary and cultural critic, has recently noted Mormon group cohesion and growth in numbers and accompanying economic and political power (90) and praised what he sees as its unusual theological power because of Joseph Smith's restoration of ancient insights into the eternal and divine nature of the self (105). He identifies Mormonism with "the American Religion" (111) and predicts that it will soon become the equivalent of a state religion in some parts of America (263) and will assume major worldwide influence and power in the twenty-first century (263–65).[3]

Such a religion might well be expected to produce a characteristic, good, possibly even great, literature—at least among its predominant cohesive group of literate members, who at this point, for historical reasons, are English-speaking. This group now totals nearly five million, a larger audience and one more coherent in powerful theological beliefs, mythic vision, and unique cultural and religious experiences than the audiences for which Chaucer, Shakespeare, or Milton wrote—indeed larger and more coherent than that available to any English or American writer until the middle of the nineteenth century.

A distinguished literature has, in fact, long been expected by Mormons themselves—even prophesied by their leaders. As early as 1857, with the Church less than thirty years old and most Mormons living at a subsistence level just ten years after the forced trek into the Great Basin wilderness, Apostle and future Church President John Taylor promised that "Zion will be far ahead of the outside world in everything pertaining to learning of every kind. . . . God expects Zion to become the praise and glory of the whole earth, so that kings hearing of her fame will come and gaze upon her glory."[4] Only thirty years after that, as part of his effort in the late 1880s to encourage creation of a "home literature" that would be by, about, and for the edification of Mormons, future Apostle Orson F. Whitney prophesied, "We will yet have Miltons and Shakespeares of our own. . . . In God's name and by His help we will build up a literature whose top shall touch heaven, though its foundations may now be low in earth."[5]

However, nearly ninety years later, another Apostle, Boyd K. Packer, quoted Whitney and expressed regret that "those foundations have been raised up very slowly. The greatest poems are not yet written. . . . The greatest hymns and anthems of the Restoration are yet to be composed. . . . We move forward much slower than need be."[6] The next year, in 1977, Church President Spencer W. Kimball—in a special issue of the *Ensign* (the official Mormon magazine) devoted to the arts—expressed similar disappointment but also continuing expectation:

> For years I have been waiting for someone to do justice in recording in song and story and painting and sculpture the story of the Restoration, the reestablishment of the kingdom of God on earth, the struggles and frustrations; the apostasies and inner revolutions and counter-revolutions of those first decades; of the exodus; of the counter-reactions; of the transitions; of the persecution days; of the miracle man, Joseph Smith, of whom we sing "Oh, what rapture filled his bosom, For he saw the living God."[7]

It is remarkable that what many see as the first major blossoming of a mature Mormon literature commenced about the time of these two statements by Elder Packer and President Kimball. It is also remarkable that the issues they raised or implied about why the prophesied success had come so slowly have continued to be central to critical debates among Mormons about the nature and quality of their writers' literary heritage and contemporary achievement. Just three years later, at the Church's sesquicentennial in 1980, I was able to celebrate what I called "The Dawning of a Brighter Day,"[8] citing a relative outpouring in the late 1970s of personal essays, dramas, and collections of poetry and fiction of increasing quality. Since then the growth in quantity of Mormon literature published (especially fiction), in readership, in publishing outlets, in critical essays and anthologies, and in participation in Mormon literature classes has been steady—and there has been, in my view, a steady increase in *quality* of writing as well.

But not everyone agrees. Richard H. Cracroft—who could be called the father of modern Mormon literary studies for his pioneering work in the early 1970s in producing the first anthologies[9] and starting the first Mormon literature classes—has strongly objected to the recent directions in most Mormon literature as being too imitative of flawed contemporary critical and moral trends and thus untrue to Mormon traditions and values.[10] In this concern, he echoes the warning and counsel of Elder Packer to Mormon artists in 1976 that too many "want to please the world" or to "be in style," and so our artistic heritage grows "ever so gradually." "Our worship and devotion will remain as unique from the world as the Church is different from the world. Let the use of your gift be an expression of your devotion to Him who has given it to you."[11]

At the same time, critics like Bruce W. Jorgensen have called for a Mormon literature that is distinguished not so much by specific doctrinal content and didactic purposes as by its powerfully conveyed love of the world God has given us and by its unusual hospitality to diversity of both content and style.[12] This stand seems to me consonant with President Kimball's call in 1977, cited above, for literature that includes the full range of Mormon experience: "struggles and frustrations; apostasies and inner revolutions and counter-revolutions . . . counter-reactions . . . persecution days . . . miracle man . . . rapture." Certainly one explanation for the general failure of Mormon literature to fulfill its expectations was that it had remained too timid, too narrowly conventional. It had been satisfied with the safe middle ground of experience and with the non-risk-taking authorial voice, so it was not courageously dealing with the extremes of "apostasy" and "rapture" that President Kimball seems to be calling for.

These two emphases—Elder Packer and Richard H. Cracroft calling for a quality of devotion, spirituality, and focus on the purposes of the restored Church and the fundamentals of the restored gospel, and President Kimball and Bruce W. Jorgensen inviting generous and realistic response to the full range of worldly and other-worldly experience—seem to me compatible, though not easily so. They provide the major poles of current critical discussion in Mormon letters and the major rubrics for describing what seems central to Mormon literature at present and throughout its history.

Issues

The debate presently articulated most forcibly by Cracroft and Jorgensen has continued for at least twenty years. In 1974, in the introduction to their landmark anthology, Cracroft and his co-compiler, Neal Lambert, wrote, "Readers must never forget that for the Latter-day Saint, his church, as the Doctrine and Covenants declares, is 'the only true and living church on the face of the whole earth,' and a literature, or a criticism of a literature, which fails to examine Mormonism on these terms is not only unfair, it is futile."[13] That same year, Karl Keller, in a roundtable in *Dialogue: A Journal of Mormon Thought* on Mormon literature, claimed that "more alarming than the paucity of qualified works of fiction in the Church is the lack of fictional exploration of the theology itself. Mormon fiction is by and large jack-fiction; it does not live by the principles of the Church. . . . With few exceptions the more removed a work of Mormon fiction is from orthodoxy, the better its art . . . , and the more narrowly orthodox its point of view, the poorer its art."[14]

Keller's trenchant metaphor, "jack-fiction," captures the paradox at the heart of this debate: everyone wants literature that is uniquely Mormon, even "orthodox"—but also *good,* that is, skillful and artful; the problem is that focusing on either quality seems to destroy the other. *Jack-fiction* derives from *jack-Mormon,* in modern times the term for someone attached, even very strongly, to Mormon culture and sometimes quite "orthodox" in moral behavior, but not really conversant with or deeply committed to the theology or an "active" participant at church. Most Mormon literature to 1974 had both failed to be good literature and had been only superficially Mormon—especially, Keller says, that which had *tried* to be most orthodox. The solution, he urged, lay in learning our own theology and dramatizing it effectively on the model of Flannery O'Connor, whom Keller quoted at length:

> I see from the standpoint of Christian orthodoxy. This means that for me the meaning of life is centered in our Redemption by Christ and what I see in the world I see in its relation to that.[15]
>
> The good novelist not only finds a symbol for feeling, he finds a symbol and a way of lodging it which tells the intelligent reader whether this feeling is adequate or inadequate, whether

> it is moral or immoral, whether it is good or evil. And his theology, even in its most remote reaches, will have a direct bearing on this.
>
> It makes a great difference to the look of a novel whether its author believes that the world came late into being and continues to come by a creative act of God, or whether he believes that the world and ourselves are the product of a cosmic accident. . . . It makes a great difference whether he believes that our wills are free, or bound like those of the other animals.[16]

Keller ended his call for a genuinely faithful Mormon literature by predicting, "When someone becomes capable of creating imaginative worlds where Mormon theological principles are concretely true, then we will have a writer of the stature of Flannery O'Connor. *Because* she was a Catholic, she said, she could not afford to be less than a good artist."[17]

Twenty years later, Keller's conditional prophecy, as well as those of Elder Whitney and President Kimball, are, I believe, beginning to be fulfilled—in the work of Orson Scott Card, Levi S. Peterson, Terry Tempest Williams, Margaret Young, and many others. Before discussing them I will describe some of the theological foundations for these fine Mormon writers' work and review their literary heritage.

Resources

Keller suggested that Mormon writers, to achieve the theological literacy needed to create their unique imaginative worlds, should read Sterling M. McMurrin's *The Theological Foundations of the Mormon Religion* (Salt Lake City: University of Utah Press, 1965), which he calls "essentially an outline of esthetic possibilities of Mormon articles of belief."[18] Though McMurrin, who builds on the work of Elder B. H. Roberts, whom many consider Mormonism's finest historian and theologian, does in fact provide a concise organization of what is most dramatic and unusual in Mormon thought, others could be added: Joseph Smith himself, especially "The King Follett Discourse";[19] sections 88 and 93 of the Doctrine and Covenants; 2 Nephi 2 and Alma 42 from the Book of Mormon; Brigham Young, in such sermons as "The Organization and Development of Man";[20] John A. Widtsoe; Joseph Fielding Smith; Hugh B. Brown; Spencer W. Kimball; Lowell Bennion; Truman Madsen; Margaret Toscano; Blake Ostler; Melodie Moench Charles; Janice Allred; and many others.

In such places are revealed and explored central Mormon ideas that are able to nourish a great literature: All human beings are fundamentally uncreated, noncontingent intelligences with infinite potential, literally gods in embryo. Like God, we are indestructible but bound forever in a real environment of spirit, element, and other beings that both limit and make demands on us and also make genuine joy and eternal progression possible as we learn to understand that environment and relate in love to those beings. Freedom is not an illusion but is of tragic proportions: God did not make us or the world out of nothing and cannot force salvation upon us, and thus our choices have real consequences for good and evil. Therefore Christ's Atonement is a paradox, involving a fortunate fall: each of us *must* lose innocence, experience opposition and sin, struggle with justice and our guilt, before we will let Christ's mercy break the bonds of justice within us and satisfy the demands of God's justice in our consciences so we can have the strength to develop in the image of Christ. Eternally separate and impenetrable as each of us is, we cannot realize our fullest nature and joy except in the fully sexual unity of an eternal marriage—an idea, together with the divine equality of the sexes, given the very highest status in the unique Mormon understanding of God being God only in the male and female oneness of Heavenly Parents.

Such ideas can be, and sometimes have been, reduced to a formal creed that tempts Mormon writers toward didacticism, but they are also an extraordinarily rich and sufficient resource—taken together with the dramatic and mythically powerful Mormon history and the ethically challenging opportunities and demands of activity, covenant-making, and charismatic experience in the Mormon lay church—for empowering the imaginative worlds of Mormon literature.

Mormon writers, then, certainly have at hand sufficient *matter* with which to produce a great literature. But does Mormonism also provide insight into the values—and limitations—of the *means* of literature: language, form, style, genres, critical perspectives? From the beginning, Mormons have produced many of their writings, including some of their best, in forms that until fairly recently have been called subliterary and generally dismissed by formalist critics: diaries, letters, hymns, sermons, histories, and personal essays. In the last twenty years, poststructuralism and various forms of ethical criticism have helped us see beyond such distinctions and provided tools for identifying and appreciating the different but equal values of all kinds of literature. In 1974, Cracroft and Lambert unapologetically filled half of their anthology with the early Mormon work in unusual genres, much of which they had recovered through their own research, and they provided useful original attempts at evaluation of these genres in their introductions and notes. Partly in response to that anthology came my own belated conversion from my training in formalism to appreciation of the literary power in unusual forms, and I began to try to develop new tools of appreciation.[21]

Mormon academic critics have been trained in and made use of all the modern theoretical approaches, from the New Criticism of the 1940s and 1950s to the postmodernism that has developed since the late 1960s,[22] and no systematic criticism has emerged that successfully identifies Mormonism with any one theory of language or poetics.

Mormon theology, in fact, encourages a remarkable and fruitful openness in relation to current controversies about the nature and power of language—and thus of human thought and literature. On the one hand, poststructuralists find much that is congenial in the Mormon sense of an ongoing, continually developing universe in which God is a genuine and nonabsolute participant, himself in important ways a creature of language and its limitations. Doctrine and Covenants 1:24 informs us that God definitely speaks to us through his prophets but does so "in their weakness, after the manner of their language," which seems to be consistent with postmodern ideas about the way language always functions relative to the worldview and rhetorical resources of the speaker and the discourse community, and there is no way to get "outside" of nature and language for an absolute and therefore universally compelling "meaning." Doctrine and Covenants 93:24 further suggests that "truth is *knowledge* of things as they are, and as they were, and as they are to come" (italics added), which can be understood as meaning that truth as we know it is always relative to the knowers involved, a position central to the thought of postmodern philosophers and literary critics.

On the other hand, in the "King Follett Discourse," Joseph Smith refers to "chaotic matter—which is element and in which dwells all the glory."[23] I understand this to mean that God and humans can bring order from a pluralistic chaos that is *potent,* genuinely responsive to our creative powers embodied in mind and language. Because God created the world that we know from such a potent chaos and because his mind and ours can make connection to each other and to the world through the powers of language, we can create metaphors that closely *imitate* experience but also increase our ability to *understand* experience. Language is ultimately tragic, because it cannot perfectly embody or communicate reality, but it is all we have and we had better respect it for what it *can* do.

A Mormon theory of language, then, can accede fully neither to a naive platonic realism nor to an absolute postmodern nominalism. It is based in *faith*—faith that God is like us, personal, embodied, creative, and language-using, closely related in mind and feelings and sufficiently expressed in our organic, changing universe to be understood, at least in part, and to be trusted; faith that while language is limited and relative, it is not merely an ephemeral human creation or an ultimately meaningless game to occupy us until final doom, but rooted ontologically and shared by God.[24]

Historical Period One: Foundations (1830–1880)

Mormon literature can be divided usefully into four periods: (1) an initial outpouring in the first fifty years, 1830-80, of largely unsophisticated writing, expressive of the new converts' dramatic symbolic as well as literal journeys to Zion and their fierce rejection of Babylon, and often intended to meet the immediate and practical needs of the Church for hymns, sermons, and tracts; (2) the creation, in the next fifty years, 1880-1930, of a "home literature" in Utah, highly didactic fiction and poetry designed to defend and improve the Saints but of little lasting worth—and also the refining of Mormon theological and historical writing into excellent and lasting forms; (3) a period of reaction, by third- and fourth-generation Mormons, 1930-70, to what they saw as the loss of the heroic pioneer vision and a decline into provincial materialism, which impelled an outpouring of excellent but generally critical works, published and praised nationally but largely rejected by or unknown to Mormons, leading some to identify this group as very similar to American literature's "lost" generation of Hemingway, Stein, etc.; and (4) a slow growth and then flowering, 1960 to the present, of good work in all genres that combines the best qualities and avoids the limitations of most past work, so that it is both faithful and critical, appreciated by a growing Mormon audience and also increasingly published and honored nationally.

It seems very important, when discussing Mormon literature, to remember that Mormonism *begins* with a book. The Book of Mormon has been vilified and laughed at by other Christians and ignored by literary scholars and critics, but it is now published in over eighty languages, over five million copies a year, and has changed the lives of millions of people. Most of these people do not think of it as *literature,* but it has the verbal and narrative power, linguistic and historical complexity, ethical and philosophical weight, and mythic structure of a great epic.

It was a non-Mormon, Douglas Wilson, who twenty-five years ago pointed out the scandal of the neglect of the Book of Mormon by the American literary establishment,[25] and that neglect still continues, even in our postmodern age of canon expansion and theoretical attempts to value all writing. But Mormon scholars have made important strides both in explicating the historical and cultural substance of this rich work[26] and in applying various forms of literary analysis to the text itself. Especially important so far have been the work of John W. Welch on the ancient Hebraic poetic form of *chiasmus* in the Book of Mormon, Bruce Jorgensen on the powerful archetypal structure of the book, and R. Dilworth Rust, who has completed a book entitled "The Book of Mormon as Literature."[27]

Joseph Smith was involved, as author or translator, in much besides the Book of Mormon, and much of that other work is also of high literary merit. Sections of the Doctrine and Covenants, such as 19, 76, 88, and 121, and his accounts of his first vision have been appreciated as fine literature as well as scripture.[28] His literate and very forthcoming letters and diaries have been definitively edited,[29] as have reports of his sermons. The sermons, recorded from memory or in longhand, are quite fragmentary and unrevealing of his literary power, except for the truly remarkable "King Follett Discourse";[30] because of the advent of shorthand we have a much fuller record of the unusually practical and personal tradition of pioneer orators influenced by Joseph Smith, especially Brigham Young.[31]

Early Mormons, like their mainly Puritan forebears, were both anxious about their salvation and moved to record evidence of their joy and success in finding it. In addition, Mormon theology inclined them to think of themselves as eternal, uncreated, and godlike beings, coming here to mortality from a premortal existence to continue working out their salvation in fear and trembling. They were encouraged by Church practice and frontier American culture to bear witness both publicly and privately about their hardships, feelings, and spiritual experiences and to take interest in their individual selves and sense of creation of those selves—so they produced, at great effort and in amazing detail, diaries and personal reminiscences.[32] Good examples of the journals, showing a wide range of sophistication and experiences, are Wilford Woodruff's nearly daily record of over sixty years,[33] which provides both a rich source of ecclesiastical and cultural history and also intimate insight into the development of an Apostle and Church President; Eliza R. Snow's "Trail Diary," our best source for the horrendous crossing from Nauvoo to Council Bluffs after the martyrdom of Joseph Smith and of the unique spiritual outpourings to the women there during the winter and spring of 1847;[34] George Laub's down-to-earth record of the momentous events of Nauvoo and the costs of discipleship for ordinary members;[35] Mary Goble Pay's reminiscence of the 1856 handcart tragedy, uniquely moving in its understated purity, which demonstrates how the character of an untrained narrator and powerful events honestly recorded can combine to produce great writing;[36] and the witty, detailed, and poignant diary of Joseph Millett, covering both his 1853 mission as a teenager to Nova Scotia and his later life as a settler in Southern Utah and Nevada.[37]

Such qualities often come through in the letters as well. Like diaries, letters provide the revealing ethical context of spontaneous, unrevised thought and day-by-day decision-making and living with consequences, as well as unequaled directness. Such directness often makes diaries and letters "truer" than the usual histories, which can be falsified by generalization—and are valuable, even understandable, only when we see in them what Stephen Vincent Benét called people's "daily living and dying beneath the sun."[38]

There were also some significant achievements in traditional literary forms in the first period. Eliza R. Snow was an accomplished versifier before she converted to Mormonism and turned her talent to long, didactic poems about Mormon history, leaders, and beliefs. She also produced some fine short lyrics and a number of hymns.[39] The poems were published in two volumes, 1856 and 1877,[40] and the hymns are still a highly valued part of the Mormon hymnal, especially "O My Father," which states the unique Mormon doctrine of a Heavenly Mother. One other book of poetry was published during this period, John Lyon's *The Harp of Zion: A Collection of Poems, Etc.* (Liverpool: S. W. Richards, 1853), and other fine hymns were written by W. W. Phelps and Parley P. Pratt.[41]

The first Mormon fiction, as well as some of the most important and literate early tracts,[42] was also written by Pratt. His "Dialogue

Eliza R. Snow

Parley P. Pratt

Photographs courtesy LDS Church Archives.

between Joseph Smith and the Devil," first published in the *New York Herald* in 1844, is, though mainly a didactic effort to improve the Mormon image and teach some doctrine to its gentile audience, very witty and imaginative in its setting, argument, and lively dialogue. His *Autobiography,* edited and published in the 1870s, long after his death, and still popular in reprints today, has sections that are carefully shaped, self-conscious personal narratives much like good short stories; and some passages, such as his description of Joseph Smith rebuking the guards in Liberty Jail, rise to great eloquence.[43]

However, though there is evidence that Mormon pioneers read fiction, even during their treks, Church leaders in this first period regularly denounced the reading of novels as a waste of time and worse, the encouragement of "lies," recommending instead sermons and histories, which dealt in truth.[44] George Q. Cannon blamed novel-reading for many of the evils which prevail in the world,[45] and the best Brigham Young could say is that he "would rather persons read novels than read nothing."[46] Such reservations were understandable in the day of cheap novels flooding Utah after the coming of the railroad—and few great classics yet available. But in the 1880s some Mormon leaders actually began, with both exhortation and example, an important movement to solve the problem by encouraging and creating fiction—and drama, poetry, and essays—that explicitly set out to teach Mormon faith and doctrine.

Historical Period Two: Home Literature (1880–1930)

In 1888, Orson F. Whitney, popular poet, essayist, and bishop of a Salt Lake City ward, expressed hope for a fine and virtuous "home literature" and then continued to try to fulfill his own hope.[47] He spoke to the Mormon youth, who, as the first generation raised in the Church, lacked their own direct conversion experience. He saw these youth as declining from the faith of their parents and vulnerable to the Protestant missionaries who were beginning to proselyte in Utah. He was joined by other leaders, such as B. H. Roberts, Emmeline B. Wells, and Susa Young Gates, and the result was a virtual flood of moralistic and faith-promoting stories that became the staple of Church periodicals like the *Juvenile Instructor,* the *Contributor,* the *Woman's Exponent,* the *Utah Magazine,* and the *Young Woman's Journal.* Such stories have continued to appear in nearly every issue of twentieth-century official magazines like the *Improvement Era,* the *Relief Society Magazine,* the *Children's Friend,* and their successors down to the present.

Poets like Josephine Spencer[48] and Augusta Joyce Crocheron produced didactic and narrative poems, Charles Walker recited his Southern Utah folk poetry, and Elder Whitney published hymns, lyric

Orson F. Whitney

B. H. Roberts

James E. Talmage

Emmeline B. Wells

Nephi Anderson

Susa Young Gates

Photographs courtesy LDS Church Archives.

poetry, and a book-length poem, *Elias, an Epic of the Ages* (New York: Knickerbocker Press, 1904). Susa Young Gates published a fairly successful novel, and B. H. Roberts wrote a novel that was turned into a play performed on Broadway in New York.[49] But the most able, prolific, and lasting in influence of the early "home literature" writers was Nephi Anderson. His *Added Upon* (1898),[50] though Anderson himself recognized its limitations and revised it twice, well fulfills his own stated criterion in an essay on "Purpose in Fiction": "A good story is artistic preaching."[51] The novel follows a woman and a man and their friends from the premortal existence through mortal life and into the postmortal spirit world, showing how their love is promised before birth and subjected to earthly vicissitudes but resolved in marriage within the restored Church, then depicting their reunion and resurrection after death. Versions of this formula were immensely popular and have endured into the present in musicals like Doug Stewart and Lex De Azevedo's *Saturday's Warrior* (1974) and Carol Lynn Pearson's *My Turn on Earth* (1977). Anderson's novel, though not his best, was the only fiction of the original home literature movement that continued to be read by a sizable Mormon audience, with some readers down to the present.

A number of works of *non*fiction written during the period, because of their intellectual and literary excellence as well as their orthodox and faith-promoting power, have continued to be valued and carefully read, such as the didactic biographies of Joseph Smith by George Q. Cannon and John Henry Evans. B. H. Roberts published stimulating, powerfully imaginative and persuasive theology (for example, *Joseph Smith the Prophet-Teacher* [Salt Lake City: Deseret News Publishing, 1908; reprint, Princeton, N.J.: Deseret Club of Princeton University, 1967]) and history (for example, *A Comprehensive History of the Church of Jesus Christ of Latter-day Saints* [Salt Lake City: Deseret News Press, 1930]) that dramatically but with amazing scholarly objectivity organized the thought of Joseph Smith and retold the history of the Saints in the Church's first century. James E. Talmage, an apostle, wrote two books, *The Articles of Faith* (Salt Lake City: Deseret News, 1899) and *Jesus the Christ* (Salt Lake City: Deseret News, 1915), that combine intellectual power with stately, moving personal testimony and have justly achieved almost scriptural status among Latter-day Saints.

The forms and formulas of "home literature" that were developed in this second period continue into the present as the kind published and encouraged by the official Mormon outlets (the *Friend, New Era,* and *Ensign,* and Deseret Book) and also those, like the *Latter-day Digest* and Bookcraft, which aspire to wide and near-official acceptance by Church leaders and general Mormon readership. Richard H. Cracroft has led the way in arguing that the future of Mormon literature depends on writers learning from Nephi Anderson's "steady progress from artless dogma to gently dogmatic art"[52] to produce a steadily more sophisticated and artful work that is still, in its direct focus on Mormon moral and spiritual values, essentially didactic.[53] But others feel that such primary emphasis on the didactic, on *teaching* through literature, is paradoxically what keeps Mormon literature from being either excellent artistically or powerful morally and spiritually.

Didacticism vs. Description

From the Roman writer Horace through English critics Sir Philip Sidney and Samuel Johnson to noted twentieth-century Americans like Yvor Winters and Wayne Booth, most students of literature have recognized that it inevitably has a problematic, integrated dual purpose and effect—to teach as well as delight—and even that all discourse is fundamentally an attempt to persuade.[54] Most have also understood that the more direct and conscious the effort to teach, the less delightful the literature—and less likely it is to succeed in persuading. On the other hand, great writers who seem to *begin* with no other purpose than telling a good and honest story, or creating interesting and complex characters—or merely powerful images and affecting rhythms and sounds—end up moving us into whole new dimensions of moral understanding and religious experience. In 1969, Karl Keller argued:

> A great work of *Mormon* literature will be like all great works of literature; it will be one that makes me wrestle with my beliefs and which stimulates me by the example of the author's own effort to re-create my own life on surer grounds of belief. . . .
>
> Perhaps when we realize that literature cannot be written or read in the service of religion, but that like religion it is an exercise in otherness, an exercise in faith, an exercise in renewing our grounds of belief, *then* we will have an important body of Mormon literature.[55]

Similarly, in 1980, Bruce Jorgensen, drawing on the criticism of Wayne Booth and Sheldon Sacks, made a persuasive case that the morality of a work of literature is most authentic and thus convincing, not in the direct preaching of an "apologue" but in the inevitable hundreds of small decisions a moral *author* makes in the process of writing a realistic "action."[56]

Orson Scott Card, one of the most able as well as successful contemporary Mormon writers, provided personal confirmation of Jorgensen's thesis when he announced in 1985 that he had long before resolved never to

> attempt to use my writing to overtly preach the gospel in my "literary" works. . . .
>
> The most powerful effects of a work emerge from those decisions that the writer did not know he or she was making, for the decision simply felt inevitable, because it was right and true. . . . [E]very human being's true faith is contained in what it does not occur to us to question.[57]

Even though since then Card has increasingly made Mormonism his *subject,* he has continued to reaffirm that position against didacticism. Tory C. Anderson, in an editorial in the second issue of the first journal devoted entirely to Mormon literature, *Wasatch Review International,* argues that, because good literature more fully and accurately imitates life in the work and thus can give us moral *experience* as well as knowledge, it can be much more effective than the more abstract forms of sermon and moralistic story at the very purposes those forms espouse—showing us how and how not to live.[58]

Historical Period Three: The "Lost" Generation (1930–1970)

The first flowering of an artistically excellent Mormon literature that was able to be published nationally and gain national recognition came in the 1930s and 40s. But its authors' very reaction against the provinciality and moralism of Mormon "home literature" tended to give it the expatriate, even patronizing, qualities and consequent rejection by many Mormons that led Edward A. Geary to dub those authors "lost."[59] The main figures were Vardis Fisher, who won the Harper Prize in 1939 for *Children of God: An American Epic* (New York: Harper and Brothers, 1939), which covers most of nineteenth-century Mormon history; Maurine Whipple, who won the Houghton Mifflin Literary Prize in 1938 and published *The Giant Joshua* (Boston: Houghton Mifflin, 1941), based on the Mormon pioneer settling of southern Utah; and Virginia Sorensen, who also began with a novel about early Mormon history, *A Little Lower Than the Angels* (New York: Knopf, 1942), but then did her best work concerning the period of her own youth in the early twentieth century, especially what many consider the best Mormon novel, *The Evening and the Morning* (New York: Harcourt, Brace, 1949) and her collection of "stories," *Where*

Nothing Is Long Ago: Memories of a Mormon Childhood (New York: Harcourt, Brace and World, 1963).[60]

Geary's pioneering work on this period identified about twenty nationally published works by a dozen authors who were alike in their essentially "regional" qualities of responding to a time of what they saw as cultural breakdown. Cracroft has praised Samuel W. Taylor's *Heaven Knows Why* (New York: A. A. Wyn, 1948) as the best Mormon humorous novel and has also identified other more recent novelists who for him fit the "lost generation" rubric.[61] Jorgensen has traced the "lost generation" characteristics in a number of expatriate Mormon short story writers of the period.[62]

It seems to me useful to identify two writers of nonfiction as part of this literary "period"; they were quite different from each other

Maurine Whipple

Virginia Sorensen

Samuel W. Taylor
Photograph by Arthur Knight

Juanita Brooks

but shared the "lost" generation impulse toward more realistic and less apologetic dealing with the Mormon past and were also to some degree rejected by Mormons. Fawn Brodie's thoroughly researched *No Man Knows My History: The Life of Joseph Smith, the Mormon Prophet* (New York: Knopf, 1945) introduced the psychological approach she became famous for. Having more the strengths of a novel than biography, it was written from the point of view that Smith was a powerful charismatic genius but also a charlatan and made him into an interesting "character" as no other book had done—but it also led to her excommunication.[63] Juanita Brooks' *Mountain Meadows Massacre* (Stanford, Calif.: Stanford University Press, 1950), the first work to deal thoroughly and openly with the most tragic event of Utah Mormon history, became the model (and Brooks the hero) for the "New Mormon History," a whole movement of less didactic biography and historiography by faithful Mormons.[64] Brooks was ostracized by many Mormons but, unlike Brodie, remained a faithful Mormon and, as her biographer Levi S. Peterson has argued, was able to provide an important moral and spiritual service for the Mormon community through her work and example.[65]

Historical Period Four: Faithful Realism (1960–Present)

Richard H. Cracroft, while recognizing some of the weaknesses of the "home literature" of Nephi Anderson, claimed (in 1985) that his work "should be instructive to modern Mormon writers" in their attempts to be "at once artistic and orthodox."[66] Edward A. Geary, while criticizing the "lost generation" for its own kind of provincialism in seeing mainly the worst of Mormonism and assuming its imminent demise, recognized the "fine artistry" of their novels, comparable with "better known works in the mainstream tradition," and claimed (in 1978) "they are the best Mormon novels we have, and we are not likely to get better ones until we learn what they have to teach."[67] Since about 1960, an increasing number of Mormon writers have indeed been able to learn from the previous periods and, I believe, have produced a literature that is both artistic and ethical, that can both teach and delight as the best literature always has, that is realistic, even critical, about Mormon experience but profoundly faithful to the vision and concerns of the restored gospel of Christ.[68]

The spiritual father of the latest period of Mormon literature is Clinton F. Larson. Larson came under the influence of the craftsmanship and the religious passion of T. S. Eliot and other modern poets in the 1930s and 1940s, mainly through his teacher at the University of Utah, Brewster Ghiselin, himself a fine young American poet. In the midst of this apprenticeship, Larson served as a missionary under the eloquent, urbane, and spiritually direct Hugh B. Brown, later an Apostle. These influences helped him depart both from the didactic and inward-looking provinciality of the first two periods and the elitist, patronizing provinciality of his contemporaries in the "lost generation." He began in the 1950s to write a unique Mormon poetry of modernist sensibility and skill but also informed and passionate faith. Grounded in knowledge of Mormon theology and history and contemporary life and thought and also devoutly part of rather than standing apart from the Mormon people, Larson was able, with intelligent discrimination, to both attack and affirm the world and also Mormon culture. Karl Keller, reviewing Larson's first collection, *The Lord of Experience* (Provo, Utah: Brigham Young University Press, 1967), in 1968, wrote that it provided the first Mormon poetry that was *real* poetry: "It does not show art filling a religious purpose but shows . . . religion succeeding in an esthetic way."[69]

Larson also helped the new tradition of "faithful" but "realistic" Mormon literature along by founding the first Mormon scholarly and literary periodical, *BYU Studies,* in 1959 and then contributing his poetry regularly to that and to *Dialogue,* which was founded in 1966. Other poets, such as his colleagues at Brigham Young University, Edward L. Hart, Marden J. Clark, and John S. Harris, and, elsewhere, Carol Lynn Pearson, Lewis Horne, and Emma Lou Thayne, developed their own styles of Mormon poetry in the 1960s and 1970s; but all were influenced by Larson, if not in style or subject matter, then in being encouraged toward the new possibility he created of poetry deeply grounded in Mormon theology and experience yet also responsive to personal vision and feelings rather than merely to didactic or institutional purposes.[70] Younger poets in the 1980s and 1990s have come even more thoroughly under the influence of contemporary American and other poets; they have produced poetry that, in its challenges to traditional forms and methods as well as its interest in current issues like feminism, multiculturalism, and postmodernist anxiety about language itself, seems to some not Mormon at all. But skilled and faithful Mormon poets who appear regularly in national periodicals, such as Linda Sillitoe, Susan Howe, Lance Larsen, and Kathy Evans, seem to others of us to be taking the faithful realism Larson first created in interesting and valuable contemporary directions.[71]

Douglas Thayer and Donald R. Marshall, who were students and later teachers at Brigham Young University, became the first to explore Clinton F. Larson's new possibility in *fiction*. Departing from the mode of expatriate Mormon writers still publishing nationally in the 1960s and 1970s,[72] they began to write skillful stories that explored Mormon thought and culture in a critical but fundamentally affirmative way. Marshall was the first to publish collections, *The Rummage Sale: Collections and Recollections* (Provo, Utah: Heirloom Publications, 1972) and *Frost in the Orchard* (Provo, Utah: Brigham Young University Press, 1977), and his range is wider, from experimental stories based entirely on such things as lists or letters to sophisticated work in point of view ("The Weekend") and symbolism ("The Wheelbarrow"). Thayer began publishing his stories earlier, in *BYU Studies* and *Dialogue* in the mid 1960s, and his influence has perhaps been wider and more lasting. As one younger Mormon writer, John Bennion, who has himself already published a fine collection that includes experimental contemporary styles and subjects,[73] has put it, "Thayer taught us how to explore the interior life, with its conflicts of doubt and faith, goodness and evil, of a believing Mormon."[74]

Conflict is, of course, the very essence of fiction, and contemporary Mormon writers have found how to reveal and explore the conflicts inherent in Mormonism's complex theology and its rich history and cultural experience. Thayer has written a fine novel, *Summer Fire* (Midvale, Utah: Orion Books, 1983), which examines the challenge and possibility of redemption in the conflict posed by an innocent and self-righteous Mormon youth's exposure to evil on a Nevada hay ranch. His second collection, *Mr. Wahlquist in Yellowstone and Other Stories* (Salt Lake City: Peregrine Smith, 1989), both exploits and exposes the romantic fallacies in male response to the seductions of wilderness which have produced a conflict, even in Mormons, between heroic manhood and the values of family and community.[75]

Levi S. Peterson, who acknowledges his debt to Thayer for teaching him to write in a simple and direct style about Mormon experience, has produced two fine collections, *The Canyons of Grace: Stories* (Urbana: University of Illinois Press, 1982) and *Night Soil: New Stories* (Salt Lake City: Signature Books, 1990), as well as a novel which some consider the best yet by a Mormon, *The Backslider* (Salt Lake City: Signature Books, 1986).[76] All of Peterson's work explores in some form the conflicts in Mormon experience and popular thought between the Old Testament Jehovah of rewards and punishments and the New Testament Christ of unconditional acceptance and redemptive love.

Mormon fiction of the past fifteen years has most fully realized the hopes of many for an excellent but genuinely and uniquely Mormon literature, with a steady increase in both quantity and quality. There are now dozens of skilled writers of a great variety of methods

Clinton F. Larson

Douglas Thayer

Lewis Horne

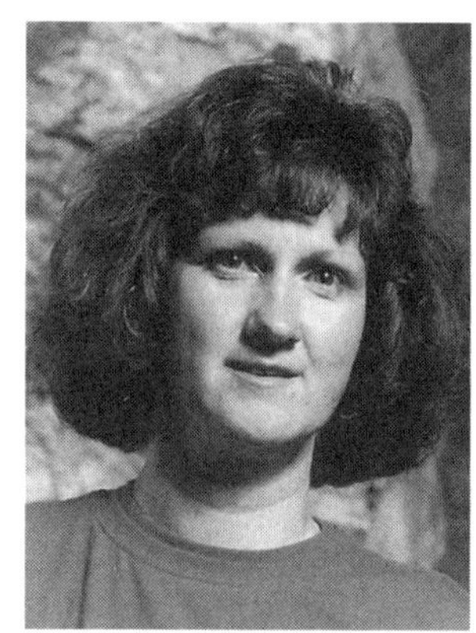
Susan Howe

John S. Harris

Edward Geary

Linda Sillitoe
Courtesy Busath Photography

Edward L. Hart

Emma Lou Thayne

Kathy Evans

Donald Marshall

Laurel Thatcher Ulrich

and perspectives: Some are continuing or improving on the "home literature" tradition, such as Shirley Sealy, Susan Evans McCloud, Jack Weyland, Brenton G. and Blaine M. Yorgason, Carol Hoefling Morris, and Gerald Lund;[77] some who are publishing excellent work nationally are to some degree expatriates and show that in their work, such as Laura Kalpakian, Judith Freeman, and Walter Kirn. But there is a large group of faithful Mormon writers of what I call the "new Mormon fiction"[78] who are both publishing nationally and gaining a growing audience of appreciative Mormon readers. Good examples are Linda Sillitoe and Michael Fillerup, both of whom explore feminism and multicultural issues from a Mormon perspective;[79] Lewis Horne and Neal Chandler, who live and write about Mormon life outside the Wasatch front;[80] and Phyllis Barber and Margaret Young, who have growing reputations for both their story collections and their novels.[81]

Perhaps the most prolific and innovative among these (certainly the most widely read and honored) is Orson Scott Card, who began as a Mormon playwright in the 1970s but then wrote traditional science fiction without Mormon reference and reached the very top of his field with Hugo and Nebula Awards two years running in 1986 and 1987. However, he turned back to openly Mormon works, beginning with *A Woman of Destiny* (New York: Berkley Books, 1984; rpt. as *Saints* New York: Tom Doherty Associates, 1988) and continuing with a fantasy series, *The Tales of Alvin Maker,* based on the life of Joseph Smith; straightforward Mormon science fiction stories in *The Folk of the Fringe* (W. Bloomfield, Mich.: Phantasia Press, 1989); a science fiction series, *Homecoming,* based on the Book of Mormon; and a novel of contemporary Mormon domestic (and spiritual) realism, *Lost Boys* (HarperCollins, 1992).

Card is the first of the latest generation of Mormon writers to have a book written about his work, Michael R. Collings's *In the Image of God: Theme, Characterization, and Landscape in the Fiction of Orson Scott Card* (New York: Greenwood Press, 1990).[82] Collings compares Card to C. S. Lewis in his skillful invention of alternate worlds in which to explore more effectively important religious questions and affirmations—what might be called, on the model of Latin American novelists, "magic realism." Card has also entered the controversy over what makes good Mormon literature, both as critic and publisher: He has started his own publishing company, Hatrack River Publications, and in the "Foreword" to his first offering, Kathryn H. Kidd's *Paradise Vue,* he offers as rationale that most Mormon novels have either "tended to be very simple-minded and presented a sugar-coated view of Mormon life" or "tended to be slow-moving, dull, and pretentious." He proposes to provide stories that "are at once fascinating and illuminating," that "give their readers . . . both entertainment and understanding."[83]

If fiction is the area where Mormons are just now beginning to fulfill the prophetic hopes for Mormon literature and to have some impact on national and world literature, it is the personal essay that seems to me to have the greatest *potential* for making a uniquely valuable Mormon contribution both to Mormon cultural and religious life and to that of others. Our theological emphasis on life as a stage where the individual self is both tested and created and our history of close self-examination in journals and testimony-bearing provide resources that have mainly been realized in great sermons[84] and various forms of autobiography but increasingly find expression in powerful informal essays and personal and family storytelling.[85]

The revered Brigham Young University English professor P. A. Christensen produced two volumes of informal essays (*All in a Teacher's Day* [Salt Lake City: Stevens and Wallis, 1948] and *Of a Number of Things* [Salt Lake City: University of Utah Press, 1962]) and various other Mormons have written effective literary, religious, and historical essays with personal dimensions.[86] However, it was Edward Geary, with "Goodbye to Poplarhaven," published in *Dialogue* 8 (Summer 1973): 56–62, who first revealed to his own community the great potential of the Mormon personal essay as an art form.[87]

Stimulated in part by *Dialogue*'s establishment in 1971 of a regular section, "Personal Voices," and the example of Geary and then others, writers developed this form rapidly. Personal essays also began to appear occasionally in *BYU Studies* and often in new periodicals like the *Ensign* (1970), *Exponent II* (1973), and *Sunstone* (1975), and by the late 1970s and early 1980s had begun to be published in edited or individual collections[88] and to receive some critical attention.[89] By the mid-1980s some Mormon writers were extending the range of the form to include diverse voices in the same essay and other elements usually confined to fiction and to consider issues like feminism and ecology—and some were occasionally published nationally.[90] One measure of the growing range and influence of the Mormon personal essay in the 1990s is the warm reception both nationally and by her own community of Terry Tempest Williams's *Refuge: An Unnatural History of Family and Place* (New York: Pantheon Books, 1991), which received excellent reviews and was awarded the Association for Mormon Letters Prize in the personal essay. Another good omen is Phyllis Barber, who won both the 1991 Associated Writing Programs Award in "Creative Non-Fiction" and a 1993 Association for Mormon Letters award for *How I Got Cultured: A Nevada Memoir* (Athens:

Darrell Spencer

Jack Weyland

John Bennion

Margaret Young

Dean Hughes

Neal Chandler

Levi S. Peterson

Gerald N. Lund

Michael Fillerup

Elouise Bell

Mary L. Bradford

Phyllis Barber
Photograph by K. C. Muscolino

University of Georgia Press, 1992), which is essentially a collection of avant garde personal essays.[91]

Drama might also be expected to be a prominent Mormon literary form, for some of the same reasons of theology and cultural history that explain the importance of the personal essay. However, despite strong support for popular dramatic productions beginning in Nauvoo and the Salt Lake Theatre and the "roadshow" tradition in twentieth-century Mormon wards,[92] as well as Crawford Gates's very popular pioneer centennial musical, *Promised Valley* (1947), it was not until the 1960s that there was much drama written by Mormons about Mormon experience. The first were mainly "closet dramas," such as Clinton F. Larson's *The Mantle of the Prophet,* and musicals, like Doug Stewart's *Saturday's Warrior* and Carol Lynn Pearson's *The Order Is Love.* By the late 1970s, however, fine Mormon dramas were being quite regularly written and produced at Brigham Young University. Of these probably the best single achievement is Robert Elliott's *Fires of the Mind,* and the finest single playwright is Thomas Rogers, who has produced plays regularly for twenty years at a consistent high quality and reached the highest level of excellence with *Huebener.*[93]

A fine tradition of one-person plays was inaugurated by James Arrington in the late 1970s with his *Here's Brother Brigham* and *Farley Family Reunion* (still regularly performed, available on video, and considered by some as perhaps the best of authentic Mormon drama).[94] The most promising younger playwrights seem to be Susan Howe (*The Burdens of Earth* and *Katy*[95]), Tim Slover (*Dreambuilder* and *Scales*[96]), Neil Labute (*In the Company of Men* and *Sanguinarians*[97]), and Eric Samuelsen (*Accommodations*[98]). (See also Michael Hicks's essay on the performing arts in this volume).

Some Mormon writers of the fourth period are achieving success, both locally and nationally, in high quality children's and young adult literature. Fine examples of the former are Steve Wunderli's *Marty's World,* illustrated by Brent Watts (Salt Lake City: Bookcraft, 1986); Phyllis Barber's *Legs: The Story of a Giraffe* (New York: M. K. McElderry Books, 1991); Catherine Hepworth's *Antics! An Alphabetical Anthology* (New York: G. P. Putnam's Sons, 1992); and Michael O. Tunnell's *three* books, *Chinook!*, *The Joke's on George*, and *Beauty and the Beastly Children* (all New York: William Morrow, 1993), which won the AML prize. Examples of the best books by Mormons for young adults are Donald R. Marshall: *Enchantress of Crumbledown* (Salt Lake City: Deseret Book, 1990); Ann Edwards Cannon: *Amazing Gracie* (New York: Delacorte Press, 1991); Louise Plummer: *My Name Is Sus5an Smith. The 5 Is Silent* (New York: Delacorte

Terry Tempest Williams
Courtesy Dennis M. Golonka

Thomas F. Rogers

Louise Plummer

Neal A. Maxwell

Chieko Okazaki

Anne Perry
Courtesy Peter R. Simpkin

Press, 1991); and Dean Hughes: *Jenny Haller* (Salt Lake City: Deseret Book, 1983) and *Go to the Hoop!* (New York: Knopf, 1993).

Prospects

The future of Mormon literature is potentially both bright and vexed. On the one hand, a number of new periodicals and presses,[99] together with increasingly popular classes in Mormon literature at Brigham Young University, are rapidly expanding the audience for good Mormon literature. Good criticism, both theoretical and practical, is regularly fostered, especially by the Association for Mormon Letters,[100] and regular book review columns[101] and even journals entirely devoted to Mormon literature are appearing. With the recent success of Orson Scott Card and Terry Tempest Williams, the national publishing market's unaccountable resistance to Mormon writing may be lessening. Anne Perry, a British convert who regularly publishes Victorian mystery novels to high critical acclaim, has recently moved from expressing her Mormon convictions only in the powerful underlying moral climate of her work to somewhat more open reference to Mormonism and is under contract for a fantasy trilogy which will deal quite directly with two women's spiritual quest.[102]

On the other hand, the potentially creative tension between the two poles of Mormons' expectations about their literature—the conflict between orthodox didacticism and faithful realism explored in the recent essays by Cracroft and Jorgensen—seems at times to be breaking down into invidious judgments, name-calling, and divisions. These divisions and exclusions have increased since the late 1970s, when Elder Packer and President Kimball encouraged Mormon writers to fulfill the prophecies of literary excellence. Even the eclectic harmony of the forums in which those leaders then spoke now seems a distant dream: Elder Packer was published in a book of essays that included Mormon critics and writers as diverse as Reid Nibley, Edward L. Hart, and Wayne C. Booth; President Kimball appeared in an issue of the *Ensign* which included (with implied approval) artists across the full range of Mormon approaches, from didactic home literature by Orson F. Whitney, Charles Penrose, and Lael J. Littke to recent realistic and experimental work by Clinton F. Larson, Emma Lou Thayne, Donald Marshall, and Orson Scott Card. Now Mormon letters seems increasingly bifurcated into mutually exclusive forums, periodicals, and presses, which I fear will impede our progress toward the rich, diverse, mutually tolerant literary community and achievements we are capable of.[103]

Mormon literature will always have a difficult burden—to describe a unique set of revealed truths and historical and continually vital religious experiences and to do so both truly and artistically. We seem to understand this better about other art forms than about literature, where the temptation is greatest to assume that a good "message" is enough. (Most Mormons can see right away that a painting of Joseph Smith's first vision done badly would demean the experience or that a clumsy or sentimental musical score on the suffering of Christ in Gethsemane would be a kind of blasphemy, but a "faith-building" story or one based on "real experience," however badly written or sentimental in its appeal, is often received uncritically.)

An increasing number of faithful Latter-day Saints are developing the skill and courage to write well in all the genres. The challenge they face—which must be faced as well by their readers, both Mormons and others—is to find ways to reach out to and unite the extremes of experience President Kimball recommended and to accept the role of art in assisting in the central human purpose Brigham Young described: "We cannot obtain eternal life unless we actually know and comprehend by our experience the principle of good and the principle of evil, the light and the darkness, truth, virtue, and holiness, also vice, wickedness, and corruption."[104]

To gain such comprehension, we must be willing, both as writers and readers, to do as Joseph Smith did—and called us to do: "Thy mind, . . . if thou wilt lead a soul unto salvation, must stretch as high as the utmost heavens, and search into and contemplate the darkest abyss, and the broad expanse of eternity."[105] A literature to match the high religious achievement of the Restoration Joseph Smith began requires both the breadth and the depth he achieved—literary skill, moral courage, and generosity—and also the spiritual passion that brought about his visions and continues to give a unique quality to the life of faithful Mormons. Mormon writers, if they are true to their sacred and powerful art of language as well as their sacred and powerful religious heritage, can aspire, Elder Packer promised in 1976,[106] to enjoy the promise by Christ to Joseph Smith: "Draw near unto me and I will draw near unto you . . . ask, and ye shall receive" (Doctrine and Covenants 88:63).

Appendix

A. General Historical and Critical Essays, Listed Chronologically

Whitney, Orson F. "Home Literature." *Contributor* 9 (June 1888): 297–302. Reprinted in *A Believing People: Literature of the Latter-day Saints,* comp. by Richard H. Cracroft and Neal E. Lambert, 203–7. Provo, Utah: Brigham Young University Press, 1975. An influential early call, by a future Apostle, for an excellent, faith-promoting literature by Mormons.

Morgan, Dale L. "Mormon Story Tellers." *Rocky Mountain Review* 7 (Fall 1942): 1, 3–4, 7. Reprinted in *Rocky Mountain Reader,* ed. by Ray B. West Jr., 404–13. New York: E. P. Dutton, 1946. A perceptive and enthusiastic review of the Mormon writers, like Fisher and Whipple, who were suddenly gaining national prominence in the 1940s—and a survey of earlier "polemical" fiction, both anti-Mormon novels and those I have called "home literature."

Cheney, Thomas E. "Latter-day Saint Literature Comes of Age." *Improvement Era* 53 (March 1950): 196–98, 214. A survey of reasons the maturing Church, with its ideals that support artistic excellence and moral purpose, can expect "in the near future" literature that "without didacticism will present . . . the good side of our culture" (214).

Mulder, William. "Mormonism and Literature." *Western Humanities Review* 9 (Winter 1954–55): 85–89. Reprinted in *A Believing People,* comp. by Cracroft and Lambert, 208–11. A perceptive review of the strengths of the unusual genres of the first period, such as diaries and letters, and the problems of the second and third periods, in trying to deal with the great epic of Mormon history (he calls for a "smaller canvas," a focus on "the experience of living things, of very particular situations"). Mulder expects the Church membership to mature in taste and "demand of Mormon writers . . . the authority of good writing, of truths made memorable."

Keller, Karl. "On Words and the Word of God: The Delusions of a Mormon Literature." *Dialogue* 4 (Autumn 1969): 13–20. A moving call, early in the fourth period, for a genuinely religious Mormon literature—not "written or read in the service of religion" (19–20) but "an exercise in faith, an exercise in renewing our grounds of belief" (20).

Jorgensen, Bruce W. "Digging the Foundation: Making and Reading Mormon Literature." *Dialogue* 9 (Winter 1974): 50–61. A substantial review of Cracroft and Lambert, *A Believing People,* confirming and extending the editors' work in "excavating" and appreciating the pioneers' foundational work, sharpening the tools for analysis of the next two periods, and perceptively praising the developing work of the "authentic voices" in the new period.

Cracroft, Richard H. "Seeking 'the Good, the Pure, the Elevating': A Short History of Mormon Fiction" (parts I and II). *Ensign* 11

(June 1981): 57-62; (July 1981): 56-61. An excellent survey of "home literature" and the "lost generation" and some contemporary period novelists, encouraging Mormon writers to a more faithful, even didactic, fiction.

England, Eugene. "The Dawning of a Brighter Day: Mormon Literature after 150 Years." *BYU Studies* 22 (Spring 1982): 131-60, complete with "Selected Bibliography." Reprinted in expanded form in *After 150 Years: The Latter-day Saints in Sesquicentennial Perspective,* ed. by Thomas G. Alexander and Jessie L. Embry, 97-146. Charles Redd Monographs in Western History, no. 3. Provo, Utah: Charles Redd Center for Western Studies, Brigham Young University, 1983. A first attempt to define literary periods for Mormon literature, including announcement of the fourth, with its special combination of strengths from the earlier ones, and a description of the resources in Mormonism for unusual and powerful content and form.

Jorgensen, Bruce W. "A 'Smaller Canvas' of the Mormon Short Story since 1950." *Mormon Letters Annual, 1983:* 10-31. Salt Lake City: Association for Mormon Letters, 1984. A thorough history of the "expatriate" writers continuing to publish nationally and of the developing fourth period writers of what I call "faithful realism," with an excellent bibliography.

Anderson, Lavina Fielding. "Making the 'Good' Good for Something: A Direction for Mormon Literature." *Mormon Letters Annual, 1984:* 150-64. Salt Lake City: Association for Mormon Letters, 1985. AML Presidential address, 1982; a survey of current Mormon fiction, including some novels still in manuscript, with a call for more daring, "fecund," and joyous work of the kind she calls "spiritual realism" (153).

Hunsaker, Kenneth B. "Mormon Novels." In *A Literary History of the American West,* ed. by Thomas J. Lyon and others, 849-61. Ft. Worth: Texas Christian University Press, 1987. A good survey of the "lost generation" and "home literature" novelists, including modern ones like Jack Weyland and Blaine Yorgason, but unfortunately quite unaware of recent developments in "faithful realism"—nothing on Thayer, Marshall, Peterson, Card, or Sillitoe.

Wilson, William A. "The Study of Mormon Folklore: An Uncertain Mirror for Truth." *Dialogue* 22 (Winter 1989): 95-110. A description of Mormon and American religious folk studies, arguing that the range should be extended, with less attention to "dramatic tales of the supernatural" (108-9) and more to "quiet lives of committed service . . . at the heart of the Mormon experience" (109). Later Wilson extended his appreciative vision to include what he calls the "family novel" (13), orally transmitted personal and group stories collected over time; see "In Praise of Ourselves: Stories to Tell," *BYU Studies* 30 (Winter 1990): 5-24.

"Literature, Mormon Writers Of." In *Encyclopedia of Mormonism,* ed. by Daniel H. Ludlow, 837-44. Vol. 2. New York: Macmillan, 1992. Short, focused entries on "Drama" (Robert A. Nelson), "Novels" (Richard H. Cracroft), "Personal Essays" (Donlu Dewitt Thayer), "Poetry" (Leslie Norris), and "Short Stories" (B. W. Jorgensen); historical and critical, with select bibliographies.

Jorgensen, Bruce W. "To Tell and Hear Stories: Let the Stranger Say." *Sunstone* 16 (July 1993): 41-50. A call to Mormon writers, but especially readers, to "be patient, longsuffering" (48), to "listen to the voice of the Other" (49), to measure Mormon literature by its unusual charity and openness.

Cracroft, Richard H. "Attuning the Authentic Mormon Voice: Stemming the Sophic Tide in LDS Literature." *Sunstone* 16 (July 1993): 51-57. A response to Jorgensen, calling for a literature that directly promotes orthodox ideals and values, which he sees as "more or less rooted in essences of spirituality shared by those" who "seek about them 'the presence of the divine,' eschewing faithlessness, doubt, and rebellion" (52).

Anderson, Tory C. "Just the Fiction, Ma'am." *Wasatch Review International* 1, no. 2 (1992): 1-9. A perceptive argument, by a younger editor and critic, that the purpose of moral teaching—and of mortal life—is best achieved not through direct preaching of propositional knowledge but through realistic imitation of life in fiction, which can give new and profitable experience more efficiently than life itself.

Mulder, William A. "'Essential Gestures': Craft and Calling in Contemporary Mormon Letters." *Weber Studies* 10 (Fall 1993): 7-25. A sympathetic survey and critique that brings up to date his 1954 essay and looks optimistically to the future—*if* Mormon writers can maintain both "a maturing craft and a strong sense of calling."

B. Important Essays on Topics or Individuals, Chronologically by Period and Subject

1. "Foundations" (1830–1880)

Wilson, Douglas. "Prospects for the Study of the Book of Mormon as a Work of American Literature." *Dialogue* 3 (Spring 1968): 29-41.

England, Eugene. "A Second Witness for the *Logos:* The Book of Mormon and Contemporary Literary Criticism." In *By Study and Also By Faith: Essays in Honor of Hugh W. Nibley on the Occasion of His Eightieth Birthday, 27 March 1990,* ed. by John M. Lundquist and Stephen D. Ricks, 91-125. Vol. 2. Salt Lake City: Deseret Book, 1990.

Cracroft, Richard H., and Neal E. Lambert. "Literary Form and Historical Understanding: Joseph Smith's First Vision." *Journal of Mormon History* 7 (1980): 31-42.

Lambert, Neal E. "The Representation of Reality in Nineteenth Century Mormon Autobiography." *Dialogue* 11 (Summer 1978): 63-74.

Jolley, Clifton Holt. "The Martyrdom of Joseph Smith: An Archetypal Study." *Utah Historical Quarterly* 44 (Fall 1976): 329-50.

Christmas, R[obert] A. "The Autobiography of Parley P. Pratt: Some Literary, Historical, and Critical Reflections." *Dialogue* 1 (Spring 1966): 33-43.

2. "Home Literature" (1880–1930)

Cracroft, Richard H. "Nephi, Seer of Modern Times: The Home Literature Novels of Nephi Anderson." *BYU Studies* 25 (Spring 1985): 3-15.

———. "The Didactic Heresy as Orthodox Tool: B. H. Roberts as Writer of Home Literature." In *Proceedings of the Symposia of the Association for Mormon Letters, 1979-82,* 32-44. Salt Lake City: Association for Mormon Letters, 1983.

3. "Lost Generation" (1930–1970)

Flora, Joseph M. "Vardis Fisher and the Mormons." *Dialogue* 4 (Autumn 1969): 48-55.

Jorgensen, Bruce. "Retrospection: *Giant Joshua.*" *Sunstone* 3 (September-October 1978): 6-8.

Wilson, William [A.] "Folklore in *The Giant Joshua.*" In *Proceedings of the Symposia of the Association for Mormon Letters, 1978-79,* 57-63. Salt Lake City: Association for Mormon Letters, 1979.

Sorensen, Virginia. "Is It True?—the Novelist and His Materials." *Western Humanities Review* 7 (1952-53): 283-92.

Bradford, Mary L. "Virginia Sorensen: A Saving Remnant." *Dialogue* 4 (Autumn 1969): 56-64.

Lee, L[awrence] L., and Sylvia B. Lee. *Virginia Sorensen.* Boise State University Western Writers Series, no. 31. Boise, Idaho: Boise State University, 1978.

Jorgensen, Bruce W. "'Herself Moving beside Herself, Out There Alone': The Shape of Mormon Belief in Virginia Sorensen's *The Evening and the Morning.*" *Dialogue* 13 (Autumn 1980): 43-60.

England, Eugene. "Virginia Sorensen as the Founding Foremother of the Mormon Personal Essay: My Personal Tribute." *Exponent II* 17, no. 1 (1992): 12-14.

Geary, Edward A. "Mormondom's Lost Generation: The Novelists of the 1940s." *BYU Studies* 18 (Fall 1977): 89-98. Also in *The Association for Mormon Letters Annual 1994,* 1:44-50. Salt Lake City: AML, 1994.

———. "The Poetics of Provincialism: Mormon Regional Fiction." *Dialogue* 11 (Summer 1978): 15-24.

Cracroft, Richard H. "'Freshet in the Dearth: Samuel W. Taylor's *Heaven Knows Why* and Mormon Humor." *Sunstone* 5 (May-June 1980): 31-37.

Peterson, Levi S. "Juanita Brooks: The Mormon Historian as Tragedian." *Journal of Mormon History* 3 (1976): 47-54. His biography is *Juanita Brooks: Mormon Woman Historian.* Salt Lake City: University of Utah Press, 1988.

England, Karin Anderson. "Feminine Voices in the Works of Juanita Brooks." In *Mormon Letters Annual, 1988-92,* 183-89 (Salt Lake City: AML, 1994).

4. "Faithful Realism" (1960–Present)

Keller, Karl. "A Pilgrimage of Awe" (a review of Clinton F. Larson's *The Lord of Experience*). *Dialogue* 3 (Spring 1968): 111-18.

Bradford, Mary L[ythgoe]. "I, Eye, Aye: A Personal Essay on Personal Essays." *Dialogue* 11 (Summer 1978): 81-89.

Jolley, Clifton Holt. "Mormons and the Beast: In Defense of the Personal Essay," *Dialogue* 11 (Autumn 1978): 137-39.

Jorgensen, Bruce W. "Element and Glory: Reflections and Speculations on the Mormon Verbal Imagination." In *Proceedings of the Symposia of the Association for Mormon Letters, 1978-79,* 65-77. Salt Lake City: Association for Mormon Letters, 1979.

———. "Romantic Lyric Form and Western Mormon Experience in the Stories of Douglas Thayer." *Western American Literature* 22 (Spring 1987): 33-49.

England, Eugene. "Thayer's Ode to a Redtail Hawk." In *Mormon Letters Annual, 1983,* 42-53. Salt Lake City: Association for Mormon Letters, 1984.

———. "Wilderness as Salvation in Peterson's *The Canyons of Grace.*" *Western American Literature* 19 (Spring 1984): 17-28.

Geary, Edward A. "Of Mormon Poesy: An Essay." In *Mormon Letters Annual 1987,* 1–7. Salt Lake City: Association for Mormon Letters, 1987.

England, Eugene. "Beyond 'Jack Fiction': Recent Achievement in the Mormon Novel." *BYU Studies* 28 (Spring 1988): 97–109.

Collings, Michael R. *In the Image of God: Theme, Characterization, and Landscape in the Work of Orson Scott Card.* Contributions to the Study of Science Fiction and Fantasy, no. 42. New York: Greenwood Press, 1990.

Mulder, William. "Telling It Slant: Aiming for Truth in Contemporary Mormon Literature." *Dialogue* 26 (Summer 1993): 155–69.

Anderson, Lavina Fielding. "Masks and Music: Recent Fiction by Mormon Women Writers." *Weber Studies* 10 (Fall 1993): 71–80.

Hogge, Robert M. "Levels of Perception in Michael Fillerup's *Visions and Other Stories.*" In *The Association for Mormon Letters Annual, 1994,* 2:154–57. Salt Lake City: AML, 1994.

Cannon, Helen Beach. "Strange Love: The Stories of Phyllis Barber." *Mormon Letters Annual, 1988–92* (Salt Lake City: AML, 1994).

C. Anthologies, Listed Chronologically

West, Ray B., Jr., ed. *Rocky Mountain Reader.* New York: E. P. Dutton, 1946. An early collection which includes work by Vardis Fisher, Maurine Whipple, George Snell, Jarvis Thurston, Dale L. Morgan, and Edward Hart. Much of this work is taken from the *Rocky Mountain Review,* which West, a Mormon teacher at the Branch Agricultural College at Cedar City, Utah, and then at the Utah Agricultural college, Logan, edited from 1937–46 and where he published many other Mormon writers, including Christy Lund Coles and Alice Morrey Bailey, and writers of future distinction, like Wallace Stegner, Brewster Ghiselin, Josephine Miles, and Langston Hughes.

Cracroft, Richard H., and Neal E. Lambert, eds. *A Believing People: The Literature of the Latter-day Saints.* Provo, Utah: Brigham Young University Press, 1974. An excellent sampling of the first three periods and the founders of the fourth, with a historical and critical general "Introduction," for each section, arranged historically and by genre, and notes on each author.

———. *Twenty-two Young Mormon Writers.* Provo, Utah. Communications Workshop, 1974. A survey of the work being done in fiction and poetry by beginning writers, mainly at Brigham Young University, who were not included in *A Believing People,* with an optimistic introduction and notes on the authors.

Peterson, Levi S., ed. *Greening Wheat: Fifteen Mormon Short Stories.* Midvale, Utah: Orion Books, 1983; distributed by Signature Books. A first gathering that shows the range and quality of fiction in the fourth period, with an introduction on the state of Mormon short stories and Peterson's principles of selection, including the authors' skill in "the conventions of modern fiction" (vii) and the stories' "moral" quality achieved through "breadth, balance, and proportion" (ix).

England, Eugene, and Dennis Clark, eds. *Harvest: Contemporary Mormon Poems.* Salt Lake City: Signature Books, 1989. With historical and critical "commentaries" by both editors and "Notes on Poets" that give extended bibliographies. Fifty-three Mormon poets, ranging from the work of Larson, Hart, Clark, and Harris in establishing the "new tradition" of spiritual realism of the past thirty years to younger poets like Evans, Howe, Larsen, and Liu, who are taking "new directions" and publishing nationally. Includes a section of "hymns and songs" by contemporary Mormons and poems about Mormonism by "friends and relations" like William Stafford, Leslie Norris, and May Swenson.

England, Eugene, ed. *Bright Angels and Familiars: Contemporary Mormon Stories.* Salt Lake City: Signature Books, 1992. With historical and critical "Introduction," a list of over one hundred "Other Notable Mormon Stories and Collections," and "Notes" on the twenty-two authors included. The authors range from "Lost Generation" writers Whipple and Sorensen to the best of a variety of "Faithful Realism," including Thayer, Marshall, Peterson, Sillitoe, Barber, Mortensen, Card, and Young.

Taylor, Curtis, and Stan Zenk, eds. *Christmas for the World: A Gift to the Children.* Salt Lake City: Aspen Books, 1991. An eclectic collection of poems, short stories, and personal essays by the full range of contemporary Mormon writers, from Whipple to McCloud and Weyland to Thayer, Fillerup, and Card.

Bell, M. Shayne, ed. *Washed by a Wave of Wind: Stories from the Corridor.* Salt Lake City: Signature Books, 1993. A collection of contemporary Mormon science fiction stories, including prizewinners like Bell, Card, and Dave Wolverton, as well as newer writers.

England, Eugene, and Lavina Fielding Anderson. *Tending the Garden: Essays on Mormon Literature.* Salt Lake City: Signature Books, forthcoming, 1995.

D. Bibliographies

For the first two periods, the best general bibliography of printed materials is Chad J. Flake, comp., *A Mormon Bibliography, 1830–1930: Books, Pamphlets, Periodicals, and Broadsides Relating to the First Century of Mormonism* (Salt Lake City: University of Utah Press, 1978) and Chad J. Flake and Larry W. Draper, comp., *A Mormon Bibliography, 1830–1930: Ten Year Supplement* (Salt Lake City: University of Utah Press, 1989), with a title index to both volumes, *A Mormon Bibliography, 1830–1930. Indexes to* A Mormon Bibliography *and* Ten Year Supplement (Salt Lake City: University of Utah Press, 1992).

Useful bibliographies can be found in connection with many of the essays cited in sections I and III above. Important manuscript holdings at various libraries are discussed in other essays in this volume. Deposits of important authors' papers and other collections of the third and fourth periods are just beginning to be made, as follows: Brigham Young University: Orson Scott Card, Dean Hughes, Clinton F. Larson, Maurine Whipple, and *Exponent II;* University of Utah: *Dialogue;* Boston University: Virginia Sorensen; Weber State University: Levis S. Peterson.

The best published source for recent Mormon literature is the "Mormon Bibliography," printed yearly in *BYU Studies* since 1960. One measure of the recent development of Mormon literature is that in the first few years the "Mormon Bibliography" was not divided into categories and from 1969 to 1975 all literature entries appeared under "Inspirational," but that since 1988 the "Arts and Literature" category has included substantial and increasing separate groupings for "Critical Essays," "Personal Essays," "Novels," "Plays," "Poems," and "Short Stories."

There is presently at Brigham Young University a complete bibliography of Mormon literature on the computer network, accessible by modem (phone the "Americana" library for instructions).

E. Periodicals and Associations That Regularly Publish Mormon Literature and Criticism, Give Prizes, and Sponsor Symposia

1. Association for Mormon Letters (founded 1976). Meets each January for a symposium of critical papers and readings and awarding of annual prizes in poetry, short story, novel, personal essays, drama, and critical essays; meets each October in a conjoint session at Rocky Mountain Modern Language Association meetings. Publishes regular volumes of papers from these meetings. To this point there have been seven: 1977 papers in *Dialogue* 11 (Summer 1978); 1978–79 in *Proceedings* (Salt Lake City: Association for Mormon Letters, n.d.); 1979–82 in *Proceedings* (Salt Lake City: Association for Mormon Letters, 1983); 1983, 1984, 1985–87, and 1988–94 in a *Mormon Letters Annual* for each of these four periods. Contact John Bennion, Dept. of English, Brigham Young University, Provo, UT 84602.

2. ***Betrachtungen* (Reflections)** (first published in 1993; quarterly). Publishes letters, reviews, and short pieces related to Mormon cultural and intellectual life, in German, French, and English. Contact Hartmut Weissman, 64 rue Albert Joly, 78000, Versailles, FRANCE.

3. ***Brigham Young University Magazine*** (formerly *BYU Today;* quarterly). Occasional personal essays and regular column of book reviews by Richard H. Cracroft. Contact James Bell, Brigham Young University, Provo, UT 84602.

4. ***BYU Studies*** (first published in 1959; quarterly). Publishes poetry, short stories, personal essays, critical essays, book reviews, and an annual "Mormon Bibliography," which includes the best current listing of all genres of literature. Contact John Welch, Brigham Young University, Provo, UT 84602.

5. **Center for Christian Values in Literature** (at Brigham Young University). Gives annual awards in fiction, poetry, and the personal essay, some of which it publishes in its journal, ***Literature and Belief*** (first published in 1981, yearly). Contact Jay Fox, Brigham Young University, Provo, UT 84602.

6. ***Dialogue: A Journal of Mormon Thought*** (first published in 1966; quarterly). Publishes poetry, short stories, critical essays, book reviews, and a large number of personal essays. Gives annual prizes in personal essay, short story, and poetry. Special issues on Mormon literature: Autumn 1969, Winter 1974, and Summer 1978. Contact Martha Bradley, P.O. Box 658, Salt Lake City, UT 84110.

7. ***Ensign*** (first published in 1971; monthly). Publishes and gives annual prizes in essays, fiction (through 1988), and poetry. Contact LDS Church, Salt Lake City, UT 84150.

8. ***Exponent II*** (first published in 1974; quarterly). Publishes poetry, many personal essays, some short fiction, and occasional reviews. Contact Sue Paxman, P.O. Box 128, Arlington, MA 02174-002.

9. ***The Friend*** (first published in 1971; monthly). Publishes essays, fiction, poetry for children. Contact LDS Church, Salt Lake City, UT 84150.

10. ***Mormon Forum*** (first published in 1993; semi-annual). Publishes letters, poetry, reviews, etc., in Japanese. Contact Jiro Numano, Kamitokimune, Kudamatusu Shi, Yamagichi Kon 744, JAPAN.

11. Mormon History Association. Sponsors annual symposium at which there are occasional sessions on Mormon literature. Gives annual awards in the writing of history and biography. Contact Craig Foster, 2470 North 1000 West, Layton, UT 84041.

12. ***Mormon Review*** (forthcoming in 1995; quarterly). To publish reviews and review-essays on all aspects of Mormon culture. Contact Gideon Burton, Dept. of English, Brigham Young University, Provo, UT 84602.

13. ***New Era*** (first published in 1971; monthly). Publishes essays, fiction, poetry for young adults. Contact LDS Church, Salt Lake City, UT 84150.

14. ***Sunstone*** (first published in 1975; bi-monthly). Publishes poetry, personal essays, fiction, plays, critical essays, and reviews. Sponsors symposia throughout the United States, where there are sessions of critical essays and readings of Mormon literature. Gives annual awards in fiction. Contact Elbert Peck, 331 Rio Grande, Suite 206, Salt Lake City, UT 84101-1136.

15. ***This People*** (first published in 1979; quarterly). Publishes profiles of authors, occasional poems and short fiction, personal essays, and a regular book review column by Eugene England. Contact Maurine Jensen Proctor, 7730 Plum Creek Ln., Sandy, UT 84093.

16. Utah Arts Council. Gives annual awards in short story, poetry, personal essay, and the novel. Contact G. Barnes, 617 East South Temple, Salt Lake City, UT 84102-1177.

17. ***Wasatch Review International: A Journal of Mormon Literature*** (first published in 1992; semi-annual). Publishes poetry, fiction, personal essays, critical essays, and reviews. Sponsors an annual "LDS Writers' Conference," together with the League of Utah Writers. Contact Tory Anderson, P.O. Box 1017, Orem, UT 84058.

18. ***Weber Studies*** (first published 1983, quarterly). Publishes poetry, fiction, personal essays, critical essays, and reviews. Special issue on Mormon literature, Fall 1993. Contact Neila C. Seshachari, Weber State University, Ogden, UT.

19. ***Zarahemla: A Forum for Mormon Poetry*** (first published in 1991; occasional). Publishes poetry and reviews of poetry. Contact Michael Collings, 1089 Sheffield Place, Thousand Oaks, CA 91360-5353.

Eugene England is Professor of English at Brigham Young University.

NOTES

[1]Jan Shipps, *Mormonism: The Story of a New Religious Tradition* (Urbana: University of Illinois Press, 1985), ix.

[2]Studies reported in *Time,* April 5, 1993, 46-47.

[3]Harold Bloom, *The American Religion: The Emergence of the Post-Christian Nation* (New York: Simon and Schuster, 1992).

[4]Cited in Spencer W. Kimball, "The Gospel Vision of the Arts," *Ensign* 7 (July 1977): 3.

[5]Whitney, "Home Literature," 300, see Appendix, A.

[6]Boyd K. Packer, "The Arts and the Spirit of the Lord," *1976 Devotional Speeches of the Year* (Provo, Utah: Brigham Young University Press, 1977), 268; reprinted in Steven P. Sondrup, ed., *Arts and Inspiration: Mormon Perspectives* (Provo, Utah: Brigham Young University Press, 1980), 5-6.

[7]Kimball, "Gospel Vision of the Arts," 5.

[8]England, "The Dawning of a Brighter Day," see Appendix, A.

[9]Cracroft and Lambert, *A Believing People,* and *Twenty-Two Young Mormon Writers,* see Appendix, C.

[10]Cracroft, "Attuning the Authentic Mormon Voice," see Appendix, A. See also his review of *Harvest: Contemporary Mormon Poems,* in *BYU Studies* 30 (Spring 1990): 119, 121-23.

[11]Packer, "The Arts and the Spirit," 10, 16.

[12]Jorgensen, "To Tell and Hear Stories," see Appendix, A; Jorgensen's essay is an expanded version of his 1991 presidential address for the Association for Mormon Letters, which responded in part to Cracroft's review of *Harvest* cited above, and Cracroft's essay, published together with Jorgensen's, is his 1992 AML presidential address, which in good part responds to Jorgensen.

[13]Cracroft and Lambert, *A Believing People,* 5, see Appendix, C.

[14]Karl Keller, "The Example of Flannery O'Connor," *Dialogue* 9 (Winter 1974): 62.

[15]Quoted in Keller, "The Example of Flannery O'Connor," 68.

[16]Quoted in Keller, "The Example of Flannery O'Connor," 68. O'Connor has also seemed to others a good model for Mormon writers: In "Digging the Foundation: Making and Reading Mormon Literature" (see Appendix, A), Jorgensen quotes her citing Aquinas that "art . . . is wholly concerned with the good of that which is made" and proposing that an art work that is "good in itself glorifies God because it reflects God" (56). In a review of Peterson's *Night Soil* (*Weber Studies* 8 [Fall 1991]: 99-100), I propose that "in Levi Peterson, Western literature and Mormon literature finally have their Flannery O'Connor" (99).

[17]Keller, "Example of Flannery O'Connor," 71.

[18]Keller, "Example of Flannery O'Connor," 69-70.

[19]Stan Larson, "The King Follett Discourse: A Newly Amalgamated Text," *BYU Studies* 18 (Winter 1978): 193-208.

[20]Brigham Young, *Journal of Discourses,* 26 vols. (Liverpool, England: R. James, 1855), 2:90-96.

[21]See Eugene England, "Great Books or True Religion?: Defining the Mormon Scholar," *Dialogue* 9 (Winter 1974): 36-49; reprinted in *Dialogues with Myself* (Midvale, Utah: Orion Books, 1984; distributed by Signature Books), 57-76.

[22]Cracroft and Lambert, basically formalists, have also been sensitive to historical and ethical approaches, as have Jorgensen and Edward Geary, who were, like them, trained in New Criticism. I have used formalist close analysis and ethical criticism based on the work of Yvor Winters, Robert Scholes, René Girard, and Emmanuel Levinas. Jorgensen and I have both used myth criticism, based on the work of Northrop Frye. Recently, Cecilia Konchar Farr has effectively used feminist criticism on Maurine Whipple's work, and she and Philip Snyder presented an illuminating post-structuralist reading of Terry Tempest Williams' *Refuge* and Thoreau's *Walden* as eco-biography at the Association for Mormon Letters symposium in January 1993, not yet published. Tom Plummer applied reader response criticism to *Refuge* in "Is There Refuge in the Text: Narrator and Reader in Terry Tempest Williams's Memoir," presented at the AML symposium in January 1994.

[23]Smith, "King Follett Discourse," 203.

[24]For a discussion of the relations between religious thought and postmodern philosophy, see James E. Faulconer, "An Alternative to Traditional Criticism," *Proceedings of the Symposia of the Association for Mormon Letters, 1979-82* (Salt Lake City: AML, 1983), 111-24; and James E. Faulconer, "Protestant and Jewish Styles of Criticism: Derrida and His Critics," *Literature and Belief* 5 (1985): 45-66; for my own reflections on these matters, more complete than my comments here, see "The Dawning of a Brighter Day," 135-36, see Appendix, A; and *Beyond Romanticism: Tuckerman's Life and Poetry* (Provo, Utah: Brigham Young University, 1991), 17-21, 207-9. Hugh Nibley, in "Genesis of the Written Word," *Temple and Cosmos: Beyond This Ignorant Present,* vol. 12 of *The Collected Works of Hugh Nibley* (Salt Lake City: Deseret Book; Provo, Utah: F.A.R.M.S., 1992), 450-90, presents evidence for a single, divinely-instituted beginning of human language.

[25]Wilson, "Prospects for the Study of the Book of Mormon," 29-41.

[26]The Foundation for Ancient Research and Mormon Studies (F.A.R.M.S.) sponsors symposia and publishes a newsletter, essays, books, and a journal, many of which are greatly helpful in seeing through to the human realities of text and writers and editor as a better basis for imaginative response to the Book of Mormon. See, for example, John L. Sorenson, *An Ancient American Setting for the Book of Mormon* (Salt Lake City: Deseret Book; Provo, Utah: F.A.R.M.S., 1985); and Sorenson, "When Lehi's Party Arrived in the Land, Did They Find Others There?" in the first issue of the new journal sponsored by F.A.R.M.S., *Journal of Book of Mormon Studies* 1 (Fall 1992): 1-34.

[27]John W. Welch, "Chiasmus in the Book of Mormon," *BYU Studies* 10 (Fall 1969): 69-84; reprinted in Noel B. Reynolds, ed., *Book of Mormon Authorship: New Light on Ancient Origins,* Religious Studies Monograph Series, vol. 7 (Provo, Utah: Religious Studies Center, Brigham Young University, 1982), 33-52; Bruce W. Jorgensen, "The Dark Way to the Tree: Typological Unity in the Book of Mormon," in *Literature of Belief: Sacred Scripture and Religious Experience,* ed. Neal E. Lambert, Religious Studies Monograph Series, vol. 5 (Provo, Utah: Religious Studies Center, Brigham Young University, 1981), 217-31; R. Dilworth Rust's book, "The Book of Mormon as Literature," is presently (1995) being considered for publication by Deseret Book and F.A.R.M.S. For an example of ethical literary criticism, based on the work of René Girard and Northorp Frye, see England, "A Second Witness for the *Logos,*" 91-125, see Appendix, B 1. Some other important and representative literary criticism of the Book of Mormon: George S. Tate,

"The Typology of the Exodus Pattern in the Book of Mormon," 245-62, and Richard Dilworth Rust, "'All Things Which Have Been Given of God . . . Are the Typifying of Him': Typology in the Book of Mormon," 233-43, both in *The Literature of Belief;* Steven P. Sondrup, "The Psalm of Nephi: A Lyric Reading," *BYU Studies* 21 (Summer 1981): 357-72; and Richard Dilworth Rust, "Liminality in the Book of Mormon," *The Association for Mormon Letters Annual, 1994* (Salt Lake City: AML, 1994), 2:207-11.

[28]James B. Allen, "The Significance of Joseph Smith's 'First Vision' in Mormon Thought," *Dialogue* 1 (Fall 1966): 29-45; Allen, "Eight Contemporary Accounts of Joseph Smith's First Vision: What Do We Learn from Them?" *Improvement Era* 73 (April 1970): 4-13; Richard H. Cracroft and Neal E. Lambert, "Literary Form and Historical Understanding: Joseph Smith's First Vision," see Appendix, B 1; Arthur Henry King, "Joseph Smith As a Writer," *The Abundance of the Heart* (Salt Lake City: Bookcraft, 1986), 197-205; and Steven C. Walker, "Doctrine and Covenants as Literature," in *Encyclopedia of Mormonism* 1:427.

[29]Dean C. Jessee, *The Personal Writings of Joseph Smith* (Salt Lake City: Deseret Book, 1984); and Jessee, *The Papers of Joseph Smith,* 2 vols. (Salt Lake City: Deseret Book, 1989, 1992). See also Joseph Smith Jr., *History of The Church of Jesus Christ of Latter-day Saints,* ed. B. H. Roberts, 2d ed. rev., 7 vols. (Salt Lake City: Deseret Book, 1971).

[30]Stan Larson, "The King Follett Discourses," see n. 19; and Andrew F. Ehat and Lyndon W. Cook, comps. and eds., *The Words of Joseph Smith: The Contemporary Accounts of the Nauvoo Discourses of the Prophet Joseph* (Provo, Utah: Religious Studies Center, Brigham Young University, 1980).

[31]The *Journal of Discourses* provides a remarkably complete record of sermons by Church leaders from 1854 to 1886. For some analysis see Eugene England, "Brigham Young as Orator and Intellectual," in *Why the Church Is As True As the Gospel* (Salt Lake City: Bookcraft, 1986), 93-108.

[32]For a general bibliography see Davis Bitton, ed., *Guide to Mormon Diaries and Autobiographies* (Provo, Utah: Brigham Young University Press, 1977).

[33]Wilford Woodruff, *Wilford Woodruff's Journal, 1833-1898 Typescript,* ed. Scott G. Kenney, 9 vols. (Midvale, Utah: Signature Books, 1983-85). See also the condensed version, *Waiting for World's End: The Diaries of Wilford Woodruff,* ed. Susan Staker (Salt Lake City: Signature Books, 1993).

[34]Published in Eliza R. Snow, *Eliza R. Snow: An Immortal, Selected Writings of Eliza R. Snow* (Salt Lake City: Nicholas G. Morgan Sr., Foundation, 1957), 292-370. For discussion of this diary's literary merit see Eugene England, "We Need to Liberate Mormon Men!" in *Dialogues with Myself,* 157-59.

[35]Eugene England, ed., "George Laub's Nauvoo Journal," *BYU Studies* 18 (Winter 1978): 151-78.

[36]Manuscript in Harold B. Lee Library, Brigham Young University, Provo, Utah; published in full as "Death Strikes the Handcart Company," in Cracroft and Lambert, *A Believing People,* 143-50, see Appendix, C.

[37]Manuscript in LDS Church Archives; published in part, with literary analysis, in Eugene England, "Without Purse or Scrip: A 18-Year-Old Missionary in 1853," *New Era* 5 (July 1975), 20-28, which was reprinted as "'The Lord Knew That There Was Such a Person': Joseph Millett's Journal, 1853," in *Why the Church Is As True As the Gospel,* 17-30.

[38]Quoted by William Mulder, in his ground-breaking critical essay, "Mormonism and Literature," 87, see Appendix, A; at that early date Mulder praised

such "unpretentious subliterature" and claimed that "it is as a collective expression that Mormon literature makes its greatest impact rather than in any single work so far by any single artist."

The best collections of letters are Dean C. Jessee, *Personal Writings of Joseph Smith;* Jessee, ed., *Letters of Brigham Young to His Sons* (Salt Lake City: Deseret Book in collaboration with the Historical Department of The Church of Jesus Christ of Latter-day Saints, 1974); Elizabeth Wood Kane (not a Mormon), *Twelve Mormon Homes Visited in Succession on a Journey through Utah to Arizona,* Utah, Mormons, and the West no. 4 (1874; Salt Lake City: Tanner Trust Fund, University of Utah Library, 1974); George S. Ellsworth, *Dear Ellen: Two Mormon Women and Their Letters* (Salt Lake City: Tanner Trust Fund, University of Utah Library, 1974); Frederick Stewart Buchanan, ed., *A Good Time Coming: Mormon Letters to Scotland* (Salt Lake City: University of Utah Press, 1988); and Constance L. Lieber and John Sillito, eds., *Letters from Exile: the Correspondence of Martha Hughes Cannon and Angus M. Cannon, 1886-1889* (Salt Lake City: Signature Books in association with Smith Research Associates, 1989).

[39]Maureen Ursenbach Beecher has published the best work on Snow's life and poetry and is at work on a biography and a complete edition of the poems. See Maureen Ursenbach Beecher, *Eliza and Her Sisters* (Salt Lake City: Aspen Books, 1991).

[40]Eliza R. Snow, *Poems, Religious, Historical, and Political* (Liverpool: F. D. Richards, 1856); and Snow, *Poems, Religious, Historical, and Political. Also Two Articles in Prose.* (Salt Lake City: Latter-day Saints' Printing and Publishing Establ., 1877).

[41]Phelps's enduring achievement is suggested by "Gently Raise the Sacred Strain," which begins each Mormon Tabernacle Choir Broadcast, and "Hosanna Anthem" ("The Spirit of God Like a Fire Is Burning"), composed for the dedication of the Kirtland temple in 1835 and still sung at all temple dedications. One of Pratt's most powerfully poetic hymns is "Father in Heaven, We Do Believe" with its remarkable metaphor for baptism, "We shall be buried in the stream / In Jesus' blessed name."

[42]For studies of Mormon tracts and other pamphlets see David J. Whittaker, "Early Mormon Pamphleteering" (Ph.D. diss., Brigham Young University, 1982); David J. Whittaker, "Orson Pratt: Prolific Pamphleteer," *Dialogue* 15 (Autumn 1982): 27–41; Peter Crawley, "Parley P. Pratt: Father of Mormon Pamphleteering," *Dialogue* 15 (Autumn 1982): 13–26; and *Scrap Book of Mormon Literature,* 2 vols. (Salt Lake City: Ben E. Rich, n.d.), which reprints many of the nineteenth-century pamphlets.

[43]"A Dialogue between Joseph Smith and the Devil" (New York *Herald,* January 1, 1844) was republished in Cracroft and Lambert, *A Believing People,* 259-65, see Appendix, C; and in *The Essential Parley P. Pratt* (Salt Lake City: Signature Books, 1990), 31–40. The *Autobiography* was first published by in 1874 and reprinted many times since, the latest Salt Lake City: Deseret Book, 1985; for a literary analysis of this work, see Christmas, "Autobiography of Parley P. Pratt," 33–43, see Appendix, B 1.

[44]See Gean Clark, "A Survey of Early Mormon Fiction" (master's thesis, Brigham Young University, 1935).

[45]"What Shall Our Children Read?" *Deseret Evening News,* April 21, 1869, 2; Elder Cannon started to publish a "Faith Promoting Series" of books in 1879, the first of which was his own account of *My First Mission;* the third, in 1881, Wilford

Woodruff's *Leaves from My Journal;* and the fifth, that same year, James A. Little's biography, *Jacob Hamblin*. These three were republished together by Preston Nibley as *Three Mormon Classics* (Salt Lake City: Stevens and Wallis, 1944).

[46]*Journal of Discourses* 9:173. See also Stephen Ken Ehat, "How to Condemn Noxious Novels, by Brigham Young," *Century 2,* vol. 1 (December 1976): 36-48.

[47]Published in the June 1888, *Contributor;* reprinted in Cracroft and Lambert, *A Believing People,* 203-7, see Appendix, C. For a more thorough review of the "home literature" period see Cracroft, "Seeking 'the Good, the Pure, the Elevating,'" 57-62, see Appendix, A.

[48]Spencer also wrote fiction; see *The Senator from Utah and Other Tales of the Wasatch* (Salt Lake City: George Q. Cannon and Sons, 1895).

[49]Susa Young Gates, *John Stevens' Courtship* (Salt Lake City: Deseret News, 1909). Roberts's play was based on his *Corianton: A Nephite Story* (1902); see Cracroft, "Seeking 'the Good, the Pure, the Elevating,'" 61, see Appendix, A.

[50]First published in 1898, with over forty reprints since, the latest is Salt Lake City: Bookcraft, 1992.

[51]Nephi Anderson, "Purpose in Fiction," *Improvement Era* 1 (February 1898): 271. Cited in Cracroft, "Nephi, Seer of Modern Times," 6-7, see Appendix, B 2. Anderson's essays seem intended to prepare a Church audience to value *Added Upon*.

[52]Cracroft, "Nephi, Seer of Modern Times," 15, see Appendix, B 2.

[53]In addition to Cracroft's "Attuning the Authentic Mormon Voice" (see Appendix, A) see the conclusion to his "Seeking 'the Good, the Pure, the Elevating,'" 61, see Appendix, A: "The future of LDS fiction will probably be closely linked with Home Literature, for the LDS writer and the LDS reader share an abiding faith and hope in eternal principle, in the possibility of billions of happy endings. . . . But the message of Mormon fiction, while inevitably moral, as is most fiction, need not be painfully blatant." Cracroft's one example, Nephi Anderson, seems to counter Cracroft's own argument, since it was his admittedly inferior novel of "artless dogma" that remained popular and influenced later "home literature"—not his more skillful "dogmatic art" in the later works.

[54]Winters, though known as a formalist "New Critic," was adamant that a poem "is a statement in words about a human experience" (11) and must be responsible to rational ethical standards; see Yvor Winters, "The Morality of Poetry" and other essays in *In Defense of Reason,* 3d ed. (Denver: Alan Swallow, 1947). Booth, a Mormon, has been an articulate opponent of some recent trends in criticism, especially its move toward opposing—or simplistically applying—ethical considerations; see Wayne Booth, *The Company We Keep: An Ethics of Fiction* (Berkeley: University of California Press, 1988). Booth has also addressed, satirically, the question of too easily applied religious didacticism, in a forum address at Brigham Young University, "Art and the Church: Or 'The Truths of Smoother,'" published in *Dialogue* 13 (Winter 1980): 9-25.

[55]Keller, "On Words and the Word of God," 19-20, see Appendix, A.

[56]Bruce W. Jorgensen, "'Herself Moving beside Herself," 43-61, see Appendix, B 3.

[57]Orson Scott Card, "SF and Religion," *Dialogue* 18 (Summer 1985): 12.

[58]Anderson, "Just the Fiction, Ma'am," 6, see Appendix, A: "The more experience I have, the more I understand this heart and soul, myself, and my fellow human beings. I have my own living experience, but good fiction expands that experience tenfold—one hundredfold—and makes it possible to apply any knowledge I have."

[59]Geary, "Mormondom's Lost Generation," 89-98, see Appendix, B 3; see also his "The Poetics of Provincialism," 15-24, see Appendix, B 3. Bruce Jorgensen first used (but did not expand upon) the phrase in "Digging the Foundation," 58, see Appendix, A: "Mormon literature may be said to have its lost or half-lost generation, and some who have not expatriated themselves have suffered mistrust and even brutal ostracism."

[60]Fisher gained much of his national prominence with work not connected with Mormonism, the Vridar Hunter tetralogy and his twelve *Testament of Man* novels, but remained to his death in 1968 best known for *Children of God;* see Flora, "Vardis Fisher and the Mormons," 48-55, see Appendix, B 3. Whipple published various articles and stories and a guidebook, *This Is the Place: Utah* (New York: A. A. Knopf, 1945), but never completed her projected trilogy that would continue *Joshua* up to the present; see Maryruth Bracy and Linda Lambert, eds., "Maurine Whipple's Story of *The Giant Joshua,*" *Dialogue* 6 (Autumn/Winter 1971): 55-62; Bruce Jorgensen, "Retrospection: *Great Joshua,*" see Appendix, B 3; and the special section of essays on Whipple in *The Association for Mormon Letters Annual, 1994.* Sorensen received two Guggenheims, but she gained greatest recognition, including the Newbery Medal, for her children's books; see Mary L. Bradford, "Virginia Sorensen: An Introduction," *Dialogue* 13 (Fall 1980): 13-16; England, "Virginia Sorensen as the Founding Foremother," 12-14, see Appendix, B 3; and the special section of essays on Sorensen in *The Association for Mormon Letters Annual, 1994.*

[61]Cracroft, "'Freshet in the Death," 31-37, see Appendix, B 3. See also Cracroft, "Literature, Mormon Writers of: Novels," in *Encyclopedia of Mormonism* 2:839, see Appendix, A. Two other important novels by Taylor are *Family Kingdom* (New York: McGraw, 1951) and *Nightfall at Nauvoo* (New York: Macmillan, 1971).

[62]Jorgensen, "A 'Smaller Canvas,'" 10-31, see Appendix, A; see also Jorgensen, "Literature, Mormon Writers of: Short Stories" in *Encyclopedia of Mormonism* 2:842-44, see Appendix, A.

[63]For a discussion of the book's many problems because of Brodie's bias, see Marvin S. Hill, "Secular or Sectarian History? A Critique of *No Man Knows My History,*" *Church History* 43 (March 1974): 78-96 and his review of the second edition, *Dialogue* 7 (Winter 1972): 72-85. Newell G. Bringhurst's "Juanita Brooks and Fawn Brodie—Sisters in Mormon Dissent," *Dialogue* 27 (Summer 1994): 105-27, explores the similarities, differences, and relationship between these two writers.

[64]For the best early essay on the problems and possibilities of Mormon historiography, see Richard L. Bushman, "Faithful History," *Dialogue* 4 (Winter 1969): 11-25, which, in an inversion of a Mormon epigram, suggests the possibility, relevant to authors of literature as well as history, that the writer's success may be related to character: "[We gain] knowledge no faster than [we are] saved." Recent collections of Mormon historiography (and some criticisms of it) of the past twenty-five years are George D. Smith, ed., *Faithful History: Essays on Writing Mormon History* (Salt Lake City: Signature Books, 1992); and D. Michael Quinn, ed., *The New Mormon History: Revisionist Essays on the Past* (Salt Lake City: Signature Books, 1992).

[65]Peterson, "Juanita Brooks," 47-54, see Appendix, B 3. Brooks has also written an excellent autobiography, *Quicksand and Cactus: A Memoir of the Southern Mormon Frontier* (Salt Lake City: Howe Bros., 1982) and edited her husband's autobiography, *Uncle Will Tells His Story* (Salt Lake City: Taggart, 1970).

[66]Cracroft, "Nephi, Seer of Modern Times," 14, see Appendix, B 2.

[67]Geary, "The Poetics of Provincialism," 24, see Appendix, B 3.

[68]Cracroft uses the term "faithful realism" to describe the recent group of Mormon novelists he most admires in his *Encyclopedia of Mormonism* essay. With his permission, I adopt it here for the entire fourth period I am attempting to define.

[69]Keller, "A Pilgrimage of Awe," 112, see Appendix, B 4. Thomas Schwartz, in "Sacrament of Terror: Violence in the Poetry of Clinton F. Larson," *Dialogue* 9 (Autumn 1974): 39–48, claims that Larson's focus on unredemptive violence in both his plays and poetry makes his work not Mormon at all; in my judgment Larson profoundly expresses a tragic sense of pain and loss in the face of the violence inevitable in a universe of law and agency, a vision fully consonant with Mormon theology. Other important Larson collections are *Counterpoint: A Book of Poems* (Provo, Utah: Brigham Young University Press, 1973) and *The Western World* (Provo, Utah: Research Division Brigham Young University, 1978).

[70]Pearson published *Beginnings* (Provo, Utah: Triology Arts, 1967); *The Search* (Provo, Utah: Trilogy Arts, 1970); and most recently, *Women I Have Known and Been* (Placerville, Utah: Aspen Books, 1992); Emma Lou Thayne, *Spaces in the Sage* (Salt Lake City: Parliament Publishers, 1971) and many other volumes, the latest being *Things Happen: Poems of Survival* (Salt Lake City: Signature Books, 1991); John B. Harris, *Barbed Wire* (Provo, Utah: Brigham Young University Press, 1974); Edward LeRoy Hart, *To Utah* (Provo, Utah: Brigham Young University Press, 1979); and Marden J. Clark, *Moods: Of Late* (Provo, Utah: Brigham Young University Press, 1979). See the "Notes on Poets" in England and Clark, *Harvest,* see Appendix, C, for more complete bibliographies of these poets (all of whom have continued publishing), as well as other important Mormon poets. A remarkable and singular achievement was R. Paul Cracroft's long Mormon epic poem *A Certain Testimony* (Salt Lake City: Epic West, 1979).

[71]See the editors' commentaries in *Harvest,* see Appendix, C, and, for a contrary view, the review of *Harvest* by Richard Cracroft, see n. 10. Linda Sillitoe has published in *Dialogue* and *Exponent II* and has a recent collection, *Crazy for Living* (Salt Lake City: Signature Books, 1993); Susan Howe has published in the *New Yorker* and *Sewanee Review;* Lance Larsen has published in the *New Republic* and *Hudson Review* and has a collection being considered for national publication; Kathy Evans has published in the *Southern Review* and *California Quarterly* and has a recent collection, *Imagination Comes to Breakfast* (Salt Lake City: Signature Books, 1992).

[72]For the best review of these writers, such as Ray B. West Jr., Wayne Carver, and David Wright (who doesn't quite fit the expatriate label but was "lost" to the Mormon literary community by his isolation and early death), see Jorgensen, "A 'Smaller Canvas,'" 10–31, and its excellent bibliography, see Appendix, A. Also see Jorgensen's "The Vocation of David Wright: An Essay in Analytic Biography," *Dialogue* 11 (Summer 1978): 38–52.

[73]John Bennion, *Breeding Leah and Other Stories* (Salt Lake City: Signature Books, 1990). A story like "Dust," in this collection, is both characteristically Mormon in its protagonist's guilt-ridden response to the apocalyptic implications of his work on nerve gases and avant garde in its uses of stylistic disjunctions Bennion learned from his teacher Donald Barthelme. Other avant garde Mormon writers include the post-modernist, occasionally minimalist, Darrell Spencer, who is publishing widely in prestigious magazines like *Epoch* and has two collections, *Woman Packing a Pistol* (Port Townsend, Wash.: Dragon Gate, 1987) and *Our*

Secret's Out (Columbia: University of Missouri Press, 1993), and Brian Evenson, who has appeared in *The Quarterly* and *Nomad* and already has a collection, *Altman's Tongue* (New York: Knof, 1994).

[74]Author's notes from a lecture by Bennion at Brigham Young University, September 1991. Thayer's very influential first collection was *Under the Cottonwoods and Other Mormon Stories* (Provo, Utah: Frankson Books, 1977).

[75]See Jorgensen, "Romantic Lyric Form," 43-47, see Appendix, B 4, and England, "Thayer's Ode to a Redtail Hawk," 42-53, see Appendix, B 4. In my judgment, Thayer's "The Redtail Hawk," *Dialogue* 4 (Autumn 1969): 83-94, reprinted in *Mr. Wahlquist,* is the finest Mormon story yet—its sophisticated use of point of view and its profound theme enable it to stand with the best American stories of the twentieth century.

[76]See England, "Wilderness as Salvation," 17-28, see Appendix, B 4, and my review of *Night Soil,* 99-100, see n. 16. Also see my essay on contemporary Mormon novels, "Beyond 'Jack Fiction,'" 98-102, see Appendix, B 4.

[77]See Eugene England's column in *This People* 11 (Fall 1990): 65-68 for a review of many current "home literature" writers and Richard Cracroft's review of Gerald Lund's *The Work and The Glory,* Vol. 1, in *BYU Studies* 31 (Summer 1991): 77-81.

[78]See Eugene England, "The New Mormon Fiction"—and also the notes on contributors and the list of "Other Notable Mormon Stories and Collections"—in *Bright Angels and Familiars,* see Appendix, C. My column for the Summer 1990 issue of *This People* describes the *annus mirabilis* of 1989-90, when nearly as much first-rate Mormon fiction was published as in the previous ten years—or the 150 years before that.

[79]Sillitoe has a novel, *Sideways to the Sun* (Salt Lake City: Signature Books, 1987), and a collection of stories, *Windows on the Sea and Other Stories* (Salt Lake City: Signature Books, 1989); Fillerup has a collection, *Visions and Other Stories* (Salt Lake City: Signature Books, 1990), and a novel, *The River* (Signature Books, forthcoming).

[80]Horne, who lives in Canada, publishes both poetry and prize-winning stories in a great variety of non-Mormon publications and now has a collection, *What Do Ducks Do in Winter?* (Salt Lake City: Signature Books, 1993); Chandler, who lives in Ohio, has a collection, *Benediction* (Salt Lake City: University of Utah Press, 1989) and has also published a play, *Appeal to a Lower Court, Sunstone* 14 (December 1990): 27-50.

[81]Barber has a collection, *The School of Love* (Salt Lake City: University of Utah Press, 1990), and a novel, *And the Desert Shall Blossom* (Salt Lake City: University of Utah Press, 1991); Young has two novels, *House without Walls* (Salt Lake City: Deseret Book, 1990) and *Salvador* (Salt Lake City: Aspen Books, 1992), and a collection, *Elegies and Love Songs* (Moscow: University of Idaho Press, 1992).

[82]For the critical writing about Card through 1990, both by Mormons and others, see Collings's bibliography. See also Eugene England, "Speaker for the Dead and the Different," *This People* 14 (Summer 1993): 41-50, and Mick McAllister, "Embracing the Other: The Beloved Alien and Other Ethical Fictions of Orson Scott Card," in *The Association for Mormon Letters Annual, 1994* 2:158-65. Card forthrightly expresses some of his views on the values and moral quality of literature in *A Storyteller in Zion: Essays and Speeches* (Salt Lake City: Bookcraft, 1993), 65-105, which also includes his important letter to *Dialogue* (Summer 1985) on "Science Fiction and the Mormon Religion," 156-61.

[83]Orson Scott Card, "Foreword," in Kathryn H. Kidd, *Paradise Vue* (Greensboro, N.C.: Hatrack River Publications, 1989), x–xi, xiii. Card seems to me too harsh in his judgments of previous Mormon novels and too impressed with the writers he is sponsoring ("I am tempted to say that now . . . the Mormon people have their Jane Austen, their Mark Twain" [xiv]). He certainly seems right about his goals, but so far he is fulfilling them best through his own writing.

[84]The sermon tradition has been powerful and influential from the first, beginning with Joseph Smith (see Ehat and Cook, *Words of Joseph Smith*) and continuing through Brigham Young (*The Discourses of Brigham Young,* ed. John A. Widtsoe) and the other pioneer orators collected in the *Journal of Discourses*. The sermons of modern Church leaders whose sermon style has been influential, notably J. Reuben Clark, David O. McKay, Hugh B. Brown, Spencer W. Kimball, Gordon B. Hinckley, Neal A. Maxwell (AML prize, 1984), Marion D. Hanks, Jeffrey R. Holland, and Chieko Okazaki (AML prize, 1993) are available in the semi-annual *Conference Reports* and conference issues of the *Ensign* and in individual collections. For an analysis of Mormon sermon style and its literary power, see Eugene England, "A Small and Piercing Voice: The Sermons of Spencer W. Kimball," *BYU Studies* 25 (Fall 1985): 77–90, reprinted in *Why the Church Is As True As the Gospel,* 125–43. Though there are as yet no collections of sermons by lay Mormons, many such sermons have been published in official and independent periodicals, particularly in the "From the Pulpit" section of *Dialogue,* and many of the best modern personal essays are reworked sermons, showing the close connection between these two forms.

[85]William A. Wilson, a distinguished American folklorist, has written persuasively about the power and value of Mormon folk literature in *On Being Human: The Folklore of Mormon Missionaries* (Logan, Utah: Utah State University Press, 1981) and "The Study of Mormon Folklore," see Appendix, A. See Wilson's essay in this volume for examples and resources for Mormon folklore, such as the work of Austin E. and Alta S. Fife and Thomas E. Cheney and the Mormon Folklore Archives at Brigham Young University and Utah State University. The special issue of the *Utah Historical Quarterly* on "Mormon Folklore" (Fall 1976) contains another foundational essay by Wilson: "A Bibliography of Studies in Mormon Folklore," 389–94.

[86]See, for instance, Hugh Nibley, *Approaching Zion* (Salt Lake City: Deseret Book and Provo, Utah: F.A.R.M.S., 1989); Dennis Rasmussen, *The Lord's Question: A Call to Come unto Him* (Provo, Utah: Keter Foundation, 1985); Neal A. Maxwell, *That Ye May Believe* (Salt Lake City: Bookcraft, 1992); Jeffrey R. and Patricia Holland, *On Earth As It Is in Heaven* (Salt Lake City: Deseret Book, 1989); and Chieko Okazaki, *Lighten Up!* (Salt Lake City: Deseret Book, 1992) and *Cat's Cradle* (Salt Lake City: Deseret Book, 1993).

[87]In their section on "The Essay" in *A Believing People,* see Appendix, C, Cracroft and Lambert included six essays that might be called informal but only one, Geary's "Goodbye to Poplarhaven," that has the literary and personally revealing qualities that mark the excellent work being done since in this important form of the fourth period. In their introduction to that section, the editors express surprise that "the essay has not been as vital a literary force in Mormondom as might be expected" (201) and predict that "the personal essay will undoubtedly assume a larger role as a vehicle for the expression of the values of a people as manifest in the individual life of a sensitive writer" (202), and indeed Geary's essay began the outpouring of work that has fulfilled that prediction. (There were a few excellent

single essays before Geary's, such as Karl Keller's "Every Soul Has Its South," *Dialogue* 1 [Summer 1966]: 72–79, and Carole C. Hansen's "The Death of a Son," *Dialogue* 2 [Autumn 1967]: 91–96, but they did not become part of a continuing body of influential work.) Geary in turn was influenced by Virginia Sorensen's collection, *Where Nothing Is Long Ago: Memories of a Mormon Childhood* (New York: Harcourt, Brace, and World, 1963), and named his own collection *Goodbye to Poplarhaven: Recollections of a Utah Boyhood* (Salt Lake City: University of Utah Press, 1985). He uses a phrase for the Mormon country skyline from Sorensen's collection (in "The Ghost") for the title of his most recent work, an experimental combination of personal reflection with natural and cultural history, *The Proper Edge of the Sky: The High Plateau Country of Utah* (Salt Lake City: University of Utah Press, 1992).

[88]The earliest collections still tended to emphasize the somewhat scholarly and formal, such as Claudia L. Bushman, ed., *Mormon Sisters: Women in Early Utah* (Cambridge, Mass.: Emmeline Press, 1976) and Vicky Burgess-Olson, ed., *Sister Saints* (Provo, Utah: Brigham Young University Press, 1978), but gradually the truly personal essay emerged in collections like Lowell L. Bennion's *The Things That Matter Most* (Salt Lake City: Bookcraft, 1978); Eugene England's *Dialogues with Myself;* Sharon Hawkinson's *Only Strangers Travel* (Salt Lake City: Bookcraft, 1984); Edward Geary's *Goodbye to Poplarhaven;* and Mary Lythgoe Bradford's *Leaving Home: Personal Essays* (Salt Lake City: Signature Books, 1987). Bradford also edited two notable collections, *Mormon Women Speak: A Collection of Essays* (Salt Lake City: Olympus Publishing Co., 1982) and *Personal Voices: A Celebration of Dialogue* (Salt Lake City: Signature Books, 1987).

[89]See especially Bradford, "I, Eye, Aye," 81–89, see Appendix, B 4; Jolley, "Mormons and the Beast," 137–39, see Appendix, B 4; Donlu Dewitt Thayer's entry on "Literature, Mormon Writers of: Personal Essays," in *Encyclopedia of Mormonism* 2:840–41, see Appendix, A; England, "The Dawning of a Brighter Day," 152–54, see Appendix, A; and England, "Virginia Sorensen as the Founding Foremother," 12–14, see Appendix, B 3. For a general introduction to the contemporary personal essay, see *The Art of the Personal Essay: An Anthology from the Classical Era to the Present,* selected and with a fine historical and theoretical introduction by Phillip Lopate (New York: Avelar Books, Doubleday, 1994).

[90]Kevin G. Barnhurst published directly Mormon personal essays, "Living without Health," *Commentary* 75 (April 1983): 33–40, and "The Lumpen Middle Class," *The American Scholar* 51 (Summer 1982): 369–79; Terry Tempest Williams published "The Clan of One-Breasted Women," which became the last chapter of *Refuge: An Unnatural History of Family and Place* (New York: Pantheon Books, 1991), in *Northern Lights* 6 (January 1990): 9–11, and in *MS* 2 (September/October 1991): 31–34. See also Eugene England, "Easter Weekend," *Dialogue* 21 (Spring 1988): 19–30, and England, "My Grandfather's Nickel," forthcoming (1995) in *Sewanee Review*. Illustrating the complex and shifting border between fiction and personal essay is the work of Pauline Mortensen, written as personal essays for her master's thesis at Brigham Young University but published as stories in various periodicals, and her collection, *Back Before the World Turned Nasty* (Fayetteville: University of Arkansas Press, 1989).

[91]Elouise Bell has published humorous personal essays regularly in *Network,* a magazine for professional women, collected in *Only When I Laugh* (Salt Lake City: Signature Books, 1990). Laurel Ulrich, who has published her personal essays regularly in *Exponent II,* which she helped found in 1974, as well as

in the *Ensign* and *Dialogue,* is working on *two* collections: Mormon personal essays, to be published by the Women's Research Center at Brigham Young University, and more general essays, to be published by Knopf, the publishers of her 1990 Pulitzer Prize winning *A Midwife's Tale: The Life of Martha Ballard, Based on Her Diary 1785-1812* (New York: Knopf, 1990). Thomas Edward Cheney has published a fine collection of folkloristic boyhood memories shaped into essays, *Voices from the Bottom of the Bowl: A Folk History of Teton Valley, Idaho, 1823-1952* (Salt Lake City: University of Utah Press, 1991).

[92]See the list of these and a fine short history of Mormon drama in Robert A. Nelson's entry on "Literature, Mormon Writers of: Drama" in *Encyclopedia of Mormonism* 2:837-38.

[93]*Fires of the Mind* was published in *Sunstone* 1 (Winter 1975): 23-93, and produced at BYU in 1974 and again in 1982, Robert A. Nelson directing. *Huebener* was produced at Brigham Young University in 1976, Ivan Crosland directing, and is published in Rogers' collections, *God's Fools: Plays of Mitigated Conscience* (N.p.: Eden Books, 1983; distributed by Signature Books) and *Huebener and Other Plays* (Provo, Utah: Poor Robert's Publishers, 1992). Frederick Bliss and P. Q. Gump (aliases for Orson Scott Card) published an early piece of useful dramatic criticism, "Mormon Shakespears [*sic*]: A Study of Contemporary Mormon Theatre," *Sunstone* 1 (Spring 1976): 55-63. Recent work suggests a growing interest in Mormon dramatic criticism: see Nola D. Smith, "Madwomen in the Attic: A Feminist Reading of *Saturday's Warrior* and *Reunion,*" in *The Association for Mormon Letters Annual, 1994* 1:139-44, and Michael Evendon, "Angels in a Mormon Gaze," *Sunstone* 17 (September 1994): 55-64.

[94]More recently Arrington has written *J. Golden* and, with Tim Slover, *Wilford Woodruff: God's Fisherman,* produced at Oxford, England, in 1987 and published in *Sunstone* 16 (February 1992): 28-48. This tradition has been further developed by Carol Lynn Pearson in *Mother Wove the Morning,* her recreation of sixteen women from history exploring the concept of a Mother God, which since 1990 has played regularly to audiences in Utah and throughout the country and is on video.

[95]*Burdens of Earth* was produced at Brigham Young University in 1987, directed by Robert A. Nelson, and published in *Sunstone* 11 (November 1987): 12-33; *Katy* was commissioned for the 1992 Brigham Young University Women's Conference and directed by Claudia Harris.

[96]*Dreambuilder* was produced at Brigham Young University in 1989, directed by John Elzen, and *Scales* was produced at Weber State University in 1981, directed by Tim Sutton.

[97]*In the Company of Men* was produced at Brigham Young University in 1992, directed by the author, and won the Association for Mormon Letters prize for 1993. *Sanguinarians* was produced at Brigham Young University and in Chicago in 1990.

[98]Produced at Brigham Young University in May 1993, directed by Thomas Rogers, and published in *Sunstone* 17 (June 1994): 30-53.

[99]In addition to the official Church periodicals, all of which continue to publish fiction, personal essays, and poetry, and the well-established unofficial journals such as *BYU Studies, Dialogue, Exponent II,* and *Sunstone,* which publish more contemporary and even experimental examples of these same forms (and, in the case of *Sunstone,* occasional dramas), new periodicals are constantly appearing, such as *This People, Zarahemla: A Forum for Mormon Poetry.* The most recent are *Wasatch Review International,* founded 1992, which is devoted entirely to publishing the best current literature and criticism, and *The Mormon*

Review, forthcoming in 1995, which will review all aspects of Mormon literature and culture.

Deseret Book and Bookcraft continue to publish mainly didactic "home literature," though they have reached for new levels of faithful realism in writers like Carroll Hoefling Morris, whose *The Broken Covenant* (Salt Lake City: Deseret Book, 1985) takes on the difficult topic of adultery, and Gerald Lund, who won the Association for Mormon Letters Awards in 1991 and 1993 for volumes one and four of his epic *The Work and the Glory* (Salt Lake City: Bookcraft, 1990–). Signature Books is the main publisher of the writers of the fourth period, though some have been published recently by the University of Utah Press and an increasing number by national publishers. Aspen Books is doing an increasing number of books by Mormon writers of all kinds, including an anthology, *Christmas for the World* (1991); Margaret Blair Young's fine novel, *Salvador;* and a forthcoming biography of Maurine Whipple and a collection of her fiction, including parts of the unfinished draft of a sequel to *The Giant Joshua.*

[100]The proceedings of this professional association contain many of the best essays in Mormon literary criticism, have appeared in seven volumes, and its regular quarterly *Newsletter* includes short reviews of most new books of Mormon literature. It also encourages Mormon writers by sponsoring regular readings of new work in members' homes and through its annual awards in the novel, short fiction, poetry, personal essay, and criticism. The Association also awards honorary life memberships, with a handsome plaque, to distinguished contributors to Mormon letters. See Appendix, E 1.

[101]See Richard H. Cracroft's regular (beginning March 1991) column, "Alumni Book Nook," in *Brigham Young Magazine* for all Brigham Young University Alumni (formerly *BYU Today*), and my "Worth Reading," which appears regularly (since 1988) in *This People.*

[102]See her very popular Victorian mystery series, which features the morally reflective Inspector Thomas Pitt and his remarkably liberated wife and co-crime-solver, Charlotte; *Bethlehem Road* (New York: St. Martin's Press, 1990) deals in part with the starving to death of a Mormon convert by her abusive, chauvinist husband, who thinks he has the right to refuse a mere woman's decision about religion.

[103]The pain this dilemma creates for many Mormon writers was expressed recently by one, who said to me, "I believe God has given me an artistic gift with which to bless the Church and the world, and I have devoted my life to developing and sharing that gift. But the official Church magazines have made it clear they do not need or want my gift to fulfill their didactic purposes, the non-Mormon journals and presses reject my efforts to express my faith through my writing as too 'religious' for their audience, and when I write for the independent Mormon periodicals and presses I am considered, by many Mormons, *persona non grata.*"

[104]*Journal of Discourses* 7:237. Elsewhere Brigham Young insisted humans must "learn the nature of mankind, and to discern that divinity inherent in them. . . . We should not only study good, and its effects upon our race, but also evil, and its consequences" (cited in Cracroft, "Seeking 'the Good,'" pt. I, 58).

[105]Smith, *History of the Church* 3:295.

[106]Packer, "The Arts and the Spirit of the Lord," 281. I feel particularly good about the prospects of Mormon literature because I have recently read, in manuscript, Douglas Thayer's new novel, "A Member of the Church." It is a splendidly skilled and moving exploration of two different kinds of moral and spiritual life in young Mormon men—one that, I believe, fulfills Elder Packer's promise.

Looking southeast along Main Street, Salt Lake City, ca. 1904. This stereoview is part of a 1904 LDS Church historical set. When "read" properly, historic photographs can be used as artifacts. Notice the clean street, modern transportation network, electrical lines, and use of a bicycle by the gentleman in the straw hat (at center right). All these symbols reflect the ideas that America was technologically advanced, democratic, and hygienically superior. Photograph by James Ricalton. Courtesy California Museum of Photography, Riverside, California.

Mormon-Related Material in Photoarchives

Richard Neitzel Holzapfel and T. Jeffery Cottle

As primary sources of historical information, photographs provide a "window on the past."[1] Only recently, however, have they been considered important historical sources. Indeed, researchers and repository staffs have only begun to appreciate the important contribution that photographs and other visual images can make to historical research.[2]

Museums, historical societies' archives, official Church repositories, university libraries, state archives, and private collections across the United States—particularly in the West—hold many photographs of interest for the Latter-day Saint historical community. In addition to preserving well-known images by celebrated photographers, these repositories also house many little-known—and essentially unused—collections containing significant images by unknown amateurs, master documentarians, and the earliest photojournalists. Some well-known repositories in Utah and Missouri, for example, contain spectacular yet rarely seen images that capture the Mormon experience.

Historians of the Mormon experience should be aware of the unique and important perspective that photographs can provide. Like other nonprint, visual images (paintings, prints, and illustrations), photographs are artifacts—part of the fabric of the past[3]—that one must learn to read.[4] Photographs depicting past events or prominent individuals provide valuable economic, social, historical, architectural, and genealogical details not available in traditional documents. In order to aid scholars in reading and using photographs of the Mormon experience, this article briefly describes the photographers who recorded Mormon life, outlines how scholars of Mormonism have used photographs, and describes the repositories that hold such photographs.

Photographers of the Mormon Experience

Researchers should be aware of the people who made photographs of priceless historical value. Mormon photographers include Lucian Foster (actively photographing between 1845–47), Marsena

Cannon (1850-60s), Charles R. Savage (1860-1906), James Shipler (1860s-1914), Charles William Carter (1864-90s), Edward Martin (1865-70s), Charles W. Symons (1867-1913), James Fennemore (1870-80s), James H. Crockwell (1880s-1900), Charles Ellis Johnson (1880s-1910s), George Edward Anderson (1880s-1928), Elfie Huntington (1892-1940), and Harold Allen (1940s-80).[5] In addition to these, other photographers also recorded people and places of interest to historians of Mormonism. Among this group of photographers are Thomas Easterly, William Henry Jackson, J. J. Reilly, Charles Wieftle, C. L. Pond, A. J. Russell, and various photographers employed by H. T. Anthony and Company. These pioneer landscape photographers passed through Nauvoo, Salt Lake City, and Utah during the nineteenth century, capturing important images that preserve the texture of Mormon life during that time.[6]

Various Scholarly Uses of Photographs

Several photographic historians have published pathbreaking works dealing with nineteenth-century photographers and Mormon historical photographs. Furthermore, numerous historians have published studies that emphasize the visual history of the Church and describe the photographers who chronicled that history. Some of the major works include George Edward Anderson and John Henry Evans, *Birth of Mormonism in Picture* (Denver: Williamson-Haffner, 1909); Rulon S. Howells, *The Mormon Story: A Pictorial Account of Mormonism* (1957; Salt Lake City: Bookcraft, 1964); Nelson B. Wadsworth, *Through Camera Eyes* (Provo, Utah: Brigham Young University Press, 1975); Rell G. Francis, *The Utah Photographs of George Edward Anderson* (Lincoln: University of Nebraska Press, 1979); Gary L. Bunker and Davis Bitton, *The Mormon Graphic Image, 1834-1914: Cartoons, Caricatures, and Illustrations* (Salt Lake City: University of Utah Press, 1983); A. J. Simmonds, *Pictures Past: A Centennial Celebration of Utah State University* (Logan: Utah State University Press, 1988); Douglas Tobler and Nelson B. Wadsworth, *History of the Mormons in Photographs and Text: 1832 to the Present* (New York: St. Martins Press, 1989); Nelson B. Wadsworth, *Set in Stone, Fixed in Glass: The Great Mormon Temple and Its Photographers* (Salt Lake City: Signature Books, 1992); Scott Facer Proctor, *Witness of the Light: A Photographic Journey in the Footsteps of the American Prophet Joseph Smith* (Salt Lake City: Deseret Book, 1991); and Bill Lee Schaffer and Jo Schaffer, "Stereo Photography in Salt Lake City," *Stereo World* 18 (July/August 1991): 4-16.

Three books by Richard Neitzel Holzapfel and T. Jeffery Cottle attempt to collect some of the earliest photographic images of Mormon historical sites. These books include *Old Mormon Palmyra and New England: Historic Photographs and Guide* (Santa Ana, Calif.: Fieldbrook Productions, 1991), *Old Mormon Kirtland and Missouri: Historic Photographs and Guide* (Santa Ana, Calif.: Fieldbrook Productions, 1991), and *Old Mormon Nauvoo and Southeastern Iowa: Historic Photographs and Guide* (Santa Ana, Calif.: Fieldbrook Productions, 1991). The books draw on the important repositories where historic photographic prints and negatives are preserved.

In addition to the foregoing, several excellent historical studies have used photographs for interpretive purposes. An early attempt to use photographs as documentary sources is Dale L. Morgan, "The Changing Face of Salt Lake City" *Utah Historical Quarterly* 27 (July 1959): 209–32. Another innovative use of photographs is Lavina Fielding Anderson, ed., *Chesterfield: Mormon Outpost in Idaho* (Bancroft, Idaho: The Chesterfield Foundation, 1982). Two essays in that book, namely Paul Anderson's "An Idaho Variation on the City of Zion" and Craig Law and Craig M. Call's "Chesterfield, 1980: A Photo Essay," use nonprint material to help illuminate the Mormon past. In addition, F. Ross Peterson's effort to collect historic photographs of the people of Chesterfield is a worthy example of what can be done to document the social history of Mormon community life.

An exciting interpretive use of photographs is Gary B. Peterson and Lowell C. Bennion, *Sanpete Scenes: A Guide to Utah's Heart* (Eureka, Utah: Basin Plateau Press, 1987). In *Sanpete Scenes,* Peterson and Bennion link text and graphics. This effort to weave the past and the present together with historic and contemporary photographs is an innovative way to present and interpret changes in Mormon society.[7]

Like *Sanpete Scenes,* Richard Neitzel Holzapfel's "Stereographs and Stereotypes: A 1904 View of Mormonism," *Journal of Mormon History* 18 (Fall 1992): 155–76, uses photographs as text. In addition, "Stereographs" interprets photographs as cultural artifacts laden with cultural meaning. "Stereographs" is the latest attempt to use nonprint materials as primary sources in Mormon historical studies.

As documentary sources and interpretative tools, photographs can provide unique details that aid historical studies. Carma de Jong Anderson's "A Historical Overview of the Mormons and Their Clothing, 1840–1850" (Ph.D. diss., Brigham Young University, 1992) is a fine example of how photographs enhance historical studies. Anderson's work uses photographs and paintings to present details about nineteenth-century Mormon culture that would be difficult to glean from other sources. Other scholars have used photographs to supply the details necessary to reconstruct the physical characteristics of well-known personalities. In the case of Mormon studies, this reconstruction has been done for Joseph Smith and Brigham Young.[8]

Repositories of Mormon-Related Photographs

Photographs are unique documents. Whereas libraries collect multiple copies of books and other published materials in relatively uniform sizes and formats, photographs differ greatly in size and format. Therefore, they are usually housed in archival collections.[9] Those collections of interest to Mormon historians vary widely in size and subject. Notwithstanding this variety, many repositories hold significant collections of great research value. These collections contain a wide range of material, such as one-of-a-kind daguerreotypes, ambrotypes, tintypes, multiproduced cartes de visite, stereographs, paper prints, and numerous fragile glass-plate negatives.[10]

Repositories of Mormon photographs are responsible for conservation, identification of images (subject and date), interpretation, and appraisal of the Saints' photographic heritage. Only after collections have been evaluated, indexed, cataloged, and placed in safe storage are they ready for use. Many Mormon-related collections are carefully organized and conserved. Others, however, hampered by insufficient funding, inadequate equipment, and a lack of suitable storage facilities, will require considerable care if they are to survive.[11]

Eliza R. Snow, Mormon poet. Mormon photographer Lucian Foster may have taken this daguerreotype in Nauvoo, ca. 1845. Snow's hairstyle and dress, including epaulet sleeves, engagements to the elbow, and tight corset, are distinctive of the 1840s. Her dress could be heavy dull silk or alpaca, a very soft cloth from Peru, made of llama's wool and silk. This image indicates what textiles were available in a frontier town like Nauvoo. Courtesy LDS Church Archives.

In addition to being aware of these difficulties, scholars should remember that historic photographs have only lately been recognized as important source documents. This late recognition means that the principles of provenance have not always been applied to photographs; hence, provenance is one of the major deficiencies of almost all photo-archive collections.

Reproduction fees at photoarchives range from five dollars to fifty dollars, with the average fee around ten dollars. Several factors may increase the fee. First, fees vary according to the size and quality of the reproduction requested. Brigham Young University's library, for example, offers four levels of reproduction quality: regular, publication, exhibit, and archival. Second, the place of reproduction may increase costs. Many institutions can reproduce items in-house. Institutions lacking such capability, however, require the help of outside studios; in such cases, the expense increases significantly. Third, rush orders usually require an additional fee. The normal time required for obtaining prints ranges from five working days to several weeks. Finally, reproduction costs are higher if the institution does not own a "negative" of the photograph.

In addition to reproduction fees, researchers who wish to publish photographs must often pay a publication fee. Use-for-publication fees range from no charge to one hundred dollars. This fee is often waived or reduced significantly for scholarly publications. Regardless of the fee amount, all large repositories require written requests for permission to publish images.

Many repositories try to take advantage of new technologies that give researchers easier and quicker access to nonprint material. Future use of CD-ROM technology in photoarchives, for example, looks very promising. CD-ROM can project a photograph's image onto a computer screen during the initial stages of research. This process will not only speed access, but will help preserve original historic photographs as they are handled less. Moreover, CD-ROM will allow material within several collections to be cross-referenced quickly and efficiently.

Repositories of particular interest to historians of the Mormon experience include the following: the Archives Division, Church Historical Department, The Church of Jesus Christ of Latter-day Saints; National Society of the Daughters of Utah Pioneers; Photographic Archives, Harold B. Lee Library, Brigham Young University; Library and Archives, Reorganized Church of Jesus Christ of Latter Day Saints; Utah State Historical Society; Special Collections, Manuscript Division, J. Willard Marriott Library, University of Utah; and Special Collections and Archives, Merrill Library, Utah State University. In these and other

Here is a sample of the variety of photographs that can assist students of the past. Each photograph must be handled with care. Photograph by Ron Read.

repositories, regular dialogue with the photoarchivist is essential. The amount of time required for staging (the time between acquisition of a photograph and its availability to researchers) can be significant, ranging from a few months to several years.

The LDS Church Archives (Salt Lake City, Utah). The LDS Church Archives employs about thirty full-time employees. Three individuals work part-time with the photoarchive section at any given time.[12] The primary focus of the collection is to document the history of the LDS Church. The archives' estimated one million images relate directly to LDS Church history. Of particular interest are the collections of Marsena Cannon, Charles Carter, and C. R. Savage and Company.

The archives is well organized. A computer system in the main reading room provides easy access to the collections. Access to photographs is based on either the image's subject or the name of the photographer. A software package, developed in-house, provides several features that help researchers cross-reference material. In addition, several staff members are highly conversant in photographic history and photographers; they can assist patrons with the preparation of captions and provide valuable documentary information about images in the collections.

In association with the LDS Church Archives, the Visual Resources Library, a division of Media Services of the Church's Audiovisual Department, is an important repository of twentieth-century Mormon photographs. The Visual Resources Library has more than 250,000 images taken by staff and free-lance photographers. The majority of these images represent contemporary Church life, leaders, and institutions. Many photographs of Church historical sites, however, are also available. Patrons can access these items through a computerized system organized by subject. Any photograph that has appeared in official LDS publications since 1985 can be accessed by either the periodical name, month, and year or by the article title and page number.[13]

National Society of the Daughters of Utah Pioneers (Salt Lake City, Utah). The National Society of the Daughters of Utah Pioneers (DUP) employs a museum staff of one full-time secretary and thirty-five part-time volunteers. Three staff members work on the photographic collection.[14] Nelson B. Wadsworth (a collector discussed later in this article) assists the DUP by making negatives of original photographs housed at the museum. Some copies of prints and portrait paintings in the DUP's collection are available at either the LDS Church Archives or the LDS Museum of Church History and Art (Salt Lake City, Utah).

The DUP collection emphasizes Utah pioneers (1847–70). More than twenty-five hundred original portraits are displayed at the DUP. During a recent review of original daguerreotypes, ambrotypes, and tintypes, the staff discovered some seventy new images—a rich and important collection that will add significant information to the early social history of Utah. Yet unknown numbers of photographs are located in several family albums housed in the museum.

Staff members are currently organizing uncataloged portrait photographs. Original portrait photographs and copies are filed with biographical information about the individual depicted. Some two thousand prints have been filed thus far in this biographical file collection. Access is possible by special arrangement with the DUP.

Brigham Young University (Provo, Utah). The Brigham Young University Library Archives and Manuscript Department has eight full-time employees and numerous part-time student employees.[15] One full-time and one part-time employee and a student lab technician maintain the photoarchive section, which houses 750,000 images. The majority of these images deal directly with Mormon history. Of particular interest are the George Edward Anderson and Charles Ellis Johnson collections.

The photoarchives includes three major areas of interest: Mormonism and the American West, arts and communication, and Brigham Young University. BYU archives recently decided to study and promote the history of photography and is preparing numerous special photographic registers and indexes. In addition, the BYU library has joined the Research Library Group, which is headquartered at Stanford University. This organization is a national networking system that offers, among other sources, archival information and photographic material to researchers nationwide.

BYU's procedure to incorporate new material into its repository begins with an overview listing, followed by an initial inventory and the development of an index. The preparation of a final register depends on the size, complexity, and significance of the collection.

Utah State Historical Society (Salt Lake City, Utah). The Utah State Historical Society has three full-time employees and one part-time employee, with one individual directly responsible for the photo-archives.[16] This repository holds approximately 500,000 photographic images, nearly half of which relate directly to Mormon history. The society offers both a large manual catalog system (based on subject headings) and a computer system that refer the researcher to numerous filing cabinets filled with mounted duplicate photographs. The society's primary emphasis is Utah history.

University of Utah (Salt Lake City, Utah). The University of Utah archives employs four full-time and two part-time employees; one employee works full-time with photographs and other nonprint material.[17] The archives houses nearly 500,000 images, approximately thirty percent of which deal directly with LDS Church history. In order of priority, the collection focuses on Utah history, Mormon history, Colorado Plateau, and Western history. The photographs are divided into subgroups by photographer, donor, or subject. Researchers can access the collection through a manual catalog system that leads to indexes of specific photographs.

RLDS Library-Archives (Independence, Missouri). The RLDS Library-Archives has four full-time employees and several volunteers.[18] One individual is directly responsible for the photographic collection. The library owns some 40,000 prints and 100,000 negatives. The threefold purpose of the library is to collect and preserve material that illustrates the early history of the Restoration; provide a history of the RLDS Church, including factions and splinter groups; and house the official papers and documents of the RLDS Church. Nearly one thousand images deal directly with the early restoration period from 1830 to 1860.

The RLDS Library-Archives has recently moved from the Auditorium into new facilities at the recently completed temple complex. User access to the collections is by a manual retrieval system (index cards) based on subjects. The archives plans to automate its system in the near future.

Utah State University (Logan, Utah). Utah State University has five full-time and six part-time employees, with one individual overseeing the photographic collection.[19] The repository emphasizes Cache Valley and southern Idaho history; it particularly focuses on the history of Logan and Utah State University. Other important emphases include the Mormons and history of the United States. The collection houses approximately 500,000 views, nearly half of which deal directly with Mormon history. Cataloging of photographs is based on the Idaho State University system, which numbers the views as they are added to the collection. Like the Utah State Historical Society, the university makes mounted copies of photographs available to researchers.

Other Important Repositories. During the past few years, several leading photoarchives and museum repositories in the United States have begun to promote an understanding of photography's role in American culture. These repositories have expanded their traditional conservation duties by offering exhibition instruction and conferences related to their holdings in addition to collecting photographs.

One example of a photoarchives that has expanded its traditional role is the California Museum of Photography (Riverside, California). The CMP's collections include many photographic images of the Mormon experience. The photographic collection is organized into three subcollections: the Bingham Collection of Technology and Apparatus, the University Print Collection, and the Keystone-Mast Collection.[20] Each subcollection has a distinct system of internal organization. Research, however, can be easily conducted across the boundaries of each group.

Of the CMP's three collections, the Keystone-Mast collection likely holds the most interest for Mormon historians. It is the largest surviving collection of American stereoscopic images published for mass markets at the end of the nineteenth century. The collection includes important stereographic sets, individual prints, and negatives relating to LDS Church history.

The LDS Museum of Church History and Art (Salt Lake City, Utah) is dedicated to exhibition and interpretation of nonprint material. Recently, the museum organized a remarkable photographic feast entitled "A Vision of Zion: Photographs of Latter-day Saint Life, 1845–1991." Under the direction of Robert Davis, this exhibition utilized more than 275 historic and contemporary photographs to interpret Mormon group life.[21] In addition to the LDS Museum, several other institutions (Brigham Young University, Springville Museum of Art, the Utah State Historical Society, and Utah State University) have prepared photographic exhibitions for the public. In several cases, these institutions have published high-quality books and guides to the exhibitions.[22]

Another important source of photographs is Nauvoo Restoration, Inc. (Salt Lake City, Utah), which maintains an archival collection. The collection focuses on Nauvoo history, particularly the documentation of Mormon period buildings and homes. Materials are organized by site, not by photographer or date. At this time, unfortunately, the collection is restricted and unavailable to researchers. This restriction applies even to those items that have been previously published.

Several repositories own smaller collections of interest to Mormon historians. The Brigham City Museum-Gallery (Brigham City, Utah), for example, houses approximately two hundred images dealing with Brigham City history. These images represent the work of Bernice Gibbs Anderson, Alma W. Compton, and Charles R. Savage. Another repository is the Springville Museum of Art (Springville, Utah), which holds a small, uncataloged collection. Also of interest is the Art Institute of Chicago (Chicago, Illinois). The Institute holds a group of architectural photographer Harold Allen's images depicting the architectural history of Nauvoo.

The Illinois State Historical Library (Springfield, Illinois) contains a large but uncataloged collection. Another historical society, the State Historical Society of Missouri (Columbia, Missouri), also has an extensive photographic collection. Researchers may borrow photographs from SHSM if duplicates or negatives exist in the society's files. In addition, the Pictorial Library of the Missouri Historical Society (St. Louis, Missouri) offers access to over 100,000 photographic images. Of particular interest are Thomas Easterly's views of Nauvoo and surrounding communities during the 1840s and 1850s.

The Western Reserve Historical Society (Cleveland, Ohio) houses a collection of nonprint materials, including some eighty thousand photographs and prints. The collection documents the history of Cleveland and the section of northwestern Ohio known as the Western Reserve. As a repository of Ohio photographs, the society holds images of interest to historians of the Mormons' Ohio period.

The International Museum of Photography, George Eastman House (Rochester, New York) holds one of the finest photographic collections in the United States. Researchers with on-line computers can access the George Eastman House's interactive catalog by special arrangement with the manager of information systems. The catalog allows researchers to access an integrated system of photographers and photographs. The system is updated on a regular basis and contains nearly five thousand more items than Andrew H. Eskind (currently the

House's manager of information systems) and Greg Drake's *Index to American Photographic Collections* (Boston: G. K. Hall, 1990). Aside from the main Mormon-related repositories, the *Index* is the best resource for identifying potential locations for research. It is arranged by photographer and by repository, but not by photographic subject. The *Index* also provides several research strategies for locating photographic collections or photographs by a particular photographer.

A number of institutions house images by important Mormon photographers. These collections range from one or two views to a dozen. The pioneering work of Charles R. Savage, for example, is represented in many collections throughout the United States. His Utah photographs can be found in Special Collections, University of Kansas (Lexington, Kansas); the Art Museum, Princeton University (Princeton, New Jersey); the Print Department, Boston Public Library (Boston, Massachusetts); Prints, Drawings and Photographs, Yale University Art Gallery (New Haven, Connecticut); the Museum of New Mexico (Santa Fe, New Mexico); and the Seattle Art Museum (Seattle, Washington).

Individual Collectors. In addition to repositories, several individuals—including E. E. Calggett, Ida Bloom, Rell G. Francis, Gary B. Peterson, Nelson B. Wadsworth, and photographic dealer William Lee—have collected photographs and original negatives of Mormon historical interest. Nelson B. Wadsworth, for example, has gathered important historic photographs, such as the Charles Ellis Johnson collection (more than 3,000 negatives), and has helped to preserve photographs in professional repositories. Wadsworth first began collecting material for the Utah State Historical Society, then for Brigham Young University's Harold B. Lee Library; he presently serves the library at Utah State University in Logan, Utah, where he is a professor.[23] He states, "Unfortunately, because of lack of funds, the majority [of the photographs and negatives], particularly the negatives, are yet uncataloged and are merely in an unused state of preservation. My philosophy has been to get them preserved and protected before someone decides to throw them away."[24] As has been noted previously, the lack of funds to which Wadsworth refers is a continual problem in the effort to preserve Mormon photographs.

Conclusion

For over 150 years, the camera has been an untiring eyewitness to the growth of Mormonism throughout the United States and the world. Photographers, for example, recorded important images of the City of Joseph as the Saints began the exodus to the Rocky Mountains. Photographers also captured the beauty of the Great Basin and recorded the ingenuity of the Saints who transformed the Mormon Corridor from a barren desert into a productive agricultural area. In addition, photographers have preserved the everyday events that lie at the heart of Mormon culture and society. Through these images, photographers have captured the indomitable spirit of the early pioneer Saints. That spirit enabled the LDS Church to thrive despite almost constant persecution, internal division following Joseph Smith's death, a long and difficult migration west, a fragile pioneer economy, and a federal campaign against the corporate Church in the 1880s.

The LDS Church's complex history means that every photograph of the Mormon experience is a historical record. Each says a little about a time and place. All are part of the rich Mormon photographic experience. For the historian who is "visually literate," historic photographs offer a valuable and largely untapped source for the study of Mormonism.

Richard Neitzel Holzapfel is Assistant Professor of Church History, Brigham Young University, and T. Jeffery Cottle is an attorney in Orem, Utah.

NOTES

[1]See Richard Neitzel Holzapfel and T. Jeffery Cottle, "The City of Joseph in Focus: The Use and Abuse of Historic Photographs," *BYU Studies* 32 (Winter and Spring, 1992): 249-68.

[2]A good bibliographic source for the history of photography is Laurent Roosens and Luc Salu, *History of Photography: A Bibliography of Books* (New York: Mansell, 1989). Roosens and Salu cover specific time periods and regions, information that can assist the Mormon historian. For a general introduction to the history of photography, see Peter Pollock, *The Picture History of Photography: From the Earliest Beginnings to the Present Day* (New York: Harry N. Abrams, 1969); Sir Cecil Walter Hardy Beaton, *The Magic Image: The Genius of Photography 1839 to the Present Day* (London: Weinfeld and Nicolson, 1975); and Baumant Newhall, *The History of Photography from 1839 to Present,* rev. ed. (New York: Museum of Modern Art, 1982).

[3]An excellent example of the use of these artifacts is Bradley B. Williams "The Image of the American West in Photography, 1839-1890" (Ph.D. diss., University of Iowa, 1984).

[4]Published photographs of many nineteenth-century Mormons are found in Frank Ellwood Esslow, *Pioneers and Prominent Men of Utah* (Salt Lake City: Western Epics, 1966); Andrew Jenson, *Latter-day Saint Biographical Encyclopedia,* 4 vols. (Salt Lake City: Andrew Jenson History Co., 1901-36); Orson F. Whitney, *History of Utah,* 4 vols. (Salt Lake City: George Q. Cannon and Sons, 1892-1904);

Marvin E. Wiggins, *Mormons and Their Neighbors: An Index to Over 15,000 Biographical Sketches from 1820 to the Present,* 2 vols. (Provo, Utah: Brigham Young University Harold B. Lee Library, 1984); and Nellie Spillsbury Hatch and B. Carmen Hardy, *Stalwarts South of the Border* (Fullerton, Calif.: Shumway, 1985).

[5]Biographical information on these photographers can be found in *The Story of an Old Album* (Salt Lake City: Daughters of Utah Pioneers, 1975); "Early Pioneer Photographers," in *Our Pioneer Heritage,* comp. Kate B. Carter (Salt Lake City: Daughters of Utah Pioneers, 1958–77), 18: 249–304; "Mirror of Zion: The Utah Photographs of George Edward Anderson," *American Heritage* 30 (June/July 1979): 28–47; John E. Carter, "Photographing across the Plains: Charles R. Savage in 1866," *Nebraska History* 71 (Summer 1990): 58–63; William Clark, "The Photographs of George Edward Anderson: Glass Plates," *Rocky Mountain Magazine* 2 (January/February 1980): 38–45; J. Kenneth Davies, *George Beard: Mormon Artist with a Camera* (Provo, Utah: By the author, 1980); Rell G. Francis, "Photography—the Modern Medium," *Beehive History* 5 (1979): 16–19 [describes George Edward Anderson]; Francis, "The Utah Photographs of George Edward Anderson," *Society* 17 (January/ February 1980): 57–61; Francis, "Views of Mormon Country: The Life and Photographs of George Edward Anderson," *American West* 15 (November/ December 1978): 14–29; William W. Slaughter and W. Randall Dixon, "Utah under Glass: An Introduction to Four Prominent Pioneer Photographers of 19th Century Utah," *Sunstone* 2 (Summer 1977): 28–39; Slaughter and Dixon, "Prominent Pioneer Photographers of 19th Century Utah," *Sunstone* 3 (November/December 1977): 13 [describes James Fennemore]; Madeline B. Stern, "A Rocky Mountain Book Store: Savage and Ottinger of Utah," *BYU Studies* 9 (Winter 1969): 144–54; Nelson B. Wadsworth, *Set in Stone, Fixed in Glass: The Great Mormon Temple and Its Photographers* (Salt Lake City: Signature Books, 1992); Wadsworth, "Through Camera Eyes: A Pictorial History of Utah and the Mormons, as Seen through the Lenses of the Frontier Photographer" (master's thesis, Brigham Young University, 1975); Wadsworth, "Zion's Cameraman: Early Photographers of Utah and the Mormons," *Utah Historical Quarterly* 40 (Winter 1972): 24–54; Wadsworth, "A Village Photographer's Dream," *Ensign* 3 (September 1973): 40–55; *Albumen Prints from the Charles Ellis Johnson Collection* (Provo, Utah: Brigham Young University College of Fine Arts and Communications, 1983); *A Woman's View: The Photography of Elfie Huntington (1869–1949)* (Salt Lake City: Springville Museum of Art and Atrium Gallery and Salt Lake Public Library, 1958); Lynn DelliQuadri and Susan F. Rossen, eds., *Harold Allen: Photographer and Teacher* (Chicago: The Art Institute of Chicago, 1984).

[6]A guide to well-known photographers is William S. Johnson, *Nineteenth-Century Photography: An Annotated Bibliography* (1839–1879) (Boston: G. K. Hall, 1990); and specifically for western photographers, Carl Mautz, *Checklist of Western Photographers: A Reference Workbook,* 3d ed. (Brownsville, California: Folk Image, 1986). For specific information on individual photographers, see Donald E. English, "William H. Jackson: Western Commercial Photographer," *Colorado Heritage* nos. 1–2 (1983); Rowe Findley and James L. Amos, "The Life and Times of William Henry Jackson," *National Geographic* 175 (February 1989): 216–54; John C. Ewers, "Thomas M. Easterly's Pioneer Daguerreotypes of Plains Indians," *Missouri Historical Society Bulletin* 24 (July 1968): 329–39; Carla Davidson, "The View from Fourth and Olive: A Remarkable Collection of Daguerreotypes by the St. Louis Photographer Thomas Easterly," *American*

Heritage 31 (December 1979): 76-93; Paul Addison Hickman, *John James Reilly, 1838-1894: Photographic Views of American Scenery* (Albuquerque: University of New Mexico, 1987); "Captain Russell and the Mormons," *Humphrey's Journal of Photography and the Allied Arts and Sciences* 20 (April 15, 1869): 320; Peter Palmquist, "C. L. Pond: A Stereoscopic Gadabout Visits Yosemite," *Stereo World* 10 (January/February 1984): 18-20; and Thomas Waldsmith, "Charles Weiftle: Colorado Entrepreneur," *Stereo World* 5 (September/October 1978): 4-11.

[7]For other examples of the use of photography in historical studies, see William E. Hill, *The Oregon Trail Yesterday and Today: A Brief History and Pictorial Journey along the Wagon Tracks of Pioneers* (Caldwell, Idaho: Aaxton Printers, 1989); Craig Law and Nancy Law, "Mormon Documentary Photography," *Sunstone* 1 (Summer 1976): 39-41; Carolyn Rhodes-Jones, "Reflections on a Rural Tradition: A Photographic Essay," *Utah Historical Quarterly* 47 (Spring 1979): 167-77; "Transcontinental Travelers' Excursions to Salt Lake City and Ogden: A Photographic Essay," *Utah Historical Quarterly* 47 (Summer 1979): 273-90.

[8]See, for example, Richard C. Ryder, "Personalities in Perspective: Brigham Young," *Stereo World* 1 (March/April 1980): 18, 28; Marba C. Josephson, "What Did the Prophet Joseph Smith Look Like?" *Improvement Era* 56 (May 1953): 311-15, 371-75; J. Lewis Taylor, "Joseph Smith: A Self Portrait," *Ensign* 3 (June 1973): 40-44; Ephraim Hatch, "What Did Joseph Smith Look Like?" *Ensign* 11 (March 1981): 65-73; and William B. McCarl, "The Visual Image of Joseph Smith" (master's thesis, Brigham Young University, 1962).

[9]Nonprint materials, including rare and little-known illustrations, paintings, prints, and other visual images, are found in several important collections. For those relating to Nauvoo, see Stanley B. Kimball, "Nauvoo," *Improvement Era* 65 (July 1962): 512-17, 548-51; and Kimball, "Nauvoo as Seen by Artists and Travelers," *Improvement Era* 69 (January 1966): 38-43.

[10]For a discussion on the dating and identification of historic photographs, see James M. Reilly, *Care and Identification of 19th Century Photographic Prints* (Rochester: Eastman Kodak Company, 1986).

[11]Robert A. Weinstein and Larry Booth, *Pioneering Work, Collection, Use, and Care of Historical Photographs* (Nashville: American Association for State and Local History, 1977), notes some of the problems facing photographic repositories.

[12]Information provided by William Slaughter and Randall Dixon, LDS Church Archives.

[13]Information provided by Bruce Pearson, Visual Resources Library.

[14]Information provided by Edith Menna, Daughters of Utah Pioneers.

[15]Information provided by Billie Plunkett and Dennis Rowley, Brigham Young University Archives.

[16]Information provided by Susan Wetstone, USHS.

[17]Information provided by Drew Ross, University of Utah.

[18]Information provided by Ronald Romig, RLDS Library-Archives.

[19]Information provided by Peter Schmid, Utah State University.

[20]See *Guide to the Collections* (Riverside: California Museum of Photography, University of California Riverside, 1989).

[21]See "Family Album: 1845-1991," *Ensign* 22 (February 1992): 26-30.

[22]A representative number of exhibit catalogs include Dennis Rowley, ed., *The Beautiful Illusion of Substance: Four Photographers and the American West: An Exhibition Selected from the Brigham Young University Photoarchives*

(Provo, Utah: Friends of the Brigham Young University Library, 1990); *Setting Sail: [The Photographs of] Franklin S. Harris* (Provo, Utah: Friends of the Brigham Young University Library, 1985); and Steven L. Olsen and Dale F. Beecher, *Presidents of the Church: An Exhibition at the Museum of Church History and Art* (Salt Lake City: The Church of Jesus Christ of Latter-day Saints, 1985).

[23]During the early years of collecting photographs, several institutions' personnel were unfamiliar with proper archival procedures required to preserve old photographs. Photographs in their custody faded; were often abraded, bent, and torn; and priceless original negative glass plates were destroyed.

[24]Douglas F. Tobler and Nelson B. Wadsworth, *The History of the Mormons in Photographs and Text: 1830 to the Present* (New York: St. Martin's Press, 1989), 8.

Restored interior store room, Newel K. Whitney Store, Kirtland, Ohio, ca. 1987. Courtesy LDS Museum of Church History and Art.

Museums and Historic Sites of Mormonism

Steven L. Olsen

Despite a trend to critically examine the cultural role of museums and historic sites and despite the anxiety of many museum professionals for the future of their institutions, public support of museums has never been better. Since the bicentennial of the American Revolution (1976), the United States has seen a renewed interest in matters historical, scientific, and cultural as reflected in levels of public and private funding, the creation or expansion of major museums and historic sites, attendance at those institutions, and the quality and number of and support for publications and audiovisual programs on American heritage. Likewise, since the Mormon sesquicentennial (1980), similar support has existed for the preservation and interpretation of Mormon heritage at museums and historic sites.

To be sure, the heritage officially celebrated by Americans and Mormons in their respective museums and historic sites is a particular kind of history. In the case of the LDS Church, emphasis is placed on events, personalities, and places central to the founding of Mormonism and the establishment of Mormonism as an important religious and social force in the world—that is, on that which justifies the creation and maintenance of a distinctive Mormon identity. This kind of history is intended to engage the visitor in a historical inquiry about the meaning of Mormonism and its place in society and in the lives of individuals.

Such an inquiry, while not as objective as some would prefer, is based on the pedagogical assumption that values (in this case, religious) are not only essential to effective interpersonal and cross-cultural communications (in this case, about the past), but also crucial elements of the past that, in and of themselves, require preservation and interpretation. From this perspective, a complete and proper understanding of a social group requires an awareness of and appreciation for the values that motivated them in the past as well as the present. Therefore, objects, exhibits, furnishings, and settings become the spatial and material symbols of a larger Mormon reality that is preserved in the past, celebrated in the present, and projected as vital for the future.

What follows is a brief description of the most important museums and historic sites of the Mormon experience. These museums and sites represent solid historical scholarship and sincere value orientation in the field of Mormon studies. These institutions are sponsored by not only LDS and RLDS headquarters departments but also state and federal government agencies and private organizations. Thus they reflect a range of interpretive emphases and preservation philosophies. In short, the kinds of historical sources and perspectives available to visitors and researchers at each site are distinctive but, for the most part, complementary.

Museums and Historic Sites of the LDS Church

Since 1869, The Church of Jesus Christ of Latter-day Saints (LDS) has had an active program for the collection of historic artifacts and works of art, as well as the acquisition of exhibition space for the public display of those collections. Utah's first museum, Deseret Museum and Menagerie, attempted to portray the Mormons as a viable social and religious group and the Intermountain West as a viable American ecosystem. To this end, Deseret Museum exhibited natural specimens of the Great Basin and cultural artifacts of Mormon pioneers. Subsequent generations of LDS Church museums—the Deseret Museum and the Bureau of Information on Temple Square—acquired collections and mounted exhibits consistent with their particular and distinctive identities.

The most recent generation of LDS museums opened in 1984. The Museum of Church History and Art in Salt Lake City was founded to educate the general public, but particularly Latter-day Saints, about the historical and artistic heritage of the Church and its members. This modern, professional, 65,000-square-foot facility is equipped with secure, environmentally controlled storage rooms for its more than 50,000 artifacts and works of art. Collections access is granted to qualified researchers through a recently completed automated catalog system.

Exhibition galleries occupy about 20,000 square feet on three floors. The main-floor gallery contains a permanent exhibit on the history of the LDS Church, focusing on central, enduring themes of Mormon identity that emerged in the several decades following the Church's founding in 1830. The second-floor galleries include permanent exhibits on the Presidents of the Church, foundations of LDS art, and temporary exhibits on a variety of historical and artistic themes. The basement includes a small gallery for temporary exhibits and a theatre for audiovisual presentations and live performances related to the museum's mission.

Museum of Church History and Art "Covenant Restored" exhibit. Courtesy Museum of Church History and Art.

Historical collections emphasize institutional and individual artifacts related to LDS Church history from 1800 to the present. Of particular significance are textiles, furniture, ceramics, coins, and tools of the pioneer period. Collections of art in all traditional media portray events and personalities in Church history and interpret values and doctrines of Mormonism. The collections include works by LDS artists C. C. A. Christensen, LeConte Stewart, Minerva Teichert, Avard Fairbanks, Wulf Barsch, Dan Weggeland, George M. Ottinger, and John Hafen. The museum also has numerous lithographs from nineteenth-century periodicals depicting the Mormon westward migration and life in Utah. In addition, the museum has an ongoing program to collect artifacts and artworks reflecting Church history and LDS beliefs and life-style in countries around the world. Of particular significance are Polynesian artifacts from the nineteenth and early twentieth centuries brought to Utah by returning Mormon missionaries and contemporary Native American art of the American Southwest collected by museum curators.

In addition to its historical museum, the LDS Church maintains a number of historic sites. These interpret events and personalities central to Mormonism's historical beginnings, including the gospel's restoration, the pioneer trek west, and the settlement of the Great Basin. Some of these sites contain restored or reconstructed buildings and period furnishings. Others are interpreted primarily with monuments or exhibits. Still others are identified only with informative markers. The first two categories of sites also have guides to assist with tours and interpretation. The following briefly describes official LDS historic sites that contain important architectural, artifactual, archaeological, or archival resources. The list is organized by the relevant historic date. Except as noted, historical research files on the restoration, furnishing, and interpretation of these sites are located at the Museum of Church History and Art or in the Archives Division of the Church Historical Department.

Joseph Smith Jr. Birthplace. From 1804 to 1806 the Smith family worked a one-hundred-acre farm several miles northwest of Sharon, Windsor County, Vermont. Here on December 23, 1805, Lucy Mack Smith gave birth to her third son, Joseph. Superficial examination of the site in 1905 revealed the location of a few of the farm structures, including the stone cellars from the homes of Solomon Mack and Daniel Mack, his son, and the fireplace hearth and stoop stones of the Joseph and Lucy Mack Smith home.

After acquiring the property in 1905, the Church erected a monument to Joseph Smith on the centenary of his birth. Since that time, the Church has landscaped the grounds to resemble a formal garden and has marked the locations of some of the original farm buildings. It has also constructed a visitors' center containing exhibits about the life and contributions of Joseph Smith.

Joseph Smith Family Farm. Between 1818 and 1830, the family of Joseph Smith Sr., lived on a one-hundred-acre farm two miles south of Palmyra, New York, along the old Stafford Road, on the Palmyra-Manchester township line. Here Joseph Smith Jr. received the earliest of his sacred experiences, the First Vision and the visitations of the angel Moroni. Here, too, Oliver Cowdery assisted Joseph and Hyrum Smith to prepare the printer's manuscript of the Book of Mormon, and the Eight Witnesses to the Book of Mormon received their special testimony.

In their time on the farm, the Smiths cleared sixty acres and planted orchards, fields, and gardens. They constructed two homes on the site, first a log home and later a frame home. With its meadows, woodlots, and "sugarbush," and its barns, granaries, fences, corrals, sheds, coopering shop, and other outbuildings and natural features, this farm conformed to the highest agricultural ideals of the period.

Sacred Grove, ca. 1980. Courtesy LDS Museum of Church History and Art.

The LDS Church acquired this property in 1907 and has since made a number of modest improvements in visitor amenities. Standing at present are the Sacred Grove (reduced in area since the First Vision) and the frame home, as modified in 1870. A focused archaeological excavation by Brigham Young University in 1982 yielded the site and layout of the log home and its well. Much additional historical research has specified the layout and general functioning of the farm during the Smiths' occupancy. However, neither the site nor its interpretation currently reflects this vast body of knowledge.

E. B. Grandin Print Shop. In 1979 the LDS Church acquired the portion of Exchange Row on Main Street in Palmyra, New York, where the Book of Mormon was first printed in 1830. Between 1979 and 1980, the LDS Historical Department conducted an extensive architectural investigation of the second and third floors and determined the layout of the 1820s printing operations. The building is not restored at present, but the first floor contains a modest exhibit on printing.

Peter Whitmer Farm, Fayette Township, New York. In 1980 the LDS Church completed reconstruction of a log home like that where Joseph Smith completed the Book of Mormon manuscript in 1829 and where he organized the "Church of Christ" in 1830. The site at present contains no other visible evidence of the historic Peter Whitmer farm. There is, however, a visitors' center containing exhibits about the formal organization of the LDS Church and its priesthood hierarchy.

Independence, Missouri, Visitors' Center. At least three religions that trace their roots to Joseph Smith claim portions of the site dedicated by the Prophet in 1831 as the "center place" for the City of Zion and location of the temple where Christ would return to earth to establish his millennial reign. On its portion, the LDS Church has erected a visitors' center. In the basement is a museum-type exhibit on the early history of Mormonism in Missouri. Completed in 1980, this exhibit focuses on the glories of the Mormon religious vision for western Missouri and on the difficulties and failures experienced in attempting to realize that vision.

Newel K. Whitney Store, Kirtland, Ohio. During the 1830s, the Whitney store served as the Church's first headquarters, residence of Joseph and Emma Smith (and birthplace of their first surviving son), first bishop's storehouse, first formal Mormon schoolhouse, and town center and post office for the emerging community of Kirtland Flats. Other historic homes and building sites surround the store, but none has been restored or reconstructed to the Mormon period. In 1988 the store received an award from President Ronald Reagan's Council on Historic Restoration for being one of the best historic restorations of the 1980s completed without use of government funds.

John Johnson Home, Hiram, Ohio. In the mid-1830s, this home served as a temporary residence of Joseph and Emma Smith, location for important Church conferences, site of crucial revelations of early Mormonism, and place of the first violent persecution of Joseph Smith. At present, only the front portion of the home has been restored to this period.

Historic Nauvoo, Illinois. From 1839 to 1846, the Mormons settled on this large bend on the Mississippi River as their gathering place and Church headquarters. At its peak, Nauvoo was one of the largest and most controversial cities in Illinois. In the 1960s, descendants of Nauvoo's initial residents began privately restoring ancestral homes. In 1963, Nauvoo Restoration, Inc., was formed to assist in this process. The LDS Church later lent financial and professional support to the massive archaeological, architectural, genealogical, historical, and other research and restoration efforts to create what has become an impressive complex of forty residential, commercial, civic, and other sites. A visitors' center contains interpretive exhibits about Mormon Nauvoo, two theatres for audiovisual and live presentations, and a genealogical research data bank. Archives of Nauvoo Restoration, Inc., are located at the Church Historical Department, Salt Lake City.

Carthage Jail, Illinois. On June 27, 1844, Joseph and Hyrum Smith were murdered here by a mob consisting of citizens from Illinois and neighboring Missouri. The LDS Church acquired this site in 1903. In 1939 the jail was partially restored and a visitors' center added with interpretive exhibits. In 1988 a thorough restoration of the jail took place and updated exhibits and audiovisual presentations were installed in the visitors' center. The site and visitors' center are surrounded by formal, gardenlike grounds.

Winter Quarters, Florence, Nebraska. During the winter of 1846–47, the first companies of Mormon pioneers established a camp on the border of the Iowa and Nebraska territories. It served for two decades as an outfitting station for Mormon immigrant trains. It was also a burial ground for several hundred immigrants, many of whom succumbed to sicknesses persistent along the Missouri at the time. With formal landscaping and a heroic monument to pioneering sacrifice, the cemetery is the current focus of historic interpretation at this site.

Beehive House, Salt Lake City. Brigham Young constructed this principal residence in 1854. It also served as the office of the Church's First Presidency during the nineteenth century. The office contains exhibits about Brigham Young, and the home is opulently furnished in the style of the 1880s. The adjoining Lion House, formerly the home of

Cove Fort entrance, ca. 1985. Courtesy LDS Museum of Church History and Art.

several of Young's plural wives and their children, preserved in high Victorian decor, is presently a public restaurant and reception center.

Cove Fort, Millard County, Utah. In 1867, Brigham Young directed Ira Hinckley to build a way station between Fillmore and Beaver to accommodate travelers along the "Mormon corridor" and protect them and local residents from potential "Indian depredations." The furnished and restored fort, reopened in 1992, includes several reconstructed outbuildings.

Brigham Young Winter Home, St. George, Utah. Late in his life, Brigham Young spent most winters in Utah's "Dixie." The Church acquired this home in 1975 and restored it to the 1870s period. The adjoining building, originally a telegraph office, contains modest exhibits on pioneer life in southern Utah.

Jacob Hamblin Home, Santa Clara, Utah. Jacob Hamblin was an early Mormon settler in Utah's "Dixie" and a lifelong missionary to the Native Americans of the Southwest. The Church acquired and restored his principal residence to the 1860s period. Outbuildings and landscaping are not restored to the historic period.

In addition to these principal historic sites, several dozen other Mormon sites are interpreted either by visitors' centers with no restored buildings or simply by a permanent identifying marker. The LDS Church also recognizes several of its ecclesiastical buildings (temples, tabernacles, and meetinghouses) as worthy of preservation from an architectural, aesthetic, or historic standpoint. These are concentrated in Utah, but stretch from New York to Hawaii, and from Alberta, Canada, to Arizona.

Museums and Historic Sites of the RLDS Church

The Reorganized Church of Jesus Christ of Latter Day Saints (RLDS) also has a historic restoration program and a modest museum program. The RLDS sites program focuses on Nauvoo, Illinois, and Kirtland, Ohio. In Nauvoo, the two homes of Joseph and Emma Smith have been well preserved, furnished, and interpreted for the public, along with Joseph's "Red Brick Store" and the extant foundations of the Nauvoo House (hotel). There is also a visitors' center where the public can receive more general information about RLDS history. A recently opened garden allows visitors easier access to the Smith Family Cemetery behind the homestead.

In Kirtland, Ohio, the major RLDS site is the Kirtland Temple, the first of its kind dedicated by the Mormons. The building has been well preserved, and a small adjoining visitors' center orients visitors to the historic and architectural significance of this structure. In Lamoni, Iowa, is Liberty Hall, the restored home of Joseph Smith III.

The RLDS Church also possesses a modest collection of historic artifacts and works of art. Some are housed at the Auditorium, Independence, Missouri; others are on display across the street in the Temple School in a museum-type exhibit area.

Mormon Sites and Museums Preserved by State and Federal Government

The Division of Parks and Recreation of the Utah Department of Natural Resources operates a series of "heritage parks," some of which are museums and some of which are historic sites. Of particular relevance to students of Mormonism is Pioneer Trail State Park at the mouth of Emigration Canyon in the foothills east of Salt Lake City. Here is found the re-creation of a stylized Mormon community pre-1869, "Old Deseret." The town consists of a variety of domestic and commercial structures from the Mormon West that have been transported to this site or reconstructed on site. Most notable are Brigham Young's "Forest Farm" home and the 1850s Social Hall, reconstructed from architectural and archaeological research. If it is completed according to its master plan, "Old Deseret" will be the most ambitious interpretation of Mormon pioneer life outside of Nauvoo, Illinois. Also at Pioneer Trail State Park is the "This Is the Place" Monument—the single most important sculpture in Utah—honoring the various groups to explore and settle the Great Basin: Mormons, Native Americans, Jesuits, and trappers.

Other Utah heritage parks of value to Mormon studies include Fremont Indian State Park west of Richfield along Interstate 70, Edge of the Cedars Museum in Blanding, the Territorial Statehouse in Fillmore, Camp Floyd and Stage Coach Inn near Fairfield, and Iron Mission State Park near Cedar City. Each has collections or sites available to the public and research files containing historical, cultural, architectural, archaeological, and/or geographical information specific to the respective locations and associated historical events. The recently dedicated monument near the site of the Mountain Meadows Massacre (1857) southwest of Cedar City is also worth a visit.

The National Park Service operates several sites in the Intermountain West that relate directly or indirectly to Mormon studies. Pipe Springs National Historical Monument in northern Arizona is a well-preserved Mormon fortification. Built in 1871, Pipe Springs has been ably furnished and interpreted by the Park Service. While its Mormon significance is not emphasized as much as that of Cove Fort, there is much of pioneer craftsmanship and life-style that can be learned from a visit to the site and from its guides. The Golden Spike National Historic Site west of Brigham City celebrates the completion of the transcontinental railroad in 1869. Mormons were a large part of the labor force for the last segment of the Union Pacific Railroad through Utah. Capitol Reef National Park in south-central Utah surrounds the early Mormon settlement of Fruita. Although Fruita is now a ghost town, the Mormon settlement of this and other towns in the region is part of the interpretation in the park visitors' center.

The Ronald V. Jensen Living History Farm documents life in early twentieth-century rural Cache Valley in northern Utah. The equipment, lifestyle, built forms, furnishings, and farming methods reflect common technology and practices of the period. As part of Utah State University, the Jensen Farm has compiled an impressive archive and library of agricultural life in turn-of-the-century Utah.

The Utah State Historical Society also has artifactual collections of importance to Mormon studies. They help document the commercial, industrial, governmental, recreational, and ethnic histories of Utah in which individual Mormons as well as the LDS Church played important roles.

Local and Private Museums and Historic Sites of the Mormon Experience

The Daughters of Utah Pioneers (DUP) has existed for nearly a century for the purpose of honoring individual pioneers and their families who settled Utah. While not exclusively oriented to Mormon pioneers, the DUP has had an aggressive campaign to preserve artifacts, documents, and sites of value to Mormon studies. DUP headquarters in Salt Lake City includes a museum containing hundreds of thousands of pioneer artifacts of every kind. Most are on public exhibit. The Pioneer Museum also contains an archive of primarily pioneer letters, diaries, and other personal documents. Collections also include thousands of photographs—mostly pioneer portraits—and a number of important works of art by pioneer artists. While its library and archive are closed to the public under current policy, a resource file is open to researchers. It contains a vast amount of information on pioneer Utah ordered topically and compiled from newspapers, pamphlets, and many other published and unpublished sources, beginning in the late nineteenth century.

The Daughters of Utah Pioneers also has more than fifty branch museums throughout Utah, containing important collections of artifacts, documents, photographs, and works of art of significance to the history of local communities.

Like the LDS Church, the Daughters of Utah Pioneers has had an aggressive site marking campaign. The DUP has published guides which direct visitors to the nearly five hundred historic markers scattered along the highways and byways of Utah.[1]

Complementing the mission and focus of the Daughters of Utah Pioneers is the Sons of Utah Pioneers. While less accomplished than the DUP in the development of museums and historic sites, the Sons of Utah Pioneers was primarily responsible for the impressive collection that currently exists as Pioneer Village at the theme park, Lagoon, north of Salt Lake City. Pioneer Village is more characteristic of a museum than a historic site, with historic-type building facades and interiors serving as period rooms and elaborate exhibit cases for numerous artifacts from the second half of the nineteenth century. These collections emphasize more the commercial and industrial activities of Utah pioneers than do the collections of the DUP Pioneer Memorial Museum.

Utah has numerous local and municipal museums featuring artifactual and artistic collections of value to students of Mormonism. Within its specific emphasis on Utah art, the Springville Museum of Art possesses works of art in all mediums that document and interpret the careers of many Mormon artists from C. C. A. Christensen to the present. The Fairview Museum currently possesses the single largest public collection of sculpture by Mormon artist Avard Fairbanks. The Wheeler Historic Farm in Salt Lake County is restored as a turn-of-the-century living history farm. Union Station in Ogden contains museums that document the influence of the railroad and gun manufacturing industries in Utah, industries in which the Mormons played a major role.

Many other museums in America, from the Smithsonian Institution in Washington, D.C., to the Gene Autry Museum in greater Los Angeles, feature Mormonism and its contribution to American culture in lesser degrees. These are too numerous to mention, but they collectively acknowledge the wider role of Mormonism in American history and the legitimacy of Mormon studies in material as well as documentary terms.

Selected Bibliography

General References

Anderson, George E., and John Henry Evans. *Birth of Mormonism in Picture.* Salt Lake City: Deseret Sunday School Union, 1909.

Anderson, Paul L. "Heroic Nostalgia: Enshrining the Mormon Past." *Sunstone* 5 (July/August 1980): 47–55.

Brigham, Janet. "Church History Sites—Separating Fiction from Facts." *Ensign* 9 (March 1979): 74-75.

Carter, Thomas, and Peter Goss. *Utah's Historical Architecture, 1847-1940: A Guide.* Salt Lake City: University of Utah Press, 1988.

Haglund, Karl T., and Philip F. Notarianni. *The Avenues of Salt Lake City.* Salt Lake City: Utah State Historical Society, 1980.

Jackson, Richard H. "Historical Sites." In *Encyclopedia of Mormonism,* ed. by Daniel H. Ludlow, 592-95. Vol. 2. New York: Macmillan, 1992.

Jackson, Richard H., G. Rinschede, and J. Knapp, "Pilgrimage in the Mormon Church." In *Pilgrimage in the United States,* ed. by G. Rinschede and S. M. Bharddwaj, 27-61. Berlin: D. Reimer, 1989.

Kimball, Stanley B. *Historic Sites and Markers along the Mormon and Other Great Western Trails.* Urbana: University of Illinois Press, 1988.

Leonard, Glen M. "New Look at LDS Historic Sites." *Mormon History Association Newsletter,* no. 42 (November 1979): 6-7.

Leone, Mark P. "Archeology as the Science of Technology: Mormon Town Plans and Fences." In *Research and Theory in Current Archeology,* ed. by Charles L. Redman, 125-50. New York: John Wiley and Sons, 1973.

Lyman, Edward Leo. *Guidebook: Mormon Historical Sites in the San Bernardino [California] Area.* Claremont, Calif.: By the author, 1991.

McCormick, John S. *The Historic Buildings of Downtown Salt Lake City.* Salt Lake City: Utah State Historical Society, 1982.

Oscarson, R. Don. *The Travelers' Guide to Historic Mormon America.* 1965. Reprint, Salt Lake City: Bookcraft, 1976.

"Pioneer Life Revisited." *Ensign* 16 (July 1986): 40-43.

Wells, Merle. "A Seven-Day Tour of Idaho's Historic Attractions." *Journal of the West* 17 (October 1978): 101-12.

Museums

Eubanks, Lila Carpenter. "The Deseret Museum." *Utah Historical Quarterly* 50 (Fall 1982): 361-76.

Jacobsen, Florence Smith. "LDS Museums." In *Encyclopedia of Mormonism* 2:971-93.

"Museum Artifacts." In *An Enduring Legacy,* comp. by The Lesson Committee, 329-76. Vol. 3. Salt Lake City: Daughters of Utah Pioneers, 1979.

Rollins, Kerril Sue. "LDS Artifacts and Art Portray Church History: The New Church Museum." *Ensign* 14 (April 1984): 44–53.

Talmage, James E. "The Deseret Museum." *Improvement Era* 14 (September 1911): 953–82.

———. "The Passing of the Deseret Museum." *Improvement Era* 22 (April 1919): 527–31.

Historic Sites and Preservation Issues

Haggerty, John W. "Historic Preservation in Utah, 1960–1980." Master's thesis, Brigham Young University, 1980.

Leone, Mark. "Why the Coalville Tabernacle Had to Be Razed." *Dialogue: A Journal of Mormon Thought* 8 (Summer 1973): 30–39.

Lyon, T. Edgar. "How Authentic Are Mormon Historic Sites in Vermont and New York?" *BYU Studies* 9 (Spring 1969): 341–50.

Wilding, D. D. "Restoring the Rexburg Tabernacle." *Snake River Echoes* 14 (Winter 1985): 122–24.

New England

Anderson, Richard Lloyd. "The House Where the Church Was Organized." *Improvement Era* 73 (April 1970): 16–25.

Beldius, Patricia. "A Monumental Race with Winter." *Vermont Life* 38, no. 1 (1983): 45–48.

Berge, Dale L. "Archaeological Work at the Smith Log House." *Ensign* 15 (August 1985): 24–26.

———. "Archaeology at the Peter Whitmer Farm, Seneca County, New York." *BYU Studies* 13 (Winter 1973): 172–201.

Ellsworth, J. Orvall. "The Birthplace of the Church." *Improvement Era* 27 (April 1924): 550–53.

Enders, Donald L. "The Sacred Grove." *Ensign* 20 (April 1990): 14–17.

———. "A Snug Log House: A Historical Look at the Joseph Smith, Sr., Family Home in Palmyra, New York." *Ensign* 15 (August 1985): 14–23.

Holzapfel, Richard Neitzel, and T. Jeffery Cottle. *Old Mormon Palmyra and New England: Historic Photographs and Guide.* Santa Ana, Calif.: Fieldbrook Productions, 1991.

McGavin, E. Cecil. "The Whitmer Home: A New Addition to the Church's Collection of Historic Places." *Improvement Era* 30 (September 1927): 1016–21.

"The Way It Looks Today: A Camera Tour of Church History Sites in New York, New England, Pennsylvania, and Ohio." *Ensign* 8 (September 1978): 33–49.

Ohio and Missouri

Dyer, Alvin R. "Bureau of Information Erected on the Site of the Liberty Jail at Liberty, Missouri." *Missouri Historical Review* 57 (July 1963): 379-88.

Holzapfel, Richard Neitzel, and T. Jeffery Cottle. *Old Mormon Kirtland and Missouri: Historic Photographs and Guide.* Santa Ana, Calif.: Fieldbrook Productions, 1991.

Parkin, Max H. "The Way It Looks Today: A Camera Tour of Church History Sites in Missouri." *Ensign* 9 (April 1979): 32-44.

"Restored Whitney Store Dedicated in Kirtland." *Ensign* 14 (November 1984): 110-11.

"The Way It Looks Today: A Camera Tour of Church History Sites in the Kirtland Neighborhood." *Ensign* 9 (January 1979): 31-48.

"Whitney Store Wins Major U.S. Preservation Award." *Ensign* 19 (January 1989): 76-77.

Illinois

Berge, Dale L. "The Jonathan Browning Site: An Example of Archaeology for Restoration in Nauvoo, Illinois." *BYU Studies* 19 (Winter 1979): 201-29.

Cannon, Janath R. *Nauvoo Panorama: Views of Nauvoo before, during, and after its Rise, Fall, and Restoration* (Salt Lake City: NRI, 1991).

Harrington, Virginia S., and J. C. Harrington. *Rediscovery of the Nauvoo Temple: Report on the Archaeological Excavations.* Salt Lake City: Nauvoo Restoration, 1971.

Holzapfel, Richard Neitzel, and T. Jeffery Cottle. *Old Mormon Nauvoo, 1839-1846: Historic Photographs and Guide.* Provo, Utah: Grandin Books, 1990.

Jacobson, Irene C. "Recent Restoration of Nauvoo, a Mormon Community in Illinois, 1839-1846." Master's thesis, Brigham Young University, 1972.

Josephson, Marba C. "Church Acquires Nauvoo Temple Site." *Improvement Era* 40 (April 1937): 226-27.

Kimball, J. LeRoy. "The Restoration of Nauvoo." *Utah Medical Bulletin* 21 (May 1973): 3-7.

Krohe, James, Jr. "A New City of Joseph." *Americana* 8 (April 1980): 56-61.

Launius, Roger D., and F. Mark McKiernan. *Joseph Smith, Jr.'s Red Brick Store.* Western Illinois Monograph Series, no. 5. Macomb: Western Illinois University, 1985.

Lund, George W. "The Challenge of Reconstructing the Red Brick Store." *Saints' Heritage: A Journal of the Restoration Trail Foundation* (1988): 75-88.

Lyon, T. Edgar. "The Current Restoration in Nauvoo, Illinois." *Dialogue* 5 (Spring 1970): 13-25.

Utah and the West

Anderson, Judy Butler. "The Beehive House: Its Design, Restoration, and Furnishings." Master's thesis, Brigham Young University, 1967.

Anderson, Lavina Fielding, ed. *Chesterfield: Mormon Outpost in Idaho.* Bancroft, Idaho: Chesterfield Foundation, 1982.

Arrington, Joseph Earl. "Brigham's Home: The Beehive House." *Sunset* 135 (September 1965): 36-38.

The Beehive House: Home of Brigham Young, Pioneer President of The Church of Jesus Christ of Latter-day Saints and Governor of the Territory of Deseret. Salt Lake City: The Church of Jesus Christ of Latter-day Saints, 1978.

Hendricks, Rickey Lynn. "Landmark Architecture for a Polygamous Family: The Brigham Young Domicile, Salt Lake City, Utah." *Public Historian* 11 (Winter 1989): 25-47.

Jacobsen, Florence S. "Restorations Belong to Everyone." *BYU Studies* 18 (Spring 1978): 275-85. [Brigham Young Home, St. George, Utah].

Peterson, Gary B., and Lowell C. Bennion. *Sanpete Scenes: A Guide to Utah's Heart.* Eureka, Utah: Basin/Plateau, 1987.

Porter, Lawrence C. "A Historical Analysis of Cove Fort, Utah." Master's thesis, Brigham Young University, 1966.

Steven L. Olsen is Manager of Operations, Museum of Church History and Art, Salt Lake City.

NOTE

[1]See "Monuments Erected by Daughters of Utah Pioneers," in *Heart Throbs of the West,* comp. Kate B. Carter, 12 vols. (Salt Lake City: Daughters of Utah Pioneers, 1939-51), 6:85-196 [marker numbers 1-87]; Carter, *Treasures of Pioneer History,* 6 vols. (Salt Lake City: Daughters of Utah Pioneers, 1952-57), 2:405-500 [markers 88-180], 6:493-547 [markers 181-233]; Carter, *Our Pioneer Heritage,* 20 vols. (Salt Lake City: Daughters of Utah Pioneers, 1958-77), 5:393-436 [markers 234-70], 20:377-464 [markers 271-396]; and The Lesson Committee, comp., *An Enduring Legacy,* 12 vols. (Salt Lake City: Daughters of Utah Pioneers, 1977-89), 10:293-332 [markers 397-433]. See also "Landmarks Saved by the Daughters of Utah Pioneers," in *Our Pioneer Heritage,* 10:497-548.

THEATRE!!

SECOND NIGHT
OF THE
SEASON.

WEDNESDAY EVENING, MARCH 12, 1862.

The Performance will commence with the Popular Historic Farce,

STATE SECRETS;
OR THE
Tailor of Tamworth.

With characteristic Music, composed and arranged expressly for this piece, by Prof. C. J. THOMAS.

Gregory Thimblewell, the Tailor of Tamworth, (with a Song) - - -	MR. H. E. BOWRING.
Robert, his Son - - - - - -	MR. R. H. PARKER.
Master Hugh Neville, (an Officer in the Army of the Parliament, commanded by General Fairfax) - - -	MR. S. D. SIRRINE.
Calverton Hal, (a Cavalier belonging to the Army of Prince Rupert) -	MR. W. H. MILES.
Humphrey Hedgehog, (a wealthy Miller and Landlord of the Black Bull Inn, in Tamworth - - - - - -	MR. P. MARGETTS.
Maud Thimblewell, (the Tailor's Wife) -	MRS. BOWRING.
Letty, Daughter of Hedgehog, (with a Song)	MISS THOMAS.

Cavaliers, Townspeople.

SENTIMENTAL SONG (Beautiful Star). -	Miss PRICE.
COMIC SONG. - - - - -	Mr. DUNBAR.

To conclude with the Favorite Comedy, in 3 Acts,

THE SERIOUS FAMILY.

Charles Torrens - - - -	MR. J. M. SIMMONS.
Capt. Murphy Maguire - - - -	MR. H. K. WHITNEY.
Frank Vincent - - - - -	MR. R. H. PARKER.
Aminadab Sleek - - - - -	MR. JOHN T. CAINE.
Danvers - - - - -	MR. R. MATTHEWS.
Lady Sowerby Creamly - - -	MRS. COOKE.
Mrs. Charles Torrens - - - -	MRS. WOODMANSEE.
Emma Torrens - - - - -	MRS. A. CLAWSON.
Mrs. Ormsby Delmaine - - -	MRS. BOWRING.
Graham - - - - - -	MISS THOMAS.

Guests, by Ladies and Gentlemen of the Company.

(The Comedy will conclude with the old English Dance, "Pop Goes the Weasel.")

Doors open at 6. Performance commences at 7.

Tickets for Sale at the Theatre Box Office after 4 o'clock on the days of Performance.

Parquette, First and Second Circles, - - - - 75cts.

Third Circle, - - 50 "

Children in arms not admitted.

One of the earliest known theater bills for the Salt Lake Theatre, 1862. Courtesy LDS Church Archives.

The Performing Arts and Mormonism: An Introductory Guide

Michael Hicks

"What many people call sin is not sin." —Joseph Smith, 1841

Joseph Smith's remark suggests the attitude of many early Mormons toward the recreations and amusements that many religious societies deplored. Brigham Young shrugged off the prevailing asceticism of his time, teaching that God had given music, dancing, and even the theater for the pleasure of his Saints. Generations of Mormons since have warmed to the performing arts—whether popular song, comic theater, recreational dancing, or the more academic forms of music, drama, and dance. In every instance, performers and creators alike seem to have fulfilled their aesthetic missions with zeal.

General Studies

The Mormon rapprochement with the performing arts is examined in a number of general studies. Two good examples are Arthur Ray Bassett, "Culture and the American Frontier in Mormon Utah, 1850–1896,"[1] and R. Laurence Moore, "Learning to Play: The Mormon Way and the Way of Other Americans."[2] Another excellent (and underappreciated) overview is William J. McNiff, *Heaven on Earth: A Planned Mormon Society.*[3] The specific contributions of women in Mormon culture are treated in Raye Price, "Utah's Leading Ladies of the Arts";[4] Jill C. Mulvay, "Three Mormon Women in the Cultural Arts";[5] and Jean R. Jenkins, "Portrait of a Lady: Kathryn Bassett Pardoe."[6] More studies in this area are forthcoming. Two other surveys, each with its particular angle of vision, are Juanita Brooks, "Culture in Dixie,"[7] and Janice P. Dawson, "Chatauqua and the Utah Performing Arts."[8] General discussions of the aesthetics of Mormon arts appear in Lorin F. Wheelwright and Lael J. Woodbury, eds., *Mormon Arts, Volume One;*[9] Steven P. Sondrup, ed., *Arts and Inspiration: Mormon Perspectives;*[10] Joy C. Ross and Steven C. Walker, eds., *Letters to Smoother, etc. . . .: Proceedings of the Fifth Annual Brigham Young University Symposium on the Humanities;*[11] and Michael Hicks, "Notes on Brigham Young's Aesthetics."[12]

Music

Understandably, music has received the lion's share of attention, since its personal and institutional uses are so many and varied. Perhaps the only way to grasp that diversity is to survey the pages of ordinary Mormon publications and diaries, where music is almost invariably mentioned, sometimes in unexpected contexts. Several diaries of nineteenth-century Mormon musicians provide wonderful glimpses of musical life, including those of Joseph Beecroft, George Goddard, and Thomas McIntyre, all of which are in the Library-Archives of the Historical Department of The Church of Jesus Christ of Latter-day Saints, Salt Lake City, Utah. The same repository also contains some essential oral histories by J. Spencer Cornwall, Evangeline T. Beesley, Lowell M. Durham, and Mary Jack. All of these are filled with anecdotes displaying the spirit of music and spirited musicians in the LDS Church.

A few good surveys of Mormon musical life have been published: Howard Swan, *Music in the Southwest, 1825–1950;*[13] Lowell M. Durham, "On Mormon Music and Musicians";[14] an entire issue of *Dialogue: A Journal of Mormon Thought;*[15] Verena Ursenbach Hatch, *Worship and Music in The Church of Jesus Christ of Latter-day Saints;*[16] and Michael Hicks, *Mormonism and Music: A History.*[17] Two dissertations are also noteworthy for their broad perspective: William Earl Purdy, "Music in Mormon Culture, 1830–1876,"[18] and Jay Leon Slaughter, "The Role of Music in the Mormon Church, School, and Life."[19]

Much of the scholarly work related to Mormon music has concentrated on the hymns—not only the plentiful catalog of hymns borrowed and derived from the Christian world at large, but also the hundreds of hymns created by and for Latter-day Saints. The earliest general treatment of the subject—and still an excellent one—is David Sterling Wheelwright, "The Role of Hymnody in the Development of the Latter-day Saint Movement."[20] An introductory survey of the history of the hymnbooks is Michael F. Moody, "Latter-day Saint Hymnbooks, Then and Now."[21] The essential hymnbook "companions"—studies of the hymns in various editions of Mormon hymnbooks—are George D. Pyper, *Stories of Latter-day Saint Hymns, Their Authors and Composers;*[22] J. Spencer Cornwall, *Stories of Our Mormon Hymns;*[23] and Karen Lynn Davidson, *Our Latter-day Hymns: The Stories and the Messages.*[24] The various editions of LDS hymnbooks, including Sunday School and Primary songbooks, may be found at the LDS Historical Department and in the Special Collections vault at the Harold B. Lee Library, Brigham Young University. The various hymnbooks and their locations are best identified through Chad J. Flake, *A Mormon Bibliography, 1830–1930: Books, Pamphlets, Periodicals, and Broadsides*

Relating to the First Century of Mormonism.[25] Many hymn texts are found in the journals of early Latter-day Saints. One excellent source of such mid-nineteenth-century manuscript hymn texts is the collection by Joel H. Johnson (LDS Historical Department).

Most scholarly studies examine the hymns from a literary perspective. Studies treating Mormon hymnody as a mirror of the symbolism, doctrine, and social concerns of the Saints include Helen Hanks Macaré, "The Singing Saints: A Study of the Mormon Hymnal, 1835–1950";[26] Michael Hicks, "Poetic Borrowing in Early Mormonism";[27] and Dean L. May, "The Millennial Hymns of Parley P. Pratt."[28]

Studying the music of the hymns is somewhat more complicated, since many tunes were passed along in oral tradition before the use of printed tunebooks in Mormondom. Two dissertations ferret out the various musical influences: Newell Bryan Weight, "An Historical Study of the Origin and Character of Indigenous Hymn Tunes of the Latter-day Saints";[29] and William Leroy Wilkes Jr., "Borrowed Music in Mormon Hymnals."[30] In any study of the sources for Mormon hymnody, one must not neglect Bruce David Maxwell's unpublished "Source Book for Hymns,"[31] of which both the LDS Historical Department and Brigham Young University have copies. Michael Moody proposed some new directions for LDS Church music in his "Contemporary Hymnody in The Church of Jesus Christ of Latter-day Saints."[32]

Other works examine the vernacular texts and music generally referred to as "folk song." A seminal treatment is Levette J. Davidson, "Mormon Songs."[33] Three subsequent studies have continued in Davidson's vein by collating transcriptions of field recordings from the hinterlands of Mormondom: Austin and Alta Fife, *Saints of Sage and Saddle: Folklore among the Mormons;*[34] Lester A. Hubbard, *Ballads and Songs from Utah;*[35] and Thomas E. Cheney, ed., *Mormon Songs from the Rocky Mountains: A Compilation of Mormon Folksong*.[36] The source recordings for these collections may be found in the Fife Folklore Archives (Utah State University, Logan, Utah), the Austin and Alta Fife recording collection and the Lester Hubbard recording collection (both in the Marriott Library, University of Utah). A sampling of such songs is found in the *New Beehive Songster.*[37]

Vernacular instrumental music has received much less attention, despite the wealth of material on the Salt Lake City Band, the Nauvoo Brass Band, and bands of the Nauvoo Legion found in the LDS Historical Department. Probably the best scholarly survey of Mormon bands remains Martha Tingey Cook, "Pioneer Bands and Orchestras of Salt Lake City,"[38] although it should be supplemented with the following articles produced under the auspices of the Daughters of Utah Pioneers:

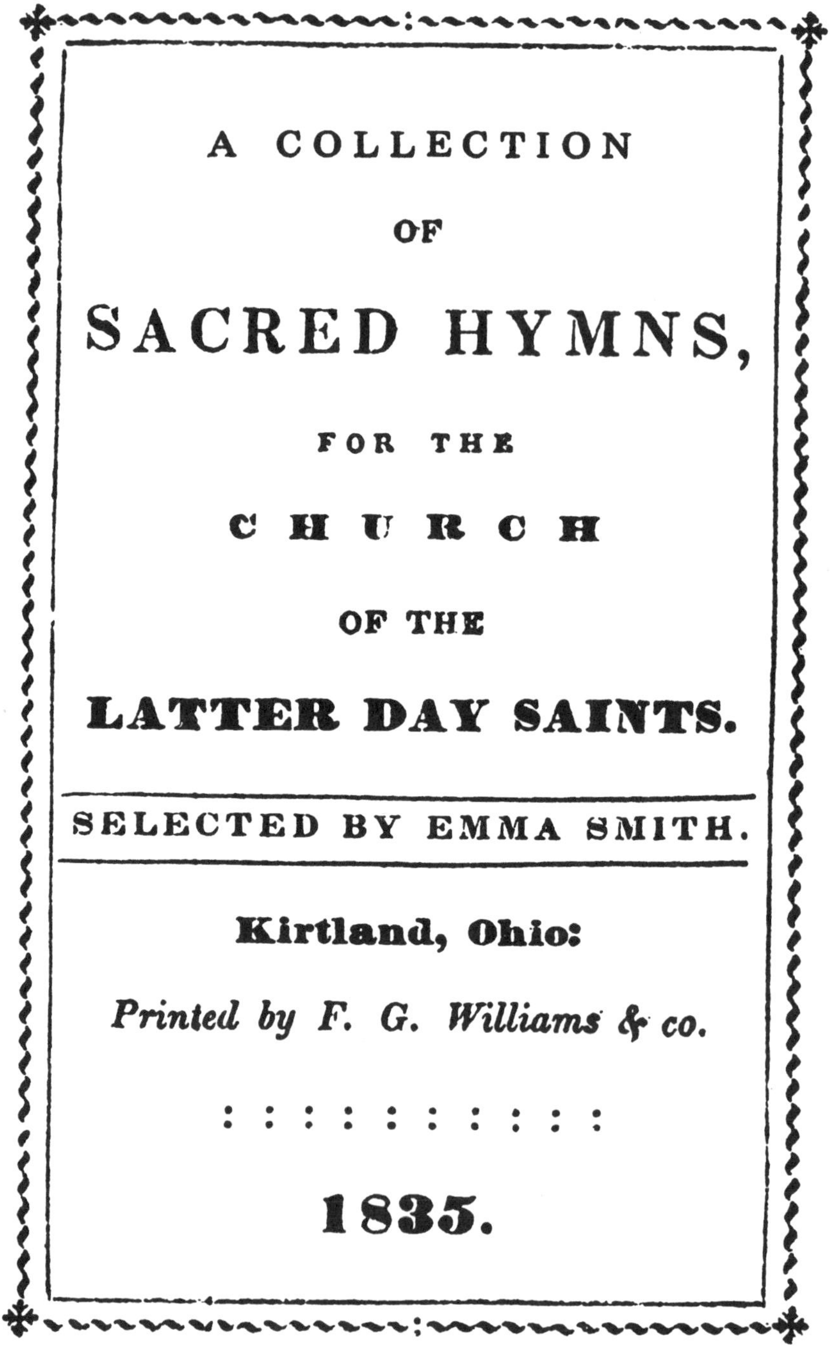

A COLLECTION

OF

SACRED HYMNS,

FOR THE

CHURCH

OF THE

LATTER DAY SAINTS.

SELECTED BY EMMA SMITH.

Kirtland, Ohio:

Printed by F. G. Williams & co.

: : : : : : : : : :

1835.

Title page of the first LDS hymnal, 1835. Courtesy LDS Church Archives.

"Bands and Orchestras of Early Days,"[39] "Bands and Orchestras,"[40] and "The Nauvoo Brass Band."[41] Kenner C. Kartchner, *Frontier Fiddler: The Life of a Northern Arizona Pioneer*[42] chronicles the upbringing and career of a fiddler in turn-of-the-century Mormon culture.

Many nineteenth-century European converts to Mormonism brought their considerable musical training to the Great Basin. They took the helm of Church music, taught Mormon youth how to sing, and, in the process, built lasting musical dynasties. For an overview of their work, see (in addition to the surveys already mentioned) "Pioneer Musicians and Composers."[43] Historiography has been especially generous to some of these musicians. Their lives and works are examined in various commemorative articles in Church magazines and in the following biographical studies: William Earl Purdy, "The Life and Works of Charles John Thomas: His Contributions to the Music History of Utah";[44] Bruce David Maxwell, "George Careless, Pioneer Musician";[45] Marion Peter Overson, "Joseph J. Daynes, First Tabernacle Organist: His Contributions to the Musical Culture of Utah and the Significance of His Life and Works";[46] Sterling E. Beesley, *Kind Words, the Beginnings of Mormon Melody: A Historical Biography and Anthology of the Life and Works of Ebenezer Beesley, Utah Pioneer Musician;*[47] Howard Hoggan Putnam, "George Edward Persy Careless: His Contributions to the Musical Culture of Utah and the Significance of His Life and Works";[48] Dale A. Johnson, "The Life and Contributions of Evan Stephens";[49] and Ray L. Bergman, *The Children Sang: The Life and Music of Evan Stephens.*[50]

Understandably, large music businesses complemented the work of these musicians. The two most informative sources about such businesses are probably the letterpress copybook of David Calder (LDS Historical Department) and the Margaret Summerhays Collection (Brigham Young University). A cottage industry in music criticism also emerged, treated in Basil Hansen, "An Historic Account of Music Criticism and Music Critics in Utah";[51] and Virgil H. Camp, "John Elliott Tullidge: The Influence of His Life and Works on the Musical Culture of Utah."[52]

The jewel of Mormon music is undoubtedly the Tabernacle Choir. Almost all of the musical sources identified in this article treat the choir to some extent. An early scholarly overview is Mary Musser Barnes, "An Historical Survey of the Salt Lake Tabernacle Choir of the Church of Jesus Christ of Latter-day Saints."[53] Two works amplify and update Barnes's work: Charles Jeffrey Calman and William I. Kaufman, *The Mormon Tabernacle Choir;*[54] and Gerald A. Petersen, *More Than Music: The Mormon Tabernacle Choir.*[55] For closer examinations of the choir, scholars should peruse several sources in the LDS Historical Department: the various repertoire lists, tour files, and minutes of the choir itself, and the twenty-volume journal of Thomas C. Griggs, which gives a candid and judicious look at the workings of the choir around the turn of the century. Much of the choir's history has been presented in works by or about its conductors. Benjamin Mark Roberts, "Anthony C. Lund, Musician, with Special Reference to His Teaching and Choral Directing,"[56] examines the choir's director in the 1920s and early 1930s (see also the Cornelia Lund Collection, Brigham Young University). J. Spencer Cornwall gives a personal account in his informative *A Century of Singing: The Salt Lake Mormon Tabernacle Choir,*[57] which may be profitably read in conjunction with Fern Denise Gregory, "J. Spencer Cornwall: The Salt Lake Mormon Tabernacle Years, 1935–1957."[58] Oral histories by Cornwall and his successor, Richard P. Condie, are in the LDS Historical Department.

The Salt Lake Tabernacle also houses one of the world's more famous organs. Donald Gordon McDonald, "The Mormon Tabernacle Organ,"[59] and Barbara Owen, *The Mormon Tabernacle Organ: An American Classic*[60] survey the organ's history. The LDS Historical Department has an extensive archive of taped broadcasts and organ recital programs from 1904 on. The organists themselves have also left several testaments of their own. The most voluble of the organists was Alexander Schreiner, regarding whom see the oral histories in the LDS Historical Department, as well as *Alexander Schreiner Reminisces,*[61] and Darwin Wolford, comp., *Selections from the Writings of Alexander Schreiner on Music and the Gospel.*[62] For a woman's perspective on life in the organ loft, consider the journals of Edna Coray Dyer (in the Howard Coray Family Collection, Brigham Young University).

Mormonism has produced its share of good composers. Copies of most of the major choral works by Evan Stephens and B. Cecil Gates, to name two, are in the LDS Historical Department; regarding Gates's work, see Lyneer Charles Smith, "Brigham Cecil Gates: Composer, Director, Teacher of Music."[63] The two most celebrated twentieth-century composers thus far have been Arthur Shepherd and Leroy Robertson. Richard Loucks surveys Shepherd's life and music in *Arthur Shepherd: American Composer.*[64] Some of Shepherd's papers are housed at the University of Utah, as is a sizable collection of Robertson's papers, including musical sketches and scores. So far, the only analytical approach to Robertson's work is Cynthia Louise Hukill, "A Stylistic Analysis of Selected Piano Works of Leroy Robertson (1896–1971)."[65] To understand how a generation of Mormon composers after Robertson saw its role and mission, see the short-lived *Notes of the LDS Composer's Association* (copies at Brigham Young University); and Merrill Bradshaw, *Spirit and Music: Letters to a Young Mormon Composer.*[66]

The Utah Symphony has always had a tenuous connection to the LDS Church. A detailed history of the symphony appears in Conrad B. Harrison, *Five Thousand Concerts: A Commemorative History of the Utah Symphony*.[67] The institution had its most prodigious growth while under the baton of Maurice Abravanel, who has left several oral histories, the most extensive of which is at the Utah State Historical Society. Abravanel's career is celebrated in Lowell M. Durham, *Abravanel!*[68] Another non-Mormon institution that helped to elevate the Mormons' musical culture of Mormondom is chronicled in Marcus S. Smith, *With Them Were Ten Thousand More: The Authorized History of the Oratorical Society of Utah*.[69]

In the twentieth century, the LDS Church took measures to insure the consistency of its musical practice and to provide technical training to aspiring sacred musicians. The minutes, correspondence, memos, bulletins, and other files of the Church's General Music Committee (and its various subcommittees) from 1920 to the present tell a detailed and often fascinating story. These are all housed in the LDS Historical Department, although access to them is generally restricted. But a good abstract of the committee's minutes from 1920 through 1962 appears in Jay Leon Slaughter, "The Role of Music in the Mormon Church, School, and Life."[70] Mormon music education receives its due in Harold R. Laycock, "A History of Music in the Academies of the Latter-day Saint Church, 1876–1926";[71] Grant Lester Anderson, "Some Educational Aspects of the Music Training Program of The Church of Jesus Christ of Latter-day Saints, 1935–1969";[72] and Donald George Schaefer, "Contributions of the McCune School of Music and Art to Music Education in Utah, 1917–1957."[73] Among manuscript sources related to the topic of music education, the most colorful is William King Driggs, "L.D.S. Church Academies Music Departments—1909 to 1921."[74] One of the finest teachers, and an eminent performer, was Emma Lucy Gates Bowen, whose substantial collection of personal papers is at Brigham Young University. Recently, some musicians have publicly lamented the decline of music training in the Church—consider Paul C. Pollei, "The Decline of Music in Mormon Culture."[75]

Even though it has a central place in Mormon worship, music has provoked some tensions in the realm of style. Those tensions fall into two main categories, the cross-cultural and the cross-generational. On the former, little has been published, although much can be learned from Murray Boren, "Worship through Music Nigerian Style";[76] and P. Jane Hafen, "'Great Spirit Listen': The American Indian in Mormon Music."[77] But in the cross-generational arena, treatises abound, among which are: Lex de Azevedo, *Pop Music and Morality*;[78] E. Lynn Balmforth,

Rock 'n' Reality. Mirrors of Rock Music: It's [sic] Relationship to Sex, Drugs, Family & Religion;[79] Darwin Wolford, *Four Messages of Rock Music;*[80] and Jack R. Christianson, *Music: Apples or Onions?: A Spiritual Approach to a Sensitive Subject.*[81]

Dance

While shunned by some denominations, dancing has been acceptable and even encouraged in the LDS Church. Although the Church has occasionally warned against the moral improprieties of specific dances—and these have changed over time—it has generally encouraged dancing both as a recreation and as an art form. The standard survey is Karl E. Wesson, "Dance in the Church of Jesus Christ of Latter-day Saints, 1830-1940."[82] Most other works deal with the nineteenth century only, putting Mormon dancing in its most positive light: Leona Holbrook, "Dancing as an Aspect of Early Mormon and Utah Culture";[83] Debra Hickenlooper Sowell, "Theatrical Dancing in the Territory of Utah: 1846-1848";[84] Ruth E. Yasko, "An Historical Study of Pioneer Dancing in Utah";[85] "Dancing—a Pioneer Recreation";[86] and "Pioneer Dancing."[87]

Dancing schools and their successors, university and college dance courses, helped dancing evolve from a pastime to a discipline—i.e., from "dancing" to "dance." This is the theme of Georganne Ballif Arrington, "Mormonism: The Dancingest Denomination."[88] There are also more specialized studies of dance training in Mormondom: Denise P. Olsen, "An Historical Overview of Modern Dance at Brigham Young University from 1875 to 1986";[89] Roxanne Smith, "The History of Ballet at Brigham Young University";[90] and Charles W. West, "A History of Folk Dancing at Brigham Young University."[91] Although training in dance has produced many exemplars of the art, so far there seem to be no in-depth treatments of individual dancers (a cursory one is Debra Sue Hickenlooper, "Sara Alexander: Brigham's Favorite Danseuse").[92]

Tension has surrounded certain kinds of dancing, as outlined in Hicks, *Mormonism and Music,* as well as in Davis Bitton, "'These Licentious Days': Dancing among the Mormons,"[93] and Gary C. Kunz, "Provo in the Jazz Age."[94] Some tensions have involved dancing as a form of expression in the international Church, particularly among those groups deemed "Lamanites"—descendants of Hebrews who migrated to the New World and Polynesia. The only official Mormon vehicle for the traditional dancing of Pacific islanders is the Polynesian Cultural Center, treated in Craig Ferre, "A History of the Polynesian Cultural Center's 'Night Show,' 1963-1983";[95] and James Whitehurst, "Mormons and the

Hula: The Polynesian Cultural Center in Hawaii."[96] With regard to the dancing of Native American Mormons, see Mary Stephanie Reynolds, "Dance Brings about Everything: Dance Power in the Ideologies of Northern Utes of the Uintah and Ouray Reservation and Predominantly Mormon Anglos of an Adjacent Uintah Basin Community."[97] Also, one should note a curious episode regarding Mormons and Native American Ghost Dance religion. On this topic see both Garold D. Barney, *Mormons, Indians, and the Ghost Dance Religion of 1890;*[98] and Lawrence G. Coates, "The Mormons and the Ghost Dance."[99]

Drama and the Theater

Like dancing, the theater enjoyed phenomenal success in nineteenth-century Mormondom, as is demonstrated in Harold I. Hansen, *A History and Influence of the Mormon Theatre from 1839-1869;*[100] Preston Ray Gledhill, "Mormon Dramatic Activities";[101] Edmund Emil Evans, "A Historical Study of the Drama of the Latter Day Saints";[102] William Henry Thorpe, "The Mormons and the Drama"[103] and "History of Drama in the West";[104] and two articles by Leland H. Monson, "Shakespeare in Early Utah"[105] and "Pioneer Interest in the Drama."[106]

Unlike many religious leaders of his day, Brigham Young encouraged theater-going as both a means of wholesome recreation and a way of learning moral values. He promoted the Deseret Dramatic Association, a semiofficial society of aspiring thespians discussed in Ila Fisher Maughan, *Pioneer Theatre in the Desert.*[107] The operating papers of the association are located in the LDS Historical Department, including minutes, letterpress copybooks, and order books.

The veritable temple of the Deseret Dramatic Association was the Salt Lake Theatre, which became a *cause célèbre* among Mormons during its sixty-six-year history—and the centerpiece of every discussion of Mormon theater since. The published books, written primarily by employees of the theater, include John S. Lindsay, *The Mormons and the Theatre;*[108] Horace G. Whitney, *The Drama in Utah: The Story of the Salt Lake Theatre;*[109] Alfred H. Lambourne, *A Play-House;*[110] George D. Pyper, *The Romance of an Old Playhouse;*[111] and Myrtle E. Henderson, *A History of the Theatre in Salt Lake City from 1850-1870.*[112] One published article augments this list: "The Salt Lake Theatre."[113] More recently, three dissertations have given thorough, scholarly perspectives: Therald Francis Todd, "The Operation of the Salt Lake Theatre, 1862-1875";[114] Roberta Reese Asahina, "Brigham Young and the Salt Lake Theater, 1862-1877";[115] and Lee E. Scanlon, "Buffalo Bill in a Boiled Shirt: The Salt Lake Theatre, 1869-1874."[116] Finally, two articles discuss the theatre's demise: Ronald W. Walker and Alexander M. Starr, "Shattering the Vase: The Razing of the Old Salt Lake Theatre";[117] and Samuel W. Taylor, "How I Destroyed the Old Salt Lake Theatre."[118]

But there was plenty of drama in other Mormon locales, as is demonstrated in a number of theses and dissertations: Courtney H. Brewer, "A History of Drama in Logan, Utah, and Neighboring Communities to 1925";[119] Beth Browning, "History of Drama in Ogden";[120] Burnett B. Ferguson, "History of Drama in Provo, 1853-1897";[121] Rue Corbett Johnson, "The History of the Drama in Corinne and Brigham City, Utah, 1855-1905";[122] Harold R. Oaks, "An Evaluation of the Beginnings, Purpose, and Influence of Drama in Ogden from 1840 to 1900";[123] Elmo G. Geary, "A Study of Dramatics in Castle Valley from 1875 to 1925,"[124] adapted into Elmo G. Geary and Edward A. Geary, "Community Dramatics in Early Castle Valley";[125] and Albert O. Mitchell, "Dramatics in Southern Utah—Parowan, Cedar City, Beaver, St. George—from 1850 to the Coming of the Moving Picture,"[126] from which derives his "Pioneers and Players of Parowan."[127]

A few biographies of actors, critics, and other participants in Mormon theatrical life have appeared: Annie Kiskadden, "The Life Story of Maude Adams and Her Mother";[128] J. Keith Melville, *The Mormon Drama and Maude Adams;*[129] Mavis Gay Gashler, "Three Mormon Actresses: Viola Gillette, Hazel Dawn, Leora Thatcher";[130] Ralph E. Margetts, "Biography of Phil Margetts, Utah Actor";[131] Derek Spriggs, "The Acting and Directing Career of Franklin Rasmussen";[132] Crae James Wilson, "The Acting and Directing Career of Moroni Olsen";[133] Sheryl Lee Wilson, "Nathan and Ruth Hale: People, Producers, Playwrights, Performers";[134] and Ted Lyon, *John Lyon: The Life of a Pioneer Poet.*[135]

As it has fostered other performing arts, the academy has been a fertile breeding ground for the theatrical arts. Mormon institutions of learning and secular institutions in Mormon country have been equally quick to sponsor dramatic productions of many sorts. The standard surveys of this topic are: Morris Martin Clinger, "A History of Theater in Mormon Colleges and Universities";[136] Randall Lee Bernhard, "Contemporary Musical Theatre: History and Development in the Major Colleges and Universities of Utah";[137] John Thomas Bidwell, "History of Theatre and Theatre Curriculum at Ricks College, Rexburg, Idaho, through 1981";[138] Charles A. Henson, "A History of the Theatre and Cinematic Arts Department: Brigham Young University 1920-1978."[139]

There are many manuscript resources for the students of Mormon theater. Various papers and account books from the Salt Lake Theatre papers are in the LDS Historical Department; the Utah State Historical Society also has a good collection of posters. The papers of theater

Salt Lake Theatre, 1870. Courtesy LDS Church Archives.

managers David McKenzie and John T. Caine are also in the LDS Historical Department. Moreover, the papers of George Pyper (University of Utah) afford scholars a great deal of material, amid which is the large, indispensable manuscript volume by H. L. A. Culmer, "Record of Performances for Forty Years in the Salt Lake Theatre from Its Opening March 8, 1862 until March 7, 1902." The journal of Elijah Larkin (the LDS Historical Department), a frequent visitor to the Theatre, gives some good on-site observations from the nineteenth century. Also, the papers of theater critic John Lyon are at Brigham Young University.

Indigenous Mormon playwriting was considerably slower in developing than indigenous Mormon music. The principal vehicles for theatrical writing have been (1) commemorative pageants that celebrate the Church's history, and (2) ephemeral road shows produced by and for the Church's youth organizations. (Collections of both are in the LDS Historical Department and Brigham Young University). Davis Bitton takes up the commemorative pageants in his article, "The Ritualization of Mormon History."[140] For scholarly treatments of the Church's best-known pageant, see Charles W. Whitman, "A History of the Hill Cumorah

Pageant, 1937-1964, and an Examination of the Dramatic Development of the Text of *America's Witness for Christ*";[141] and Richard N. Armstrong and Gerald S. Argetsinger, "The Hill Cumorah Pageant: Religious Pageantry as Suasive Form."[142] An even more specialized study of a Mormon commemorative play is Patrick Debenham and W. Hyrum Conrad, "Tamiris Pioneers *Promised Valley*"[143] (on the influence of dance director Helen Tamiris). Meanwhile, the literary content of Church-sponsored stage events, particularly the youth-oriented, are examined in Gary L. Stewart, "A Rhetorical Analysis of Mormon Drama";[144] and T. Leonard Rowley, "The Church's Dramatic Literature,"[145] adapted from his "A Critical and Comparative Analysis of Latter-day Saint Drama."[146]

A small movement toward creating a distinctive Mormon theater blossomed in the 1960s and early 1970s. This movement extended the commemorative tradition of Mormon theater with more profound dramatizations and characterizations drawn from Mormon scripture and history. One of its most avid participants was Lael J. Woodbury, from whom came two seminal articles, both published in *BYU Studies:* "A New Mormon Theatre"[147] and "Mormonism and the Commercial Theatre."[148] Unfortunately, much of the Mormon dramatic literature since then, even if performed, remains unpublished. Among the more notable published works are: Orson Scott Card, "Father, Mother, Mother, and Mom";[149] Robert Frederick Lauer, "The Beehive State";[150] Susan Howe, "Burdens of Earth";[151] and two collections by Thomas F. Rogers—*God's Fools: Plays of Mitigated Conscience*[152] and *Huebener and Other Plays*.[153] Two notable one-man plays have been recorded, both for Covenant Recordings in Salt Lake City: James W. Arrington and Bruce Ackerman, *J. Golden;*[154] and James Arrington and Tim Slover, *Wilford Woodruff: God's Fisherman*.[155] Antedating all of these—and inspiring many of them—is Clinton F. Larson, *The Mantle of the Prophet and Other Plays*.[156] Finally, to sample more commercially oriented Mormon theater from this period, one should examine the videotape of the phenomenally popular musical by Doug Stewart and Lex De Azevedo, *Saturday's Warrior*.[157] Aspects of that musical are critiqued in Nola Diane Smith, "Saturday's Women: Female Characters as Angels and Monsters in *Saturday's Warrior* and *Reunion*."[158]

As with the other arts reviewed here, Mormon drama has experienced its share of tensions, as it grapples both with the demands of gospel morality and the changing fashions of the theater. Some of the broader issues are outlined in Ronald Wilcox, "Morality or Empathy? A Mormon in the Theater."[159] The clash of racial stereotypes is discussed in Michael Hicks, "Ministering Minstrels: Blackface Entertainment in Pioneer Utah."[160] Alan Frank Keele, "Trailing Clouds of Glory?

Bad Drama May Be Blasphemous,"[161] is a polemic on the low quality of recent Mormon drama, as is Frederick Bliss and P. Q. Gump, "Mormon Shakespears [*sic*]: A Study of Contemporary Mormon Theatre."[162]

Conclusion

If the foregoing outline of sources on Mormonism and the performing arts seems at all tidy, beware. Any earnest researcher must face the daunting fact that sources concerning music often cross over into theater, dancing into music, theater into dancing, and so forth. I have tried to sketch the larger branches of research into these topics. But artists of all genres form a peculiar and often intimately connected community whose work is destined to interweave. Because the performing arts are often difficult to disentangle, a real grasp of any one of them probably must be holistic—earned by the researcher's willingness to delve into mounds of interrelated sources in hopes of finding the perfect detail that can illuminate so much.

Michael Hicks is Associate Professor of Music at Brigham Young University, Provo, Utah.

NOTES

[1]Arthur Ray Bassett, "Culture and the American Frontier in Mormon Utah, 1850-1896" (Ph.D. diss., Syracuse University, 1975).

[2]R. Laurence Moore, "Learning to Play: The Mormon Way and the Way of Other Americans," *Journal of Mormon History* 16 (1990): 89-106.

[3]William J. McNiff, *Heaven on Earth: A Planned Mormon Society* (Oxford, Ohio: Mississippi Valley Press, 1940).

[4]Raye Price, "Utah's Leading Ladies of the Arts," *Utah Historical Quarterly* 38 (Winter 1970): 65-85.

[5]Jill C. Mulvay, "Three Mormon Women in the Cultural Arts," *Sunstone* 1 (Spring 1976): 29-39.

[6]Jean R. Jenkins, "Portrait of a Lady: Kathryn Bassett Pardoe," *Exponent II* 3 (June 1977): 9.

[7]Juanita Brooks, "Culture in Dixie," *Utah Historical Quarterly* 29 (July 1961): 254-67.

[8]Janice P. Dawson, "Chatauqua and the Utah Performing Arts," *Utah Historical Society* 58 (Spring 1990): 131-44.

[9]Lorin F. Wheelwright and Lael J. Woodbury, eds., *Mormon Arts, Volume One* (Provo, Utah: Brigham Young University Press, 1972).

[10]Steven P. Sondrup, ed., *Arts and Inspiration: Mormon Perspectives* (Provo, Utah: Brigham Young University Press, 1980).

[11]Joy C. Ross and Steven C. Walker, eds., *Letters to Smoother, etc. . . .: Proceedings of the Fifth Annual Brigham Young University Symposium on the Humanities* (Provo, Utah: Brigham Young University Press, 1981).

[12]Michael Hicks, "Notes on Brigham Young's Aesthetics," *Dialogue* 16 (Winter 1983): 124–30.

[13]Howard Swan, *Music in the Southwest, 1825–1950* (San Marino, Calif.: Huntington Library, 1952).

[14]Lowell M. Durham, "On Mormon Music and Musicians," *Dialogue* 3 (Summer 1968): 19–40.

[15]*Dialogue* 10 (Spring 1975–1976).

[16]Verena Ursenbach Hatch, *Worship and Music in The Church of Jesus Christ of Latter-day Saints* (Provo, Utah: M. Ephraim Hatch, 1968).

[17]Michael Hicks, *Mormonism and Music: A History* (Urbana: University of Illinois Press, 1989).

[18]William Earl Purdy, "Music in Mormon Culture, 1830–1876" (Ph.D. diss., Northwestern University, 1960).

[19]Jay Leon Slaughter, "The Role of Music in the Mormon Church, School, and Life" (D.M.E. diss., Indiana University, 1964).

[20]David Sterling Wheelwright, "The Role of Hymnody in the Development of the Latter-day Saint Movement" (Ph.D. diss., University of Maryland, 1943).

[21]Michael F. Moody, "Latter-day Saint Hymnbooks, Then and Now," *Ensign* 15 (September 1985): 10–13.

[22]George D. Pyper, *Stories of Latter-day Saint Hymns, Their Authors and Composers* (Salt Lake City: Deseret Book, 1939).

[23]J. Spencer Cornwall, *Stories of Our Mormon Hymns,* 2d ed. rev. (Salt Lake City: Deseret Book, 1963).

[24]Karen Lynn Davidson, *Our Latter-day Hymns: The Stories and the Messages* (Salt Lake City: Deseret Book, 1988).

[25]Chad J. Flake, *A Mormon Bibliography, 1830–1930: Books, Pamphlets, Periodicals, and Broadsides Relating to the First Century of Mormonism* (Salt Lake City: University of Utah Press, 1978).

[26]Helen Hanks Macaré, "The Singing Saints: A Study of the Mormon Hymnal, 1835–1950" (Ph.D. diss., University of California at Los Angeles, 1961).

[27]Michael Hicks, "Poetic Borrowing in Early Mormonism," *Dialogue* 18 (Spring 1985): 132–42.

[28]Dean L. May, "The Millennial Hymns of Parley P. Pratt," *Dialogue* 16 (Spring 1983): 145–50.

[29]Newell Bryan Weight, "An Historical Study of the Origin and Character of Indigenous Hymn Tunes of the Latter-day Saints" (D.M.A. diss., University of Southern California, 1961).

[30]William Leroy Wilkes Jr., "Borrowed Music in Mormon Hymnals" (Ph.D. diss., University of Southern California, 1957).

[31]Bruce David Maxwell, "Source Book for Hymns," unpublished (1982), copies located at the LDS Church Archives and at the Harold B. Lee Library.

[32]Michael Moody, "Contemporary Hymnody in the Church of Jesus Christ of Latter-day Saints" (D.M.A. diss., University of Southern California, 1972).

[33]Levette J. Davidson, "Mormon Songs," *Journal of American Folklore* 58 (October–December 1945): 273–300.

[34]Austin Fife and Alta Fife, *Saints of Sage and Saddle: Folklore among the Mormons* (Salt Lake City: University of Utah Press, 1956).

[35]Lester A. Hubbard, comp. and ed., *Ballads and Songs from Utah* (Salt Lake City: University of Utah Press, 1961).

[36]Thomas E. Cheney, ed., *Mormon Songs from the Rocky Mountains: A Compilation of Mormon Folksong* (Salt Lake City: University of Utah Press, 1981).

[37]*The New Beehive Songster, Vol. 1: Early Recordings of Pioneer Folk Music,* Okehdokee Records, Okla. 75003; *New Beehive Songster: Volume 2 New Recordings of Utah Folk Music,* comp., ed., and produced by Hal Cannon, Jan Harold Brunvand, and Tom Carter, Okehdokee Records, Okla. 76004.

[38]Martha Tingey Cook, "Pioneer Bands and Orchestras of Salt Lake City" (master's thesis, Brigham Young University, 1960).

[39]"Bands and Orchestras of Early Days," in *Heart Throbs of the West,* comp. Kate B. Carter, 12 vols. (Salt Lake City: Daughters of Utah Pioneers, 1939-51), 4:117-44.

[40]"Bands and Orchestras," in *Our Pioneer Heritage,* comp. Lesson Committee, 20 vols. (Salt Lake City: Daughters of Utah Pioneers, 1958-77), 20:69-132.

[41]"The Nauvoo Brass Band," in *An Enduring Legacy,* comp. Kate B. Carter, 12 vols. (Salt Lake City: Daughters of Utah Pioneers, 1978-89), 4:85-136.

[42]Kenner C. Kartchner, *Frontier Fiddler: The Life of a Northern Arizona Pioneer,* ed. Larry V. Shumway (Tucson: University of Arizona Press, 1990).

[43]"Pioneer Musicians and Composers," in *An Enduring Legacy* 6:45-84.

[44]William Earl Purdy, "The Life and Works of Charles John Thomas: His Contributions to the Music History of Utah" (master's thesis, Brigham Young University, 1949).

[45]Bruce David Maxwell, "George Careless, Pioneer Musician," *Utah Historical Quarterly* 53 (Spring 1985): 131-43.

[46]Marion Peter Overson, "Joseph J. Daynes, First Tabernacle Organist: His Contributions to the Musical Culture of Utah and the Significance of His Life and Works" (master's thesis, Brigham Young University, 1954).

[47]Sterling E. Beesley, *Kind Words, the Beginnings of Mormon Melody: A Historical Biography and Anthology of the Life and Works of Ebenezer Beesley, Utah Pioneer Musician* (n.p.: By the Author, 1980).

[48]Howard Hoggan Putnam, "George Edward Persy Careless: His Contributions to the Musical Culture of Utah and the Significance of His Life and Works" (master's thesis, Brigham Young University, 1957).

[49]Dale A. Johnson, "The Life and Contributions of Evan Stephens" (master's thesis, Brigham Young University, 1951).

[50]Ray L. Bergman, *The Children Sang: The Life and Music of Evan Stephens* (Salt Lake City: Northwest Publishing, 1992).

[51]Basil Hansen, "An Historic Account of Music Criticism and Music Critics in Utah" (master's thesis, Brigham Young University, 1933).

[52]Virgil H. Camp, "John Elliott Tullidge: The Influence of His Life and Works on the Musical Culture of Utah" (master's thesis, Brigham Young University, 1957).

[53]Mary Musser Barnes, "An Historical Survey of the Salt Lake Tabernacle Choir of The Church of Jesus Christ of Latter-day Saints" (master's thesis, University of Iowa, 1936).

[54]Charles Jeffrey Calman and William I. Kaufman, *The Mormon Tabernacle Choir* (New York: Harper and Row, 1979).

[55]Gerald A. Petersen, *More Than Music: The Mormon Tabernacle Choir* (Provo, Utah: Brigham Young University Press, 1979).

[56]Benjamin Mark Roberts, "Anthony C. Lund, Musician, with Special Reference to His Teaching and Choral Directing" (master's thesis, Brigham Young University, 1952).

[57]J. Spencer Cornwall, *A Century of Singing: The Salt Lake Mormon Tabernacle Choir* (Salt Lake City: Deseret Book, 1958).

[58]Fern Denise Gregory, "J. Spencer Cornwall: The Salt Lake Mormon Tabernacle Years, 1935-1957" (D.M.A. diss., University of Missouri-Kansas City, 1984).

[59]Donald Gordon McDonald, "The Mormon Tabernacle Organ" (master's thesis, Union Theological Seminary, 1952).

[60]Barbara Owen, *The Mormon Tabernacle Organ: An American Classic* (Salt Lake City: The Church of Jesus Christ of Latter-day Saints, 1990).

[61]Alexander Schreiner, *Alexander Schreiner Reminisces* (Salt Lake City: Publishers Press, 1984).

[62]Darwin Wolford, comp., *Selections from the Writings of Alexander Schreiner on Music and the Gospel* (Orem, Utah: Cedar Fort, 1991).

[63]Lyneer Charles Smith, "Brigham Cecil Gates: Composer, Director, Teacher of Music" (master's thesis, Brigham Young University, 1952).

[64]Richard Loucks, *Arthur Shepherd: American Composer* (Provo, Utah: Brigham Young University Press, 1980).

[65]Cynthia Louise Hukill, "A Stylistic Analysis of Selected Piano Works of Leroy Robertson (1896-1971)" (D.M.A. diss., University of Missouri, 1988).

[66]Merrill Bradshaw, *Spirit and Music: Letters to a Young Mormon Composer* (Provo, Utah: Brigham Young University Press, 1976).

[67]Conrad B. Harrison, *Five Thousand Concerts: A Commemorative History of the Utah Symphony* (Salt Lake City: Utah Symphony Society, 1986).

[68]Lowell M. Durham, *Abravanel!* (Salt Lake City: University of Utah Press, 1989).

[69]Marcus S. Smith, *With Them Were Ten Thousand More: The Authorized History of the Oratorical Society of Utah* (Salt Lake City: Actaeon Books, 1989).

[70]Jay Leon Slaughter, "The Role of Music in the Mormon Church, School, and Life" (D.M.E. diss., Indiana University, 1964).

[71]Harold R. Laycock, "A History of Music in the Academies of the Latter-day Saint Church, 1876-1926" (D.M.A. thesis, University of Southern California, 1961).

[72]Grant Lester Anderson, "Some Educational Aspects of the Music Training Program of The Church of Jesus Christ of Latter-day Saints, 1935-1969" (master's thesis, Brigham Young University, 1976).

[73]Donald George Schaefer, "Contributions of the McCune School of Music and Art to Music Education in Utah, 1917-1957" (master's thesis, Brigham Young University, 1962).

[74]William King Driggs, "L.D.S. Church Academies Music Departments—1909 to 1921," manuscript in Special Collections and Manuscripts, Brigham Young University.

[75]Paul C. Pollei, "The Decline of Music in Mormon Culture," *Sunstone* 16 (September 1992): 11-14.

[76]Murray Boren, "Worship through Music Nigerian Style," *Sunstone* 10 (May 1985): 64-65.

[77]P. Jane Hafen, "'Great Spirit Listen': The American Indian in Mormon Music," *Dialogue* 18 (Winter 1985): 133-42, adapted from her "A Pale Reflection: American Indian Images in Mormon Arts" (master's thesis, Brigham Young University, 1984).

[78]Lex de Azevedo, *Pop Music and Morality* (North Hollywood, Calif.: Embryo Books, 1982).

[79]E. Lynn Balmforth, *Rock 'n' Reality. Mirrors of Rock Music: It's [sic] Relationship to Sex, Drugs, Family & Religion* (Salt Lake City: Hawkes, 1971).

[80]Darwin Wolford, *Four Messages of Rock Music* (Rexburg, Idaho: By the author, [1970]). An interesting, extended chronicle (257 pp.) of a group of LDS young adults who were followers of the Grateful Dead rock band is a senior honors thesis: Delilah, Samson, Dew Jack Straw, and Sugaree, "The Bus Came By and I Got on, That's Where It All Began" (Brigham Young University, 1991).

[81]Jack R. Christianson, *Music: Apples or Onions?: A Spiritual Approach to a Sensitive Subject* (Orem, Utah: JMC Publications, 1984).

[82]Karl E. Wesson, "Dance in The Church of Jesus Christ of Latter-day Saints, 1830–1940" (master's thesis, Brigham Young University, 1975).

[83]Leona Holbrook, "Dancing as an Aspect of Early Mormon and Utah Culture," *BYU Studies* 16 (Autumn 1975): 117–38.

[84]Debra Hickenlooper Sowell, "Theatrical Dancing in the Territory of Utah: 1846–1848," *Dance Chronicle* 1, no. 2 (1978): 96–126.

[85]Ruth E. Yasko, "An Historical Study of Pioneer Dancing in Utah" (master's thesis, University of Utah, 1947).

[86]"Dancing—a Pioneer Recreation," in *Treasures of Pioneer History,* comp. Kate B. Carter, 6 vols. (Salt Lake City: Daughters of Utah Pioneers, 1952–57), 2:345–404.

[87]"Pioneer Dancing," in *An Enduring Legacy* 4:345–83.

[88]Georganne Ballif Arrington, "Mormonism: The Dancingest Denomination," *Century 2,* vol. 5 (Fall 1980): 42–56.

[89]Denise P. Olsen, "An Historical Overview of Modern Dance at Brigham Young University from 1875 to 1986" (master's thesis, Brigham Young University, 1987).

[90]Roxanne Smith, "The History of Ballet at Brigham Young University" (master's thesis, Brigham Young University, 1986).

[91]Charles W. West, "A History of Folk Dancing at Brigham Young University" (M.R.E. field project, Brigham Young University, 1970).

[92]Debra Sue Hickenlooper, "Sara Alexander: Brigham's Favorite Danseuse," *Exponent II* 3 (June 1977): 10.

[93]Davis Bitton, "'These Licentious Days': Dancing among the Mormons," *Sunstone* 2 (Spring 1977): 16–27.

[94]Gary C. Kunz, "Provo in the Jazz Age," *Sunstone* 9 (January–February 1984): 33–38. See further, Kunz, "Provo in the Jazz Age: A Case Study" (master's thesis, Brigham Young University, 1983).

[95]Craig Ferre, "A History of the Polynesian Cultural Center's 'Night Show,' 1963–1983" (Ph.D. diss., Brigham Young University, 1988).

[96]James Whitehurst, "Mormons and the Hula: The Polynesian Cultural Center in Hawaii," *Journal of American Culture* 1 (Spring 1989): 1–5.

[97]Mary Stephanie Reynolds, "Dance Brings about Everything: Dance Power in the Ideologies of Northern Utes of the Uintah and Ouray Reservation and Predominantly Mormon Anglos of an Adjacent Uintah Basin Community" (Ph.D. diss., University of California–Irvine, 1990).

[98]Garold D. Barney, *Mormons, Indians, and the Ghost Dance Religion of 1890* (Lanham, Md.: University Press of America, 1986).

[99]Lawrence G. Coates, "The Mormons and the Ghost Dance," *Dialogue* 18 (Winter 1985): 89-111.

[100]Harold I. Hansen, *A History and Influence of the Mormon Theatre from 1839-1869* (Provo, Utah: Brigham Young University Press, 1967). See also Noel A. Carmack, "A Note on Nauvoo Theater," *BYU Studies* 34, no. 1 (1994): 94-100.

[101]Preston Ray Gledhill, "Mormon Dramatic Activities" (Ph.D. diss., University of Wisconsin, 1950).

[102]Edmund Emil Evans, "A Historical Study of the Drama of the Latter Day Saints" (Ph.D. diss., University of Southern California, 1941).

[103]William Henry Thorpe, "The Mormons and the Drama" (master's thesis, Columbia University, 1921).

[104]"History of Drama in the West," in *Heart Throbs of the West* 4:77-116.

[105]Leland H. Monson, "Shakespeare in Early Utah," *Improvement Era* 63 (October 1960): 718-21, 763-64.

[106]Leland H. Monson, "Pioneer Interest in the Drama," *Improvement Era* 67 (April 1964): 264-65, 290, 292.

[107]Ila Fisher Maughan, *Pioneer Theatre in the Desert* (Salt Lake City: Deseret Book, 1961), derived from her "History of Staging and Business Methods of the Deseret Dramatic Association, 1852-1869" (master's thesis, University of Utah, 1949).

[108]John S. Lindsay, *The Mormons and the Theatre* (Salt Lake City: Century Printing, 1905).

[109]Horace G. Whitney, *The Drama in Utah: The Story of the Salt Lake Theatre* (Salt Lake City: Deseret News, 1915).

[110]Alfred H. Lambourne, *A Play-House* (n.p., n.d.).

[111]George D. Pyper, *The Romance of an Old Playhouse* (Salt Lake City: Seagull Press, 1928).

[112]Myrtle E. Henderson, *A History of the Theatre in Salt Lake City from 1850-1870* (Evanston, Ill.: n.p., 1934).

[113]"The Salt Lake Theatre," in *Our Pioneer Heritage* 5:213-60.

[114]Therald Francis Todd, "The Operation of the Salt Lake Theatre, 1862-1875" (Ph.D. diss., University of Oregon, 1973).

[115]Roberta Reese Asahina, "Brigham Young and the Salt Lake Theater, 1862-1877" (Ph.D. diss., Tufts University, 1980).

[116]Lee E. Scanlon, "Buffalo Bill in a Boiled Shirt: The Salt Lake Theatre, 1869-1874," (Ph.D. diss., Brigham Young University, 1979).

[117]Alexander M. Starr and Ronald W. Walker, "Shattering the Vase: The Razing of the Old Salt Lake Theater," *Utah Historical Quarterly* 57 (Winter 1989): 64-88.

[118]Samuel W. Taylor, "How I Destroyed the Old Salt Lake Theater," *Dialogue* 23 (Summer 1990): 134-37.

[119]Courtney H. Brewer, "A History of Drama in Logan, Utah, and Neighboring Communities to 1925" (Ph.D. diss., Brigham Young University, 1972).

[120]Beth Browning, "History of Drama in Ogden" (master's thesis, Brigham Young University, 1947).

[121]Burnett B. Ferguson, "History of Drama in Provo, 1853-1897" (master's thesis, Brigham Young University, 1952).

[122]Rue Corbett Johnson, "The History of the Drama in Corinne and Brigham City, Utah, 1855-1905" (master's thesis, Brigham Young University, 1954).

[123]Harold R. Oaks, "An Evaluation of the Beginnings, Purpose, and Influence of Drama in Ogden from 1840 to 1900" (master's thesis, Brigham Young University, 1962).

[124]Elmo G. Geary, "A Study of Dramatics in Castle Valley from 1875 to 1925" (master's thesis, University of Utah, 1953).

[125]Elmo G. Geary and Edward A. Geary, "Community Dramatics in Early Castle Valley," *Utah Historical Quarterly* 53 (Spring 1985): 112-30.

[126]Albert O. Mitchell, "Dramatics in Southern Utah—Parowan, Cedar City, Beaver, St. George—from 1850 to the Coming of the Moving Picture" (master's thesis, University of Utah, 1935).

[127]Albert O. Mitchell, "Pioneers and Players of Parowan," *Utah Humanities Review* 1 (January 1947): 38-52.

[128]Annie Adams Kiskadden with Verne Hardin Porter, "The Life Story of Maude Adams and Her Mother," *Green Book Magazine* 11-13 (June 1914-January 1915).

[129]J. Keith Melville, *Feminine Contributions to Mormon Culture: The Mormon Drama and Maude Adams* (Provo, Utah: Extension Publications Division of Continuing Education, Brigham Young University, 1965).

[130]Mavis Gay Gashler, "Three Mormon Actresses: Viola Gillette, Hazel Dawn, Leora Thatcher" (master's thesis, Brigham Young University, 1970).

[131]Ralph E. Margetts, "Biography of Phil Margetts, Utah Actor" (master's thesis, University of Utah, 1950).

[132]Derek Spriggs, "The Acting and Directing Career of Franklin Rasmussen" (master's thesis, Brigham Young University, 1971).

[133]Crae James Wilson, "The Acting and Directing Career of Moroni Olsen" (Ph.D. diss., Brigham Young University, 1981).

[134]Sheryl Lee Wilson, "Nathan and Ruth Hale: People, Producers, Playwrights, Performers" (master's thesis, Brigham Young University, 1973).

[135]T. Edgar Lyon Jr., *John Lyon: The Life of a Pioneer Poet* (Provo, Utah: Religious Studies Center, Brigham Young University, 1989).

[136]Morris Martin Clinger, "A History of Theater in Mormon Colleges and Universities" (Ph.D. diss., University of Minnesota, 1963).

[137]Randall Lee Bernhard, "Contemporary Musical Theatre: History and Development in the Major Colleges and Universities of Utah" (Ph.D. diss., Brigham Young University, 1979).

[138]John Thomas Bidwell, "History of Theatre and Theatre Curriculum at Ricks College, Rexburg, Idaho, through 1981" (master's thesis, Brigham Young University, 1982).

[139]Charles A. Henson, "A History of the Theatre and Cinematic Arts Department: Brigham Young University 1920-1978" (Ed.D. diss., Brigham Young University, 1980).

[140]Davis Bitton, "The Ritualization of Mormon History," *Utah Historical Quarterly* 43 (Winter 1975): 67-85.

[141]Charles W. Whitman, "A History of the Hill Cumorah Pageant, 1937-1964, and an Examination of the Dramatic Development of the Text of *America's Witness for Christ*" (Ph.D. diss., University of Minnesota, 1967).

[142]Gerald S. Argetsinger, "The Hill Cumorah Pageant: Religious Pageantry as Suasive Form," *Text and Performance Quarterly* 9 (April 1989): 153-64.

[143]Patrick Debenham and W. Hyrum Conrad, "Tamiris Pioneers *Promised Valley*," *Encyclia* 68 (1991): 327-45.

[144]Gary L. Stewart, "A Rhetorical Analysis of Mormon Drama" (Ph.D. diss., University of Iowa, 1968).

[145]T. Leonard Rowley, "The Church's Dramatic Literature," *Dialogue* 4 (Autumn 1969): 129-38.

[146]T. Leonard Rowley, "A Critical and Comparative Analysis of Latter-day Saint Drama" (Ph.D. diss., University of Minnesota, 1967).

[147]Lael J. Woodbury, "A New Mormon Theatre," *BYU Studies* 10 (Autumn 1969): 85-94.

[148]Lael J. Woodbury, "Mormonism and the Commercial Theatre," *BYU Studies* 12 (Winter 1972): 234-40.

[149]Orson Scott Card, "Father, Mother, Mother, and Mom," *Sunstone* 2 (Summer 1977): F1-F16.

[150]Robert Frederick Lauer, "The Beehive State," *Sunstone* 13 (December 1989): 22-44.

[151]Susan Howe, "Burdens of Earth," *Sunstone* 11 (November 1987): 12-33.

[152]Thomas F. Rogers, *God's Fools: Plays of Mitigated Conscience* (Provo, Utah: Thomas Green Taylor, 1983).

[153]Thomas F. Rogers, *Huebener and Other Plays* ([Provo, Utah]: Poor Robert's Publications, 1992).

[154]James W. Arrington and Bruce Ackerman, *J. Golden* (Salt Lake City: Covenant Recordings, 1983).

[155]James Arrington and Tim Slover, *Wilford Woodruff: God's Fisherman* (Salt Lake City: Covenant Recordings, 1988); also published in *Sunstone* 16 (February 1992): 28-48.

[156]Clinton F. Larson, *The Mantle of the Prophet and Other Plays* (Salt Lake City: Deseret Book, 1966).

[157]Doug Stewart and Lex De Azevedo, *Saturday's Warrior* (Hollywood: Bob Williams Productions, 1989).

[158]Nola Diane Smith, "Saturday's Women: Female Characters as Angels and Monsters in *Saturday's Warrior* and *Reunion*" (master's thesis, Brigham Young University, 1992).

[159]Ronald Wilcox, "Morality or Empathy? A Mormon in the Theater," *Dialogue* 2 (Spring 1967): 15-27.

[160]Michael Hicks, "Ministering Minstrels: Blackface Entertainment in Pioneer Utah," *Utah Historical Quarterly* 58 (Winter 1990): 49-63.

[161]Alan Frank Keele, "Trailing Clouds of Glory? Bad Drama May Be Blasphemous," *Sunstone* 6 (July-August 1981): 47-51.

[162]Frederick Bliss and P. Q. Gump [Orson Scott Card], "Mormon Shakespears [*sic*]: A Study of Contemporary Mormon Theatre," *Sunstone* 1 (Spring 1976): 54-66.

Resources for the Study of Science, Technology, and Mormon Culture

Richard F. Haglund Jr. and Erich Robert Paul

> If one of our Elders is capable of giving us a lecture upon any of the sciences, let it be delivered in the spirit of meekness—in the spirit of the holy Gospel. If, on the Sabbath day, when we are assembled here to worship the Lord, one of the Elders should be prompted to give us a lecture on any branch of education with which he is acquainted, is it outside the pale of our religion? I think not. . . . If an Elder shall give us a lecture upon astronomy, chemistry, or geology, our religion embraces it all. It matters not what the subject be, if it tends to improve the mind, exalt the feelings and enlarge the capacity. The truth that is in all the arts and sciences forms a part of our religion.
>
> —Brigham Young[1]

Despite the prominent role played by science and technology in shaping the modern world, and notwithstanding the manifold professional achievements of Mormon practitioners of science and technology, surprisingly few studies have analyzed the interaction of science and technology with Mormon culture. Resources and index materials for the study of the impact of science and technology on the Mormon community are scattered and often unpublished. In an effort to encourage more systematic investigations of the impact of science and technology on the beliefs, practices, and culture of the Latter-day Saints, the following commentary tries to summarize what is now available and to categorize the most significant areas for fruitful investigation.

In this essay, we define *science* as the study of natural phenomena with little regard to their utility, and *technology* as the application of scientific principles to the solution of more or less practical problems. While these definitions are too coarse for intricate distinctions between "pure" versus "applied" science, they are consistent with much current discussion about the spectrum of scientific and technological activities. Our discussion is in five parts: (1) a general survey of works that describe the relationship between science and technology, on one hand, and Mormon theology and culture on the other. The next four sections summarize (2) books and periodicals about

Mormon scientists and about science; (3) sources in books and periodicals about technology and Mormon technologists; (4) sources in specialized bibliographies relevant to science, technology, and Mormon culture; and (5) special collections of material related to these topics. Interwoven are references to some of the major works from outside the Latter-day Saint community providing background and perspective on issues in science, religion, and technology in general.

Science, Technology, and Mormon Culture

Like every other institution in the modern world, the LDS Church exists in a cultural setting permeated by the forces of science and technology. Far from ignoring these forces, leaders of the Church have contended from the beginning that scientific truth was part of the gospel.[2] John Henry Evans, who wrote the first sympathetic biography of Joseph Smith published by a non-Mormon press, first made the significant *intellectual* content of the restored gospel clear and highlighted the progressive character of the Prophet's thinking.[3] Joseph Smith's influence on the hospitable attitude toward intellectual activity generally and scientific thought in particular is detailed in B. H. Roberts's *Joseph Smith: The Prophet-Teacher*.[4] As for science's inseparable companion, technology, Brigham Young and all the presidents of the Church have asserted that technology is part of the revealed knowledge which God intended to improve the lot of men and women in a general way[5] and especially to aid in spreading the gospel message.[6] Indeed, to the extent that science and technology are embraced humbly and employed for the benefit of humankind, the modern prophets have viewed such truths as being harmonious with the gospel and helpful in understanding the design and purpose of the universe.

By comparison with other religious denominations, the Latter-day Saint community has not only produced an unusually large number of scientists for its size,[7] but also managed to retain the commitment and activity of a large proportion of those scientists.[8] Sterling McMurrin noted in 1959 and Robert Miller affirmed in 1992 that this well-documented hospitality of Mormon culture toward science and technology was firmly rooted in Mormonism's revealed theology. That theology accentuates the temporal and spatial connectedness of God to his creations, encourages the study of all truth as part of the gospel, affirms the continuity of matter and spirit, and posits an active partnership between God and humanity in the redemption of the world.[9] On numerous occasions since the Church was organized in 1830, its leaders have publicly corroborated this positive attitude toward science and technology.[10]

While LDS leaders have usually had a positive attitude, relations between science and religion in general have sometimes been difficult. Indeed, the tension between the scientific and religious views of human origins, human nature, and human potential has sometimes seemed irreconcilable. Individual church members and the Church as an institution have occasionally wrestled with the ideas, theories, implementation, and cultural side effects of science and technology. The two examples usually cited are: First, in 1911 ecclesiastical leaders became concerned that the zealous advocacy of evolutionary ideas and antireligious sentiments might weaken students' commitment to the gospel at Brigham Young University.[11] Second, in the early 1930s, several General Authorities carefully considered the possibility of life and death on this earth before Adam and Eve, but their discussions left unanswered questions.[12] These cases showed that some of the newer scientific theories—particularly those related to atheistic cosmogony and the naturalistic theories of evolution—were incompatible with revealed truth. Similarly, many current technological issues, particularly those concerning medical powers to alter, end, or lengthen life, are a source of increasing concern for individual Mormons and for Church policymakers.

Discomforts over specific doctrinal issues and ethical ramifications of scientific developments are only two of the forces which have eroded the historically favorable attitudes of Mormons toward science and technology, as Sessions and Oberg have suggested in a recent essay.[13] This erosion parallels a similar trend in American society, marked by the emergence of a strong evangelical movement and a general feeling that science and technology are responsible for environmental and social problems.[14]

Sources of Epistemological Tension. The intellectual, spiritual, and doctrinal tensions that Latter-day Saints feel about science and technology come from many sources, just as similar tensions do for believers in other religious communities.[15] One major LDS concern is *epistemological,* having to do with the modes of knowing and understanding in science as compared to those of religion. Mormon theology places primary emphasis on revelation received through authoritative priesthood leaders, where such scientific paradigms are developed principally through public discourse and debate. Disputes about the process of creation, the extent to which human behavior is actually governed by free will, and the origins of humankind are seemingly unavoidable. While science discovers its universe piecemeal, continually revising, correcting, and redrawing the picture, Mormon theology provides a relatively broad picture summarized in key revelations.

Mormons expect enlightenment to come primarily from meditation on or research consistent with the principles embodied in those revelations. For any Latter-day Saint, whether or not a professional scientist or technologist, any attempt to accommodate both of these profoundly different approaches to knowledge of the universe and humanity's place in it is guaranteed to challenge both faith and reason.

Out of the tension between scientific thought and the desire for faith-promoting attachment to their religious community, Mormon scientists and technologists have produced a large body of literature, mostly in the form of essays focusing on the reconciliation of personal piety with a scientific vocation. Elder John A. Widtsoe, for example, a member of the Quorum of the Twelve, wrote a major series of brief essays for the *Improvement Era* in the period from 1938 through 1952. The wide-ranging collection was later published in book form.[16] Elder Widtsoe had earlier penned two books on the relationship between science and the restored gospel as instructional manuals for the youth of the Church.[17] Elder Joseph F. Merrill, likewise of the Quorum of the Twelve and an engineer by profession, delivered a series of radio broadcasts—later published in book form—for the youth of the Church on science and religious faith.[18]

Biographical essays, such as recent studies of James E. Talmage[19] and of John A. Widtsoe,[20] frequently present the lives of Latter-day Saint scientists as a kind of Pilgrim's Progress in which the resolution of the tension between faith and reason is a major part of the protagonist's life work. Two of the most famous Mormon scientists, Henry Eyring and Harvey Fletcher, have been described in this vein.[21] Autobiographies (such as those of John A. Widtsoe[22] and Henry Eyring[23]) offer similar opportunities for individuals to share insights gained from examining their faith in the light of scientific knowledge. A series of essays based on this approach to science, technology, and religion was published in *The Instructor* during the late 1960s.[24] More recently, physicist Robert Fletcher has described both the similarities and contrasts between the ways he learned truth in the laboratory and through Church service.[25] Elder Russell M. Nelson, a member of the Quorum of the Twelve Apostles and a renowned heart surgeon, has also written autobiographically about his experiences with questions of scientific reason and religious faith.[26]

In controversial areas, noted Latter-day Saint scientists have frequently attempted to reconcile the insights of science with religious revelations. Often, these works were published either in official Church publications or with the explicit encouragement of the First Presidency. John A. Widtsoe's *A Rational Theology*[27] and *In Search of*

Truth,[28] Joseph F. Merrill's *The Truth-Seeker and Mormonism*,[29] and Frederick J. Pack's (a geology professor and theistic evolutionist) *Science and Belief in God* are typical examples from the first half of the century.[30] In the late 1950s, responding to Joseph Fielding Smith's scripturally based *Man, His Origin and Destiny*,[31] Paul A. Green compiled a group of essays to show that faithful Church membership and a scientific vocation are compatible.[32] Some of the main points of Green's book were later portrayed in a film designed particularly for Latter-day Saint students and youth leaders. At about the same time, Lowell Bennion wrote a more general discussion setting the character of scientific truth in context with religion, philosophy, and the arts;[33] a similar work was later written by University of Utah geneticist Frank Salisbury.[34] These works are typically based on the premise that the restored gospel embraces all truth; therefore, any apparent conflicts can be resolved by either increased knowledge or a broader perspective. This viewpoint leads naturally to the idea that both science and religion represent converging or parallel, though by no means equivalent, paths to truth.[35]

While most Latter-day Saints probably accept the foregoing approach, the intellectual pluralism it implies is not always favorably received. Furthermore, the view, relatively common in an earlier day, that science might actually bolster faith[36] is likely regarded with suspicion by many contemporary Latter-day Saints. This suspicion can probably be blamed on two factors: first, a naive, idealist view of the nature of "reality" underlying scientific results;[37] and second, a concern that laypersons may lose faith in fundamental gospel principles due to their inability to resolve technical disputes about current scientific findings.

Some authors have approached the epistemological reconciliation of science and religion by trying to show that revealed truths of the gospel can be harmonized with scientific principles. One example is John A. Widtsoe's classic *Joseph Smith as Scientist*, in which a comparative study of scientific and religious truths provides a reassuring glimpse of similarities as well as the familiar differences.[38] Another example is David Bailey's modern comparison of science and religion, which surveys current ideas on relativity, quantum theory, and molecular biology, and outlines points of consonance and dissonance with relevant Latter-day Saint doctrines.[39] Possible approaches to epistemological reconciliation are as varied as the individuals who propose them. Past proposals, however, have been essentially personal reconciliations; they have offered solace and insight but little systematic aid for those trying to locate the historical and philosophical roots of differences or conflicts. Moreover, comparisons of gospel truths and scientific principles have often turned on the temporary positions taken by science or on partially understood gospel principles. Therefore, such comparisons are rapidly outdated as either scientific inquiry or religious understanding matures. For example, Widtsoe compares the "light [which] proceedeth forth from the presence of God to fill the immensity of space" (D&C 88:12) with the lumeniferous ether.[40] Contemporary readers will not find this comparison convincing because the ether has been discarded as a bulwark of electromagnetic theory.

Sociological Causes of Tension. Another cause of tension lies in the character of religious and scientific communities. In religious communities, ecclesiastical authority is believed to be conferred by God through the call to service and the receipt of inspiration; the acceptance of that authority is part of the faith by which members of religious communities live. In the scientific community, the community's assessment of the virtuosity of individual scientists in carrying out experiments or constructing new theories underlies personal authority. For religious communities, authority is defined by revelation, scripture, theological principles, and by the authority or stature of an interpreter of doctrine. For science, authoritative knowledge is recognized by the degree to which it conforms to prevailing scientific paradigms;[41] personal authority and stature are conferred by demonstrated virtuosity in working within that paradigm or reshaping the paradigm to bring greater unity to the scientific view of nature. In religion, personal spirituality, revelation, prophetic or other charismatic gifts, and faithful service generally are the hallmarks of community recognition; this recognition gives great weight to cumulative, normative experiences that are consistent with eternal or universal truths. In science, the expectation is that today's experts will be turned out by tomorrow's new discoveries;[42] thus, relentless self-criticism and the high value accorded to originality and novelty are built into the procedures by which scientists evaluate one another's work. Willingness to submit to this process is part and parcel of the "social contract" which sustains the community of scientists and defines membership in it.[43]

The social structure of the scientific community and its habitual modes of communication complicate the task of understanding how science and technology have affected Mormon culture. Scientists and technologists communicate primarily in specialized journals, books, and conference proceedings. That literature is highly stylized, and even according to some of its practitioners does not represent the true character of scientific thought.[44] Recent studies of the history of science have also shown that the Baconian model of science as a largely inductive enterprise built on observations and experiment is incomplete in fundamental ways.[45] Instead, science appears to progress by a complex interplay of experiment and theory, strongly influenced by metaphysical and even aesthetic preconceptions. The growth of theory in physics, chemistry, and now in biology has been built much more on a search for meaning and comprehension. This search has been conducted in ways that are difficult to explain to people outside the scientific community and often seem to contradict the reverence for the "stubborn, irreducible facts of nature" on which science has supposedly been built.[46] Compounding all of these problems is the fact that scientists are, as a rule, not skilled at communicating the cultural significance of their work to nonspecialists,[47] though attempts to do so are increasing in number and in effectiveness. These sociological circumstances have been equally present among Latter-day Saint scientists and technologists.[48]

As in the past, General Authorities with scientific or technological training and experience continue to build bridges of understanding between the scientific and ecclesiastical communities. Among the present Quorum of the Twelve Apostles, Elders Russell M. Nelson and Richard G. Scott carry on a long tradition of men who have given up scientific careers to become Church leaders. When General Authorities like Elders Nelson and Scott have written explanatory material about specific doctrinal points relating, for example, to questions about evolution, creation, or medical ethics, their expertise has helped them to deal with the perceived epistemological problems of authoritative interpretation. Furthermore, the fact that a General Authority might hold membership in the religious and scientific communities may also serve to legitimize both approaches to truth in the minds of those dealing with any apparent conflicts between scientific and religious claims.[49]

Through the first half of this century, influential scientists in the Church, including members of the Quorum of the Twelve Apostles, made persistent attempts through books and Church periodicals to present the inner workings of science.[50] With the increasingly rapid pace of scientific and technological advances, however, and given the increasing administrative demands on the Twelve and other General Authorities in a truly worldwide Church organization, the days when ecclesiastical leaders could take time to educate the Church membership about these issues are probably gone, never to return.

In recent years, relatively few articles about science have appeared in official Church publications. Some writers have suggested that the decline in such articles and the perceived influence of conservative views about the age of the earth and evolution signal a "Mormon retreat from science."[51] This, however, is an oversimplified view of a complex issue. Mainstream scientific points of view continue to be printed in the *Ensign* in response to queries about the age of the earth,[52] and the articles about controversial issues in the *Encyclopedia of Mormonism* follow a moderate course.[53] Serious discussion of this question is overdue, but scholarly studies based on something more than anecdotes will have to await more citation analysis than has yet been done.

Rhetorical and Linguistic Sources of Tension. Many of the tensions between science or technology and religion appear to result from *rhetorical* and *linguistic* differences between the scientific and religious communities, differences which are by no means unique to Latter-day Saints. For example, in a recent address, Elder Russell M. Nelson of the Council of the Twelve, after speaking in detail about the intricate regulatory system of the human body and the astonishing reach of the laws of genetics, noted that

> some without scriptural understanding . . . have deduced that, because of certain similarities between different forms of life, there has been a natural selection of the species, or organic evolution from one form to another. Many of these people have concluded that the universe began as a "big bang" that eventually resulted in the creation of our planet and life upon it. To me, such theories are unbelievable! Could an explosion in a printing shop produce a dictionary? It is unthinkable! Even if it could be argued to be within a remote realm of possibility, such a dictionary could certainly not heal its own torn pages or renew its own worn corners or reproduce its own subsequent editions![54]

These remarks are intended, of course, for a general audience and, in context, are part of a strong testimony about the essentially divine origin of humanity and the purposefulness of creation. To the casual listener, these statements might suggest an antiscientific bias which is clearly not intended, since the logic of the entire presentation turns on the results of intricate scientific analysis.

What statements about scientific models—such as the explosion in the print shop—imply is the fact that the rules of science explicitly disallow elements of the Divine. No matter how much individual scientists may believe in God—and many do—they know that because of their colleagues' widely differing beliefs, science works as well as it does only by relying on experiments or logical demonstrations that are potentially verifiable and tentatively accepted by participants in the discussion. An initial qualitative model ("an explosion in a printing shop") may seem implausible at first. Indeed, a tremendous weight of criticism has been laid by scientists themselves on the now-outmoded Darwinian model of natural selection by random variation.[55] However, by asking questions that can be analyzed in a *quantitative* fashion—"How much explosive?" "How heavy are the fragments?" "Do the fragments interact with one another during or after the explosion?"— scientists can evaluate, discard, and possibly improve the model. Indeed, the purpose of a scientific model may be as much to stimulate this kind of evaluative dialogue as to explain or predict natural phenomena. However peculiar laypersons may deem the idea of starting with models that seem to make no sense, scientists are often able to move forward by starting with just such simple-minded efforts and then applying the standard tools of logical and mathematical analysis to see where the models break down. In such a way, troublesome questions at the current interface between science and theology can be addressed. In addition to scientists' presentations, many historians and philosophers of science are now actively contributing to the understanding of science—its nature, its inner workings, and its relationship to society and culture.[56]

Resources in Science and Mormonism

The doctrinal warrant for Latter-day Saint interest in science is rooted in modern revelation. "The Glory of God is intelligence," proclaims the Doctrine and Covenants, that is, "light and truth" (D&C 93:36). This truth is defined in latter-day revelations as knowledge of reality: "And truth is knowledge of things as they are, and as they were, and as they are to come" (D&C 93:24). That knowledge of the truth is critical both here and hereafter is clear from the promise that "whatever principle of intelligence we attain unto in this life, it will rise with us in the resurrection. And if a person gains more knowledge and intelligence . . . than another, he will have so much the advantage in the world to come" (D&C 130:18–19). For many Latter-day Saints, as for the seventeenth-century astronomer Johannes Kepler, the celestial harmonies of the universe are tangible evidence of the order, balance, and creative energy of God. "[A]ny man who hath seen any or the least of these [kingdoms] hath seen God moving in his majesty and power" (D&C 88:47). Scriptural injunctions to look heavenward and into nature for evidence of God's handiwork have doubtlessly had a strong influence on decisions by Latter-day Saints to take up scientific careers.

In surveying current book and periodical resources related to science and Mormon culture, we consider four general categories of science: (1) *astronomy and cosmology,* the study of the universe of which our world is a part; (2) the *earth and planetary sciences* which focus on the origin, structure, composition, and dynamics of our planet and our solar system; (3) *life sciences,* which emphasize the origin, behavior, and dynamics of plants and animals; and (4) the *materials sciences,* such as physics and chemistry, which embrace the composition, structure and behavior of the fundamental particles that comprise nuclei, atoms, molecules, and larger aggregations of matter.

Astronomy and Cosmology. Astronomy and cosmology have been of interest to Church members because of these disciplines' relation to questions about the origin and age of the universe and about the plurality of worlds. Not surprisingly, among the earliest recorded articles from Church publications are several dealing with "signs in the heavens," "plurality of worlds," and the "regeneration and eternal duration of matter."[57] After the Saints had settled in Utah, this interest continued unabated, to the point that "The Astronomer and His Work" was considered important enough to be featured in *The Juvenile Instructor.*[58] Orson Pratt, in his *Key to the Universe, or a New Theory of Its Mechanism,* undertook to show mathematically how Newtonian mechanics could be extended to the motion of the ether and tried to solve certain puzzling aspects of planetary motion.[59]

Since the earliest years of the Restoration, Latter-day Saints have expressed a deep interest in cosmology (the structure of the universe) and cosmogony (the origins of the universe). These interests have found their central focus in Mormon ideas dealing with "worlds without number" and the "plurality of worlds" as expressed in numerous doctrinal sources such as the Pearl of Great Price. The historical and scientific significance of these ideas about many worlds, both within and beyond the LDS context, are a central theme in Erich Robert Paul's *Science, Religion, and Mormon Cosmology.*[60] Throughout the nineteenth and well into the twentieth centuries, the idea of the plurality of worlds resonated with popular cultural paradigms of the times.[61] The visions of the Prophet Joseph Smith on this question are well documented in his writings and in Latter-day Saint scriptures,[62] and Orson Pratt and others made frequent reference to the plurality of worlds in their sermons and writings. As links have grown stronger between modern theories of the universe's origins and of the possibility of life elsewhere in the universe (exobiology), scientific interest in the plurality of worlds has been revived. That interest is now being fostered through a high-technology search for extraterrestrial intelligence.[63]

Earth and Planetary Science. The creation of the earth and the place of that creation in the plan of salvation have been matters of great interest both to Mormon scientists and to the general membership of the Church. As noted by F. Kent Nielsen and Stephen D. Ricks in the *Encyclopedia of Mormonism,*[64] the critical feature of all scriptural accounts of creation is their focus on the earth serving as a testing place for Heavenly Father's children prior to its eventual transformation into a celestial body. This sense that the earth itself partakes of a divine destiny forms the basis for a unique Latter-day Saint approach to science as well as to problems of the environment discussed later in this essay. The gradual deletion of this divine purpose from scientific accounts of creation is one of the hallmarks of the emerging modern worldview which some Latter-day Saints find problematic.[65] These LDS concerns may profitably be compared with Protestant perspectives that take into account historical change in the sociology of knowledge and the effect of those changes on the dialogue between religion and science.[66]

Beyond making cogent statements—derived from both scripture and modern revelation—of *why* the earth was created, Mormon scientists and laypersons have tried to understand *how* the process of creation unfolded and how that process relates to the history of the earth and the solar system as seen by scientists. Until relatively recently, most members of the Church seemed content to accept the conventional old-earth estimates of geology.[67] W. W. Phelps's 1844 estimate is quoted by Bruce R. McConkie, for example, as giving a "true and authentic" approximation of 2.555 billion years for the age of the world.[68] We do not know whether Phelps intended this estimate to be the age of the earth, the solar system, the universe, or of the materials used to create the world (in the now quite discredited scenario which postulated that the earth was created from pieces of other earths). Nevertheless, Apostle and geologist James E. Talmage held in 1931 that a creation occurring several billion years ago was harmonious both with scriptures and modern revelation.[69] LDS doctrine clearly rejects the idea that the world was created *ex nihilo.*

Despite the history of old earth ideas in the Church, not to mention the even longer estimates by geologists, some Mormons have been attracted to creationist perspectives which grow out of young-earth theories and the evidence which purports to underpin them. The origins of this attraction seem to be the same as they are among Christian fundamentalists: a desire to demonstrate that the literal King James translation of the Genesis account of creation is an appropriate basis for the interpretation of geological evidence.

Within the fundamentalist community, the conceptual foundations of the creationist approach were outlined in 1923 by George McCready Price in his *The New Geology.*[70] Price's text was widely used in many fundamentalist colleges; during the 1920s, it found its way into the hands of Joseph Fielding Smith, then a member of the Quorum of the Twelve Apostles. *The New Geology* postulated, among other things, that the fossil record of geological strata arose from the rapid deposition of sediment following the Noachian flood. Along with substantial quotations from both scripture and previous Church leaders, Elder Smith used *The New Geology* to challenge the position—supported by James E. Talmage[71] and Elder B. H. Roberts of the Seventy—that an old-earth geology and belief that some life and death occurred on this earth before Adam were compatible with the scriptural record.[72] The public and private debate among the General Authorities of the Church was ended by direction of the First Presidency in 1931, only to begin again after the publication of Joseph Fielding Smith's *Man, His Origin and Destiny* in 1954.

At a time when most Mormon scientists went to great lengths to distance themselves from the age-of-the-earth controversy, Melvin Cook, an internationally recognized explosives expert and professor of metallurgy at the University of Utah, emerged as an ardent and vocal supporter of a young-earth geology and a fossil record determined by the Deluge. Cook's strong support and his unimpeachable scientific credentials were convincing for many lay Mormons trying to sort out the conflicting views of the experts. His two books on the topic, one for Mormon audiences and one for a more general readership,[73] attempt to provide scientific grounds for bolstering the literal reading of the book of Genesis espoused in Joseph Fielding Smith's *Man, His Origin and Destiny.* Cook, who wrote a laudatory introduction to *Man, His Origin and Destiny,* has particularly focused on concerns about the various radiological dating methods upon which old-earth chronologies are based.[74] While Cook has explicitly rejected certain aspects of creationist dogma, including the idea of a creation *ex nihilo,* he has continued to champion other features of creationist thought, notably the idea of a very young earth.

Central to all discussions of the age of the earth have been the methods of geology and the apparent conflict between these methods and a literal reading of Genesis (although differences between Genesis and the accounts in the Pearl of Great Price are significant). William Lee Stokes, a geologist from the University of Utah, wrote a detailed study (1979) of the elements of the biblical creation narrative and the revelations in the Pearl of Great Price.[75] Stokes suggests that modern science has much interesting material to contribute to an understanding of the creation narratives; he also notes the potentially negative impact of creationist teachings on both science and Latter-day Saint theology. Geneticist Frank Salisbury wrote about the Mormon creation narratives in a similar vein (1976), but with somewhat more emphasis on biology.[76] Recent *Ensign* articles intended for the general membership of the Church have reinforced more conventional scientific views about the age of the earth[77] and the time required for the earth's creation.[78] Thus far, Latter-day Saint scientists have made only one attempt (1979) to deal with the scientific questions surrounding the chronology of creation in a comprehensive way.[79] Among the topics treated by specialists in this work are the accuracy of radio-carbon dating, dendrochronology, fossil records, and archaeomagnetic dating. However, the emphasis in these studies is clearly on reconciliation of theological—rather than scientific—issues related to dating objects of ancient origin.

Life Sciences. Complicating the question of the age of the earth is the temporal sequence of various life forms on this planet. Mormon theology posits a unique understanding of creation wherein all life, whether plant, animal, or human, participates in the divine plan to redeem the world.[80] This theology has especially significant implications for Latter-day Saint attitudes toward animal life and the environment; references relating to this particular topic are described under the heading *Engineering Sciences* in a later section of this essay. All of these sources emphasize that men and women play a central role as the only beings created in the image of God and as those charged with stewardship over all other life on earth.

The most voluminous literature about the life sciences and Mormonism revolves around Darwin's theory of evolution. Mormon responses to Darwin's *The Origin of Species,* published in 1859, began in earnest soon after the book was published.[81] In 1931, the First Presidency plainly stated that a clear division of labor and opinion exists between religion and science:

> Upon the fundamental doctrines of the Church we are all agreed. Our mission is to bear the message of the restored gospel to the world. Leave geology, biology, archaeology and anthropology, no one of which has to do with the salvation of the souls of mankind, to scientific research, while we magnify *our* calling in the realm of the Church. . . . Upon one thing we should all be able to agree, namely, . . . "Adam is the primal parent of our race."[82]

Because evolutionary ideas have so often been linked with both biological questions about the origin of life and great issues of human behavior and responsibility,[83] the Darwinian view of evolution has been widely debated. In addition, the Darwinist worldview conflicts with Mormon theology of the atonement and eternal progression.

In many respects, the Latter-day Saints' debate over evolution has paralleled that which occurred among the Protestant churches.

In both cases, the chief concern has been to defend the unique status of man and woman as special creations. The position of several LDS Church leaders has been summarized in Bruce R. McConkie's *Mormon Doctrine.*[84] Furthermore, believing Latter-day Saints and their Protestant brethren and sisters have sometimes attacked evolution as "false science," charging that it was not only in conflict with the Bible but that it actually hindered the progress of biological science.[85] While scientifically trained observers would consider this charge baseless,[86] it does have a foundation in the Baconian tradition of science as a systematic induction of facts from nature. Indeed, those who oppose evolution as false science are probably repelled by the strong theoretical aspect of evolutionary thought. This theoretical cast was a feature of science that Bacon did not foresee; it was increasingly characteristic, however, of nineteenth- and twentieth-century physics and chemistry.[87]

The ideas that humans existed before Adam or that men and women are directly descended from lower forms of life are clearly inconsistent with biblical teachings about the creation and with the presumed degeneration of humanity after the Fall. This idea of pre-Adamic "humanids" on this planet was one of the reasons Joseph Fielding Smith considered B. H. Roberts's writings problematic, notably Roberts's massive work, *The Truth, the Way, the Life,* which has been characterized as "a kind of historical notebook of science and Mormon theology."[88] While Roberts did not believe in human evolution, he did believe that "humanid" creatures existed before Adam. These creatures, according to Roberts, were all destroyed along with all other forms of life during a worldwide cataclysm. The Garden of Eden, Roberts argued, was not created until after the cataclysm.

In the 1920s, polarization in American society about the nature of evolutionary science and its impact on religious doctrine and feelings led to a hardening of positions on both sides of the issue.

> One contemporary observer blamed the creation-evolution controversy in part on the "intellectual flapperism" of irresponsible and poorly informed teachers, who delighted in shocking naive students with unsupportable statements about evolution. It was understandable, wrote an Englishman, that American parents would resent sending their sons and daughters to public institutions that exposed them to "a multiple assault upon traditional faiths."[89]

Latter-day Saint parents, like other religiously minded people concerned about the faith of the younger generation, were equally disturbed about attacks on religion in the name of science. Regrettably, as scientists have changed the framework of the theory of evolution,[90] and as sociologists and sociobiologists have groped toward a scientific justification for ethical and moral behavior,[91] these developments—distinctly more reconcilable with Latter-day Saint theology—have not been widely known in the Mormon community.

In a 1984 *Ensign* article, Elder Boyd K. Packer provided a valuable and comprehensive discussion about human origins and destiny, reaffirming the unique status of men and women as the only creatures made in the image and likeness of deity.[92] In 1990, he reiterated these basic elements in the divinely ordained plan of salvation and stated: "If you respect the truths of moral and spiritual law, you are in little danger for your soul in any field of study."[93] Thus, believing Latter-day Saints feel comfortable pursuing scientific studies based on evolutionary theories while simultaneously respecting the revelations that teach the unique status of humankind and the eternal purposes for which God created the earth. Indeed, the theory of evolution can be taught in Brigham Young University's life science departments in tacit acknowledgment that no other theoretical framework for the scientific study of life from the level of molecular biology on upward makes sense.[94] At the same time, however, most Brigham Young University students, according to a recent survey cited by Numbers, reject the idea that human life could have evolved from "lower species."[95]

As of this writing, the 1909 and 1925 expositions of the First Presidency on the origins of humankind and on evolution remain the official position of the Church. These positions are detailed in Duane Jeffery's historical summary of the Church's official reactions to evolutionary theory.[96] In 1992 the Board of Trustees of Brigham Young University (which includes the First Presidency and seven members of the Quorum of Twelve Apostles) approved the distribution of a packet containing the statements on evolution by the First Presidency, noting that "various views have been expressed by other Church leaders on this subject over many decades; however, formal statements by the First Presidency are the definitive source of official Church positions."[97] In a cover letter, professor William Evenson noted that those who prepared the packet for the Board of Trustees wished "to avoid the implication that a greater sense of unanimity or resolution of this topic exists than is actually the case, and we are eager to avoid contention."[98]

Recent accounts of the origins of life appear to be much more complex than the basic Darwinian paradigm of evolution. This complexity opens the door once again for people to reconcile the doctrine of special creation of humanity with modern scientific ideas.[99] The Darwinian paradigm was based on the twin pillars of natural selection and branching speciation. Natural selection was viewed as the force that drove a wedge between members of a common ancestral species to produce the branching evident in nature. Darwin's work was based to a significant degree on the idea that selection could occur in any direction. However, as modern genetics and molecular biology have developed, Darwin's simple picture has been increasingly revised. During the Darwin centennial year Vasco Tanner published in *BYU Studies* a review of the changes in the Darwinian theory of evolution,[100] and in 1993 geneticist Eldon Gardner outlined the salient distinctions between conventional evolutionary theory and scriptural teachings about human origins.[101] In 1979 a number of Latter-day Saint scholars addressed issues relating to human origins as seen both through the lens of LDS theology and from the perspective of modern biology.[102] Certainly, recent experiments have shaken the naive confidence that the mysteries of life's origins would be resolved by biochemistry and molecular biology.[103] The very uncertainty of science at this time is grounds for confidence that room exists for both faith and reason.

Of potentially tremendous importance to the origins debate is a constellation of ideas evolving from scientists' understanding of complex, nonlinear systems. These systems exhibit a behavior referred to as "self-organization,"[104] and surprisingly, such an evolution of order from chaos has now been demonstrated in various chemical, biological, and ecological systems.[105] The ideas of complex system theory are certain to have dramatic effects on scientific concepts of natural selection, and at least one author has suggested that self-organization accounts for the origin of life.[106] None of this discussion has yet been interpreted within the framework of Latter-day Saint theology.

Materials Sciences. Embracing both the oldest (chemistry and metallurgy) and the newest (elementary-particle physics) sciences, the study of the structure, properties, and processing of matter has attracted the attention of numerous LDS scientists. From its earliest days, Mormon theology took a radical position in opposition to traditional Christianity on the origin and nature of matter.[107] Joseph Smith firmly rejected the traditional matter-spirit dualism of Thomas Aquinas's Neoplatonic synthesis with Christianity. The Prophet posited that the spirit is as tangible as matter, though not as readily perceptible; that both spirit and matter are eternal; and that the earth and its inhabitants were not created *ex nihilo* but through an organization of pre-existing matter.[108] These doctrines were elaborated by Parley P. Pratt[109] and by his brother Orson.[110] Current scholarship suggests that Orson's systematic elaborations of these doctrines owed much to the free-ranging thought of his older brother, and that both were in the intellectual and spiritual debt of the Prophet Joseph Smith.[111]

With the development of the special theory of relativity and of quantum physics in the early twentieth century, the basic concepts of matter and energy and their indestructibility—as described by early Church leaders—seemed to be strongly confirmed.[112] Since that time, however, the materials sciences have developed the concepts of quantum theory into a broad-ranging complex of computational and experimental techniques. These techniques have not only explained and exhibited the structure of matter down to atomic (even subatomic) scales, but have made possible the creation of designer materials at the molecular and macromolecular scale. Because the materials sciences study the attributes of existing matter rather than the origins of matter, the materials sciences have caused little controversy in the Church. Moreover, practical applications have given the materials sciences preferred status as a partner in the generation of useful technology. Thus, the opinions of materials scientists on science and religion seem to have found general acceptance within the Church as well.

Henry Eyring, arguably the most famous of all Mormon scientists, is an important example of a materials scientist who frequently expressed his opinions about science and religion even when his opinions clearly differed from those of some Church leaders. During his tenure at the University of Utah (1946–81), Eyring was an influential and active figure in Church circles. This influence seems to have been due not only to Eyring's personal connections with Church leaders, but also to his superb sense of institutional diplomacy and the moderate, generous tone in which he couched his writings about science and religion.[113] Even while vigorous antievolutionary and anti-old-earth campaigns were waged by Joseph Fielding Smith and Bruce R. McConkie, among others, Eyring maintained an audience among all interested parties. Through frequent speeches and many articles in Church magazines (later collected in *The Faith of a Scientist*),[114] Eyring provided a glimpse into his basis for belief and some helpful perspectives on science as an intellectual community. Elder Mark E. Petersen of the Quorum of the Twelve Apostles—one of the more conservative members of that body in his approach to science and religion issues—had 110,000 copies of the book distributed to students in the 1960s. This illustrates Eyring's influence and also the willingness of Church leaders to support a tolerant stance on scientific issues as long as that stance was consistent with a firm commitment to basic Mormon doctrine.

Future Latter-day Saint scientists working in the materials sciences will likely have many opportunities to provide their disciplinary perspectives on issues of creation and evolution, especially as the materials sciences are now becoming tied in to other traditionally separate branches of science, including cosmology and molecular biology. This more unified description of nature should have significant ramifications for certain issues in the areas of science and theology. Two examples of this trend are worthy of note.

The first example concerns the marriage of elementary particle physics with cosmology, the whimsically named "Glorious Revolution" of 1977 out of which a unified theory of electromagnetic and weak nuclear forces emerged. This unified theory is the cornerstone of the so-called "standard model," including the Big Bang. The "Glorious Revolution" was based on a worldwide effort of theorists and experimentalists to understand the forces which hold protons, neutrons, and other subatomic particles together. Their efforts led to virtually complete acceptance of a Big Bang theory of creation grounded on a unified, experimental, and theoretical picture of the way the tiniest building blocks of matter could have been forged in the incredibly hot, dense matter at the dawn of creation.[115] For many scientists, the success of the so-called "standard model" represented both a confirmation that the universe did indeed have a beginning and a clear signal that science could never penetrate to the final secret of that beginning:

> It is not a question of another year, another decade of work, another measurement or another theory; at this moment it seems as though science will never be able to raise the curtain on the mystery of creation. For the scientist who has lived by his faith in the power of reason, the story ends like a bad dream. He has scaled the mountains of ignorance; he is about to conquer the highest peak; as he pulls himself over the final rock, he is greeted by a band of theologians who have been sitting there for centuries.[116]

Fifty years ago, Elder Widtsoe might well have greeted the foregoing announcement as leaving a door open once again for divine action. Contemporary scientists have also seen a new opportunity for a reconciliation between the revealed insights of religion and the latest findings of science.[117] However, some Latter-day Saints are concerned that the Big Bang theory might be used as yet another attempt to explain the universe without explicitly acknowledging the hand of the Creator, but the two are not mutually exclusive.

Another facet of the materials sciences which is likely to receive greater prominence in the future is the theory of complex systems applied to materials, known in the vernacular as chaos theory. The theory of complex systems began with Poincaré and his study of complex planetary orbits at the turn of the century. His beautiful mathematics of chaos received new life through Edward Lorenz and others' study of fluid dynamics and meteorology. As chaos theory begins to infiltrate condensed-matter physics and chemistry, it seems destined to link with molecular biology to change scientific understanding of evolution. The theory of complex systems describes the behavior of particles and systems of particles whose response to forces is nonlinear, that is, not strictly proportional to the magnitude of the force. Complex systems, such as molecules reacting with each other on metal surfaces, show a sensitive dependence on initial conditions which makes predicting their future behavior impossible even though their trajectories are perfectly deterministic.[118] This breakdown of the historical link between determinism (lawful behavior) and predictability is certain to force a re-evaluation of much of the metaphysics underlying twentieth-century science.

Hence, from the scientific point of view, the universe appears to be significantly more interesting than we might have guessed from the classical picture of an ensemble of atoms relentlessly dissipating life-giving and creative energy in obedience to the Second Law of Thermodynamics.

> Thoughtful physicists concerned with the workings of thermodynamics realize how disturbing is the question of, as one put it, "how a purposeless flow of energy can wash life and consciousness into the world. . . . Thermodynamic entropy fails miserably as a measure of the changing degree of form and formlessness in the creation of amino acids, of microorganisms, of self-reproducing plants and animals, of complex information systems like the brain. Certainly these evolving islands of order must obey the Second Law. The important laws, the creative laws, lie elsewhere."[119]

It is the qualitatively new picture of the world—a world which includes such phenomena as creativity, self-correction and self-replication—that is the hallmark of the "new science" of nonlinear materials science.

Resources on Technology and Mormonism

If the motivation for doing science is to *know,* then the driving force behind technology is to *do* in a practical way that which scientific knowledge makes possible. The divine injunction to Adam to "replenish the earth, and subdue it," and the warning that "in the sweat of thy face shalt thou eat thy bread," are only two of the bases for the assumption that practical knowledge is relevant to the gospel and to many praiseworthy applications in Mormon culture. If science presents problems for religion because its models appear to contradict revealed theological principles, technology causes difficulty for the believer because of its practical, ethical challenge: shall we do, must we do, all of what we *can* do?

Technology is more than "applied science." Technology emphasizes materials processing, the organization of the means and forces of production, and the relationship of both of these to economic growth and societal benefit.[120] Within the framework of the restored gospel, the revealed principles of consecration and stewardship[121] stand out as peculiarly relevant to technology and Mormon culture. Thus, studies of technology and Mormonism involve the practical effects of science on humankind and the discharge of humankind's stewardship over the earth. For the purposes of this review, we consider the engineering sciences, the agricultural sciences, and the health sciences.

Engineering Sciences. Engineering in all of its branches—biomedical, chemical, civil, electrical, environmental, materials, and mechanical, among others—deals with the practical necessities of life: shelter, transportation, communication, energy, and a livable environment. Latter-day Saints have distinguished themselves in many branches of engineering, from mining and sugar-beet refining to space exploration. Contrary to popular opinion, the Mormon rapprochement with technology began even during the earliest days of Latter-day Saint colonization of the western United States,[122] and continued with enthusiasm thereafter. Some of the enthusiasm for technology undoubtedly sprang from the need for practical gadgetry for farms and factories; nevertheless, the principle of stewardship clearly had a large impact on the drive to improve the material surroundings of Zion through technology. Regrettably, little of this story has been told.

The growth of sheer technological capability through the various branches of engineering raises a host of questions related to the quality of human life. While serving as presidents of the Church's European Mission in the 1920s and 1930s, Elders Talmage, Widtsoe, and Merrill came face to face with a ruthless technological scientism that empowered both fascism and communism without any vestige of moral restraint.[123] These Mormon scientists with ecclesiastical responsibilities, like many scientists of the day, were forced to give up earlier beliefs that aligned science with truth and human progress.

The atomic bomb detonated over Hiroshima in 1945 forced Latter-day Saints, as it did the scientific community, to confront those forces in human society which seem to impel us to use "every gadget that is technically possible, no matter how murderous it is."[124] The impact on Utah's industry of one such potentially destructive weapons technology—the intercontinental ballistic missile and the rocket engines which propel it—was discussed in 1962 by Leonard Arrington and Jon Perry.[125]

An apparently unexplored chapter on Mormons involved in the technology of modern weaponry is the story of John Moses Browning, the inventor of the machine gun. Browning's father Jonathan, a convert to the Church and neighbor to Brigham Young and Heber C. Kimball in Nauvoo, eventually settled in Ogden, Utah, where John Moses was born in 1855. The younger Browning's career as designer and builder of small arms began when he was a teenager in his father's gunsmithing shop. He served a mission in the southern states (late 1870s) and remained devoted to the Church even after he rose to prominence as an inventor of modern firearms.[126]

The computer has had and continues to have an enormous impact on Church programs and capabilities. James B. Allen, in a 1983 essay about the introduction of computing machinery into the Church, has raised numerous generic issues about our ability to keep cultural and theological bearings fixed while using new technologies to magnify ecclesiastical stewardships.[127] According to Allen, the Church has rarely been at the forefront of technological change, and thus far the Church has made no systematic effort to incorporate technology planning into its programs.[128] Nevertheless, several areas of computer research have been strongly supported at Brigham Young University, including computer-assisted textual analysis and translation.[129] Furthermore, outside the sphere of Church activities and programs, Mormon technologists have generated major developments in computer software and hardware and have created innovative applications for computers in other fields, such as medicine and design. Several of the most important of these computer technologists have contributed their papers to collections described later in this essay.[130]

The deleterious consequences to the earth's environment of human technological progress have been amply documented, as have their political and scientific ramifications.[131] Twentieth-century environmental movements in the Americas and Western Europe have frequently identified the Judaeo-Christian ideal of human dominion over the earth as the destructive rationale for plundering the environment. Environmentalists, for this reason, are often hostile toward the scientists who make new technology possible and toward religious believers who, in environmentalists' minds, have sanctioned technological application. As Ian Barbour in 1980 has pointed out, however, many features of Jewish and Christian belief support a rational environmental philosophy if people choose to emphasize them.[132] These features include the ideas of unity with God's creation (well-known in mystical thought) and biblical ideas about stewardship that are prominent in LDS revelation (Doctrine and Covenants 78, 82, 83).

Mormon attitudes toward the environment have followed the mixed attitudes of the general culture. Numerous scriptural injunctions familiar to Mormons, however, suggest that an ecological ethic based on stewardship is appropriate because the earth belongs not to humans, but to God. In an important essay in 1972, Hugh Nibley called attention to Brigham Young's prescient, or more properly, prophetic, application of the concept of human stewardship over the earth to the need for environmental consciousness.[133] Going far beyond simple ideas of conservation (which of themselves would have been astonishing in the days of the frontier), Young called for an environmental ethic in which men and women acted as partners with God in re-creating and enhancing the natural world for the blessing of God's children. Young's ethic is reminiscent of other environmental concepts based on cultural and theological ideas stretching back to the Greeks.[134] This notion of stewardship anticipated some of the environmental ideas that appeared a hundred years later in the writings of, among others, microbiologist René Dubos.[135]

The development of the Mormon environmental ethic can be seen in attempts to regulate mining in Utah. Mining and metallurgy were two of the earliest industries in Utah, and the social consequences of these activities sometimes attracted unfavorable attention from Church authorities. By the late 1850s, the problems of mining had brought into being a relatively coherent Church policy on mining. The policy was designed to lead to "orderly, balanced development of local resources by a unified people for the support of a permanent society."[136] The resulting interplay between economic incentive and community values has been documented in many studies of Church history, beginning with Leonard Arrington's *Great Basin Kingdom.* However, little attention has been paid to the role of Church members in the scientific and technological innovations associated with the mining industry, particularly with respect to fulfilling the ideals of the Mormon environmental stewardship.[137]

An important part of environmental thinking concerns human attitudes toward animals. Mormon thought in this area has been directly guided by the concept of stewardship, and runs against the grain of typical frontier behavior in the United States. As shown in several studies, notably those by Gerald Jones,[138] Mormon doctrine clearly teaches a high level of responsibility for human conduct toward animals. In modern revelation, "the beasts of the field and the fowls of the air . . . [are] ordained for the use of man for food and for raiment, and that he might have in abundance." These creatures are not to be killed wantonly, however, for "wo be unto man that sheddeth blood or that wasteth flesh and hath no need" (D&C 49:19, 21).

Agricultural and Food Sciences. The agricultural and food sciences have direct relevance to the ability of people to meet their needs for daily bread. While Latter-day Saint scripture proclaims that "the earth is full, and there is enough and to spare" (D&C 104:17), food scarcity and famine continue to be among humankind's many unresolved problems. Deeply ingrained in the Mormon tradition, of course, is Isaiah's ancient vision of making the "desert blossom as the rose,"[139] a vision that nineteenth-century Mormon pioneers transformed into reality in the Great Salt Lake valley. That vision and heritage have been the starting point for significant Mormon involvement in the agricultural sciences of irrigation, crop and soil chemistry, and farm management.[140] Many of the important early developments in irrigation and other aspects of agricultural science are described in John A. Widtsoe's autobiography,[141] Arrington and Bitton's sesquicentennial history of the Church,[142] and professional agricultural journals.[143]

While modern agricultural science has made abundant food production possible, Latter-day Saint scriptures and the warnings of the prophets suggest that the ability to distribute food equitably and generously is a much larger issue. The questions of population and the ability of the earth to feed its population are critical to Mormons' approach to the developing nations of the world. Phillip Low[144] and Sylvan Wittwer[145] have pointed out that the earth's carrying capacity is presently vastly underutilized largely because of an inability to find politically and socially acceptable mechanisms for producing a more equitable distribution of existing resources.

Health Sciences. The most persistent LDS emphasis on medical science seems to have been related to the Word of Wisdom (D&C 89).[146] The largest number of printed works concentrate on medical reasons for abstinence from alcohol, tobacco, tea, and coffee,[147] or on the consequences of the observance of the Word of Wisdom for the public health of Mormon society.[148] Still unexplored to a significant degree are the medical benefits of the "positive" side of the Word of Wisdom, such as eating meat sparingly and basing the diet on whole grains.[149] These aspects of the Word of Wisdom can be expected to attract more attention as the effects of diet on health become more interesting to medical practitioners.

Mormon belief in the healing power of priesthood blessings has created some ambivalent attitudes among Church members about the relative merits of faith versus medical knowledge. Some descriptions of a crucial boyhood operation performed on the Prophet Joseph Smith suggest that divine providence might have an influence on medical knowledge and practice.[150] The best-known scriptural prescription for treating those without sufficient faith to be healed recommended herbs and other mild remedies (D&C 42). This scriptural prescription produced an interesting diversity of herbal medicine among the Latter-day Saints.[151]

Two major book-length works on medical practice and cultural attitudes among the Mormons have appeared in recent years: one in 1981 by Robert Divett[152] which followed up on a pair of related essays,[153] and the other in 1991 by Lester Bush.[154] The Bush study emphasizes traditional Mormon concerns about wellness, death, dying, sexuality, and healing, largely in historical context. The book suggests that in most areas, the challenges to Mormon beliefs posed by modern, high-technology medical practice have largely been resolved in favor of rational, indeed liberal, use of modern medical knowledge. Studies of the spread of medical ideas and knowledge in pioneer days in Utah[155] highlight a growing preference for applying the remedies of medicine and public health as far as these were perceived to be effective.[156] The tension between faith in priesthood blessings and in the increasingly powerful techniques of modern medicine, however, was a difficult matter to resolve; this tension can be seen from Eric Bluth's 1993 history of the smallpox-vaccination question in Utah.[157] The quite pragmatic approach advocated by Brigham Young—namely, to avail oneself of both the blessings of God and of the best medical remedies available[158]—seems now to be favored by the Latter-day Saint community, guaranteeing high support for modern health practices.[159]

Infant and child care have always loomed large in Latter-day Saint culture; they have been described in detail in both official and unofficial sources.[160] Biographical essays in *Mormon Sisters*[161] chart the careers of Patty Sessions and Ellis Shipp, famous LDS midwife and doctor, respectively, whose medical training was beautifully augmented by their deep spiritual convictions.[162] These two healthcare workers represent the hundreds of women who served, in Claudia Bushman's words, as "mystics and healers" in Utah's pioneer days.[163] Many of the Mormon midwives and women medical doctors were sent on missions to the best available schools of the time by the leaders of the Church with the specific charge to augment their medical training with profound spiritual conviction.[164] Related questions of what has come to be known as reproductive medicine—a complex set of issues relating to birth control, abortion, and medical ethics in the context of human sexuality—have also been addressed recently by Lester Bush.[165]

More controversial medical subjects, however, have also been examined in recent years. The new possibilities of biotechnology in the service of medicine raise a host of ethical issues that many Mormons and their neighbors of other faiths must address.[166] The epidemic spread of acquired immune-deficiency syndrome (AIDS) has created ambivalent attitudes in the general population, an ambivalence which is based on the presumption of guilt—much like biblical leprosy—associated with contracting the disease.[167] Closely related to the question of AIDS is the issue of the biological roots of homosexuality.[168] Fueled by rapidly increasing knowledge about the biochemistry of thought and behavior, the debate over whether homosexuality is a learned or willed behavior, or whether it is partially conditioned by genetic or biochemical factors, poses significant challenges for Church members. A clear proscription against homosexuality, as articulated in both the scriptures and the entire Judaeo-Christian tradition, has been affirmed by Church leaders. In light of the clear "Thou shalt not," a major issue for Latter-day Saints concerns how to understand and deal practically and sympathetically with those who have homosexual leanings. Scientists have not yet unsnarled the tangle of possible biological dysfunctions or malformations,[169] genetic deficiencies, and environmental influences that lead to homosexual behavior. The issue, however, will be difficult for Latter-day Saints, a difficulty complicated by the Church's long-standing and often legitimate concern about the excesses and fads of the social sciences.[170] Should a clear connection between homosexuality and genetic deficiency be discovered, the entire complex of issues surrounding attitudes toward unborn children—in the areas of abortion, fetal-tissue research, and in utero surgical and medical intervention—will have to be reconciled with doctrines already and still to be revealed through the prophetic direction that Latter-day Saints accept as binding.

Bibliographical Resources on Science, Technology, and Mormonism

A few bibliographies can guide the researcher into specialized material about science, technology, and Mormonism. These bibliographies include the *BYU Studies Index 1959–1991,* which contains categories in science and philosophy and is available on computer microdiskettes in keyword-searchable formats; the twenty-year index to *Dialogue: A Journal of Mormon Thought,* also with separate categories for science, medicine, and philosophy; and a bibliography compiled by James B. Allen, Ronald W. Walker, and David J. Whittaker entitled *Studies in Mormon History,*[171] which will be published soon. *Studies in Mormon History,* a two-volume work, is a detailed and comprehensive guide to historical studies of Mormonism. As such, *Studies in Mormon History* contains only those items on science, technology, and their practitioners deemed worthy of historical significance. The extensive bibliographical essay by Paul[172] and the shorter essay by Oberg and Sessions[173] give selected, critical reviews of key works. The former emphasizes cosmology and evolution, while the latter deals with more general problems of reconciling scientific and religious points of view in a Mormon context.

The most extensive bibliography on science, technology, and Mormon culture is still unpublished. During the 1980s, Robert L. Miller, then archivist for the Science, Medicine and Engineering Collection at the University of Utah, compiled a 342-page typescript entitled "Science/Mormonism Bibliography." The journals and newspapers Miller canvassed were all produced within the Latter-day Saint community (though not all were Church publications). The publications include *Evening and The Morning Star, Messenger and Advocate, Times and Seasons, Latter-day Saints Millennial Star, Journal of Discourses, Deseret News, Deseret News Magazine, Deseret News Weekly, Juvenile Instructor, Women's Exponent, Contributor, Parry's Literary Magazine, Normal, Young Women's Journal, Improvement Era, Ogden Standard Examiner, Salt Lake Tribune, Provo Herald, Utah Educational Review, Utah Historical Quarterly, Ensign, New Era, Friend, BYU Studies, Church News, Dialogue, Sunstone,* and *Journal of Mormon History.* Included also are articles from less well-known journals as well as unpublished talks, including archival material, from a variety of influential lay and ecclesiastical Latter-day Saint thinkers. Books dealing directly with both scientific and theological issues have also been included.

The Miller bibliography lists the articles, books, and talks in three chronological divisions: (1) 1830–1900; (2) 1901–89; and (3) 1830–1989. Parts (1) and (2) are arranged in order of the year in which the article, book, or talk appeared, and within each year alphabetically by the author or by title if no author is given. Part (3) reorganizes the first two parts alphabetically. Part (1) is comprehensive and can therefore be used with confidence by the researcher. Part (2) is not comprehensive, but still represents a helpful starting point for the serious scholar. The bibliography is not annotated; it is a simple but exceedingly useful compilation of publications. It is currently available in the special collections departments at both the University of Utah and Brigham Young University, although researchers must retrieve the cited materials for themselves.

A simple reading of the Miller bibliography reveals interesting aspects of the resources question. One aspect is the timelessness of certain questions. For instance, the *Improvement Era* of March 1918 contains an article by geologist Frederick J. Pack on the question "Should Latter-day Saints Drink Coca-Cola?" No corresponding article appears seventy years later on the test marketing of caffeine-free Coca-Cola Classic in the Intermountain West.

In the early years (pre-1850) of the bibliography, a large number of articles reflect the thought of leading Church authorities, including Parley P. Pratt, Orson Pratt, Brigham Young, and Joseph Smith. Some of these writings address particular controversies, such as evolution or the age of the earth, but the majority of the articles focus on parallels between gospel principles and the discoveries of science, especially physics and astronomy. These discoveries were generally seen as supportive of the conceptual framework of the Restoration. By the early 1970s, however, a number of quite different tendencies appear in the Miller bibliography (always allowing for the fact that its accuracy and completeness are not known for that period). First, the general run of articles in official Church publications is overwhelmingly reactive, dealing with perceived conflicts either between the gospel and scientific discovery or between orthodox Church behavior and a worldview purportedly supported by science. Most of the works dealing with controversial issues are found in unofficial publications. Many of the writers of these works are outside the circle of Church authorities, and few of the pieces are written by the most widely recognized scientists in the Church. The problems and opportunities associated with this "unsponsored sector" of Mormon thought and writing have been discussed elsewhere.[174] The point of this observation is simply to note that quasi-official commentary on science and religion, which appeared so frequently in the Church magazines in the 1930s, 1940s, and 1950s, has now been replaced by largely unofficial commentary.

Another observation from the Miller bibliography is the surprising degree to which the printed material continues to follow the lines of classic debates on evolution and creation that began over a hundred years ago. Mormon scientists, on the one hand, have attempted to relate the continuing discussion of evolution and creation to current scientific thinking.[175] Ecclesiastical leaders, on the other hand, have reaffirmed historic points of doctrine—as reflected, for example, in messages from the First Presidency[176]—while noting that science and religion play distinct roles in the human search for meaning.

Special Collections on Science, Technology, and Mormonism

Brigham Young University, the University of Utah, Utah State University, and the Historical Department of the Church all have special collections relating to science, technology, and Mormon culture. While these collections are by no means comprehensive, they do form an important starting point for any serious investigation. Most of the university collections are primarily based on affiliations with their respective institutions or the state of Utah; significant opportunity exists, therefore, for more general initiatives and collections on themes of general interest.

Brigham Young University Collections. The Special Collections and Manuscripts Division of the Harold B. Lee Library at Brigham Young University has a number of important collections. The collection has no strong focus apart from the fact that most materials come from scientists, engineers, or physicians who have had Brigham Young University affiliations as students or faculty. One of the important major collections is the collected papers of James E. Talmage. From his earliest days as a youthful instructor at the Brigham Young Academy, Talmage liked to be called a chemist, despite his formal training in geology. The Talmage Collection includes classroom notes and texts from Talmage's student days at Lehigh and Johns Hopkins Universities, diaries, papers from Deseret Museum, and some documents from his career as a consulting geologist.[177] Another important collection is the Harvey Fletcher Collection. The collection has about sixty storage boxes of materials relating to Fletcher's career, representing almost all of his career except the Bell Laboratories manuscripts. (The University of Utah has Bell Laboratories manuscripts in photocopy.) Other collections include the papers of Carl F. Eyring and of Franklin S. Harris, both noted agricultural scientists. The Harris memorabilia include thousands of photographs from his trips to the Soviet Union and around the world beginning in the 1920s. The collection also contains the writings of Vasco Tanner. Tanner, who taught zoology at Brigham Young University for forty years and died in the late 1960s, kept a voluminous record of his network with the larger scientific community and contributed an important evaluation of the status of Darwinian approaches to biology. BYU's zoology department had a number of well-known faculty, including Eldon Beck and Herbert Frost, whose papers are also available. Papers of other faculty members include those of biochemist Clark J. Gubler; physicists John Hale Gardner, Wayne B. Hales and Phillip J. Hart; physical chemist Tracy Hall, who contributed works on the synthetic diamond and related high-pressure research; James J. Christensen, chemical engineer and codiscoverer of techniques to filter out trace elements in water; Richard R. Lyman, who was the Utah State Engineer before his call to the Council of the Twelve Apostles; Caleb Tanner and E. O. Larsen, well-known civil engineers, the latter having designed and constructed Deer Creek Dam in Provo Canyon; and Joseph K. Nicholes, a chemist for whom a professorship is named.

Other acquisitions of note include the Eugene Thompson Collection, which contains photocopies of most of the extant official letters and documents relating to Church doctrine and evolution. The Special Collections and Manuscript Division also has the Centennial History Collection, a Brigham Young University institutional file that describes the major achievements of the period 1875 through 1975, including histories written by the various departments and colleges in the 1970s. The collection is available in University Archives, as are the centennial history project research files.

University of Utah Marriott Library Collections. The Manuscript Division at the University of Utah has a collection of papers, books, and diaries of a number of prominent Latter-day Saint scientists, engineers, and physicians, particularly those who have had affiliations with the University of Utah. The Utah Collection emphasizes the papers and memorabilia of prominent Utah-related scientists and entrepreneurs, constituting a record of Utah's heritage in the development of science, medicine, and technology. Most of the collections are cataloged on-line on OCLC and RLIN and are thus searchable by electronic means. The university has no plans at present, however, to make the collection materials themselves electronically accessible.

Most of the collections received to date have been cataloged, and a draft index describes the contents of each collection. The collections include significant personal and technical papers of the following prominent Mormon scientists and technologists (their order is strictly alphabetical): Alan Ashton, former professor of computer science at Brigham Young University and former chief executive officer of software company WordPerfect; Melvin Cook, former professor of metallurgy and director of research at the University of Utah, and founder of IRECO, a pioneering firm in the commercial explosives industry; Ralph V. Chamberlin, a biologist and one of those first recruited to and then dismissed from Brigham Young University in the evolution controversy of 1911; David C. Evans, University of Utah professor of computer science, computer entrepreneur, developer of computer drafting systems; Henry Eyring, theoretical chemist, discoverer of reaction rate theory, University of Utah faculty member and administrator; Philo Taylor Farnsworth, television inventor; Harvey Fletcher, researcher at Bell Telephone Laboratories and later professor of physics at Brigham Young University, often called the "father of stereophonic sound"; James C. Fletcher, scientist, university president, aerospace entrepreneur, and formerly head of the National Aeronautics and Space Administration; Eldon John Gardner, Utah State University geneticist and author of numerous essays on the theory of evolution as it relates to Mormon theology; William R. Gould, formerly a mechanical engineer and later chief executive officer of Southern California Edison, an important innovator both in environmental protection and in the electrical power industry; George R. Hill, formerly EIMCO Professor of Chemical and Fuels Engineering at the University of Utah, and former director of the U.S. Office of Coal Research; Frederick J. Pack, Deseret Professor of Geology at the University of Utah; Ellis Shipp, early Utah physician trained at Temple University, Philadelphia; James Edward Talmage, geologist, University of Utah professor, and later a member of the Quorum of the Twelve Apostles; and a number of important contemporary figures in the biomedical sciences, such as John A. Dixon, R. Adams Cowley, and Ewart Swinyard. Many of the collections include personal memorabilia, photographs, unpublished documents, journals, lecture notes, and correspondence, in addition to published papers.

Aside from the foregoing, the university has other collections relating to the practice of medicine in rural Utah, the development of mineral resources, and water projects in the state of Utah. An extensive collection of tape-recorded interviews includes comments by University of Utah faculty members on issues related to Mormonism and science and to relations between Latter-day Saints and others on the campus. Particularly prominent in these interviews are questions related to attitudes about the theory of evolution and to science and religion issues as these were explored on the University of Utah campus.

Utah State University Collections. Through the 1930s, Utah State University, formerly the Utah State Agricultural College, was the cradle of scientific agricultural studies in the Intermountain West, and its alumni have distinguished themselves internationally in both academic and government posts. The Utah State University Archives and Special Collections division has many important papers and collections concerning water engineering and agricultural studies. In addition, individual colleges also maintain collections of material from their own faculties. Joel Edward Ricks has compiled an important summary of the 1888–1938 period for Utah State University.[178]

The Archives and Special Collections Division has all of Elder John A. Widtsoe's presidential papers stemming from the era of his scientific investigations of dry farming and his energetic attempts to develop extension agriculture services in Utah (1907–16). The Water Research Laboratory, the center of irrigation engineering studies at Utah State, has also contributed a large collection of papers. The collection includes the papers of Orson Winso Israelsen, a distinguished professor in the Department of Agricultural and Irrigation Engineering at Utah State University, whose classic *Irrigation Principles and Practices* was translated into a dozen languages. The Division also has manuscripts and papers of faculty and alumni who have made significant contributions outside the University, such as George Dewey Clyde, who served on the staff of the Agricultural Experiment Station and as a faculty member of the College, later as Dean of Engineering, and eventually as Governor of Utah.

Both the University of Utah and Utah State University have played significant roles in space research and engineering in Utah. While many of the documents from the Utah State projects are presently under confidentiality restrictions and therefore have not yet been cataloged, a history of the projects has been published.[179] Faculty publications in all areas are cataloged on-line and logged in alphabetical order. The catalog, of course, contains no explicit indication of religious affiliation. Here, the researcher interested specifically in Mormon scientists would need to develop that information through other sources.

Historical Department of the Church Collections. The Historical Department of the Church has not purposely set out to develop an archive focusing on science and technology. The department nevertheless contains a comprehensive collection of books, magazines, and journals relevant to this topic in its general collection. Archival material on individuals has been collected and cataloged, but normally only if an individual has been an ecclesiastical leader or became prominent in the history of the Church. Important material on Orson Pratt, for instance, is only available in the Historical Department. Access to these materials is open to anyone with a demonstrated scholarly purpose consonant with the current Church guidelines for research.

Conclusions

The foregoing survey of the literature on science, technology, and Mormonism discloses a number of important resources and trends. First, a surprising amount of material exists, but much of it is scattered through unofficial sources that are not generally known outside a relatively small community of scholars. Even those resources in libraries remain largely unanalyzed and unexplored. Most of the collections are also based on institutional or geographical connections rather than thematic areas for scholarly inquiry. Therefore, much work remains in both of these areas. And in all cases, much more attention needs to be given to the activities of Mormon scientists and technologists living outside the Intermountain West who now vastly outnumber those whose activities have brought them into association with Utah universities.

A first critical project is to develop a complete and computerized bibliographical resource. In scientific and technological fields, the rapid growth of literature—usually exponential, with a doubling time measured in periods of ten to twenty years[180]—testifies to the importance of wide dissemination of material for critical analysis and discussion. The doubling time of literature on science, technology, and Mormonism appears, even from the incomplete record of Miller's "Science/Mormonism Bibliography," to be somewhere between fifty and one hundred years. This doubling time testifies to the relative lack of scholarly activity on the subject. Though incomplete, Robert Miller's bibliography still seems to be a useful starting point for this project, and we hope that this work will find the support necessary for its swift completion.

For Latter-day Saint scientists and technologists, the need for more information represents a signal opportunity to develop once again a corpus of literature that will explain science and technology to the Latter-day Saint layperson. Outside the Church, the present is a golden age of science-writing for the general public; we think of Lewis Thomas, Stephen Hawking, Isaac Asimov, Robert Jastrow, and Henry Petroski, among others. Inside the Church, on the other hand, people have scarcely been touched by the impulse to explain in ordinary English the substance of science's deepest explorations of nature and their significance for Latter-day Saint belief and practice. Church members, of course, now live in countries with the widest possible range of scientific and technological sophistication, and with cultural perspectives on science which range from enthusiasm to deep suspicion. However, we suspect that the hunger for science writing, especially as its findings may relate to Church doctrine and practice, will always be great.

The biggest unfilled need for knowledge about science and technology appears to be in the area of ethics. For the typical Latter-day Saint, technology's seemingly inexorable modification of social and family ties is very real. Yet Mormons talk and write relatively little about the impact of modern medical practice on their perceptions of death and dying, to say nothing of the historic Mormon theology of stewardship as it relates to agriculture, animals, and the environment. Virtually no systematic studies exist for the Latter-day Saint scholar or layperson comparable to the immense body of religious and secular commentaries on social responsibilities of scientists, or about the impact of technology on the temporal and spiritual welfare of Latter-day Saints and others. Thus far, we have no Jacques Ellul, Leo Marx, or Lewis Mumford among the Mormons.

While the need for specific bibliographical resources is great, the greatest need is for a renewal of the confidence that earlier Latter-day Saint scholars seem to have felt in relating the changing interpretations of science to the eternal perspectives of the gospel. The changes in attitudes among Church members toward science parallel the ups and downs of their attitudes about intellectuals in general, as Davis Bitton demonstrated a quarter century ago.[181]

Given that "opposition in all things" seems to be part of the human condition, the current situation probably should not be surprising. We believe, however, that the pendulum has now swung away from equilibrium. Science will not go away, and technology will continue to shape the fabric of society. Both science and technology are vast and successful enterprises, explaining many of the mysteries of this wondrous universe in which we live and using that knowledge for the benefit of humankind. Many scientists and technologists, both those inside the Church and out, can find evidence of the Divine in nature even as they employ their most sophisticated tools to forge an entirely scientific explanation of their findings. Science has historically been overwhelmingly a liberating, democratizing, healing force in human society. Furthermore, as we have pointed out in the case of evolution, the self-correcting impulses of science appear to lead back, in the end, to a picture of the universe that is generally consistent—in many fascinating respects—with the picture revealed by Latter-day Saint prophets and scripture. Treating science and scientists as the enemies of true religion will not help Latter-day Saints comprehend how scientific understanding relates to the revealed words of the scriptures. If for no other reason than the fact that the origins of modern science are deeply rooted in the religious values that undergirded the Protestant Reformation and, *mutatis mutandi,* the Restoration, science and technology should be viewed as a vital part of the underpinnings of Mormon culture.

A century ago, the conflict paradigm for the relationship between science and religion was propounded by Andrew D. White and John W. Draper.[182] That paradigm was based on what Latter-day Saints would properly consider an incomplete view of religious faith and on what a modern scientist would view as an extremely naive picture of the character of science and scientific knowledge. Ironically, many

Mormons have accepted the conflict model despite the long history of conciliatory statements by the great majority of Church authorities and in the face of overwhelming evidence that conflict is neither inevitable nor productive.[183] At the same time, another paradox exists: Mormon acceptance of and optimism about technology remains high though certainly not uncritical,[184] even as troubling questions are being raised about technology's impact on human society and culture outside the Church.

As scientists have tried to justify their work to an increasingly skeptical public, they have become much more sophisticated in their perception of science as a cultural and intellectual enterprise. Recent scholarship in the history and sociology of science has softened some of the most naive and notorious conceits about the extent to which the results of scientific inquiry reflect reality. At the same time, studies of science by historians and sociologists have demonstrated that science is in fact a human enterprise in which loose ends and untidy conclusions are part and parcel of the business.[185]

> if truth is a number
> not only is it never
> in the back of the book
>
> but it never comes out even
> ends in a fraction
> cannot be rounded off.
>
> Approximation
> was the first art.
> It is the only science.[186]

If science is only an approximation, and if God has yet to reveal "many great and important things pertaining to the Kingdom of God,"[187] we have the glorious option of exploring many ways, including both the scientific and the religious, to find our bearings in the cosmos.

The most important resource for the study of science, technology, and Mormon culture would be a recovered sense of confidence in the power of the human mind, guided by the divine spirit of God, to answer in the affirmative the ancient question, "Canst thou by searching find out God?" (Job 11:7) Latter-day Saint history and the beginnings of a literature about science, technology, and Mormon culture suggest that these endeavors, like everything else that is praiseworthy, lovely or of good report, lead—if sometimes by circuitous routes—back to the traces left by a loving Creator on his creations. "Ye have," as the Book of Mormon prophet Alma wrote, "all things as a testimony unto you" that "there is a God and that Christ shall come" (Alma 30:39-41).

Richard F. Haglund Jr., is Professor of Physics at Vanderbilt University, Nashville, Tennessee; Erich Robert Paul was the Joseph Priestly Professor of the History of Science and Professor of Computer Science at Dickinson College, Carlisle, Pennsylvania. Erich Paul died on October 12, 1994.

This work owes much to many. It is a great pleasure to thank Jenny Broadbent (Marriott Library of the University of Utah), for sharing the still unpublished index to the library's collection; Hollis Johnson (Indiana University), for helpful leads, especially in the areas of technology, astronomy, and cosmology; Robert Miller, for access to his unpublished bibliography on science and Mormonism and for helpful suggestions on the text and references; Robert Parson (Utah State University Library), for information on the library's collections related to water projects, agriculture, and space science in Utah; Sterling B. Weede (North Carolina State University), for his recollections of prominent Latter-day Saints in the food and agricultural sciences; and David J. Whittaker (Brigham Young University), for the material about the BYU special collections, for helpful criticism of first drafts, and for his seemingly endless store of information about important sources.

NOTES

[1]Brigham Young, *Journal of Discourses,* 26 vols. (Liverpool: F. D. Richards, 1855-86), 1:334-35 (December 5, 1853).

[2]Erich Robert Paul, "Science and Religion," in *Encyclopedia of Mormonism,* ed. Daniel H. Ludlow, 5 vols. (New York: Macmillan, 1991), 3:1270-72.

[3]John Henry Evans, *Joseph Smith: An American Prophet* (New York: Macmillan, 1933). Republished by Deseret Book (Salt Lake City, 1989).

[4]B. H. Roberts, *Joseph Smith: The Prophet Teacher* (1908). Republished with an introduction by Sterling McMurrin (Princeton, N.J.: Deseret Club of Princeton University, 1967). In this work, Roberts used the term "eternalism" to describe the philosophical character of Joseph Smith's thought and revelations.

[5]See, for example, John A. Widtsoe, *How Science Contributes to Religion* (Salt Lake City: n.p., 1927), a course of study for the Church's Mutual Improvement Association. An important general work on this topic by a Latter-day Saint scientist is that of Franklin S. Harris with Newburn I. Butt, *Scientific Research and Human Welfare* (New York: Macmillan, 1924).

[6]Spencer W. Kimball, "When the World Will Be Converted," *Ensign* 4 (October 1974): 2-14.

[7]Kenneth R. Hardy, "Social Origins of American Scientists," *Science* 185 (1974): 497-506. For earlier studies, see E. L. Thorndike, "The Production, Retention and Attraction of American Men of Science," *Science* 92 (August 16, 1940): 137-41; see also Thorndike's "The Origin of Superior Men," *Scientific Monthly* 56 (May 1943): 424-33.

[8]Robert L. Miller, "Science and Scientists," in *Encyclopedia of Mormonism* 3:1272-75. This unusual pattern of activity was noted by Thomas F. O'Dea in *The Mormons* (Chicago: University of Chicago Press, 1957), 238-39. It has been

substantiated in recent studies as well. See David John Buerger, "Highly Educated Mormons Are More Religious, Study Shows," *Sunstone* 10 (March 1985): 51; and Brent Harker, "Academic Minds, Religious Hearts," *BYU Today* 39 (April 1985): 16.

[9]Sterling M. McMurrin, *The Philosophical Foundations of Mormon Theology* (Salt Lake City: University of Utah Press, 1959); and Miller, "Science and Scientists," 1272.

[10]See, for example, a number of statements quoted in David H. Bailey, "Scientific Foundations of Mormon Theology," *Dialogue* 21 (Summer 1988): 61-80; and Paul, "Science and Religion," 1271-72.

[11]Gary James Bergera, "The 1911 Evolution Controversy at Brigham Young University," in *The Search for Harmony: Essays on Science and Mormonism*, ed. Gene A. Sessions and Craig J. Oberg (Salt Lake City: Signature Books, 1993), 23-41; and Richard Sherlock, "Campus in Crisis: BYU in 1911," *Sunstone* 4 (January-February 1979): 10-16.

[12]Richard Sherlock, "We Can See No Advantage to a Continuation of the Discussion: The Roberts-Smith-Talmage Affair," *Dialogue* 13 (Fall 1980): 63-78. See James B. Allen, "The Story of *The Truth, the Way, the Life,*" in B. H. Roberts, *The Truth, the Way, the Life* (Provo, Utah: BYU Studies, 1994), clxxxv-clxxxviii.

[13]Gene A. Sessions and Craig J. Oberg, "The Mormon Retreat from Science," editors' introduction to *The Search for Harmony: Essays on Science and Mormonism,* v-xxii.

[14]The intellectual positions taken by evangelical Christians are complex and have evolved over time. For instance, it is only in the last several decades, with the establishment of the Creation Research Society (1963), that evangelicals relinquished a more liberal view of the age of the earth and adopted a literal 6,000-year period. See Ronald L. Numbers, *The Creationists* (New York: Alfred A. Knopf, 1992), chs. 6-9; and Erich Robert Paul, *Science, Religion, and Mormon Cosmology* (Urbana: University of Illinois Press, 1992), 180-81.

[15]For a survey of the relationship between science and religion from a general Judaeo-Christian perspective, see Ian G. Barbour, *Religion in an Age of Science* (New York: HarperCollins, 1990).

[16]John A. Widtsoe, *Evidences and Reconciliations*, 3 vols. (Salt Lake City: Bookcraft, 1943, 1947, 1951). The currently available volume is John A. Widtsoe, *Evidences and Reconciliations*, arr. G. Homer Durham (Salt Lake City: Bookcraft, 1987).

[17]John A. Widtsoe, *Science and the Gospel* (Salt Lake City: General Board, YMMIA, 1908); and Widtsoe, *How Science Contributes to Religion.*

[18]Merrill, a member of the Engineering faculty at the University of Utah before his call to the Quorum of the Twelve Apostles, received a doctorate in physics from Johns Hopkins in 1899. Joseph F. Merrill, *The Truth-Seeker and Mormonism* (Independence, Mo.: Zion's Printing and Publishing, 1946), is a collection of radio addresses.

[19]John R. Talmage, *The Talmage Story: Life of James E. Talmage—Educator, Scientist, Apostle* (Salt Lake City: Bookcraft, 1972). See also Dennis Rowley, "Inner Dialogue: James Talmage's Choice of Science as a Career, 1876-1884," *Dialogue* 7 (Autumn 1970): 3-12.

[20]Dale LeCheminant, "John A. Widtsoe: Rational Apologist" (Ph.D. diss., University of Utah, 1977).

[21]Edward L. Kimball, "Harvey Fletcher and Henry Eyring: Men of Faith and Science," *Dialogue* 15 (Autumn 1982): 74-86; and Steven H. Heath, "The

Reconciliation of Faith and Science: Henry Eyring's Achievement," *Dialogue* 15 (Autumn 1982): 87-99.

[22]John A. Widtsoe, *In a Sunlit Land* (Salt Lake City: Deseret News Press, 1952).

[23]Henry Eyring, *The Faith of a Scientist* (Salt Lake City: Bookcraft, 1967).

[24]Among numerous possible examples, one can list the following articles: Frank B. Salisbury (geneticist), "Our Organized Universe," *Instructor* 102 (June 1967): 226-29; Thomas J. Parmley (physicist), "Proclaim the Handiwork of God," 102 (July 1967): 272-74; Henry Eyring (chemist), "Obedience is the Price of Freedom," *Instructor* 101 (1966): 166-67; and H. Tracy Hall (materials scientist), "A Scientist Looks at the Miracles of Jesus," *Instructor* 101 (March 1966): 86-87.

[25]Robert C. Fletcher, "One Scientist's Spiritual Autobiography," in *A Thoughtful Faith,* ed. Philip L. Barlow (Centerville, Utah: Canon Press, 1986), 127-36.

[26]Russell M. Nelson, *From Heart to Heart: An Autobiography* (Salt Lake City: By the author, 1979). In criticizing the thesis of a book in which the author claims that English physicist Michael Faraday's deep religious commitment must have influenced his scientific activities, Charles Tanford (who is not LDS) used the example of his mentor, Henry Eyring. Observing that Eyring was a devout Mormon and a brilliant scientist, Tanford states that nothing in Eyring's professional writings or classroom presentations would suggest that his religion directed his scientific pursuits (Charles Tanford, "Religious Resonances," *Nature* 351 [1991]: 705).

[27]John A. Widtsoe, *A Rational Theology* (Salt Lake City: Deseret News, 1915).

[28]John A Widtsoe, *In Search of Truth* (Salt Lake City: Deseret Book, 1930).

[29]Merrill, *The Truth-Seeker and Mormonism.*

[30]Frederick J. Pack, *Science and Belief in God* (Salt Lake City: Deseret News Press, 1924).

[31]Joseph Fielding Smith, *Man, His Origin and Destiny* (Salt Lake City: Deseret Book, 1954).

[32]Paul A. Green, ed., *Science and Your Faith in God* (Salt Lake City: Bookcraft, 1958). Chapter authors include Henry Eyring, Harvey Fletcher, Franklin S. Harris, Joseph F. Merrill, Frederick J. Pack, and John A. Widtsoe.

[33]Lowell L. Bennion, *Religion and the Pursuit of Truth* (Salt Lake City: Deseret Book, 1959), especially chapters 2, 3, 5, and 9. See also Bennion's "The Uses of the Mind in Religion," *BYU Studies* 14 (Autumn 1973): 47-55.

[34]Frank B. Salisbury, *Truth by Reason and by Revelation* (Salt Lake City: Deseret Book, 1965). The book was reviewed by F. Kent Nielsen in *BYU Studies* 7 (Autumn 1965): 87-88.

[35]R. Grant Athay, "Astrophysics and Mormonism: Parallel Paths to Truth," in *The Search for Harmony,* ed., Sessions and Oberg, 249-56.

[36]Richard F. Haglund Jr., "Science and Religion: A Symbiosis," *Dialogue* 8 (Fall 1973): 23-40.

[37]Erich Robert Paul, "Science: Forever Tentative?" *Dialogue* 24 (Summer 1991): 119-26.

[38]John A. Widtsoe, "Joseph Smith as Scientist," *The Improvement Era* 7 (November 1903-October 1904): 1-8, 81-86, 161-67, 241-47, 337-44, 401-9, 501-9, 561-70, 699-705, 737-42, 897-902. See also Widtsoe's book *Joseph Smith as Scientist: A Contribution to Mormon Philosophy* (Salt Lake City: General Board, YMMIA, 1908). The current edition was published in Salt Lake City by Publishers Press in 1990.

[39]Bailey, "Scientific Foundations of Mormon Theology."

[40]Widtsoe, *Joseph Smith as Scientist,* 29 and chs. 1-4. See also Paul, *Science, Religion, and Mormon Cosmology,* 158.

[41]In the history of science, the word *paradigm* has come to have a technical meaning as that body of data and theory which comprise the accepted description of phenomena at any given time. Scientific revolutions are thus seen as devolving from a paradigm shift. The concept was first elaborated by Thomas Kuhn, *The Structure of Scientific Revolutions*, 2d ed. (Chicago: University of Chicago Press, 1970).

[42]Richard F. Haglund Jr., "Is There a Cure for Authoritarianism in Physics?" in *By Study and Also by Faith: Essays Honoring Hugh Nibley,* ed. John M. Lundquist and Stephen D. Ricks, 2 vols. (Salt Lake City: Deseret Book; and Provo, Utah: F.A.R.M.S., 1991), 2:438-55.

[43]Michael Polanyi, *Science, Faith and Society* (Chicago: University of Chicago Press, 1964). See also Polanyi's *The Tacit Dimension* (Gloucester, Mass.: Peter Smith, 1966).

[44]Among the more interesting papers written on this aspect of science is Sir Peter Medawar, "Is the Scientific Paper Fraudulent?" reprinted in *The Threat and the Glory: Reflections on Science and Scientists,* ed. David Pyke (New York: HarperCollins Publishers, 1990).

[45]Jacques Barzun, *Science: The Glorious Entertainment* (New York: Harper and Row, 1967).

[46]Stephen G. Brush, "Should the History of Science Be Rated X?" *Science* 183 (March 3, 1974): 1164-67; and Richard S. Westfall, "Newton and the Fudge Factor," *Science* 179 (1973): 751-58.

[47]The most familiar discussion of this problem is C. P. Snow's classic *The Two Cultures: And a Second Look* (Cambridge: Cambridge University Press, 1969). Another engaging presentation is Jacob Bronowski's dialogue "The Abacus and the Rose," in his *Science and Human Values,* rev. ed. (New York: Harper and Row, 1965).

[48]In addition to specific attempts to deal with science in the context of Latter-day Saint religion, important essays on the popularization of science exist within the Mormon community. Several of these essays on scientific and technological topics are found in *BYU Studies* and are listed in the *BYU Studies* index volume, *BYU Studies* 31 (Fall 1991).

[49]For a personal example of the importance of this factor, see Richard Pearson Smith, "Science: A Part of or Apart from Mormonism?" *Dialogue* 19 (Spring 1986): 106-22.

[50]From the numerous sources, we cite the following representative examples. First, during the 1880s and 1890s, James E. Talmage authored a series of articles in *The Contributor* on everything from "The Microscope" and "Living Lights of the Air" to "Flies and Gnats." Second, the *Juvenile Instructor* of 1892 (27:589-90, 638-39) lists a fairly technical article by John Ritchie Jr., "The Astronomer and His Work," which describes in detail the tools and models of astronomy in that era. Third, a series of articles on famous universities in the *Juvenile Instructor* begins with a piece by Lewis T. Cannon, "The Massachusetts Institute of Technology," *Juvenile Instructor* 29 (1894): 468-72. Other institutions profiled in the same series included the University of Michigan, Harvard University, and Cornell University. Fourth, Franklin S. Harris and N. I. Butt penned a series of six articles entitled "Heroes of Science" on the lives of Liebig, Henry, Bunsen,

Welsbach, Röntgen, and Helmholtz, in *Improvement Era* 27 (serialized in the June-December issues of 1924); the series continued in 1925 with studies of Mendel, Goodyear, Lister, Mme. Curie, Bell, and Edison. Franklin S. Harris continued into the 1960s with the latest news about science and technology in his *Improvement Era* column "Discovering Our Universe."

[51]See, for example, Oberg and Sessions, "The Mormon Retreat from Science," editors' introduction to Oberg and Sessions, *The Search for Harmony,* v-xxii. See also Erich Robert Paul's review essay of Oberg and Sessions in *Sunstone* 18 (April 1995): 74-78.

[52]Morris S. Petersen, "Fossils and the Scriptures," *Ensign* 17 (September 1987): 28-29.

[53]"Evolution" 2:478; "Science and Religion" 3:1270-72; and "Science and Scientists" 3: 1272-75.

[54]Russell M. Nelson, "The Magnificence of Man," *Ensign* 18 (January 1988): 64-69.

[55]For example, Sir Fred Hoyle observes that "A junkyard contains all the bits and pieces of a Boeing 747, dismembered and in disarray. A whirlwind happens to blow through the yard. What is the chance that after its passage a fully assembled 747, ready to fly, will be found standing there? So small as to be negligible, even if a tornado were to blow through enough junkyards to fill the whole Universe." *The Intelligent Universe* (New York: Holt, Rinehart and Winston, 1983), 19.

[56]One of the more accessible guides to this material, particularly that relating to cosmology and creation, is the bibliography in Paul, *Science, Religion, and Mormon Cosmology,* 246-57.

[57]See "Signs in the Heavens," *The Evening and the Morning Star* 2 (December 1833): 116; and Paul, *Science, Religion, and Mormon Cosmology,* 106-7, 122.

[58]John Ritchie Jr., "The Astronomer and His Work," *The Juvenile Instructor* 27 (October 1, 1852): 589-90, 638-39.

[59]Orson Pratt, *Key to the Universe, or a New Theory of Its Mechanism,* second edition adapted from the first European edition (Salt Lake City: Historian's Office, 1879).

[60]Erich Robert Paul, *Science, Religion and Mormon Cosmology* (Urbana: University of Illinois Press, 1992).

[61]In recent years, several scholars have explored the plurality of worlds in the broader European and Anglo-American context. See Steven J. Dick, *Plurality of Worlds: The Origins of the Extraterrestrial Life Debate from Democritus to Kant* (New York: Cambridge University Press, 1982); and Michael J. Crowe, *The Extraterrestrial Life Debate, 1750-1900: The Idea of a Plurality of Worlds from Kant to Lowell* (New York: Cambridge University Press, 1986).

[62]R. Grant Athay, "Worlds without Number: The Astronomy of Enoch, Abraham, and Moses," *BYU Studies* 8 (Spring 1968): 255-69; and R. Grant Athay, "Astrophysics and the Gospel," *New Era* 2 (September 1972): 14-19.

[63]See Hollis R. Johnson, "Civilizations Out in Space," *BYU Studies* 11 (Autumn 1970): 3-12; and Erich Robert Paul, "Extraterrestrial Intelligence and Mormon Cosmology," in *Science, Religion, and Mormon Cosmology,* 192-227.

[64]F. Kent Nielsen and Stephen D. Ricks, "Creation, Creation Accounts," in *Encyclopedia of Mormonism* 1:340-43, including the references therein. A related article by Keith Norman, "Adam's Navel," *Dialogue* 21 (Summer 1988): 81-97, gives detailed comparisons of the Mormon creation narratives with those of the Old Testament and the ancient Near East.

[65]F. Kent Nielsen, "The Gospel and the Scientific View: How the Earth Came to Be," *Ensign* 10 (September 1980): 67–72.

[66]A. R. Peacocke, *Creation and the World of Science* (Oxford: Clarendon, 1979). This book is an adaptation of the author's Bampton Lectures, the stated purpose for which is "to confirm and establish the Christian Faith."

[67]An authoritative summary of this point of view is that of the Apostle James E. Talmage, "The Earth and Man," *Deseret News* Church Section, November 21, 1931, 7–8.

[68]Paul, *Science, Religion, and Mormon Cosmology*, 183. Phelps's original estimate comes from *Times and Seasons* 5 (January 1, 1844): 759. This number is precisely 7,000 (earth-years since creation) times 365 (days/earth-year) times 1,000 (earth-years/divine day). Whether the foregoing calculation was the basis for Phelps's estimate is not known. See Bruce R. McConkie, *The Mortal Messiah: From Bethlehem to Calvary*, 4 vols. (Salt Lake City: Deseret Book, 1979–81), 1:29.

[69]Talmage, "The Earth and Man."

[70]George McCready Price, *The New Geology: A Textbook for Colleges, Normal Schools, and Training Schools; and for the General Reader* (Mountain View, Calif.: Pacific Press Publishing Association, 1923).

[71]Elder Talmage's ideas and the questions about scriptural accounts of the creation raised by the fossil record have been described in Petersen, "Fossils and the Scriptures," 28–29. A more general account of creationist ideas in the framework of the scientific issues is given in Numbers, *The Creationists*, 308–14.

[72]Numbers, *The Creationists*, 306–14.

[73]Melvin A. Cook, *Science and Mormonism* (Salt Lake City: Deseret Book, 1967); and Cook, *Prehistory and Earth Models* (London: Max Parrish, 1966).

[74]Melvin A. Cook, "Where is the Earth's Radiogenic Helium?" *Nature* 179 (1957): 213. More than four decades later, this question turned up as central to the controversy over so-called cold fusion. See S. E. Jones, E. P. Palmer, J. B. Czirr, D. L. Decker, G. L. Jensen, J. M. Thorne, S. F. Taylor, and J. Rafelski, "Observation of Cold Nuclear Fusion in Condensed Matter," *Nature* 338 (1989): 737–40. Later, Cook expanded on his concerns about radiological and other dating schemes in "Do Radiological Clocks Need Repair?" *Creation Research Society Quarterly* 5 (October 1968): 70, a publication of the evangelical Creation Research Society.

[75]William Lee Stokes, *The Creation Scriptures: A Witness for God in the Scientific Age* (Bountiful, Utah: Horizon Publishers, 1979).

[76]Frank J. Salisbury, *The Creation* (Salt Lake City: Bookcraft, 1976)

[77]In the "I Have a Question" section of the *Ensign*, Morris Petersen answered the following question: "Do we know how the earth's history as indicated from fossils fits with the earth's history as the scriptures present it?" Petersen, a Brigham Young University professor, professional geologist, and stake president, advanced the view that the earth is billions of years old and rejected the view of Mormon creation-science advocates that the earth was created in either six days or six thousand years (*Ensign* 17 [September 1987]: 28–29).

[78]In the "I Have a Question" section of the *Ensign*, Thomas R. Valletta answered the following question: "Does Abraham's usage of 'time' lead us to understand that the Creation was not confined to six 24-hour days as we know them?" Valletta, an institute instructor in the Church Educational System, wrote that the term *day* is "used in scripture to indicate the period wherein the labor of God is performed" and that "each 'day' may not even be of the same length" (*Ensign* 24 [January 1994]: 53–54).

[79]Wilford M. Hess and Ray T. Matheny, eds., *Background for Man: Preparation of the Earth,* vol. 1 of *Science and Religion: Toward a More Useful Dialogue* (Geneva, Ill.: Paladin House Publishers, 1979).

[80]This view is stated in numerous places in modern scriptures (see, for example, Doctrine and Covenants 77) and clarified authoritatively by the First Presidency of the Church in two doctrinal expositions: "The Origin of Man," by Joseph F. Smith, John R. Winder, and Anthon H. Lund (1909); and "'Mormon' View of Evolution," by Heber J. Grant, Anthony W. Ivins, and Charles W. Nibley (1925). These two documents are partially reproduced in the *Encyclopedia of Mormonism* 4:1665–70. See also note 176 for the original citations.

[81]George Q. Cannon, "Origin of Man," *Latter-day Saints' Millennial Star* 23 (October 1861): 651.

[82]Statement by Heber J. Grant, Anthony W. Ivins, and Charles W. Nibley, First Presidency Minutes, April 7, 1931. Quoted by William E. Evenson, "Evolution," in *Encyclopedia of Mormonism* 1:478.

[83]The response of social scientists to the Darwinian paradigm has been described at length by Robert J. Richard, *Darwin and the Emergence of Evolutionary Theories of Mind and Behavior* (Chicago: University of Chicago Press, 1987).

[84]Bruce R. McConkie, *Mormon Doctrine,* 2d ed. (Salt Lake City: Bookcraft, 1966), 247.

[85]Clark A. Peterson, *Using the Book of Mormon to Combat Falsehoods in Organic Evolution* (Springville, Utah: Cedar Fort, 1992).

[86]See the review of Clark Peterson's book by Michael F. Whiting, "Lamarck, Giraffes, and the Sermon on the Mount," in *Review of Books on the Book of Mormon* 5 (1993): 209–22.

[87]Ronald L. Numbers, "The Creationists," in *God and Nature: Historical Essays on the Encounter between Christianity and Science*, eds. David C. Lindberg and Ronald L. Numbers (Berkeley: University of California Press, 1986), 398–99.

[88]Roberts's motivation and approach to the problem of reconciling the gospel with philosophy and science have been described by Truman G. Madsen in *Defender of the Faith: The B. H. Roberts Story* (Salt Lake City: Bookcraft, 1980), ch. 17. See also Truman G. Madsen, "The Meaning of Christ—*The Truth, the Way, the Life:* An Analysis of B. H. Roberts' Unpublished Masterwork," *BYU Studies* 15 (Spring 1975): 259-92. "The Truth, the Way, the Life" was not published in Roberts's lifetime because a few parts of it were not approved by the Reading Committee of the Quorum of the Twelve Apostles, one member of which was Elder Joseph Fielding Smith. Roberts chose to leave the work unpublished rather than correct or change it. The manuscript, together with several introductory essays, was published twice, separately, in 1994. B. H. Roberts, *The Truth, the Way, the Life: An Elementary Treatise on Theology,* ed. John W. Welch (Provo, Utah: BYU Studies, 1994); and B. H. Roberts, *The Truth, the Way, the Life,* ed. Stan Larson (San Francisco: Smith Research Associates, 1994).

[89]Numbers, "The Creationists," 398.

[90]See, for example, the report of the debate at the famous 1980 Chicago conference on whether microevolution—the well-studied evolution *within* species—can lead to macroevolution (change from one species to another). The short answer, according to Roger Lewin's report, was "No." See his "Evolutionary Theory under Fire," *Science* 210 (1980): 883–85.

[91]James Q. Wilson, *The Moral Sense* (New York: Free Press, 1993), especially p. 140.

[92]Boyd K. Packer, "The Pattern of Our Parentage," *Ensign* 17 (November 1984): 66-69.

[93]Boyd K. Packer, "The Law and the Light," in *To Learn with Joy,* ed. Monte S. Nyman and Charles D. Tate (Provo: Religious Studies Center, Brigham Young University, 1990), 10.

[94]Stuart A. Kauffman, *The Origins of Order* (New York: Oxford University Press, 1993), especially chapter 1. The question of evolution in a cosmological setting is discussed by Sir Fred Hoyle in *The Intelligent Universe* (New York: Holt, Rinehart and Winston, 1984).

[95]Numbers, *The Creationists,* 308. The percentage of students who do *not* believe that human life evolved from "lower animals" rose from 36 percent in the mid-1930s to 81 percent in 1973.

[96]Duane E. Jeffery, "Seers, Savants, and Evolution: The Uncomfortable Interface," *Dialogue* 8 (Fall/Winter 1973-74): 41-75.

[97]*Evolution and the Origin of Man,* informational packet distributed at Brigham Young University, October 1992.

[98]Brigham Young University *Daily Universe,* November 12, 1992, 3. Professor Evenson was Dean of the College of Physical and Mathematical Sciences and a professor of physics at the time he made this statement. See also Evenson, "Evolution," in *Encyclopedia of Mormonism* 2:478; and Evenson, "Science: The Universe, Creation, and Evolution," in B. H. Roberts, *The Truth, the Way, the Life: An Elementary Treatise on Theology,* ed. John W. Welch (Provo, Utah: BYU Studies, 1994), cxi-cxxix.

[99]A. R. Peacocke, *God and the New Biology* (London: J. M. Dent, 1986).

[100]Vasco M. Tanner, "Charles Darwin after One Hundred Years," *BYU Studies* 2 (Fall-Winter 1959-60): 43-53. The complete body of Tanner's papers is currently being organized for scholarly use at Brigham Young University's Harold B. Lee Library.

[101]Eldon J. Gardner, "Organic Evolution and the Bible," in *The Search for Harmony,* 189-222.

[102]Wilford M. Hess, Raymond T. Matheny, and Donlu D. Thayer, eds., *The Appearance of Man: Replenishment of the Earth,* vol. 2 of *Science and Religion: Toward a More Useful Dialogue* (Geneva, Ill.: Paladin House Publishers, 1979).

[103]See John Horgan's review, "In the Beginning . . .," in *Scientific American* 264 (February 1991): 116-25.

[104]Stuart A. Kauffman, "Antichaos and Adaptation," *Scientific American* 265 (August 1991): 78-84; Per Bak and Kan Chen, "Self-Organized Criticality," *Scientific American* 264 (January 1991): 46-53.

[105]For a summary, see Ilya Prigogine and Isabelle Stengers, *Order out of Chaos: Man's New Dialogue with Nature* (New York: Bantam Books, 1984), particularly p. 190.

[106]Kauffman, *Origins of Order,* chapters 2-4.

[107]David M. Grant, "Matter," in *Encyclopedia of Mormonism* 3:868-69.

[108]Doctrine and Covenants 93:29-35; 131:7-8. See also the reports of the "King Follett Discourse" given by Joseph Smith on April 7, 1844, as recorded by various Church members. The reports are reproduced in Andrew F. Ehat and Lyndon W. Cook, comps. and eds., *The Words of Joseph Smith: The Contemporary*

Accounts of the Nauvoo Discourses of the Prophet Joseph, Religious Studies Monograph Series, vol. 6 (Salt Lake City: Bookcraft, 1980), 340-62.

[109]Parley P. Pratt, *Key to the Science of Theology* (Liverpool: Franklin D. Richards, 1855) and *The Millennium and Other Poems: To Which Is Annexed a Treatise on the Regeneration and Eternal Duration of Matter* (New York: W. Molineux, 1840). A detailed discussion of the significance of Pratt's early influence on the systematization of Mormon theology is given by Peter Crawley, "Parley P. Pratt: Father of Mormon Pamphleteering," *Dialogue* 15 (Autumn 1982): 13-26.

[110]Orson Pratt, *The Absurdities of Immaterialism* (Liverpool: R. James, 1849). For an analysis, see David J. Whittaker, "Orson Pratt: Prolific Pamphleteer," *Dialogue* 15 (Autumn 1982): 27-41.

[111]The most comprehensive analysis of the Pratt brothers' interest in science and Mormon metaphysics is that of Erich Robert Paul, *Science, Religion, and Mormon Cosmology,* chapter 6. While other studies of the Pratts' work had explicated their views, few had done so within the context of nineteenth-century scientific and philosophical thought. For an early view of this problem of scientific context, see Erich Robert Paul, "Early Mormon Intellectuals: Parley P. and Orson Pratt, a Response," *Dialogue* 15 (Autumn 1982): 42-48.

[112]The metaphysical character of quantum mechanics has been discussed in particularly accessible fashion by Nick Herbert, *Quantum Reality* (Garden City, N.Y.: Anchor Books, 1985).

[113]See, for example, correspondence related to questions of evolution and creation between Eyring, Smith, and Elder Adam S. Bennion of the Council of the Twelve, in Steven H. Heath, "Henry Eyring: Mormon Scientist" (master's thesis, Brigham Young University, 1980), 158.

[114]Henry Eyring, *The Faith of a Scientist* (Salt Lake City: Bookcraft, 1967).

[115]Steven Weinberg, *The First Three Minutes* (New York: Basic Books, 1975); see also Andrew Pickering, *Constructing Quarks: A Sociological History of Particle Physics* (Edinburgh, Scotland: Edinburgh University, 1984), for a discussion of the personal networking which was involved in the marriage of cosmology and particle physics in the reincarnated "Big Bang" theory. For a less jubilant perspective, see Sir Fred Hoyle, *Facts and Dogmas in Cosmology and Elsewhere* (Cambridge: Cambridge University Press, 1982).

[116]Robert Jastrow, *God and the Astronomers* (New York: W. W. Norton, 1978), 116.

[117]An important perspective here is that of a nuclear physicist turned Anglican priest, John C. Polkinghorne, in his *Science and Creation: The Search for Understanding* (Boston: New Science Library, 1988).

[118]A popular history of the evolution of chaos theory is given by James Gleick, *Chaos: Making a New Science* (New York: Viking, 1987). A slightly more technical account by one of chaos theory's most acclaimed creators, but still accessible to the general reader, is that of David Ruelle, *Chance and Chaos* (Princeton, N.J.: Princeton University Press, 1991).

[119]Quoted in Gleick, *Chaos,* 308.

[120]David S. Landes, *The Unbound Prometheus: Technological Change and Industrial Development in Western Europe from 1750 to the Present* (Cambridge: Cambridge University Press, 1969); Leo Marx, *The Machine in the Garden: Technology and the Pastoral Ideal in America* (New York: Oxford University Press, 1964); and Lewis Mumford, *The Myth of the Machine: Technics and Human Development* (New York: Harcourt Brace Jovanovich, 1967).

[121]Leonard J. Arrington, Feramorz Y. Fox, and Dean L. May, *Building the City of God: Community and Cooperation among the Mormons* (Salt Lake City: Deseret Book, 1976).

[122]Thomas G. Alexander, "Wilford Woodruff, Intellectual Progress, and the Growth of an Amateur Scientific and Technological Tradition in Early Territorial Utah," *Utah Historical Quarterly* 59 (Spring 1991): 164-88.

[123]Paul, *Science, Religion, and Mormon Cosmology,* 162-64.

[124]Hannah Arendt, *The Human Condition* (Chicago: University of Chicago Press, 1958), 3.

[125]Leonard J. Arrington and Jon G. Perry, "Utah's Spectacular Missiles Industry: Its History and Impact," *Utah Historical Quarterly* 30 (Winter 1962): 2-39.

[126]*The National Cyclopaedia of American Biography,* 62 vols. (New York: James T. White, 1929), 20:8-9; see also John Browning and Curt Gentry, *John M. Browning, American Gunmaker* (Garden City, N.Y.: Doubleday, 1964).

[127]James B. Allen, "Testimony and Technology: A Phase of the Modernization of Mormonism since 1950," in *After One Hundred Fifty Years,* ed. Thomas G. Alexander and Jesse L. Embry (Provo, Utah: Charles Redd Center for Western Studies, Brigham Young University, 1983), 171-207.

[128]Allen, "Testimony and Technology," 201.

[129]During the late 1970s, Brigham Young University developed a machine translation project. The intent was to translate the Church's English-language publications into French, Spanish, Portuguese, and Italian from a central location. With the advent of the microcomputer, however, the project was disbanded. The project's mainframe computer was later used as one of the first pieces of equipment in Brigham Young University's Humanities Research Center, an enterprise that has developed many innovations for computer-aided humanities and foreign language education. (The foregoing information was provided by Charles D. Bush of Brigham Young University's Humanities Research Center.)

[130]See the heading *Special Collections on Science, Technology, and Mormonism* in this article.

[131]Robert C. Paehlke, *Environmentalism and the Future of Progressive Politics* (New Haven, Conn.: Yale University Press, 1989).

[132]Ian G. Barbour, *Technology, Environment, and Human Values* (New York: Praeger, 1980). See also Lewis G. Regenstein, *Replenish the Earth: A History of Organized Religion's Treatment of Animals and Nature* (London: SCM Press, 1991). The second of these has a chapter devoted to Mormon beliefs in this area.

[133]Hugh Nibley, "Brigham Young and the Environment," in *To the Glory of God,* ed. Truman G. Madsen and Charles O. Tate (Salt Lake City: Deseret Books, 1972), 2-29. See also Hugh Nibley, *Brother Brigham Challenges the Saints,* eds. Don E. Norton and Shirley S. Ricks, vol. 13 of *The Collected Works of Hugh Nibley* (Salt Lake City: Deseret Book and Provo, Utah: F.A.R.M.S., 1994), 3-101. Important historical studies of the environment history of the Mormons are William W. Speth, "Environment, Culture, and the Mormons in Early Utah: A Study in Cultural Adaptation," *Yearbook of the Association of Pacific Coast Geographers* 29 (1967): 53-67; Richard H. Jackson, "Righteousness and Environmental Change: The Mormons and the Environment," in *Essays on the American West, 1973-1974,* ed. Thomas G. Alexander, Charles Redd Monographs in Western History, no. 5 (Provo, Utah: Charles Redd Center for Western Studies, Brigham Young University, 1975), 21-42; Dan L. Flores, "Islands in the Deseret: An Environmental Interpretation of the Rocky Mountain Frontier" (Ph.D. diss., Texas A&M University

College Station, 1978); Flores, "Zion in Eden: Phases of Environmental History of Utah," *Environmental History* 7 (Winter 1983): 325–44; Flores, "Agriculture, Mountain Ecology, and the Land Ethic: Phases of the Environmental History of Utah," in *Working on the Range: Essays on the History of Western Land Management and the Environment,* ed. John R. Wunder (Westport, Conn.: Greenwood Press, 1985), 157–86; Jeanne Kay and Craig J. Brown, "Mormon Beliefs about Land and Natural Resources, 1847–1877," *Journal of Historical Geography* 11 (July 1985): 253–67; and Thomas G. Alexander, "Stewardship and Enterprise: The LDS Church and the Wasatch Oasis Environment, 1847–1930," *Western Historical Quarterly* 25 (Autumn 1994): 341–64.

[134]The classic text summarizing attitudes toward nature is Clarence J. Glacken, *Traces on the Rhodian Shore: Nature and Culture in Western Thought from Ancient Times to the End of the Eighteenth Century* (Berkeley: University of California Press, 1967). In an American context, the basis for an environmental ethic is described in Roderick Nash, *Wilderness and the American Mind,* 3rd ed. (New Haven, Conn.: Yale University Press, 1982); and Nash, *The Rights of Nature: A History of Environmental Ethics* (Madison: University of Wisconsin Press, 1989).

[135]See, for example, René Jules Dubos, *Reason, Awake: Science for Man* (New York: Columbia University Press, 1970); and his earlier related work *The Dreams of Reason: Science and Utopias* (New York: Columbia University Press, 1961).

[136]Leonard J. Arrington, *Great Basin Kingdom: An Economic History of the Latter-day Saints 1830–1900* (Lincoln: University of Nebraska Press, 1966). First published by Harvard University Press in 1958.

[137]George R. Hill is among the Latter-day Saints whose active involvement in the modern mining industry is part of Utah's history. An extensive collection of documents from his career is found in the University of Utah collection described on pp. 587–88 of this essay.

[138]Gerald E. Jones, "The Gospel and Animals," *Ensign* 2 (August 1972): 60–65; and Gerald E. Jones and Scott S. Smith, *Animals and the Gospel: History of Latter-day Saint Doctrine on the Animal Kingdom* (Thousand Oaks, Calif.: Millennial Productions, 1980). On the larger American context, see Jones, "Concern for Animals as Manifest in Five American Churches: Bible Christian, Shaker, Latter-day Saint, Christian Scientist, and Seven-Day Adventist" (Ph.D. diss., Brigham Young University, 1972).

[139]Isaiah 35:1.

[140]Dean L. May, "Agriculture," in *Encyclopedia of Mormonism* 1:27–29.

[141]John A. Widtsoe, *In a Sunlit Land: The Autobiography of John A. Widtsoe* (Salt Lake City: Deseret News, 1952), chapters 9, 11, and 17.

[142]Leonard J. Arrington and Davis Bitton, *The Mormon Experience: A History of the Latter-day Saints* (New York: Alfred Knopf, 1979), 311–18.

[143]John Bradshaw and Norma Yourchik, "Mormons, Soil-Water Stewards for More Than a Century," *Soil Conservation* 28 (1962–63): 239.

[144]Phillip Low, "Realities of the Population Explosion," *Ensign* 1 (May 1971): 18–27.

[145]Sylvan H. Wittwer, "Food Production, People, and the Future," *BYU Studies* 16 (Summer 1976): 641–59. At the time this article was written, Wittwer was on the faculty of Michigan State University, an institution at which numerous Latter-day Saint scholars were trained in the agricultural sciences.

[146]For discussion of the history of the Word of Wisdom in general, see Thomas G. Alexander, "The Word of Wisdom: From Principle to Requirement," *Dialogue* 14 (Fall 1981): 78-88; and Lester E. Bush Jr., "The Mormon Tradition," in *Caring and Curing, Health and Medicine in the Western Religious Traditions,* ed. Ronald L. Numbers and Darrel W. Amundsen (New York: Macmillan, 1986), 397-420. See also Bush, "The Word of Wisdom in the Nineteenth Century," *Dialogue* 14 (Fall 1981): 47-65; and Paul H. Peterson, "An Historical Analysis of the Word of Wisdom" (master's thesis, Brigham Young University, 1972).

[147]Roger R. Williams, "Tobacco and Alcohol," *Ensign* 7 (April 1977): 57-60; and Clifford J. Stratton, "The Xanthines: Coffee, Cola, Cocoa, and Tea," *BYU Studies* 20 (Spring 1980): 371-88.

[148]Paul S. Bergeson, "Infants and the Word of Wisdom," *Ensign* 7 (April 1977): 54- 59.

[149]Lora Beth Larson, "The Do's in the Word of Wisdom," *Ensign* 7 (April 1977): 46-53.

[150]See the following articles by LeRoy S. Wirthlin: "Joseph Smith's Surgeon," *Ensign* 8 (March 1978): 58-60; "Joseph Smith's Boyhood Operation: An 1813 Surgical Success," *BYU Studies* 21 (Spring 1981): 131-54; "Nathan Smith (1762-1828): Surgical Consultant to Joseph Smith," *BYU Studies* 17 (Spring 1977): 319-37.

[151]Richard C. Poulsen, "Some Botanical Cures in Mormon Folk Medicine: An Analysis," *Utah Historical Quarterly* 44 (Fall 1976): 379-88; Norman Lee Smith, "Herbal Remedies: God's Medicine?" *Dialogue* 12 (Autumn 1979): 37-60; and Norman Lee Smith, "Why are Mormons so Susceptible to Medical and Nutritional Quackery?" *Journal of Collegium Aesculapium* 1 (December 1983): 29-44.

[152]Robert T. Divett, *Medicine and the Mormons: Introduction to the History of Latter-day Saints Health Care* (Bountiful, Utah: Horizon Publishers, 1981).

[153]Robert T. Divett, "His Chastening Rod: Cholera Epidemics and the Mormons," and "Medicine and the Mormons: A Historical Perspective," *Dialogue* 12 (Autumn 1979): 6-16 and 16-25, respectively.

[154]Lester E. Bush Jr., *Health and Medicine among the Latter-day Saints: Science, Sense and Scripture* (New York: Crossroads, 1991).

[155]Blanche E. Rose, "Early Utah Medical Practice," *Utah Historical Quarterly* 10 (1942): 14-33. A number of documents, including journals and unpublished family histories from prominent Utah medical families, are found in the Utah Science, Medical, and Engineering Archives at the University of Utah.

[156]Sherilyn Cox Bennion, "The *Salt Lake Sanitarian*: Medical Advisor to the Saints," *Utah Historical Quarterly* 57 (Spring 1989): 125-27; Lester E. Bush Jr., ed., "On Mormonism, Moral Epidemics, Homeopathy, and Death from Natural Causes," *Dialogue* 12 (Winter 1979): 83-89; Valerie Florance, "Healing and the Home: Home Medicine in Pioneer Utah," in *From Cottage to Market: The Professionalization of Women's Sphere*, ed. John R. Sillito (Salt Lake City: Utah Women's Historical Association, 1983), 28-46; Linda P. Wilcox, "The Imperfect Science: Brigham Young on Medical Doctors," *Dialogue* 12 (Fall 1979): 26-36; and Joseph L. Lyon and Steven Nelson, "Mormon Health," *Dialogue* 12 (Fall 1979): 84-96.

[157]Eric L. Bluth, "Pus, Pox, Propaganda and Progress: The Compulsory Smallpox Vaccination Controversy in Utah, 1896-1901" (master's thesis, Brigham Young University, 1993).

[158]John A. Widtsoe, ed., *Discourses of Brigham Young* (1954; Salt Lake City: Deseret Book, 1978), 162-63.

[159]Bush, *Health and Medicine among the Latter-day Saints,* 93-107.

[160]Claire Wilcox Noall, "Mormon Midwives," *Utah Historical Quarterly* 10 (1942): 84-144. See also Clair Wilcox Noall, "Utah's Pioneer Women Doctors," *Improvement Era* 42 (January, March, May, June, and August 1939): 16-17, 51-54, 144-45, 180-82, 274-75, 332-33, 372, 462-63, 501-5.

[161]Chris Rigby Arrington, "Pioneer Midwives," in *Mormon Sisters,* ed. Claudia L. Bushman (Cambridge, Mass.: Emmeline Press, 1976), 43-65.

[162]Claudia Bushman, "Mystics and Healers," in *Mormon Sisters,* 1-24.

[163]Bushman, "Mystics and Healers."

[164]Arrington, Pioneer Midwives," 56-58, 60-61; Bush, *Health and Medicine*, 94-95; and Arrington and Bitton, *The Mormon Experience,* 227-28.

[165]Lester E. Bush Jr., "Ethical Issues in Reproductive Medicine: A Mormon Perspective," *Dialogue* 18 (Summer 1985): 41-66.

[166]A sketch of the major problem areas in biomedical technology is given by James L. Farmer, William S. Bradshaw, and F. Brent Johnson, "The New Biology and Mormon Theology," in *The Search for Harmony,* 17-22.

[167]Steven J. Sainsbury, "AIDS: The Twentieth-Century Leprosy," *Dialogue* 25 (Fall 1992): 68-77.

[168]R. Jan Stout, "Sin and Sexuality: Psychobiology and the Development of Homosexuality," *Dialogue* 20 (Summer 1987): 29-43.

[169]Duane E. Jeffery, "Intersexes in Humans: An Introductory Exploration," *Dialogue* 12 (Fall 1979): 107-13.

[170]Neal A. Maxwell, "Some Thoughts on the Gospel and the Behavioral Sciences," *BYU Studies* 16 (Summer 1976): 589-602.

[171]James B. Allen, Ronald W. Walker, and David J. Whittaker, comps., *Studies in Mormon History* (Urbana: University of Illinois Press, forthcoming).

[172]Erich Robert Paul, *Science, Religion, and Mormon Cosmology,* 237-57.

[173]Craig J. Oberg and Gene A. Sessions, "Science and Mormonism: A Review Essay," in *The Search for Harmony,* 283-90.

[174]Arrington and Bitton, *The Mormon Experience,* chapter 18.

[175]Richard Sherlock, "A Turbulent Spectrum: Mormon Reactions to the Darwinist Legacy," *Journal of Mormon History* 5 (1978): 33-59; and Farmer, Bradshaw, and Johnson, "The New Biology and Mormon Theology," 71-75.

[176]Joseph F. Smith, John R. Winder, and Anthon H. Lund, "The Origin of Man," *Improvement Era* 13 (November 1909): 75-81; and Heber J. Grant, Anthony W. Ivins, and Charles W. Nibley, "'Mormon' View of Evolution," *Improvement Era* 28 (September 1925): 1090-91.

[177]The Deseret Museum is discussed in Steven L. Olsen's essay "Museums and Historic Sites of Mormonism" elsewhere in this volume.

[178]Joel Edward Ricks, *The Utah State Agricultural College: The Last Fifty Years, 1888-1938* (Salt Lake City: Deseret News Press, 1938).

[179]Doran J. Baker, "On the History of Upper Atmospheric and Space Research in Utah," *Encyclia: The Journal of the Utah Academy of Sciences, Arts and Letters* 63 (1986): 39-47.

[180]Derek J. de Solla Price, *Little Science, Big Science* (New York: Columbia University Press, 1986); and John Ziman, *The Force of Knowledge* (Oxford: Oxford University Press, 1968).

[181]Davis Bitton, "Anti-Intellectualism in Mormon History," *Dialogue* 1 (Autumn 1966): 111-33; and Leonard Arrington, "The Intellectual Tradition of the Latter-day Saints," *Dialogue* 4 (Spring 1969): 13-26.

[182]Andrew D. White, *History of the Warfare of Science with Theology* (London: Macmillan, 1896); and John W. Draper, *History of the Conflict between Religion and Science* (London: Henry S. King, 1875).

[183]David C. Lindberg and Ronald L. Numbers, "Beyond War and Peace: A Reappraisal of the Encounter of Christianity and Science," *Church History* 55 (September 1986): 338-54. An exposition in the Latter-day Saint context is Richard F. Haglund Jr., "Science and Religion: A Symbiosis," *Dialogue* 8 (Autumn/Winter 1973): 23-40.

[184]Todd Britsch, private communication.

[185]Jerome R. Ravetz, *Scientific Knowledge and Its Social Problems* (Oxford: Clarendon Press, 1971).

[186]John Stone, "Even Though," *American Scholar* 49 (Summer 1980): 336.

[187]Article of Faith 9 in Pearl of Great Price, Joseph Smith—History.

Sources for Mormon Visual Arts

Richard G. Oman

Defining Mormon Art

What is Mormon art? As curator of acquisitions at the Museum of Church History and Art, I have struggled with this question for over a quarter century. For me the question is not simply academic; it affects acquisition recommendations that I must make regularly. And I am still not sure I have a succinct answer. Nevertheless, a few important issues must be addressed in defining Mormon art.

First, the simple equation of "Utah art" and Mormon art raises more questions than it solves. While in the past the majority of Mormons lived in Utah, today over four-fifths of the Church's membership does not live in Utah, and over three-fourths of all new growth in the Church is taking place outside the United States.[1] Furthermore, not all artists living in Utah are Mormons. Since any definition of Mormon art that comprehends only Utah is already inaccurate and will become increasingly inaccurate in the future, the definition of Mormon art must be inclusive enough to include Mormon artists from throughout the world.

The geographical and cultural diversity among Latter-day Saints engenders diversity of styles and media among Mormon artists. Traditional western definitions of "fine art" that focus on oil painting and bronze or marble sculpture are simply not broad enough to cover the creations of contemporary Mormon artists. However, if Mormon art is simply defined as art done by Mormons in any style and in any medium, the definition becomes so general that it lacks sufficient parameters to have any meaning. What then *is* a good working definition of Mormon art?

For this essay, "Mormon art" is art done by Mormons that relates thematically to the artists' Mormon faith, history, experience, and community. This definition is elastic and is enriched, not threatened, by stylistic and cultural diversity. Within this definition, however, not all art done by Mormon artists is Mormon art; hence, some artists and some works do not appear in this essay. A few pieces with non-Mormon themes are included in order to place a particular Mormon artist in clearer context. Only the most prominent of the over one thousand known Mormon artists are mentioned.

In addition to understanding the foregoing definition of Mormon art, readers should know that this essay is intended only as a broad overview presenting brief descriptions of artists and their works. A thorough treatment of Mormon art history would require multiple volumes. Furthermore, unlike narrative history, art history's documents are the *objets d'art* themselves. Hence, rather than provide exhaustive analysis, I chose to briefly describe the numerous "documents" of Mormon art history. As a final note, readers should also be aware that this essay's main focus is on sculpture and painting, although some folk art is mentioned. Certain objects of folk material culture, such as pottery, pine furniture, and quilts, are also addressed in Carol Edison's essay in this volume.

Sculpture

The last quarter of the twentieth century has brought about a great increase in the number of LDS sculptors with many smaller pieces—some of which are overtly LDS in subject matter—being done for private collectors. But the religious sculptural tradition among the Latter-day Saints has usually focused on four main areas: Angel Moroni statues for the tops of temple spires, huge baptismal fonts with life-sized oxen (also in temples), symbolic and narrative sculpture on temple exteriors, and commemorative sculpture that usually celebrates important events in Church history and often marks important Church historic sites.

Early Mormon Sculpture. Sculpture has played an important role in the LDS Church since the Nauvoo period. The earliest LDS sculptors were English convert/emigrants William Player (1793–1873), Charles Lambert (1816–92), and Harvey Stanley (born about 1811 in Ohio). All three of these carved the Nauvoo Temple's baptismal font oxen and sun-, moon-, and starstones (symbolizing the three degrees of heavenly glory). The sunstones carved for this temple are unique pieces of early LDS sculpture. Only two originals survive: one in the state park in Nauvoo and the other in the Smithsonian Institution. An exact replica sunstone, hand-carved in the same stone, is on permanent exhibit at the Museum of Church History and Art (hereafter "Church museum").

In Salt Lake City, William Ward (1827–93), an architectural draftsman and stonecarver from England, assisted Truman Angell during the early construction of the Salt Lake Temple. One of Ward's finest remaining pieces is the gravestone of Thomas Tanner, the head blacksmith during the temple construction. (Ward even signed the gravestone.) The original, which was beginning to crack and flake badly, is now being preserved in the Church museum.

Above the door of Brigham Young's Lion House (which was designed by Ward) is perhaps Ward's most well-known piece of sculpture, the stone lion. Unfortunately, the stone of this piece is badly weathering and flaking, and the facial details of the lion are almost gone.

Perhaps the finest work of stone sculpture from the pioneer period of Utah is not in Utah. The "Utah Stone" is placed in the Washington Monument in Washington, D.C., along with others submitted by each state or territory at the time of the monument's construction. William Ward created Utah's stone using oolite—a soft, cream-colored stone—from Manti. Superbly carved with a beehive, the "All-seeing Eye," the word *Deseret,* and other distinctively Mormon symbols, it remains embedded in an interior wall of the Washington Monument and is still in very good condition.

In early Salt Lake City, sculpture was supported by Brigham Young as well as the Church. The arched gate to the Young farm, the Eagle Gate, was graced with a wooden, copper-covered sculpture of a large eagle perched on a beehive. Today, a replica of the sculpture surmounts an enlarged gate spanning State Street in Salt Lake City, while the original is on display in the Daughters of Utah Pioneers Museum (DUP museum) up the street. The symbol of the eagle on the beehive was not simply a decoration for Brigham Young's family compound; it was also the symbol of the Territory of Deseret, the Territory of Utah, and eventually the state of Utah, as manifested on the state seal. The eagle, the symbol of the United States, was added to link together state and nation. Another carved beehive was placed on the cupola of one of Brigham's homes; it remains in its original location, and the home is still known as the Beehive House.

Emigrant Furniture Makers. The Eagle Gate and Beehive House sculptures were carved by Ralph Ramsey (1824–1905), a cabinetmaker and woodcarver converted in England. Ramsey also carved the decorative casing for the pipes of the original Salt Lake Tabernacle organ. The organ is still intact in its original location, although the casing has been expanded around it several times.

Other works by Ramsey are still extant though secular. Among these are a magnificent newel post and banister—the finest examples of interior decorative woodcarving from pioneer Utah—at the Devereaux House in downtown Salt Lake City. The Daughters of Utah Pioneers museum (Salt Lake City) contains a magnificent carved bed by Ramsey. In Richfield, Utah, Ramsey's home still stands and is currently being used as the local historical museum. The home contains some of Ramsey's well-crafted fireplace mantles. One of his most dramatic pieces of exterior architectural ornamentation is in the small Mormon pioneer settlement of Snowflake, Arizona: a prominent pioneer home sports a life-sized wood carving of a horse's head surrounded by a huge horseshoe. The wide distribution of Ramsey's work reflects the nineteenth-century Mormon pattern of "calling" families to settle new colonies.

Ramsey was not the only convert furniture-carver from England. In the later nineteenth century, David Hughes (1847–1923) came to Utah, where he taught cabinetmaking at the Utah State Agriculture College (now Utah State University) in Logan. In addition to furniture, he also carved figureheads for ships. In the Church museum is a charming bas-relief portrait, apparently based on a Maudsley profile, that Hughes made of Joseph Smith. The portrait is surrounded with elaborate carvings, including an eagle with outstretched wings and two American flags. The side profile of the Prophet shows the unmistakable simplification of anatomy frequently seen in ships' figureheads.

Twentieth Century. While the works of Hughes, Ramsey, and other English emigrant artisans shaped the Mormon sculptural tradition during the Church's first half-century, a second major tradition began with the completion of the Salt Lake Temple. Utahn Cyrus Dallin (1861–1944), who had studied sculpture in Paris, was asked by Wilford Woodruff to sculpt the angel Moroni statue that caps the tallest spire of the Salt Lake Temple. This beaux arts–style sculpture has become the most recognized and copied piece of sculpture in the Latter-day Saint tradition. Today, various versions of this piece cap the towers of many LDS temples. Dallin was also commissioned to create a Church monument to Brigham Young; it was placed at the intersection of Main and South Temple streets in Salt Lake City.

Dallin grew up in Springville, Utah. His parents and grandparents were English converts who emigrated to Utah but eventually became disaffected from the Church. Dallin was blessed as a baby but was never baptized. He spent most of his career in Boston, although he frequently returned to Springville to visit his mother and his family home. In Boston, Dallin obtained virtually all of the major commissions for public sculpture of his time. He sculpted John Winthrop in front of the State House, Paul Revere at the Old North Church, Massasoit at Plymouth Rock (copies of this piece grace the grounds of the Utah state capitol and Brigham Young University), and a mounted Indian entitled *Appeal to the Great Spirit* that appears in front of Boston's Museum of Fine Arts. In addition to these works, Dallin built his reputation on depicting the American Indians whom he had known as a boy growing up in Springville. Dallin's life-sized bronze equestrian figures can be found in Chicago (Grant Park); Kansas City (Penn Valley Park); Philadelphia (Fairmont Park); and Vienna, Austria.[2]

Two other sculptors with LDS roots, brothers Gutzon (1867–1941) and Solon (1868–1922) Borglum, also made a major impact on the history of early twentieth-century American sculpture. The Borglums lived for a time in the Bear Lake Valley of Utah and Idaho before moving to Ogden. Their parents, Danish convert/emigrants, eventually became disenchanted with the Church and moved to the Midwest, where Gutzon and Solon came of age. Gutzon is best known for the presidential sculptures on Mt. Rushmore and the Stone Mountain Memorial to the Confederacy outside of Atlanta. In addition, his *Mares of Diomedes* is housed in the Metropolitan Museum, and his portrait head of Abraham Lincoln is displayed in the rotunda of the national Capitol.

Solon's pieces, though less monumental, also deal with American history, especially the American cowboy. Many of these works are in public collections, such as the Detroit Institute of Arts; the Joslyn Art Museum in Omaha, Nebraska; the Thomas Gilcrease Institute in Tulsa, Oklahoma; and the Whitney Gallery of Western Art in Cody, Wyoming.

The next major sculptor from the Mormon tradition was Brigham Young's grandson Mahonri Young (1877–1957). Mahonri Young studied in Paris, where he was strongly influenced by the famous sculptor Auguste Rodin. Young spent most of his life thereafter in New York City, where he taught at the Art Student's League for many years. But he also created four major religious monuments in Salt Lake City: the Seagull Monument; the full, standing bronze portraits of Joseph and Hyrum Smith on Temple Square; and the "This Is the Place" Monument at the mouth of Emigration Canyon east of Salt Lake City. This last piece, the largest sculptural monument in Utah, marked the centennial of the Mormon pioneers' entry into the Salt Lake Valley. Among Young's major pieces outside of Utah is the seated figure of his grandfather Brigham in the rotunda of the Capitol in Washington, D.C.

In New York City, Mahonri's work can be seen at the American Museum of Natural History. He made several trips to the American Southwest and created life-sized bronze figures of members of the various Native American tribes from the area. Other Young pieces are displayed in the Metropolitan Museum of Art.

The largest collection of Mahonri Young's work is at Brigham Young University. Ernest L. Wilkinson, while president of the university, purchased this collection from the Mahonri Young family estate. In addition to the Brigham Young University collection, West High School (Salt Lake City) has several of Young's life-sized figures displayed on large buttresses. Collections of smaller pieces can be found at the Church museum, the Springville Museum of Art (hereafter "Springville museum"), and the Utah Museum of Fine Arts.

Avard Fairbanks (1897–1987), another Utah sculptor who studied in Paris before World War I, also left a major legacy to Mormon arts. Fairbanks has probably done more overtly LDS pieces of sculpture than any other Mormon sculptor. Two of his finest early works are in the Springville museum: *Mother and Child* (white Carrera marble) and *Spring* (bronze). This last figure is a superb piece of art deco sculpture.

Among Fairbanks's earliest and best works is the elaborate frieze around the top of the Hawaii Temple in Laie. This piece was a collaboration with Fairbanks's older brother, J. Leo (1878–1946). Leo designed the frieze; young Avard did the sculpting. The frieze forms a bas-relief around the four sides of the top of the temple. Each side represents a period from Church history: the Old Testament, the New Testament, the Book of Mormon, and latter days (basically Joseph Smith's first vision to the present). With dozens of figures, this elaborate frieze is the single most thematically elaborate sculptural program ever undertaken by an LDS sculptor. Other major sculptures by Fairbanks at the Hawaii Temple include the baptismal font and twelve oxen, *Hawaiian Motherhood,* and *Lehi Blessing Joseph.* Only Temple Square in Salt Lake City and the Nauvoo sculpture garden can compare with the Hawaii Temple as a major focus of exterior LDS sculpture.

Among Fairbanks's other major LDS pieces is *Youth and New Frontiers,* which was originally created for the Mormon exhibition at the Chicago World's Fair in 1933. Other LDS pieces include the Aaronic Priesthood Restoration Monument on the bank of the Susquehanna River near Harmony, Pennsylvania; the Winter Quarters Cemetery monuments near Omaha, Nebraska, which include *A Tragedy of Winter Quarters,* the entrance panels, and the *Honor Roll* panel; the *Mortal Moroni* on the grounds of the Manti Temple; the *Eternal Family* at the Provo City Hall; the *Restoration of the Aaronic Priesthood by John the Baptist,* the Three Witnesses Monument, and the Nauvoo Bell campanile bas-relief, all on Temple Square; and the *Restoration of the Melchizedek Priesthood* Monument, the *First Vision* (marble), and a life-size portrait of the young Joseph Smith at the Church museum. At Brigham Young University, Fairbanks sculpted the two bas-relief panels, *Lehi-Nephi* and *Mormon-Moroni,* which flank the south entrance to the Harold B. Lee Library.[3]

In 1946, Fairbanks was asked by A. Ray Olpin, then president of the University of Utah, to return to Salt Lake City and create the department of fine arts at the University of Utah. While there, Fairbanks influenced a whole generation of LDS artists; among the most noteworthy were Ortho Fairbanks (a nephew), Edward Fraughton, and Grant Speed. Being a strong advocate of the traditional classical academic tradition in sculpture, Avard fought as a rearguard against abstract art during his years on the faculty.

The Fairbanks family produced several artists of considerable talent. Avard's father, John B., was one of the art missionaries the Church sent to Paris to prepare to paint murals in the Salt Lake Temple. Avard's older brother, J. Leo, studied art in the eastern United States and Paris and later founded the art department at Oregon State University. Avard's son Justin sculpted the new eagle and beehive to replace Ralph Ramsey's original for the Eagle Gate. Another of Avard's sons, Johnathan, became curator of American art at the Museum of Fine Arts in Boston. Avard's nephew Ortho became a sculptor of some note in both Utah and Arizona. Ortho's most significant Mormon monuments are the Karl G. Maeser Monument at Brigham Young University and the Eliza R. Snow Monument, which stands in front of the Daughters of Utah Pioneers Museum in downtown Salt Lake City.

Edward Fraughton (1939–), a native of Park City, Utah, is one of Avard Fairbanks's most well-known students. Among Fraughton's most prominent Mormon pieces is the Mormon Battalion Monument in a park near "Old Town" San Diego, California. In Utah, he created the monument *All Is Well* for the Brigham Young Family Cemetery in Salt Lake City. At Temple Square is his fine portrait bust of Truman Angell, the architect of the Salt Lake Temple. One of Fraughton's most monumental pieces is the state symbol of Wyoming, a heroic-sized rider and bucking horse entitled *The Spirit of Wyoming.* This monument stands on the grounds of the state capitol in Cheyenne. Most of Fraughton's work centers around nineteenth-century western themes of cowboys, Native Americans, and mountain men. The majority of his sculptures are table-sized bronze pieces that are sold to private collectors.

D. J. Bawden (1956–), a Salt Lake City artist, was influenced by Avard Fairbanks and Ed Fraughton. His major Mormon pieces have centered on Joseph Smith. His extensive research has made his bronze busts probably the most accurate images ever created of the Prophet, of whom no known photographs exist. His work is in the collection of the Church museum.

Torlief Knaphus (1881–1965), a convert/emigrant from Norway, created several significant Mormon pieces. For example, Knaphus made a monument for Temple Square depicting the most dramatic epic of the pioneer trek west: the sufferings and faith of the handcart pioneers. Knaphus also created a major monument of Moroni and the Gold Plates that was placed on the crest of the Hill Cumorah, near Palmyra, New York. For the Cardston Temple in Alberta, Canada, Knaphus created a bas-relief, *Christ and the Woman at the Well.* A casting of this piece is on the front of the Edgehill Ward chapel in Salt Lake City. Knaphus also sculpted the baptismal font and oxen for the Cardston Temple. These oxen have become the prototype for many temple-font oxen.

Millard Malin (1891-1975), a contemporary of Knaphus, created the angel Moroni statue on the Los Angeles Temple and sculpted the temple's baptismal font with its twelve oxen. The oxen supporting this font are full of baroque movement and are among the most expressive ever done for a temple baptismal font.

Karl Quilter (1929-) has for many years taught seminary classes in the Church Educational System. As a sculptor, his most significant creations have been statues of the angel Moroni that are cast in fiberglass and mounted on the tops of many modern temple spires.

Art and Belief Movement. Beginning in the early 1970s, some LDS artists, notably several on the Brigham Young University art faculty at the time, developed what has come to be known as the "art and belief movement." Much of this group's art used contemporary artistic styles to focus on LDS themes. An early focal point for exhibition was the Mormon Arts Festival, which was held each spring for several years at Brigham Young University.

Among the leading sculptors in this art and belief movement were Franz Johansen (1929-), Dennis Smith (1942-), Trevor Southey (1940-), Dallas Anderson (1931-), Frank Riggs (1922-), Neil Hadlock (1944-), Frank Nackos (1939-), and Peter Myer (1934-). Each of these artists attempted to create works of art expressing important aspects of LDS theology, history, and lifestyle. Among the most powerfully religious pieces by these artists are Johansen's *The Rod and the Veil* and Southey's *The Moment after the Restoration of the Melchizedek Priesthood*. Both of these pieces are now in the Church museum. Johansen also created a huge bas-relief which forms the facade above the entrance doors of the museum. Neil Hadlock's finest work as part of this tradition is a piece called *The Scapegoat.* Frank Nackos's major piece, *The Tree of Knowledge,* is placed just north of the Harold B. Lee Library at Brigham Young University. Among Dallas Anderson's best LDS pieces is a standing portrait of Joseph Smith.

Most members of the art and belief group have not continued to produce significant works of thematically LDS art. Several years ago, Dallas Anderson left the art faculty at Brigham Young University and moved to southern California, where he now creates sculptures to decorate the Crystal Cathedral, the spectacular modern church building in Garden Grove commissioned by the Reverend Robert Shuler. Frank Nackos, Neil Hadlock, and Frank Riggs have all moved toward mostly

Franz Johansen (1928–), *The Rod and the Veil.* Bronze, 84" x 99 1/2", Utah, 1975. Johansen taught sculpture and served as chairman of the art department at BYU for many years. This sculpture combines symbolism from the Book of Mormon, early Church history, and contemporary life.

abstract works with little or no LDS religious meaning, works that are virtually indistinguishable from the general sweep of formal abstract sculpture anywhere else in the nation. Other group members have built regional reputations as sculptors. For a few years, however, the art and belief movement did focus on LDS faith and culture. The major exception to the group's move away from religious subjects has been Franz Johansen. Among his works are huge medallions on the doors of the Washington, D.C., Temple.

Probably the best known sculptor in the art and belief group is Dennis Smith (1942–) of Alpine, Utah. Much of his fame resulted from his creation of almost all the pieces in the Monument to Women sculpture garden in Nauvoo, Illinois. Commissioned by the Relief Society to commemorate the 125th anniversary of that organization's founding, the sculpture garden was the most ambitious Church-sponsored sculptural program in the second half of the twentieth century. The project consisted of several life-size bronze statues of women involved in traditional roles. Several of these works are also displayed in the Church Office Building plaza in Salt Lake City.

Smith also created much sculpture depicting childhood, some of which he used to illustrate *Star-Counter* (Provo, Utah: Trilogy Arts, 1970), a book of his poetry. This book and his sculptures of childhood did much to spread his reputation among a broad segment of American Latter-day Saints, particularly those who attended Brigham Young University during the 1960s and 1970s. Smith also received many public and commercial commissions for his sculptures of childhood and families. A typical example of these childhood scenes is a life-size bronze at the entrance of the Springville museum. Smith's most dramatic work is a huge piece he did for the foyer of the new Primary Children's Hospital in Salt Lake City. His fanciful flying machines, frequently with skinny, long-legged boys at the controls, have also been very popular. Some of these pieces can be seen in the lobby areas of the Salt Lake International Airport.

The childhood sculptures are a corollary to Smith's sculptures in Nauvoo. They catch the wonder and joy of preadolescent boys and girls and reflect an idealized childhood that is part of how Latter-day Saints (particularly those from the Intermountain West Mormon cultural region) feel about a happy, secure childhood. Taken together with the Monument to Women pieces, the childhood sculptures reflect the idealized Mormon idea of motherhood and family. In more recent years, Smith has attempted to turn his talents to painting, but with much less success. Nevertheless, the genuine affection that literally hundreds of thousands of Latter-day Saints have for the Monument to Women and the childhood pieces has guaranteed Smith's fame as an artist among many Mormons of modern times.

As mentioned previously, not all the sculptures in Nauvoo were done by Dennis Smith. Florence Hansen (1920–), a Utah sculptor whose work consistently focuses on LDS women, created the sculpture of Joseph Smith and his wife Emma, the first president of the Relief Society. Another work by Hansen, *Expulsion from Missouri,* depicts Emma fleeing through a winter storm with her small children. A small bronze, *Emigrants,* which shows a young Scandinavian couple waiting by their trunk, represents the tens of thousands of Mormon converts who emigrated from Europe to the United States and gathered to Zion in the nineteenth century. In *Teaching with Love,* Hansen shows a young mother teaching her little daughter the violin. All of these small bronzes are in the Church museum collection.

Gary Price (1955–), like Dennis Smith, has done works depicting childhood. He has also created bronze figures for fountains. Some of his secular work can be seen at the Springville museum. His more religious pieces include a bust of Christ and an environmental pioneer scene complete with covered wagon, oxen, people, and a hill. The Church museum has both of these religious works.

Bronze. James Young (1937–) has taught for many years at the College of Eastern Utah in Price. He is best known for his bronze sculptures depicting mule-drawn mining cars that describe an earlier age of coal mining in the area in which he lives.

In Arizona, Clyde Morgan (1942–) has been developing a reputation for his bronze sculptures. One of his most outstanding pieces is the Vietnam War Memorial on the grounds of the Utah state capitol building.

Jerry Anderson (1935–), currently living in the small village of Leeds near St. George, Utah, is another artist who creates bronze sculptures. The campus of Southern Utah State University in Cedar City has two of his large baroque pieces and the Dixie College campus in St. George has one. Both of the sculptures at Southern Utah State University deal with Mormon history, depicting a survivor of a handcart company and the heroic efforts to build the school.

L'Deane Trueblood (1928–), also living in the St. George area, sculpts in the classical tradition. Working mostly in bronze, she has created many fine portrait busts. One noteworthy piece is her equestrian sculpture of Jacob Hamblin, which is held by the Church museum.

Clayton Robbins (1919–) lives in the Salt Lake Valley and works primarily in bronze. Stylistically, his work falls into the area of classical realism. Thematically, his sculptures are usually portraits and figures, frequently of children.

Laura Lee Stay (1958–) has created one of the most powerfully religious female sculptures, *Woman of Reverence.* This bronze sculpture is in the collections of both the Church museum and the Springville museum.

Brent Gehring (1942–) is capable of working in both the classical realist tradition and the more abstract mannerist style. The Church museum has his portrait bust of early LDS Church leader Heber C. Kimball. Among his more abstract works is *Antidote for Nostalgia,* which deals with the great difficulty the pioneers had in farming the hot, arid, unyielding land of the Great Basin.

Stanley Wanlass (1941–), a native of Lehi, Utah, has become best known for his sculptures of classic automobiles in colored patinated bronze. These works depicting the American love affair with the automobile have been exhibited in both the United States and Europe. His most significant historical monument, which commemorates Lewis and Clark, is at Fort Clatsop State Park near Astoria, Oregon.

American West. Clark Bronson (1939–) and his nephew Johnathan Bronson (1952–) create works depicting the distinctive animals of the American West. Clark, who currently lives in Bozeman, Montana, is one of this country's foremost wildlife sculptors. His works are mostly table-sized bronzes of elk, bears, eagles, and other wild animals.

Stanley Johnson (1939–) of Mapleton, Utah, also works in the tradition of realistic bronzes depicting the epic of the American West. His two finest pieces are *Eagle Boy* and *Minitari Warrior.* Examples of his work are in the collections of both the Springville museum and the Church museum. *Minitari Warrior* is a fine depiction in bronze of a painting by George Catlin of the same subject.

Peter Fillerup (1953–), originally from Cody, Wyoming, but now living in Heber City, Utah, is primarily a sculptor of themes from the American West. Most of his works depict cowboys, mountain men, and Native Americans. His largest work is *Steamboat,* the mascot of the University of Wyoming Cowboys. This heroic-sized rider and bucking bronco graces the university campus in Laramie. Another campus mascot, *The Jayhawk,* is on the campus of the University of Kansas in Lawrence. At Philmont, the huge Boy Scouts of America ranch in New Mexico, stands his large bronze sculpture of a boy scout. Fillerup has also done several major religious works, among them an eight-foot marble statue of Christ for the Biblical Arts Center in Dallas, Texas. His small bronze of Porter Rockwell is in the collection of the Church museum.

Grant Speed (1930–) epitomizes the American western movement. Speed originally came from west Texas, where he worked on the family cattle ranch. He was a member of Brigham Young University's rodeo team, then became a professional bronc rider for several years. After numerous broken bones, Speed decided to sculpt broncs instead of riding them. He studied with Fairbanks at the University of Utah before becoming a professional artist. Among other places, his works can be seen in the Cowboy Artists of America Museum in Kerville, Texas. He has served as president of the Cowboy Artists of America, probably the most exclusive group of contemporary western artists.

Native American. Oreland Joe (1958–) a Southern Ute/Navajo living near Shiprock, New Mexico, is one of the most respected Native American sculptors. He works in stone, especially alabaster and marble, and centers on the theme of the Native American family, primarily mother and child.

Harrison Begay (1961–) is a Navajo from Arizona married to a Santa Clara Pueblo from New Mexico. As is customary in these matrilineal societies, the Begays moved to the Santa Clara Pueblo, where Begay quickly learned the blackware pottery tradition of his wife's people. Begay is rapidly becoming one of the more significant Native American artists in the American Southwest. He has broadened the Pueblo pottery tradition by using the techniques and materials of blackware pottery to create sculptures of freestanding figures. Among his finest work of this type is the subtle yet powerful *Last Supper* in the collection of the Church museum. This multifigured work is one of the finest contemporary religious sculptures by a Mormon artist. Begay is currently creating a large blackware pot with a bas-relief of Lehi's dream of the tree of life for the Church museum. Begay's in-laws, Andy and Marsha Padilla, and his wife's grandparents, Eugene and Isabelle Naranjo, are also very competent sculptors in the artistic traditions of their native pueblo. A fine nativity created by the Padillas and a delightful Noah, family, ark, and animals made by the Naranjos and their children are both in the Church museum.

Another Latter-day Saint Native American artist of growing national and international reputation is Lowell Talishoma (1950–), a Hopi from Second Mesa, Arizona. After spending most of his youth in Utah in the Indian Placement Program, he returned to the Hopi Reservation, where he has become well-known as one of the finest contemporary kachina carvers. While most of his carving is done in traditional cottonwood root, he has cast some of his more recent work in bronze. A superb rooster kachina carved from cottonwood root is part of the collection of the Church museum.

Wood. Jan Fisher (1938–) served on the art faculty of Brigham Young University—Hawaii Campus for many years. He has done several significant sculpture commissions in Hawaii. Epanaia Christy (1921–) and Mataumu Alisa (1942–), two Polynesian Latter-day Saints living in Hawaii, are also significant sculptors. Christy is a native Maori from New Zealand and Alisa is a native Hawaiian.

Roger Otis (1945–), from upstate New York, studied woodcarving and furniture making at the Rochester Institute of Technology's College of Fine and Applied Arts. Since his graduation, however, he has devoted his energies to wood sculpture. His work is on exhibit at Wright Patterson Air Force Base Museum in Dayton, Ohio, and the Burnett Park Zoo in Syracuse, New York. His most significant LDS piece to date is a life-size sculpture of Queen Esther from the Old Testament, a depiction based on a painting of the same subject by Minerva Teichert. This large wood sculpture was created for the second Churchwide International Art Competition and received a purchase prize from the Church museum.

John Taye (1946–), originally from Minnesota, graduated from the Otis Art Institute in Los Angeles and is on the art faculty at Boise

State University. His preferred medium of sculpture is wood, and his work has been featured in several one-man shows in Idaho, Utah, Montana, and California. Some of his work includes highly realistic depictions of the old animal skulls frequently found bleached in the deserts of the West. His basswood sculpture entitled *Reading the Bible,* which features a female figure in a chair reading the scriptures, is in the collection of the Church museum.

International. Victor de la Torres (1929–), a native of Ecuador who now lives in Caracas, Venezuela, is a full-time professional artist. Most of his work is sculpture done in wood. He has carved portrait busts of all the presidents of the Church along with large bas-reliefs depicting passages from the Book of Mormon. His *Lehi's Vision of the Tree of Life* is on exhibition at the Church museum.

From Kinshasa, Zaire, comes the work of Bob Tshipepele-Kande (ca. 1950), who works in the traditional African medium of wood. The Church museum has his delightful sculpture *Mouptees,* which depicts a seagull with a cricket in its mouth. The artist, never having seen a seagull, has created one that looks more like a black parrot. The piece is superbly carved and finished in polychrome. The story of the great nineteenth-century Mormon pioneer miracle of the seagulls and the crickets has gone to Africa and then come back to Salt Lake City with a fresh artistic interpretation.

The two major visual art forms in Indonesia are batiks and wood sculpture. Raharjo (c. 1950–), a professional sculptor from the island of Java, has sculpted a large bas-relief panel in wood of Joseph Smith and the Nauvoo Temple. This panel is in the collection of the Church museum.

Painting

The history of Mormon painters begins in Nauvoo in the 1840s—the second decade following the establishment of The Church of Jesus Christ of Latter-day Saints. Two factors explain the early development of an artistic tradition within the small, new church on the American frontier: foreign missionary work and the desire of new converts to emigrate to the main body of the Saints. Without these two factors, the Mormons would likely have had virtually no early art tradition because almost all Mormon painters during the Church's first half-century were born in Europe. The only major exception to this European tradition was Pennsylvania-born George M. Ottinger.

The British Beginnings. The first LDS painters, both English converts, were Sutcliffe Maudsley (1809–81) and William Major (1804–54). Maudsley painted the earliest portraits among the Mormons:

primitive but accurate profiles of members of the Smith family in Nauvoo. As of this writing, the only public institution with Maudsley's works is the Church museum, which has several portraits depicting Joseph Smith.

Major, who crossed the plains in 1848, was the earliest painter in Utah. Unfortunately, he died while serving a mission to his native England and left few works. His most famous painting, begun in Winter Quarters and completed in the Salt Lake Valley, depicts Brigham Young and his family in the stagelike interior of an English mansion. This painting attempts to transplant to the American frontier a British art tradition that goes back to Gainsborough; *Brigham Young and His Family* is in the collection of the Church museum. Two of Major's small landscapes, depicting Fillmore and Parowan, Utah, are part of the furnishings of Brigham Young's Beehive House. The Daughters of Utah Pioneers museum (Salt Lake City) has a charming Major oil portrait of Brigham Young with a cocked hat and a full military uniform. The Springville museum has two small watercolor drawings of Indian chiefs, Washaki of the Shoshoni and Parishort of the Corn Creek band of the Paiutes.

Robert Campbell (1810–90), *General Joseph Smith Addressing the Nauvoo Legion.* Watercolor and ink on paper, 16 1/4" x 11 1/2", Illinois, 1845. Campbell drew on his experiences in Nauvoo to create this earliest narrative painting of Church history by a Mormon artist.

In 1853 another English convert painter, Frederick Piercy (1830–91), journeyed to Utah. He made detailed sketches and watercolors along the way to illustrate a Mormon emigrant guidebook, *The Route from Liverpool to Great Salt Lake Valley* (Liverpool, 1855). This visual record is the earliest surviving series showing the entire Mormon route west. Many of Piercy's original watercolor paintings and drawings are in the Boston Museum of Fine Arts and the Missouri State Historical Society. The Church museum has examples of most of the published engravings that were made from his paintings and drawings.

Over the next quarter of a century, Utah's painting tradition was enriched by many more British converts. Most had limited formal education and modest art training in England, but in a raw, new land their works were well received. Almost all the painted landscapes of the mountains and Great Salt Lake are in the exaggerated and romantic styles then popular in England; these paintings reflect the religious faith of the painters, who saw the face of the Lord in nature and Zion in the purity of the western wilderness. The painters were particularly captivated by the biblical imagery that linked mountains and the Lord's holy temple. Almost none of the extant works by these early British artists are genre historical subjects. One exception is Scottish convert/emigrant Nathaniel Spens's rendition of *The Deacon Jones' Experience,* held by the Springville museum. But this humorous painting is not an original; it is actually a copy of an earlier British painting by Archibald Willard.

The major exception in the area of historical painting by British convert/emigrant artists is the work of William Armitage (1817–90), who was born and trained in London. Armitage's style shows the strong influence of the Royal Academy's interest in dignified portraiture and historical subjects, although Armitage's work is a somewhat primitive and old-fashioned version of that tradition. His religious masterpieces are *Joseph Smith Preaching to the Indians* and *Christ's Appearance to the Nephites.* These huge paintings, the largest easel paintings done in nineteenth-century Utah, originally hung in the Salt Lake Temple. The Joseph Smith painting is currently on exhibit at the Church museum, while the painting of Christ and the Nephites has recently been restored and reinstalled in the Salt Lake Temple.

Reuben Kirkham (ca. 1835–86) and John Tullidge (1836–99) were two other early English convert/emigrant landscape painters. Kirkham settled in Logan, where he helped paint some of the original murals in the Logan Temple. Like William Major, he died in his fifties, and very little of his work is extant. A dramatic scene he rendered of Logan Canyon is in the Church museum. The Springville museum has the largest and probably the finest remaining painting by Kirkham, *Sunset in Blacksmith Fork Canyon, Logan; 1879.*

Tullidge grew up in the southern English coastal city of Weymouth, where his home was practically on the beach. His father (also named John) was a musician and a graduate of Eton College. His brother, Edward, was a reporter, historian, poet, playwright, and publisher. With this kind of family background, it is not surprising that John was enamored with English Romanticism. He was very fond of painting dramatic mountain canyon scenes with waterfalls. Good examples can be seen in both the Church museum and the Springville museum. He also created dramatic seascapes of ships in storms, undoubtedly based on memories of his childhood years by the sea. The Church museum has a fine seascape done by Tullidge in the 1890s, thirty years after he had emigrated from England.

A strong cultural conservatism is evident in the works of these early artists. While they had permanently left England, they retained English ideas as an important part of their worldview. Biblical allusions to nature as a symbol of purity and religious power reinforced this English Romanticism. For example, nineteenth-century English poetry, mostly in the form of lyrics for hymns, drew heavily on religious imagery that linked mountains, the concept of Zion, divine protection, and the presence of the Lord. A good example of such a hymn is "O Ye Mountains High," by London-born Charles W. Penrose.

Another significant English convert/emigrant painter, George Beard (1855–1944), settled in the small northern Utah village of Coalville. Beard, who had spent his boyhood near romantic Sherwood Forest in rural Nottingham, loved to roam the Uintah Mountains. Several mountains and lakes in this remote range were named by Beard. He was also an active photographer, mostly of mountain scenes. Most of his paintings were also mountain scenes, done in a greatly exaggerated romantic style. One of his finest mountain landscapes is in the old co-op store building—which Beard managed for many years—on Coalville's main street. Another such landscape is in the collection of the Church museum. North Summit High School in Coalville also has a very fine collection of Beard's paintings, including a very interesting piece showing a wagon train, tiny and distant, going by the cliffs of the Green River.

The most prominent English convert painters from this period were Alfred Lambourne (1850–1926) and Henry Lavender Adolphus Culmer (1854–1914). Culmer received by far the most national recognition, primarily through his large paintings of the canyons and deserts of southern Utah, which paintings were published in the March 1907 issue of the *National Geographic Magazine.* Brigham Young

University has a huge, superb Culmer painting of Shoshoni Falls on the Snake River. The Utah State Historical Society and the Utah State Fine Arts Collection, administered by the Utah Arts Council, each have fine paintings of Utah's southern canyons and deserts. The Church museum has two major pieces by Culmer: a small oil of Shoshoni Falls, and a large painting of Black Rock and the Great Salt Lake.

Alfred Lambourne was a romantic's romantic. He "homesteaded" a desert island in the middle of the Great Salt Lake so that he could write poems and paint sunrises and sunsets. Two of his finest Great Salt Lake scenes are in the Church museum, along with several other smaller pieces. The Springville museum also has some small pieces. Lambourne's two masterpieces, however, were done for the Salt Lake Temple, where they still hang. These represent the culmination of the wedding of English Romanticism with Mormonism, and it is not coincidental that both these works communicate religious events in terms of romantic landscapes. The first painting, which depicts Adam-ondi-Ahman, represents the beginning and ending of human history. The second, depicting the Hill Cumorah, represents the restoration of the gospel to the earth. Two paintings almost identical to these are housed in the Church museum.

The Early Scandinavian Tradition. Contemporary with the early British artists in Utah were the Scandinavian convert painters who focused on historical and genre painting rather than landscapes. The leaders of this tradition in pioneer Utah were Carl Christian Anton Christensen (1831–1912) from Denmark and Danquart Weggeland (1827–1918) from Norway. Both were trained in the Royal Academy of Art in Copenhagen at a time when genre painting and local and regional historical painting were strongly encouraged as a cultural bulwark against advancing German cultural and military aggression.

Christensen's "Mormon Panorama" is the most significant series of LDS historical paintings to survive from the nineteenth century. It includes twenty-two tempera paintings, each eight feet by ten feet, recounting the pre-Utah history of the Church in epic dimensions. The Christensen family donated the paintings to the Church via Brigham Young University. Several paintings from this series are on exhibition in the permanent historical gallery of the Church museum. Christensen's two finest easel paintings are *Handcart Pioneers,* displayed in the Church museum, and *Reunion of the Saints,* displayed at the Daughters of Utah Pioneers museum (Salt Lake City). Christensen also created a series of oil paintings depicting early scenes from the Book of Mormon. Most of these are in the collection of the Church museum, with the balance in the collection of Pioneer Village (owned by the Lagoon Corporation) in Farmington, Utah.

Other small historical pieces by Christensen are in the collections of the Utah Museum of Fine Arts ("Utah museum"), the Springville museum, and the Church museum. The charming painting *Home Sweet Home,* which is in the collection of the Utah museum, probably depicts Christensen's home in the Sanpete Valley. Among the rarest of Christensen's small pieces is a watercolor painting of a ship at sea—almost certainly the ship on which Christensen and his wife crossed the Atlantic. This work is probably the only original painting by a Mormon artist of an emigrant ship chartered by the Church. On such ships, tens of thousands of Mormons gathered to Zion from Europe. This piece is on permanent exhibition in the historical gallery of the Church museum along with two small oil paintings of the Mormon Battalion.

Christensen helped convert Danquart Weggeland, who became the other major Scandinavian painter in pioneer Utah. While Christensen settled in Sanpete Valley in central Utah, most of Weggeland's Utah experience was in Salt Lake City, with the exception of a short period pioneering on the shore of Utah Lake near Lehi. Some of Weggeland's finest work—his two largest pioneer trek paintings, *The Pioneers of*

C. C. A. Christensen (1831–1912), *Handcart Pioneers.* Oil on canvas, 25 3/8" x 38 5/16", Utah, 1900. A native of Denmark, Christensen pulled a handcart across the plains in 1857. Christensen and Weggeland were the most consistent narrative painters among the pioneer generation of LDS artists.

1847 Crossing the North Platte and *The Mormon Battalion,* and two fine small paintings of the territorial prison—are at the Daughters of Utah Pioneers museum (Salt Lake City). The paintings of the prison were undoubtedly done to celebrate the Mormon men who had been sentenced to prison for practicing polygamy.

The Church museum has several portraits by Weggeland, including a portrait of Carl Christensen's wife; some studies of Norwegian peasants dressed in traditional costumes; and several pioneer scenes, including one with a wagon train crossing the mountains and another with a handcart company. This latter scene is particularly noteworthy because of the obvious European (and particularly Scandinavian) dress of the pioneers. The pictures of Salt Lake City include one of Weggeland's home on Fourth South and a charming ice skating scene. The Church museum also has New Testament scenes from the passion of Christ; early scenes of the St. George Temple, where Weggeland painted the early temple murals; a painting depicting a small harbor in northeast England where Weggeland stopped for two years to paint portraits while he saved money to make the trip to Utah; a fine little oil painting of Weggeland's homestead at Pelican Point on the shore of Utah Lake; and a landscape of Bishop Madsen's Provo farmstead, site of an annual LDS Scandinavian reunion for many years.

Lagoon's Pioneer Village has a fine Weggeland genre scene of a pioneer homestead and several of his paintings depicting scenes from the Book of Mormon. The Springville museum also exhibits a very fine Weggeland pioneer homestead. In addition, the museum's painting of a gypsy camp in Utah shows a Mormon village in the background.

Samuel Hans Jepperson (1855–1931) came to Utah with his Danish parents when he was a young child, yet the Scandinavian tradition of historical genre painting still influenced him. While quite naive in technique, his paintings have a gentle charm and capture the early history of Provo and Utah Valley like Christensen's did for Sanpete County. The best collection of Jepperson's paintings is in the Daughters of Utah Pioneers museum in Provo.

Jacob Johannes Martinus Bohn (1823–1900), a native of Aalborg, Denmark, was a painter and a poet. He translated most of the lyrics in the first Danish edition of the Church hymnal. Only a few of his paintings remain. Those that do are copies of a series of paintings by Hungarian artist M. Munckasy. This is the same series that Weggeland copied for the passion of Christ. Bohn's paintings graced the chapels of the central Salt Lake valley for many years. Today, Bohn's *Christ before Pilate* hangs in the Murray North Stake Center. The artist is buried nearby in the Murray City Cemetery.

To group early LDS artists in Utah by nation of origin may seem odd, especially when many of them had lived in Utah for many years, thousands of miles from their native lands, and had even come to Utah as children. But the vast cultural melting pot of pioneer Utah did not operate nearly as fast as one might assume. The Scandinavians had their own Utah newspaper, the *Biekuben,* well into the twentieth century. Scandinavians frequently settled together; indeed, Sanpete Valley has long been recognized as a focus of Scandinavian culture in pioneer Utah. But even Salt Lake City had its "Danish Ward" (the Second Ward), where Dan Weggeland went to church with his family. On the front wall of the interior of the Second Ward chapel (built in 1907 and recently restored) on the corner of 500 East and 700 South, hangs a large Weggeland copy of Leonardo's *Last Supper*.

The British Saints likewise continued their cultural traditions. For example, Edward Tullidge, the brother of John, wrote an epic play about the life of Oliver Cromwell. Edward also published a literary magazine, *Tullidge's Quarterly,* almost thirty years after leaving England. The majority of the magazine's articles concerned news, literature, and commentary about Great Britain, although local history was also included.

The Lone American. The only American-born painter in the early period was George M. Ottinger (1833–1917), a native of Philadelphia. His works include both historical and landscape paintings and have a wide range of thematic content. He painted, for example, two townscapes of an English emigrant barber's ancestral village of Putney. One of these pieces, depicting the village church, is in the Church museum. Ottinger also created a fine painting depicting a Civil War battle; it hangs in the Lion House in downtown Salt Lake City. Inspired by the Book of Mormon's focus on the pre-Columbian inhabitants of this hemisphere, Ottinger was fond of depicting romantic scenes from the late Aztec Empire. The Springville museum and the Church museum both have examples of these works.

In addition to the foregoing, Ottinger painted portraits, though not all of the same quality. His single best portrait is of Brigham Young; it is held in the collection of the Church museum. Springville has a charming self-portrait of Ottinger in his uniform as the Salt Lake City fire chief.

Artistically, Ottinger's two most delightful pioneer paintings are *The Immigrant Train* (Springville museum) and *The Water Witch* (Church museum). One of Ottinger's largest historical paintings, *The Mormon Battalion,* is also in the Church museum. In addition, the Church museum has two small oil paintings that Ottinger made while he crossed the plains in a Mormon wagon train in 1861: one

George M. Ottinger (1833–1917), *Chimney Rock*. Oil on canvas, 6 1/4" x 13", Nebraska Territory, 1861. Ottinger was the lone American among early British or Scandinavian pioneer painters in Utah. Ottinger created this painting when traveling by wagon train to Utah.

depicts a circle of wagons at sunset near Chimney Rock, and the other portrays wagons at the ferry on the Green River of Wyoming. Along with the paintings by Piercy, these are virtually the only paintings of Mormon pioneers crossing the plains that were done by Mormon artists while on the trail west. All other paintings on the subject by Mormon artists, including those who had crossed the plains themselves, were produced many years later.

Paris. As previously mentioned, in 1890 the Church called several promising artists to go to Paris to study painting so they could return and paint the murals in the Salt Lake Temple. These artists were set apart as art missionaries by the First Presidency of the Church. The Church also financed their travel, living expenses, and tuition. In exchange, the missionaries were credited with repayment as they painted the temple murals. Immediately after being set apart, John Hafen (1856-1907), Lorus Pratt (1855-1923), and John B. Fairbanks (1855-1940) left for Paris, where they were soon joined by Edwin Evans (1860-1946). They formally studied academic figure at the Academie Julian in Paris; impressionism they picked up from more informal contacts in France.

The largest paintings of the art missionaries adorn the walls of the Salt Lake Temple. Three problems exist, however, for those who wish to study these works for their historical value: (1) access is strictly limited; (2) the paintings are unsigned and in some cases are collaborations by several artists; and (3) the murals have been "repaired" over the years with heavy overpainting. Due to these problems, researchers are probably limited to several large oil "sketches" of some of the murals, particularly those of John Hafen, that are held in the collections of Brigham Young University and the Church museum.

The three finest collections of the art missionaries' work are at the Springville museum, Brigham Young University, and the Church museum. The Springville museum has a fine cityscape of Springville by Hafen; one of John Fairbanks's finest paintings, a sunset scene looking over Utah Valley and Utah Lake; and a nice little harvest scene in Cache Valley by Lorus Pratt. Brigham Young University's finest Mormon works by Hafen are a series he did to illustrate the classic LDS hymn of the plan of salvation, "O My Father." The Church museum has two fine portraits by Hafen and numerous large landscapes. But the museum's finest Hafen piece is his masterpiece, *Girl with Hollyhocks.* This painting depicts the artist's daughter in the family's backyard surrounded by hollyhocks. It is one of the most moving paintings ever done by an LDS artist in depicting a father's love. The Church acquired its large Hafen collection around the turn of the century when Church leaders agreed to support Hafen and his family in exchange for paintings. Hafen's large impressionist landscapes have decorated Church headquarters for many decades. Several are now on exhibit in the Church museum.

One of the Church museum's most interesting paintings is John Fairbanks's *Magdalena River Valley in South America.* This valley marked the end of the trail for a Brigham Young University expedition, led by Benjamin Cluff, to search for Book of Mormon lands. Fairbanks was the painter who accompanied the expedition to visually record its findings.

Paintings in the Church museum by Lorus Pratt, another art missionary, include portraits (including one of President John Taylor), pioneer scenes (a covered wagon descending Provo Canyon), a large threshing scene in the Salt Lake Valley, and numerous other works.

Upon his return from Paris, Edwin Evans began teaching at the University of Utah, where he served as the chairman of the art department for many years. The largest collection of Evans paintings is at Lehi High School (in Evans's hometown of Lehi, Utah), but these do not necessarily represent his best work. One of Evans's favorite themes was cattle, which he herded as a young boy. His finest painting, a genre scene with a calf, is at Brigham Young University. The Church museum also has a good Evans painting of cows by the Jordan River.

The art missionaries are remembered for their unique calling as well as for their works. Other Utah artists, however, preceded them to Paris. Among these were James Harwood (1860–1940), John Clawson (1858–1936), sculptor Cyrus Dallin, and Herman Haag (1871–95).

John Hafen (1856–1910), *Girl with Hollyhocks.* Oil on canvas, 36" x 41", Utah, 1902. Hafen was an "art missionary," sent to Paris to study art in preparation for painting the murals in the Salt Lake Temple. This Impressionist painting depicts the artist's youngest daughter in the backyard of the family home.

Herman Haag is represented in the Church museum by two major works. One is a large charcoal drawing of Christ and John the Baptist, for which the artist won an award while studying in Paris. The other piece is a medium-sized oil painting of Nephi slaying Laban. This painting, almost proto-cubist in style, is the first painting ever done by a Mormon artist on this Book of Mormon subject. Upon his return from Paris, Haag also taught at the University of Utah. He is another painter who left few works due to an early death.

John Willard Clawson (1858–1936), a grandson of Brigham Young, was born in the Beehive House. His first art studies were with George M. Ottinger at the University of Deseret. In 1881, "Will" and his new bride traveled to New York City, where he studied at the National Academy of Design. He went to Paris in 1889 (a year before the arrival of the art missionaries) to study at the Academie Julian, where James Harwood was already studying. After returning from Paris, Will supported himself (rather handsomely) as a portrait painter—mostly in California. Some of his finest portraits are of LDS General Authorities; these are in the Church museum.

The aforementioned James Taylor Harwood came from an LDS background but was not himself a baptized Mormon. Nevertheless, he created some significant works of Mormon art. Among them are two superb, large, religious paintings: *Come Follow Me* (depicting Christ calling Peter as an Apostle) in the Church museum and *Christ and the Ages* at Brigham Young University. In addition to these pieces, he created numerous paintings depicting Mormon pioneers and significant pioneer landmarks. Among the best of these are pioneer paintings at the University of Utah and the Salt Lake Public Library, as well as a fine painting of the public works blacksmith shop in the Church museum. Harwood's *The Gleaners,* a harvest scene done in France, seems to be an updated version of Ruth and Naomi gleaning the fields of Boaz; it is in the collection of the Church museum. Most of Harwood's works are landscapes. Fine examples are in the Church museum, Brigham Young University, the University of Utah, and the Springville museum. Straightforward portraits by Harwood are less common, but the Church museum has two fine portraits of Harwood's wife, Harriet.

All the art missionaries and most of the others that went to Paris returned to Utah to paint and teach—and they sent their best students to Paris to study. This second wave included Mahonri Young (1877–1957), Donald Beauregard (1884–1914), and Lewis Ramsey (1875–1941). Mahonri Young returned to Utah and then went to New York City, where he taught at the Art Student's League. He developed a national reputation, primarily as a sculptor and graphic artist. The largest collection of his painting and graphic works is at Brigham Young University. This collection includes prints, drawings, oil paintings, and watercolors. The Church museum has two fine oil paintings, both of which depict scenes of the Navajos in the Southwest.

Donald Beauregard spent most of his short artistic life in New Mexico. A wealthy patron there took a liking to his work and supported him for a number of years. He made important contributions to the early Santa Fe tradition, and most of his extant works hang in the Art Museum of New Mexico in Santa Fe. These works include a series of murals depicting the life of St. Francis; they decorate the walls in the museum's theater. One of the galleries is totally dedicated to his works. Beauregard stayed in Salt Lake City only briefly before moving on to California; consequently, in Utah his works are quite rare in public collections. The best of these is in the Territorial State House Museum in Fillmore, the artist's hometown.

Lewis Ramsey studied in Chicago, New York, and Boston before finally going to Paris. Upon returning to Salt Lake City, he taught art at the LDS University (later the LDS Business College). Many of his early works were portraits; several can be seen at the Church museum. His masterpieces of Mormon art, however, are all various versions of Moroni delivering the golden plates to Joseph Smith. These paintings are all done in a competent impressionistic style. Examples of this work can be seen in the Salt Lake City Eleventh Ward Chapel, the Portland Temple, the Chicago Temple, and the Church museum. Much of Ramsey's later work was devoted to canyons of southern Utah and desert scenes in California, where he eventually settled.

Two other artists in the LDS Paris tradition deserve mention here. Alma B. Wright (1875–1952) painted portraits and landscapes, and his works are found in most of the major public collections in Utah. However, his most significant LDS paintings are murals in the Cardston Temple.

Lee Greene Richards (1878–1950) became the preeminent portrait painter in Salt Lake City during the first few decades of the twentieth century. The Church museum has a large collection of Richards's portraits of Apostles. The Springville museum has a superb allegorical painting by Richards of a young woman (his daughter) looking down Emigration Canyon as the wagon trains roll down into the Salt Lake Valley. Richards's most monumental LDS paintings are the large murals and paintings in the Cardston, Mesa, and Idaho Falls temples.

The New York Tradition. With the coming of World War I, the focus for post-Utah training shifted from Paris to New York City and the Art Student's League. Among the most significant early LDS artists within this tradition were Mabel Frazer (1887–1982) and Minerva Teichert (1888–1976), two of the most stylistically aggressive LDS painters of the twentieth century.

Mabel Frazer spent most of her career on the art faculty of the University of Utah. Her finest Mormon painting is a scene depicting a pioneer farmer plowing with his oxen while seagulls hover overhead. This work is in the Church museum, which has numerous Frazer pieces. The Springville museum has several landscapes by Frazer, including a fine painting depicting the desert country of the Arizona Strip. Frazer also did many paintings depicting pre-Columbian ruins in Mexico and Guatemala; they were done in preparation for a large mural depicting the artist's vision of people from the Book of Mormon. This mural was painted in her ward chapel near the University of Utah.

Many of the small and medium-sized paintings of the ruins are in the Church museum.

Minerva Teichert's work celebrates the Mormon experience through narrative art. One of her favorite sayings was, "When the story is told, the picture is finished." She began studying art in San Francisco and Chicago before going to New York City, where she studied with Robert Henri at the Art Student's League. Upon her return to Idaho and, later, Wyoming, she raised a large family while helping her husband farm, homestead, and ranch. She became active in local politics, accepted responsible positions in her ward, and created an incredible number of historical and genre paintings that depicted "her people": Mormon pioneers, Oregon Trail pioneers, fur trappers, Native Americans, contemporary western ranchers, and men and women from the scriptures (mostly the Book of Mormon). The two most significant collections of her work are at Brigham Young University (whose president, Franklin S. Harris, accepted her paintings in lieu of tuition for her children) and the Church museum. She also painted the huge murals covering the walls of the "World Room" in the Manti Temple, as well as significant paintings in the Montpelier Stake Tabernacle; the Cokeville, Wyoming, chapel; and the old North Cache High School building.

Minerva K. Teichert (1889–1976), *Covered Wagon Pioneers, Madonna at Dawn.* Oil on canvas, 72" x 132", Wyoming, 1936. After receiving art training in New York, Teichert returned to the West, where she spent her life documenting in art pioneer history and her Mormon faith. Many of her paintings focus on women.

The art career of LeConte Stewart (1891–1990) roughly paralleled Teichert's, which is fortunate since both lived long, rich, productive lives. Each sought to celebrate their Mormon faith and tradition, but each did so in very different ways. Stewart celebrated the pioneer Mormon landscape that remained in northern Utah into the last quarter of the twentieth century. The indelible stamp of the Mormon pioneers on the landscape was evident in their barns, villages, homesteads, and fields edged with poplar trees. Stewart carefully recorded this gentle fusing of Mormons with the land. Today's onrush of urbanization has almost eliminated this landscape, and Stewart's paintings will increasingly become superb documents of visual history as well as outstanding works of art. Collections of his works can be seen in virtually every major public art collection in Weber, Davis, Salt Lake, and Utah counties. In Kaysville, where Stewart made his home, the city library has a gallery with a permanent exhibition of his work. The Church museum has a large collection and once mounted a major retrospective which included a catalog. Stewart also painted murals in the Hawaii, Cardston, and Mesa temples.

The Twentieth-Century Utah Tradition. In Cache Valley, a fine tradition developed in the first half of the twentieth century among the Utah State University art faculty. This group included Henri Moser (1876–1951), Calvin Fletcher (1882–1963), and Everett Thorpe (1907–). Moser focused on the Mormon landscape of Cache Valley; his works can be found in most of the major public collections in Utah. Fletcher created both landscapes and genre. Perhaps his finest works were murals in the Logan Temple, which were removed when the temple was renovated and are now in storage at the Church museum. There are large collections of his work at Utah State University and Brigham Young University. Thorpe also did landscapes but is perhaps best known for his portraits, genre, and historical paintings. His work can best be seen at Utah State University and some chapels in Logan.

In more recent years, other Utah State University faculty—Harrison Groutage (1925–), Gael Lindstrum (1919–), and Glen Edwards (1935–)—have added to the Cache Valley tradition. Utah State University has examples of their works. In addition, the Church museum and the Springville museum have works by Lindstrum and Groutage. Lindstrum painted mostly in watercolor, but the Church museum has a fine oil depicting Brigham Young's winter home in St. George. Edwards's work has a strong narrative content, usually focusing on nineteenth-century western themes. Groutage's best-known LDS paintings are dramatic panoramas of Cache Valley, with the Logan Temple as the focal point.

Joseph A. F. Everett (1883–1945) was best known for his small pastoral water colors of the Salt Lake Valley. His major LDS paintings decorate the World Room of the Idaho Falls Temple, where he depicts the settling of the valleys of the Mormon mountain west. Everett also painted murals in the World Room of the St. George Temple.

The next major leaders in Mormon painting were Arnold Friberg (1913–), from Illinois, and Alvin Gittens (1922–81), a convert from England. Both taught at the University of Utah. Friberg's most significant commissions include a dozen paintings depicting events from the Book of Mormon; they are now published in all missionary editions of the Book of Mormon. As a result, they have become very important visual precedents for a whole generation of Mormon artists, especially those who are converts to Mormonism. Other works by Friberg include scenes for Cecil B. DeMille's film *The Ten Commandments*[4] (for which he was nominated for an Academy Award), a large series on the Royal Canadian Mounted Police, and portraits of Great Britain's Prince Charles and Queen Elizabeth II. Much of his current work consists of American frontier west scenes. The only major public collection of Friberg's work is in the South Visitors' Center on Temple Square, where his Book of Mormon paintings are displayed.

Alvin Gittens was best known as a portrait painter and a teacher. He put his students through rigorous courses in anatomy and perspective at a time when other art schools were emphasizing the easier road of expressionism. Gittens was the region's preeminent portrait painter until his death. The finest collection of Gittens portraits is owned by the University of Utah, but the Utah Arts Council has a few of his paintings, as does the Church museum.

Brigham Young University's answer to Gittens as a portrait painter was Roman Andrus (1907–). Andrus did religious works in addition to portraits. His most powerful religious work is probably the dynamic painting of the Book of Mormon prophet Abinadi. Brigham Young University has the best collection of Andrus's religious works.

Robert Shepherd (1909–91), a Salt Lake City native, painted superb temple murals in the Idaho Falls, Manti, and Los Angeles temples. The Church museum has a large collection of Shepherd's original temple mural drawings. Shepherd's murals reflect three totally different styles. The Idaho Falls Garden Room murals are done with soft pastels and a flat, graphic, art-deco style that seems to be influenced by the early classic Walt Disney full-length cartoon movies. The Manti Garden Room murals, with their dreamy blues, show the unmistakable influence of the work of Maxfield Parrish. The Los Angeles World Room murals show the influence of the strong, bold, almost cubistic surfaces of Maynard Dixon.

In the early 1970s, as mentioned in this essay's section on sculpture, a group of LDS artists began to form at and around Brigham Young University; these artists were interested in exploring the interface between their religious faith and their art. The leading painters of this group were Gary Smith (1942–), a convert from Oregon; Dennis Smith (1942–) and William Whitaker (1943–), both of Utah; James Christensen (1943–), from California; and Trevor Southey (1940–), a convert from Rhodesia (now Zimbabwe). Several have gone on to build national reputations, and most have continued to paint some overtly LDS pieces. The best public collections of these artists' work can be found at Brigham Young University, the Springville museum, and the Church museum. Of special note are a large collection of Trevor Southey etchings and engravings (Church museum), his *Eden Farm* (Springville museum), and a series on the LDS plan of salvation (BYU). A fine collection of Gary Smith's work can be seen at Brigham Young University and the Church museum. A major book has appeared on the recent work of James Christensen. Vern Swanson of the Springville museum has an ongoing research and publishing interest in this group of artists.

Among other LDS painters still producing, Robert Marshall (1944–), originally from Mesquite, Nevada, has spent many years as the head of the Brigham Young University art department. He has done some fine symbolic LDS paintings that focus on the sacrament and the Resurrection. Brigham Young University, the Springville museum, and the Church museum all have examples of his work. Bruce Smith (1936–), also on the Brigham Young University art faculty, has done some fine symbolic LDS paintings that sometimes place biblical themes in the present. Two of his finest religious pieces are *The Return of the Prodigal Son* and *Jacob and Leah,* both in the Church museum.

Al Rounds (1954–), a prolific watercolorist living in the Salt Lake Valley, has built a large following for his finely crafted, somewhat sentimental landscapes, many of which depict significant LDS historic sites. Many of his paintings have been reproduced for covers and inside covers of the *Ensign.* Most of his paintings are in private collections; however, the Church museum has a huge watercolor depicting a hill scene in England with two early LDS missionaries.

Frank McEntire (1946–), a convert to the Church and originally from Texas, also makes his home in the Salt Lake Valley. McEntire's work focuses on abstract symbolism that draws heavily from pseudotribal sources. He has exhibited paintings at the Springville museum and the Salt Lake Art Center.

Shana Cook Clinger (1954–), one of Gittens's best students and his heir apparent, paints mostly portraits. She has also painted some allegorical paintings depicting LDS women's themes. Nancy Glazier (1947–), now living in Montana, has become one of the leading wildlife painters in the United States. Two of her best LDS paintings also use wildlife elements; *The Lamb and the Lion* and *Latter-day Daniel* are both in the Church museum. Another LDS woman, Jeanne L. Clark (1925–), currently on the faculty at Brigham Young University, paints brilliantly colored, somewhat abstract canvases depicting families. She is rapidly gaining a regional reputation for her work. Brigham Young University, the Springville museum, and the Church museum all have examples of her work. Rose Ann Petersen (1935–), from Bountiful, Utah, has created many works of LDS art that use symbols linking Latter-day Saints and the Old Testament. Her work is represented in the Church museum.

Greg K. Olsen (1958–) has done many tightly painted works depicting children and families as well as some major works depicting events from the scriptures. One of his finest early religious paintings is *The Transfiguration of Christ,* which hangs in the Seattle Temple. He is currently being commissioned by the Church to do a series depicting Old Testament events.

Contemporary Americans. Clark Kelly Price (1945–), from Star Valley, Wyoming, has built a regional and national reputation for his realistic paintings of western Americana. His ability to depict people and animals lends itself to works with a strong narrative content. Among his LDS paintings are *Noah and the Ark, Daniel in the Lions' Den,* and *Early LDS Missionaries before the King of Tonga,* all in the Church museum collection. Other LDS artists from Wyoming include Harold (1918–) and Glen (1946–) Hopkinson, father and son. Both work in the western genre area. Their LDS works focus on the Mormon pioneer experience. An LDS chapel in Cody, Wyoming, now used as a visitors' center, has paintings by the Hopkinsons depicting the LDS settlement of the Big Horn Valley of Wyoming. Another LDS painter in Cody is Mel Fillerup (1924–), who also does western genre works with occasional LDS pioneer themes. In Jackson, Wyoming, James Wilcox (1941–) has a large commercial art gallery and paints the dramatic landscape of the Teton Range.

In Rexburg, Idaho, Ricks College has created an art tradition among its faculty. Best known is Del Parson (1948–), formerly of the faculty, and his widely reproduced portrait of the Savior in red. Parson has since moved to St. George, Utah, where he teaches at Dixie College. Del's father, Oliver (1916–), is also a painter of note and served as chairman of the Ricks College art department for many years. Don Ricks (1929–) and his son Douglas (1954–), both from Rexburg, paint the LDS landscape of the Upper Snake River Valley and the surrounding mountains as well as western genre scenes.

In Utah County, Michael Coleman (1946–) and John Jarvis (1946–) work as wildlife and western artists. Coleman has built a major national and international reputation; unfortunately, except for a few early works depicting rural scenes in Utah, none of his work is thematically LDS. Jarvis, on the other hand, has painted some fine works depicting LDS homesteads. His LDS masterpiece is his large gouache *Jacob Hamblin and Chief Tuba* (Church museum). Gary Kapp (1942–), another Utah Valley artist, has done several large paintings of scenes from the Book of Mormon. He paints in a tightly narrative style. While his Book of Mormon works have been reproduced in the *Ensign,* they are in private collections.

In Midway, Robert Duncan (1952–), who began his career painting nineteenth-century Native American genre scenes, has now focused on mostly twentieth-century genre scenes depicting LDS farming and ranching families. Most of his works focus on the interaction of different generations within a family. Much of these paintings' content is based on his personal experiences with his grandfather on the family ranch in Big Piney, Wyoming. This particular focus springs directly from his LDS beliefs about the eternal nature of the family.

Valoy Eaton (1938–) and David Arnsbrach (1948–) are painters of note in Vernal, Utah. Eaton paints gentle rural scenes, frequently focusing on the family working together in a garden. An early painting by Eaton depicts two young Native American priests blessing the sacrament. This is one of the few paintings that depicts this sacred ordinance and also one of the only paintings depicting any aspect of the Indian Placement Program. The painting is part of the Brigham Young University art collection. Arnsbrach is best known for his representations of early Vernal history, including a fine painting of the Uintah Stake Tabernacle, the LDS architectural masterpiece of the Uintah Basin.

Judith Mehr (1951–), originally from California but now living in the Salt Lake Valley, has created several major LDS paintings depicting activities from the lives of LDS women. Among these activities are family gardening, food storage, and homemaking. While gardening is a part of the culture of the American West, it received special emphasis for Mormons during the administration of President Spencer W. Kimball. Works of Mehr, Eaton, and Duncan reflect the response of LDS artists to that imperative. Mehr's most ambitious painting, a large mural depicting Christ and genealogy work, hangs in the foyer of the Family History Library in Salt Lake City. The Church museum has a good collection of her work.

In Arizona, Howard Post (1948–) has created LDS genre pieces depicting home teaching, family reunions, and a private moment of a Relief Society teacher and a member of her class. Post's works can be found in the Church museum and have also been reproduced in the *Ensign*. Another LDS artist living in Arizona is Bart Morse (1938–), who teaches art at the University of Arizona. In the Church museum collection are two LDS pieces by Morse: one depicts the Little Cottonwood granite quarries used during the building of the Salt Lake Temple; the other is a graphic piece depicting the capstone laying ceremony for the Salt Lake Temple.

Judith Campion (1935–) of Seattle, Washington, is a gifted portrait artist who frequently works with graphite on paper. Her portrait of Spencer W. Kimball (in the collection of the Church museum) splendidly captured the sparkling personality of this humble modern prophet.

Originally from the eastern United States, LDS convert Paul Forster (1923) served on the art faculty at Brigham Young University for a time. He also spent several years living in New Mexico. Among his most powerful LDS works is a painting of the First Vision that includes the spirit of the adversary with whom Joseph battled. This piece is part of the collection of the Church museum. Forster also painted murals in the London, New Zealand, and St. George temples. Like Forster, Kent Goodlife (1946–) also taught on the Brigham Young University art faculty. He is best known for his meticulously rendered drawings. Several of his figure studies depict the Savior.

Ken Baxter (1944–), a Salt Lake City native, is primarily a landscape artist working in an impressionistic style. While he has painted many nineteenth-century scenes of Salt Lake City, his finest LDS painting depicts an emigrant ship at twilight loading Latter-day Saints at the Liverpool docks. This work is in the Church Area Offices in Manchester, England. Richard Murray (1948–), also of Salt Lake City, is another impressionist landscape artist. Very few of his works have any overtly LDS content; however, he did create a superb historical painting displayed in the Church offices in Manchester, England. The painting depicts the first LDS missionaries in Great Britain as they enter the town square in Preston on a rainy afternoon in 1837. Frank Magleby (1928–), a longtime art faculty member at Brigham Young University, also painted a scene from the 1837 mission. Specifically, Magleby's 1987 painting of the John Benbow farm focuses on the pool where Wilford Woodruff baptized hundreds of former United Brethren into the Church.

Farrell Collett (1907–), of Ogden, taught art for many years at Weber State University, where the art building is named after him. While he is best known for his realistic wildlife paintings (particularly of cougars), he has also painted a series depicting the Mormon pioneers and the settlement of Utah. These pieces are part of the Weber State University collection.

Lucy Leuppe McKelvey (1946–), *Echoes of the Ancient Ones.* Fired clay, 12 3/4" x 11 1/2", New Mexico, 1988. McKelvey is the leading contemporary Navajo potter. In this piece, she uses traditional Southwest Native American iconography to tell the story of the Book of Mormon.

In the American Southwest, as a result of missionary work going back to the 1860s, thousands of Native Americans have joined the Church. Many of the finest Hopi artists are LDS. Among the most prominent are potters Fannie Nampeyo Polacca (ca. 1900–1987), Helen Naha (1922–), Joy Navasie (1919–), Rodina Huma (ca. 1950–), and Thomas Polacca (1934–); kachina carvers Lowell Talishoma (1950–) and Emil Pooley (1908–); and father and son silversmiths Wayne (1923–79) and Phil Sekaquaptewa (1948–), Michael Sockyma (1942–), and Trinidad Lucas (ca. 1968–). Among the Navajos, Robert Yellowhair (1937–) of Snowflake, Arizona, is a professional painter, as is William V. Hatch (1955–) of Fruitland, New Mexico. Lee Yazzie (1946–) is a leading jeweler and Lucy McKelvey (1946–) has a national reputation as a potter. Leta Kieth (1923–) from Chilchinbito is a fine weaver of pictorial rugs. Vera Spencer (1964–), from Sanders, Arizona, is another outstanding LDS Navajo weaver. Among the Maricopas, Ida Redbird (1888–1971) is perhaps their most famous potter. Among the Santa Clara Pueblos, Christina (1892–1980) and Terrisita Naranjo (1919–) have national and international reputations as potters. Other potters among the Santa Claras are members of the Eugene and Isabelle Naranjo family; the Andy and Marsha Padilla Family; and Harrison Begay, a Navajo who is married to a daughter of the Padillas.

Among the strongly LDS works of art by these artists are two rugs, *Missionaries in Monument Valley* and *The Mesa Temple,* by Leta Kieth. Other works include a pot, *The Book of Mormon,* by Lucy McKelvey, and a pot by Thomas Polacca that depicts the conversion and religious life of his grandfather. Robert Yellowhair has painted *Lehi's Vision of the Tree of Life,* and Ivy Norton (1910–) has created a beehive basket using traditional Hopi coiled basket techniques. *Beehive Concho Belt* by Michael Sockyma, *The Three Degrees of Glory* by Phil Sekaquaptewa, and *The Salt Lake Temple* by Trinadad Lucas are three fine LDS pieces in silver by Hopi Latter-day Saints. All of these works are owned by the Church museum.

The Late Twentieth-Century International Tradition

Since pioneer times, LDS artists have continually been drawn to Utah from outside the United States. Brigham Young University has become an important focus for this artistic immigration. Three of the most recent art faculty immigrants are Wulf Barsch (1943–) and Hagen Haltern (1947–), both from Germany, and Søren Edsberg (1945–), from Denmark. Barsch, a winner of the 1975–76 Prix de Rome, has built a national reputation with his strong, geometric, semiabstract paintings

Wulf E. Barsch (1943–), *Alpha and Omega.* Oil on paper, 60" x 28", Utah, 1984. In this painting, Barsch, a native of Bohemia, represents the relationship between earth life and the plan of salvation. The drab, gray room symbolizes this world without the gospel's perspective.

that often include LDS themes. The Church museum has a large collection of his prints and several of his larger paintings. Brigham Young University, the Springville museum, and the Utah Arts Council also have collections of his work. Søren Edsberg has built a European reputation for his strongly stylized geometric paintings that also have strong LDS overtones. Haltern is best known for his graphite drawings; the Church museum has a small but superb piece depicting the prophet Jeremiah. Haltern has also done more abstract symbolic religious pieces that are in the Brigham Young University collection. Besides being a visual artist, Haltern is also interested in writing about his theories of LDS art.

In the 1950s, Richard Burde (1912-) emigrated to Utah from his native Germany. Burde was trained in Dresden before World War II. His work reflects much of the historical Northern European art tradition, particularly the baroque art of the seventeenth century. Burde may be the most prolific LDS painter of scriptural themes to date; he has painted scores of paintings depicting scenes from the Bible. The Church museum has several of his pieces, including *The Return of the Prodigal Son, Christ Washing the Feet of the Apostles,* his large masterpiece *Christ on Calvary,* and *Joseph Smith* (depicted as a German scholar).

Ljiljana Crnogaj Fulepp (1952-), a convert from Zagreb, Croatia, now lives in Arizona. Her most accomplished art media are Gobelin tapestry embroidery and traditional back-painted glass from Croatia. The Church museum has four of her LDS pieces, including *Joseph Smith, The Second Coming of Christ, Missionaries Preaching in a Croatian Village,* and *An Early Baptism Near Belgrade.*

Not all European LDS painters have come to the United States. Pino Drago (1947-) of Italy; Johan Bentin (1936-) of Denmark; and Knud Edsberg (1911-), the father of Søren, also from Denmark, are among a growing community of European LDS artists. Each is represented in the

Church museum collection with works that are deeply religious. Drago and Bentin's works are highly symbolic. Knud Edsberg specializes in genre and very traditional portraiture. The Church museum has a collection of his portraits of several Apostles as well as some of his paintings about families.

In Austria, Rosalina Lipp (1927–) has a reputation as one of the country's finest folk painters. She specializes in traditional furniture painting. Besides teaching in government-operated folk art schools, she has also been an official folk art ambassador for her nation to Belgium, Switzerland, Germany, and France. Her major LDS piece is a large painted armoire that depicts missionaries, the Salt Lake Temple, the First Vision, the angel Moroni, and the restoration of the priesthood. This piece is on exhibit at the Church museum.

Latin America and the Caribbean have also produced a significant number of important LDS painters, the most prominent being Mexico's

Erick Duarte (ca. 1965–), *Ready for Covenant.* Pastel on paper, 30 1/2" x 40 1/2", Guatemala, 1990. Gift of the Silver Foundation. Like many contemporary LDS artists, Duarte paints the story of missionary work from a convert's point of view. This painting was an award winner in the second Churchwide art competition sponsored by the Museum of Church History and Art.

Jorge Cocco (1936–), Panama's Antonio Madrid (1949–), Chile's Jose R. Riveros (ca. 1940–), Guatemala's Erick Duarte (ca. 1965–), and Haiti's Henri-Robert Bresil (1952–). Riveros's *Amumu Petu: Go Ye Therefore* won the award of excellence and a purchase prize at the second Churchwide art competition at the Church museum. All of these artists have produced important LDS paintings using artistic approaches totally different from their fellow LDS artists in Utah. Cocco and Madrid, for example, look to Spain for stylistic models. Bresil draws on the bright and exuberant folk tradition from Haiti. His *Alma Baptizing in the Waters of Mormon* is in the Church museum collection. The Church museum has works by all of these artists.

Cuna Indians, *Moroni Raising the Title of Liberty*. Cloth, 20" x 16", Panama, before 1990. Gift of Elder and Sister Ted E. Brewerton. These appliqué and reverse appliqué textile panels are the main traditional art of the Cuna Indians. This *mola* is based on Book of Mormon paintings by Arnold Friberg. Folk artists throughout the Church frequently base their paintings on images they see in Church publications.

Among the LDS folk painters from Latin America, Estelle Estrada (1969–), from Guatemala City, and Joselito Jesus Acevedo Garcia (1965–), from Huancayo, Peru, have both produced works with charm, honesty, insight, and religious conviction. Estrada's *The Gospel Comes to the Lamanites* and Joselito Garcia's *The Lamanites Shall Blossom as a Rose* are both part of the collection of the Church museum. One of the finest LDS Latin American artists, Juan Escobedo (1946–), who is originally from San Luis Potosi, now lives in Nevada. His bright, exuberant works capture the vibrant folk art tradition of his native Mexico. His *Joseph Smith and the Tree of Life* is part of the collection of the Church museum.

Juan Zarate (1930–) lives in Guatemala, where textile weaving is the main national art form. Zarate lives in the highlands town of Momostenango, spins and prepares his own yarn (some of it dyed with local indigo), and weaves heavy wool blankets on an ancient Spanish colonial loom. LDS themes are often woven into these blankets. Zarate has

Joni Susanto (1961–), *The First Vision*. Textile, 28 1/2" x 36", Java, Indonesia, 1990. Susanto learned batik, the national art form of Indonesia, from his father-in-law. Susanto is a full-time professional batik artist and a convert to the Church.

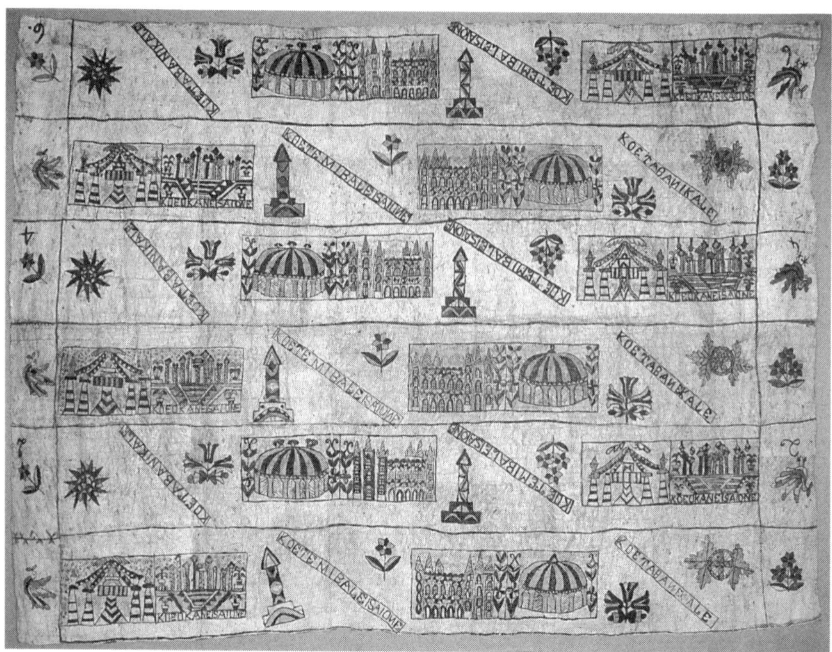

Va Va'u District Relief Society, *Temple Square Tapa Cloth*. Tapa cloth, 123" x 80", Tonga, 1936. The Relief Society in Tonga used pictures of Temple Square in designing this tapa cloth. The Salt Lake Temple, Tabernacle, Tabernacle organ and choir seats, Eagle Gate, and the Seagull Monument are depicted.

been an official art ambassador of his nation in international artist exchanges. The Church museum has a Zarate blanket depicting the angel Moroni in the center.

In the South Pacific, Rei Hamon (ca. 1915–), a Maori from New Zealand, is building a reputation as an environmental artist. His tight stipple drawings express his spiritual attachment to the land, plants, and native animals of New Zealand. In some of his art, he depicts the spirits of the departed trees that the English settlers have almost eliminated from many parts of the land. The scripture in Moses 3:5, which describes the spiritual creation of all living things, comes to mind as one studies some of Hamon's work. The Church museum has a small collection of his pieces.

In Indonesia, where batik is the preeminent art form, Hadi Pranoto (1937–) and his son-in-law, Joni Susanto (1961–), from Yogyakarka, Java, are recognized batik artists. The Church museum has a significant collection of their batiks depicting early LDS history as

Lawrence Enigiator, *The Family*. Okheum wood, 48" x 24" x 16", Nigeria, 1993. Enigiator sculpted this piece in the traditional style of Benin. Note the Book of Mormon carried by a family member. This sculpture received a purchase award at the Third International Art Competition, sponsored by the Museum of Church History and Art.

well as contemporary LDS scenes. In Sierra Leone, Africa, Emil Wilson (ca. 1955–), a recent LDS convert, is also a noteworthy batik artist. The Church museum has a collection of over twenty of his batiks with LDS themes ranging from biblical scenes and early Church history to scenes from Wilson's LDS branch in Freetown.

Although the LDS Church is relatively young, with beginnings on the American frontier, Mormon artists have been and remain amazingly international. While their art encompasses many styles, its unity comes through shared religious beliefs and through recurring LDS religious themes. The lack of an official liturgical art has kept Mormonism from forcing its artists into narrow stylistic traditions. This has been especially significant as the Church has expanded into many different cultures. Some of the aesthetic constants that seem to be continually expressed by Mormon artists are the narrative and symbolic traditions in art, a reverence for nature, a lack of nihilism, respect for the human body, a strong sense of aesthetic structure, and rigorous craftsmanship.

Mormon Pine Furniture

One of the most distinctive folk art traditions during the western pioneer period of nineteenth-century Mormonism was the creation of furniture. Most of the furniture makers were British and Scandinavian convert immigrants. A few were from the eastern states. Missionary work and the nineteenth-century practice of gathering brought skilled LDS furniture makers to Utah, then dispersed them to small, remote communities. The nineteenth-century emphasis on self-sufficiency, culminating in the creation of the United Orders and Mormon cooperatives, kept the tradition alive even after the coming of the railroad.

The furniture these artisans made was usually of pine, although some other local woods such as box elder and poplar and a few rare pieces of imported hardwoods were used. The pine resulted in more heavily proportioned furniture to compensate for the weakness of the soft wood. The furniture was invariably painted. A favorite form of finishing was to "hand grain" with paint to simulate the grain pattern and color of the more exotic hardwoods. Sometimes solid colors, such as reddish brown, black, and blue, were used on minor pieces.

Pine furniture throughout the Mormon settlement area used three distinctive stylistic traditions. The Brigham City style developed because of a United Order furniture factory there. The Public Works in Salt Lake, developed as part of the support facility for the building of the temple, produced its furniture according to another distinct tradition. Finally, Sanpete County's tradition reflected the large Scandinavian population in that area.

The serious study must examine the pieces of furniture themselves. The best public collections of Mormon pine furniture are mostly at restored historic sites such as the Beehive House, Cove Fort, the Jacob Hamblin Home, Pipe Springs, the Brigham Young Winter Home, and the Brigham Young Forest Farm House (at Pioneer Trails State Park). The major museum collections are at the Church museum, Lagoon's Pioneer Village (this collection was purchased from the Sons of Utah Pioneers), the Daughters of Utah Pioneers museum in Salt Lake City, the Territorial Statehouse in Fillmore, and the Brigham City Museum. Two collections are particularly noteworthy. First, Pipe Springs was furnished almost exclusively with Mormon pine pieces from southern Utah, so it gives a very good picture of the artistry of that region of the state. Second, the Church museum has the best collection of Salt Lake Public Works furniture. William Bell, a London furniture maker, was the superintendent of the Public Works and put his English stamp on its furniture.

Printed material on Mormon pine furniture is quite limited. For that reason, scholarly works about pine furniture are described here rather than in the bibliography appended to the end of this article. The best published analysis of Mormon pine is an essay by Nancy Richards, "Mormon Craftsmen in Utah," in *Utah Folk Art: A Catalog of Material Culture,* ed. Hal Cannon (Provo: Brigham Young University Press, 1980), 61-90. Connie Morningstar's *Early Utah Furniture* (Logan: Utah State University Press, 1976) lacks the level of analysis of Richards's work, but contains some very useful information. Morningstar has included the names and sometimes a very short biographical note for more than one hundred furniture makers. She has also included a fairly complete bibliography of published sources and unpublished theses as of 1976. A third book that deals with Mormon pine is the catalog *Frontier America: The Far West* (Boston: Museum of Fine Arts, 1975). The catalog contains a chapter by Elizabeth Sussman on furniture (155-96). This chapter is superficial in its overall analysis of Mormon pine; nevertheless, it contains several photographs of Mormon pine along with some good captions.

The most recently published information on Mormon pine is in the August 1991 issue of *Country Home Magazine.* Despite the fact that this is a publication from the popular rather than the scholarly press, the articles on Mormon pine, "At Home in the Promised Land" and "Latter-day Legacy," contain excellent color photographs and are good general introductions to Mormon pine furniture.

The best scholarly work on Mormon pine is Thomas Carter's "Building Zion: Folk Architecture in the Mormon Settlements of Utah's Sanpete Valley, 1849-1890" (Ph.D. diss., Indiana University, 1984). "Building Zion" traces much of the Sanpete furniture tradition back to its Scandinavian roots. Carter does not deal with the full range of Mormon pine, but he eloquently reminds us that each branch of the Mormon pine tradition deserves a similar study.

Another avenue of research that must be explored is the biographies of the furniture makers themselves. Morningstar gives us a hint of what is available. The Family History Library and other archives must be researched for additional biographical information.

Since much pine furniture was made in cooperative shops and factories, the Mormons' unique and religiously driven economic environment must be studied. Two of the best introductory sources on this subject are Leonard J. Arrington, *Great Basin Kingdom: An Economic History of the Latter-day Saints, 1830-1900* (Cambridge, Mass.: Harvard University Press, 1958), and Leonard J. Arrington, Feramorz Y. Fox, and Dean L. May, *Building the City of God: Community and Cooperation among the Mormons,* (Salt Lake City: Deseret Book, 1976).

Mormon Quilts

Unlike the home production of pine furniture, quilting has continued among Latter-day Saints in the western heartland (those areas settled by Mormons in the nineteenth century). Quilting was artistic and frugal, practical and celebratory, individually creative and communal, and innovative and traditional. Some of the kinds of quilting that Mormon women have developed include bishop's quilts (made to honor or thank bishops), missionary quilts, family history quilts, temple quilts, blessing quilts, scouting quilts, celebration quilts, and ward quilts.

A major public collection is in the chain of Daughters of Utah Pioneers museums throughout the state; the main museum in Salt Lake City has an especially good collection. Another major public collection of Mormon quilts is housed in the Church museum. Other Church historic sites also have good collections; these include collections at the Beehive House; the Brigham Young Winter Home; the Jacob Hamblin Home; Nauvoo; and the sites in the Palmyra, New York, area. Utah State University is also beginning to collect Utah (but not necessarily Mormon) quilts. Pioneer Trails State Park, Pioneer Village at Lagoon, the Territorial Statehouse in Fillmore, Pipe Springs National Historical Monument, and the Layton City Museum also have collections.

Of the foregoing collections, the Church museum has the most intensive focus on collecting quilts that are distinctively LDS in function and iconography. This museum also has the most active quilt-collecting program. The current collection includes over 250 quilts at the museum and historic sites. Included are quilts brought to Utah by pioneer emigrants, others made in the Mormon intermountain region in the nineteenth and twentieth centuries, quilts from Polynesia (particularly Tahiti and Hawaii), and Mormon centennial and sesquicentennial pieces.

The Utah Quilt Guild has been involved for a number of years in building an archive of antique quilts in Utah. The guild photographs the quilts and determines the provenance of each one. A very significant contribution of this program is its catalog of private quilt collections, which greatly adds to the historical resources available to the study of this art form.

Major Public Collections of Mormon Art

There are several major public collections of Mormon art: the Museum of Art, Brigham Young University (Provo, Utah); the Springville Museum of Art (Springville, Utah); the Utah State Arts Council (Salt Lake City); the Utah Museum of Fine Arts (on the campus of the University of Utah); the Utah State Historical Society (Salt Lake City); the Daughters of Utah Pioneers museum in Salt Lake City (there are many branch museums of the DUP throughout Utah, but few have significant art collections compared to the Salt Lake City museum); Pioneer Village at Lagoon (Farmington, Utah); the Museum of Church History and Art (Salt Lake City); the Lion House (Salt Lake City); the Beehive House (Salt Lake City); the Nora Eccles Harrison Museum (on the campus of Utah State University); Weber State University (Ogden, Utah); Pioneer Trails State Park (Salt Lake City); Territorial Statehouse (Fillmore, Utah); Ricks College art department (Rexburg, Idaho); Brigham Young

University—Hawaii Campus (Laie, Hawaii); Missouri Historical Society (Columbia); Museum of Fine Arts (Boston); Joslyn Art Museum (Omaha); the Smithsonian Institution (Washington, D.C.); and the Church visitors' centers, particularly those on Temple Square in Salt Lake City; in Cody, Wyoming; in New York City; and near San Diego.

Natural history museums with major collections of folk art by LDS artists can be found in various locations, including Arizona, New Mexico, and the Smithsonian. Most of the art is Hopi pottery, Navajo weaving, and Pueblo pottery. In order to access these collections, the researcher needs to know the names of the artists.

The Springville museum, particularly under the current director, Vern Swanson, is building a very fine collection of Utah art. This collection is being assembled primarily along stylistic rather than thematic lines. Therefore, while the collection contains a fine overview of Utah art, the Mormon content is still embryonic. A significant recent development at Springville is an annual Christmas exhibition, where artists are encouraged to do religious and seasonal fine art. Religious themes are also starting to appear in the annual Spring Salon exhibition, giving Springville the potential to enlarge the Mormon content of its collections.

The Daughters of Utah Pioneers and the Utah State Historical Society collections have some very good pre-1930 Mormon pieces. However, neither of these institutions seems to have actively built its art collection for the last half-century.

The Utah State Arts Council was one of the earliest state art councils in the nation. Its collection of Utah art, though one of the largest, has few pieces with much Mormon content. In terms of recent collecting (the last half-century or so), the arts council seems to specifically avoid acquiring works of art with any Mormon or religious content. The exception has been the broader collecting philosophy of the council's folk art section.

The university-related collections generally focus on works of art produced by their own faculty, with Mormon content being of secondary importance to the main aim of documenting the stylistic traditions of the artists. However, collections of contemporary Mormon art by LDS artists living outside Utah can be found at Ricks College and BYU—Hawaii.

The Church museum has by far the most comprehensive collection of Mormon art. The collection includes both traditional Mormon fine art and folk art from the pre-Utah period and the entire history of Utah. It also includes Mormon folk art and fine art from the rest of the United States and abroad. With contemporary Church demographics and current growth patterns, the international aspect of Mormon art will become increasingly important. A constant series of changing exhibitions and art competitions that focus on various Mormon themes and geographical areas regularly add to the Churchwide dimension of the Church museum.

Four factors explain the Church museum's extensive collection of Mormon art. First, over the years the Church has directly commissioned many works of art to meet Church needs; these have relied heavily on narratives with LDS content. Second, the curators, with the strong support of Historical Department and General Authority directors and advisors, have actively sought out works of art with overtly LDS content from the United States and abroad. Third, the Churchwide art competition has directly aided in the acquisition of works of art with LDS themes. Finally, the Church museum has occasionally commissioned works of art, virtually all of which have had LDS content.

The LDS temples contain major collections of Mormon art, but these collections are not available for viewing or research by the general public. Among the LDS temples with the finest collections are those in Salt Lake City, Manti, Cardston, Idaho Falls, Mesa, Los Angeles, and Hawaii. Some of the more recent temples also have a few works of Mormon art. The recent temples, however, generally hold framed prints of Mormon art; the remainder of the art consists of original works that have little or no Mormon content.

Major Document Collections

Primary written document collections are not as common in Mormon art history as they are in other areas of Mormon studies. Several facts explain this situation. First, until the last ten or twenty years, archives have more often focused on religious, political, economic, and educational leaders of the Mormon community. Few scholars were doing research in the area of the visual arts among the Mormons, so archivists did not work to fulfill demands that did not exist. In addition, visual artists usually do not write very much; their preferred means of expression is in the creation of their art rather than written commentary, journals, and letters. Two of the most significant departures from this pattern are the writings of C. C. A. Christensen and John Hafen.

Many of the written documents that do exist are produced by people other than the artists—for example, critics who publish reviews of exhibitions in newspaper articles. Several important collections of these documents exist. One is the Salt Lake artists' newspaper clipping scrapbook, which can be found in Special Collections at the Salt Lake Public Library. This collection contains *Deseret News* and *Salt*

Lake Tribune clippings from the first half of the twentieth century. A second valuable collection is the George Dibble Collection, housed in Special Collections at the University of Utah's Marriott Library. George Dibble was on the art faculty at the university for many years and was also the art critic for the *Salt Lake Tribune.* His art columns contain a wealth of information about artists he knew personally.

Of note at Weber State University's Special Collections is the Elizabeth Stewart Collection; it contains news clippings and articles that cover the years from 1914 through 1957. Artists discussed include Dallin, Weggeland, Fairbanks, Ottinger, Folsom, Young, and Lambourne. Another item of importance at Weber State is the Farrell Collett collection.

Like Weber State, Utah State University also has some good document collections in its Special Collections at the Merrill Library. The collections focus on former art faculty at Utah State University.

The Western Americana Collection at the Harold B. Lee Library of Brigham Young University contains primary research material on over two dozen historical Utah artists. The best document collections deal with the lives of Mahonri Young and John Hafen. The archives also has some of Bent F. Larsen's papers; Larsen was one of the earlier university faculty members to envision a need to document the history of Mormon art. The extensive document collection of LDS artist Jack Sears is concerned mostly with documenting the life of Sears's good friend Mahonri Young. The library has an oral history of Roman Andrus, who served on the Brigham Young University art faculty for many years. In the large photoarchives of the university, two major collections stand out: one, done by John B. Fairbanks, deals with the Cluff Expedition that traveled to northern South America looking for the civilizations of the Book of Mormon; the other is the work of pioneer photographer George Edward Anderson. The BYU Museum of Art has its extensive collection of original works of art entered on a computer catalog system.

A small but well-organized research section has been established in an upstairs room in the Springville museum. It includes mounted photographs of art by many Utah artists, as well as looseleaf notebooks of clippings and other published research on Utah artists.

Because of the extensive patronage of the visual arts by the Church, the Church Historical Department Archives and Library cannot be overlooked in any serious research into the comprehensive history of Mormon art. The art historical crown jewels of the archives are the complete papers of Carl Christian Anton Christensen, primarily assembled by Richard Jensen of the Smith Institute at Brigham Young University. While some of the original writings are in Danish, most have been translated into English by Orson West, a native Dane. The collection includes much of Christensen's poetry and journals, as well as the original scripts that accompanied the presentation of "The Mormon Panorama" series described earlier in this essay. Christensen's work is significant because he was easily the most important early LDS historical painter. Letters to and from the First Presidency and the "art missionaries" in Paris are also key documents in the archives. In addition, there is a small but growing collection of oral histories on LDS artists; among these are Matthew Heiss's fine interviews with Trevor Southey, Thomas Polacca, and Iris Youvella. The Journal History of the Church is another useful tool in studying the history of Mormon art. This "journal" is a scrapbook selection of newspaper clippings and journal entries arranged chronologically. A fairly good index exists for this work.

The Church Historical Department Archives has over one hundred thousand historical photographs. Among the most historically and artistically significant photographs by an LDS photographer are those of Springville's George Edward Anderson. In addition, the Church Historical Department Library staff has carefully indexed Church periodicals. Of particular note are the writings of John Hafen in the *Juvenile Instructor* and a long run of short articles on LDS art and artists in the *Relief Society Magazine*. The library's extensive book collection on Mormon history also has significant bits and pieces of information on the history of Mormon art.

The Church museum maintains a small library on art and material culture as well as a slide collection of works in its collection. It employs a full-time art librarian, along with several regular volunteers. In addition to printed and photographed work, the museum has a computer catalog of its extensive art collection. A file on LDS artists, containing institutional records and research on over twelve hundred individuals, has been assembled primarily by me as senior curator at the museum. It represents one of the few archival records on non-Utah LDS artists and is virtually the only one on non-American LDS artists. However, because these are the working files of the museum, they are not available for public research.

Conclusion

At its interpretive core, Mormon art deals with Mormon themes. Such themes have been the unifying thread in the Mormon artistic tradition for more than a century-and-a-half. As the Church becomes increasingly international and cross-cultural, Mormon themes will become the only threads that hold this tradition together. Furthermore, international expansion and the need to rewrite cultural history to include such expansion will render traditional categories of painting and sculpture insufficient to describe the vast sweep of the Mormon art tradition. Hence, future art historians will require much broader aesthetic training if they wish to do a comprehensive history of Mormon art. In addition to such training, art historians will need to understand the visual language of artists from many cultural backgrounds. Such understanding can come through iconography studies, which have become ever more significant in identifying cohesion within a tradition.

As I ponder the increasing balkanization of culture in the United States and abroad, the Latter-day Saint experience offers some promising areas of cultural inquiry. Can unity among people of substantial ethnic diversity reach down to their deepest spiritual core? What insights into the Mormon experience will new Mormons bring with them? What impact will these increasingly diverse aesthetic, intellectual, and spiritual insights have on the direction of Mormon art?

Artistic unity for diverse Mormons requires more than a once-a-year folk arts festival in a city park. Such unity in diversity is an artistic response to a set of shared assumptions about the nature of God, the individual, the family, humanity, and history. Individual Mormons' different cultural backgrounds will result in different mediums, techniques, styles, and even some differences in iconography. But the profundities of the visual discussion will be shared by Mormons no matter what culture they come from. Mormons see the world and each other differently than people who are not Mormons. This worldview appears in Mormon art. One of the great challenges to scholars is to articulate the visual expression of this spiritual and historical core of the Mormon people.

Select Bibliography

The following is a select bibliography of works about LDS art. Works listed are categorized as either books and manuscripts, journal articles, theses and dissertations, or key periodicals. The list of theses and dissertations focuses almost exclusively on works done at Brigham Young University (Provo, Utah), the University of Utah (Salt Lake City), and Utah State University (Logan). While these three universities have not produced all the theses and dissertations on LDS art, they certainly have produced the vast majority.

Books and Manuscripts

Andrew, Laurel B. *The Early Temples of the Mormons: The Architecture of the Millennial Kingdom in the American West.* Albany: State University of New York Press, 1978.

Barsch, Wulf. *In the Desert—a Stranger in a Strange Land.* Provo, Utah: By the author, [1984].

Bashore, Melvin L., comp. *Index to Art Works in LDS Church Periodicals.* Salt Lake City: Church Library, The Church of Jesus Christ of Latter-day Saints Historical Department, 1979.

Broder, Patricia Janis. *Bronzes of the American West.* New York: Harry N. Abrams, 1973.

Bunker, Gary L., and Davis Bitton. *The Mormon Graphic Image, 1834-1914: Cartoons, Caricatures, and Illustrations.* Salt Lake City: University of Utah Press, 1983.

Burke, Dan E. *Utah Art of the Depression: An Exhibition from the Utah State Fine Arts Collection.* Salt Lake City: Utah Arts Council, 1986.

Cannon, Hal, comp. *The Grand Beehive.* Salt Lake City: University of Utah Press, 1980.

Cannon, Hal, ed. *Utah Folk Art: A Catalog of Material Culture.* Provo, Utah: Brigham Young University Press, 1980.

Carlson, John F. *Carlson's Guide to Landscape Painting.* 1958. Reprint, New York: Dover Publications, 1973. A frequent source for LeConte Stewart, for whom Carlson was the most influential teacher.

Carter, Kate, ed. *Pioneer Quilts.* Salt Lake City: Daughters of Utah Pioneers, 1979.

Davies, J. Kenneth. *George Beard: Mormon Pioneer Artist with a Camera.* N.p., [1980].

Davis, Carolyn O'Bagy. *Pioneer Quiltmaker: The Story of Dorinda Moody Slade, 1808-1895.* Tucson, Arizona: Sanpete Publications, 1990.

Davis, Robert O. *LeConte Stewart: The Spirit of Landscape.* Salt Lake City: The Church of Jesus Christ of Latter-day Saints, 1985.

Dawdy, Doris Ostrander. *Artists of the American West: A Biographical Dictionary.* 2 vols. Chicago: Swallow Press, 1974-81.

Department of American Decorative Arts and Sculpture. *Frontier America: The Far West.* Boston: Museum of Fine Arts, 1975.

Eastwood, Laurie Teichert, and Robert O. Davis. *Rich in Story, Great in Faith: The Art of Minerva Kohlhepp Teichert.* Salt Lake City: The Church of Jesus Christ of Latter-day Saints, 1988.

Fairbanks, Eugene F. *A Sculptor's Testimony in Bronze and Stone: The Sacred Sculpture of Avard T. Fairbanks.* Salt Lake City: Publishers Press, 1972.

Francis, Rell G. *Cyrus E. Dallin: Let Justice Be Done.* Springville, Utah: Springville Museum of Art, 1976.

Fox, Sandi. *Quilts in Utah: A Reflection of the Western Experience.* Salt Lake City: Salt Lake Art Center, 1981.

Gerdts, William H. *Art across America: Two Centuries of Regional Painting.* Vol. 3 of *The Far Midwest, Rocky Mountain West, Southwest, Pacific.* New York: Abbeville, 1990.

Gibbs, Linda Jones. *Harvesting the Light: The Paris Art Mission and Beginnings of Utah Impressionism.* Salt Lake City: The Church of Jesus Christ of Latter-day Saints, 1987.

———. *Masterworks.* Salt Lake City: Museum of Church History and Art, 1984.

Graham, Mark, and Cathy Graham. *The Seal of Moroni.* New York: C. and M. Graham, 1979.

Hamon, Rei. *The Art of Rei Hamon.* Auckland, New Zealand: Collins, 1980.

Harthorn, Sandy, and Kathleen Bettis. *One Hundred Years of Idaho Art, 1850–1950.* Boise, Idaho: Boise Art Museum, 1990.

Hartman, Russell P., and Jan Musial. *Navajo Pottery: Traditions and Innovations.* Flagstaff, Arizona: Northland, 1987.

Harwood, James Taylor. *A Basket of Chips: An Autobiography.* Ed. by Robert S. Oplin. Salt Lake City: Tanner Trust Fund, University of Utah Library, 1985.

Haseltine, James L. *One Hundred Years of Utah Painting.* Salt Lake City: Salt Lake Art Center, 1965.

Hedgpeth, Don. *From Broncs to Bronzes: The Life and Work of Grant Speed.* Flagstaff, Arizona: Northland, 1979.

Held, John Jr. *The Most of John Held Jr.* Brattleboro, Vermont: Stephen Greene Press, 1972.

Henri, Robert. *The Art Spirit.* Philadelphia: J. B. Lippincott, 1923. Minerva Teichert referred to Henri, her most influential teacher, as her mentor and even named her first child after him.

Horne, Alice Merrill. *Devotees and Their Shrines: A Hand Book of Utah Art.* Salt Lake City: Deseret News, 1914.

Jacka, Jerry D., and Lois Jacka. *Beyond Tradition: Contemporary Indian Art and Its Evolution.* Flagstaff, Arizona: Northland, 1988.

Jensen, Richard L., and Richard G. Oman. *C. C. A. Christensen 1831–1912: Mormon Immigrant Artist.* Salt Lake City: The Church of Jesus Christ of Latter-day Saints, 1984.

Kaysville Art Club. *Pioneers of Utah Art.* Ed. by Elsie S. Heaton. Logan, Utah: Educational Printing Service, 1968.

Lambourne, Alfred. *Scenic Utah: Pen and Pencil.* New York: J. Dewing, 1891.

LeFree, Betty. *Santa Clara Pottery Today.* School of American Research Monograph Series, no. 29. Albuquerque: University of New Mexico Press, 1975.

Lund, Grant L. "Christ and the Creative Individual: A Study of the Interrelationship of Learning, Creating, Art, and Life." 1980. Manuscript held in Special Collections, Harold B. Lee Library, Brigham Young University, Provo, Utah.

McEntire, Frank. *Dreams and Shields, Spiritual Dimensions in Contemporary Art.* Salt Lake City: Salt Lake Art Center, 1992.

Maxwell Museum of Anthropology. *Seven Families in Pueblo Pottery.* Albuquerque: University of New Mexico Press, 1974.

Monrad, Kasper. *Danish Painting, the Golden Age.* London: The National Gallery of Art, 1984. Gives an artistic and cultural context for early LDS Scandinavian artists such as C. C. A. Christensen and Dan Weggeland.

Morningstar, Connie. *Early Utah Furniture.* Logan, Utah: Utah State University Press, 1976.

Nibley, Hugh, and Robert O. Davis. *Wulf Barsch: Looking toward Home.* Salt Lake City: [Wulf Barsch], 1985.

Olpin, Robert S. *Dictionary of Utah Art.* Salt Lake City: Salt Lake Art Center, 1980.

———. *Jos. A. F. Everett, 1883-1945.* Salt Lake City: Salt Lake Art Center, 1988.

———. *Waldo Midgley: Birds, Animals, People, Things.* Salt Lake City: Utah Museum of Fine Arts, University of Utah, 1984.

Olsen, Steven L. *Presidents of the Church: An Exhibition at the Museum of Church History and Art.* Salt Lake City: Church of Jesus Christ of Latter-day Saints, 1985.

Oman, Richard G. "Artists, Visual." In *Encyclopedia of Mormonism,* ed. by Daniel H. Ludlow, 70-73. Vol. 1. New York: Macmillan, 1992. (Hereafter referred to as *Encyclopedia of Mormonism.*)

———. "Sculptors." In *Encyclopedia of Mormonism* 3:1285-86.

Paxman, Shirley Brockbank. *Homespun: Domestic Arts and Crafts of Mormon Pioneers.* Salt Lake City: Deseret Book, 1976.

Peacock, Martha Moffit. "Art in Mormonism." In *Encyclopedia of Mormonism* 1:73-75.

Robertson, Edna, and Sarah Nestor. *Artists of the Canyons and Caminos: Santa Fe, the Early Years.* Layton, Utah: Gibbs Smith, 1976.

Rowley, Dennis. *A Step Beyond: Artists' Archives and the Creative Process, an Exhibition in Special Collections and Archives and Manuscripts.* Provo, Utah: Friends of the Brigham Young University Library, 1987.

Rowley, Dennis, and Diane R. Parkinson, comps. *Register of the John Hafen Collection Mss. 356.* Provo, Utah: Division of Archives and Manuscripts, Harold B. Lee Library, Brigham Young University, 1988.

St. James, Renwick, ed. *A Journey of the Imagination: The Art of James Christensen.* Trimbull, Conn.:Greenwich Press, Ltd., 1994.

The Salt Lake Temple: A Monument to a People. Salt Lake City: University Services, 1983.

Samuels, Peggy, and Harold Samuels. *Contemporary Western Artists.* Washington, D.C.: Judd's, 1982.

———. *The Illustrated Biographical Encyclopedia of Artists of the American West.* Garden City, New York: Doubleday, 1976.

Schwarz, Ted. *Arnold Friberg: The Passion of a Modern Master.* Flagstaff, Arizona: Northland, 1985.

Sondrup, Steven P., ed. *Arts and Inspiration: Mormon Perspectives.* Provo, Utah: Brigham Young University Press, 1980.

South, Will. *James Taylor Harwood, 1860–1940.* Salt Lake City: Utah Museum of Fine Arts, University of Utah, 1987.

Springville Museum of Art. *Women Artists of Utah.* Springville, Utah: Springville Museum of Art, 1984.

Stewart, Zipporah L. *Door to Noisemakers Inn.* Published by the author, n.d.

Swanson, Vern G. *Sculptors of Utah: An Art Exhibition at the Springville Museum of Art.* Springville, Utah: Springville Museum of Art, 1983.

Swanson, Vern G., Robert S. Olpin, and William C. Seifirt. *Utah Art.* Layton, Utah: Gibbs Smith, 1991.

Teichert, Minerva Kohlhepp. *Selected Sketches of the Mormon March.* N.p., n.d.

———. *A Romance of Old Fort Hall.* Portland, Ore.: Metropolitan Press, 1932. A folk account of the people who lived in the Fort Hall, Idaho, area around 1900, where Minerva Teichert grew up. A good source to understand some of Teichert's passion for recording the pioneer experience.

Trenton, Patricia, and Peter H. Hassrick. *The Rocky Mountains: A Vision for Artists in the Nineteenth Century.* Norman: University of Oklahoma Press in association with the Buffalo Bill Historical Center, 1983. Contains an interesting section on Frederick Piercy.

Wheelwright, Lorin F., and Lael J. Woodbury, eds. *Mormon Arts, Volume One.* Provo, Utah: Brigham Young University Press, 1972.

Wunderlich, Rudolf G., and Peter Hassrick. *Michael Coleman.* Lincoln: University of Nebraska Press, 1978.

Journal Articles

Allen, James B. "Education and the Arts in Twentieth-Century Utah." In *Utah's History,* ed. by Richard D. Poll and others, 587-608. Provo, Utah: Brigham Young University Press, 1978.

Allen, James B., and John B. Harris. "What Are You Doing Looking up Here? Graffiti Mormon Style." *Sunstone* 6 (March/April 1981): 27-40.

Arrington, Harriet Horne. "Alice Merrill Horne, Art Promoter and Early Utah Legislator." *Utah Historical Quarterly* 58 (Summer 1990): 261-76.

Arrington, Harriet Horne, and Leonard J. Arrington. "Alice Merrill Horne, Cultural Entrepeneur." In *A Heritage of Faith: Talks Selected from the BYU Women's Conferences,* ed. by Mary E. Stovall and Carol Cornwall Madsen, 121-36. Salt Lake City: Deseret Book, 1988.

"The Arts." Special issue of the *Ensign* 7 (July 1977): 6-11.

Bradley, Martha S. "Mary Teasdel, Yet Another American in Paris." *Utah Historical Quarterly* 58 (Summer 1990): 244-60.

Bradley, Martha S., and Lowell M. Durham Jr. "John Hafen and the Art Missionaries." *Journal of Mormon History* 12 (1985): 91-106.

Bradshaw, Merrill. "Reflections on the Nature of Mormon Art." *BYU Studies* 9 (Autumn 1968): 25-32.

Carmer, Carl. "A Panorama of Mormon Life." *Art in America* 58 (May-June 1970): 52-65. [Re: C. C. A. Christensen's art.]

Davis, Robert O. "'I *Must* Paint.'" In *Rich in Story, Great in Faith: The Art of Minerva Kohlhepp Teichert,* Museum of Church History and Art, 12-14, 29-44. Salt Lake City: The Church of Jesus Christ of Latter-day Saints, 1988.

[Derr], Jill Mulvay. "Three Mormon Women in the Cultural Arts." *Sunstone* 1 (Spring 1976): 29-39.

Dillingerger, Jane. "Mormonism and American Religious Art." *Sunstone* 3 (May/June 1978): 13-17.

Eastwood, Laurie Teichert. "My Mother—Minerva Kohlhepp Teichert." In *Rich in Story, Great in Faith: The Art of Minerva Kohlhepp Teichert,* Museum of Church History and Art, 1-11. Salt Lake City: The Church of Jesus Christ of Latter-day Saints, 1988.

Evans, David W. "Early Mormon Artist Proclaimed 'Art Discovery of 1970.'" *Improvement Era* 73 (May 1970): 18-29. [C. C. A. Christensen.]

Ewers, John C. "Cyrus E. Dallin, Master Sculptor of the Plains Indian." *Montana: Magazine of the West* 18 (1968): 35-43.

Fletcher, Dale T. "Art and Belief: A Group Exhibition." *Dialogue: A Journal of Mormon Thought* 2 (Spring 1967): 48–52.

Florence, Giles H., Jr. "Harvesting the Light: The 1890 Paris Art Mission." *Ensign* 18 (October 1988): 35–41.

Haseltine, James L. "Mormons and the Visual Arts." *Dialogue* 1 (Summer 1966): 17–29.

Hinton, Wayne K. "Mahonri Young and the Church: A View of Mormonism and Art." *Dialogue* 7 (Winter 1972): 35–43.

"Images: Fine Arts Competition, 1987." *Ensign* 18 (February 1988): 34–41. Reproduction of winning paintings submitted to the Church's first international art competition.

Janetski, Joyce Athay. "Louis Comfort Tiffany: Stained Glass in Utah." *Utah Preservation/Restoration* 3 (1981): 20–25.

Johnson, Marian Ashby. "Minerva's Calling." *Dialogue* 21 (Spring 1988): 127–43.

———. "Minerva Teichert: Scriptorian and Artist." *BYU Studies* 30 (Summer 1990): 66–70.

Kelley, Brian. "The Martyrdom as Seen by a Young Mormon Artist." *New Era* 3 (December 1973): 20–30.

Kimball, Spencer W. "The Gospel Vision and the Arts." *Ensign* 7 (July 1977): 2–5.

Leonard, Glen M. "Sculpture from the Church's Second International Art Competition." *Ensign* 21 (August 1991): 42–47. Photographs of winning sculptures in this competition.

Myer, Peter, and Marie Myer. "New Directions in Mormon Art." *Sunstone* 2 (Spring 1977): 32–64. A fairly comprehensive article on the avant-garde in 1970s Mormon art.

Oman, Richard G. "Baskets and Dancing Blankets." *Ensign* 7 (July 1977): 74–79. Perhaps the earliest article on non-Western LDS art.

———. "Henri-Robert Bresil's *Alma Baptizing in the Waters of Mormon*." *BYU Studies* 32, no. 3 (1992): 101–2. Discusses the work of an LDS artist from Haiti.

———. "LDS Southwest Indian Art." *Ensign* 12 (September 1982): 33–48.

———. "Lehi's Vision of the Tree of Life: A Cross-Cultural Perspective in Contemporary Latter-day Saint Art." *BYU Studies* 32, no. 4 (1992): 5–34. The most extensive article to date dealing with the cross-cultural and non-Western aspects of LDS art.

———. "Quilting Sisters." *BYU Studies* 33, no. 1 (1993): 145–50.

———. "Rei Hamon." *Ensign* 9 (October 1979): 19–23.

———. "Sculpting an LDS Tradition." *Ensign* 20 (October 1990): 38–43.

Oman, Richard, and Susan Oman. "A Passion for Painting: Minerva Kohlhepp Teichert." *Ensign* 6 (December 1976): 52–58.

Packer, Boyd K. "The Arts and the Spirit of the Lord." *BYU Studies* 16 (Summer 1976): 575–88.

Pinborough, Jan Underwood. "Minerva Kohlhepp Teichert: With a Bold Brush." *Ensign* 19 (April 1989): 34–41.

"Pioneer Art and Artists." In *An Enduring Legacy,* comp. by Lesson Committee, 233–72. Vol. 7. Salt Lake City: Daughters of Utah Pioneers, 1977–89.

"A Portfolio of Mormon Painters." *Ensign* 7 (July 1977): 39–56.

Richards, Heber G. "George M. Ottinger, Pioneer Artist of Utah: A Brief of His Personal Journal." *Western Humanities Review* 3 (July 1949): 209–18.

Roberts, Allen D. "Art Glass Windows in Mormon Architecture." *Sunstone* 1 (Winter 1975): 8–13.

"Sand and Sea and the Gospel Net: Art of Clark Kelley Price." *Ensign* 17 (February 1987): 34–37.

Smith, Dennis. "Drawing on Personal Myths." *Dialogue* 20 (Fall 1987): 109–14.

"The State of the Arts: Four Views." *BYU Today* 38 (June 1984): 18–24.

South, Will. "The Federal Art Project in Utah: Out of Oblivion or More of the Same?" *Utah Historical Quarterly* 58 (Summer 1990): 277–95.

Swanson, Vern G. "Mormon Art and Belief Movement." *Southwest Art* 21 (December 1991): 66–70. Deals with some of the Utah County visual artists who spearheaded the first Mormon Arts Festivals held at Brigham Young University in the early 1970s.

Walker, Ronald W., and D. Michael Quinn. "'Virtuous, Lovely, or of Good Report': How the Church Has Fostered the Arts." *Ensign* 7 (July 1977): 80–93. A good historical overview of Church support for the arts.

Wilson, Laurie. "The Nauvoo Monument to Women: A Photo Essay." *Ensign* 7 (March 1977): 28–31. See also Janet Bringham. "Nauvoo Monument to Women." *Ensign* 8 (September 1978): 72–75.

Wooley, Athelia T. "Art to Edify: The Work of Avard T. Fairbanks." *Ensign* 17 (September 1987): 34–38.

Young, Levi Edgar. "The Angel Moroni and Cyrus Dallin." *Improvement Era* 56 (April 1953): 234–35, 268.

Young, Mahonri Sharp. "Mormon Art and Architecture." *Art in America* 58 (May-June 1970): 66–69.

Zobell, Albert L., Jr. "Cyrus Dallin and the Angel Moroni Statue." *Improvement Era* 71 (April 1968): 4–7.

Theses and Dissertations

Andersen, Velan Max. "Arnold Friberg, Artist: His Life, His Philosophy and His Works." Master's thesis, Brigham Young University, 1970.

Bassett, Arthur Ray. "Culture and the American Frontier in Mormon Utah, 1850–1896." Ph.D. diss., Syracuse University, 1975.

Bunnell, Max Edwin. "A Study of Bent Franklin Larsen as Artist and Educator." Master's thesis, Brigham Young University, 1962.

Christensen, Carl Landus. "An Analysis of Visual Religious Symbols Appearing in the *Improvement Era, Ensign,* and *New Era* Published by The Church of Jesus Christ of Latter-day Saints." Master's thesis, Brigham Young University, 1974.

Conant, William Lee Roy. "A Study of the Life of John Hafen, Artist, with an Analysis and Critical Review of His Work." Master's thesis, Brigham Young University, 1969.

DeGraw, Monte B. "A Study of Representative Examples of Art Works Fostered by the Mormon Church with an Analysis of the Aesthetic Value of These Works." Master's thesis, Brigham Young University, 1959.

Dickson, Mamie Platt. "The Work of LeConte Stewart, Painter, Lithographer, Etcher, and Designer." Master's thesis, University of Utah, 1955.

Faulkner, Don Charles. "Alpine Art Colony." Master's thesis, University of Utah, 1975.

Hafen, P. Jane. "A Pale Reflection: American Indian Images in Mormon Arts." Master's thesis, Brigham Young University, 1984.

Hague, Donald Victor. "The Life and Work of Lynn Fausett." Master's thesis, University of Utah, 1975.

Heimdal, Stuart P. "Four Paintings, Illustrating Significant Historical Events from the Life of Abraham, as Contained in the Pearl of Great Price." Master's thesis, Brigham Young University, 1968.

Hinton, Wayne K. "A Biographical History of Mahonri M. Young, A Western American Artist." Ph.D. diss., Brigham Young University, 1974.

Hopkin, Elizabeth B. "A Study of the Philosophical and Stylistic Influence of Jean-Francois Millet on Mahonri M. Young from 1901 to 1927." Master's thesis, Brigham Young University, 1990.

Janetski, Joyce Athay. "A History, Analysis, and Registry of Mormon Architectural Art Glass in Utah." Master's thesis, University of Utah, 1981.

Knapp, Alma J. "The History of Cyrus Edwin Dallin, Eminent Utah Sculptor." Master's thesis, University of Utah, 1948.

Knapp, Lamont Poulter. "The History of Solon Hannibal Borglum." Master's thesis, University of Utah, 1950.

Larsen, Lila Duncan. "H. L. A. Culmer, Utah Artist and Man of the West, 1854–1914." Master's thesis, University of Utah, 1987.

Leek, Thomas A. "A Circumspection of Ten Formulators of Early Utah Art History." Master's thesis, Brigham Young University, 1961.

McCarl, William B. "The Visual Image of Joseph Smith." Master's thesis, Brigham Young University, 1962.

MacFarlane, Donald A. "An Analysis of Mahonri M. Young as a Draftsman." Master's thesis, Brigham Young University, 1969.

Miller, Marilyn. "The Artist and Her Work: Visual Images from the Words of Isaiah." Master's thesis, Brigham Young University, 1971.

Moss, Edwin G. "Heaven-Hell Series." Master's thesis, Utah State University, 1973.

Myer, Peter Livingston. "An Interpretation of Events in the Life of Christ." Master's thesis, University of Utah, 1959.

Needham, S. Eugene. "Chosen People." Master's thesis, Utah State University, 1981.

Nielsen, Emma Cynthia. "The Development of Pioneer Pottery in Utah." Master's thesis, Brigham Young University, 1963.

O'Brien, Terry John. "A Study of the Effect of Color in the Utah Temple Murals." Master's thesis, Brigham Young University, 1968.

Ostler, Barbara Boyer. "Lee Greene Richards: Portrait Painter." Master's thesis, University of Utah, 1991.

Prestwich, Larry Berg. "A Visual Interpretation of Events and Personalities from the Book of Mormon." Master's thesis, Brigham Young University, 1966.

Proctor, Peggy H. "Publication Design for the Youth of The Church of Jesus Christ of Latter-day Saints." Master's thesis, Brigham Young University, 1973.

Schlinker, Lori. "Kitsch in the Visual Arts and Advertisement of The Church of Jesus Christ of Latter-day Saints." Master's thesis, Brigham Young University, 1971.

Sisemore, Claudia. "Alvin Gittens, Realist." Master's thesis, University of Utah, 1976.

Smedley, Delbert Waddoups. "An Investigation of Influences on Representative Examples of Mormon Art." Master's thesis, University of Southern California, Los Angeles, 1939.

Smith, Bruce Hixson. "A Brief Inquiry into the Character and Purpose of Art." Master's thesis, University of Utah, 1969.

South, William Robert. "The Life and Art of James Taylor Harwood, 1860–1940." Master's thesis, University of Utah, 1986.

Southey, Trevor. "A Survey to Determine the Public Responses and Attitudes toward the First Festival of Mormon Art at Brigham Young University." Master's thesis, Brigham Young University, 1969.

Swensen, A. John. "A Study of the Artistic Philosophy of Mahonri Mackintosh Young." Master's thesis, Brigham Young University, 1971.

Taylor, James Harvey. "A Study of Early Utah Water Color Painting." Master's thesis, Brigham Young University, 1974.

Thorpe, Everett C. "A Mural for the Logan Tabernacle." Master's thesis, University of Utah, 1954.

Trimble, Roxie Dale. "Four Utah Mormon Artists as Authors." Master's thesis, Brigham Young University, 1982.

Van Stipriaan, Dorothy. "Biographical Dictionary of Utah Artists." Master's thesis, Case Western Reserve University, 1959.

Wardle, Marian Eastwood. "Minerva Teichert's Murals: The Motivation for Her Large-Scale Production." Master's thesis, Brigham Young University, 1988.

Weaver, Max D. "The Development and Transition of the Art of Calvin Fletcher from Naturalism to Abstraction during the Period 1895–1953." Master's thesis, Utah State Agricultural College, Logan, 1955.

Webb, Terry Douglas. "Mormonism and Tourist Art in Hawaii." Ph.D. diss., Arizona State University, 1990.

Yonemori, Shirley Kazuko. "Mahonri Mackintosh Young, Printmaker." Master's thesis, Brigham Young University, 1963.

Key Periodicals

American Indian Art Magazine
BYU Studies
Dialogue: A Journal of Mormon Thought
Ensign
The Improvement Era
The Juvenile Instructor
The Relief Society Magazine
Southwest Art Magazine
Sunstone
This People

Richard G. Oman is Senior Curator, Museum of Church History and Art, Salt Lake City.

NOTES

All photographs used in this article are courtesy Museum of Church History and Art.

[1]Daniel H. Ludlow, ed., *Encyclopedia of Mormonism,* 5 vols. (New York: Macmillan, 1992), 4:1518–36.

[2]An excellent biography of Dallin exists: Rell G. Francis, *Cyrus E. Dallin: Let Justice Be Done* (Springville, Utah: Springville Museum of Art, 1976).

[3]Figures of honored citizens of Oregon, Wyoming, and North Dakota by Fairbanks are in the national Capitol rotunda. George Washington University, in Washington, D.C., has several monumental bronze portrait heads of George Washington by Fairbanks, as does the Washington state capitol in Olympia, Washington. Ancient Sparta is the site of Fairbanks's *Lycurgus the Lawgiver.* After the placing of this piece, Fairbanks was knighted by King Paul of Greece.

[4]*The Ten Commandments* is held in the DeMille Collection at Brigham Young University Archives.

Part V:

Conclusion

The Records of Mormon History: Additional Guides and Repositories

David J. Whittaker

Introduction

Mormon Americana has brought together a large number of authors to describe both repositories with Mormon material and specific topics of importance to students of the Latter-day Saint experience. However, as wide as we have cast our nets, we still could not cover all the libraries or topics that would be of interest to all researchers of Mormon history and culture. This concluding essay surveys additional guides and repositories, acknowledging that even with this additional information, our efforts remain incomplete.

General Guides to Manuscript Collections

In 1961 the Library of Congress began the first systematic effort at bibliographic control of manuscripts throughout the country. Now a multivolume guide, the *National Union Catalog of Manuscript Collections* (Washington, D.C.: Library of Congress, 1962–), commonly known as NUCMC, describes collections that have been reported by various repositories. Indices by subject first appeared in 1964; the 1991 index is the most recent.

Computer databases such as RLIN (Research Libraries Information Network) and OCLC (Online Computer Library Center) are very valuable resources for researchers and can be accessed at most major libraries. Such bibliographical databases are essential tools of the serious scholar.

In 1961 the National Historic Publications Commission issued Philip M. Hamer's *A Guide to Archives and Manuscripts in the United States* (New Haven: Yale University Press), which provided a detailed survey of about thirteen hundred repositories. Organized by state and city within the state, the guide also provided a subject index. A second edition was published in 1988: *Directory of Archives and Manuscript Repositories in the United States* (Phoenix, N.Y.: Oryx Press). A useful guide to state, county, and local historical societies is Donna McDonald, comp., *Directory of Historical Societies and Agencies in the United States and Canada,* 11th ed. (Nashville: American Association for State and Local History, 1978). See also Modoc Press, comp., *Special Collections in College and University Libraries* (New York: Macmillan, 1989); Mary Ellen Gleason, ed., *Religious Archives in the United States and Canada: A Bibliography, 1958–1981* (Chicago: The Society of American Archivists, 1984); and Andrea Hinding, ed., *Women's History Sources: A Guide to the Archives and Manuscript Collections in the United States* (Boston: R. R. Bowker, 1979).

Beginning in 1939, the Works Progress Administration funded the writing of histories and archival guides to most states. A guide to these is provided by Loretta L. Hefner, comp., *The WPA Historical Records Survey: A Guide to the Unpublished Inventories, Indexes, and Transcripts* (Chicago: The Society of American Archivists, 1980). The Utah Historical Records Survey produced three volumes: *Inventory of Church Archives of Utah,* vol. 1 (History and Bibliography of Religion; 121 pp., June 1940), vol. 2 (Baptist Church; 70 pp., August 1940), and vol. 3 (Smaller Denominations; 72 pp., February 1941). See also *Utah: A Guide to the State* (New York: Hastings House for WPA, 1941).

All of these sources are of value to Mormon scholars. As Latter-day Saints can be found in all the states, one never knows what treasure will be found where, although the preponderance of material is located in states where the Mormons have had a significant historical experience: New York; Ohio; Missouri; Illinois; Iowa; and the western states of Utah, Idaho, Arizona, Nevada, and California. Theses and dissertations on Mormon historical topics have been written at colleges and universities from coast to coast; at last count there have been almost three thousand produced. A beginning guide is *A Catalogue of Theses and Dissertations concerning The Church of Jesus Christ of Latter-day Saints, Mormonism and Utah* (Provo, Utah: College of Religious Instruction, Brigham Young University, 1971).

Another useful bibliographical guide which has numerous Mormon and Mormon-related items is John M. Townley, *The Trail West: A Bibliography-Index to Western American Trails, 1841–1869* (Reno, Nev.: Jamison Station Press, 1988). Joseph Sabin, and others, *Bibliotheca Americana: A Dictionary of Books Relating to America, from Its Discovery to the Present Time,* 29 vols. (New York: By the author, 1868–1936) is essential for printed items, especially when used with John Edgar Molnar, *Author-Title Index to Joseph Sabin's Dictionary of Books Relating to America,* 3 vols. (Metuchen, N.J.: Scarecrow Press, 1974). An extremely useful reference work for broader research is

Francis Paul Prucha, *Handbook for Research in American History: A Guide to Bibliographies and Other Reference Works* (Lincoln: University of Nebraska Press, 2nd ed., revised, 1994).

Libraries in the East

The National Archives and the Library of Congress in the nation's capital hold Mormon material and references in significant quantities. The National Archives holds the following: Utah territorial and army records; records of Utah-federal relations; Department of the Interior General Land Office records; federal census records of Utah; and federal district court records, including those dealing with the polygamy cases of the late nineteenth century. Useful aids for the serious researcher are *Guide to the National Archives* (Washington, D.C.: National Archives and Record Service, 1974), *Selected List of Publications of the National Archives and Records Service* (Washington, D.C.: National Archives and Records Center, 1973 [and later editions]), "Photographs Relating to Utah and the Mormons in the National Archives" (Salt Lake City: LDS Historical Department, n.d., mimeographed), and *List of National Archives Microfilm Publications in the Regional Archives Branches* (Washington, D.C.: National Archives and Records Center, 1975). Specific Utah records are held by the Region 8 Archives, Federal Records Center, in Denver, Colorado. A useful tool in researching these records is Robert Svenningsen and Enid T. Thompson's *List of National Archives Microfilm Publications Region 8* (Denver: Federal Records Center, 1969).

In addition to its extensive collection of published material, the Library of Congress has copies of Mormon manuscript items. Diary material can be located through A. Jeff Simmonds, *Index to Names in the Library of Congress Collection of Mormon Diaries,* vol. 1, no. 2 (Logan: Utah State University Press, Western Text Society, 1971). In 1973, Kathy Cardon prepared a "Register of the Library of Congress Collection of Mormon Diaries" (typescript; copy in Historical Department, LDS Church), which is a guide to the library's thirteen reels of microfilm. Because of its role as a place of deposit for the Federal Writers' Project, the library contains transcripts of some four hundred Mormon diaries, journals, and autobiographies. A good account by one major participant is Juanita Brooks, "Jest A Copyin'—Word F'r Word," *Utah Historical Quarterly* 37 (Fall 1969): 375-95.

For other source material in federal government records, see Dee Leon Storrs, "Index to Mormons and Mormonism and Related Topics as Contained in the Congressional Globe, (1833-1873), Thirty-Third to Forty-Second Congress" (master's thesis, University of

Washington, 1957); Carol W. Christensen, *Mormons and Mormon History as Reflected in U.S. Government Documents, 1830–1907* (Washington, D.C.: U.S. Department of Health, Education, and Welfare, National Institute of Education, 1977); and Susan L. Fales and Chad J. Flake, comps., *Mormons and Mormonism in U.S. Government Documents* (Salt Lake City: University of Utah Press, 1989). The value of the United States' presidential libraries must also be considered for material on Mormons who have served in presidential cabinets or in other high-level capacities. For example, the Brigham Young University Archives has the papers of Utah Congressman Arthur V. Watkins, but noticeably absent are his papers relating to Indian policy matters of the 1950s, when he co-sponsored several pieces of termination legislation; thus, Watkins's oral history interview in the Eisenhower Library (Abilene, Kansas), which interview includes information on his attitudes toward Native Americans, is of value.

Other Eastern repositories of great value to scholars of Mormonism include the American Antiquarian Society, the Harvard University libraries, and the Cornell University library. Founded in 1812, the American Antiquarian Society (Worcester, Massachusetts) is the oldest national historical society in the United States. Especially rich in printed material (books, broadsides, pamphlets, maps, newspapers, and almanacs), the library holds the largest single collection of imprint material relating to American history. Through its program on the history of books in American culture, the society encourages scholars to use its rich holdings to more fully document and interpret the cultural role of books and other forms of printed material in American history. While the study of the larger American context for early Mormon publishing has only begun in Mormonism, these collections have potentially great value. Specific manuscript items of interest to researchers of Mormonism include the following: the papers and sketches of David Augusta Burr, which cover the Utah War period when David accompanied his father, David H. Burr, the surveyor general of Utah (1855–57), out west; the journal of Reverend George Moore, a Unitarian clergyman in Quincy, Illinois, during the Nauvoo period (December 27, 1840–May 12, 1845), which contains scattered references to Mormons, including an account of a personal visit with Joseph Smith in Nauvoo on June 3, 1842; and the letters of Hiram S. Rumfield to his wife, in which he describes his experiences and observations among the Mormons in Utah Territory when he worked as the assistant treasurer for the Overland Mail Company (1861–65).

The libraries of Harvard University contain a variety of items dealing with Mormon history. For example, they hold the research files of the *People of Rimrock* project,[1] a comparative study of cultures in the Four Corners area of northeast Arizona; this study launched the careers of a number of scholars who have continued to show interest in Mormon studies (for example, Robert Bellah and Thomas O'Dea). The libraries hold several other important collections: the Corinne Marie (Tuckerman) Allen Papers, 1896–1927 (in the Schlesinger Library), which include correspondence relating to the Utah Congress of Mothers and other organizations in Salt Lake City on topics of social welfare, humanitarian work, and educational reforms (Allen's husband was a congressman from Utah in 1896–97); and the Edward Palmer Collection (acquired only in part by the Houghton Library from an auction in 1914), which contains notes, newspaper clippings, and observations made in southern Utah and northern Arizona in the 1870s on such topics as Indians, Mormon settlements, legal disputes, weather, and personal explorations.[2]

The Boston Public Library has a few rare Mormon imprints, and the library of Boston University has the diaries and papers of Virginia Sorensen, a major Mormon writer. The New York Historical Society has several items, including the diary of Leopold Bierwirth, a New York City merchant who recorded his train trip to San Francisco in 1872. Bierwith's diary includes long descriptions of his visits among the Mormons in Salt Lake City. See further Arthur J. Breton, *A Guide to the Manuscript Collections of the New York Historical Society,* vols. 1 and 2 (Westport, Conn.: Greenwood Press, 1972). The library of Duke University in Durham, North Carolina, has the papers of Alfred Cumming, the Utah territorial governor between 1857 and 1861.

The Cornell University library (Ithaca, New York) has established a collection emphasizing material on the Burned-Over District of western New York, a collection that is bound to contain early Mormon references and provide a broader context for the experiences of the founders and early converts of the Church. For descriptions of other collections, such as the David Augusta Burr papers (which contain his diary of an 1855 trip to Utah and an 1858 letter with detailed information on the state of affairs in Utah during the Utah War), see Kathleen Jacklin, ed., *The Collection of Regional History and University Archives: Report of the Curator and Archivist, 1962–1966* (Ithaca, N.Y.: Cornell University Libraries, 1974). Other collections, such as those at Oberlin College (Oberlin, Ohio) and the Alexander Campbell Archive in the T. W. Phillips Memorial Library, Bethany College (Bethany, West Virginia), also contain material with possible important Mormon connections. The Oberlin library, for example, owns the original Solomon Spaulding manuscript.[3]

The collections at the Western Reserve Historical Society (Cleveland, Ohio) contain important documents as well. For example, the papers of A. C. Williams contain letters of Arthur B. Deming, an ardent anti-Mormon who was active at the turn of the century. See further Kermit J. Pike, *A Guide to the Manuscripts and Archives of the Western Reserve Historical Society* (Cleveland: The Western Reserve Historical Society, 1972). See also Stanley B. Kimball, "Sources on the History of the Mormons in Ohio: 1830–1838 (Located East of the Mississippi)," *BYU Studies* 11 (Summer 1971): 524–40.

Midwest Collections

The University of Michigan at Ann Arbor has two libraries of interest. The first is the William L. Clements Library of Early Americana, whose strength for LDS history is primarily in the area of imprints, including a fine collection of early editions of the Book of Mormon. The library also holds the Lewis Cass Papers, which contain several James J. Strang letters; the notes of Henry Halkett, which document his visit with Joseph Smith in May 1844; the Kane Papers, consisting of 176 items of family correspondence between the children of John K. Kane (1795–1858), the most important being the letters of Thomas L. Kane in the 1850s; and other Mormon references scattered throughout the library. A useful reference to the library is Arlene Phillips Shy and Barbara A. Mitchell's *Guide to the Manuscript Collections of the William L. Clements Library* (Boston: G. K. Hall, 1978). The Bentley Historical Library, which is the university's other library of interest to scholars of Mormonism, focuses on the Michigan historical collections and the university's own archives. Specific collections with Mormon references include the Whittemore Family Papers; the Charles M. Cleveland Family Papers; an Elon John Farnsworth letter of April 8, 1859, discussing army life in frontier Utah; an 1842 letter mentioning a sermon preached by Joseph Smith (see the Warner Wright Goodale Papers); and photocopies of a letter of James J. Strang to Governor John S. Barry in 1851. The Clarke Historical Library of Central Michigan University (Mount Pleasant) also contains Mormon-related materials.

The Chicago Historical Society has a large collection of Mormon manuscripts. "Mormons and Mormonism," a fifty-six-page descriptive inventory of the Mormon collection, was prepared in September 1962, and additions have been made since that time. The researcher must be aware that these Mormon items are in various departments of the society: manuscripts are in the archives and manuscripts department; broadsides are in the prints and photographs department; newspapers, periodicals, books, and pamphlets are in the library; and artifacts are in the decorative and industrial arts department. Especially focused on the Mormons' sojourn in Illinois during the 1840s, the collections cover the period from 1832 to 1954 and consist of about 175 items. These are very important to students of early Mormon history. The earliest Mormon material (1832-40) includes two letters of Joseph Smith to his wife Emma (June 6, 1832, and January 20, 1840); a stock ledger and index to the ledger of the Mormons' Kirtland Bank, 1836-37; an Orson Pratt letter of October 20, 1840, from Edinburgh, Scotland, describing his missionary work there; about ninety items of Illinois material primarily concerned with the growing conflict between the Mormons and their neighbors; a variety of original items on the events leading to Joseph Smith's death in June 1844; correspondence of James J. Strang to Emma Smith dated February 22, 1846; and material relating to the "Kinderhook Plates" of 1843, including one of the original plates. Additional material concerns the succession crisis, the trek westward, and a variety of topics in Utah history. The serious researcher will want to study the inventory prepared by the society.

The Joseph Regenstein Library of the University of Chicago formerly held two original manuscript leaves of the Book of Mormon; they were sold to the Historical Department of the LDS Church in 1984. Nevertheless, the library retains the Amos Davis account book (1839) for a Nauvoo, Illinois, mercantile establishment (a microfilm copy is in the LDS Church Historical Department). For a description of about half of the Western Americana books given to the Newberry Library (Chicago) in 1964, many of which concern Mormons, see Colton Storm, comp., *A Catalogue of the Everett D. Graff Collection of Western Americana* (Chicago: University of Chicago Press, 1968). The Garrett Theological Seminary at Northwestern University houses the Kimball Young Collection, including his important research on Mormon plural marriage.

The important microfilm collection at Southern Illinois University is described in Stanley B. Kimball, *Sources of Mormon History in Illinois, 1839-48: An Annotated Catalog of the Microfilm Collection at Southern Illinois University*, 2d ed. (Carbondale-Edwardsville: Southern Illinois University, 1966). See also John C. Abbott, "'Sources of Mormon History in Illinois, 1839-48,' and a Bibliographic Note," *Dialogue: A Journal of Mormon Thought* 5 (Spring 1970): 76-79; and Paul D. Spencer, "Mormon Acquisition, Mormon-Related Manuscripts," *Journal of the Illinois State Historical Society* 64 (Spring 1971): 91-99. See also Victoria Irons and Patricia C. Brennan, *Descriptive Inventory of the Archives of the State of Illinois*

(Springfield: Illinois State Archives, Office of the Secretary of State, 1978), which indicates Mormon material in record groups of the attorney general (101.8; 101.9; 954.12) and other areas.

Manuscript repositories in Missouri are surveyed in Stanley B. Kimball, "Missouri Mormon Manuscripts: Sources in Selected Societies," *BYU Studies* 14 (Summer 1974): 458-87. Also of value is Cecil A. Snider, comp., "A Syllabus on Mormonism in Illinois from the Angle of the Press: Newspaper Source Materials, 1838-1848," 8 vols. and index (Iowa City, Iowa: n.p., 1933), available in Special Collections, Brigham Young University. The State Archives of Missouri (Jefferson City) has prepared a guide to the microfilm collection of its Mormon War papers: "Guide to the Mormon War Papers, 1838-1841," *Archives Information Bulletin* 2, no. 4 (October 1980). The State Historical Society of Missouri and the University of Missouri (Columbia) have a number of valuable items scattered throughout their manuscript collections. The National Historic Trails Museum (Independence) is creating a major research library that will include journals of the overland trails. The ongoing inventory of these records includes Mormon and Mormon-related records. Also of great value for these narratives are Merrill J. Mattes, *Platte River Road Narratives: A Descriptive Bibliography of Travel over the Great Central Overland Route to Oregon, California, Utah, Colorado, Montana, and Other Western States and Territories, 1812-1866* (Urbana and Chicago: University of Illinois Press, 1988), a guide to 2,082 items; and Lannon W. Mintz, *The Trail: A Bibliography of the Travelers on the Overland Trail to California, Oregon, Salt Lake City, and Montana during the Years 1841-1864* (Albuquerque: University of New Mexico Press, 1987), which focuses on published items. See also Henry R. Wagner and Charles L. Camp, *The Plains and the Rockies: A Critical Bibliography of Exploration, Adventure and Travel in the American West, 1800-1865,* ed. Robert H. Becker, 4th ed., rev. and enl. (San Francisco: John Howell Books, 1982).

In Iowa, the State Historical Society (Des Moines) and the library at Graceland College (Lamoni) are important repositories. The Iowa State Historical Society has Charles B. Thompson's manuscripts relating to his church's troubled Iowa years as well as the important Strangite records: the Strangite Apostolic Ministry Book, the "Chronicles of Voree," and the "History of Warren Post." The collection at the RLDS Graceland College is described in Paul M. Edwards, "The Restoration History Manuscript Collection," *Annals of Iowa* 47 (Spring 1984): 377-81.

The Kansas Historical Society (Topeka) holds the Isaac McCoy Papers which contain letters addressing the Mormon attempts to do missionary work among Native Americans on the Missouri frontier in the 1830s. The Nebraska State Historical Society (Lincoln) has the papers of John Finch Kinney, the chief justice of Utah Territory (1854–56), which include correspondence with Brigham Young, Daniel H. Wells, George A. Smith, and Wilford Woodruff.

For a description of the Mormon material in the American Home Missionary Society Collection at the Amistead Research Center (New Orleans), see Roger Launius, "The American Home Missionary Society Collection and Mormonism," *BYU Studies* 23 (Spring 1983): 201–10; and Launius, "American Home Missionary Society Ministers and Mormon Nauvoo: Selected Letters," *Western Illinois Regional Studies* 8 (Spring 1985): 16–45. See also *A Guide to the Microfilm Edition of the Papers of the American Home Missionary Society, 1816 (1826–1894) 1936* (Glen Rock, N.J.: Microfilming Corporation of America, 1975 and 1987).

Western Repositories

The American Heritage Center at the library of the University of Wyoming (Laramie) has acquired a large number of collections, western and otherwise, during the last decades. Most are yet to be inventoried and cataloged, but there are sure to be Mormon collections among those gathered by Gene Gressley's collecting net. A brief overview is given in Gressley, "The American Heritage Center: A Resource as a Resource," *Annals of Wyoming* 64 (Winter 1992): 22–26.

The western history department of the Denver Public Library (begun in 1929 and established as a separate department in 1934) has a number of Mormon items, including a Frank J. Cannon letter copybook, 1899–1902; the Josephus Hatch papers, including his 1852 overland diary from Iowa to Salt Lake City; and the Spalding family scrapbooks (five volumes) relating to John Franklin Spalding, who was bishop of the Episcopal Church in Colorado, and Franklin Spencer Spalding, who was bishop of the Episcopal Church in Utah. The scrapbooks (volumes 3 and 4) contain correspondence and newspaper clippings relating to Franklin's work *Joseph Smith Jr., as a Translator* (1912). More generally see Alys H. Freeze, "The Western History Collection of the Denver Public Library" *Great Plains Journal* 11, no. 2 (1972): 101–15.

The State Historical Society of Colorado has a few Mormon items, the most extensive of which are the papers of Frank J. Cannon, democratic senator from Utah and son of George Q. Cannon. This collection is described in Susan A. Nieminen, *An Inventory of the Papers of Frank Jenne Cannon 1859–1933* (Denver: State Historical Society of Colorado, 1969). The University of Colorado at Boulder also has a number of Mormon items in its western historical collections (established in 1918). See Ellen Arguimban, comp., and John A. Brennan, ed., *A Guide to Manuscript Collections* (Boulder: Western Historical Collections, University of Colorado, 1982). See also John A. Brennan, "The University of Colorado's Western Historical Collections," *Great Plains Journal* 11, no. 2 (1972): 154-60. All the repositories in Colorado attempt to document the larger history of the region, including mining, merchandising, and ranching, activities that involved Mormons—often from the earliest years of settlement.

The Idaho State Historical Society (Boise) and the Eli M. Oboler Library at Idaho State University (Pocatello) house a variety of items related to the LDS experience in that state. The Fred T. Dubois collection in the Oboler Library documents Dubois's public career, including his years as an Idaho senator, his opposition to Mormon polygamy, and his role in the attempts to unseat Utah Senator Reed Smoot in 1903. Especially valuable are the large number of pioneer life stories, copies of which have been deposited in both libraries. These stories have recently been studied in Susan Hendricks Swetnam, *Lives of the Saints in Southeast Idaho: An Introduction to Mormon Pioneer Life Story Writing* (Moscow: University of Idaho Press; Boise: Idaho State Historical Society, 1991).

Additional repositories in Utah have material worth noting. The Daughters of Utah Pioneers maintain in Salt Lake City a museum and archives which houses a number of significant items. Many of these manuscript items have appeared in the various lessons prepared by the Daughters of Utah Pioneers and have been published in several series: Kate B. Carter, comp., *Heart Throbs of the West*, 12 vols. (Salt Lake City: DUP, 1939-51); Carter, comp., *Treasures of Pioneer History,* 6 vols. (Salt Lake City: DUP, 1952-57); Carter, comp., *Our Pioneer Heritage*, 20 vols. (Salt Lake City: DUP, 1958-77); The Lesson Committee, *An Enduring Legacy,* 12 vols. (Salt Lake City: DUP, 1977-89); and The Lesson Committee, *Chronicles of Courage,* 4 vols. (Salt Lake City: DUP, 1990-93), which series is ongoing. The Daughters of Utah Pioneers Library is staffed by volunteers, and access to the collections is generally limited to DUP members; however, the Historical Department of the LDS Church has been microfilming various items which can be used at the Historical Department Reading Room.

The library of Southern Utah University (Cedar City) has several significant collections, including the papers of William Palmer and Charles Kelley, students of Utah history. Another significant—but less accessible—collection is the privately owned Wilford C. Wood collection. For a description (236 pages), see LaMar C. Berrett, *The Wilford C. Wood Collection: An Annotated Catalog of Documentary-Type Materials in the Wilford C. Wood Collection* (Bountiful, Utah: Wilford C. Wood Foundation, 1972).

The *Guide to Archives and Manuscript Collections in Selected Utah Repositories: A Machine-Readable Edition* (Salt Lake City: Utah State Historical Society, 1991) is a bibliographical guide to 12,440 records in ten Utah repositories. This guide is available for purchase on computer disks. A good review of the project is provided by Susan L. Fales in *Journal of Mormon History* 19 (Spring 1993): 173–75. Max J. Evans provides a good overview of Utah public libraries in "A History of the Public Library Movement in Utah" (master's thesis, Utah State University, 1971).

There are several repositories in Arizona that Mormon scholars will wish to visit. The Special Collections in the library at the University of Arizona (Phoenix) has the extensive Udall family collections. The Udall collections include the papers and journals of David K. Udall (1851–1938), founder of St. Johns, Arizona; the Levi Stewart Udall (1891–1960) papers are also available. In addition, the library holds the manuscript minute book of the "Little Colorado Stakes of Zion," covering conferences held from 1878 to 1886 at Sunset, Brigham City, St. Joseph, and other Mormon settlements in Arizona Territory; the papers of Lot Smith (1830–92), which cover the period from 1855 to 1889 and include letters from Brigham Young and Wilford Woodruff when Smith was president of the Little Colorado Stake; and a collection of photocopied journals and letters dealing with the Mormon settlements in Arizona, especially those at Joseph City and other points along the Little Colorado River.

The Arizona Historical Society (Tucson) also holds important Mormon and Mormon-related material. These include the Frederick Samuel Dellenbaugh Collection's sixty-two manuscript volumes, which contain fourteen notebooks of the artist and topographer on Major John Wesley Powell's second Colorado River expedition (1871–72) plus material Dellenbaugh gathered on Mormon exploration and settlement of Utah; the Joseph Fish Collection, which includes a copy of the autobiography of this early Mormon settler of Utah and Arizona and a 1906 "History of Arizona," considered the first consecutive history of Arizona Territory; the Joseph Neal Heywood family collection, which includes the diaries of Joseph's father, John N. Heywood Sr., a Mormon bishop in Nevada and Arizona, and the diaries (1900–1948) of Heywood Jr.; the papers of James Warren Lesueur, president of the LDS Arizona Temple from 1927 to 1944; the Joseph Harrison Pearce collection, documenting the life of a man who was the first forest ranger in Arizona (supervising the Black Mesa Forest Reserve), a special policeman on the Apache White River Reservation from 1905 to 1907, and a detective for the Livestock Sanitary Board from 1913 to 1915; and the Ammon M. Tenney collection, including eight diaries covering his pioneering life in Arizona (1858) and in Mexico (1890–1910). For a more complete guide, see Charles C. Colley, comp., *Documents of Southwestern History: A Guide to the Manuscript Collections of the Arizona Historical Society* (Tucson: Arizona Historical Society, 1972).

A useful survey of repositories containing manuscripts that document the history of Nevada, where the Mormons have had a presence since the 1850s, is Robert D. Armstrong, comp. and ed., *A Preliminary Union Catalog of Nevada Manuscripts* (Reno: University of Nevada for the Nevada Library Association, 1967). This useful survey describes fifty-nine repositories in twenty-three states, including Utah.

The library of the University of Oregon (Eugene) holds several Mormon-related collections. These include the papers of Sylvester Mowry, the majority of which are copies of letters describing railroad escort duty in Washington Territory (1853) and life in Salt Lake City in Colonel Edward J. Steptoe's command (1854–55); the papers and journals of Claton Silas Rice, a home missionary for the Congregational Church in St. George and Cedar City (1908–18); the diaries of Heber Hyder Davis from his LDS mission to England (1899–1901); the papers of Henry Davidson Sheldon, which contain some 5,163 letters, many in correspondence with Kimball Young, a Mormon sociologist; and the Joseph Lane papers (1852–81), including his correspondence with Jacob B. Backenstos (sheriff of Hancock County, Illinois, in the 1840s and friend of the Mormons; he later settled in Oregon) when Lane was Oregon's territorial governor. For a more complete guide, see Martin Schmitt, comp., *Catalogue of Manuscripts in the University of Oregon Library* (Eugene: University of Oregon, 1971).

Many of the libraries in California have collections that contain Mormon material. In addition to the collections in the Bancroft and Huntington libraries, the serious student will consult the libraries of the California Historical Society and the libraries of the University of California system; for example, UCLA holds the Lamoni Call papers.

The researcher will also wish to consult catalogs of manuscript dealers and auctions to discover collections that have surfaced over the years. Examples include Herbert S. Auerbach, *The Distinguished Collection of Western Americana: Books, Newspapers and Pamphlets, Many Relating to the Mormon Church*, 2 pts. (New York: Parke-Bernet Galleries, 1947–48); Edward Eberstadt and Sons, *Utah and the*

Mormons . . . Rare Books, Manuscripts, Paintings, etc., offered for sale by Edward Eberstadt and Sons (New York: [1956]); Charles L. Woodward, *Bibliothica-Scallawagiana. Catalogue of a Matchless Collection of Books, Pamphlets, Autographs, Pictures, etc. Relating to Mormonism and the Mormons* (New York: n.p., 1880); and *"The Auerbach Collection": Manuscripts and Other Selections from the Herbert S. Auerbach Collection of Western Americana* (Northampton, Mass.: L & T Respess Books, 1992).

While the great bulk of material on Mormon history is in repositories in the United States, the researcher should not ignore libraries in Canada (especially in Alberta) or Europe. For the British Library, see David J. Whittaker, *Mormon Americana: A Bibliographical Guide to Printed Material in the British Library Relating to The Church of Jesus Christ of Latter-day Saints* (London: The Eccles Centre for American Studies, The British Library, 1994).

Concluding Comments

We have come a long way since S. Lyman Tyler discussed "The Availability of Information concerning the Mormons," *Dialogue* 1 (Autumn 1966): 172–75. Professional archivists have more fully begun to discuss the role of religious archives,[4] and the professionalizing of Mormon repositories has resulted in more adequate bibliographical control and cataloging.

The Latter-day Saints have a dynamic, living faith, and historical records are only a partial index to the inner spirit of the movement. The Mormons have been serious record keepers, following the counsel of a prophet-historian in the Book of Mormon who spoke of a function of such activity as "enlarg[ing] the memory of this people" (Alma 37:8). While the Mormons' most significant purpose in record keeping was to enlarge their *own* memories of the covenants they had made with their God and the experience they had had with their neighbors, these records can also enlarge the memory of anyone who seeks to understand the experiences of those who have laid the foundation for what some see as a new world religion.

NOTES

[1]See Evon Z. Vogt and Ethel M. Albert, eds., *People of Rimrock: A Study of Values in Five Cultures* (Cambridge, Mass.: Harvard University Press, 1966). The study examined the communities of Zuñis, Spanish-Americans, Mormons, and Texas homesteaders.

[2]I am grateful for the assistance of Joel Pulliam, an LDS student at Harvard University, for sharing with me his preliminary survey on which I have drawn for this information.

[3]Until its discovery in the 1880s, the Spaulding manuscript was claimed to be the real source for the Book of Mormon. See the essay by Lester E. Bush Jr., "The Spalding Theory Then and Now," *Dialogue* 10 (Autumn 1977): 40–69.

[4]See, for example, the discussions in Robert Shuster, "Documenting the Spirit," *The American Archivist* 45 (Spring 1982): 135–41; James M. O'Toole, "What's Different about Religious Archives?" *Midwestern Archivist* (1984): 91–101; O'Toole, "Things of the Spirit: Documenting Religion in New England," *The American Archivist* 50 (Fall 1987): 500–17; Peter J. Wosh, "Bibles, Benevolence, and Bureaucracy: The Changing Nature of Nineteenth Century Religious Records," *The American Archivist* 52 (Spring 1989): 166–78; and Shuster, "'Everyone Did What Was Right in His Own Eyes': Fundamentalist/Evangelical/Pentecostal Archives in the United States," *The American Archivist* 52 (Summer 1989): 366–75.

Subject Index

R

S

T